CHINA, JAPAN, KOREA
and MONGOLIAN REPUBLIC
CONIC PROJECTION
SCALE OF MILES
0 100 200 300 400 500
SCALE OF KILOMETRES
0 100 200 300 400 500
Capitals of Countries
Provincial Capitals
Trade Routes
International Boundaries
Provincial Boundaries
Canals
10,000
5,000
2,000
1,000
500
Sea Level
Below Sea Level
100
Altitudes in Feet
Depths in Fathoms
Copyright by C.S. HAMMOND & CO., N.Y.
0574
W9-AGT-771
SEA OF JAPAN
SEA OF OKHOTSK
YELLOW SEA
EAST CHINA SEA
SOUTH CHINA SEA
HOKKAIDO
HONSHU
SHIKOKU
KYUSHU
KOREA
JAPAN
FORMOSA
TAIWAN
REPUBLIC OF THE PHILIPPINES
LUZON
HEILUNGKIANG
KIRIN
LIAONING
ANTUNG
JEHOL
KIANGSU
CHEKIANG
FUKIEN
ANHWEI
SHANTUNG
NANKING
SHANGHAI
TIENTSIN
TOKYO
Yokohama
Yokosuka
Nagoya
Kyoto
Osaka
Kobe
Sakai
Wakayama
Okayama
Hiroshima
Kure
Shimonoseki
Moji
Kokura
Yawata
Fukuoka
Sasebo
Nagasaki
Kumamoto
Kagoshima
Kanazawa
Niigata
Sendai
Aomori
Hakodate
Sapporo
Otaru
Muroran
Asahigawa
Kushiro
SEOUL
P'yongyang
Pusan
Taegu
Inch'on
Kaesong
Ch'ongjin
Wonsan
Vladivostok
Khabarovsk
Blagoveshchensk
Harbin
Tsitsihar
Changchun
Kirin
Mukden
Fushun
Anshan
Yingkow
Antung
Port Arthur
Talien
Tsingtao
Tsinan
Hangchow
Soochow
Wusih
Chinkiang
Foochow
Amoy
Taipei
Tainan
Keelung
Chinwangtao
Shanhaikwan
Naha
Okinawa Gunto
RYUKYU IS.
BONIN ISLANDS
VOLCANO IS.
Iwo Jima
DAITO ISLANDS
KURIL IS.
Tropic of Cancer
Bashi Channel
Balintang Channel
Korea Strait
Tsugaru Str.
La Perouse Str.
HONG KONG
Pratas I.
Cheju-do (Quelpart I.)
Gulf of Chihli
Mouth of Hwang Ho 1938 - 1947
Hangchow Bay
Peter the Great Bay
E. Korea Bay
Korea Bay
Ullung-do

VAN NOSTRAND POLITICAL SCIENCE SERIES

Editor

FRANKLIN L. BURDETTE
University of Maryland

LONDON, K.—*How Foreign Policy Is Made*

PLISCHKE, ELMER—*Conduct of American Diplomacy*

DIXON, R. G., JR. and PLISCHKE, ELMER—*American Government: Basic Documents and Materials*

SPROUT, HAROLD and MARGARET—*Foundations of National Power,* 2nd Ed.

LANCASTER, LANE W.—*Government in Rural America,* 2nd Ed.

TORPEY, WILLIAM G.—*Public Personnel Management*

JORRIN, M.—*Governments of Latin America*

PLISCHKE, ELMER—*International Relations Basic Documents*

LINEBARGER, P.M.A., DJANG, C., and BURKS, A. W.—*Far Eastern Governments and Politics*—CHINA AND JAPAN, 2nd Ed.

GOODMAN, WILLIAM—*The Two-Party System in the United States*

WATKINS, J. T., IV, and ROBINSON, J. W.—*General International Organization*

FAR EASTERN GOVERNMENTS AND POLITICS

CHINA AND JAPAN

PAUL M. A. LINEBARGER

Professor of Asiatic Politics, The School of Advanced International Studies, The Johns Hopkins University, Washington, D.C.

DJANG CHU

Sometime Associate Professor of Political Science, The Comparative Law School, Soochow University, China, and Special Lecturer, The School of Advanced International Studies, The Johns Hopkins University, Washington, D.C.

ARDATH W. BURKS

Associate Professor of Political Science, Rutgers University, New Brunswick, N.J.

SECOND EDITION

D. VAN NOSTRAND COMPANY, INC.

PRINCETON, NEW JERSEY

TORONTO LONDON

NEW YORK

D. VAN NOSTRAND COMPANY, INC.

120 Alexander St., Princeton, New Jersey
257 Fourth Avenue, New York 10, New York
25 Hollinger Rd., Toronto 16, Canada
Macmillan and Co., Ltd., St. Martin's St., London, W.C. 2, England

All correspondence should be addressed to the principal office of the company at Princeton, N. J.

Published simultaneously in Canada by
D. VAN NOSTRAND COMPANY (Canada), LTD.

Library of Congress Catalogue Card No.: 56-12290

PRINTED IN THE UNITED STATES OF AMERICA

Preface to the Second Edition

This work is a revision of the original edition of 1954. At this time it has seemed more important to take care of the dramatic events in the Communist world and Japan's continued healing from a great defeat than to retrace historical fundamentals. Accordingly, the modern parts of each section—on Nationalist China, Communist China, and post-treaty Japan—have been revised to bring political developments down to the summer of 1956, and the new Chinese Communist Constitution has been added to the appendices. A few of the more irritant errors or points of unnecessary controversy have been ironed out.

Some of the most pressing issues can be followed only in the newspapers and in popular, official, or scholarly journals. The authors have striven, not always successfully, to reconcile political judiciousness with an awareness of the contemporary scene.

Of China, it can almost be said that in these unsettled years there are never enough books. Chinese change continues at an ominous pace. This carries out an old prediction. John W. Foster wrote in 1903 about the prescient prophecy of the Sino-Manchu bannerman, Wên Hsiang, who was one of the few farsighted officials at the court of the Empress Dowager:[1] "Wensiang, the wisest and most farseeing Chinese statesman of modern times, was accustomed to say to foreign diplomats and others who urged speedy reforms: 'You are all too anxious to awake us and start us on a new road, and you will do it; but you will all regret it, for, once awaking and started, we shall go fast and far,—farther than you think, much faster than you want.'" This development rings loud today from the expert propaganda radios of Peking and the jetworthy airfields of Fukien.

The therapy of hate is, among all parts of mankind, a ready though costly cure for the deeper ailments of the body physical, politic, or spiritual. Of this remedy, the Chinese Communists are still making dangerously liberal use. The xenophobia and autocracy of the Chinese Communist leadership, though tempered with contact inside the Communist and Asian worlds, still

[1] John W. Foster, *American Diplomacy in the Orient,* Boston, 1903, p. 434.

represent a large uncertainty in the problem of peace. Perhaps the further future will be able to see that sometime in the 1950's or 1960's the largest human decision of our time was taken, unwittingly and unnoticed. If the fever of revolution, the spasm of near-insanity, of belief, of cruelty, which has characterized Chinese mass revolts in the past applies to this case (People's China), the cycle of revolution may proceed as it has in the past toward the pacification and the rehumanizing of Chinese culture. Chinese habits might engulf Communism; Communism may, contrariwise, still engulf China. This is indeed a larger question than the problem of Mao, the embarrassed antipope in a Communist creed which has just voted a more presbyterian form of government.

Nationalist China remains important not only in its own right, but as the residual legatee of all the mainland's troubles. In his Double Ten (October 10) speech of 1955 President Chiang made the explicit point that the Nationalists had to remain a purely Chinese political and moral force if they were to win China at all. They had to win alone, politically, or not win. This affirmation, together with the reassurances carried by Vice President Nixon in July, 1956, froze the suspended Chinese civil war in its lengthening expectancy.

In Japan, the 1956 election of a less than two-thirds conservative majority in the House of Councilors, while no disaster, was a warning that the "politics of waiting" might not necessarily go well in that country. The Japanese have no clear opportunity to grow within the bloc of anti-Communist nations. Until their international role and their domestic economy promise them a future which is both honorable and reasonable, protests from the Left and from the eccentric Right can be expected. The relative cordiality and sanity of official American-Japanese relations after a decade of forced intimacy is a tribute to the decency of both peoples, and a demonstration of the adequacy of both their governments.

This work has continued the story, but the story goes on. The Ryukus or the Spratlys may make world history before this book is printed again. Only fundamentals endure, and fundamentals in Far Eastern politics can be defined as such because they too grow and change. For the rest of our years, Chinese and Japanese politics remain a factor in the personal lives of Americans. It is perhaps sad that uncertainty should create interdependence when decades of peace did not, but both the uncertainty and the interdependence are massive facts.

P.M.A.L.
July, 1956 D.C.
A.W.B.

PREFACE TO THE FIRST EDITION

This book presents the governments of China and Japan. These governments in their present form are the successors of other, past governments which—when interpreted—explain a great deal of the continuity of civilization in China and Japan and of the background to the present-day political behavior of Chinese and Japanese. Furthermore, a study of the governments of China and Japan in the past is illuminating not only as to the present character and intentions of the leaders and followers in these two countries, but as an explanation of the relationships of each country with the other and with other Asian and Western powers in the past.

This is a study in comparative government, historically applied. It is not a political history. Bibliographical footnotes in the appropriate sections of the book will give the reader a considerable number of leads from which he can follow political history as such.

The reason for this is a simple one. There are many excellent political histories of Japan and almost as many of China in various Western languages. On the other hand, it is rare for these two countries to be described in a comparative government text. So far as the authors know, this is the first serious work in comparative government which covers both China and Japan without attempting to cover all the major nations of the world; it is also the first, so far as they know, to attempt to present the comparative government pattern of each country by displaying well known governments which have existed one after the other.

The purpose of the authors is, in the first instance, to fill a long-empty gap in the field of political science textbooks. They hope that their colleagues in the teaching profession will welcome this book as a work on Far Eastern politics, supplementing the many basic introductions to the politics and area study of the Far East which already exist. They hope that, as such, it will serve either as an introductory guide to the Far Eastern tradition of the governing of men, or as an advanced survey, based on Far Eastern language materials, for the specialist in area studies.

In the second place, the authors hope to be of service to the general reader—particularly to the general reader who wants to go behind the way things seem today and to find out how political customs and political habits came to be what they are. This purpose will be fulfilled if these portrayals of ancient and modern Chinese and Japanese governments are accepted for what they are: descriptive presentations of actual systems of government, with some reference to the historical events which led to the foundation of each system and to its supersession by another.

PAUL M. A. LINEBARGER
DJANG CHU
ARDATH W. BURKS

March, 1954

Acknowledgments

THIS volume was originally planned and initiated by an agreement between the publishers and the authors in December, 1948. Since that time all the authors have become indebted to the Editor of the Van Nostrand Political Science Series, Franklin L. Burdette, Department of Government and Politics, University of Maryland, for his interest in the project, his guidance, and his cooperation.

Since the book was initiated, all of the authors have visited the Far East. Linebarger has made five trips on various errands. Burks has since spent fifteen months in the Far East, twelve of which were in Japan, most of them at the University of Michigan Center for Japanese Studies at Okayama. Space forbids a detailed listing of the countless number of Far Eastern government servants and scholars, as well as American colleagues, scholars, and friends, resident in the Far East, who freely offered insights and suggestions which eventually affected the authors' views. Needless to say, however, the opinions set forth are entirely the unofficial views of the authors and they alone stand responsible for them.

Linebarger wishes specifically to acknowledge his gratitude to teaching colleagues in The School of Advanced International Studies of The Johns Hopkins University. He pays tribute to the patient aid of Mr. John Carr of the Alderson Reporting Service, in transcribing drafts of the volume.

Both Djang and Burks are deeply indebted to Mr. Howard Linton who, as friend and Librarian, East Asian Institute, Columbia University, gave selflessly of his time in order to aid in the search for primary Far Eastern materials.

Burks wishes specifically to thank Dr. Hugh Borton, Director, East Asian Institute, Columbia University, and Dr. Robert E. Ward, Associate Director, Center for Japanese Studies, for their careful reading of and suggestions on the section on Japanese Government and Politics. Present and former colleagues, Dr. L. Ethan Ellis, Chairman, and Dr. Henry R. Winkler, History Department, Rutgers University; and Dr. Richard Edwards, Associate Professor of Political Science, Lafayette College, read portions of the Japan section and made valuable suggestions. Finally, Burks has added one more item to his long-standing debt of gratitude to members of the Japan Section, Division of Orientalia, Library of Congress, Washington, D.C.—Dr. Edwin G. Beal, Jr., Mrs. Katsuyo Takeshita, and Mr. Andrew Kuroda—for their indefatigable and friendly aid in searching for primary Japanese materials. The usual and familiar "last but not least" acknowledgment must be divided, as was the authorship of this volume, among the three long-suffering wives of the authors—Dr. Genevieve Collins Linebarger, Jane Chu Djang, and Jane Lyle Burks—all of whom cheerfully withstood the arguments, compromises, and eventual proofs. Especially to Jane Burks, Djang and Burks are grateful for extensive retyping in the final draft stage. This debt the authors want to repay, however inadequately, by dedicating this volume to their wives.

The three authors believe that this work is a genuine composite of their joint efforts. It is inevitable that the authors' points of view should in all three cases be colored by actual experience, as well as by the more commonly recognized procedures of research, reading, note-taking, and interviews. The authors hope to have been honest in expression of points of view on events which have been highly controversial, in academic no less than in political circles. The authors will be indebted to those readers who will be so kind as to advise them of errors or of serious omissions in the book as it now stands; they may be reached in care of the publishers.

PAUL M. A. LINEBARGER
DJANG CHU
ARDATH W. BURKS

Contents

APPENDICES

CHINA

JAPAN

PART
ONE

The Government and Politics of China

A NOTE ON CHINESE AND JAPANESE NAMES

Chinese and Japanese personal names are given in the conventional form, with the family name preceding the given name, *except* where Chinese or Japanese authors have had their works published in English. In such cases, bibliographic citations follow the order of names as given on the title pages and are often listed according to Western usage.

Chinese and Japanese place names—as well as other Chinese and Japanese words—follow (in Chinese) the Wade-Giles and (in Japanese) the Hepburn systems of transliteration, *except* for a few Chinese place names which have become more commonly familiar in Chinese Postal system spellings.

CHAPTER
ONE

Political Evolution In Old China

In China as well as in the Western World, the myth of Chinese antiquity is very important. Chinese civilization falls short—by several thousand years—of being the first known civilized community. If the fall of Egypt is dated from the death of Cleopatra, Egypt at its death was perhaps older than China is now. The important living fact about Chinese antiquity is this: China is older than any other human community now in existence. The myth of age runs through Chinese views of China no less than through Western views of China.

If the Chinese think that China is the oldest nation on earth and take pride in that assumption, without bothering to define the terms *old* or *nation,* present-day Chinese belief in China's antiquity must still be reckoned a force on the international scene.

The Popular Chinese Cosmogony. From a scientific point of view, the historical facts concerning China's origin are perhaps less important in modern politics than the Chinese myths about their own origin. In both the Nationalist and Communist periods of modern China, the Chinese have defended irrational or legendary elements in their own culture, whenever those elements could contribute to a vigorous revolutionary or anti-foreign propaganda campaign. It is paradoxical to see a Chinese atheist rejecting Christianity as myth and then presenting Chinese mythology as a defense of wise atheist patriotism.

The Communist regime has not been in power long enough to make plain its own party line concerning the reconciliation of Chinese traditions to the international Communist ideology. The China of the 1950's entered a community of Communist states which were already in existence, a community heavily overbalanced by the avowed primacy of Russia in that system. So it has become familiar for Americans to hear day by day that a

Russian was the first discoverer of the telegraph, the balloon, the automobile, the printing press, or the like. China's Communist regime has not been in power long enough to show whether the Chinese outdo the Russians in their claims of pioneering in the fields of invention and discovery. If they ever do compete, the Chinese have the richer body of legends from which to draw, as well as the longer span of history. On the other hand, the Chinese may be sophisticated enough to let the Russians claim the discovery of North America, the invention of the sewing machine, the manufacture of the first bicycle, and so on, and support the Russians with that very special Chinese talent which can be called the *mockery of assent*—the capacity, more developed in Chinese than among other peoples, to deride a fellow human being by agreeing with him so expressionlessly that he never quite knows whether he is being mocked or not.

Although the Chinese mock other people readily, they are themselves thin-skinned when mocked from the outside. Accordingly, very little has been heard in recent times concerning the Chinese traditionalist view of the creation of the universe from chaos. Such a view answers the child's question, "Daddy, where did the world come from?" Every culture has its own cosmogony. It would be impossible to understand the American Declaration of Independence or the assumptions made by the Constitution of the United States concerning human faith if one did not have at least a nodding acquaintance with the story of Adam and Eve as told in Genesis. Similarly, the Chinese superstitions about the origin of their own world and of themselves have the importance which self-description plays in any culture. They have another importance to be detailed at greater length in the description of Confucius (pages 25-27). The Chinese, more than any other people, use their history to control their present; history became in the Confucian world, which lasted from about the time of Christ to the beginning of the twentieth century, a pretty overt instrument of ideological control. One of the parts of that instrument was the creation of an official past more reasonable and more literate than the manufactured past which has been developed by each modern totalitarian state, but which, in its own way, performed a comparable function.

An intelligent but illiterate Chinese peasant, born in the 1880's, would be about seventy years old at the present time. Such a man would, in his own lifetime, have seen China changed from one civilization into another. It would be difficult to know what such an old man really thinks of the Communists and their theories. Depending on his economic status and his personal role in the revolution, he may or may not support the present Communist government. One thing, however, is certain about him: the world is not what he thought it was in his childhood. When this hypothetical peasant was young, he was probably told a fairy story about the primal man named P'an Ku, who reduced the Universe out of chaos. P'an Ku separated the heavens from the earth, created the great mountains and the immense rivers, and gave life to living organisms.[1]

Even among the ordinary Chinese farmers and workers, this myth never had the tragic majesty, the undertones of touchingly profound allegory, which attach themselves to the Hebrew legend of Adam and Eve. P'an Ku was neither blessed nor profane, neither lucky nor unlucky, neither clean nor guilty. He bequeathed humanity, even in Chinese legend, nothing more than the mere fact of existence. No modern Chinese believes seriously in the P'an Ku story, and it is likely that even in the nineteenth century very few Chinese paid serious attention to a giant alleged to have lived a quarter of a million years ago.

Much more to the point is the more modest legend of China's origin, which still affects a great deal of Communist and Nationalist foreign policy, still makes *jus sanguinis* rather than *jus soli* the working foundation for China's approach to the problems of citizenship and international war, and may color the long-range assimilation of the Communist concepts of history to a living Chinese civilization.

Much more plausibly than with the P'an Ku story, the Chinese accept the legend that a semi-human, semi-divine Emperor named Huang Ti was the common ancestor of the Chinese people. To Huang Ti are attributed the chieftancy of the primal Chinese tribe, the courageous leadership of the first Chinese in battle, and the invention of the compass. His wife is described in legend as having been the first human being to rear silkworms and to teach the common people the art of sericulture. One of Huang Ti's subordinates is credited with the invention of Chinese calendars and another with devising the ideographs which are the characteristic Chinese method of writing. The historicity of Huang Ti—the Chinese term means literally "The Yellow Emperor"—has not been demonstrated. A sumptuous mausoleum which supposedly contains his remains is located in the district of Sian and for centuries received annual sacrifices from the official representatives of the Chinese Imperial Government. Modern Chinese historians usually comment that the Yellow Emperor was in all probability the symbolic personification of an era in which the first beginning of Chinese civilization was made and consolidated. Along with the Yellow Emperor, various other legendary heroes helped set the tone for later Chinese politics. The Emperors Yao and Shun play comparable roles in Chinese legend—both in the living legend of the twentieth century and in the earlier legend accepted by Confucius as a foundation to history. To them can be assigned positions in popular Chinese thinking comparable to those occupied by Noah and his sons in European and American thought.

None of the Chinese religions or superstitions possess a cosmogony as

[1] It is interesting to compare this Chinese cosmogony with the indigenous cult of Japan, the legendary basis and modern significance of which is described on pp. 261-266, especially fn. 5.

important in its relation to everyday behavior as the Hebrew-Christian cosmogony.

The Chinese in modern times have neither barriers to new beliefs nor supports for ancient faith comparable to the major religions of the West. In this respect, China is in marked contrast to India, where the Hindu religion permeates the archaic civilization and presents serious problems in the conduct of modern Indian life. It must be credited to a weakness of Chinese civilization that there is very little Chinese spirituality of characteristically Chinese origin that can support those Chinese who wish to resist Communist secularism. On the other hand, the Chinese come to modernity whether Communist or democratic, with very few drags on their capacity to absorb and to accept modern ways of thinking. The Chinese tradition, when divested of superstitious trappings, leaves the modern Chinese with a pleasant sense of self-importance; the loss of the superstition does not involve any deep spiritual loss.

The Hsia and Shang Dynasties. The Hsia dynasty lies at the threshold between legend and possible historicity. There have been no demonstrable excavations of Hsia relics and no physical substantiation of a specifically Hsia-type culture. Its traditional dates, 2205-1766 B.C., are computations as fanciful as Bishop Usher's calculation of the beginning of the world according to the Old Testament. (He fixed the date as being on a designated morning in the month of October, 4004 B.C.)

The next dynasty, the Shang, sometimes called the Yin, is traditionally ascribed to the years 1766-1122 B.C. Within the past fifty years the existence of a great city of Shang has been confirmed by discoveries as dramatic as the excavations of Heinrich Schliemann at Troy. Just as Schliemann discovered Troy as a physical city after it had been lost for more than 2,000 years, modern Chinese archaeologists dug into the traditional "Mounds of Yin" in Honan province and discovered, point by point, confirmation for most of the traditional historiography. About three fourths of the names of the legendary Shang rulers have been taken out of legend and confirmed as definite historical data from contemporaneous physical sources.[2]

These dramatic excavations of Shang relics provide confirmation of the location and form of the oldest known Chinese political and social system. Chinese society was already on a patriarchal pattern. The chief occupations of the Shang people were farming, fishing, and hunting. They made excellent earthenware and bronze vessels. The elaborateness of their religious ceremonies is demonstrated by the great number of sacramental objects dug out in the Mounds of Yin.

According to both legend and archaeology, the army of Shang was well

[2] The dramatic story of the rediscovery of Shang has been best told in H. G. Creel's readable and popular work, *The Birth of China,* New York, 1937; see also Chap. IV, "Antiquity: To the Fall of Shang" by L. Carrington Goodrich, in H. F. MacNair, Editor, *China,* Los Angeles, 1946; Tung Tso-pin, "Ten Examples of Early Tortoise-shell Inscriptions," *Harvard Journal of Asiatic Studies,* Vol. II, Nos. 1 and 2 (June, 1948).

organized. Cavalry and chariots determined the predominant patterns of warfare.

The political organization of the Shang dynasty is still relatively uncertain. It would appear that the Shang people comprised the strongest of many Chinese tribes existing in that period. The Shang kingdom had conflicts with the people called Chou and with the nomads whose descendants were called Huns by the Westerners.

The Shang political entity existed amid a number of other states; whom these comprised and where they were located seem less certain. At the head of the Shang states was a king or *wang* whose religio-political duties were not subdivided. Unlike ancient Israel, in which prophets and kings were sharply distinguished, the most archaic Chinese *wang* never left room for priestly or kingly rivals. Succession in the office of *wang* went from older brother to younger; in the absence of a brother it went from father to son.

Shang history has not been given the hundred and fifty years of modern political reviews to which Near Eastern history has been subject.

Chinese accounts of Shang antiquity are colored by specialized interpretations as peculiar as medieval Christian paintings of Old Testament stories. It is as dangerous to understate the civilization and extent of Shang rule as to overstate it. At a minimum it seems safe to assume that the particular Shang state is the predecessor-state of modern China chiefly because early Chinese history was written by people who lived under an organized monarchy and who, in attempting to explain their own past, extrapolated their own institutions and ways of thought retroactively. At the least there was a great city which had arisen from trivial foundations; at the most there was a very early but already sophisticated monarchy.

The Chou Dynasty. With the arrival of the Chou dynasty (ascribed to the years 1122-255 B.C.), archival history itself is reached. The latter part of the Chou is as definite and historic year for year as the same period in Rome. The beginnings of the Chou are cloudy. A large amount of specific detail provided by traditional Chinese historiography makes the material concerning early Chou history difficult to handle, since the natural suspicion is raised that extremely minute descriptions of events, personalities or institutions are more a credit to the inventiveness of the historian than to his care in appraising source materials.

By the traditional history, the Chou period marked the inauguration of a specific feudal system. The founder of the dynasty, the Emperor Wu, is described as conquering Shang and fifty other tribes. After the conquest he is further described as appointing a number of noblemen to head the various feudal states which had served as "screen and fence" to the outer frontiers of the Empire. Some 1,600 Imperial clansmen and ministers were thus selected to man the feudal system. If their ranks are translated into the nearest European terms, the five grades can be described as Duke, Marquis, Earl, Viscount, and Baron. A Duke or Marquis was allotted a territory of a hundred square *li*. (The *li* can be roughly computed as a third of a mile.) An Earl received seventy square *li*. A Viscount or a Baron controlled fifty square *li*. Feudal lords who received territories of less than fifty square *li* did not maintain direct contact with the Emperor, but were vassals to the outer feudal lords. Within this loose feudal system the Emperor himself made a tour of inspection throughout the Empire every five years. The feudal lords were required to attend the court from time to time to give an account of their stewardship. When the Emperor found that a particular domain was especially well governed, its lord was granted more land and an official promotion. If a domain was found to be in disorder, the incompetent lord was punished or deprived of his land.[3]

Another traditional aspect of the Chou political system has played an important role in Communist and Nationalist propaganda in modern times. This is the so-called *ching t'ien* or well-field system, which was much publicized and praised by the Confucianists of later ages as an ideal economic system. (One effect was felt in Japan and is described on pages 285-286. The Japanese Sinified their system of land tenure, or at least imitated what they thought was the ideal system.) Although the traditional accounts of the system are not always consistent, enough evidence has been found to ascertain that some sort of a well-field system did actually exist in the Chou period. According to the traditional account, cultivable land was divided into nine equal parts, each part containing one hundred *mou*. (A *mou* is approximately one sixth of an acre.) Eight of these nine parts were assigned one each to a family and were called private fields, the ninth field being cultivated by the eight families in turn for the benefit of the lord to whom the land ultimately belonged. By this measure, not more than one ninth of the total working time of any Chinese family had to be dedicated to the state. This figure is considerably lower than the most extreme reactionary would demand under the present-day American tax system, where approximately a third of the working time of employed adults is applied to the payment of taxes. Needless to say, very few Chinese periods ever reached this ideal. Neither under the empires of later periods nor under the Nationalists and Communists of the present age have the Chinese peasants paid less than a fourth or a third of their work as taxes or rent; very often the able-bodied farmer had to pay as much as two thirds or three quarters of his total produce. The ideal of the *ching t'ien* system set up a measure which across the centuries was capable of inspiring profound discontent. Under the legendary accounts of this system, every able-bodied male over the age of twenty was obliged to till the land until he was sixty, whereupon he returned the land to the lord and enjoyed a pension issued by the government. Orphans, the disabled, the aged, and the insane received government care. Improbable though this Utopia may appear to us, its appearance in early

[3] Ch'en Ku-yüan, *Chung-kuo fa-chih shih* (A history of Chinese law and institutions), Shanghai, 1934, pp. 142-143.

Chinese history has provided a canon of criticism to the Chinese peasant.[4]

If one guesses at the probabilities of Chou conditions, it seems reasonably certain that the feudal system represented a marked advance in the earliest Chinese methods of government. When the first few Chou emperors ruled, their power and influence were still strong. Their system may have had the attractiveness and capacity of an innovation. As the Imperial descendants became decadent and indulged in luxuries or as the feudal lords became more settled in their position and acquired more power, the fiefs acquired greater independence and the subordinate lords became jealous of one another. In 771 B.C. wild tribes from the West invaded the capital, and the dynasty almost came to an end. A new Emperor of the House of Chou moved the capital eastward to Loyang. Despite the change, the Imperial power was on the wane. The feudal states surrounding the new capital competed in building up strong armies, each for the aggrandizement of itself. The influence of the central court became practically nonexistent, like that of the last of the Holy Roman emperors, and their Germanic and Italian fiefs.

Two points that are curiously interesting when seen with Western eyes stand forth quite sharply in the early history of Chou. Twenty-nine centuries before the birth of Jean Jacques Rousseau, the Chinese found themselves the possessors of a *theory of revolution* so coherent and so explicit as to affect their history down to the present day. As it developed from the time of Chou, the theory held that only virtuous rulers could retain the *t'ien ming* (Mandate of Heaven). Those who had lost the mandate to rule had neither the moral superiority to stave off, nor the right to suppress, rebellion. This doctrine emerged clearly in Confucian political thought and, later, as an important check on the absolute power of the Emperor (as such, it is discussed on page 53).

We may never know how much of this theory of revolution is genuinely contemporaneous with the foundation of Chou; its attribution to the beginning of Chou power is beyond cavil. The other striking point among the Chou contributions to subsequent Chinese history was the development about the middle of the first millenium B.C.—2,000 years, that is, before the Treaty of Westphalia—of a reasonably coherent system of *kuo*—a term usually translated into the bald English equivalent of "nation" or "state." In other words, the national and international world which underlies most present-day American experience arrived on the Chinese scene about 2,600 years ago and departed about 2,200 years ago.

In neither respect—the possession of a theory of revolution or working experience with power politics between nations—was China unique among the ancient civilizations of mankind. Many other ancient civilizations possessed comparable doctrines or underwent similar experiences. The peculiar thing about the Chou contribution was the explicitness of the traditions

[4] Cf. Tsui Chi, *A Short History of Chinese Civilization*, New York, 1943, Chap. IV.

which arose from these experiences and the continuity of the process of government from Chou times to the present.

Histories of China pay a great deal of attention to the remarkable contributions of philosophy to Chinese civilization in the Chou period. Some of these contributions are discussed later so as to put the Confucian tradition of government into context. (See pages 25-29.) The Confucian tradition itself made no immediate impact on the pattern of social classes under government or of the power structure within government, but the spirit of Confucianism exerted a long, sustained, and overwhelmingly important pressure which, although oblique, was more important than any other pressure in the long span of China's history. With reference to the *process* of government, one can say that the Confucian tradition sophisticated the Chinese to a degree which has never been excelled by any other political system, ancient or modern. Confucianism instituted something very close to articulate ideological control. Confucianism more than any other philosophy of government answers the preponderant question, "If governments truly govern only those actions of men which are in violation of the ideas of men—if, furthermore,

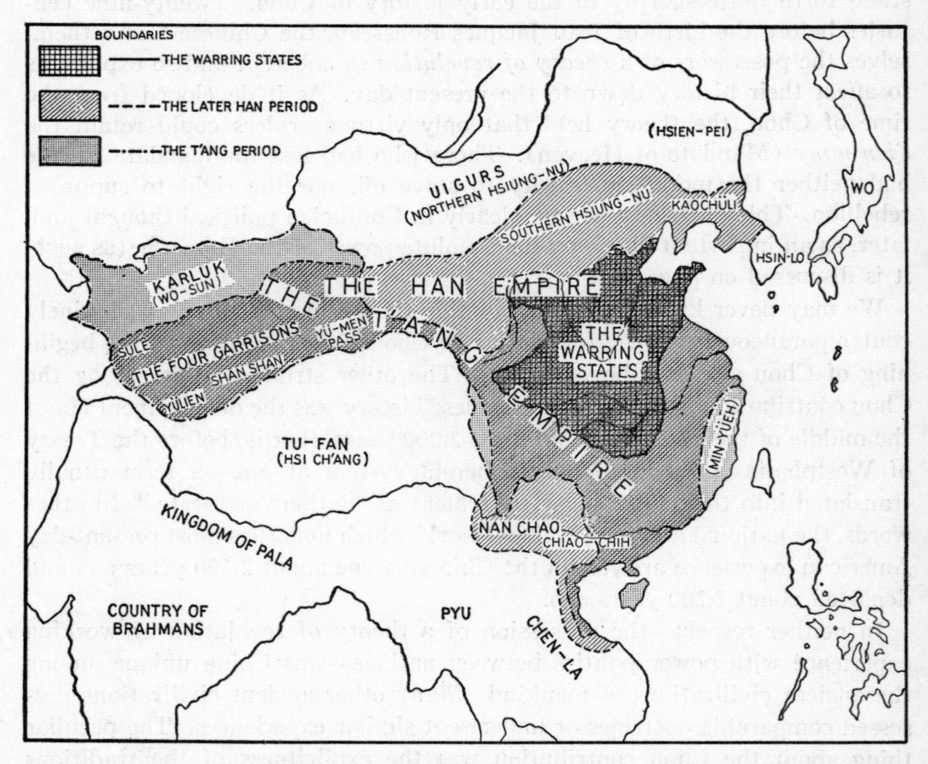

The Expansion of the Chinese Empire showing three different stages: The Period of Warring States (circa 330 B.C.); The Later Han Dynasty (circa A.D. 100) and The T'ang Dynasty (circa A.D. 750)

the ideas of men, both rulers and ruled, are the final instrumentalities of power and direction in human life—if the nurture of ideas is more fundamental than the most solemn or sovereign proclamation of law—if these are true, how can the rulers rule the ideas within their own minds, rule the minds of their contemporaries, and rule the minds of men not yet born so as to insure harmony, justice, and serenity in human society?" At the present time, every civilization in the world is seeking a political answer to this or to similar questions. Sociologically speaking, the Confucianists came closer to accomplishing that which others later sought, the withering away of the state and the substitution therefor of a system of indoctrination too purposeful to be called mere education and too sustained to be designated propaganda.[5]

Unification and Utopia. The fiefs of the early Chou became the *kuo* of the middle Chou period. These *kuo* can be called proto-nations in that they were states which possessed most, but not all, of the characteristics of the modern national state. Operationally their behavior differed very little from that of the nation-states of the Western World in the eighteenth, nineteenth, and twentieth centuries. They had the equivalents of League of Nations and United Nations systems, their counterparts to NATO and ANZUS, their realpolitic and their idealistic ventures. They met a doom which has often been foretold for our world of nation-states: one nation cruel, selfish, brave, and militant swallowed all the others.

The conqueror was Ch'in (255-206 B.C.). The politics of Ch'in in the last part of the Chou period are reminiscent of the rise of Prussia among German states. Competent ruler, realistic fighting, audacious generalship, and a dogged, consistent search for power led Ch'in to victory. The Ch'in king who set himself up as *de facto* First Ruler of Mankind adopted measures of unification so stringent that their imprint can still be seen on the Chinese today. He tried to destroy the present so as to insure the future of his own posterity. In order to achieve his near-totalitarian tyranny he sought to build an intellectual barrier against the past and a physical barrier against the northern barbarians. He ordered the burning of books in an effort to destroy China's cultural heritage so that posterity might think that he himself was the originator of all the Chinese civilization. The title he took for himself was more arrogant than that of any Caesar, Kaiser, or Czar; he called himself merely *Shih-huang-ti*—the *First* Emperor. He ruthlessly burned all the political and ethical classics and, according to traditional history, buried alive any scholar who dared criticize his policy. He issued stern laws, increased the severity of punishments, enforced drastic labor and

[5] Fifteen years ago one of the authors of this book attempted to explore some aspects of this problem in a survey of the role of politics in Chinese life. This was Paul Linebarger's *Government in Republican China,* New York, 1938. The same author is preparing a reissue of that book largely rewritten in the light of the subsequent experiences and misadventures of the Chinese people in the field of politics and of the author's own opportunities to reconsider some basic aspects of the problem on the basis of his personal experiences in Chinese affairs, as well as the developing scholarship of the field.

military conscriptions, terrorized the populace so that everyone denounced everyone else, and made education the business of his all-powerful government. It was not his fault that he did not exceed, in tightness of control, the totalitarianism of a Hitler or of a Stalin. He did all he could, given the means at hand. In place of an Iron Curtain he built a stone wall against the world outside—the Great Wall of China, much of which endures to this day. (Subsequent rulers maintained the wall and added to it; the First Emperor was the one who got the foundations laid.) To build this wall he used up human lives by tens and hundreds of thousands. The gigantic task was rushed to completion far ahead of any Soviet or Nazi timetable.

Chinese historians got their quiet, mocking revenge on the First Emperor by calling him *Ch'in-shih-huang-ti*—that is, they called him the *Ch'in* First Emperor, not the *First* Emperor. The term which is rendered "emperor" in English had not been borne by mortal men before, since the Chou rulers called themselves Sons of Heaven. Not only in title were there striking differences between the feudal system of the Chou dynasty and the totalitarian system of the Ch'in dynasty. The Chou represented a paternal system of government under which the Son of Heaven and the feudal lords equally shared the responsibilities of government, while the power of the latter system was concentrated in the personal hands of the Emperor alone. The First Emperor used assassination, abduction, predetermined death penalties, and the massacre of political unreliables without hesitation or mercy.

In the field of local government the First Emperor and his son ruled over a system of regions or *chün* to take the place of the former feudal *kuo*. There were 36 regions throughout the empire; each was governed by an official directly appointed by the Emperor. Uniformity was indeed the chief characteristic of the *chün*. It was in this period that the standardization of Chinese characters occurred, all the local variations of the language being reduced to a single official vocabulary and style. Everything was standardized on a world-wide basis for the entire Chinese world, all the way down to the gauges of the wagon wheels, so that carts could traverse the length and breadth of China without having to be adapted to different breadths for the stone tracks which provided ancient China with its crude but usable predecessor of the railroad. Localism and particularism were savagely repressed. Communications facilities throughout China were built up. The people were disarmed, allegedly for their own protection, and out of the impounded weapons the metal was smelted down and cast into twelve colossal figures.

It is a common belief in China that governments built on sheer force and based on intimidation alone are not destined to last long. After the death of the First Emperor in 210 B.C., revolt broke out as a result of the people's reaction against totalitarianism, and the Empire fell to pieces. The Great Ch'in Dynasty, which was designed by its cruel and ambitious empire builder to last for "10,000 generations," actually lasted only fourteen years (after the *Ch'in-shih-huang-ti* assumed the title, Emperor).

When the Ch'in fell, the *kuo* could not be reconstituted. The reigning houses had been extirpated, the scholastic and administrative elites had been massacred or had disappeared, the very boundary stones had been carried away. The Chinese world had accomplished unification, although at a fearful price. Once achieved it was impossible to go back to the disorderly but happy-seeming age of the proto-nations.

The Han dynasty floated to power on a tide of blood. With the Han there began a tendency which lasted a thousand years and more, the slow rise of oligarchy. Since the Han dynasty (206 B.C. to A.D. 220) came to power as a reaction of the common people against the oppressiveness of the Ch'in, it therefore attempted to be traditionalist and, although militant in foreign policy, was rather careful in its domestic measures concerning the Chinese people.

The Han dynasty was interrupted by a short-lived and illegitimate dynasty called the Hsin-ch'ao, or New Dynasty, set up by the usurper and socialist Emperor, Wang Mang. Member of an Empress' family, he set himself up as Emperor in order to abolish slavery, private property, money, private trading, mass warfare, and conventional education. He terrorized all China with his fanatical utopian measures, which were well meant, but cruelly carried out. He was killed and was superseded by a prince of the legitimate Han house. A distinction is made between the two halves of the Han dynasty, the period before Wang Mang being called the Former Han and the period after Wang Mang being called the Later Han.

During the Han dynasty the power of the Emperor was limited by the dominance of strong ministers. The actual power of the court was grasped by Imperial relatives, especially by the relatives of the Empress or the Empress Dowager (since these came from outside the palace walls and could be counted on to have practical connections with the working politics of the country). Following the practice of the Ch'in dynasty, the Han court vested the major portion of responsibilities of the state in the office of the Chancellor, who was usually an Imperial in-law. Besides the Chancellor there was also a Marshal, who was in charge of military affairs, and an Imperial Recorder, who served as State Secretary to the Emperor. These three officials together were called the Three Lords; on behalf of the Emperor they exercised a part or even the whole of his titulary monarchial power. The excessive power vested in the hands of the chancellors frequently led to usurpation and intrigue.

Further Imperial Development. By the end of the Later Han dynasty the ruling Emperor had become a figurehead. Actual political power had fallen into the hands of strong military leaders who committed themselves to perpetual warfare and to a diplomacy of intrigue. The greatest of all Chinese novels—*The Romance of Three Kingdoms,* which to this day provides the source for most of the stories shown in old-fashioned Chinese grand opera and which is said to be better known than any other novel in the world—is based on the story of three provisional kingdoms, one of which was led by the chivalrous warrior who claimed to be the successor king to the fallen house of Han.

Out of the chaos attending the fall of Han, out of internecine strife and senseless bloodshed, the Tsin (or Chin) dynasty (A.D. 265-420) arose. The Tsin was characterized by the rise of powerful, interlinked families. Preponderant influences of the big family groups were so overwhelming that no emperor dared make an appointment without the consent of the great families. The rise of this new aristocracy was an accidental by-product of a civil service system which required that local officials throughout the country recommend capable men to hold government positions; this system inevitably promoted the interests of the important families, since only the members or relatives of influential families obtained recommendation and appointment. Gradually political power flowed from court out to the countryside, from the one Imperial family to the great landlord families. For more than three hundred years—during the Tsin dynasty, the interregnum of six dynasties which followed the Tsin, and the rise of Sui (A.D. 581-618) which preceded the T'ang (A.D. 618-907)—the influence of the great families continued while the titular remaining families rose and fell. This situation was not curtailed until the T'ang dynasty appeared, re-establishing a *bona fide* civil service examination and once again demanding the criterion of actual personal merit for official appointment and promotion.

Palace eunuchs became another political force arising during the Sui and T'ang. Their power, although unsuspected, was entirely understandable. Proximity to the Imperial person gave them a leverage on government which was sure to appear as soon as the Emperor himself became of superlative importance in the pattern of government. In our own time the right of direct access to the President of the United States has become one of the most critical perquisites of high American administrative office, despite the fact that the United States is a democratic republic in which the President, regardless of overcommitment of his time, still sees a great deal of the public. This right of access increases in importance when the executive is sacred, cut off from the public by ceremonial and excessive protection and removed from everyday life by the establishment of a cloud-cuckooland of interminable niceties and elegant recreations within the palace walls. The eunuchs, castrated late in adolescence, were far from being the rolypoly comedy characters so familiar to the readers of American cartoons. Instead they were astute, selfish men, driven by a greed for power and wealth. Their ready access to the household life of the Emperor enabled them to out-maneuver ministers and court officials. At the end of the T'ang dynasty the eunuchs virtually seized the Emperor's person and bid him issue orders in accordance with their wishes.

Generally speaking, the eleven centuries from the Ch'in dynasty through the T'ang represents a transitional period from feudalism to absolute monarchy, in so far as the structure of the government is concerned, but qualified throughout by the pervasive Confucian doctrines of ideological control. During this long transitional epoch, although the government remained monarchial in form, the actual operation of government was by turns monopolized by various categories of persons—Imperial relatives, military men, influential families, or court eunuchs—who at one time or another usurped the power of the Emperor. Not until the Sung dynasty (A.D. 960-1279) did the powers of state become so firmly lodged in the hands of the Emperor that an actual working monarchy could be said to prevail at all times.

Nevertheless the T'ang dynasty is a turning point in Chinese history so far as the administrative system of government is concerned. The T'ang exemplar in government provided a pattern, in form and terminology at least, for Japanese government.[6] The T'ang model of government gave political expression to *la Chine joyeuse* so deftly characterized by Father Leon Wieger, S. J. Under the T'ang the Chinese established patterns of artistic, literary, and political exuberance which gave expression to a very rich flowering of a great culture.

The founding Emperor of the T'ang, posthumously called T'ai Tsung, was credited with many political innovations. Most significant among these was the introduction of a civil service examination system. Those civil service examinations were conducted as early as the Sui dynasty, and, although crude counterparts of examinations can be traced as far back as the Han, it fell to the first T'ang ruler to make this the main means for recruiting administrative officials.[7] T'ang adaptation of civil service techniques as a *sole* channel for official position marks the arrival of the first true bureaucracy to be developed by mankind. This system revolutionized the method of government and laid the foundation of government by the merit system.

Civil service examinations were held publicly and regularly. The subjects on which candidates were examined were varied, sensibly chosen, and arduously demanding.[8] At the time of its institution, the T'ang examination system bore a reasonable applicability to everyday life; as centuries passed the content of the examinations was to become more stereotyped, less real-

[6] See Chap. 11, pp. 279-280, "The T'ang Exemplar in Japan."

[7] Homer Dubs in his monumental translation of *The History of the Former Han Dynasty by Pan Ku*, Baltimore, 1938, 1944, tells the story of the fussy Han Emperor who very carefully provided the concubines in his harem with graded ranks and titles, thus anticipating Waacs, Waves, and maybe Marines by many centuries. One of the present authors spent a hilarious afternoon with Dubs at Duke University many years ago trying to decide whether an upper-grade sweetie should be promoted to a darling J.G. or to a Yummy, probationary. Dubs ended up using somewhat more serious English for the translation of these piquant Han titles which had lain forgotten in the archives for 2,000 years.

[8] Baron Robert des Rotours in his *La Traité des Examens*, Paris, 1932, and in his *Traité des Fonctionnaires et Traité de l'Armée*, Leyden, 1947; and Otto Franke in his *Geschichte des chinesischen Reiches*, Berlin, 1936, Vol. II, pp. 530-549, provide more detailed descriptions of this system. Baron des Rotours has given a virtual lifetime to the study of the T'ang. His presentation opened the door into a whole new world.

istic, and more demanding of useless rhetoric and the memorizing of long-forgotten practices.[9]

Separation of powers in the administrative establishment was also an innovation by the T'ang rulers. In the central administration there were three administrative divisions (*shêng*) that were responsible for the enforcement of their respective duties. These were:

1. the Division of Ministers (*Shang-shu-shêng*), the executive branch of the government controlling the six administrative departments;
2. the Division of the Secretariat (*Chung-shu-shêng*), an agency that drafted laws and orders and recorded the merits and punishments of officials; and
3. the Division of the Palace (*Men-hsia-shêng*), responsible for editing the imperial history and conducting ceremonial rites. The heads of these three divisions, while in conference, constituted a Privy Council that assisted the Emperor in making important decisions. However, it became unfortunate although common practice to have one person carry the titles of all three division heads, thus concentrating all administrative power into his own hands. The six working level administrative departments were those of Civil Affairs, Rites, War, Punishments, Revenue, and Public Works. Originated in the Sui dynasty and elaborated in the T'ang, this system remained in force until the end of the Manchu dynasty on December 31, 1911, and was reconstituted in Manchukuo by the Japanese, so that its final fall in Manchuria came in 1945. The basic administrative organization of the T'ang can best be illustrated by Chart 1.[10]

In the field of local government the T'ang dynasty differed from its predecessors in that it created an over-all supervisory local government unit called *tao* or "circuit" above the traditional *chou* or "prefecture" and *hsien* or "district." Strictly speaking, the *tao* was not a part of local government but was rather a unit linking the central government to the local authorities. The T'ang Empire was, as a whole, first divided into ten and later into fifteen circuits, each headed by a governor whose duty it was to supervise the administration of all local government components within his jurisdiction. Under each circuit there were a number of prefectures and under the prefecture, the districts. In the thirteenth year of Chen Kuan (A.D. 639) there were 350 *chou* (prefectures) and 1,555 *hsien* (districts).[11]

The earlier T'ang emperors succeeded in enforcing a complete separation between the military and civil administration. At this time there was an

[9] The subjects examined included mathematics, law, philosophy, literature, classics, and political affairs which represented the total sum of learning and scholarship in that period. See Ch'en, *op. cit.*, pp. 214-215.

[10] Adopted from Hsü Ch'ung-hao, *Chung-kuo chêng-chih kai-yao* (Outline of Chinese political system), Chungking, 1943, pp. 14-15; see also Kao I-han, *Chung-kuo nei-ko chih-tu chih yen-ke* (The evolution of the cabinet system in China), Shanghai, 1926; Li Chün, *Chung-kuo tsai-hsiang chih-tu* (The institution of premiership in China), Shanghai, 1947, Chap. III.

[11] Ch'en, *op cit.*, pp. 166-167.

effective standing army, divided into 600 units, one third stationed in the environs of the capital and the remainder scattered throughout the Empire at strategic and frontier points. The interference of military officers in local affairs was strictly forbidden. The army was under the jealous control of the central government. About the middle of the dynasty the talented but

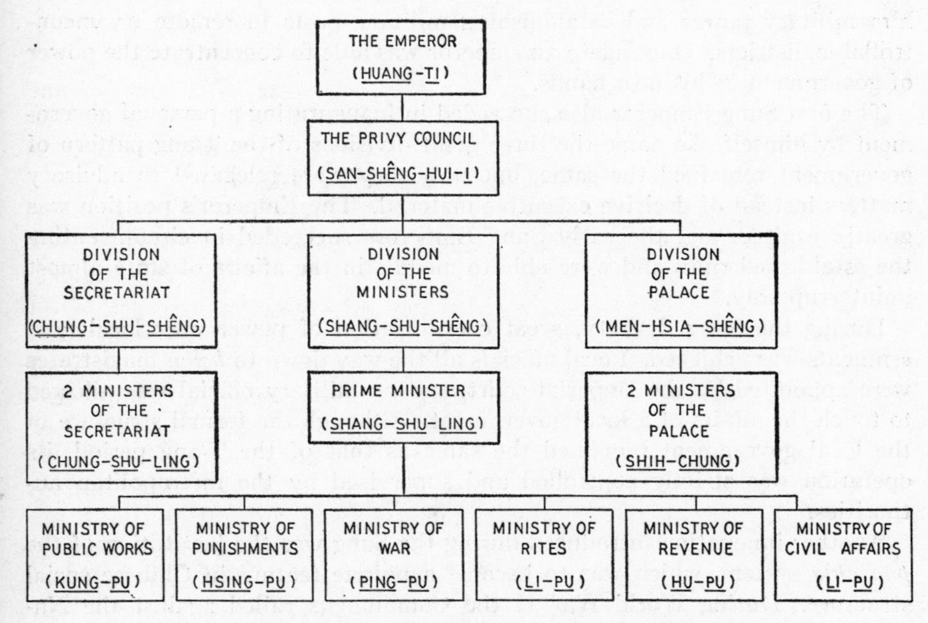

CHART 1—Policy-making Organization Under the T'ang Dynasty

ill-starred traitor, An Lu-shan, launched a rebellion of such terrifying proportions that the complete military collapse of the T'ang seemed only a matter of time. Although he suffered violent death at the hands of his own son in 757, his disorder triggered an endless succession of further rebellions. The army was being influenced more and more by the palace eunuchs. Local military commanders became so independent as to arrogate to themselves the authority of civil administration in their particular localities. No dynasty could survive such conditions long. The glorious T'ang, having set a high watermark for one very special kind of civilian, secular, beautiful, and creative civilization, collapsed in whining confusion and raving turmoil.

Monarchy in China, Sung to Ch'ing.[12] The weakness of the later part

[12] The best source materials on the history of Chinese political institutions are to be found in the *Chih-kuan chih* (Treatise of offices) in the various dynastic histories. Most of these histories were compiled by Imperial order. Since T'ang there was the tradition of compiling the history of the preceding dynasty officially by its successor. Other sources are Chi Yün *et al.*, *Li-tai chih-kuan piao* (Tables on offices in the various dynasties) and *Chiu-t'ung* (Nine complete works). Among the useful general works in Western languages are H. Cordier, *Histoire générale de la chine,* 4 Vols., Paris, 1920-21; L. C. Goodrich, *A Short*

of the T'ang dynasty was demonstrated by the independence of local military commands. These reduced the central power to a minimum. The first Emperor of the Sung dynasty (A.D. 960-1279) was a military leader himself; he realized from his own experience that the existence of autonomous military commands was a standing threat to the Empire. By a clever psychological maneuver he succeeded in persuading his generals to surrender to him military power and in abolishing military posts in remote or uncontrollable districts. Once again an emperor was able to concentrate the power of government in his own hands.

The first Sung Emperor also succeeded in inaugurating a personal government by himself. In name the three great divisions of the T'ang pattern of government remained the same, but now they were relegated to advisory matters instead of decisive executive material. The Emperor's position was greatly exalted, and the early Sung Emperors succeeded in circumventing the established rules and were able to meddle in the affairs of state almost uninterruptedly.

During the Sung dynasty, great concentration of power over local governments was achieved. Local officials all the way down to *hsien* magistrates were appointed by the Imperial court, and no military official was allowed to touch the affairs of a local government. Although the formal structure of the local government remained the same as that of the T'ang period, its operation was strictly controlled and supervised by the metropolitan authorities.

Another innovation introduced during the Sung was the institution of the *pao chia* system, which was to become a unique feature in Chinese social structure. During World War II the Communists railed against the Nationalists for allegedly reconstituting the old *pao chia* as a reactionary measure; when the Communists came to power they instituted, under still another name, a much more onerous one. (See page 232.)

Under the original Sung arrangements every group of ten families formed a *pao,* every fifty families formed a "great *pao,*" and every five-hundred families a "head *pao.*" The headmen of the *pao chia* organization were trained by regular army officers. Each family with more than one male member sent an adult male to serve in the system, which became a collective responsibility device and a local defense unit as well.[13]

Despite the tremendous concentration of power by the Sung and the practice of personal absolutism by the Sung emperors, the dynasty gradually lost its vigor. Weak emperors succeeded one another. In 1127 the house of Sung was forced to move its capital to the city now called Hangchow under pressure of the Golden Tartars. The rise of Mongol power inundated both the

---

History of the Chinese People, New York, 1943; and K. S. Latourette, *The Chinese, Their History and Culture,* New York, 1949.

[13] The earliest evidence of the Japanese counterpart *(tonarigumi)* is summarized on pp. 269-270; see especially fn. 15.

Tartars and the native Sung dynasty. By 1279 China was under Mongol control.

In modern terms the immense power of the Mongols and their swift fall can be explained to Western laymen by saying that for some purposes Mongol authority was never more than "consolidation government" in the technical military sense of that term at its best. Before their conquest of China the Mongols lived by hunting and the tending of herds. They were organized under tribal systems. They possessed hardihood, intelligence, and mobility; and they had the capacity to outrange the most advanced military technology of their rivals. When the Mongol rulers came to China, they found that the Chinese political system offered them more power and greater stability than did their own. The Mongol rulers themselves turned to Chinese civilization as being more inviting, more secure, and more luxurious than their own. Characteristic Mongol procedures, such as the election of the ruler at a mass meeting of magnates, were superseded in favor of hereditary monarchy on the Chinese pattern. The Mongols became Chinese for some purposes and remained Mongols for others. They never became Chinese enough for their Mongolian origin to be forgotten; they did not stay Mongol enough to overawe China with their exterior resources of military power held in reserve. Their dynasty, called Yüan in Chinese, was short-lived (A.D. 1279-1368).

In the sphere of central administration the Mongols further modified the Chinese system by increasing the centralization of power in the hands of a single official. The three-division system employed by the T'ang and Sung dynasties was abolished. All executive functions were vested in a Central Secretariat (*Chung-shu-shêng*) which had control over governmental affairs and public officials. The position of Grand Secretary (*Chung-shu-ling*) was usually held by the heir designate; he in turn was assisted by two separate prime ministers, the Prime Minister of the Left and the Prime Minister of the Right. A number of assistants in the Secretariat attended to the routine administrative requirements of government. Besides the Grand Secretary there was a Privy Council (*Shu-mi-yüan*) which was responsible for military and strategic affairs of the state, and a Censorate (*Yü-shih-t'ai*) which exercised supervisory functions over government officials. Chief Mongol innovation in the field of local administration was the *shêng* or province. Some of these provinces, appreciatively called countries by Marco Polo, survive with their Mongol outlines as Communist provinces at the present time. The provincial system as a whole was retained in modern times by the Nationalists contrary to the wishes of Sun Yat-sen. From the Nationalists it has been continued with modifications by the Communists. The original Mongol stamp is still quite clear. Since the Mongols were the conquerors of an alien population they were obsessed by the idea of revolt and did everything possible to create safeguards against rebellion. One such safeguard was the enforcement of a rigid scheme of local government, the most complicated China had ever seen. Counting the province and going downward, there were five different grades of local government: the *shêng* (province), the *lu* (region), the *fu* (circuit), the *chou* (prefecture), and the *hsien* (district or county).

At the inauguration of the Yüan dynasty the Chinese portion of the Mongol Empire was divided into eleven provinces. All high government officials were non-Chinese—Mongols, Arabs, Central Asians, and even the Italians of the Polo family—assisted in each case by Chinese employees. A local militia system was set up similar to the *pao chia* of the Sung. Under this system five families constituted a *lin,* five *lin* made a *pao.* Within a *pao* or a *lin* everyone was responsible for the action of everyone else and, if any rebellion or conspiracy occurred, all members of the group were punished for the misdeeds of the one.

The Mongols haughtily enforced racial distinction measures against the Chinese. The conquered natives were forbidden to keep arms. The streets of Peking were broadened and laid out in a rectangular design for the same reason that Major Pierre l'Enfant designed the streets in Washington, D.C.: if the local populace became unruly, artillery batteries could blow them out of the main streets and cavalry charges could bottle them up block by block for subjugation or massacre. Mongol garrisons were stationed in strategic points throughout the country. Racial discriminations were applied against persons of Chinese race and language, persecution was frequent, and indignities common. The Mongol campaigns against Japan (see pages 306-307), Java, and Burma drew heavily on China for support; and the Mongols, who tore the soul and hope out of medieval Muscovy, were unable to remain in China for a full century. A rebel leader, an ex-priest, lascivious and audacious beyond all belief, exploited the people's resentment against foreign domination and won a quick victory in an amazingly short period of time.

This man, the founder of the Ming dynasty (A.D. 1368-1644) was ruthless in temperament and powerful by sheer personal capacity. He ruled with a strong hand and crushed his political opponents mercilessly. Having a high opinion of himself he lifted the idea of absolute monarchy to its fullest extent, almost reaching the solipsist paranoid lunacy of that Khmer Emperor who discovered his own inward emotions—*le moi-subtil,* as the French archaeologists so neatly translated—to be the guiding principle of the universe, and who embodied his crazy daydreams in immortally beautiful, gigantic works of consummate architectural art. The Ming founder did not leave palaces or monuments behind, but he did leave titles. The Emperor himself became the decisive force in Chinese politics. In no other time in China's history had the personal aptitude of a single person played so dominant a role in the affairs of the Chinese world.

The central administrative system of the Ming dynasty differed radically from the systems of its predecessors. The executive function was concentrated in the Emperor's own hands. He was assisted by six Grand Secretaries who individually served the sovereign as advisers. They also served as the heads of the six ministries and were responsible for administrative matters of the government.

The censorial system reached its maturity under the Ming. The Board of Censors (*Tu-ch'a-yüan*) was endowed with substantial powers of impeachment and supervision. The censorate became an instrument of monarchial control as well as a guarantee of clean, effective administration.

Under the Ming the *pa ku* or "eight-legged essay" was introduced as the sole subject for all civil service examinations. Rigid and elegant in form and hypnotically difficult to master, the eight-legged essay was such—so hoped the Ming emperors—that the talented men of China would waste their time and energy in an elegant, but useless, accomplishment, and would thus be unable to allow themselves the luxuries of independent thought and rebellious activity. The examination rules also became more rigid and elaborate and the merit system as a whole gained more prestige and prominence under the Ming than it had ever enjoyed before.

The Ming devised a system of three tiers to handle their local administration. During most of the period, the country was divided into fifteen *shêng* (provinces) largely taken over from the Mongols. These *shêng* were further subdivided into nearly 300 prefectures and these again into 1,171 districts.

Provincial government was collegial in form: boards, not individuals, ran each province. Executive, judicial, and financial matters in each province were handled by three separate Imperial appointees. Each was independent of the other, but a decision, to be binding, had to be reached by all three. Under the collegially governed provinces the prefectures and districts each had a single responsible head who was an Imperial appointee and was allowed a specified number of assistants.

The Ming dynasty provides what can probably be described as China's most perfect instance of an absolute monarchy along Ottoman or French lines. The system insured a certain amount of security and prosperity when the monarch himself happened to be a strong personality, but it became a wretched system indeed when the control of the whole Chinese system fell into the hands of a weakling. The later Ming emperors made use of their power to satisfy their personal whims—extraordinary whims they were, too—rather than to carry out the rigorous duties which should be expected of a conscientious monarch. The Ming house collapsed amid charges of venality, which for sheer grandeur have exceeded anything known in Italian or American politics. The Imperial family had become rotten. The system itself was so close to being reasonably good that it was adopted by China's last monarchial house with only minor changes. This house was a foreign one, the Manchu or Ch'ing dynasty which came to power in 1644 and fell in 1912. The last Ch'ing monarch is a Soviet state prisoner somewhere in Siberia. Since the Ch'ing was the immediate precursor of the modern republican and Communist governments, it is worth extended consideration in its own right (see Chapter 3).

Before moving on, it is well to recapitulate the political evolution of Old China. Perhaps most important in this evolution is the obvious age of China, in terms of continuity in way of life and antiquity of political institutions. The Chinese cosmogony, stripped of superstition, reveals a secular attitude, rather than deep, unchanging religious beliefs which might affect everyday behavior and political development. Very early China produced a sophisticated sense of monarchy; by the Chou period, China had also developed a right of rebellion. Like other great cultures, the Chinese early passed through its own peculiar experiênces with feudalism, nation-states, and unification by blood-and-iron. Specific political ideologies and institutions began to emerge at the time of Han and were more fully articulated during the dynasties of Sui and T'ang. Most remarkable was the development of a civil service, a true bureaucracy, which will bear further examination. Central organization was matched by systems of local government. There followed further development and refinement of monarchy in the great Sung, Yüan, and Ming dynasties.

Before turning to a discussion of China's last dynasty, the Ch'ing, it is therefore necessary to include some discussion of the Chinese society underneath the various systems of monarchy which made the structure so little and the personality so much when matters of high decision were involved.

CHAPTER TWO

The Chinese Society Beneath the Confucian State

FROM the point of view of the modern student of politics, the most important feature about old China lay not in the particular structure of the political system—neither in the way laws were made nor in what they contained—but in the relationship of the political system as a whole to the rest of the society.

Within the framework of the Confucian ideology Chinese social life as a whole acquired a momentum which, in some respects, was more persistent than any known in a comparable Western state. Even in those periods of Western history in which governmental functions were reduced to an apparent minimum, government played a greater part in everyday life than did its equivalent in China.

Empire or Pseudomorph. One of the authors of this book raised the serious doubt some fifteen years ago that the processes called "government" in the West and "government" in China were similar in more than name. Certainly many of the difficulties between the Ch'ing dynasty and the Western states arose from fundamentally incompatible assumptions concerning the relationship of government to the rest of society.

The statement made fifteen years ago still holds:

> Government in China was an auxiliary activity, the reserve power of a hierarchy given to the pursuit of different ends. The officials were teachers first and magistrates afterward; the emperor was a supreme model first and a ruler afterward; the people were shamed, and punished only when they were shameless. Such was the ideal theory upon which the Chinese built their world society. The facts were rarely as bright as they might have hoped; the reserve power never disappeared. . .
>
> As a state, as an all-embracing control institution, the old Chinese

hierarchy was a pseudomorph—it looked like a state but was not really one.[1]

The Traditional Society. Chinese society can be characterized with several safe generalizations. It can be described as continuous in many respects from the beginning of the Han dynasty 202 B.C. to the end of the Ch'ing A.D. 1912. In its economy it was predominantly agrarian. In its class structure it was what has been called a "gentry state," the social and psychological equivalent of an agriculturally based bourgeois, but not the economic equivalent of the modern middle class state. Strategically China consisted of several major plains and a vast amount of mountain country in which individual communities lived not far above a level of autarchy.

In social organization Chinese society was rich in the tightness and comprehensiveness of its extra-political facilities. In demographic terms the Chinese population was characterized by a high birth rate and a high death rate, a state of affairs which David Riesman has correctly, although sweepingly, described as inclining a group toward a traditionalist culture. It should be noted that, although the birth rate was high, previous to Ch'ing dynasty times the mortality rate too remained high. Thus it was not until Ch'ing times that the population of China grew to such vast proportions.

Intellectually, the Confucian ideology which gained ascendancy in the Han dynasty constituted the undisputed foundation of Chinese political thinking. Educationally, the gentry class was a ruling class of scholars. By tradition and by processes of intellectual and governmental discipline, this class more than any other sustained the tradition and the moral code of the scholastic empire and maintained the reservoir of personnel for the official

[1] Paul M. A. Linebarger, *Government in Republican China,* New York, 1938, pp. 19-21. Professor Linebarger continued: "The necessity for government did not always proceed from the frailties of the governed. The Confucian system, although worthy of its great esteem, was marked by the difficulties which attend all human organization. Corruption and tyranny appeared, and were not by any means negligible. In many cases it may be supposed that a system of laws would have provided redress for persons treated arbitrarily or unjustly; but if one is to judge by experience in the West, even law brings with it other types of injustice peculiar to itself. In China some of the most benevolent and effective emperors advocated at times a government of rules and not of men, in order to check the caprice and the oppression of officials; yet the role of law in China, in contrast to the part it has played in the West, remained slight. The West affords instances of effective political work outside legal systems, while the Chinese have produced law codes of considerable breadth and significance. Nevertheless, the power of Chinese government aside from law is just as clear as the Western development of government within law.

"The old Chinese system was based upon control through ideas, control exercised through the maintenance of clear notions of right and wrong, as founded in certain well-established common-sense traditions. The world of fact and the world of right and wrong were bound together, and the whole ideology was one of general and all-pervasive order. While the Western impact was felt cumulatively through the nineteenth century, the Chinese world of fact went down into the limbo of myth in a disestablished few generations, and with it went the compulsion which Confucian common sense had exerted. The consequent development of new ways of acting, which had nothing to do with traditional control, upset the entire scheme. When the system of ideological guidance began breaking down, there was a stampede to get away from it. Men no longer trusted it, no longer trusted the tameness of their neighbors. A new wildness, a savagery armed with science, had come with the aliens from beyond the seas. It was the old hierarchy to which men turned, calling it *the state.*"

hierarchy. Economically, local self-government was to a high degree the rule. At its best such self-government was relatively democratic, operating through guilds and family systems. The stability of the almost endless succession of small communities accounted for the relative security and efficiency of local affairs in China.

Seen in contrast with other cultures, the localization and stability of Chinese life cost an immense price in economic opportunity and in keen, legally sophisticated justice. Artistically and literarily, Chinese culture was a forced growth within the limits of the Confucian tradition, as we shall see.

For better or for worse, this society, which can be tagged "old China," is the largest social and political organization the human race has ever brought forth. Several billion human beings lived and died within its confines. If the benefits and faults of this society are contrasted with those smaller and more tumultuous civilizations which coexisted with it in the Middle East and in the European world, it can be said that Chinese life never reached the aesthetic productivity of an Athens, the spiritual force and élan of early Islam or of Gothic Catholicism, never obtained the self-destroying capacity for stupendous growth which developed in the economic and technological system of early modern Western Europe. Chinese life over the centuries averages out as the most civilized to exist anywhere in the two millenniums since Christ. China offered a rich and elegant continuity and security. Chinese life delivered immense humaneness and great rewards within the limits of safety. But China never departed enough from normality and decency to enjoy the shocking but creative extremes so often found in the Persian, Arab, and Christian worlds.

The apparent capacity of Chinese society to rejuvenate itself and to keep on going appeared limitless. Some sort of a Chinese crisis would probably be occurring in Chinese society today even had the Western World not invaded the Far East militarily, religiously. technologically, and economically; but it is by no means certain that this crisis would have reached the depths or the seriousness of the present Chinese revolution, whether in its Nationalist or Communist phase. The old China which we know was weary, corrupt, but it was not dead or dying until Christianity, gun boats, machine production, and mass transportation upset the economic and technological universe of the Chinese. The China we know is a China suffering gigantic trauma from clash of cultures, our Western culture as against old Chinese culture, which started a hundred years ago; the wounding, the goading, the stimulating, and the changing processes of this clash are not yet at an end.

The Confucian Ideology.[2] Although the political and ethical system

[2] For discussions on Confucian ideology, the following works in English are outstanding: J. K. Shryock, *The Origin and Development of the State Cult of Confucius,* New York, 1932; Lin Mou-sheng, *Men and Ideas, An Informal History of Chinese Political Thought,* New York, 1942; H. G. Creel, *Confucius, the Man and the Myth,* New York, 1949; Hu Shih, "The Establishment of Confucianism as a State Religion during the Han Dynasty," *Journal of the North China Branch of the Royal Asiatic Society,* 1929, pp. 20-41. Among

of Confucius (traditionally dated 551-479 B.C.) was the fundamental dogma of Chinese politics from the middle of the former Han dynasty to the end of the nineteenth century, Confucianism at its inception had rivals in the pre-Ch'in era. At the time Confucianism began, there were various schools of Chinese thought: the Astrologers, the Taoists, the Logicians, the Legalists, the Mohists, and others, each as prominent as Confucianism in those brilliant but turbulent days of the fighting *kuo*. Confucianism was somewhat more lucky than the others in surviving the book burning undertaken by the First Emperor. The person most responsible for making Confucianism into a state philosophy, therewith letting other schools of thought lapse into oblivion, was Tung Chung-shu (179-104 B.C.), who was the Chief Minister of the great Military Emperor, Wu Ti, of the former Han dynasty. In the teachings of Confucianism, Tung found ideas which could be exploited for the support of monarchy and legitimacy. He was the founder of the system whereby only Confucianists were accredited scholars and thus permitted to join the government bureaucracy. His performance went a long way toward establishing the scholastic state which was to prevail for two thousand years.

What attracted the Han monarchists to Confucian teaching was Confucius' doctrine of the stratification of people into different social classes; his tolerance of just enough mobility to keep those classes stable, and the indoctrination of role-consciousness were probably strong compelling forces. Under this system the obedience and contentment of the people were deemed supreme moral virtues. Confucian ethics did not regard man as an isolated individual or permit him unprescribed freedom in the pursuance of private interests, but required him to fulfill his manifold social obligations in a manner peculiar and appropriate to his own social status.

The Confucian conception of the relationship between the individual and society was defined essentially in terms of duties rather than of rights. The doctrine of the inalienable rights of the people was not to be found in the Confucian tradition. The Confucian code instead stressed the theory of the inalienable duties of the people and the rightfulness of government by an intellectual and moral elite. The code underscored the idea of the moral duties of the individual toward society promising that, when each man fulfilled his duty toward himself, his family, the state, and the world, a Great Harmony would prevail, radiating cultural glory and insuring peace. Hence, the end of human existence was neither the fulfillment of individual life nor the glory of the state; it was the maintenance of a special, prescribed kind of civilization.

The Confucian ideal of good government put great emphasis on the per-

---

Chinese books the following are important: Fung Yu-lan, *Chung-kuo che-hsüeh shih* (this book has been translated by Derk Bodde into English under the title *A History of Chinese Philosophy,* Princeton, Vol. I, 1939; Vol. II, 1953); Tao Hsi-shêng, *Chung-kuo chêng-chih ssŭ-hsiang shih* (A history of Chinese political thought), 4 Vols., Chungking, 1942; Hsiao Kung-ch'üan, *Chung-kuo chêng-chih ssŭ-hsiang shih* (A history of Chinese philosophy), Shanghai, 1945-46.

sonal character of the ruler rather than on the legal system on which the structure of government was built. Law and order were supposed to be enforced not by external compulsion but by inner discipline. In order to achieve good government it was necessary for the ruling class to lead an exemplary life for the common people to follow. The standard of *chün-tzŭ* was set up for the entire scholar-gentry class. They should represent the highest type of morally integrated individuals upon whom both political and social responsibilities were to fall.

Confucian government was therefore authoritarian. It emphasized social status. It disregarded individual rights. It inculcated belief in moral control. All these fitted perfectly with the monarchical system which successive Chinese ruling families endeavored to build and to appropriate. Hence, it was not without reason that Confucian concepts, almost to the exclusion of the philosophies of other schools, should have dominated Chinese political theory for more than twenty centuries.[3]

Confucianism dominated the political scene, in theory; actually, even the Confucian tradition was greatly influenced by the notions of other schools of thought. Ideally, according to the Confucian tradition, government remained in reserve; practically, it became a fine mixture of administrative machinery affected by Legalist theory. A fixed body of Law, impartially administered, does not fluctuate as does the character of princes, according to Legalist thought.

The Scholar-Gentry Tradition.[4] From the former Han dynasty onward, the Confucian classics were made the cornerstone of Chinese scholarship and bureaucracy. They became the key to officialdom. Since only Confucianists were admitted as scholars, therewith obtaining civil service appointments, first by the process of recommendation and later by systems of examinations, Confucian literati monopolized statecraft and administration. Their economic and political capacities became the dominant factor in the political side of Chinese culture. The Confucian theory of social stratification comprised the foundation of Chinese bureaucracy. The stratification was carried to an extreme by Confucius' disciple, Mencius, who divided the people into two categories, the ruling and the ruled. Mencius said, "Some labor with their minds and some labor with their physical strength. Those who labor with their minds govern others. Those who labor with their strength are governed by others. Those who are governed by others support the governing few, and those who govern others are supported

[3] Nor is it any surprise to find, early in Japan's history, an intrusion of Confucian concepts (see Chap. 11, pp. 275-276, "The Confucian Concepts in Japan") indeed centuries later in Tokugawa Japan, hierarchical concepts of Neo-Confucianism, fitted perfectly the shogunal usurpation (Chap. 13, pp. 312-315, "Tokugawa Neo-Confucianism").

[4] For the development of the scholar-gentry tradition, see S. W. Williams, *The Middle Kingdom, a Survey of the Geography, Government, Literature, Social Life, Arts and History of the Chinese Empire*, 2 Vols., London, 1883, Vol. I, Chap. 8; Latourette, *op. cit.*, Vol. II, Chap. 17; Chêng Ho-shêng, *Chung-kuo chin-shih shih* (History of modern China), Chungking, 1945, Chap. 14; Ch'en Kung-lu, *Chung-kuo chin-tai shih* (History of modern China), Shanghai, 1935, Chap. 15.

by the governed many." According to the Confucian dictum, the ruling class should be composed of a small number of scholars who, by virtue of talent and training, constitute the cream of society. They should distinguish themselves from the common herd by their superior knowledge and their exemplary conduct. Assuming positions as the arbiters of morals and the administers of justice, they should not be punished or humiliated by virtue of measures which could be applied only to the common people.

Thus old China, existing in a balanced equilibrium and (relative to its various contemporaneous societies) a placid quietude, was strictly molded on the Confucian pattern. At the top of the social scale the scholar-gentry class enjoyed the products of the work of the toiling many. This class developed a way of life that was artistic and sophisticated, yet in many ways unrealistic and unproductive. Chinese cilivization in its grand tradition was proudly adorned by many exquisite and superb works of literary, graphic, and plastic art, but the culture was in the main static, lacking the creative spirit and dynamic force of the pre-Han periods. The common peasants existed. They scarcely lived in the modern sense of the term. The happiness of the peasants at their low economic level can be taken as a political punishment or an economic crime, depending upon the point of view of the modern beholder. In either case, poverty and happiness have both been taken for granted by the peasants in China for the past fifty generations. They accepted their low level of income; they tolerated what looks like oppression to us; they were sustained by a fatalistic philosophy.

The recruitment of the ruling class was mainly through the system of civil service examinations. This system had, of course, its weaknesses. From the period of the Sui dynasty through Sung to the decadence of Ch'ing, some candidates cheated, bribed the readers, or even, as sons of high officials, took easier tests. During the decline of the Ch'ing, lower offices were sold by the government. Yet, even in the worst periods, only a minority obtained status fraudulently. Only by years of painful study plus a pretty good margin of luck could a scholar expect to pass these examinations. Once a man passed the examination of the first grade he acquired the educational equivalent of our college degrees, the social standing of a member of the ruling class, and the honor and privileges of a literatus in the legal and administrative setup. When fortunate enough to be appointed to official position he became a member of the implicit brotherhood of the "wearers of the official girdle," attainment of which was the dream and aspiration of every school boy in China.

Appointed officials in old China knew one another or knew about one another somewhat after the fashion that West Pointers and Annapolis men keep track of each other in our society. The names and standings of all officials were listed in the periodic publications, *Chin-shen ch'üan-shu* (The complete record of the girdle wearers). It was a great honor to have one's name listed in that book. Once within the charmed circle of officialdom, the normal incumbent concentrated his attention on climbing the ladder of bureaucracy. Taken at large, the scholar bureaucrats formed a body of men mutually inclined to protect one another and attempted to regard the common people as a source of profit rather than a trust. Yet certain rules of conduct were necessary to imbue the officials with some sense of balance and character; otherwise their immoderateness and greed might have jeopardized the security of the reigning family.

Below the rank of regularly appointed officials there were a large number of hangers-on around each *yamen,* which can be roughly translated as "county courthouse." *Yamen* runners performed the functions of police, local interpreters, administrative and judicial collectors, and court attendants. Not actual members of the officialdom, these marginal public servants were also inadequately paid by government and had to extort a decent living, when they could obtain it, by milking the population. The ordinary peasants and workers suffered more from the oppression of these subordinates, if oppression is measured by the amount of irritation involved, than from the regularized oppression of their superiors.

Unsuccessful civil service candidates turned themselves into village teachers or into personal secretaries of officials, since persons who had once studied the Confucian classics considered it beneath their dignity to pursue occupations such as commerce, artisanship, or manual labor. These unsuccessful scholars were poorly paid for their work, but they were unwilling to relinquish their pretensions of being members of the scholar-gentry class.

Many modern Chinese, quite apart from whether they are Nationalists or Communists in outlook, believe that the construction of the scholar-gentry class robbed Chinese society of its richest talents by diverting promising and energetic people from the pursuance of useful occupations. Abstention from manual labor became the conventional mark of social distinction, an index of respectability and an evidence of superior achievement. Consequently the talents of the Chinese were drawn almost completely to the relatively nonproductive occupations of learning the classics and administering the *status quo.*

Labor for Rice and Study for Office. Under monarchical rule the vast majority of the Chinese therefore concentrated their efforts upon one of the two strenuous pursuits, "labor for rice or study for office." Out of countless millions only a few thousands were lucky enough to get official position. According to the 1812 edition of *Ta-Ch'ing hui-tien* (The collected institutes of the great Ch'ing),[5] the government of China comprised 8 viceroys, 15 governors, 19 finance commissioners, 18 judicial commissioners, 82 circuit intendants, 182 prefects, 1,836 sub-prefects, 178 canton officials, and 1,293 district magistrates. At the most there were an equal number of metropoli-

[5] *Ta-Ch'ing hui-tien* was the nearest approach to written constitutional law as the term is understood in the West. It defined political organizations and their functions and described ceremonial rites and political regulations. It was published in six editions, the first in 1690 and the last in 1908.

tan officials at the court in Peking. The number of public functionaries, therefore, was extraordinarily small—by modern standards grossly inadequate—for the administration of so vast a territory and so enormous a population.

Inevitably the greater part of everyday Chinese affairs could not be conducted by the government, but was handled by a variety of institutions such as clans, village associations, and guilds. The clan was formed by a group of families with a common ancestry and a common surname. The eldership of the clan was assumed by the most senior and therefore the most respected person of the clan. In title and very often in fact he had full control over his clansmen. The division of the people into clans was more marked in the southern provinces than in the north. In the south it was not uncommon for clans to dominate whole communities and even to engage on occasions in private wars with one another. When a clan member committed a serious crime the elder of the clan was empowered to punish him, even to the extent of the death penalty. Only when the clan did not punish did the government intervene, not to punish the individual, but to punish the clan for having failed to carry out its disciplinary duties. In the north the clan was comparatively more loosely organized; its functions lay more in the direction of commemorating ancestors and maintaining a common reserve fund for the relief of clan members. The clan system was a product of a loosely governed society where legal protection for the individual was virtually unobtainable. Clan organization was therefore both juridically and economically inevitable.

Next to the clan in importance was the village association. Each *hsien* comprised a number of villages, most commonly twenty or thirty, and was ruled by a magistrate appointed by the central government. The magistrate had functions of overseership far above the level of workaday life. In modern eyes his role is reminiscent of the tasks assumed by British district commissioners in nineteenth-century India or by Colonial officials in Central Africa at the present time, wherein a single European takes on economic, legal, political, and moral responsibilities for thousands of natives scattered across a substantial reach of territory. *Hsien* reached down far, but not far enough to *govern* everyday life. Hence, the villages had to be self-governing and the kind of government which emerged in each village reflected the temperaments and capacities of the inhabitants as well as the balances of personalities and groups within the village. Some were just, some despotic. Some villages came close to a democracy of the New England town meeting kind, while others were as brutally oppressed as the worst of the slave plantations in the early West Indies. As long as they did not make trouble or call attention to themselves, the government looked at them little and cared about them less.

Most commonly the village was a local self-contained and self-governed unit headed by a village elder who was chosen in an informal election by the principal persons in the community. Whereas (by prescriptions of law) the district magistrate was also an outsider, the village elder was a local man holding office during good behavior and receiving whatever remuneration his fellow villagers could and would give him. The main duties of the village elder consisted of supervising public order, overseeing the general welfare, and acting as a liaison between the villagers and the representatives of the *hsien*. Since he was not officially appointed by the government there was no force of law behind his authority; nevertheless, his orders were generally observed and his decisions enforced.

Law was expensive, remote, and hazardous: within the village litigation was to a large degree replaced by arbitration and compromise. When disputes of a minor character arose between villagers, the village elder would conduct a public hearing in the village tea house. Often the onlookers served as a sort of *ad hoc* and informal jury to decide the case. The losing party was obliged to pay whatever compensation or fine the elder might impose on him and was also expected to stand treat for the refreshments of everyone in the tea house at the time of the hearing. Since the *yamen* bailiffs were petty tyrants, it was only natural for the common people to avoid suits at law if they possibly could, and the tea house arrangement provided a convenient means to that end. At least nine village disputes out of ten were settled in this way. Now and then the village elder himself could be dishonest, extortionate, or cruel, but the very informality of his position made him vulnerable to conspiracies against him. Village self-government tended to be reasonable and mildly democratic in tone simply because it depended on a degree of popular assent; otherwise, its decisions had no force.

Guilds. The *hui* were self-governing units in cities playing the role which villagers did in rural areas. Often translated by the English term "guild," the *hui* was actually a more comprehensive and varied kind of organization. Three preponderant kinds of *hui* were the professional guilds, the native guilds, and the secret sects. Professional guilds were based on occupational lines and can be further subdivided into craft guilds and merchant guilds. As a rule, each was organized to maintain a monopoly over its specific trade or profession, to prevent competition, to determine prices and wages, and to fix a standard of quality for work or wares. Furthermore, they established private courts of their own to settle disputes among members, imposing fines when necessary. They also established trust funds to take care of unemployment, illness, burial funds, or other extraordinary needs of their members. Each guild had a patron saint often drawn from Buddhist or Taoist theology, very frequently a prominent figure in local legend, preferably some personage possessing a vague connection with a profession. The patron saint of the theatrical guild, for instance, was Emperor Hsüan Tsung of the T'ang because of his love for theatrical performances. Associated with the guild system was an apprentice system through which young learners indentured themselves to a master craftsman for a certain number of years without pay.

Upon fulfillment of the required service and accomplishment of the expected skills the apprentice became a full-fledged member of the regular guild.

The *hui-kuan* or "native guilds" were a symbol of real social, cultural, and economic regionalism in China. Strangers in a given place banded together for protection against the natives, particularly against local, rapacious officials. In this way, too, people manifested their sentimental attachment to the old home town with which the family, by tradition, identified itself. Those who moved off the countryside set up clubs based upon home localities; these afforded companionship, solace, protection, and economic opportunities. To this day clubs of this kind are important in such non-Communist Chinese cities as Hongkong, Singapore, and San Francisco. Native guilds were found in Peking and in all the provincial capitals, as well as in most of the big trading cities. In Peking in the nineteenth century almost every province had a *hui-kuan*. Many of the larger and more prosperous districts had their own *hui-kuan*. The club houses of the *hui-kuan* were erected at the expense of prosperous persons from the particular locality who resided in the city in which the guild was located. It is as though all the former residents of Sunbury, Pennsylvania, who moved to Washington, D.C., clung together for loyalty and fellowship and managed to build a structure comparable in size, cost, and function with the usual Masonic Shrine or Odd Fellows Hall. In Ch'ing China the most imposing buildings in each provincial capital next to the governor's fortified palace and the examination halls were the native guild buildings. Some *hui-kuan* buildings were adorned with beautiful gardens. Each *hui-kuan* provided free lodging for traveling or visiting members of the native community; often such visitors were candidates for the metropolitan or provincial examinations. Sometimes, if things went poorly with them, they would drop in "for a little while" to await a governmental appointment and would end up waiting months or years. The *hui-kuan* obviously had to provide traveling expenses for stranded fellow natives as well as coffin space for those who died away from home. In old China native loyalties to the place of origin were so high that important dignitaries and prosperous businessmen were virtually compelled to help their fellow natives either by placing them in minor administrative positions or by lending them money to tide them over their difficulties; the native guilds were therefore only one among several socially required modes of expressing sentimental attachment to one's native area.

Secret Societies. Secret societies have been prevalent in China throughout Chinese history; they flourished particularly in the Ch'ing period, finally covering the entire length and width of the empire. Cloaked under the robe of religious and fraternal interests, secret societies challenged the authority of the government whenever opportune occasions arose. They were the forerunners of the political parties which existed in Republican China (1912-1928), since most of them originated as revolutionary institutions dedicated to the overthrow of oppressive governments in the nineteenth-century Manchu rule. The secret societies suffered constant persecutions, were denied able leadership by the scholastic bureaucracy which tempted and recruited men of intellectual capacity, and were considered outcasts by polite society: it was thus easy for them to degenerate into gangs of desperadoes and evildoers. The secret societies had strict regulations for their own members and were in a position to inflict drastic and terrifying punishment on individual members who dared to defy the regulations. Within gangdom, generosity toward fellow members was a cardinal rule. Outside the limits of the secret society, almost anything was legitimate loot. Under the Ch'ing such societies as the Elders, the Triads, the Little Daggers, the Lotus, and the Righteous Harmony Fists (named "Boxers" by Westerners) were common among the people. These organizations flourished despite cruel suppressive measures directed against them by the authorities.[6]

The composite effect of high ideological control by a deliberately nurtured tradition, *laissez-faire* in politics, and nonpolitical administration by family, village, and *hui,* was to reduce the functions of formal government below any known Western minimum. Thus there was fulfilled the ancient Chinese teaching that the people were best governed when they were least governed. The official government supported such irreducible services as collection of taxes, over-all maintenance of public order, provision of courts for some litigation, and defense of the frontiers. Even in these minimal services the Imperial authorities relied heavily upon local guilds and villages for their cooperation and assistance. Most protection, welfare, and insurance services were performed by villages or guilds. Loosely organized and independent of law, these organizations could not be destroyed by formal decrees nor erased by a change in political leadership. The fact that they were for the greater part popularly supported made them a redeeming feature in a society governed by a political system which was *pro forma* autocratic.

The Economy of Old China. China's pre-modern economy had been extraordinarily self-sufficient prior to the period of the Western impact. Although various portions of the country were frequently ravaged by famines, pestilence, or insurrection, China as a whole had never depended upon foreign imports for existence, even for sustenance of a single economic function. There was no foreign trade, as such, only tribute payments and gifts in return from the Emperor. In terms of food and clothing the Chinese had been reasonably successful in solving their own economic problems. The Imperial government left the people alone, and the people, thrifty, hardheaded, patient, took reasonably good care of themselves. The government controlled the coinage of currency, the operation of public granaries, and the monopolies of salt and iron. Aside from these the populace was left to itself

[6] For more detailed descriptions of the traditional Chinese society, see P. M. A. Linebarger, *Government in Republican China,* Chap. 6; A. H Smith, *Village Life in China,* New York, 1899; J. S. Burgess, *The Guilds of Peking,* New York, 1928; H. B. Morse, *The Gilds of China,* London, 1909; M. C. Yang, *A Chinese Village,* New York, 1945.

in pursuing most economic activities. Regulations and interference, when they came, came from the guilds, not from the government. In old Chinese parlance the population was divided into four classes. These were, in the order of their dignity and honor, *scholars, farmers, laborers, merchants.*[7] Scholars at the top of the list were considered the finest product of society. Members of the officialdom were drawn exclusively from this class. Since it cost a great deal of money to become a scholar, almost all scholars were members of the scholar-gentry class with monied families behind them. Almost all, but not all: there were enough exceptions to give many Chinese the illusion of equality of opportunity for gifted persons, since brilliantly promising children were from time to time supported by their native villages, their guilds, or private philanthropists long enough for them to skip the gentry class and go directly from one of the lower categories of society into officialdom.

Next in importance to scholars, in terms of social prestige, were the farmers. For immemorial ages China had been dependent upon agriculture. The empire derived its major revenues from land taxation. The scholar gentry was supported by rents paid by farmers. The intellectuals saw, readily enough, that the country could not long exist without the toil of the farmers. This appreciation was expressed by land and revenue policies which (in form, at least) favored the farmers over the other classes of society. Merchants and laborers were commonly thought of as being dispensable or unimportant except for times of emergency.

Old China had no large industry, although there were heavy concentrations of local handicrafts. Wealth was not to be found through industrial investment, but was concentrated most frequently in land, jewels, and bullion. Surplus wealth was almost inevitably invested in land. Landlords ranged from the big absentee landowners who possessed hundreds of thousands of *mou* of land, down to petty proprietors who cultivated part of their own land and rented the rest to tenants. In the late nineteenth century, big landowners were more commonly found in the northern provinces than in the provinces south of the Yangtze River. This phenomenon was due to the fact that the southern provinces were ravaged by the ferocious economic experiments of the T'ai-p'ing rebels (A.D. 1850-1865) who applied a rough Christian agrarian socialism and broke up large private holdings of land. The fighting incident to suppression of the T'ai-p'ing was so bloodthirsty

[7] For an intriguing debate involving the relative dignity of such classes and, indeed, the entire role of the government in the economy, see *Discourses on Salt and Iron, A Debate on State Control of Commerce and Industry in Ancient China,* translated from the Chinese of Huan K'uan with Introduction and Notes by Esson M. Gale, Leyden, 1931. The place of the merchants at the bottom of the scale reflected the physiocratic tinge which is traceable to the beginnings of Confucian thought. It must be remarked that another sequence ran, first, scholars; second, farmers; third, laborers and merchants; fourth, degraded professions. The degraded professions were those which by tradition or supervision were regarded as filthy or inhuman. Prostitution, barbering, play acting, and soldiering were pre-eminent among the degraded professions.

on both sides that most of the southern provinces were devastated and wasteland was abundant. In some cases, landowners voluntarily implored the local authorities to declare their land ownerless, since they could not obtain tenants and did not wish to meet the tax bills on the land.

There were great discrepancies in the amount of rental paid and the treatment of tenants by landlords in various localities. Generally the amount of rental varied from one third to two thirds of the total yearly crop, depending on a variety of factors, such as the productivity of the land and the amount of seeds and fertilizers provided by the landowner. In some instances tenants were required to perform manual service in the landlord's households. The local custom and the disposition of particular landlords added further variations to the conditions of the tenant. As a general rule landlords maintained a close association and personal relationship with local officials. If a landlord chose to be oppressive, there was usually no remedy available to the peasant other than public opinion. When the tenants failed to pay rent because of famine or misfortune, it was not uncommon for them to sell their children—children thus sold became indentured servants or prostitutes. There was, however, a strong undercurrent of popular sentiment against large landholding. When a member of a decaying family wanted to sell land, it was necessary for him first to obtain the consent of his fellow clansmen. Furthermore, according to tradition, the seller of land could also go back to the purchaser for more money if he was still in distress after the deal was completed. The purchaser thus never quite knew how much a piece of land would ultimately cost him. This practice and many other local traditions held landlordism in check to a considerable degree.

Land Taxes. In Ch'ing dynasty, under practices originally laid down by the T'ang, the land tax was paid in two installments. The first installment was called the *ch'ien-liang* or "cash for crops" levied in cash from the ninth month of the lunar calendar onward. The second installment was called *ts'ao-mi* or "transported rice" and was paid in rice by the eight provinces situated along the Grand Canal, land in the other provinces paying cash. This levy was collected from the twelfth month of the lunar year onward. In each instance a certain number of days were prescribed for the actual payment of the levy. A penalty of one fifth was imposed on persons who failed to pay within the prescribed time limit. Each district had a cadastral registry or record of landownership; this was supposed to be kept up to date in the registrar's office of the district (*hsien*) headquarters. The land records got into very bad confusion in the nineteenth and early twentieth century. This arose in part from the unfortunate practice of letting the office of registrar become quasi-hereditary, since tradition permitted only one family to record all land titles in the district and to monopolize the fees attendant upon transfers of land.

Because of the vast geographic range of the empire and the extreme difficulties to be found from the jungles of the Indo-Chinese border to sub-arctic

North Manchuria, the methods of cultivation and kinds of crops varied in the extreme. The Huai River was the demarcation line so far as the agricultural pattern was considered. South of the Huai River there was abundant rainfall, permitting two crops a year. In some localities in Southwest China three crops a year were not uncommon. These warm moist river basins were used predominantly for the rice crop, to which wheat, beans, corn, and other crops were supplementary. North of the Huai River, where chillier weather forestalled a two-crop system, farmers planted wheat, cotton, maize, millet or *kao-liang*.

Farm Life. The Chinese farmer rarely became a peasant in the sense of being the semi-slave familiar from our pictures of European barons or Hindu Zemindars. Even at its worst he felt himself to be a yeoman. Though his life was strenuous and hard, though his working day during the busy season ran to more than fourteen hours, and though his women and children on occasion had to get out in the fields and help, the farmer had a considerable sense of self-reliance. When the busy season was over many energetic farmers turned to handicrafts in order to bring in surplus income. The womenfolk reared silk worms, gathered the cocoons, and spun cloth. The men did their own building, maintenance, well digging, and carpentry. In modern eyes the hard work and frugal living paid off in nothing more than grinding poverty. Occasional trips to fairs and markets constituted the only recreation of the farmer. He did not even have the Sunday off which the Christian religion offered to Westerners. Education was beyond the reach of the vast majority of the rural population. Only occasionally did a well-to-do farmer send one of his sons to school.

Much of Chinese farming was on marginal land, so far as rainfall, terrain, and soil were concerned. This accounted in part for the low standard of living. Also, conservativeness concerning methods of production and population pressure were more obvious reasons for the farmers' pitiable situation.

Laborers. In the traditional social scale, laborers ranged below farmers. Since the modern factory system was not introduced into China until the nineteenth century, most laborers in old China were handicraft workers, farm hands, and domestic servants. The various kinds of handicraft occupations, commonly known as "the thirty-six trades," included carpenters, masons, cooks, blacksmiths, and many others. Each trade in each district had its own guild. When a farm family had too many children and the land could not support them all, one of the children would be sent out to learn a trade. Thirteen to sixteen years was considered an appropriate age for becoming an indentured apprentice. During his apprenticeship the learner served his master very much like a domestic servant. He learned his trade first by observing and only later by practice, and he received no pay. After specified number of years of apprenticeship the apprentice was ready to qualify as a master craftsman himself.

Among laborers farm hands were the worst off. Unskilled agricultural labor had no guild, and the itinerant farm worker was considered an available extra body—no more. Farm hands were hired by rich farmers on a yearly basis, obtaining board and lodging and a nominal pay of ten to twenty taels of silver. Farm hands earned so little that it was difficult for them even to become tenants.

Although slavery had been abolished in China many centuries back, servants, either salaried or indentured, were very common. Even the poorer middle class people could afford an abundance of servants. Stable rural districts produced such an unceasing overflow of population that there was a constant migration of people born in the countryside, but proceeding to the city in search of work as domestic servants. Their lives were in general easier than the lives of farm hands, but their social position was extremely low. Even the poorest Chinese usually preferred to stay on the most miserable of farms rather than become a servant.

The Merchants. Traditionally the merchants belonged to the lowest group in the social scale. Since this tradition existed in the eyes of the literati and since the merchants actually lived with a considerable degree of comfort and had their own social life within their own circles, they did not mind being looked down on. The Confucian exquisites maintained that nothing new was actually created by trading, but the merchants engaged in the hard-headed problems of practical business knew better. The gap between theory and practice was immense. Merchants played an important role in China's economy from Han times onward, and, although the intelligentsia thought of the scope of business as being limited, China's trading and merchandising activities have also been described as vigorous, aggressive, well organized, and profitable by the Arab, Italian, Portuguese, and other Western visitors to China.

The most important business activities, such as salt and canal transportation, were monopolized by the government, but even where government enjoyed a nominal monopoly the servicing businesses to the main government business were generally performed by private merchants on a subcontract basis. The merchants' activities started with the trading of clothing, household wares, and foodstuffs. Often the merchant lived in his shop. Even today, for example, Chinese bookbinders are probably cooking their suppers on the charcoal stoves used during the day to heat the stamps or to cook the library paste. At night they and their families would sleep on the books, on the work tables, under the tables, or in the corners of the room.

In China across the ages, Confucianist governments looked with disfavor on merchandising. Little was done to encourage it. Heavy duties were placed on customers. The entirely normal reaction of the businessman was to resort to illegality and to bribe his fair share of opportunity when he could not obtain it by law. This gave the merchants the reputation of being cunning and untrustworthy.

Although despised by the other classes of people, merchants were usually much better off financially than either farmers or workers. Some merchants attained immense wealth and world-wide prominence. Many of the more prosperous ones purchased official titles from the government and became factors in local politics.

From the beginning down to the present day, Chinese business has been handicapped by inadequate monetary systems. Silver bullion and copper coins were commonly used as legal tender. The unit of silver was the Chinese ounce ("tael" in English) ; the standard coin was the round coin with the square hole, called "cash" in the English language as it is used in China. The exchange rate between taels and cash varied from time to time. In the last days of the Manchu dynasty one silver tael equaled 800 cash. Rice was priced at 2,000 cash per picul, meat at 60 cash per catty, and vegetable at 3 or 4 cash per catty.[8] At this price range the salary of a village teacher was about 50 to 60 taels a year, barely enough for him to support his family if both the cost and the standard of living were low. Within each local area old-fashioned Chinese banks similar to our small loan firms made loans to craftsmen and merchants at rates of 2 or 3 per cent per month and up. Pawn shops were even more respectable than banks and advanced small loans on secure collateral, such as clothing, tools, and household effects.[9]

Politics, Policy and Art. The society of "old China" possessed to a superlative degree the quality of *coherence*. In this it was not peculiar, save for the pervasiveness of related motives and themes interlacing political behavior, literary art, the graphic arts, and the plastic arts. Almost all major civilizations, at their time of florescence, show an interrelationship between the formal political system of public life, the policies adopted or prescribed by that political system, the social life existing within the framework of the political, and the artistic product—whichever art it may be—of that social system. Even when old China was dying, Havelock Ellis, a British student of social life, best known for his pioneer work on sex, noted in Peking a rhythmical coherence, a harmony of over-all human experience, which he sensed in no other contemporary culture.[10]

In the Western World the everlasting divorce which has prevailed since the Reformation—the divorce of spiritual sanction from political purpose—gives no ground for the assumption that in our time or in the time of our children there will be a serious reunion of man's view of the universe as he may express it through religion, his view of collective experience as he may express it through the purposive processes of government, and his view of the world immediately around him as he may express it in art. The art of the

[8] One picul (133.3 pounds) equaled 100 catties (1.3 pounds each).

[9] On the economic life of the Chinese people in the later days of the Ch'ing dynasty, the following books may be consulted: A. H. Smith, *op. cit.;* F. H. King, *Farmers of Forty Centuries, or Permanent Agriculture in China, Korea and Japan,* Madison, 1911; Ch'en, *op. cit.,* Chap. 15; Chou Ku-ch'eng, *Chung-kuo t'ung-shih* (A general history of China), 2 vols., Shanghai, 1935, Chap. 12.

[10] Havelock Ellis, *The Dance of Life,* London, 1928.

United States, literary or graphic, is very little related to government of the United States.

This was not true of civilizations such as the Athenian, the Roman, the Cambodian, or the old Chinese. Scholarship and art bore a definite relationship to government. The effectiveness and creativeness of government was reflected age by age by corresponding riches in the field of artistic accomplishment. Only in two of the many periods of Chinese history is there to be found the phenomenon which surrounds American and European private lives today—the reconciliation of political purposelessness or decline with sustained artistic creativeness. Until the time of the warring *kuo* (sixth, fifth, fourth, and third centuries before Christ) and in the Southern Sung period (twelve and thirteen centuries after Christ) the Chinese did have weak government and great art. Save for these periods, the rule generally held true that political creativeness and buoyancy were reflected in the creation of distinctive styles and new considerations in scholarship, philosophy, literature, poetry, painting, architecture, and the other arts.

From a modern point of view the scholars of old China had very little time to pursue practical and useful knowledge. They were obliged by the Confucian traditionalism to concentrate in their study of the classics and to write the elegant, but incredibly difficult, eight-legged essays.

The eight-legged essay, developed in the Ming dynasty, was a stereotyped literary form containing eight paragraphs, each paragraph running between 360 and 720 words. Each paragraph had to have a prescribed type of beginning and an equally prescribed ending. The fifth and sixth paragraphs had to be rhythmically arranged in four and six word phrases. The topics of the essays were inevitably selected from the *Four Books* and *Five Classics*.[11]

Most of the Confucian scholar bureaucrats knew very little about branches of knowledge other than the classics. Even some of the highest and most accomplished degree holders possessed only scanty information on actual events in Chinese history or on the practical usages of Chinese government. Their minds were often so hypnotized by the classics that they really believed everything in the pre-Ch'in era to be a golden example fit for incorporation in the everyday life of their times. Many such obstinate classical scholars attained high government positions; their cultivated ignorance cost the government dear in population and prestige.

In the old China of the last several centuries the over-all literature was expressed in three different styles: the polite style (*p'ien-t'i-wen*), the classical style (*wen-yen-wen*), and the vernacular style (*pai-hua-wen*). The polite style was written in rhythmic phrases of four or six Chinese mono-syllabic

[11] The list of classical books of the Confucian School varied at different times. However, since Sung, the number of classical works has been fixed at nine and in two groups. The *Ssŭ-shu,* or the Four Books include the *Lun-yü,* or Analects, the *Ta-hsüeh,* or Great Learning, the *Chung-yung,* or Doctrine of the Mean, and *Meng-tzŭ,* or the Discourses of Mencius. The *Wu-ching*, or the Five Classics are the *I-ching,* or Classic of Changes, the *Shu-ching,* or Classic of History, the *Shih-ching,* or Classic of Poetry, the *Li-chi,* or Record of Rites, and the *Ch'un-ch'iu,* or Spring and Autumn Annals.

ideographs. It was used in official proclamations, ceremonial essays, and the literature of eulogy. The classical style usually appeared in the form of a condensed allusive difficult prose. It was used for the writing of historical documents and political essays. The vernacular style was the most popular of all. Scholars who failed their examinations often turned to writing novels as a medium of self-expression. From the Yüan dynasty down through the Ch'ing, Chinese productivity in this field was rich and varied. Among the most famous Chinese novels are the *Hung-lou-mêng,* the sensitive and romantic portrait of an official family interwoven with delicate love stories and realistic petty intrigues; the *San-kuo-chih yen-i,* or Romance of Three Kingdoms; the *Shui-hu,* an adventurous story of rebellion and brigandage; and that great classic of Chinese pornography, *Chin-p'ing-mei.* All of these are available in English translations.[12]

The translation of Western books into Chinese was first undertaken by Jesuit missionaries. By 1664, the Jesuits had published more than 150 books on various scientific subjects.[13] The Jesuit effort did not arouse a serious Chinese response. The Imperial Russian government sent a large collection of Russian and European books to Peking in the early nineteenth century; no one at the court bothered to study them. Only after military and naval defeats did the officials and scholars of the Ch'ing bother to turn to Western scholarship. By the end of the nineteenth century European-language materials were being translated in quantity. After China's defeat by Japan in 1895, inbound translations reached fluid proportions. They have remained a factor in Chinese cultural life ever since. The Communist triumph of 1949 has merely substituted the translation of materials in Communist form for the translation of the cultural products of the West.

In the fields of art and architecture, accomplishments varied dynasty by dynasty. T'ang, Sung, and Ming paintings are of particular importance. Porcelain in China has always been a superlatively important art; in many respects the finest porcelains thus far produced by mankind can be ascribed to the eighteenth-century rule of Ch'ien Lung. Chinese architecture never achieved great variety of style or mastery of varied forms as did its Western counterpart. China has no Chartres to contrast against an Acropolis. In many respects the architecture of old China is reminiscent of the official buildings in Washington, D.C.: Chinese structure possessed a dependable but modest amount of beauty; it could be counted on to be lovely but rarely stirred, shocked, or quickened the deepest capacity of the human imagina-

[12] In the field of literature, a few important general surveys may be consulted: H. A. Giles, *A History of Chinese Literature,* New York, 1901; A. Wylie, *Notes on Chinese Literature,* Shanghai, 1902; F. Brinkley, *China: Its History, Arts and Literature* (Oriental Series, Vols. IX-XII, 1902); Hu Shih, *Wu-shih-nien chung-kuo chih wen-hsüeh* (Fifty years of Chinese literature), Shanghai, 1932. An excellent survey of translation works of Chinese literature, both classic and modern, is J. R. Hightower, *Topics in Chinese Literature,* Cambridge, 1950. This book gives an annotated bibliography of all important translations in Western languages.

[13] See P. Eckel, *The Far East Since 1500,* New York, 1947, p. 66.

tion. Whatever the Chinese lacked in architecture, they more than made up in interior decoration, in clothing, and in gardening. Even amid the decay and troubles of the twentieth century much of China is still beautiful, with a beauty deriving as much from the deft artistic certainty of the human touch as from the natural picturesqueness of a great part of the Chinese terrain.

Having traced the political evolution of old Imperial China and having related its developing political institutions to the Chinese society as a whole, beneath the Confucian state, we can now turn to China's last great dynasty, the Ch'ing or Manchu. From several points of view, China under Manchu rule is an important subject to the understanding of modern Chinese politics and government. On the international level, the autocracy superimposed on democracy which was old Imperial China met the power of the West during the Manchu rule. Judged by the last two centuries of Manchu dominance, Imperial government and the loose society beneath proved hopelessly inadequate in the face of repeated blows and pressing demands. On the other hand, judged by three centuries of Manchu leadership, the Ch'ing dynasty was among China's greatest and most influential. It must always be remembered that basic characteristics of both the long past and of the short past survive even today.

CHAPTER THREE

The Manchu Empire of China

PRESENT-DAY Chinese leaders, both Nationalists and Communists, have had to manipulate the human material bequeathed them by the immediate past. Indeed, they were themselves part of that human material, subject to the inescapable limitations and advantages, visible or invisible, which accrued to them from the culture to which they were born. Behind the image of Stalin, ultramodern leader of a revolutionary Communist world, there lurks the face of the tense young seminarian named Djugashvili. Comparably behind the modern physician democrat, Sun Yat-sen, there was always to be seen the practical mind of the peasant boy from the mother land of emigration and rebellion, Kwangtung. Both Chiang Kai-shek and Mao Tse-tung, of China today, are bone, nerve, muscle, and brain, the product of an old China which no Chinese could either recreate or forget.

How Russian is the Soviet Union? How Chinese is Red China, or for that matter, Nationalist China? Questions such as these require not only an understanding of the far past, but a command of the recent past as well.

The absurdities of China in the *Tuchün* period (about 1916-1930) become understandable fallibilities when they are contrasted with the Manchu Empire, corrupt at its heart even though reformed at the center, which fell in 1912. Most Chinese leaders today were born in the last years or months of "old China." Old China does not mean the China of Confucius, but the China of the Manchus, of the Empress Dowager, of gunboat diplomacy, of the Boxer Rebellion, of the Open Door, of railroad building, of Japanese invasions, of exchanges in money and communications, and of the arrival of the press. Nations with good foundations do not need revolutions. Behind the Bolshevik revolutions there lay the long dry rot of the Romanovs, behind Hitler, the centuries of a Germany with inadequate political form, and behind modern Nationalist and Communist China, the Manchus. Britain, America, Japan, Switzerland, and similar nations have not needed revolutions: their immediate past has been strong enough to support the foundations of the present system.

Manchu Ghosts in the Chinese Present. Although present-day Chinese institutions bear no outward resemblance to those of the past, many present political trends and practices actually owe their form and tenor to traditional patterns which have long been discredited or discarded. By the scale of two millenniums Chinese Imperial government was good. By the scale of two hundred years Chinese Imperial government was hopelessly inadequate to meet the shocking demands imposed upon it by the physical arrival of the Western World in the Far East, not to mention the psychological and intellectual demands which such a bouleversement entailed.

Four of the most obvious Chinese political characteristics inherited from the past have been:

a government of men,
a politics of ethics and not of law,
intermingling of the legislative, executive, and judicial powers, and
implicit emphasis on the ideological power of government.

Personal Government. Taking the first, one can say that the traditional Chinese political system was fundamentally a pattern of personal relations. A people conditioned by two millenniums of monarchical and scholastic bureaucratic rule were apt to confound institutions with men. Everyday Chinese life often presents examples of cultural realism to be found only among trained anthropologists or sociologists in the West. The Chinese often see through the custom or the office to the man and the role he is playing.

This intuitively realistic attitude toward life implies a recognition of the fact that institutions are always reducible to the individuals who portray them, to be strengthened by strong-willed and powerful personalities or to be weakened by timid defensive men. Furthermore, a respect for personal authority was considered not merely a cardinal principle of Confucian ethics, but a workable criterion of good human conduct. In family, as well as in government, the Chinese felt themselves to be ruled by persons, not by rules.

Evidence for this can be found in the fact that for a highly developed civilization China had a singularly crude judicial structure and no legislative system of importance. This point can become more plain if one contrasts American and Chinese behavior under conditions of terrifying stress, for example, during the present Sino-American struggle in Korea. The Americans within their military and political structures of government responded with a frenzy of policy making, drafting and revising papers, regulations, and policies by the bushel. The Chinese reshuffled a few men and sacrificed both lives and property without too much of an inclination to meddle with their own rules.

Politics and Ethics. Perhaps it is a little misleading to say that the Chinese have traditionally confused *politics* with *ethics*. It certainly is untrue if one takes these two terms in their ordinary Western meanings, since both politics and ethics are specialized fields capable of clean-cut, sharp, documented definitions. The statement is true if the two terms are polarized —politics being taken as a precise system of exercising governmental control in society and ethics being taken as an imprecise, diffused horse-sense way of deciding things without splitting hairs or looking to the rules. The Chinese can be said to have sought harmony between men by recourse to nonspecialized standards and judgments, whereas most of the Western civilizations (of the past as well as of the present) have placed strong reliance on the compartmentalization of social standards and the definition of exact legal, ethical, and reasonably useful formulas.

By Confucian doctrine political goodness was merely one of the common components of human goodness. The ruling personnel of a society had to prove themselves morally outstanding in all respects if they were to expect obedience in political respects. A magistrate was guided less by legal codes than by his own moral aptitudes in deciding cases involving disputes. However, this did not necessarily mean that there was a state of lawlessness; the ancient but unbroken rules of propriety were both firm in their general content and resilient in each particular application. Like some fanatical modern political ideologists, they transcended all legal codes and regulations. The traditional Chinese political system was ethical in the sense that it was vague, realistic in the sense that it judged the rule of men and did not permit intelligent, just, or perceptive men to escape their human and emotional responsibilities behind a screen of arbitrary verbal definitions. An American judge can hang a murderer with whose point of view he feels a lurking sympathy; a Chinese judge would acquit the murderer on the basis of a man-to-man appraisal that there was something wrong with the law in requiring a sentence of death.

The Whole Power of Government. Thirdly, in the traditional Chinese political system no distinction was made between the legislative, executive, and judicial powers of government. The whole power of government was vested in the person of the Emperor. He in his turn delegated a part of his authority to his ministers. The old Chinese Empire was stained throughout by the paternalistic biases of Chinese family life; the Chinese were driven at all times by the inescapable analogy of ruler and the people on the one hand, as against the patriarch and the members of his family on the other.

No restraint was put on the father in the patriarchal family other than the expectation that, if he went completely mad or became utterly oppressive, somebody somehow would get around to doing something about it. In political form there was no limitation on the power of the Emperor and hence no idea of the separation of powers in the old Chinese political system. The function of protest and remonstrance, left to the adults at large and shared on occasions by servants and children within the family system, had its counterpart in the office of censors. Censors were vested with the power to remonstrate against the wrongful acts of the Emperor, but they could do nothing but remonstrate. Their complaints had no legal effect. The doctrine of *ultra vires* is not found in Chinese thought.

Shifting Forms and Steadfast Men. During the past hundred years China has undergone many political changes, promulgated many constitutions, and adopted a variety of forms of government. At times this strikes the Western beholder as being tantamount to chaos. China seems both kaleidoscopic and quick-changing, hopelessly beyond the reach of any ordinary intelligence. The problem is not as difficult as it seems. The changes in form occur rapidly *precisely because they do not matter in Chinese life.* The transition in the character of the personal leadership to be found in Chinese politics has been much slower and is much more intelligible than the apparent change in Chinese political institutions. From rebel Hung Hsiu-ch'üan, and his adversary, the Viceroy Tsêng Kuo-fan, down to the Marxist Mao Tse-tung, and the revolutionary conservative Chiang Kai-shek, is much less of a transition than the apparent institutional contexts would suggest.

Personal leadership transcending government, diffusely ethical rather than precisely legal standards, and the wholeness of the power of government have remained fundamental principles in Chinese politics under all political systems. The pretenses of the early Peking republic to a three-power system and the attempts of the Nationalists to set up a five-power system were in their way less realistic than the Communist reversion to a one-power system of government which happens to be Marxist and Chinese attainment. Put it more bluntly:

In Western nations the leader obtains office. In China the leader leads; once in power he creates offices for himself and his followers.

Where does power come from if not the office?

Not from law, not from structure, not from title or delegation, but preeminently from the explicit or hidden continuation of the Confucian assumptions concerning ideological control.

Persistent in Chinese politics of the late Manchu and Republican periods has been the attempt to establish a rule of law modeled on the Western conception of the state. Each group of leaders has attempted to pretend that its group-leadership was not decisive, that the new system mattered, not the men who ran it. In each instance the behavior of the leaders contradicted the things which they said. The implicit Confucian idea that law was a by-product of ideology has been almost indestructible. The more desperately one group tried to improve on its predecessors, the more illusory the structure of government has appeared.

In each of the fundamental instruments of government promulgated by successive regimes the professed political belief of the ruling circle was inevitably displayed in the most prominent places. Inevitably the dignity and permanence of law have been sacrificed to the political expedients which put them in place. The content of Confucianism is gone, but the *processes* of Confucian thinking—the *ways* in which a Confucianist thought rather than *what* he thought have survived almost without change. The content of Confucian ritualism is obsolete; modern political doctrines have taken its place. A modern Chinese Communist judge on the mainland decides cases by applying principles of political dogma just as his predecessors did when they used their moral aptitudes instead of a definite set of laws.

Manchu Inheritance. The Meiji Emperor of Japan bequeathed to modern Japan the vision of a romantic reconstituted monarchy arising from the sleep of ages and leading a great, unique nation to world power. His contemporary, the Empress Dowager Tz'ŭ Hsi bequeathed to China a weariness with the long past and a positive contempt for the recent past. The Manchu inheritance is therefore a set of habits, not a group of structures.[1]

The political habits of modern China are of course post-Manchu habits: but they rest on the world as it was under the Manchu emperors of China. Some features of old China run back to the ages before Confucius, some to the times of the fighting *kuo*. most of them to the immediate past. A half century of revolution and reform has destroyed the old system but has not yet replaced it. Chinese political habits have changed somewhat between the 1850's and the 1950's, but the change is much less than it seems. The Manchu structure is important for what it failed to do and for the residue of habits which it has left in the Chinese political mind.

Authority of the Manchu Emperor. The Manchu structure of government was patterned after the established system of the Ming (A.D. 1368-1644) which—as pointed out on pages 20-21—had brought monarchical institutions to their acme and had increased the power and prestige of the Chinese Emperor beyond all precedent. So strong was the Ming structure that it readily obtained the admiration of the early European visitors, themselves subjects of monarchs, who enhanced its representation in the Western World.

When the Manchus reached the decisive point in their long drawn out conquest of China in 1644 they found that the political institutions of the Ming were worth preserving, since these institutions could reinforce Manchu rule over an alien people. Shrewd Manchu leaders knew that as long as the fabric of government and the methods of administration remained unchanged the common people would find their daily lives unaltered and would thus accept the conquest. They were right in their estimate of the situation; the masses of people, as opposed to the armed forces of the Ming

[1] The contrast—between China and Japan—is of course not confined to the late nineteenth century. Twelve hundred years before Meiji, and Tz'ŭ Hsi, Japan looked to the future while China already gloried in her past. The respective roles are described on pp. 270-271.

and to a handful of conspiring and opportunistic leaders, offered no serious opposition.

Although culturally inferior to the Chinese, the Manchus were able to govern a highly sophisticated and well-organized people simply by leaving a going concern as untouched as possible. The invaders pretended that they had entered Peking at the invitation of a Ming general, the later infamous Wu San-kuei, to punish the rebels who had caused the death of the last Ming Emperor; they were thus in a position to contend that they had won the throne from the rebels and not from the Ming. This intelligent sophistry rendered many of the Confucian-minded officials of the Ming dynasty conscience-free to join the new Manchu rulers and enabled the invaders to inherit the Ming institutions completely staffed without much opposition.

Unfortunately for themselves the Manchus were alien. They had to choose between maintaining their own nationality at the risk of offending the Chinese and losing power at some long-to-be-dreaded but uncertain date, or to abandon their nationality, become Chinese, and sacrifice the glory of their conquest. They chose to remain Manchu.

Remaining Manchu meant staying foreign.

Staying foreign meant maintaining the fact of conquest, however much the forms of constitutionality might gloss it over.[2] The Manchu high command put strong garrisons at a number of strategic points throughout China. These garrisons were stationed in separate quarters, segregated from the Chinese; they constituted a permanent force independent of the regular Chinese armed forces. These Manchu garrisons degenerated completely after generations of corruption and inactivity. Unlike the garrisons of British forces stationed in India for almost the same length of time, they were not rotated to their homeland enough to maintain their fighting qualities or their sense of identity.

Another Manchu device was a deliberate introduction of racial discrimination. Under prescribed formulas civil offices were reserved to Manchus on a racial basis in such a way as to provide a counterweight to Chinese in the bureaucracy and to effect a balance between the two races. Since it was hopeless to expect the Manchus to acquire the degree of efficiency which the Ming had demanded of the Chinese, Manchus did not need to go through the vigorous examination system. The practical effect of this was not expected by the founders of the system: the Manchu members were, precisely because they were less trained, usually inferior to their Chinese colleagues. Aside from the racial discrimination in garrisons and in the bureaucracy, the Manchus were able to continue most of the Ming processes of government.

Political Powers of the Emperor.[3] The essential characteristic of the

[2] This decision was made evident by a proclamation, issued by the Prince Regent of the conquering Manchu in 1644; see Hsiao I-shan, *Ch'ing-tai shih* (History of Ch'ing dynasty), Chungking, 1944, pp. 23-24

[3] Detailed descriptions of the power exercised by the Manchu Emperor are to be found in the following: H. S. Brunnert and V. V. Hagelstrom, *Present Day Political Organization*

Chinese monarchy was the unlimited authority of its Emperor. His position has very few analogies, say, with the Pharaohs of Egypt or the Grand Incas of Pre-Columbian Peru. He ruled a vast empire by inherited prerogative, although inheritance was never on the basis of primogeniture, thus leaving most of the emperors a pretty wide choice of sons, since polygamy prevailed. Once in office his powers knew no limit, other than the psychological limits of the personalities with whom he chose to surround himself. Along with political power, he enjoyed the prestige of supreme moral and intellectual leadership. His very mistakes in writing led to modifications of the dictionary. His name was so sacred that the ideographs with which it was written had to be expunged from everyday use.

Earlier dynasties had maintained certain inhibitions on the Emperor: unwritten constitutional regulations, Confucian doctrines of moderation, a public opinion which could be activated by crisis, and the frank admonition of his ministers of state. These faded. The principle of the Emperor's unlimited authority was carried by the Ming to an extreme. Moral and legal limitations were swept aside. The emperors became absolute despots.[4]

The first Ming Emperor abolished the premiership and substituted a Grand Secretariat. In so doing he appropriated all the power of the Premier to himself and divided the workaday functions of that office among several Grand Secretaries. The same Emperor with hellish foresight reintroduced and modified the civil service examination in rigid and schematic form, inventing the eight-legged essay as a means of stifling the imaginations of unborn generations of men. By making their studies so hard that they had no time for real-life public affairs, he smothered the probability of rebellious activity on the part of scholars. The Manchu emperors, taking the Chinese dynastic title, Ch'ing, eagerly acquired all the institutional authority of the Ming emperors. Influenced by the ruthless practices of their own nomadic people and the personal energy of the founders of the dynasty, they exalted the power of the Manchu emperors of China to a position even higher than that carried by their native predecessors.

The early Manchu emperors exercised not only the usual prerogatives of the Chinese sovereign, but they concentrated into their own hands the powers of appointment and removal for all official posts and, making sure that social degradation reinforced political subjection, they degraded their subordinates from the proud status of functionaries of state to the status of

---

of China, Shanghai, 1912, Part I; Hsieh Pao-ch'ao, *The Government of China (1644-1911),* Baltimore, 1925, Chap. II; W. F. Mayers, *The Chinese Government,* Shanghai, 1897, Part I; S. W. Williams, *The Middle Kingdom,* London, 1883, Vol. I, pp. 394-407; Hsiao I-shan, *op. cit.,* Chap. 3.

[4] Perhaps this was a trauma on the Chinese political system comparable to the damage done the Russian political system by the same injurious element—the common factor of Mongol conquest. The Mongols perfected few ideas but obedience; obedience they did teach with the bloody and unforgettable example of their success. Russia became absolutist as the Mongol power ebbed. That the Ming, who succeeded the Mongols in China, should have been absolutistic too is surely more than an empty coincidence.

nu ts'ai (slaves). This was the term Manchu dignitaries used in referring to themselves when addressing the Emperor.

As a result Manchu emperors were less apt to listen to the exhortation of their subordinates about good government or against the wanton use of power. The Manchus thus broke the democratic and popular threads which had been woven into the traditional Chinese monarchical system. They lost the advantages of tinge of democracy, and they gained little but the perilous freedom of encompassing their own doom the more swiftly. The final fall of the Manchus, although it came about through revolutionary moments which in turn developed from the Western impact, was long anticipated by the whimsical and witless use of power by emperors who were so powerful that they could not be taught to govern themselves.

Generally speaking the Manchu Emperor, like his Chinese predecessors, was vested with all legislative, executive, and judicial powers. He exercised these powers with a free hand. So immense was the volume of state business that he necessarily had to delegate a great deal of the use of that power to his ministers, but the Manchus never tolerated interference with the principle that the power of the Emperor, when he chose to exercise it, was unlimited. In the field of legislation he issued edicts and rescripts which became the law of the land. The Emperor's writ was so wide that it covered all aspects of human activity and ran throughout the extent of the Chinese and Manchu domain—a combined Empire which extended from the Northeastern provinces (Manchuria) to the Bay of Bengal and the Gulf of Siam, from the unknown Pacific to the Russian frontier.

The only limitation on Imperial legislation was the requirement that the ruler's edicts should not contradict those of his own ancestors. Even this was not a written rule, and willful emperors were free to break established precedent. The body of laws called *Ta-Ch'ing lü-li* (Statutes and rescripts of the great Ch'ing dynasty),[5] which for all practical purposes served as the civil and penal code of the Empire, was subject to frequent alterations by the Emperor who could issue an edict whenever he chose. His words were law, and no legal right could be held in opposition to his pleasure.

With respect to the executive power the Chinese language did not even have the term "executive." According to Confucian logic, the oneness of political authority in a state was to be compared to the oneness of the sun in the universe. The Emperor was the fountain of honor and privilege, the creator of services, the examiner of talents, the head of the armed forces, and the dispenser of tax revenues. Patently, it was impossible in actual practice

[5] *Ta-Ch'ing lü-li* was first published in 1647. Revised editions were promulgated at frequent intervals. An extensive collection of notes, comments, and cases illustrating the application of the law was appended to the 1799 edition. The body of laws was grouped under the following major headings: general, civil, physical, ritual, military, criminal, and laws relating to public works. The English translation by Sir Thomas Staunton was published in 1810 with the Chinese title romanized as *Ta Tsing Leu Lee.* The French translation came out somewhat belatedly in 1924 by the Catholic father Guy Boulais (under the title of *Manuel du Code Chinois,* Shanghai, 2 vols.).

for even a Chinese Emperor to handle such vast amounts of state affairs with his own eyes and hands. Consequently it was physically necessary for him to share a part of his powers with his ministers: he could either delegate, or else they had to usurp.

The judicial power of the Emperor was absolute and final; he was seen as the source of law and mercy. No one could maintain a claim against him nor question the validity of his decisions. He alone served as a final court of appeal. Theoretically he could be approached to rectify any injustice occurring within his domain. A few energetic emperors actually undertook the personal management of judicial trials which were important or picturesque, but these occasions were rare. It was necessary for the Emperor's personal interest to be piqued or for the entire empire to face grave consequences, in order to bring direct Imperial participation.

Beyond these institutional functions the Emperor was vested with a strong extralegal authority which he exercised by virtue of his position. He was the head of the official state religion, Confucianism, and honorary head of every other tolerated religion within his empire (since Confucianism was orthodox and all other faiths fell into the category of either licensed or prohibited heresy). The position of the Chinese Emperor was as paradoxical as if George I had insisted on being not merely head of the Anglican Church, but chief of the illegitimate Catholic Church of England, Chief Rabbi of the Jewish Community, Chief Imam of all Moslems in his domain, and Supreme Hindu for his Indian dominions. He was the arbiter of morals. He alone was qualified to offer sacrifices to a deistic but capricious divinity called Heaven; *per contra* he had to assume personal responsibility to his people for such calamities as earthquake, flood, and drought. Public fortune was considered a consequence of his virtue, but just as inevitably public misfortune was attributed to his wickedness. He was also supposed to be the moral and intellectual leader of the nation.

With the very nature of government ability on so personal a foundation, the character and aptitude of the Emperor became the chief criteria for the measurement of administration. The monarchs of the Manchu line are to be characterized not so much by the categories "progressive" and "conservative," or "good" and "vicious," but "strong" and "feeble." Extraordinary physical, moral, and intellectual strength was a character of the two greatest emperors of the Ch'ing line, K'ang Hsi and Ch'ien Lung; feebleness, personal viciousness, and stupidity beyond belief were characteristic of many of the emperors of the last part of the line. Within such an Empire there was no legal safeguard against the misuse of unlimited power, no outlet (such as Japan possessed) for unused political power. The only palliative for which men could hope was the reasonableness and moderation of the Emperor—or his death and a new Emperor.

Limitations on the Imperial Power. However absolute and unlimited the power of the Emperor might appear, in actual application it had practical limitations.

In the first place the Emperor himself, a human being, was bound by traditions and precedents as well as the established rules of the dynasty in which he had been brought up from infancy and childhood. He too was a member of the Confucian family. The Confucian dictum of filial piety did not allow him in his minority to make exceptions. Even after he came to power he had to maintain the form of obedience to his ancestors. Time and again some weak and ignorant old woman emerged from life-long seclusion as the one force in China superior to the Emperor; the mother of the reigning Emperor was the one human being beyond his reach and outside his authority. If an Emperor issued a decree which contradicted his ancestors' laws, no matter how degrading or unjust those laws may have been, he was sure to encounter routine objections from his ministers who, as good Confucianists, would respectfully but insistently exort him with the endless whine:

"The established rules of Your Majesty's Ancestors. . . ."

Only a pugnacious and imaginative emperor dared break tradition and adventure into the field of practicing political reform.

Secondly, a limitation was placed on the Emperor by the bulk of state business and the sheer size of his domain. He had to delegate his authority to his subordinates in the capital as well as in the provinces. This delegation of power was officially recognized by the *Ta-Ch'ing hui-tien* (Collected institutes of the great Ch'ing), which provided that all important matters must be submitted to the Emperor for approval, while minor duties are to be performed by the departments directly.

Even under the limits of this judicial delegation the powers of subordinate officials were in theory advisory, although extensive and absolute in practice in the instance of such officers as the viceroys of major provinces. Actions of all officials could be repudiated at the pleasure of the monarch and could be withdrawn at his will.

Apart from these regular instituted central and local officials, to whom delegation of the power of the Emperor was a necessary concomitant of function, there were groups of people who often usurped the Imperial power surreptitiously. These fell into four outstanding categories: matrimonial relatives of the Emperor; maternal relatives of the Emperor; court stewards; and eunuchs. The maternal relatives enjoyed the occasional advantage of access to his mother who was usually a widow (in rare cases an Emperor retired and let his son reign). The matrimonial relatives of the Emperor were even more dangerous. Chinese emperors had large harems. The importance of the women in the harem ranged upward from the status of slave girl to a position equal or superior to that of the Emperor. Yehonala, the ignorant but strong-willed Manchu girl who later ruled China with the title of the Empress Dowager Tz'ŭ Hsi, became important because she was a clever manipulator who had won the Emperor's affection. Whole cliques in the capital centered around this favorite or that potential favorite of the Emperor, precedence being determined partly by the Emperor's erotic caprice and partly by the record of the women in bearing sons.

Benefiting from study of Chinese history, replete with tragic examples of petticoat politics and eunuch usurpation, the early Manchu emperors tried to make specific provisions to protect their heirs against these dangers. Under the prescribed Manchu rules the Imperial clansmen were kept permanently disarmed and were required to reside in Peking. Relatives of the Emperor were disqualified from participation in politics, and palace eunuchs were forbidden to meddle in any business beyond their household tasks. These measures worked well for the first hundred and fifty years.

Thirdly, there was a check on the Emperor provided by the established procedures and offices of the Censorate. The Chinese term for censor, *yü-shih,* originally designated an Imperial historian whose duty it was to record the speeches and deeds of the emperors. In so doing the historian inevitably accepted the responsibility of criticizing the ruler for improper speech or for his misconduct. The role of the *yü-shih* was later extended to include criticism of the conduct of all officials, whatever their grade.

The censors over the ages made themselves useful to the rulers not merely as critics of the Emperor's own conduct, but as "eyes and ears" whereby the Emperor could spy on the mandarins.[6] Under despotic rulers only those censors who had a willingness to die for justice, a passion for the public weal, or a burning desire for posthumous fame would dare to incur the imperial displeasure by criticizing something which the Emperor had done. Supposedly invested with special and limitless freedom of speech, many a censor died because he tested the principle too far. Subtle emperors, instead or martyrizing impudent censors, disgraced them or mocked them.

Wise and prudent emperors tried to make the best of the censorial institution, accepting pertinent criticism and avoiding lines of conduct which might invite an uproar from the whole body of censors. Only a foolish emperor, however, would let the censors say anything any time; to do so would be to encourage impertinence and to endanger the realm with a spirit of feeble meekness.[7]

Fourthly, the most important check on the absolute power of the Emperor was the pressure of public opinion. Usually public opinion represented the views of the literati and the gentry. Only on extreme occasions when human

[6] The term, *mandarin,* of uncertain origin, quite possibly Portuguese, is the European sobriquet for the scholar bureaucrats of the old Chinese civil service. Since the first European advisors to China came from monarchies hereditary with aristocracies imbedded in their social systems, they found it difficult to understand the role of a man who was neither a priest nor a noble and yet who assumed many of the roles and capacities of each.

[7] A scholarly description of the development of the Chinese censorate, with an explanation of its connection with the modern control function, is to be found in Richard L. Walker, "The Control System of the Chinese Government," *The Far Eastern Quarterly,* Vol. VII, No. 1 (November, 1947).

lives or the most cherished superstitions were in danger, did the quiet masses of China break into uproar. An informed and educated public opinion was a necessary palliative to autocracy in a country which lacked legal safeguards against despotism. The continuity of the scholar bureaucrats as a class explains perhaps the relative continuity of Chinese civilization as against the successive civilizations which rose and fell in Southeast Asia and in India.

The Manchu dynasty on frequent occasions used atrocious methods to suppress public opinion, inflicting unbelievable cruelties on persons who dared to protest, yet on other occasions emperors bowed to public demand and made amend for their own wrongful conduct. Behind this balance between Emperor and opinion there lay the implicit threat—the deepest of all balances in the Chinese constituent system—that the people had a moral right and a political duty to dispose of a sovereign who became tyrannical and oppressive.

Unlike the Japanese dynasty which had been unbroken since prehistoric times, each Chinese dynasty owed its own mandate to rule to a successful exercise of the right of rebellion and the transfer of the sovereign authority by popular action. In Chinese parlance this was the *t'ien ming,* the "Mandate of Heaven" and a mystical entity in quasi-religious Confucian thought. (In modern terms it is nothing more than the plebiscite of assent daily given by all peoples to any government which exists among them.)

The Confucian theory assumed that only virtuous rulers could retain the *t'ien ming,* and those who lost had neither the ability nor the right to suppress a rebellion. The ultimate sanction of rebellion served as the Chinese warning to any emperor who, despite his possession of unlimited power, was tempted to behave like some of his colleagues among other Oriental despots or the Russian czars. The content of the Confucian teaching made many emperors more humane and democratic than Westerners are likely to imagine. Hence, although there was no juridical safeguard against the misuse of unlimited Imperial power, these extralegal limitations made the unqualified autocracy of the Manchus a tolerable, if not an entirely satisfactory, system of government.

Policy Formulation for the Dragon Throne. In the contemporary American sense of the term "policy," there was no policy in old China. The major social, economic, or political choices which face Americans and other Westerners today could not be made because the alternatives did not present themselves. To expand or not to expand, to make power-political decisions affecting national survival, to move for or against segregations of races, to introduce or to reject new and basic labor guarantees—such issues never arose within the framework of the inclusive Confucian ideology. What we call "policy" was for the greater part predetermined by the education of the Emperor and of his officials, by the social and intellectual environment which surrounded them, by the momentum of a civilization which appeared to them and to the rest of the world to have greater stability than any other civilization on earth.

To the Manchus, reigning as the Ch'ing dynasty, problems of policy were matters which had to be settled at the beginning of the contest and at the final consolidation of their occupation of China. Once firmly in power they too could join their predecessors in the perpetuation of an almost policy-less administration. This repose, such as it was, did not last for long. The sleighs of the Russians, the ships of Britain, kept increasing their pressure, minute at first but at flood proportions at the end, at the northern and southern extremes of the Empire.

Policy became more and more important whether the Manchus and Chinese liked it or not.

Throughout the period there was of course a sustained minimum of policy decisions which had to be faced, economical and political decisions for which no standard operating procedure was available within the confines of the Confucian classics. From the onset of their reign the Manchu emperors themselves stirred up the necessity for policy by attempting to maintain a two-race segregated empire, keeping one foot in their original homeland of Nomadic, semi-civilized Manchuria and the other in the immensely larger, wholly settled realm of China.

When the Manchu conquerors entered Peking they knew that their own people, although brave soldiers, were novices in the art of government. Whether Manchu or Chinese, an emperor had to exert his authority through the instrumentalities of mandarins, who, subject only to restraints from above, were irresponsibly powerful within the limits of their several jurisdictions. The Manchus found the bureaucracy of their Ming predecessors, composed of the literati class, an extremely valuable instrument for the administration of conquered people. The initial Manchu conquest was characterized by efficiency, the effectual and thrifty use of terror, and relative swiftness. Once in power, the Manchus moved rapidly to restore the whole machinery of the Ming government. The only serious changes, as mentioned above, consisted of the establishment of Manchu garrisons at strategic points and the reservation of key policy posts for persons of Manchuria.[8]

Several outstanding features of this Sino-Manchu bureaucracy warrant attention.

First, under the paternalistic autocracy of old China, no clearly subdivided political power was allocated to a specific political organization. There were vaguely written terms of reference such as the duties and responsibilities of each government department as outlined in the *Ta-Ch'ing hui-tien*, but no

[8] On the early situation which led to the policy of establishing Manchu garrisons at strategic points, there are Chêng Ho-shêng, *op. cit.*, Vol. II, Chap. 9; Chin Chao-feng, *Ch'ing-shih ta-kang* (Outline of the history of the Ch'ing dynasty), Shanghai, 1935, Chap. II, pp. 363-371; Hsiao I-shan, *Ch'ing-tai t'ung-shih* (General history of the Ch'ing dynasty), Shanghai, Vol. I, pp. 464-476; E. Haenisch, *Bruchstücke aus der Geschichte Chinas unter der Mandschu-Dynastie*. II. *Der Aufstand des Wu San-Kuei, aus dem Shêng-wu-chi übersetzt.* (*T'oung Pao,* March 1913, pp. 1-130).

prescriptions operated against the authority of the Emperor. The exact, necessary sphere of authority of each organization actually depended more on the personal relationship prevailing at a given time between the heads of various component fractions of government and the Emperor or his household than on written regulations or rules.

Secondly, the operation of government was divided so as to insure checks and balances between the central and local governments and between the various branches of administrative service rather than for the application of swift efficient administration. It was more to the interests of the new emperors to remain in power than to give good government (good government, although a goal, was always a second-choice goal). Since the main interest of the Manchu house was to keep the reigning family on the Throne and to drain the wealth of the provinces for the support of the court in Peking, it was urgently necessary to secure protective devices through which any potential excess of independence on the part of Imperial ministers could be checked and the interests of the reigning family safeguarded. Rarely did constructive policies originate from the central administration in Peking.

Peking usually eschewed policy. The metropolitan officials were usually content with the routine business of approving or disapproving measures reported from viceregal or provincial headquarters. Characteristic Chinese bureaucrats possessed small capacity for initiative; they reserved their energy for intriguing and personal politics, at which they excelled.

Thirdly, the Chinese bureaucracy was recruited almost exclusively among the literati who came preponderantly from the gentry class. There was thus a sense of comradeship within the service; conspicuously lacking was corresponding sense of trust for the common people with whose welfare the service was charged. The core of the administration, the highest posts, were open only to metropolitan graduates; the circle was tighter; both the comradeship and the rivalry were limited to the apex of the pyramid. Scholarship rather than action kept driving Chinese bureaucrats away from creative political functions toward sterility and formalism.[9]

[9] In its own interest this portion of Chinese administrative history is of only passing concern to the modern American, however exciting it may seem to the specialized historian of Far Eastern affairs. At the risk of stating the obvious it must be pointed out that this bureaucracy is not interesting for its sake alone, but for our future as well. In some respects the Americans of the middle twentieth century are fortunate to live in a world in which they cannot afford to decay; whether we like it or not the challenge of the Politburo bid for world power compels us to keep our economic, military, and propaganda fronts in operation. Living amid danger and turmoil as we do, it is easy to think that world peace will bring relief to the anxieties and problems which beset us. The Manchu Empire is a realistic and horrible demonstration of historic truth that peace engenders problems no less oppressive than the problems of war. Indeed, peace can sometimes be more nightmarish than war, because people are at least willing to do something about a war situation, whereas a peace situation can be corrupt, frustrated, and disappointing beyond belief, and yet remain beyond the capacity of any man, however hopeful or honest, to alter. The problems of the Manchu bureaucracy are not very important in the 1950's; it is dreadfully possible that these problems may recur in the human race of the 2050's, when and if the dead hand of the world-wide *status quo* uses the psychological and sociological pretext of "no war, ever again" to set itself against reform, vitality, development, changing, or intelligent response to the most elementary of problems. Any imaginative reader can see that

The metropolitan administration of Peking can be categorized as comprising two levels of organization: the policy-determining group of agencies and the routine administrative agencies.

Among the policy-determining agencies the most important organization was the Grand Secretariat, *Nei-ko*. The Grand Secretariat was instituted by the Mings in 1382 as a substitute for the ancient premiership; it was retained by the Manchus. Grand Secretaries, six in number, possessed supreme advisory power and exalted privilege of free access to the Emperor, but they lacked those powers of actual decision and high prestige which had been enjoyed by the premiers of earlier dynasties. Under the Ch'ing three members of the Grand Secretariat were Manchus and three Chinese, two of each being regular and one an associate.

The office of Grand Secretariat was the highest step in the bureaucratic ladder. Appointment to that office was the aspiration of all entrants into public service. The Grand Secretaries were appointed only from the rosters of Ministers of Departments, Censors-General, or Viceroys. They usually held concurrent posts. Besides acting as political advisor to the Emperor each had a variety of state functions to perform. Each was burdened with the duties of drafting edicts, making notes on the memorials presented by officials, taking custody of the Imperial seal, and a variety of ceremonial duties. Collectively their responsibility was to help the Emperor in the general management of state affairs.

Another important metropolitan organ was the Council of State (*Chün-chi-ch'u*). This agency was formed in 1730 as an emergency organization to help in the suppressing of a rebellion. Its original object was the handling of military matters, but it soon came to deal with all important state affairs. As specified in the *Ta-Ch'ing hui-tien,* its duties were "to write Imperial edicts and decisions, and to determine such things as may be of importance to the Army and to the nation, in order to aid the sovereign in regulating the machinery of affairs."[10] Thus the Council of State took over part of the responsibility originally vested in the Grand Secretariat, although it never shared the high degree of prestige enjoyed by the Grand Secretariat. The Councilors were held ready for audience at any time, took charge of the writing of rescripts and the keeping of memorials, and made recommendations to the Emperor on the appointment of all important government officials. Briefly stated, the duty of the Councilors was to give general assistance and advice to the Emperor on all matters of state.

The number of members of the Council of State varied according to the pleasure of the Emperor. They were drawn from the ranks of princes of

---

within the limits of our own American society we have at least the seeds of orthodoxy, conformity, and decay. The parallel between the Manchu-Chinese past and the European-American future is not a certain one. It is a serious enough potentiality to be of interest to anyone who is willing to look beyond the strategy of today to the world which all of us wish, one way or another, to bequeath to our grandchildren.

[10] *Ta-Ch'ing hui-tien* (1908 edition, Shanghai), *chüan* 3.

blood, ministers and vice-ministers of the six departments, and the chief officers of all other metropolitan courts or boards. The usual number of Councilors was five or six with a Manchu in the senior-most position. Below the Councilors there were 32 Secretaries of the Council who were drawn from lesser officials of the various metropolitan courts and were nicknamed the "Little Councilors." Because of the importance of their work and their access to key personages, the Secretaries of the Council were usually regarded as men on the way up in the Imperial administration. Secretaryship was an almost sure sign of future favor and promotion.

The third predominant facility in the metropolitan administration was the Censorate (*Tu-ch'a-yüan*). The Censorate was composed of two principal and four assistant Censors-General, 24 departmental censors, 56 provincial censors, 2 censors for the Imperial clansmen, and 10 for the metropolitan city of Peking.[11] Since the Censorate had a long tradition in China and reflected the trend of public opinion toward government, it occupied an important position in the political system.

Apart from the traditional censorial duty of remonstrating to the Emperor for his own misconduct, the Censorate was vested with responsibilities of supervising government officials in the performance of their official duties and the conduct of their private lives, and in auditing the accounts of the metropolitan Department of Revenue and the revenue agencies of the several provinces. The Censorate also supervised the construction of public buildings, the damming of rivers, and the direction of charitable enterprises.[12] Some members of the Censorate even performed judicial functions in conjunction with other judicial organizations.

The Grand Secretariat, the Council of State, and the Censorate formed a triad of agencies which were vested with important deliberative and advisory functions. In Manchu China they were the highest governmental bodies, directly assisting the Emperor in basic decisions. Other organizations were far more routine in character, some of them regular government departments performing long-established administrative functions, whereas others were irregularly instituted organs in charge of certain specific responsibilities or Imperial household duties. For both categories of agencies it must be remembered that the pattern of the Emperor as exemplified in the Dragon Throne, by which he was obliquely mentioned, had become a force almost as decisive in the Chinese monarchy as the personal rule of Louis XIV.

Regular Administrative Organizations. At the core of the routine

[11] Hsieh, *op. cit.*, p. 88.

[12] The responsibility of the Comptroller of the Army as it has developed since the end of World War II bears many significant parallels to the Chinese Censorate. The responsibilities of the Comptroller's office overlap to a very high degree with those of the old Chinese Censorate when one allows for the difference in technology, language, and culture. The responsibility of the Chinese Censorate for charitable works is for instance paralleled by the duties of the Comptroller of the Army with respect to unappropriated funds of the Army—the various welfare, semi-private, corporate, and other funds which come not from revenue, but from the inevitable money-making activities attendant upon Army housekeeping and philanthropy.

administration there were six administrative departments (sometimes translated as boards) inherited from the Ming system with little change in their organization or functions. Each department was headed by two ministers and four vice-ministers, assisted by bureau directors, secretaries, and comptrollers. The departments were charged with the responsibility of carrying on the routine administrative business of the largest Empire in the world.[13]

The Department of Rites (*Li-pu*) was concerned with ritual observances, educational matters, and state protocol. The most important work of the Department of Rites pertained to education and to literary examinations. Since the agency was the chief ceremonial facility of the government, foreign embassies fell within its province, but foreign embassies were merely one among many ceremonial details to be handled. Others were sacrificial ceremonies, the official forms for on-the-record meetings between officials, and official dress designs.

Another *Li-pu* (sounds almost the same as the above but written with different ideographs) was the Department of Civil Service. This was concerned with the duties of recommending to the Emperor suitable incumbents to offices, conferring titles, ranks and rewards, granting of leaves of absence, and making of regulations concerning civil service examinations. Functions of the Department were distributed among its bureaus: Bureau of Appointments, Bureau of Titles, Bureau of Examinations, and Bureau of Records.

The Department of Revenue (*Hu-pu*) with its 14 bureaus organized on a territorial basis was empowered to regulate taxes and duties, to take the census, to examine expenditures, and to audit the central and provincial treasuries. Furthermore, this Department was also given the responsibilities of regulating currency and coinage, standardizing weights and measures, and supervising commercial intercourse, both domestic and foreign.

The Department of Military Affairs (*Ping-pu*) was entrusted with the development, direction, and maintenance of the army and navy, the handling of military commissions and commands, and the building of the national development. The four bureaus in this Department were the Bureau of Military Selection, Bureau of Statistics, Bureau of Communications, and Bureau of Supplies.

The Department of Justice (*Hsing-pu*) was charged with the duties of drafting regulations pertaining to the application of laws, granting of pardons, hearing of special evidence, and the final determination of the scales of fines and punishments. Noteworthy is the fact that it had no network

[13] The Manchu Empire had a population on the border of 300,000,000 at the time that George Washington was President of the United States. At the time the United States had a population in the neighborhood of 4,000,000 and the United Kingdom a population of 6,000,000 or 7,000,000. The Manchu Empire was consequently about 75 times the size of Washington's America and about the size of 40 United Kingdoms as of 1800. See John K. Fairbank, *The United States and China,* Cambridge, 1948, pp. 139 ff. The population growth of the Western powers has very sharply reduced the gap between China and other states. Problems of sheer administrative volume which were important to the Manchus are important to us Americans today, in a way that could not be imagined by the officials in Washington's, Madison's, or Jefferson's administration.

of prosecuting attorneys since the unitary powers of Chinese magistrates precluded the necessity of a separate attorney and judge in the same court. This Department had in its charge all the judicial and administrative work of the Empire and in special circumstances served as a court of appeal.

The Department of Public Works (*Kung-pu*) was assigned the regulation and erection of public buildings, mausolea, highways, canals, bridges, and dikes, the procurement of weighing and measuring devices, and the building of ammunition depots. This Department was also divided into four bureaus: Bureau of Imperial Mausolea, Bureau of Construction, Bureau of Weights and Measures, and Bureau of Rivers and Canals.

Manchu Foreign and Colonial Offices. After the Treaty of Tientsin in 1858 the Western powers obtained the privilege of having their diplomatic representatives reside in Peking. To meet this unprecedented contingency, the Manchu government established the Office of Foreign Affairs (*Tsung-li ya-mên*). This was first organized on a commission basis, its members numbering as high as eleven, holding other substantive posts. Forty years later the *Tsung-li ya-mên* was replaced by a modern Department of Foreign Affairs (*Wai-wu-pu*).[14]

The Manchu Colonial Office is of importance because of the perennial problem of China's relationship to its inland dependencies. Called *Li-fan-yüan,* it was instituted for the government and the direction of external frontiers, the supervision of such internal frontiers as the unassimilated aborigines or the wandering tribes, the regulation of the governments of the Nomads, and the management of tributary states. All outlying territories and dominions which were not yet qualified to assume the status of province came under the supervision and guidance of this Colonial Office. The President and his two Vice-Presidents were either Manchus or Mongols. The work of the Office was divided among six different bureaus, treating such matters as boundaries, titles of nobility, official appointments, the reception of visiting princes from Inner and Outer Mongolia, the organization of the Manchu military cadres called banners, and the relay of communications throughout the Colonial Empire.

Other Metropolitan Organs. The *Han-lin-yüan* usually translated as the "Academy of Letters" was the personnel pool at the apex of the entire scholastic bureaucracy. In theory this organization assembled the most accomplished personalities of China; from its membership the Emperor selected his most responsible officers. The members when in inactive or reserve status spent their lives studying somewhat after the manner of the Institute for Advanced Study located at Princeton, New Jersey. In other words, there was the speculation that the members would perform some kind of serious and valuable scholastic work; there was also the opportunity for

[14] In the last days of Ch'ing dynasty other modern ministries were added in 1906: a Ministry of Education *(Hsüeh-pu),* a Ministry of Agriculture, Industry, and Commerce *(Nung-kung-shang-pu),* and a Ministry of Posts and Communications *(Yu-Ch'uan-pu).*

stimulation through conferences and discussions; but there was no curriculum or degree and no schedule requirements. Occasionally the *Han-lin-yüan* as a body was given archival or literary functions, such as supervising the publication of a series of government documents or the editing of a group of literary works. Only those scholar bureaucrats who had passed the final, highest metropolitan examinations were made members of the academy. Two presidents appointed for life exercised a loose supervisory control over the studies of the members. Below the presidents there were four grades of officers with five persons in each office, and an unlimited number of members.[15]

From the above it can be seen that the metropolitan administration under the Manchus was so instituted as to preserve the entire power of government in the hands of the Emperor, since all important governmental organizations were either pure advisory organs, administrative agencies, or machineries of political control, and there were no institutions that possessed responsible executive authority like the premiership of Sung or Yüan dynasties. The result was that efficient government was insured only when energetic monarchs were ruling with strong hands, while misgovernment and corruption prevailed when the Dragon Throne was occupied by weaklings.

General Features of Local Administration. In approaching the subject of provincial and local government in old China one must keep in mind the axiom—stated above and here demonstrated—that the level of government in China was lower than anywhere else in the civilized world. In other words, the process which we call "politics" secured external development and inward stability at a smaller expenditure of man-lives, a smaller percentage of total income, than any medieval or modern Western state has done. Within the limits of the Confucian ideological system there was neither room for government nor need for the government beyond an unbelievably low minimum.

Quantitatively speaking, the low level of governmental activity in all aspects of the Chinese political system contributed to some very special features concerning the relationship of local government to the metropolitan

[15] Among other institutions of the metropolitan administration the following may be mentioned:

i. Office of Transmission *(T'ung-chêng-ssŭ)* had the duty of opening, recording, and transmitting to the Council of State all memorials received from the provinces.

ii. Grand Court of Revision *(Ta-li-ssŭ)* exercised a general supervision over the administration of the criminal law.

iii. The four minor courts: (a) Court of Sacrificial Worship *(T'ai-ch'ang-ssŭ)*; (b) Court of Imperial Stud *(T'ai-p'u-ssŭ)*; (c) Court of Imperial Entertainments *(Kuang-lu-ssŭ)*; and (d) Court of State Ceremonial *(Hung-lu-ssŭ)*.

iv. Imperial Board of Astronomy *(Ch'in-t'ien-chien)*.

v. The Imperial Household *(Nei-wu-fu)* was divided into seven departments. These were: (a) Treasury of the Privy Purse *(Kuang-ch'u-ssŭ)*; (b) Pay and Commission Office for the Household Brigade *(Tu-yu-ssŭ)*; (c) Office of Worship, Ceremonial, and Control of Eunuchs *(Chang-I-ssŭ)*; (d) Pasturage Department *(Ch'ing-fêng-ssŭ)*, (e) Collectorate of Rents for Banner Property *(K'uai-chi-ssŭ)*; (f) Office of Works *(Ying-tsao-ssŭ)*; and (g) Judicial Department *(Shen-hsing-ssŭ)*.

See Mayers, *op. cit.*, Part II; Hsieh, *op. cit.*, Chap. 10.

authorities. Chief among these were the following four points: local autonomy, checks and balances, minimum administration, and what can be called "social delegation."

First, the local government occupied a semi-autonomous status in relation to the central authorities. The particular legal relationship cannot be described in satisfactory terms as either *unitary,* or as *federal,* since in the field of personnel the central government maintained absolute power, but in the matter of processes the local governments were left almost untouched. As long as the local governments furnished their quota of rice or bullion in taxes for the maintenance of the Imperial court, as long as they avoided outrage to the general scheme of Confucian morality and presented no notorious cases of criminality or misfortune, as long as they supported the vague general policies of the central administration, as long as peace and order made it unnecessary for the central authorities to bother with them, as long as they depended upon their own resources of intelligence and man power to keep themselves inconspicuous, they were free from interference from the central government. So wide was their latitude in the exercise of local powers that, prior to the establishment of the Office of Foreign Affairs, the conduct of diplomatic relations was considered a local matter entirely subject to local initiative and of interest to Peking only in the form of long delayed euphuistically worded reports.

Secondly, the principle of checks and balances was carried to extreme so far as the control of local government personnel was concerned. Local officials all the way down to the *hsien* magistrates were appointed by metropolitan authorities. No person was allowed to serve in his native county or province, so that the psychological relationship of a government official resembled the consular relationship in modern Western life more than the mayoral relationship. At his best the local official was regarded as "that nice outsider" and not as "one of our leading citizens."

So jealous was Peking in its monopoly of the appointing power that, although the provincial authorities might make recommendations, the actual orders of appointment and dismissal had to go through Peking itself. The appointment for each post was made for a term of three years; no person could ever be appointed to serve in the province of his birth. These regulations were designed to make sure that no local official would either start with strong enough connections to obtain an improper degree of influence, or stay long enough in the community to acquire a dangerous measure of leadership.

There were further checks and balances. Local officials were given the power not only to supervise their subordinates: they were frequently encouraged to impeach one another or their superiors. For instance, the Viceroy (*Tsung-tu,* sometimes translated as Governor-General) was given the *ex officio* title of Deputy Censor-General and therewith, beyond his authority of maintaining a strict control over provincial officials, was also vested with the power to impeach other viceroys or even ministers of the central government.

Thirdly, local government functions—apart from functions required by the central government such as the collection of revenue and the maintenance of peace—were limited to a minimum. These were the settlement of legal disputes, the conduct of public construction and relief work, and the maintenance of ritual or educational facilities. There were neither definite regulations governing these activities nor assured funds to finance them. Hence, the personal integrity and ability of local officials were the determining factors of the success or failure of local government enterprises. Since these activities were not mandatory, the scope of local functions was so flexible as to permit local officials to undertake them or not. Not even the pressure of public opinion could demand the performance or the omission of a specific project which might come into question in a particular district. For both people and officials the highest criterion of behavior was to escape Imperial notice, to avoid making trouble, to make sure that official displeasure would neither punish the community nor blight the ear of the scholar bureaucrat to whom the community was entrusted.

Fourthly, unrecognized by the Chinese themselves, there was a principle which has been rediscovered by the modern totalitarian states—a principle which can be called "social delegation," comprising the delegation to non-governmental groups of minor or specific government functions. The family, the village, and the *hui* did most of the jobs that are performed in the United States by school districts, by county boards, and by city mayors or commissions.

The Ch'ing Provinces. For the purpose of administration the Ch'ing Empire was divided into 18 provinces (*shêng;* during the later Ch'ing, the number was increased to 22). These 18 provinces were further subdivided into 185 prefectures (*fu*) and 1,545 districts or counties (*hsien*). Other levels of subdivisions included such local units as circuits (*tao*), subprefectures (*chou*), and cantons (*t'ing*). The circuits were in most cases *ad hoc* local units concerned with special functions such as those pertaining to the administration of customs, the salt monopoly, the transportation of tribute grain or military matters. The subprefectures and cantons were special local units which were too big to be classified as *hsien* and had not yet attained the status of prefectures. Generally speaking, units of local administration were divided into three well-filled layers—provinces, prefectures, districts.

The Viceroy was the highest civil official in local administration. Eight viceroyalties, each controlling from one to three provinces, covered most of China. The duties of the Viceroy consisted of the plenary control of government affairs, the supervision of all inferior officials, and the command of all "Chinese-race" military forces within his jurisdiction. The Provincial Governor (*Hsün-fu*) had a similar control over his province, but to an inferior degree. Theoretically, the Governor was under the control of the

Viceroy. In actual practice the viceroyalties did not encompass *all* the Chinese provinces, so that all provinces had governors, but only some of the provinces had viceroyalties between the governors and the Dragon Throne. Whenever the dual administration was present there was apt to be considerable rivalry between the Viceroy and the Governor as each had the power to memorialize the throne and each could impeach the other. This dual authority was further evidence of the application of the principle of checks and balances.

Provincial administrative functions were divided among several commissioners who were independently appointed by the metropolitan government and responsible to the Emperor. This is one more instance of excessive provincial authority during the Manchu regime. The Finance Commissioner (*Pu-chêng-shih-ssŭ*) was provincial treasurer and concurrently head of the civil service. The Judicial Commissioner (*An-ch'a-shih-ssŭ*) was charged with supervision over all civil and criminal cases and acted as a final court of appeal for cases arising within the provinces. The Educational Commissioner (*T'i-hsüeh-shih*) was not, strictly speaking, a provincial, but was appointed by the Emperor for the specific purpose of conducting civil service examinations and supervising educational affairs in the province.

Below the commissioners were the Circuit Intendants (*Fên-hsün-tao* or colloquially, *Tao-t'ai*). These were *ad hoc* local officials performing functions in specially designated areas. The territory under their control usually comprised several prefectures. Their number per province was indefinite. They occupied an intermediary position between the Governor and the Prefect. Their titles varied according to the functional nature of their work—such as the Salt Gabelle, grain transportation, military affairs, customs, waterways, communications and posts.

Next to the Circuit Intendants were the Prefects (*Chih-fu*), who ruled over prefectures. A prefecture in turn was composed of subprefectures, cantons, and districts or *hsien*. The Prefect was the supervising official of the largest political division within the province: each province had from 7 to 13 prefectures. Scarcely an independent administrator, his duties resembled those of a liaison officer between the Governor and the District Magistrate. The *chou* and *t'ing* were headed by *chih-chou* and *t'ing-shih* and were used to supplement the prefectural structure when necessary.

The most important local government unit was the district. The district magistrate was called *chih-hsien* officially in Ch'ing times and *hsien-chang* in modern popular parlance. The District Magistrate was regarded as the "father and mother official" of a district; theoretically it was up to him to look after the people under his jurisdiction as though they were the children of his own family. The theory was one thing, the practice quite different. Because of his intimate contact with the people the Magistrate was usually the most oppressive and feared official in the entire bureaucracy.

His duties were threefold: the collection of taxes, the settlement of litigation, and the maintenance of peace and order.

In performing his functions the District Magistrate was the final emissary of the government to the people. It was he who had to get things done. Like a bad parent in our own civilization, he asked of his children chiefly that they not bother him or get him into trouble. He *had* to forward the taxes which were collected, he *had* to keep the district quiet, and he *hoped* to get promoted onward and upward without arousing notice or displeasure. Unlike his very colleagues at the provincial level, he had no other scholar bureaucrat sharing his power or watching him. The situation was ready-made for the application of local tyranny should the Magistrate temperament so warrant.

Under the Magistrate there were a number of minor officials, whose status was comparable to the noncommissioned officers of Colonial African troops

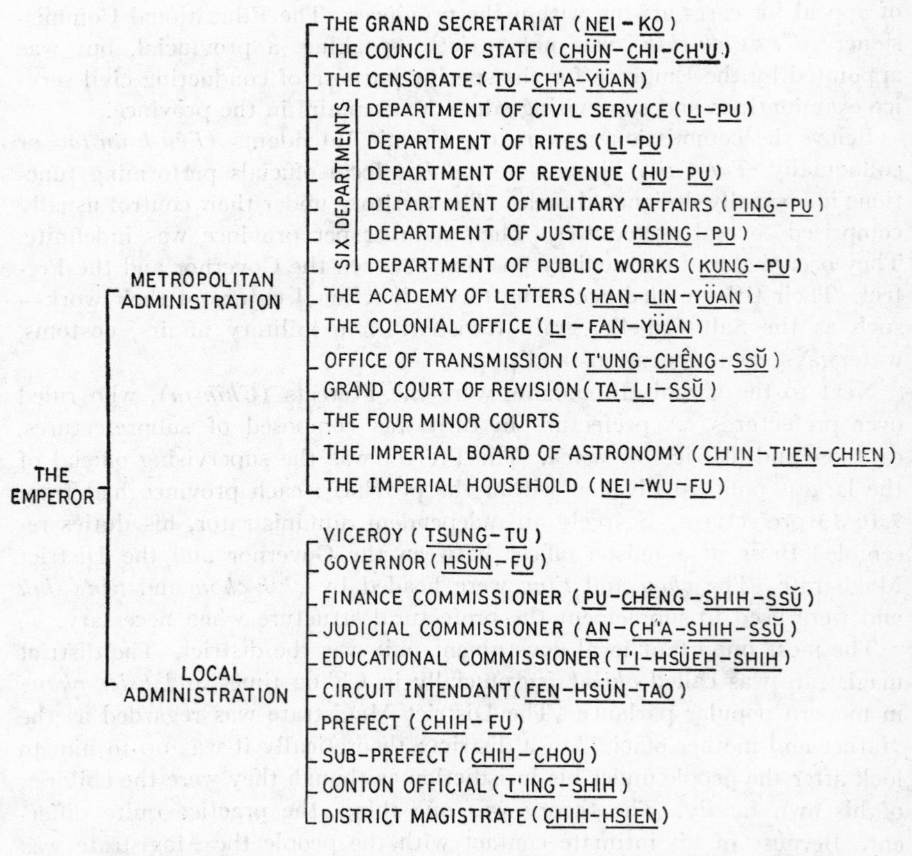

CHART 2—Organization of the Metropolitan Administration and Local System of Government (The Last Fifty Years of Ch'ing)

today when all the commissioned officers are Europeans. They had status, but not much status. They were local people. They were not scholar-bureaucrats, not gentlemen, and yet they were expected to carry out those functions of government which most irritate or inflame the people. Registrars, jail wardens, *hsien* superintendents of schools, treasury keepers, granary keepers, bailiffs, and the like could exercise a tremendous influence for good or bad.

Chart 2 presents the organization of the metropolitan administration and the local system of government systematically on the basis of the last fifty years of the Ch'ing dynasty.

Civil Service and Literary Examinations.[16] As pointed out previously, the absolute autocracy of the government of old China was made tolerable by a civil service system which possessed certain inherent democratic or popular strains. If democracy is regarded as comprising four pre-eminent ideas—equalitarianism, free social and political mobility up and down the scale, popular government, and representative government [17]—it can be said that the scholastic bureaucracy offered no equalitarianism, some free mobility, and a mild response to the demands of popular government, and more than a trace of representative government through its selection of candidates from all of China.

The underlying principle of the Civil Service system was that equal opportunity should be offered to all persons who could qualify themselves intellectually. The basic supposition was that intelligence recognized no caste and that therefore young men of talent, regardless of family connection or social position, should be allowed to climb the bureaucratic ladder through free competition in a series of literary examinations.

The old civil service examination system had been stereotyped by the first Ming Emperor. Throughout Ming and Ch'ing examinations were held at regular intervals and became the main channel *for persons of Chinese race* to obtain government posts. There were still some, of course, who succeeded by recommendation alone, by inheritance, and even by outright purchase. Yet the procurement facility by examination kept going, rallying talented men of the realm to the support of the dynasty. Relative to other branches and practices of government, there was at least an attempt to guard

[16] There is a wealth of treatises and material on civil service and literary examinations in the Ch'ing dynasty. Outstanding accounts are given in Hsieh, *op. cit.*, Chap. 6; W. F. Mayers, *op. cit.*, Chap. IX; Etienne Zi, *Pratique des Examens Littĕraires en Chine* (Varieties Sinologiques No. 5, Shanghai, 1894). For Chinese source materials, see *Ta-Ch'ing hui-tien* (1908 edition) *chüan* 33; Wang Hsieh-chien, *Tung-hua-lu* (Annals and memoirs of the Ch'ing dynasty), Peking, 1884. Excellent descriptions of the examination system in Chinese are to be found in Chu P'eng-shou, *Chiu-tien pei-cheng* (Anecdotes of the Ch'ing dynasty), Peiping, 1941, Vol. 4; Chang Chung-ju, *Ch'ing-tai k'ao-shih chih-tu tzŭ-liao* (Readings on the examination system of the Ch'ing dynasty), Shanghai, 1932.

[17] An extensive discussion of the limitations of the idea of democracy as applied to the old Chinese situation can be found in P. M. A. Linebarger's, *The Political Doctrines of Sun Yat-sen,* Baltimore, 1937, pp. 29-52 and 89-96.

against corruption and malpractice. The Manchu Civil Service did of course fail in the end, but it was the last institution to fail.

Education and Civil Service. Under the Ch'ing as in previous dynasties, the content and direction of education was under the rigid control of the government, even though the educational facilities were for the greater part private.

State rules existed only for those who already had relatively severe preliminary training. Before entering government-sponsored schools or the private academies organized by exceptional scholars on an informal basis, the prospective student had to have the most difficult part of the work behind him.

Memorizing the Confucian classics was the corner-stone of all education. Can the modern reader appreciate what this chore meant? How many present-day American students could even guess what it would mean to memorize the corpus of material larger than the New Testament? How many sane people today have memorized 80,000 consecutive words of any text whatever?

This much must be said of Confucian orthodoxy: at its worst it was humane in content. At its most rigid it still gave responsibility to the individuals. Even at its most confining the literary material of the Confucian canon was extraordinarily beautiful.

These things cannot be said for the intellectual melange thrust upon the unfortunate student who aspired to the higher posts of the Kuomintang bureaucracy. Still less does it apply to the candidates for high office in Communist China. Confucianism at its worst was a sterile humanism, but it was at least humane. At its most vulgar, its most credulous, it still carried —as the vehicle of its orthodoxy—works of tremendous and self-refreshing literary importance. The endless jargon of present-day Communism in China is neither humane, nor beautiful, nor literary. It resembles Confucianism only in one all-important respect. It, too, stifles the human mind.

Some decades or centuries from now a future America may find itself obliged to adopt the educational procedure carried out with considerable success by Confucianist China. The reform would consist of making all college degrees an act of the central government, of commissioning all successful competitors in government service (whether civil or military, active or reserve), and of thus standardizing the educational standards of the country while automatically giving the governmental facilities first priority in the procurement of talented persons. The inevitable by-product of such a procedure—which could be either dreadful or desirable, depending upon one's point of view—would be the procuring and deactivating (generation after generation) of all of the potentially active, unorthodox, or rebellious minds of the country. Everyone with enough talent to pass the examinations would automatically acquire some kind of status in the government. The status could be imperiled by unorthodoxy or disloyalty, the standards for which would be described by the administration in power. Revolutions are rarely led by stupid or uneducable men. Under such a system almost all intelligent men would be bought up by the government as soon as they reached maturity.

This is just about what happened in China.

Under the old examination system, young Chinese men took the district examination offered by the Commissioner of Education in their province. They might try as early as their late teens, competing with other previously unsuccessful candidates who were still trying in their forties or fifties. The successful candidates were given the title *hsiu-ts'ai* (cultivated talents) and became students of the district academy. The academy was not a college in the Western sense of the term. It had no buildings. There was no curriculum. It was loosely administered by the governmentally-appointed instructors.

This first step up, attainment of the *hsiu-ts'ai,* was the decisive honor or disappointment of a scholar's life. He was entitled to wear a blue gown. He was elevated above the common herd. He passed immediately beyond the reach of ordinary law and everyday punishments. No local magistrate could punish him until he was first expelled from the academy. He might get only starvation wages, but this economic poverty was offset by immense benefits of status-privilege. The only Western equivalent was priestly ordination in the Middle Ages. Most important of all, the *hsiu-ts'ai* was entitled to compete in the provincial examination and thus had a right to ascend the ladder of officialdom from within the walls.

In each province a provincial examination was held triennially. Students of all the districts within the province, after passing several preliminary examinations, were permitted to participate in the provincial examination. Successful candidates emerging from this examination became *chü-jên* (appointed persons). This degree not only entitled the holder to participate in the next higher examinations, the metropolitan ones, but it automatically placed him on an availability roster for comparatively important government appointments. The difficulty of these triennial examinations can be understood if one notes that approximately one out of every 300 participants passed the examination. This calculation is somewhat misleading in that unsuccessful candidates usually came up again in the next examination.

Most arduous of the examinations were the metropolitan ones. The examination itself consisted of three successive sessions similar to, but more difficult than, the provincial examination. Successful candidates—usually one out of every ten eligible—were awarded the degree *kung-shih* (presented scholars). Under the Ch'ing dynasty, for example, 112 regular and special metropolitan examinations were given over a span of 260 years, and a total of about 25,000 metropolitan degrees were awarded.

Men who passed the *kung-shih* were at the top. Once they got through the basic examination they were presented to the Emperor for the final palace examination. The Emperor himself was the examiner. Actually this did not confer any new degrees, but was designed to divide the successful candidates into three classes.

The first three individuals in each group comprised the first class, the next one fourth of the total were the second class, and all the others were in the third class. After the palace examination all candidates became *chin-shih* (accomplished scholars), but those of the first two classes—the three best in each triennium, plus the top 25 per cent—were assigned to the *Han-lin-yüan* (The Academy of the Forest of Pencils or, more simply, The Academy of Letters) as editors or compilers. Since only a little more than a quarter of the metropolitan graduates were eligible for positions in this Academy, membership in the Academy was the highest of all high positions scholastically. Assignment to the Academy was the dream of all scholars, young and old.

During the Manchu reign matters pertaining to the civil service examination were assigned to the Department of Rites. In actuality all examinations were conducted by specially appointed officials and the Department had only routine supervisory responsibilities. Powers of appointment into the working civil service were however reserved to the Department of Civil Service. There is recorded in the paragraphs of the great Ch'ing code, the *Ta-Ch'ing hui-tien,* a set of elaborate civil service laws and regulations usually applied with faithfulness and regularity by the Department. Briefly stated, these provisions specified two kinds of appointments, one special and the other general. Special appointments were made by the Emperor himself. General appointments were made upon recommendation of the Department of Civil Service in the name of the Emperor. Lower ranks than these, officials of the seventh rank and below, were directly appointed from the scholastic rosters by the various departments concerned.

There were several ways in which a person could get himself appointed to a working post in officialdom. The natural and proper way was to pass the examination and bide his time. A second way, less meritorious, was to apply for specially designated positions through the moral claim of extraordinary service rendered the dynasty by the applicant's relatives. A third method was through the recommendation of high dignitaries on the claim (specious or not) of having special talents or possessing extraordinary capacity for civil or military affairs. The fourth and less worthy alternative, was through purchase.

According to tradition, officials who were appointed by virtue of their possession of either the metropolitan or provincial degrees were considered as having "arrived through the honored channel" (*chêng-t'u ch'u-shen*) and were allowed to reach the highest positions of the hierarchy.

Not all persons with degrees were assured positions. Eligibility implied no legal claim to office. Just as only one in a hundred competitors ever obtained any degree whatever, only one out of every several scores of graduates was awarded an actual official position. The pressure from below was immense, and the places at the top few. The lure of great reward immobilized tens and hundreds of thousands of literate men, while it was actually awarded to few.

Only a few insignificant posts were given to relatives of high dignitaries as a recognition of distinguished service rendered by the latter. No person who had real confidence in his talent sought appointment through hereditary means, since this meant a blind-alley career. Worthy men preferred to seek the position through their own efforts in the competitive examination. The other alternative of special recommendation was tolerated in the civil service system as a means whereby key persons in the heights of the bureaucracy were granted the legal power to secure helpers whom they regarded as personally trustworthy or to show extraordinary favor to deserving subordinates. In good times this procedure was not abused. Despite the exceptions made for special promotion by recommendation, all such recommendations had to be subjected to a screening process by the Department of Civil Service before the name of the Emperor was attached to the appointment, thus making it official.

The sale of office reached so fine and high a point in China that from time to time it was legalized. This was done on the ingenious theory that if offices were going to be peddled the revenue might as well go to the Empire instead of the peculators. The Manchus legalized this practice and used it whenever they had an extraordinary need for revenue. During the T'ai-p'ing rebellion receipts from the sales of public offices became a regular support to the Imperial treasury; the volume of this outrageous traffic was so great that it actually disrupted the proper functioning of the Civil Service system. This practice often brought unworthy and even uneducated men to officialdom.

Since the posts which were sold often comprised powers amounting to jurisdiction over life and death, the common people suffered boundless injustice and the net effects on the welfare of the government were much worse than those accruing from the sale of commissions in his Britannic Majesty's forces at the time of American War for Independence.

Rank and Reward in the Scholastic Bureaucracy. The hierarchy of Manchu officialdom followed the Chinese traditional pattern, dating back to T'ang, of nine ranks, each with two grades. This applied to both civil and military offices. Each rank had a regular grade and an accessory grade. The preoccupation of each official, once appointed, was to climb the bureaucratic ladder. Generally speaking, the term of office was three years. In theory and most of the time in practice, the incumbent could not stand still in a designated position: he had to go up, down, or out. Renewal of appointment was rare. The normal process was promotion, demotion, or compulsory retirement. The evaluation of merits and demerits of all officials was made by the Department of Civil Service with the exception of those officials of the third rank or above who followed a rigorous system in drafting their own service records and submitting them to the Emperor for review.

Apart from immense prestige enjoyed by the mandarin class there were real economic privileges attached to public office. Of an official's potential income, his normal salary was in most cases a small fraction. Rather, as in the case of the U.S.S.R. at the present time, legal salaries were modest in contrast to the equally legal, but less publicized, allowances which went with each rank. A man on the equivalent of a one-hundred-dollar-a-month salary might have allowances which would give him a purchasing capacity twenty times as great. Over and above the small legal salary and the generous legal allowance, illegal incomes were almost always possible. The amount of illegal income depended upon the time, the place, and the individual. Often honest men were driven into accepting illegal incomes simply because the practice had become common. There were few safeguards against illegal practices on the part of the officials. Chinese auditing was extremely elementary.

These irrational financial arrangements gave rise to official corruption. Corruption was almost taken for granted. In the everyday conversation of educated men all government posts were classified as good or bad, depending upon their lucrativeness. It must not be inferred that no good men ever entered the service of the government or that no just deeds were performed for the populace by the servants of the Emperor. Many upright men retired from important posts penniless; thousands of them discharged their functions to the satisfaction of the people, keeping their pilfering civilized in manner and moderate in amount.

Nevertheless, the kind, benevolent efforts of ten officials could be undone by one corrupt, cruel functionary whose oppression and mendacity became legend, never to be forgiven or forgotten. A large portion of the new arrivals in officialdom, having spent the better part of their lives in memorizing high-flown ideals and mastering intricate formal literary style were prepared to be sincere and honest. It was the half-paid semi-official retainers and underclerks to be found around every *yamen* in China who showed the newly arrived official the ropes and taught him—if he had the least propensity in that direction—how to be a thief in a few simple lessons. Very often the sincere and honest intentions of the newly appointed scholar-officials would be neutralized in short order by such an environment. A few public functionaries were wicked at the outset by sheer inclination; most of them who became corrupt were influenced by the circumstances of everyday official life. A common epigram ran, "a man who accumulates a hundred thousand taels in three years can be considered an honest magistrate." Since a hundred thousand taels in 1750 had the purchasing power of several million dollars today, this was probably a gross exaggeration. Exaggeration or not, it reflected the popular distrust of officials' conduct.

Manchu Governmental Characteristics. The Manchu or Ch'ing dynasty was the last historic period of old China. It was therefore doubly important in that it was not only representative of its predecessor dynasties, but significant in that it was this reign rather than others which gave foreign nations their impression of Chinese politics and their evaluation of Chinese culture. How good was the Ch'ing regime?

It would be unfair to say that the Manchu government was corrupt and inefficient throughout its rule. During the first hundred or hundred and fifty years of the dynasty it achieved a level of prosperity markedly higher than that of contemporary Europe—higher perhaps than of any other portion of the world of that time with the exception of Japan. The main aim of the Manchu court was nevertheless revealed by its manifest policies—to keep the throne as long as possible and to raise the power of the Emperor as far as it could be raised.

From this corrupting premise in the basic Manchu theory of government there sprang surreptitiously corollaries which in the long run ruined both China and the Manchu dynasty which ruled China. Is it not important that the China which did meet the Western World was a demoralized, disaster-ridden country, not a magnificent Asian state at the height of its political vigor? Manchu weaknesses left their impress not only on China, but on world history. The three ineradicable stigmata of Manchu rule were *suspicion, reaction,* and *corruption.*

The first and most outstanding feature of the Manchu institution of government was the profound suspiciousness of the rulers—their suspicion of the conquered people, of the assimulated Chinese officials, of their own kinsmen. When the Manchus first occupied the Chinese throne they issued strict orders to prohibit miscegenation between Manchus and Chinese in an attempt to preserve the racial integrity of their much out-numbered tribes. This regulation had the long-run effect of preventing the infusion of new blood into long decaying families and of insuring the sociological stagnation of the Manchu garrisons which were stationed "in perpetuity" in the strategic centers of the conquered Chinese Empire.

The racial arrogance of the Manchus gave them identity and brought them hatred. Hitherto cosmopolitan and tolerant, the Chinese were whipped up into a consciousness of race which, carried over into the Nationalist and Communist periods of modern times, gives Chinese politics the racial tone reminiscent at its worst of Hitlerism. The China which had assimilated Jews, Arabs, Turks, Huns, and Mongols, not to mention the rag, tag, and bobtail of a thousand other races, became acutely conscious of itself as a race, merely because the Manchus imported the concept *race* and enforced it with knives and whips. The flare-up of Chinese racialism led inevitably to an underground ferment of conspiracy.

It is difficult to say which came first, Manchu suspicion or Chinese resentment, Manchu repression or the Chinese underground. Each justified and stimulated the other. Two hundred years and more of clandestine political struggle were waged in China down to the horrible months of the Spring of 1912 when the Chinese ended the racial problem with wholesale massacres of Manchus.

Suspicion left its mark on the administrative services as well. The administrative attempts to maintain a balance between the races led to the appointment of both Chinese and Manchu officials in the same service or in the same locality. This check and balance technique weakened the efficiency of administration and bequeathed to modern China the political concept that it was better to have a trustworthy government than to have a good one. Just as the Indonesians of today maintain the whole gamut of weird Dutch administrative habits bequeathed them by their former Colonial masters, just as the Indians conduct their state with an incredible pattern of modified British customs, Nationalist and Communist China are, whether they like it or not, reflections of the Manchu practice. The Manchus departed from the check and balance system after the T'ai-p'ing rebellion. Suspension of the bad habit stopped their aggravation but did not remove their imprint.

Even among the Manchus, suspicion prevailed. Imperial clansmen and the maternal relatives of the Emperor were sharply excluded from important positions. In theory, this was designed to prevent factions from arising within the groups of Imperial clansmen and relatives. Actually, the result was the stultification of the ruling house, the exclusion of able ambitious clansmen from public service. Rarely, if ever, in history has a strain of livestock had courage and initiative bred out of it as thoroughly as these qualities were bred out of the reigning Manchu family.

A reactionary outlook was the second characteristic of the Manchu government. Since the Manchus were ignorant of the art of statecraft when they first occupied the periphery of China and established a government in the Chinese form in 1625, they depended both before and after the conquest very heavily on Chinese ministers. Legend credits these Chinese ministers with devising for the Manchus a set of suicidal laws which made the corruption and collapse of the Manchu reign completely inevitable. It is not at this date possible to prove that the Chinese quislings who served the Manchus so disastrously were in fact cloaked patriots, but it is easy to read into the laws the intent, now quite apparent, of destroying the Manchu Throne. In effect these laws made life too easy for the Manchus, so easy that the Manchus could not help their remote but inescapable undoing. Overprotection, reaction, suicide—this was the grand formula of three centuries reduced to a phrase.

The spirit so brilliantly evident in the Japanese reigning family at the time of the Meiji Emperor—an eagerness to serve the past by meeting the present and thus guaranteeing the future—was completely lacking in the Imperial house of Manchus. Only one Emperor, the unfortunate Kuang Hsü, undertook reform for a hundred days in 1898, but his family and his tradition were against him. Reaction begets revolution; it is certain that the sustained ferment of modern China is owing in large measure to the endless reaction of Manchu rule.

Corruption has always been common in China. Under the Manchus it became monstrous in volume and refined in its oppression. The much-publicized corruption of the postwar Kuomintang was child's-play in comparison with the legalized thievery of the Manchu dynasty. In the later days of the Manchus the entire officialdom achieved so barefaced and sustained a volume of corruption that the cancer outgrew the organism, the thefts exceeded the revenue, the malpractices outweighed the process of government itself.

Corruption begot hypocrisy. Official salaries were kept exceedingly low. So artistic was the rascality of the Manchu bureaucracy that the lavish allowances accompanying these pretentiously humble salaries were even given the special official label, "An allowance for the avoidance of avarice." Officials who were not cut in on the legal diversion of revenue inevitably devised their own extralegal methods.

When American officials denounced the corruption of Kuomintang China they may have thought that they were denouncing Chiang Kai-shek and his immediate lieutenants. In fact they were attacking governmental habits which were ineradicably imprinted on the Chinese personality long before George Washington took oath of office as first President of the United States. The Nationalists succeeded brilliantly as long as they were not in power. It was wryly remarked of Sun Yat-sen that he was a great president whenever he was not in office. It was not the modern period, but the Manchu reign which taught the Chinese that protest was honorable and government dishonorable, administration contemptible, and conspiracy heroic. When the Nationalists took power some of them became thieves. It was easy in the light of Chinese tradition for the populace to consider that they had all become thieves. The outside world complained of Nationalist China when it was looking at the monstrous ghost of the Manchus. How much the Manchu heritage will affect the Communists is still uncertain. The formula, suspicion-reaction-corruption, is tragically well suited to any administration in China. A revolutionary ideology and an awkward economic system may compel the Communist leaders to make themselves good administrators, if they are to survive at all. The Communist press already gives much evidence of surrender of Communist bureaucrats to the impetus of the corrupt traditions of old China. The Manchu realm is forty years dead and the last Manchu Emperor a Russian prisoner in Siberia, but the problems characteristic of the Manchu period persist in China.

It was, then, indeed unfortunate that it was Manchu China—demoralized, disaster-ridden, suspicious, reactionary, and corrupt—which faced rebellion from within and the approaching power of the West outside, during the nineteenth century. China was under further disadvantage in dealing with the sea-coming barbarians. China had traditionally developed a far-reaching system of intracultural relations of her own in East Asia. This system, typically built around the Confucian concept of a family of nations, was ill-suited for adjustment to the impact of the West, with its vigorous, demanding, and sovereign nation-states.

CHAPTER FOUR

Old China's Colonial Empire and the Chinese Family of Nations

THE old Chinese political system included three distinct elements:

1. *the inner empire* inhabited by the Chinese;
2. *a colonial empire,* including a number of border areas and non-Chinese enclaves; and
3. *a Chinese family of nations,* an outer group of peripheral dependent states comprising most of the world known to the Chinese.

Across the centuries of China's history the relationship among these three types of territories played a varying but almost always significant role in the dynamics of Chinese politics. From Han down to the present, the border areas have been centers of Chinese strategic thinking.

The immense continuities of Chinese history can be readily appreciated when one observes that in Homer Dubs' magisterial translation of *The History of the Former Han Dynasty by Pan Ku* the Chinese officials of the two centuries immediately preceding the time of Jesus Christ were as much preoccupied with Sinkiang as are the Communist bureaucrats of today. The presence of the Chinese People's Volunteer Forces in Korea is motivated by Red China's contribution to the Communist cause, but it is certainly concurrently motivated by Chinese political and military considerations which have not changed in the last 2,000 years. One need only turn the pages of China's history to pick up the old theme: China claimed her manifest destiny, whenever it was physically possible for the Chinese to do so, against Burma, Siam, Indo-China, Korea, Tibet, and any other peripheral territories within reach.

Past and present meet, furthermore, in the Chinese concept of the inherent and proper inequality of nations. In old Chinese thinking any supposition of the equality of states was as outrageous and unnatural an idea as the hypothesis of the equality of individual persons within the family or the community. To old China, states were naturally unequal and China itself, being, in their opinion, the largest and most civilized community of mankind, was first and always the superior of all other states. The idea of an equal China dealing with an equal Japan was provocative and stupid, in the opinion of the Japanese militarists, during the period 1931-1945; to the Japanese of that period, Japan, not China, was the successor to China as a leader of the natural and Heaven-decreed Far Eastern family of nations.[1] What shocked the Japanese a few years ago may annoy the Chinese of tomorrow; if one considers the past, it is difficult for China and Japan to be friendly nations unless one of them is clearly and unmistakably a subordinate of the other.

Continuing Importance of the Patterns. The problems of the concentric structuring of an old Chinese Empire—an inner Chinese core, an outer ring of possessions, an outmost family of patron-and-client states—would be important only in the eyes of historians if the political habits, the semantic drives, and the sense of appropriateness bequeathed to the Chinese past were not communicated to the present. If there were any expectation among Western observers that modern China would behave in colonial, frontier, and foreign matters different from its Imperial predecessors, these doubts should have been dispelled by the spectacle of Nationalist China, weak and war-ridden as it was, attempting to raise a boundary issue with British Burma over a slice of uninhabited and uninhabitable jungle territory in the very midst of World War II, or the sight of Communist China acting as the patron state for a necessarily dependent Communist North Korea.

Not only is the old Chinese pattern important for an understanding of Far Eastern politics: like so much of the sophisticated, cosmopolitan, and prematurely modern Chinese past,[2] archaic Chinese precedents are in many curious respects highly pertinent to the American future. If we Americans are moving into the kind of world—bureaucratic, civilian, global, educated—which China has had in large measure since the Sung dynasty (A.D. 960-1279), it may be that the Chinese experience, through the familiar cycle of feudal decentralization, through the system of sovereign nation-states, and into an advanced relationship—a family of nations—can become more

[1] For a description of the ill-fated Japanese scheme of a Far Eastern family of nations, see Chap. 19, pp. 435-438, "GEACPS."

[2] Professor Charles Sidney Gardner once commented that if the term "modern" is attached solely to societies into which mechanical power has entered as a determining technological factor, China is still not "modern." If, on the other hand, the term "modern" (with somewhat finer discrimination of cultural and political factors) is attached to those politico-social entities which possess (1) bureaucracy instead of feudal chivalry, (2) paper money, (3) administration by means of printed documents and a standard operating procedure involving the keeping of a large mass of written records, by such criteria, China has been modern since about A.D. 1000.

important to America than the experience of the Bourbon, the Stuart, or the Hanoverian kings.

The Inner and Outer Empires. The Chinese language has no word which is the exact equivalent of the English word "Chinese," although for modern purposes the Chinese call their country *the Central Nation* (*Chung Kuo*), and for everyday use the Chinese call themselves either the people of *Han* in North China (where the *Han* dynasty flourished) or of *T'ang* in South China (where the highest cultural development was reached under the T'ang dynasty). A Chinese will therefore call himself a *han jên, t'ang jên,* or a *chung-kuo-jên.* The empire actually inhabited by the *han-jên* themselves can be called the Inner Empire; in some books it is called "intramural China" because it lay mostly within the Great Wall. The immediate colonial empire of China added up in the sixteenth and nineteenth centuries to a territory considerably larger than that of China proper. Thus, for example, Herman Moll's Map of the World (London, 1719) shows "Eastern or Chinesian Tartary" as covering most of what we today term the Soviet Far East and as being larger in geographic extent than the China of his time.

To both the Chinese and the more cultivated Westerners who visited the Far East, the dependencies and non-Chinese enclaves within China, which together comprised much more territory than Chinese China, seemed relatively unimportant and were comparatively unknown. The Chinese Moslem minorities, the aboriginal tribes of South and Southwest China, the Mongols within China's border area, and the Manchus, were most of the time unable to integrate themselves into independent states and were subjugated by overwhelming Chinese influence. From within the old Chinese Empire the various categories of problems presented by the different types of non-Chinese areas under Chinese jurisdiction were so dissimilar as to require unrelated Chinese administrative responses. The Chinese government had no uniform device for handling relationships with non-Chinese. Each case was taken largely on its merits, each group handled in the light of its particular history and traditions, and each group was administered by an organ of the government interested in territories of that particular status. According to the regulations recorded in the pages of the *Ta-Ch'ing hui-tien,* Mongolian, Mohammedan, and Tibetan tribes were to fall under the general jurisdiction of the Colonial Office (*Li-fan-yüan*). Miscellaneous aboriginal tribes were left under the jurisdiction of the Department of Military Affairs (*Ping-pu*). Vassal states, under which all foreign nations, including some of the European monarchies, were comprised, were controlled, in so far as their presumed relationship to the Imperial court was concerned, by the Bureau of Reception (*Chu-k'o-ssŭ*) of the Department of Rites (*Li-pu*).[3]

The Chinese World Concept. In order to understand the relationship between China and these diverse political entities, it is necessary to examine

[3] *Ta-Ch'ing hui-tien* (1690 edition), *chüan* 72.

the old Chinese concept of world organization. Archaic Chinese international relations (from the Han through the Sung periods) were conducted on a basis of inequality: the inequality did not depend solely on the fact that China was militarily stronger than her neighbors, but on the fact that the Chinese, most of the time rightly, considered themselves to be more "civilized" than the persons of other nations with which they came in contact. Chinese superiority in the Chinese mind depended upon cultural excellence, not upon strategic power; Chinese superiority in the minds of neighboring peoples depended on strategic power, reinforced by cultural superiority.

The term *"Chung Kuo"* (Central Country, Middle Kingdom) sufficiently reflects this basic Chinese feeling of superiority over peoples whom the Chinese called *i* or barbarians. To the Chinese, their own country was located at the middle of the world and was surrounded by uncivilized peoples, the barbarians of the four corners, the *man, i, jung, ti* of the South, East, West, and North, respectively. Collectively, these inferior, non-Chinese peoples, were called the *ssŭ-i,* or the four kinds of barbarians.[4] It is not difficult to explain the Chinese reasons for differentiating foreigners on the basis of their geographical locations.

Throughout the long history of China the Chinese never encountered any other people whom they were willing to consider their equals in cultural matters, even though from time to time the Chinese were subdued by peoples who had to be recognized as the military superiors of the Chinese. The Chinese committed against Japan and Korea the kind of unwitting and interminable injustice which North Americans so often commit against Mexico: the Chinese never admitted that the Japanese or Koreans were more civilized than themselves, even at those times or in those respects in which Korean or Japanese superiority might seem readily demonstrable to the eyes of an impartial Western or Indian scholar.

The idea of Chinese superiority was sustained throughout the centuries by the belief that China was superior most of the time and in most respects to most of her neighbors, and from the further fact that the Chinese possessed a very strong notion of their own factual excellence from the very beginning of their nation. The most primitive Chinese agrarian society of the Shang centered in the Yellow River basin was under constant pressure from the nomadic peoples of the North. This continued in the Chou period. Trade and diplomatic relations with the peoples of the West were established by Chinese adventurers early in the Han dynasty; it is entirely possible, as Homer Dubs points out, that a platoon of captive Roman legionaries marched with serried shields through the Han capital of ancient Loyang. The chief Han expansion was toward the South, where immense Chinese conquests followed by rapid Chinese settlement almost doubled the ter-

[4] J. K. Fairbank and S. Y. Teng, "On the Ch'ing Tributary System," *Harvard Journal of Asiatic Studies,* Vol. 6, pp. 137-140.

ritorial extent of what had been China through most of the Chou and Ch'in periods. (See the map on page 10, showing the expansion of the Empire from Chou to T'ang.) This Han expansion had phases of advance and retreat. Not until the combined Chinese-Mongol-Arab-Persian expeditionary force of Kublai Khan expelled the ancestors of the present-day Siamese from Yunnan did China proper take on the geographic shape it has today. In the Chinese dynasty which succeeded the Mongols, the Ming, the fantastic eunuch admiral, Chêng Ho, made several expeditions with heavy Chinese naval forces into the Indian Ocean. His ventures, undertaken between A.D. 1403 and 1433, involved as many as 60 vessels and 27,000 men, secured the titular subjugation of Malacca and Ceylon, and established a ceremonial but unenforced claim of Chinese jurisdiction in East Africa.

From such a variety of contacts, there developed in the Chinese mind some basic assumptions. First, the barbarians of the four corners of the world were different from one another, and hence each kind of barbarian should be treated in a particular way. Second, all the barbarians were inferior to the Chinese because they did not have the intellectual or ethical comprehension needed for adherence to the Chinese way of life, more specifically the Confucian code of personal and familial conduct. Third, it was a tremendous privilege for barbarians to have contact with the Chinese court and to obtain thereby a facsimile of culture, so to speak, a capacity to partake in the highest of human virtues at second hand by shining with the reflected light of China.

No matter how the vicissitudes of China's exterior relations went, the Chinese themselves had to make a distinction between those nations which were in point of fact independent of the practicable reach of Chinese authority and those other persons physically close enough and strategically so closely placed as to fall within the actual perimeter of Chinese military and political control. Although the Chinese scholars pretended that all the nations of the world revolved about China, in point of fact it was necessary to draw a short distinction between remote or titular vassals, whose relation to China—at the least—involved nothing more than the presentation of ceremonial tribute to China and the acceptance of formal investitures in China for their governments, on the one hand, and the immediate dependencies, which amounted to colonial possessions, on the other.

Governments of the Chinese Dependencies.[5] When the Manchus occupied the Chinese Throne from 1644 onward, they adopted *in toto* the Chinese ideology of world organization. Almost verbatim they mimicked the Ming practices in conducting relations with the peoples to the south and southwest of China. On the other hand, for the territories northeast

[5] See H. S. Brunnert and V. V. Hagelstrom, *Present Day Political Organization of China*, Shanghai, 1912, pp. 441-477; Hsieh Pao-chao, *op. cit.*, Chap. 4; O. Lattimore, *Inner Asian Frontiers of China* (American Geographical Society Series No. 21) London and New York, 1940; S. W. Williams, *op. cit.*, Vol. I, Chap. 4; Chêng Ho-shêng, *op. cit.*; Hsü Ch'ung-hao, *Chung-kuo chêng-chih kai-yao* (Outline of Chinese political system), Chungking, 1943.

of China—whence they themselves came—north of China, and west of China, they maintained part of their original Manchu procedures and outlook, since the Manchus had had contact with the peoples of Mongolia and Chinese Turkestan long before the Manchu conquest of China. So important was the special relationship between Manchus and Mongols that the original Manchu Central Administration had a Mongolian Office (*Mêng-ku Ya-mên*).

Only in 1638 did the Manchus establish a Colonial Office (*Li-fan-yüan*), allocating its control over the relationships between the Central Manchu government at Mukden and the governments of local administrative units which were denominated *fan* (frontier areas, or dependencies).[6]

In this original Mongol establishment there were four frontier areas considered as *fan*—Mongolia, Chinese Turkestan (Sinkiang), Kokonor, and Tibet. Since the frontier territory of Manchuria was in formal political theory the Conqueror of China, it could not be the inferior of China and, from the Manchu, although not from the Chinese, point of view, remained a sort of home empire for the Manchu rulers until 1907; at that time even the Manchus gave up pretending that they really ran China and organized Manchuria into the Eastern Three Provinces. Chinese Turkestan acquired its name of Sinkiang (Hsin-chiang, or New Dominion) in 1884. In the same year Kokonor was organized into a Chinese-type province under the name of Chinghai. Formosa survived the fall of Ming China to the conquering Manchus in much the way that Nationalist Formosa has survived the fall of mainland China to the Communists. A Ming loyalist, Chêng Ch'êng-kung, known as *Koxinga* in Western maritime history, drove out the Dutch and made Formosa an anti-Manchu survivor state which held out for thirty-nine years. In 1683 his descendants finally reached an agreement with the Manchus, surrendering the territory. The island was first made a part of Fukien Province, a province in its own right from 1885 to 1895, an independent and unrecognized republic for a few weeks in 1895 (the second republic ever set up by the Chinese, the first having been a short-lived experiment in Borneo, modeled on the Dutch translation of the American Constitution), a Japanese possession from 1895 to 1945, and a Chinese Nationalist province from 1945 onward. When converted into border provinces these new provinces were administered by the same administrative procedures and patterns as other provinces and hence must be excluded from consideration with the colonial dependencies. (See the map on page 81, showing the Manchu Empire with its dependencies.)

Mongolia. Both geographically and administratively Mongolia was long divided into two separate units, Outer Mongolia and Inner Mongolia. Outer Mongolia was divided into four regions, subdivided into twelve leagues. These leagues, composed of 16 tribes, were again divided into 117 banners. Inner Mongolia being a smaller district was under close control of the central government and was divided into 6 leagues, 23 tribes, 48 banners.

[6] Brunnert and Hagelstrom, *op. cit.*, pp. 160-161.

Local government in Mongolia was carried on by the Mongols themselves, without much interference from the Chinese metropolitan authorities. The real administrative units were the league and the banner. The league was a princely appanage formed by a group of banners which were bound together by common ties of race, history, and circumstance. For each league there was a Captain-General, who was elected at a triennial meeting of the

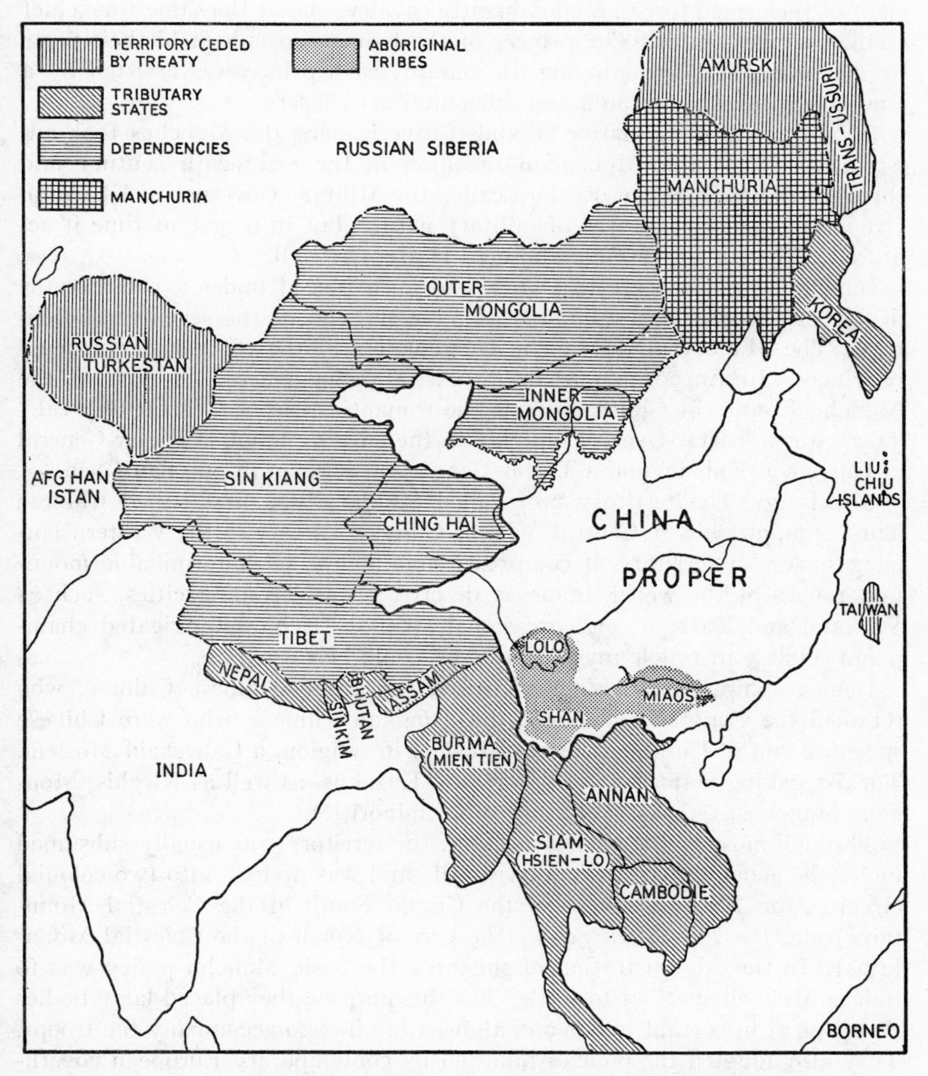

The Old Chinese Empire (The Ch'ing Period, circa 1760) showing the extent of conquests and tributaries and the distribution of aboriginal tribes in the middle of the eighteenth century

prince rulers of the banners. The triennial meeting itself was held for the discussion of judicial affairs involving members of different banners, economic problems confronting the whole league, and administrative obligations, such as the taking of the census. In Outer Mongolia, the election of the captain-general required confirmation by the Manchu Emperor of China; in Inner Mongolia, the Emperor appointed the captains-general directly. For each league the captain-general was primarily a commander-in-chief of the armed forces, predominantly cavalry, and at the same time chief civilian administrator. The princes of the banners usually held their posts by virtue of heredity, enjoying life tenure; each prince was assisted by a staff consisting of adjutants and other military officers.

In addition to these native administrative leaders, the Manchus took advantage of an Outer Mongolian rebellion in the eighteenth century and thenceforth appointed an overlord called the Military Governor of Uliasutai. Originally this position was of military nature, but in course of time it acquired authority for revenue and civil matters as well.

Inner Mongolia, closer to China, had been placed under a considerable degree of Chinese local administration by the end of the seventeenth century. The Manchus put Manchu commanders in the three Inner Mongol provinces. In European parlance, these Manchu generals, a part of the Manchu Empire of China, enjoyed the romantic title of "Tartar-General." There was a Tartar-General of Jehol in the City of Jehol, a Tartar-General of Chahar in Kalgan, and a Tartar-General of Suiyuan in Suiyuan Chên.

Sinkiang. The territory now called Sinkiang was first called Chinese Turkestan, or Chinese Central Asia, or Chinese Tartary in the Western languages. A vast territory, it comprised some of the most formidable mountain ranges of the world, immense deserts, historic trading cities, such as Yarkand and Kashgar, and occasional strips of rich, well-irrigated champaign country in which any kind of crop could be raised.

Demographically, Sinkiang comprised the purely Chinese Chinese, who retained the Confucian ideology, the Tungkan Chinese, who were Chinese speaking and of Chinese race but Moslem in religion, a Caucasoid Moslem, Turki-speaking majority of Uighurs and Kazakhs, as well as Kirghis, Mongols, Manchus, Uzbeks, and a few other minorities.

Through most of the Ch'ing dynasty, the territory was usually subsumed under the general geographical term "Ili" and was divided into two colonial circuits: the *T'ien-shan nan-lu* (the Circuit South of the Celestial Mountains) and the *T'ien-shan pei-lu* (the Circuit North of the Celestial Mountains). In the administration of this area the basic Manchu policy was to induce Mongolian tribes to settle. For this purpose they placed large bodies of troops at important points and allowed families to accompany the troops. They also adopted the policies followed by contemporary European governments in colonial enterprises in that they transported convicts to plow up new farm land and to bring uninhabited areas under cultivation. Both the

North Circuit and South Circuit were under the control of a Tartar-General residing at Ili.

The Ili headquarters was created in 1762 by Emperor Ch'ien Lung and was vested with both civil and military authority. The Tartar-General was assisted by two counselors to take cognizance of civil affairs and 34 residents scattered across his jurisdiction over both Circuits. Under the command of the Tartar-General during Manchu times was a huge army. Since this was a strategic protective course, most of the soldiers of the army had their families with them and were officially assigned to farming as well as to their military duties.

The Northern Circuit was more effectively controlled by the Manchu court than was the Southern Circuit, because of its more readily accessible geographic position and its greater ethnic homogeneity. Most local administration of the non-Chinese elements of the population was controlled by chieftains (*begs*), rulers acknowledged by the clan. Even as late as the Nationalist period in Chinese history, some hundreds of these rulers were recognized by the Chinese authorities as kinglets. These chieftaincies were hereditary, but subject to the control of the Tartar-General. In the Southern Circuit the inhabitants were mostly Moslems, less inclined to accept Manchu rule than their northern neighbors. Although nominally the Southern Circuit was just as much under Manchu Chinese control as the Northern, local chieftains were chosen by the tribes themselves and exercised their authority with a minimum of interference from Manchu officials.

Turkestan enjoyed a period of independence under Yakub Beg in the 1870's. The British went so far as to send an informal diplomatic representation to his court. The Manchus put down this insurrection very coolly, but found themselves threatened with the possibility of British aggression from the south and Russian aggression from the north. In an attempt to intensify the control over the area they constituted the greater part of the Tartar-General's command of Ili into the province of Sinkiang in 1884.[7]

Kokonor. Through the greater part of the Manchu rule, Kokonor, known in the Chinese language as Chinghai, was under the control of an Imperial Resident in Sining (*Sining pan-shih ta-ch'en*), with control over the military forces as well as the civil affairs of the tribes. *De facto* administration was carried out for the greater part by Mongol and Moslem local authorities. The Mongolian section was inhabited by five tribes, which were further subdivided into 29 banners. Like the banners of Mongolia, each banner had a prince-ruler; unlike Mongolia the banners were not combined into leagues nor did they elect their captains-general. The Mohammedan portion of the population was divided into 40 tribes, each tribe under its own *beg*.

Tibet. Peoples of Tibetan origin raided deep into China as early as the fourth and fifth centuries after Christ. The Tibetans began to achieve po-

[7] Djang Chu, "War and Diplomacy Over Ili," *The Chinese Social and Political Science Review*, Vol. XX, No. 3 (October, 1936).

litical organization and to maintain regularized relations with China in the T'ang period. In the thirteenth century Tibet became a vassal of the Mongol Empire of China, and after the Mongols fell from the Chinese throne the native Chinese Ming emperors maintained the suzerain claims of their Mongol predecessors, and the Manchus in turn took over the Ming claim. Chinese interference with Tibet was at a minimum until 1694, when a struggle between the temporal and secular powers in Lhasa brought about direct Chinese intervention.

The Manchu Chinese Emperor, K'ang Hsi, suppressed the struggle, vesting final spiritual power in the hands of the Dalai Lama. He reserved all temporal power to his own representatives, the Imperial Residents in Tibet (*Chu-tsang ta-ch'en*) of which there were two—an Imperial Resident of Interior Tibet and an Imperial Resident of Ulterior Tibet. Each Imperial Resident was assisted by four counselors of state, nominated by himself and appointed by the Manchu-Chinese Emperor or from among the superior military officials of the Tibetan army. The Imperial Resident himself was vested with supreme command of both the Chinese garrison troops and the Tibetan soldiery. Consequently, he commanded (in theory at least) the entire Tibetan civil administration: this included the appointment of officials to local units, the control of the basic means of communications, the regulation of trade and of passports, the audit of the accounts of the Lama hierarchy and the collection of taxes. From the Manchu-Chinese point of view, Tibet was divided crudely into battalions (*ying*) of which there were 165, each under the command of a *ying* commander appointed by the Imperial Resident for a term of three years. Secular power was vested by both Tibetan authority and Chinese pretension in the Dalai Lama and the Panchan Lama, each independent of the other, and both under the fairly complete control of the Imperial Residents. For two hundred years most of the Dalai Lamas were appointed to their offices when they were children of less than two or three years of age, by means of sacred horoscope and other rituals.

Manchu Colonial Policies. Fundamental Manchu policies toward administrative dependencies were displayed in two repeated series of measures. One was toleration, in which the original form of government was left intact, but placed under fairly strict supervision by the Manchu Chinese Residents or Tartar-Generals. The other was separation, whereby Chinese were split off from Mongols, Mongols from Moslems and Tibetans, and Tibetans from Chinese, so that the Manchus could sustain their policy on the basis of divide-and-rule.[8] Each dependent area had a traditional local government and appointive structure, dependent upon Peking. Although the local administration exercised a considerable degree of self-government, the powers of the Imperial Residents or Military Commanders were never restricted from Peking. The constitutional framework of the Manchus did not go to the

[8] Hsieh, *op. cit.*, pp. 336-338.

lengths of precision worked out by the British Raj in India, when it came to dividing the authority of the Supreme Power from that of the local authorities.

Manchu colonial policy varied consequently in a manner quite tragically inherited by the Chinese republic: a strong colonial ruler sent out from the Chinese metropolitan capital would interfere readily with local affairs and increase the degree of Chinese influence, sometimes benevolently and sometimes with oppressiveness or malignity, while a weak appointee would let both Chinese authority and local order deteriorate into uproar or chaos. Browbeating and timidity followed one another with lamentable regularity.

In Manchu times, the colonial dependencies were required to send to the Imperial court native products. These were sent as a sign of submission in the form of tribute bearing at regular intervals. Although the quantity and value of the physical tribute were negligible, the bearer had to be a high noble of the territory in question and the concept behind the system involved great significance—the visible demonstration of Manchu-Chinese supremacy. The higher nobles of these colonial areas were required to pay personal visits to Peking at fixed periods. Further, to strengthen the relationship between the central court and the nobility of these various dependencies, marriages between Manchu aristocrats and local nobility were arranged from time to time, and the title of Imperial Attendant (*Ch'ien-ch'ing-kung hsing-tsou*) was given to young colonial nobles on special occasions, in an effort to induce from them a higher degree of loyalty.

Since the Manchus were a minority in China, having won against military odds of more than 400 to 1, they had to play the policy of divide-and-rule through to the bitter end. Fundamental in this policy was the exclusion of Chinese from the dependencies as far as practicable, so that it would be possible to play one league against another. For the entire colonial system between 1644 and 1911, almost all the Imperial appointees were of the Manchu race. Communication between Chinese and colonials was rigorously forbidden, save for strictly licensed commerce. Intermarriage and Chinese emigration were repeatedly prohibited by Imperial decrees. Colonial immigration was equally prohibited. When Mongols on special occasions were permitted to come into China, they were required to come through specifically designated routes, and their passports were examined repeatedly. Tibetans were flatly ordered to stay on their side of the frontier and were told to have no commercial transactions with the Chinese. (Inevitably the Chinese corrupted the Manchu officials on the spot, and developed an illegal trade sustained through bribery or indifference.)

Neither Imperial China nor Republican China developed a satisfactory colonial policy. The racial discrimination shown by Chinese against their subject peoples was one of the strong points of Communist criticism until the Communists themselves took over China. This lack of understanding between Chinese and the subject peoples can be blamed, at least in part, on the Manchu policy of creating misunderstandings so as to prevent a common front of the various nationalities of the Greater China against Manchu rule.

The Aboriginal Enclaves.[9] In present-day world politics the true "forgotten man" of international affairs is probably the non-Chinese inhabitant of China—the tribesman whose people lived in China before the Chinese arrived. These aboriginal people number many millions; some of them are more numerous than some of the smaller European nationalities. Communists and Protestants are about the only outsiders who pay much attention to them, the Protestants supplying them with hospitals and Bibles, and the Communists with propaganda. Most of the non-Chinese descendants of the aboriginal inhabitants of Central and South China were driven in times past to the poorest and loneliest terrain of their former homes and are consequently hillbillies to the nth degree. Poverty, shame, disease, superstition, quarrelsomeness, and opium have either cut their population totals down or kept them in bondage to their own ignorance.

The preponderant enclaves of the aboriginal population are in present-day Southwestern China. Centuries ago these non-Chinese peoples were pushed out of the Yangtse Basin and present-day South China. Their original possession of the land is mirrored in the place names: the Chinese provinces of Kwangtung and Kwangsi, for example, refer to a lapsed kingdom of Kwang, divided after Chinese conquest into East Kwang and West Kwang. Just as Manhattan, Connecticut, and Massachusetts attest to the aboriginal possession of these American territories, although no American Indians are evident in their governments today, pre-Chinese names make it possible, along with Chinese annals, to track the long-completed Chinese wars of conquest. Some of the pre-Chinese peoples escaped into Indo-China and Burma. One such people, the *Thai,* still teaches the legend of its long-lost Chinese homeland in the public schools of Siam. The greater part of the aboriginal tribes were probably absorbed by the Chinese. It is only the remnants who inhabit the enclaves and maintain their own languages in the high hills of Yunnan, Kweichow, Kwangsi, and Szechuan.

In Manchu times these non-Chinese people caused a great annoyance to Chinese local administration in the border areas. Sometimes they amounted to a threat. Since they were different from the Chinese in both speech and customs, the aborigines came into incessant conflicts with the Chinese; on the Chinese side, constant Chinese encroachment on the land, together with commercial chicanery contributed to the friction. Traditional Chinese attitudes toward the aborigines were contemptuous and pitiless. The Chinese never failed to exploit them. On the other hand, it must be pointed out that aborigines, once assimilated into Chinese culture, Chinese education, and the Chinese system of family names, were treated without any further racial

[9] Brunnert and Hagelstrom, *op. cit.,* pp. 438-439; Ch'en Han-shêng, *Frontier Land Systems in Southernmost China,* New York, 1949; Ch'i Yün-shih, *Huang-ch'ao fan-pu yao-lüeh* (History of feudal tribes of the Ch'ing dynasty), Chekiang, 1845.

discrimination. It was only the ones who stayed un-Chinese who were persecuted. The Chinese authorities in the old days made little attempt at a serious ethnological classification. The basic Chinese method was based crudely on geographical location and the people were called the *Miao,* the *Shan,* and the *Lolo.* The Miao were concentrated in the border areas of the provinces of Kwangsi, Kweichow, and Szechuan; the Shan occupied the southern and western part of Yunnan; the Lolo lived in the mountains of Szechuan and Yunnan.

Although these tribes resided within Chinese territory they were not subject to Chinese law or administration. For centuries they had their own tribal government and administered their own affairs. Whenever it was feasible, the Chinese policy was one of assimilation, expulsion, or extermination; but when the countryside was too poor, the hills too high, the mountain valleys too remote to make it worthwhile to capture them, kill them, or wipe them out, the Chinese played one side against the other. In order to soothe them the Chinese bestowed official titles on tribal chieftains. During the Manchu dynasty, the title of Pacification Commissioner (*Hsüan-wei-shih*) and other titles varying from the third to the seventh bureaucratic rank were designated for the various grades of tribal chieftains.

Not only did the aborigines suffer from Chinese oppression and neglect; they suffered even more from their own chiefs. The tribal chieftains usually possessed absolute power over their own people and were often corrupted by having access to the seamy side of Chinese culture, such as gambling, extravagance, alcoholism, or drug addiction.

In 1726 local conflicts between Chinese and aborigines became acute. In consequence, the Viceroy, O-Erh-t'ai, pointed out the necessity of incorporating tribal territories into the regular Chinese administrative districts and replacing tribal administration with a systematic scheme of government. This process was denoted by the phrase, "placing the native districts under regular administration" (*kai-t'u kuei-liu*), and carried out very vigorously.[10] In many instances, military force was needed, but in the following fifty years not less than fifty new Chinese sub-prefectures were carved out of former tribal territories. These newly organized territories were ruled by hereditary chieftains, who received the titles of Native Prefect (*T'u-fu*), Native Sub-Prefect (*T'u-chou*), or Native Magistrate (*T'u-hsien*) and were governed on much the same basis as the regular local units. Once this wave of reform passed there still remained a large amount of population and territory never incorporated in local Chinese administration and still ruled by native chieftains. The more remote tribes were under the normal control of the Department of Military Affairs, but the actual governing consisted of nothing more than the maintenance of a tributary relationship under which the more eminent local chieftains were required to send to Peking a prescribed amount of native products at regular intervals.

[10] Chêng, *op. cit.*, pp. 548-561.

The Confucian Family of Nations.[11] Very different was the pattern employed by the Chinese Empire for dealings with civilized and power states outside China. The Chinese used all possible skills of political warfare, propaganda, and visual ceremony to impose on themselves and on outsiders the myth of Chinese universal empire. They made it a first condition for dealing with China that the outsiders accept a tributary obligation.

In the instance of civilized people, such as the Annamites, the Koreans, the Japanese, and later, the Europeans, the Chinese went to considerable lengths to put on a good show. In political theory their justification for this arrogant assumption of Chinese supremacy was the argument that anyone who was civilized enough to deal with China should be civilized enough to see the superiority of Chinese civilization to his own. Contrariwise, anyone so blind as to be unable to perceive the superiority of Chinese civilization to his own civilization was manifestly not morally fit or politically dependable enough to deal with the Chinese. Not until the English and French took Peking and burned the summer palace in 1850 did the Chinese back down from this fundamental principle, and not until the English and French with American, Japanese, German, Russian and Italian help, took it again in 1900, did the Chinese begin to be sincere in realizing that small arms and machine guns were as valid an expression of "civilization" as formal ceremonies and stereotyped classical essays.

Western historians of the Far East are quick to point out the ignorant, naïve pretensions of the Chinese court in the nineteenth century; most of them neglect a working international system, the Confucian Family of Nations, which antedated the Western community of nations by some centuries and which had functioned as well as, if not better than, its Western counterpart. It must be pointed out that a political phenomenon in decline is easy to deride and that foreign visitors who see the ignominious end and collapse of a political institution are often unable to appreciate what that institution must have been at the height of its credibility, feasibility, and power.

The Confucian Family of Nations consisted of China, at the center, and all nations civilized enough to have regular diplomatic relations with China —diplomatic meaning "tributary" in the established Chinese terms. This international system maintained a very considerable degree of order, pro-

[11] See M. Frederick Nelson, *Korea and the Old Orders in Eastern Asia,* Baton Rouge, 1945; Fairbank and Tseng, *op. cit.,* pp. 135-246; J. K. Fairbank, "Tributary Trade and China's Relations with the West," *Far Eastern Quarterly,* Vol. I, pp. 129-149; H. B. Morse, *The International Relations of the Chinese Empire,* London, 1918, Vol. II, pp. 340-341; Chêng, *op. cit.,* pp. 563-567; Hua Ch'i-yun, *Chung-kuo pien-chiang* (Chinese frontiers); *Ta-Ch'ing hui-tien* (1908 edition), *chüan* 39. The official accounts of the Chinese conquests carried out in the western part of the empire in the eighteenth and nineteenth centuries are to be found in the following two voluminous works compiled by the order of the imperial court: *P'ing-ting Chun-ke-erh fang-lüeh* (An official account of the conquest of Jungria 1700-1765), 1770, 100 bks., edited by Fu Hêng; *P'ing-ting Kan-su Hsin-chiang hui-fei fang-lüeh* (An official account of the conquest of the Mohammedans in Kansu and Chinese Turkistan 1855-1883), 1896, 320 bks., edited by Li Miu-chen.

moted commerce much of the time, and allowed a fair amount of cultural interchange. Far less exploitive and aggressive than the power exercised by Christian monarchies over non-Christian peoples, the Confucian Family of Nations in most cases left to the dependent nations a maximum of autonomy consistent with the maintenance of domestic and international order. The relationships between China and the dependent countries are difficult to express in Western terms. The early American diplomats in Peking and Seoul almost went out of their minds trying to give juridical definition to ill-defined but very tangible evidences of Chinese power over Korea, a power which, from the Chinese point of view, implied no corresponding responsibility on the part of China. The closest Western terms are "suzerain" for the paramount power, and "vassal" for the dependent power, but these are only approximate.

The suzerain and vassal relationship between China and Southeast Asia existed as early as the Han dynasty, but the zenith of the tributary activity was not reached until after the exploits of the eunuch admiral, Chêng Ho. In the Ming dynasty, even Japan and the Philippines were listed as Chinese vassals. The Manchus attempted to list all countries having relations with China as vassals but developed, under pressure or practicality, a new category of countries—the "trading nations." This list included Japan, the Philippines, Cambodia, Spain, Holland, and Java. Counterbalancing this, the 1899 edition of the *Ta-Ch'ing hui-tien* listed as vassals Korea, the Kingdom of Liuchiu (which had already been annexed to Japan and given the name Ryukyu), Annam-Tongking, Laos, Siam, the Sultanate of Sulu (already divided between Spain and Holland), and Burma. The relationship in the Confucian Family of Nations between the patron state of China and the client states around China's periphery was subject across the centuries to constant change. Even at any one time there were differences in the degree of dependence of the various subordinate states. Thus the relationships of Korea and Annam to China were closer than those of Burma or Sulu. Siam broke off the tributary relation in 1882, and in the following decade British authority covered Burma and French authority covered Annam-Tongking and Laos.

So tenuous was the pattern of superordination and subordination that the Chinese attempted to treat the first British diplomatic missions as tribute-bearing delegations. Some of the earlier European Missions went through the Chinese formulae rather than lose contact with China altogether. The Portuguese, the Dutch, and the Papacy let their representatives go through ceremonial submission to the Chinese Emperor, presumably on the entirely practical assumption that a ceremony in Peking had no effect on the real state of affairs in Europe and that, if the Chinese were foolish enough to want to consider themselves lords of the world, the more fools they. The Russians, on the other hand, neatly avoided the difficulty by allowing their diplomats to crawl as inferiors before the Chinese Emperor in state ceremonies, so long as the Chinese (who had no intention whatever of sending diplomats to St. Petersburg) agreed that if a Chinese representative ever did show up at the Court of the Czar he would perform wholly comparable ceremonies.

The practical pattern of diplomatic relations within the Confucian Family of Nations was formalized by ritual regulations which required a ceremony of submission. These regulations prescribed minute requirements and prohibitions which each tribute-bearing mission should follow, and elaborated in detail a Chinese ceremony of investiture for each new ruler as a recognition of the supremacy of the Chinese Emperor as overlord. Tribute-bearing missions were required at regular intervals. Liuchiu sent tributes yearly, Koreans once in four years, Annam once in two years, Siam once in three years, Sulu once in five years, and Burma once in ten years. The routes whereby these missions should travel were also specified. The envoys from Korea were to enter the Chinese Empire at Fenghuangch'eng, those from Liuchiu by way of Foochow, those from Annam by way of Kweilin, those from Siam by way of Canton, those from Sulu by way of Amoy, and those from Burma by way of Yunnanfu (Kunming).

When the tribute-bearing mission reached Chinese territory, the Viceroy of the province concerned was required to memorialize the Imperial court to this effect. The mission was escorted step by step all the way across China. Chinese banners, prominently displayed, told the onlookers of the origin and nature of the mission. When the tributary mission arrived in Peking it had to file a petition with the Department of Rites, asking for examination of its credentials; the examination involved detailed scrutiny of the accreditation of the envoy and a careful inventory of the tributes.

The envoy himself was given laborious rehearsals in the court etiquette, an incredibly pompous ceremony involving performance of the kowtow (*k'o-t'ou*), an act which required that he kneel on the floor and touch his forehead to the ground three times in assent to his country's subjection to the Chinese Emperor, as Lord of the World. Once this was over, the envoy was entertained at banquets in the presence of the Emperor. He and his staff were usually luxuriously entertained; they were given return gifts, for the ruler of their country, as well as personal gifts for themselves. A certain amount of private trading and sightseeing was also tolerated. The local diplomatic group was under close guard for the purposes of protection and surveillance throughout its sojourn in China. The tribute items were also specified for each country. They consisted of native products which did not constitute any significant material gain to the Imperial Chinese Treasury. Objects of real value were often presented on special occasions, such as the Emperor's birthday, majority, or marriage, but these were considered as expressions of loyalty from the vassal nations rather than an actual obligation. The value of these tributes was usually balanced by the return gifts made by the Chinese to the vassal ruler and to the members of his mission.

Parenthetically, it must be remarked that the museums of Peking are much the richer because of this system. One of the most spectacular collections of antique European clocks to be found anywhere in the world was gathered in the Forbidden City, the old Imperial Palace.

Under the screen of this tributary system, practical diplomatic relations were carried out within the Confucian Family of Nations. The contribution in ceremony and tribute was rewarded on the part of China by assurance of protection and recognition. Often this protection was very practical; the Chinese from time to time sent land forces or naval forces to the aid of their vassals and, on other occasions, the threat of Chinese intervention was enough to deter an outsider from invading a vassal. The Chinese by this system not only made their borders secure, but the Chinese emperors enhanced their own prestige in the eyes of the Chinese people. It made the Chinese, both literati and the populace, believe that the Chinese ruler was ruler of the world.

The system of investiture involved a very curious combination of processes which we call "diplomatic recognition" in international law, and "constitutional validation" in the municipal law of Western states. Investiture by the Dragon Throne not only insured the new ruler the recognition of other vassal states, but it also implied the guarantee of the morality and legitimacy of his own position within the country over which he ruled. The Chinese often withheld investiture from tyrants who had gained their thrones by *coup d'état,* murder, or other immoral processes. On occasion Chinese forces intervened in the vassal country in order to restore the rightful ruler or a rightful claim to the Throne. The ceremony itself involved an extremely complicated process. The vassal ruler had to send a mission requesting Imperial Letters Patent. The mission had to be examined in Peking and, after elaborate interrogation, a decision made at the Chinese court for or against issuance of the letter. If issuance was decided upon, the Chinese Emperor sent an envoy to the vassal. The envoy carried the patent of appointment or confirmation to the capital of the vassal state. There he was received with great ceremony involving an exchange of gifts comparable to the exchange at Peking. After the Chinese envoy returned to China it was up to the newly invested ruler to send the second mission to Peking expressing his thankfulness at having been invested. This involved a third round of exchange of gifts and ceremony.

Not only did the tributary system provide a working scheme of diplomatic relationships, but it also served the practical purpose of regulating international trade. Since China had traditionally discouraged trade with foreigners, adventurous merchants from Central Asia on many occasions disguised themselves as tributers, in order to pass through the Chinese borders. Among historians there is ground for suspicion that a rascally Armenian or Levantine may have passed himself off on the Han Emperor as a personal representative of Marcus Aurelius, in order to do business in the fabulous silk market of China.

The commercial motivation is very plain in the case of those missions which arrived with a large number of merchants and huge quantities of merchandise, all of which could be traded free of customs' duties, and exempt from the normal regulations. The tribute regulations provided that foreign merchants accompanying the tribute-bearing envoys should pay duty, but exceptions were often made. The envoys themselves were permitted to sell merchandise on their own private accounts, at the Residence for Tributary Missions, for five days without paying duties. This was permitted, providing it was carried out under the supervision of Chinese officials, who also acted as agents for the envoys if the envoys desired to make purchases in China. It took only a little greasing of the officials' palms to do very good business indeed. Foreign envoys were specifically prohibited from buying weapons, contraband, history books, and atlasses, or books pertaining to geography. These exclusions were not serious enough to impair the practical value of the trade. The willingness of the vassals to continue the tributary relationship—particularly in the case of states as far away as the Sultanate of Sulu—must be attributed in great part to the trading advantages which the tribute missions obtained.

From the above description it is clear that the relations between China and her vassal states were not contractual, but obligatory. These rested on custom, not on legal covenant. There was no treaty or agreement of any sort at the foundation of these relationships. A Western observer summed up the situation correctly in 1883:

> The inference is that the relationship of suzerain and vassal was, as far as legal phraseology may be applicable to such a state of affairs, a relationship at will merely. It was begun at will, continued at will, and therefore it would follow, was terminable at will. Neither side had pledged itself to do anything in regard to the other and, consequently, could not be regarded as guilty of any breach of contract in refusing to conform any longer to the traditional usage.[12]

China's policy toward her vassal states was different from that toward her colonial dependencies. The Chinese appointed no residents in these vassal states (except for emergency cases, such as Korea in the 1880's), assessed no taxes, proclaimed no laws, and appointed no officials. The Chinese had built their patriarchal system on a loose legal scale. Although the vassal states were of no actual value to China, they served as active buffers between China and the outside world.[13]

The Breakdown of the Inner and Outer Empire. Seen outward from Peking, the Chinese Empire comprised a world organization until it broke

[12] G. Jamieson, "The Tributary Nations of China," *The China Review,* (October, 1883), p. 95.

[13] T. Dennett, *Americans in Eastern Asia,* New York, 1922, p. 422.

down in the latter part of the nineteenth century. In Chinese eyes, China was surrounded by vassal states as a patriarch was surrounded by his family. The actual binding force of this world organization was neither physical strength nor legal obligation, but common cultural interests. The Chinese sense of superiority did not grow out of imagination or self-assertion alone, but was the natural result of China's position—one immense nation, surrounded by many small ones—together with the acute Chinese self-awareness of their cultural heritage and their moral doctrines. The Chinese system routed most of Northeast Asia into a homogeneous unity. The actual condition of the Chinese Empire a century ago was well described by G. H. Blakeslee in the following terms:

> She [China] has been the planet, the powerful civilized and cultural empire, surrounded by a circle of admiring satellite kingdoms, Korea, upon the northeast, the Tartar families on the north, Kashgar and Samarkand upon the west, Tibet in its Himalayan clouds and snows, at the southwest, Burma and Siam at the south, Annam and Cochin-China, trailing off from her southern frontier, and those tiny and inoffensive specks which lie, like a fringe, off to the east, making the eastern limits of the China sea, and known as the Liuchiu Islands, these formed a system, an Oriental world, of which the Chinese Empire was the center. They flattered her by the most delicate and subtle form of flattery, imitation. They copied her form of civilization, modelled their governmental systems after hers, borrowed her religions, adopted, in several instances, her written language, gained their knowledge of arts and literature from her, and all of them deferred and appealed to her as final authority. . . . She was arbiter of their disputes, whether domestic or international. She aided each, at times, to quell insurrection by the force of her arms.[14]

The traditional policy of China had been one of making the near happy and the distant contented. The Confucian doctrine was that "all men within the boundaries of the Four Seas are brethren." Although the relationship between China and her vassal states might have originated either in military conquest, cultural influence, or voluntary submission, all states were alike allowed to assert their own right of self-government. There had been an extension of the traditional patriarchal system on an international scale. However, the cultural relationship between China and her vassal states had been very close. In most cases, these states followed the Chinese pattern of governmental structure and social system, not by purposeful effort but rather through cultural influence. In the case of Korea and Annam, the borrowing of written language probably had a great deal to do with the sinification process, with obvious impacts on their political development. While China derived no actual benefit in asserting overlordship over these states, their loss to Western powers constituted a potential menace to the Empire. They

[14] G. H. Blakeslee, *China and the Far East,* New York, 1910, p. 32.

were buffer states, important to China when the latter got entangled in modern international politics; their loss deprived China of comfortable cushions.

In the last quarter of the nineteenth century, the influence of the competing Western Community of Nations disturbed the *status quo* of the Far East and pulled the vassal states away from China. In a crucial period of fifteen years, the Chinese lost all their vassal states—the Liuchiu to Japan in 1881, the Indo-Chinese states to France in 1885, Northern Burma to Great Britain in 1886, and Korea along with Siam to the Western System as such, the last two having proclaimed their complete independence of China. The significance of this process did not arise from China's great material losses, but from the breakdown of the traditional ideology and the practical foundations of Chinese superiority.

The story of China's dependencies was equally tragic. When the isolationist policy of the Manchu Government failed to keep the Western powers away from the Chinese ports, the Manchus belatedly realized the folly of their traditional policy toward China's colonial empire. When it was almost too late, the Manchus attempted to incorporate the dependent territories into China proper, replacing the policy of separation with that of assimilation.

After long military occupation by Czarist Russia and Japanese military forces, Manchuria was made into three eastern provinces of China in 1907. The provinces of Sinkiang and Chinghai were organized in 1884. Inner Mongolia was finally converted into the provinces of Suiyuan, Chahar, Ninghsia, and Jehol. These Manchu and Chinese policies did not stop outside encroachment.

Russia pushed the gate open in Chinese Turkestan, seizing part of Ili in 1881; Russians, both Czarists and Bolshevik, successfully infiltrated Outer Mongolia. Japan obtained Korea's independence of China only to convert Korea into a protectorate ten years later and to use Korea as a springboard into Manchuria. Great Britain stepped into the Forbidden Land of Tibet. These frontier troubles might have been avoided if the Manchus had had a more enlightened colonial policy and had succeeded in attaching the dependencies to the metropolitan homeland with a real community of interest and a sense of political participation.

Not much more can be said of the official Manchu and Chinese government policies toward the aboriginal tribes. After centuries of Chinese rule there was little left to show the presence of the Chinese except poverty and disease. No serious attempt had been made to promote the economic welfare of the aborigines or to give them educational advancement. Nothing but Chinese military superiority kept the tribes from revolt.

The breakdown of the Chinese Empire was the visible phenomenon resulting from the breakdown of the Chinese political ideology under the overwhelming pressure of a Western impact on all aspects of culture. The

Manchus who had entered China as proud foreigners, ended as the most reactionary and most Chinese portion of the entire Chinese bureaucracy, sticking desperately to precedent and attempting to ignore outside affairs. Nothing short of successive invasions by British, French, and other Western troops—invasions on a very massive scale, involving the piecemeal surrender of Chinese sovereignty and the near breakup of China's territory—made the Manchus abandon their pretensions and undertake a new appraisal of the situation. The Manchus changed too late to do any effective reform.

The Western Impact on Culture, Government, and Ideas. The tragedy of modern China has arisen from the fact that this oldest society in the modern world has been the focus of two massive social forces simultaneously. From the beginning of the nineteenth century, Manchu China began to feel the familiar, yet nonetheless wrenching, effect of decline, disorder, and rebellion. Feeble attempts at reform by the Manchus did have an effect, not in the direction of reforming China, but in precipitating a cycle of revolution which, in one guise or another, Nationalist or Communist, still goes on in China.

By the middle of the nineteenth century, China began to feel the full energy of a process which is called, in smug certainty, Westernization. An old and continuous culture, articulated politically as an autocracy superimposed on a democracy, moved from rebellion not to *a* revolution, but to a whole series of revolutions often superimposed, one on another. For more than a hundred years China telescoped a revolution in her system of interstate contacts, a revolution against an alien dynasty, an abortive revolution to parliamentary democracy, a nationalist revolution, and a communist revolution. Meanwhile, below the surface of political forms, there continued a social revolution, an intellectual revolution, and the delayed reaction of industrial revolution, which began to alter the economic foundations of China.[15]

From one point of view, the Western impact meant the forcing open of the old orders in Eastern Asia. From a Western viewpoint, China was drawn into the destiny of the Western nation-state system. In either case, China began to take at first a passive and later an active part in international relations. Ever since, all wars between Western and Far Eastern nations have involved the so-called Chinese question. Since the 1930's, the Chinese themselves have become active participants in the struggle for the control of China, and the nature of their governments has determined in part the effectiveness of their adaptation or resistance.

Too often, however, Chinese success has been judged on the organizational level, in terms of the governments which have attempted to ride out the

[15] John King Fairbank, in his chapter on "The Western Impact," in *The United States and China,* for example, discusses China's "demographic mystery." Centuries of internal peace under the Manchus and probably the importation of new crops into China's agrarian economy, allowed a doubling or quadrupling of population between 1650 and 1850, *before* Western contact and industrialization really got started.

storm of revolutions. Judged by Western or Chinese standards, Westernization of Chinese government has been at best only a mixed failure. It remains to be seen whether the present communist experiment will result in primarily a Western-type state; in primarily a Chinese-type ideological control, with a state on the side; or in an amazing amalgam of traditional Chinese and true Marxist thought—the actual withering away of the state.

One other aspect of the Western impact has been well described in the literature on the modern transformation of China, but has been less often linked to the Chinese tradition of the governing of men. Pre-Manchu and post-Manchu China have both made striking contributions to the politics of ideological control. Here too, Westernization has been a powerful force. Indeed, of the three aspects of the Western impact—on China's diplomacy, on China's government, and on Chinese ideas—the last is the most important.

Certainly China's grudging retreat, in the nineteenth century, from the Confucian concept of a Family of Nations is a familiar story. It has been well told in various textbooks and from various points of view.[16] Technically, the old orders began to give way when China signed with Russia her first modern treaty (Nerchinsk, 1689), in which China, like any other state, tried to demarcate her land frontier. It is significant that this treaty also regulated overland trade, allowed the Russians the right to send a mission to Peking, and from the beginning put Russians on a footing different from that of any other foreigners. In fact, long before Nerchinsk there had arisen the troublesome problem of dealing with these other, sea-coming barbarians.

Western states, other than Russia, approached China by sea and for the purpose of trade. These facts presented the participants two puzzles. The defenses of Manchu China, comfortably built into the Family of Nations, were largely geared to the land frontiers of Inner Asia. Traditional concepts thus had to be amended. From the Western point of view, sixteenth and seventeenth century adventurers discovered in East Asia a vast new continent for the opportunities of commerce, just as their contemporaries were responding to the challenge of the Western Hemisphere. The difference lay in the fact that East Asia already had a mature and complex political and economic life of its own.[17] Before the middle of the eighteenth century,

[16] See, for example, M. J. Bau [Pao Ming-ch'ien], *The Foreign Relations of China,* New York, 1922, written from a Chinese point of view; Dennett, *op. cit.*, carefully written from American sources; H. F. MacNair and Donald F. Lach, *Modern Far Eastern International Relations,* New York, 1950. a mature study for advanced students; E. H. Pritchard, *Anglo-Chinese Relations during the Seventeenth and Eighteenth Centuries,* Urbana, 1929, a specialized study; Harold M. Vinacke, *A History of the Far East in Modern Times,* New York (5th edition), 1950, the work of a distinguished political scientist, who ties together the international relations and the impact on Far Eastern governments; and Paul E. Eckel, *The Far East Since 1500,* New York, 1947. a good, general history text.

[17] It must be remembered that before the Portuguese effort to reach the East by sea, Ming expeditions under the eunuch admiral, Chêng Ho, moved into and across the Indian Ocean toward the West. The motive was doubtless a combination of the political desire to

China cautiously permitted, rather than actively encouraged, the entrance of foreigners. After the Portuguese first arrived in 1516, other foreigners came by sea in search of trade: the Spanish (1575), the Dutch (1604), the English (1637), and the Americans (1784). Meanwhile, the Chinese limited access to the Empire through Canton and Macao, a restriction which continued until the middle of the nineteenth century. Experiment and some bitter experience, rather than hostility, kept the Empire otherwise closed. Any attempt to establish permanent political contact at Peking was met coldly. All emissaries were regarded as mere tribute-bearers.

Western force then came to China as the hand of iron wrapped in the velvet glove of trade. Between 1840 and 1860 two wars were fought by the British, one with the help of the French, to convert tribute status to treaty trade. The Chinese insisted upon calling the first the Opium War, but historians have concluded that opium was the occasion, not the cause, of the war of 1840-42. The Treaty of Nanking, 1842, the supplementary agreement of the Bogue, and succeeding American and French arrangements were the levers which pried open Chinese stubbornness toward the sea-coming barbarians. Deliberate misunderstanding on the part of the Chinese, however, inevitably led to forceful redefinition of trade relations in the Treaties of Tientsin, 1858, and the invasion in 1860 of Peking itself, by Western force in the form of an Anglo-French expedition. During this period, for different reasons the Russians and Americans appeared as the friends of China, substituting pacific negotiation for forceful persuasion. Nevertheless, through the technique of the so-called most-favored-nation clause, China was steadily forced to substitute for the diplomatic inequality of the old Family of Nations system, a new diplomatic inequality of contact with the West. China struggled with the handicap of unequal treaties from that time until 1943.

In a very practical sense, the period 1840-1860 saw more than Western force invading China. Western government came too, since extraterritoriality placed Westerners in China solely under the jurisdiction of their own representatives. In addition, through usage Westerners also obtained footholds on Chinese soil in the form of settlements, concessions, and treaty ports. Finally, there was a by-product in Chinese government: trade and especially missionary zeal led to movement by foreigners throughout the Empire, and the demand for the protection of the life and property of foreigners. This called for increased and unprecedented Imperial intervention in regional affairs. The chain reaction had begun.

Until the expedition directed at Peking, the Western powers had dealt with only local authorities. From 1860 to 1875, representatives from the West continued to apply pressure for their common interest—the ending of China's seclusion, short of the destruction of China itself. In true Western

---

extend the suzerain-vassal relationship and incidental commercial reasons. See Fairbank, *op. cit.*, pp. 120-127.

fashion, the symbol of the underlying diplomatic issues was the attempt to secure an audience with the Emperor himself. The Chinese added to Western frustration by failure to define, in terms understandable to Western practices, their curious suzerain-vassal relationship with border areas. Brash exaggeration of Chinese right led to Western application of force; disclaimer of responsibility for vassal nations hastened the day of separation. Within China proper, individual relations with foreigners were, if anything, less harmonious than were official relations. The Tientsin massacres and the Margary murder in Yunnan brought prompt Western retaliation and served to begin the cycle of foreign pressure and anti-foreignism, which Chinese feel to some extent to this day.

With the coming of the West, the old governing traditions of East Asia were threatened in at least two ways. The proselytizing energy of Western culture broke down, in large part, the assumptions of universality and superiority upon which Chinese tradition rested, and within which the scholar-officials operated. More directly, a loose Chinese society and an isolated, jealously independent Japanese offshoot were threatened by strong, effective Western states. The Japanese response—often referred to as miraculous modernization and *Westernization*[18]—startled the world and offered an example for China. But China had a governmental problem on a far wider scale.

The first impact of the West on Chinese government was seen in the belated reforms of the Manchu dynasty itself, reforms which were too little and too late. Government in the new Chinese world after the fall of the Manchus grew out of the background of the past and the necessities of the present. Slowly, painfully, the Chinese drew from the misfortunes of the years since 1911 a small body of political methods—some Western—which were, from time to time, workable. Chinese political development was emergent, not planned. From anti-Manchu rebellion, the Chinese moved to revolution and to the failure of Western parliamentary democracy in the Phantom Republic of 1912-1928. The full cycle back to autocracy was completed only after the Chinese moved through a second, armed revolution, nationalism, war, civil war, to communism.

Despite governmental instability, China felt the Western impact on several levels which might be called political. With increased trade, it became possible for many Chinese to become wealthy and powerful outside their own country, either in treaty ports or overseas. Among such Chinese there developed a group—with the power of wealth and new family connections—which became determined to overthrow the Manchus, to modernize China, and to bring their country in line with the outside world. They built up a knowledge of modern business, of European languages, of literature, and of

[18] In Chaps. 14 and 15 of Part II, it is suggested that even in the case of Japan, *Westernization* is not an apt word for this remarkable emergence of East Asia's first Nation-State. The Japanese success may well have been a result of a selective *Japanization* of Western imports.

politics. They provided a new elite. They wanted nothing short of a revolution in China. It was Sun Yat-sen who showed them the way.

The Chinese of the nineteenth century could be forgiven for identifying Western political power with military force; rarely did they see one without the other. Actually, China's own T'ai-p'ing Rebellion (1850-1865) provided the first realistic test of Manchu military power and uncovered two startling facts. Both rebel successes and Manchu victory proved that the real forces were no longer regular troops, banner or Green Standard, but militia organized on a conscription basis. Furthermore, Chinese military techniques —Manchu or rebel—were obsolete. Western equipment, leadership, and training, although marginal, made any Chinese army more effective. Blind to these obvious facts, Manchu military leadership drifted and delayed until the crowning insult of the first Sino-Japanese War (1894-1895). Once again the margin of victory was Western military techniques, this time wielded by the sea-dwarfs of Japan. Serious military reform then began in the late nineteenth century, too late to allow the Manchus to stave off revolution, but not too late to introduce militarism into Republican China as a factor of government.

The foreign impact was felt more slowly in the economic, as compared with the governmental life of China. In the 1870's a railway was opened from Shanghai to Wusung. Although a tiny project and abortive, it was the beginning of a significant development. The revolution in Chinese communications moved into the fields of steam navigation and telegraphy. In the last decade of the nineteenth century, the foundations were laid for the Han Yang Iron Works, which were to become the largest industrial enterprise of its kind in China proper.

Turning to the realm of ideas, there is no better example of pervasive Western influence than the advent of Christianity in China. The first period of Roman Catholic activity in China extended from the thirteenth to the sixteenth century, culminating in the unflagging efforts of St. Francis Xavier. His work, and that of his successor, Matteo Ricci, illuminated the difference in attitudes of Westerners and Chinese. The Jesuits were moderately successful because they became almost thoroughly Sinified, dressing the gospel in sixteenth-century Chinese classics. The Chinese, in turn, learned much of Western science, particularly mathematics, astronomy, and geography. Yet after two hundred years of exposure, Chinese literati were perhaps less influenced by Western learning than were their European counterparts by the discovery of Asia.[19]

The first phase of Christian activity in China came to a close when religious issues merged with political issues, in the Controversy of Rites (1724),

[19] The Chinese impact was fully felt in the eighteenth-century Enlightenment, when the writings of Voltaire and Rousseau heightened the prestige of China in Europe. The full force of the Chinese exemplar was felt, however, in the writings of the Physiocrats, including Dr. Quesnay, who published in 1767 *Le despotisme de la Chine.* See Lewis A. Maverick, *China: A Model for Europe,* San Antonio, 1946.

which the Chinese settled by banning most missionary activity. At that time, the issue was not religious *per se* but involved a struggle over internal control of all ideas, including religion. The Chinese quite understandably insisted upon Imperial authority in all fields of ideology, education, and government by propaganda. Thereafter a few missionaries remained underground, but Catholic missions did not regain lost ground until they rode in again with the sea-coming merchants and were protected behind the unequal treaties. Even then, positive advances were more marked in educational work. Applied Christianity, and Christianity by personal example, were more important than the gospel. Dictionaries were drawn up, and the difficult Chinese language mastered. The missionaries began the work of translating foreign books, by no means all religious works, into Chinese. In 1872, China's first educational mission went abroad. The intellectual isolation of the Chinese began to break down.

With the establishment of American and British Protestant missions in the nineteenth century, Christianity became a positive conditioning force for a democratic ideology in Asia. With the presence of Christianity in China, the merchant and overseas Chinese counter-elite was swelled by the addition of men with a new moral certitude and ability to attack the traditional institutions of the Empire. In Chinese political experience, there have been no genuine Christian democratic party, no real Christian army, no government openly Christian in policy. Yet Sun Yat-sen was a Christian, as were the founder of the National Government, Chiang Kai-shek, and countless numbers of reformist and republican leaders. In essence, Christianity spelled modernization and Westernization to many Chinese. In more direct effects, Christianity attempted to soften and justify Western imperialism; it brought scientific, as well as moral intervention; it developed on-the-spot examples of Western ways of life; it gave the Chinese know-how in Western organizational techniques. Perhaps the greatest tribute of all to the lasting effect of Christianity on China is the rigorous and ruthless rooting out of Christian influence, identified as Western, cultural imperialism, by the Chinese Communists.

In the later history of the Western impact on Chinese ideas, Marxism too came with money, goods, treaties, and arms, reaching China first by the sea route as did most Western innovations. But its position almost from the beginning reflected an earlier land contact and the fact that Russia is China's greatest neighbor, that the Russo-Chinese frontier is one of the longest in the world.

Even in the realm of language, the development of colloquial style and mass education has meant that, despite the use of ideographs, the Chinese may reach levels of literacy approximating those achieved by Western states. During the awful convulsions of revolution and counterrevolution in modern China, many Chinese must have read in their own language only of the utter confusion which Western science has helped bring. Others have read into Chinese history only a hatred of the oppressive past and a hope for a scientific, modern, and Westernized China, different from the West only in being more modern than Europe and America. Most Chinese simply became aware of the West, and the fact that China has not adopted enough of it to make all traditions outmoded; nor has tradition survived to such an extent as to make everything Western ridiculous.

The prologue to modern revolution in China was the tradition and practice of rebellion. Rebellion approached revolution in the great T'ai-p'ing upheaval, led by the so-called Christian Rebels. Although this was the first rebellion wherein Western ideas and Western interference were significant factors, Christianity itself was only an accidental element. More significantly, the T'ai-p'ings reflected reaction against the alien Manchus and the inherent weakness of China's last dynasty. For these reasons, and also because the T'ai-p'ings opened up amazing experiments in social action, their rebellion and their government are worthy of re-examination as the pilot in the cycle of China's continuing revolutions.

CHAPTER
FIVE

The Government of the Christian Rebels, 1850-1865

DURING the past one hundred years, stupendous Chinese revolutions have succeeded one another with such shocking military violence, such dreadful political tumult, that the very magnitude of the disaster has kept outside observers from seeing the dynamics at work in Chinese society. Any one of the several Chinese revolutions is in its individual right as historic an event as the European liberal outbreaks of 1848, the Japanese Meiji Revolution of 1867, or the Turkish nationalist revolution of 1923. Many observers, non-Marxist as well as Marxist, and many scholars, Western as well as Chinese, have maintained that there is a thread of continuity in these convulsions.

Continuity in Revolutionary Convulsions. The great Christian or T'ai-p'ing Rebellion of 1850-1865 was, in many respects, the parent phenomenon of the Chinese People's Republic. Each was a response to intolerable economic conditions within China. Each was provoked by the immediate circumstances of foreign war, a war against England in the one case and a war against Japan in the other. Each was led by brilliant native leadership attempting to bring into China a vital, outside ideology, which seriously threatened the traditional Chinese way of life—then it was Christianity, now it is Marxism.

Chinese classical historians unanimously condemned T'ai-p'ing leaders as fanatic and bloodthirsty mobsters, calling them "Long-haired Bandits" and emphasizing their wanton destruction of property and indiscriminate killing. One century after their dramatic success and ultimate failure, however, they were heralded as patriotic revolutionaries by the Nationalists, and as forerunners of socialism by the Chinese Communists. In the early 1930's there was a sudden development of interest by Chinese scholars in historical materials on the T'ai-p'ing Rebellion, with perhaps tacit encouragement by the government. It was during this period that a large number of important documents were discovered and many books, sympathetic to the anti-Manchu stand of the T'ai-p'ing leaders, were written. After the Chinese Communists came to power, the T'ai-p'ing Rebellion was re-examined as a great socialistic experiment. Leaders of the Rebellion were exalted to the status of national heroes, as unselfish lovers of the people. One of the conquerors of the T'ai-p'ings, Tsêng Kuo-fan, was styled as a national traitor, a leader of reactionaries. Numerous plays and skits, portraying the righteousness and unselfishness of the T'ai-p'ing movement, have been written and presented in an effort to change popular conceptions of a long-forgotten native revolution. Recently an exhibition of T'ai-p'ing relics was presented in Nanking. From an ideological viewpoint alone, the Christian Rebellion of one hundred years ago plays a significant role in modern Chinese politics.

The Western scholar must, of course, cautiously skirt the deliberate reintroduction for propaganda purposes of T'ai-p'ing leaders and ideas into the dynamics of modern revolution. Nevertheless, the T'ai-p'ing Rebellion—in depth, fury, and scope—demands attention. It was one of the truly great convulsions of world history. It was, in many respects, the pilot which illuminated and lit the flames of modern Chinese revolutions.

It reflected the traditional cycle of internal conquest, decline, and rebellion. It began as an anti-dynastic protest against alien (Manchu) domination. It demonstrated, both in victory and defeat, the inherent weaknesses of China's last dynasty and forecast its fall. It contained overtones of foreign influence and reactions against foreign interference.

When one considers that T'ai-p'ing leaders undertook novel social and economic experiments practically without foreign ideological help, save for a scanty and perverted knowledge of Christianity, he is not surprised to find the Chinese people later willing to give any kind of revolution a fair trial.

Immediate Historical Background. After the signing of the humiliating Treaty of Nanking in 1842, the inefficiency and incompetence of the Manchu Government were brazenly exposed. Both the common people and the gentry began to feel insecure against enemies as formidable as the "Western Ocean Barbarians." The government's internal rottenness, and its weakness in the face of a foreign danger, precipitated among the populace a passionate yearning for social change and an intense hate for rulers who were themselves foreign in origin. The people of South China who possessed a long tradition of turbulence and rebellion, who more than other Chinese knew something of the outside world, and who were the last and most resistant Chinese to have been conquered by the Manchus in the 1600's, were the ones first to turn to open insurgency. Not without historical background, the provinces of Kwangtung and Kwangsi developed into hotbeds of revolution.

The T'ai-p'ing outbreak, a spectacular conspiracy and revolt of Christian desperadoes, arose from economical depression catalyzed by political instability. The process of convulsion was not wholly new. Chinese history itself was an alternating cycle of peace and convulsion. An old popular saying warned that Heaven decreed "A small turbulence every thirty years and a big uproar every hundred years."

The demographic pressure behind the political show is more revealing than the popular tradition, considered alone. The truth was that whenever peace appeared the population grew, but the cultivated land did not grow. The livelihood of the workers of the land became increasingly difficult. Destitution at an almost predictable margin led to disorder and rebellion. The reign of Ch'ien Lung (1736-1795) was a golden period in which the population was sparse, production abundant, cultural attainment high, and political vitality readily apparent. After the reign of Chia Ch'ing (1796-1820) pervasive unrest began to disturb the tranquility throughout the realm. The population was growing, but the land was not stretching to accommodate the increased number of human beings whose lives depended upon every single plot. According to Hsiao I-shan, the population increased to about 400,000,000 by the time of the Opium War—three times the probable population at the beginning of Ch'ien Lung's reign.[1] The economic pressure resulting from overpopulation was further aggravated by concentration of landholding and a high interest rate. The resulting socio-economic inequalities, amounting to a chronic outrage, were the chief motive force of all the rebellions.

During the Opium War, the Manchus lost sight of their own original military policy. In a belated and shortsighted attempt to defend their coastal frontier against possible British naval attack, they hastened to distribute a large number of weapons among Chinese groups in the population, instead of rousing the Manchu bannermen from their centuries of torpor, modernizing them, and putting them into battle. The total and humiliating defeat of the Chinese-Manchu forces by the British wherever they met, led to the scattering of these weapons among unauthorized persons.

The addition during the next decade of these two forces—(1) oppressed people, (2) brand new guns—was as predictable as the meeting of fire and gunpowder. Large-scale piracy broke out on the coast. Piracy it may have been in economic terms, but it was fighting, Chinese successfully fighting Manchus for the first time in eight generations, so far as the masses of South China were concerned. Unlike Joseph Fouche, who said, "It is more than a crime; it is a political mistake," the Manchus never realized what they themselves had done; although weak, they became more oppressive, obtaining a false sense of security by enhancing their absolutism. From within their high-walled paradise of Peking, the Manchu court dignitaries could not understand the seriousness of their position until the revolt had spread over half of China.

The leader of the rebellion was Hung Hsiu-ch'üan, an unfortunate by-product of the regular examination requirements. Hung started as a tal-

[1] Hsiao I-shan, *Ch'ing-tai shih,* cited, p. 162.

ented village boy, born in 1813, who initiated his classical studies in 1820. He took the provincial civil service examinations and failed. Undeterred, he went back to studying, prepared himself well, took the examinations again in 1837, and—failed. He had read a few Christian tracts by a native Chinese Protestant in 1833, but did not pay much attention to them. He became extremely ill, and while ill, met Jehovah, the Lord God, about whom he had read in the queer foreign tracts, at which he had glanced passingly some years before. In 1837 Hung began to suspect that it was not himself who was wrong, but the examination system, and with it the Empire. Within the theater of his own disturbed brain, Hung began to act out a tragi-comic drama which did not end until millions of people had drowned in blood. Hung discovered that God the Father had found in himself, Hung, a new and better manifestation of the Christian Trinity: God the Little Brother.

Never before, perhaps, in the history of the world, has flunking a student had such dire consequences. The improved Christian Trinity—God the Father, Jehovah; God the Son, Jesus Christ; God the Little Brother, Hung Hsiu-ch'üan—caught the peasant imagination as no Jesuit or Methodist ever caught it. Hung had a little Protestant instruction from one Issacher Roberts, an American Baptist Divine, tilling the unpromising spiritual soil of Canton city. It is not known whether Hung offered Mr. Roberts the opportunity of worshiping the Younger Brother of Jesus Christ. It is certain that the new leader not only professed to invite Western spiritual sympathy, but took few steps to obtain it. No foreign preachers or followers were involved in this weird Christianity at its outset.

In 1848 Hung inaugurated the *Shang-ti hui* or "The Association for Worshiping God." He deliberately called God by the archaic Chinese term "*Shang-ti,*" instead of calling God by the term used by the Catholics under ancient Ch'ing Imperial license, "*T'ien-chu.*" "*Shang-ti*" can be rendered back into English as "the Ruler on High" while "*T'ien-chu*" can be rendered "the Lord of Heaven." The difference, although verbal, was significant. Hung deliberately defied the legal authority of the Manchus in proclaiming the worship of an unregistered God, and expressively attributed to God as he knew Him a name not authorized by the scholastic bureaucracy.

Almost from the outset the God Worshipers began drilling and doing their best to learn what they could about infantry tactics for small mobile bodies of men. They knew that their inspired leader and their strange new God would bring them to an irreconcilable clash with Manchu authority. They were joined at the very beginning by some practicing bandits and by some semi-bandit Triads, members of a secret society which preached expulsion of the Manchus and expropriation of the profiteers. By 1850 the insurrection was well under way. Hung Hsiu-ch'üan had delirious fits in which God visited him. Hung graphically described God as an old man with a golden beard, wearing a black robe, very majestic in appearance, and overpowering in presence, who demanded that Hung exterminate all Demons and kill all those who worshiped idols. The insurrection began to spread, radiating outward from the rough, hilly countryside of Kwangsi and spreading over county after county, with both speed and violence.

In 1851 Hung proclaimed himself the Celestial King or *T'ien-wang* of the Great Peace or *T'ai-p'ing*. He proposed to be not only the Son of God in the next world, but the Ruler of Mankind in this world. Enthroning himself he issued governmental edicts and army banners inscribed with the words "Heavenly Father, Heavenly Elder Brother, and Heavenly King of Great Peace of the Celestial Kingdom."

The T'ai-p'ing revolutionary force spread with incredible speed, beside which the successes of the Bolshevik revolution in 1917 seemed like slow motion; after all, the Marxists had had seventy years of revolutionary conspiracy and agitation behind them, while Hung had less than two years of political organization. Under the strange hypnotism of Hung's fantastic but deadly serious religion, the peasants of South China launched an anti-Manchu and anti-idolatrous campaign. The Manchu garrison forces, weakened by years of venality and idleness, were no match for fanatics who were certain of victory in this world and Heaven in the next. From the occupation of the City of Yungan in the summer of 1851 to the capture of Nanking in the spring of 1853 the T'ai-p'ing armies spread over seven southwest provinces like a chain reaction. The only military parallel to the T'ai-p'ing success to be found in the West is Napoleon's triumph in reasserting his authority over the French Military Forces and the French State during the Hundred Days.

Military History. The Heavenly Kingdom was founded in Nanking in 1853, and Hung Hsiu-ch'üan began to weary of being a God and spent more time in his harem. The most spectacular of all T'ai-p'ing military successes came later in 1853, when a raiding party crossed four heavily settled metropolitan provinces, capturing 26 cities in less than four months, only to meet defeat within 20 miles of Tientsin and 100 miles from Peking itself. With this the military triumphs ceased. (See the map of T'ai-p'ing T'ien-kuo, on following page.)

The T'ai-p'ing Empire negotiated at arms' length with the Protestant and Catholic powers, whose representatives the T'ai-p'ing leaders welcomed as *hsiung-ti* or "junior brothers" in the Faith of Jesus Christ, as improved by Mr. Hung. The Westerners were as much affronted by the erratic theology of the T'ai-p'ing as by its revolutionary threat to sound business and for ten long tormenting years, two impotent empires—the worn-out Manchus and the burnt-out revolutionaries—faced one another from their respective capitals of Peking and Nanking. Slowly the contributions of the better elements in the native Chinese military service, raising an all-Chinese levy of trained irregulars, plus the addition of Western volunteers, teaching Western military skill to a composite force of adventurers and Chinese, began to turn the balance of power in favor of Peking. One American, Frederick Townsend Ward of Massachusetts, became a minor Manchu-sponsored god, after commanding the pro-Manchu volunteer force and dying from a gun-shot wound while avoiding a T'ai-p'ing surprise attack. Another American, H. S. Burgevine, having wearied of being an English instructor at the University of North Carolina, left Chapel Hill for the battlefields of the Yangtze mouth. He decided to double-cross both the Manchus and the Rebels and to make himself in his own right the Emperor of China; to this day no one knows how he met his death, but his naked body was found in a

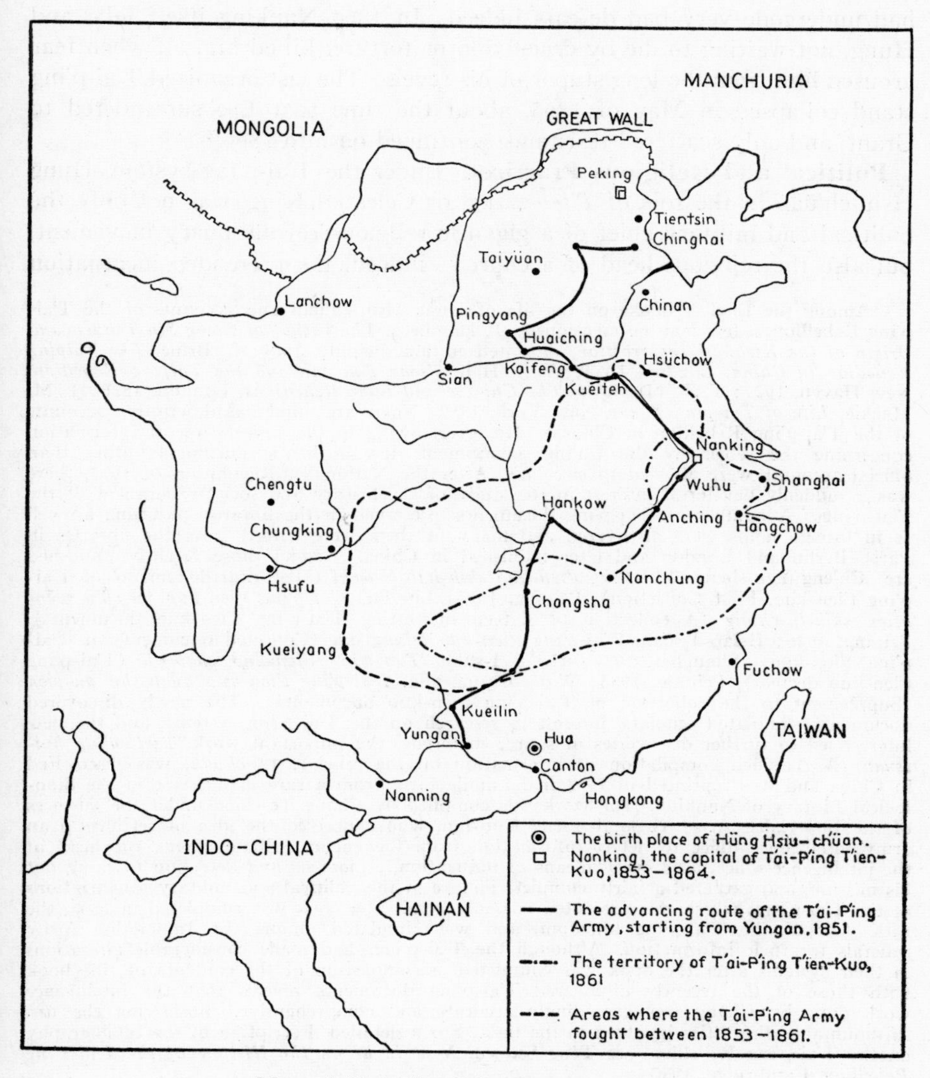

Map of T'ai-p'ing T'ien-kuo 1851-1864

canal. Final command of the Western adventurers was taken by Major Charles George Gordon, of the British Army, and led to final success by him. By 1863 the T'ai-p'ing leadership had worn itself out; so too had the T'ai-p'ing army, which at its height had numbered three and a half million. Hung himself lapsed into a career of debauchery, which would shame the eyes of an Apuleius or Boccaccio. His Ministers committed themselves to desperate feuds and violent interpersonal rivalries. Sober Imperial viceroys raised immense levies of Chinese forces, converging on Hung along a line marked out in broadest terms by the Yangtze River. By 1864 the T'ai-p'ing army had undergone very bad defeats indeed. In 1864 Nanking itself fell; and Hung, not waiting to die by crucifixion or torture, killed himself when fear aroused him from the long stupor of his revels. The last organized T'ai-p'ing stand collapsed in May of 1865, about the time that Lee surrendered to Grant, and only scattered resistance continued on into 1866.[2]

Political and Religious Practices. Under the T'ai-p'ing system, Hung Hsiu-ch'üan in the role of *T'ien-wang,* or Celestial King, was not only the political and military chief of a gigantic religious revolutionary movement, but also the religious head of a church—indeed, the pretended incarnation

[2] Among the English books on the life of Hung Hsiu-ch'üan and accounts of the T'ai-p'ing Rebellion, a few may be mentioned: T. Hamberg, *The Vision of Hung Siu-Tshuen and Origin of the Kwangsi Insurrection,* reprinted edition, Peiping, 1935; L. Brine, *The Taiping Rebellion in China,* London, 1862; W. J Hail, *Tseng Kuo-fan and the Taiping Rebellion,* New Haven, 1927; T. T. Meadows, *The Chinese and their Rebellions,* London, 1856; J. M. Mackie, *Life of Tai-ping Wang,* New York, 1857. There are numerous descriptive accounts of the T'ai-p'ing Rebellion in Chinese. However, owing to the suppression of information concerning the rebels by the Ch'ing government, few authentic documents other than official accounts were allowed to circulate. After the Nationalist Revolution of 1927, there was a suddenly developed interest in the study of the history and social experiment of the T'ai-p'ings. A number of T'ai-p'ing documents, preserved in the libraries in China as well as in foreign lands were discovered and many of them were copied from the libraries in Paris, Berlin and London and later published in China. Among those recently published are: Ch'êng Yen-shêng, *T'ai-p'ing t'ien-kuo shih-liao ti-i-chi* (Historical documents of T'ai-p'ing t'ien-kuo, First Collection), Peiping, 1925; Liu Fu, *T'ai-p'ing t'ien-kuo yu-ch'ü wên-hsien shih-lu-chung* (A collection of sixteen interesting T'ai-p'ing t'ien-kuo documents), Peiping, 1926; Hsiao I-shan, *T'ai-p'ing t'ien-kuo ts'ung-shu* (Collected documents of T'ai-p'ing t'ien-kuo), Shanghai, 1936; Hsiao I-shan, *T'ai-p'ing t'ien-kuo chao-yü* (T'ai-p'ing t'ien-kuo decrees), Peiping, 1935; Wang Chung-min, *T'ai-p'ing t'ien-kuo kuan-shu pu-pien* (Supplement to the collection of T'ai-p'ing t'ien-kuo documents). The newly discovered documents stimulated scholars' interest in research on the T'ai-p'ing systems, and the new interest led to further discoveries of source materials. An important work, *Tsei-ch'ing hui-tsuan* (A classified compilation of information on the rebels), 12 *chüan,* was discovered in China and was reprinted in 1932 in facsimile form from a rare manuscript in the Sinological Library of Nanking. The work was compiled by Chang Te-chien under the auspices of the Imperialist Army General Tsêng Kuo-fan, who conceived the idea of setting up an army intelligence office to detect information from the enemy. Chang, being the head of the intelligence office, used every means of infiltration, espionage, and detection to carry out his mission, and gathered a fairly complete picture of the political and military organizations of the T'ai-p'ings which was presented in book form. The book was completed in 1855, the fifth year of the T'ai-p'ing kingdom, and was circulated among the Imperialist Army generals for their information. Although the T'ai-p'ings had made considerable alterations in their systems after the book was completed, a comparison of the contents of this book with those of the recently discovered T'ai-p'ing documents reveals that the intelligence work done by Chang was exceedingly accurate and comprehensive, considering the unsurmountable difficulties involved in the task. For a detailed description of the bibliography on the T'ai-p'ing Rebellion, see Teng Ssu-yu, *New Light on the History of the T'ai-p'ing Rebellion,* Cambridge, 1950.

of God to that church. In his double role of spiritual and temporal ruler of China, Hung set out to reorganize the nation, on supposedly Christian principles. From his edicts and essays we can see that such Christian notions as salvation, the creation of the world according to Genesis, the Sermon on the Mount itself, the doctrine of the Resurrection of the Soul and the concept of a day of final judgment were all present. Hung knew the words of Christianity, but he somehow seems to have missed the almost timeless and irresistible mystic of its spirit.

Perhaps he was blinded by his own half-insane conviction of his status as the Son of God Himself. He made his lieutenants in the rebellion into great state officers, calling each one a king or *wang,* but he and his kings used their newly adopted religion to influence the immense masses of ignorant people, and his pretensions always trembled on that same borderline which marks off interior conviction from outward show. No one will ever quite know how much the T'ai-p'ing leadership believed of its own ideology. The vulnerability of the T'ai-p'ing version of Christianity is attested by the fact that, after the immense rebellion collapsed, no T'ai-p'ing church, no matter how small or how clandestine, survived anywhere in the world.

The T'ai-p'ing faith used temporal power to enforce religion, so much so that the religious merits of the case had little chance to survive the collapse of the military and administrative machines supporting the faith. The rise of the T'ai-p'ings was thrilling. Their rule was dreary. In T'ai-p'ing territory, everybody was supposed to go to church every week. Everyone had to perform the required religious ceremony, a caricatured adaptation of Catholic and Buddhist ceremonial. In the weekly religious meetings, T'ai-p'ing officials were both administrators and preachers. Religious essays written by Hung and others were read aloud or used as the text for sermons. There were also hymns written in a colloquial style, so as to render them readily understandable to the common people. Hung's convictions and teachings were, at first, cordially received by his immediate followers in Kwangsi, where the movement started, but as millions upon millions of people were conquered by the T'ai-p'ing army in its northward march, the T'ai-p'ings spread themselves too thin and were unable to indoctrinate the tradition-conscious population, despite the heavy penalties which they imposed on unbelievers.[3]

Furthermore, T'ai-p'ing zeal against idolatry included the wanton destruction of temples and opposition to ancestor worship; this irritated the populace and aroused distrust and enmity. If Hung had obtained, as he never did, some idea of the Christian faith as it has been practiced at its very best in the Western World, he might have introduced a major new rage among mankind; the worship of a real and personal God certainly filled a spiritual need in China. The promotion of universal love was as applicable

[3] P'êng Tsê-I, *T'ai-p'ing t'ien-kuo ke-ming ssŭ-ch'ao* (Revolutionary thought of the t'ai-p'ing t'ien-kuo), Shanghai 1946, pp. 70-81.

to China as it has been to any other country. The T'ai-p'ing leadership met too many political exigencies and had too little Christian doctrine to apply. The religious movement betrayed itself as a huge hoax, and the revolutionary reformers constructed a corrupt theocracy.[4]

T'ai-p'ing Economic Reform. In agrarian reform also the T'ai-p'ings started out with ambitious and far-reaching designs, but, because of the short duration in which their reforms were carried out, the practical value of their work has never been fully realized or appreciated.[5] As revealed in the document *T'ien-ch'ao t'ien-mou chih-tu* (Land system of the celestial dynasty), this reform was modeled on the legendary "well field" system of the Shang.

As adapted by the T'ai-p'ing Empire, this system required that all land be public land and that all produce go to the public granary. The old, the weak, and the disabled were cared for by the government; sickness was provided for, in theory, by an all-encompassing scheme of medical insurance. Weddings and funerals were given financial assistance by the authorities. All persons, both men and women, between sixteen and fifty years of age were given public land and told to work it. The proceeds of their labor went to the public treasury. Each person was expected to hold back only the amount of foodstuffs needed for his or her own survival.

The tillable land was divided into nine grades, according to its productivity. In order to insure fairness in distribution, the land each person received was necessarily a combination of the various grades. Theoretically no individual was allowed to own private property; the land allotted was not the personal estate of the tiller. His only rights were those of tilling it and of withdrawing enough for his own survival.

Apart from the basic occupation of farming, each person was required to

[4] T'ai-p'ing social and political conceptions were clearly revealed in documents, edicts, and books, which were distributed to followers. Among these, a few may be mentioned:

T'ai-p'ing chao-shu (T'ai-p'ing decrees), written by Hung Hsiu-ch'üan in 1845-1846, claimed God to be the "Heavenly Father," Jesus Christ the "Heavenly Elder Brother," and kinship to both for himself with title of "Younger Brother of Jesus Christ."

Ch'ing-pan hsin-li tsou (A memorial requesting the adoption of a new calendar) presented a combination of the traditional lunar system, which was based on a 28-day month and a 13-month year, and the Western solar system. Imposition of this calendar by the T'ai-p'ings, for a period of no less than 14 years, caused a deep psychological reaction among subjects. Revision of the names of days interfered with daily habits, many of which were centuries old, and proved to the people of South China that something fundamental in their lives had been changed.

Ch'in-ting shih-chieh t'iao-li (Regulations governing official ranks) and *Ying-chieh kuei-chên* (The recruitment of talented man) were two important documents which bore upon the administrative system. The former was a collection of regulations governing the selection, rank, duties, and responsibilities of public functionaries, while the latter was written in the form of a dialogue between the Kan Wang, the T'ai-p'ing Imperial Examiner, and a hypothetical former Ch'ing official, who sought office in the new regime, concerning the civil service and the administrative policies of the new revolutionary government.

The study of source material such as these makes the modern observer realize that T'ai-p'ing strength was not derived solely from religious fanaticism or military power, but also from the political and social reforms which the T'ai-p'ings carried out very vigorously.

[5] Cf. G. E. Taylor, "The Taiping Rebellion, Its Economic Background and Social Theory," *The Chinese Social and Political Science Review,* Vol. XVI (1932), pp. 544-614.

take up handicraft work or animal husbandry in order to increase production. The products thus obtained were considered to be the public property of the community. The theoretical system underlying this scheme was a principle of communal wealth based, in its turn, on Hung's interpretation of the Christian principle of universal love. All persons within the Celestial Kingdom were considered to be members of a single immense family, living under the benevolent guidance of the Heavenly Father above the sky and the Heavenly King in Nanking. They were all expected to work on public land, to cease selfishness, to share the things of this life joyously, and to divide up profits and comforts.

Admirable as these schemes may have been, their actual operation was rarely encouraging. Recent research by modern Chinese scholars indicates that the communal system applied only for a limited time and only in a few localities. The T'ai-p'ings abolished or modified their own system when they realized that passive resistance or noncooperation would be the response of the common people to any open attempt at enforcement. The primitive socialism of the T'ai-p'ings was more negative in disposing of unwelcome landlords and driving out the Manchu and Chinese tax officials, than positive in creating new economic order.[6]

The paleo-communist economic arrangements of the T'ai-p'ing system did apply to the military forces. After the occupation of Nanking, the rural areas around the capital were organized on a military basis. In this part of China the communal system applied as late as 1856. Even when discarded otherwise, it continued with the army. All booty gathered by officers and men was required to be turned over to the public treasury. For violation, there was only one punishment: decapitation. This was probably done for the purpose of maintaining military discipline rather than in the interests of social justice. However, in 1854, a Western observer reported that at Nanking the communist system was enforced and that "the system of public granaries and the community of goods sufficiently account for the almost entire absence of shops and trade."[7]

Other Reforms. Strange indeed was the T'ai-p'ing reform of the status of women, for which there was little Chinese precedent and not much in contemporary Christian practice in the West. During the period of conquest, women were needed for the performance of sundry duties in the army. Many of the peasant wives who had followed the T'ai-p'ing camp since the

[6] Lo Erh-kang, *T'ai-p'ing t'ien-kuo shih-kang* (Outline history of the t'ai-p'ing t'ien-kuo), Shanghai, 1937, pp. 90-98.

[7] Cited in Brine, *op. cit.*, p. 233. Another private description recorded that "when the T'ai-p'ings occupied a city, they asked the local officials to make complete survey of all the land in the District. The land was left to the tillers and the landlords were not allowed to collect rent. . . . Fortunately, there had been a good harvest the autumn before the T'ai-p'ings arrived, and the ordinary people were able to pay all the taxes required. The only people who were hard pressed were the refugees who had come into the city without obtaining jobs or bringing tools, and the landlords whose livelihood had depended on the land rent." Hsieh Hsing-yao, *T'ai-p'ing t'ien-kuo ts'ung-shu shih-san-chung* (Collection of thirteen T'ai-p'ing documents), Peiping, 1938, Vol. I, Part 2, p. 10.

early days in Kwangsi became seasoned travelers. However, promiscuity developed. In order to head off general sexual immorality, the T'ai-p'ing authorities set up special encampments for women under the command of women officers.

Once the regime was established in Nanking, special civil service examinations for women—the first of their kind in China—were opened and the successful candidates were given secretarial posts. Strict orders were issued against the long-established Chinese habit of footbinding (a disgusting but universal stylish habit of breaking the arches of the feet of infant girls, so that the adult female foot would be three inches in length). Women with bound feet were forced to do hard work as a kind of penance. Along with footbinding, prostitution was prohibited. Although all these reforms failed in the end, and although most of them were enforced for only a very short while, the fact that they should have emerged from a purely Chinese movement is startling and indicative of the deeply revolutionary temper of at least a part of the Chinese population one hundred years ago.

Other T'ai-p'ing reforms were carried out with varying degrees of success. Opium smoking and tobacco smoking were both punishable with death. For a little while the prohibition was actually carried out. In Hung's own personal writings and utterances, the prohibition of opium seems to have been one of his fundamental policies. Once he wrote a stanza which showed his resentment of opium:

> The opium pipe is like a gun
> With which you wound yourself;
> How many heroes are stretched
> Dying upon their pillows! [8]

Some modern Chinese historians credit the T'ai-p'ings with founding the movement for a popular and intelligible Chinese literary style. Other modern writers deny this. It is true that almost all T'ai-p'ing orders and edicts were written in a colloquial style. Often, T'ai-p'ing state documents included so many queer expressions and so many odd mannerisms that they were difficult to understand even when they were written. The likeliest explanation lies in the fact that most of the insurgent leaders were illiterate; they therefore used the colloquial style because it was the only Chinese writing that they could understand. They might have mistrusted the usual classical Chinese which had been employed for the purposes of government, since they themselves would have been in the position of issuing orders which they could not fully comprehend. The T'ai-p'ing linguistic reforms seem to be the obvious result of their educational handicaps, rather than a purposive attempt on the part of the T'ai-p'ing leaders to bring about a literary revolution.[9]

[8] Hamberg, *op. cit.*, p. 47.

[9] Lo Erh-kang, *Hung Hsiu-ch'üan chuan* (A short biography of Hung Hsiu-ch'üan)

The T'ai-p'ing Administrative Hierarchy. With the T'ai-p'ing triumph, uneducated insurgents who had never studied the art of government and who knew nothing of the jurisprudence and equity of other lands, undertook to set up consistent, effective control over more than 200,000,000 people. This was a tremendous task. They began well. Intelligently, they introduced a social system as revolutionary as that of any other great political reform in history. In some respects they anticipated our own highest levels of modernity. If the T'ai-p'ing experiment had only lasted longer it might have turned China into a Christian revolutionary commonwealth with effect on world history so important and far-reaching as to be unimaginable. The failure of the experiment was not inherent in the system; it was due to inadequate knowledge, scandalous conduct, and lack of sincerity on the part of the leaders.

Politically, the T'ai-p'ing system was marked by several characteristics. First, no distinction was made between the civil and military departments of government. All officials in the metropolitan area, in the army, or in local administration, were in one and the same administrative hierarchy, and all of them were entrusted with both civil and military duties. Second, women were permitted to hold responsible positions, not only in the court, but also in the army. Theoretically there was complete equality between sexes. Third, the T'ai-p'ing tried to introduce a revolutionary examination system; after they took Nanking they made an attempt to obtain intellectuals to fill administrative positions. Fourth, the T'ai-p'ing introduced the principle of hereditary positions in an effort to keep tempestuous faction-ridden leaders loyal to their posts. Official posts were considered to be rewards for merit. An official rank could be inherited either by the incumbent's descendants or by his widow.

The T'ien-wang, or Celestial King, was the only ruler since the despotic First Emperor of the Ch'in who did not assume the title of Emperor. The title itself was adopted after Hung fabricated an incredible fable for the benefit of his followers, according to which God mysteriously left a slip of paper with the inscription "The Celestial Kingdom of Great Reason, the Sovereign Ch'üan" in Hung's home, as an indication of what God wished Hung to call himself upon assuming office. As *T'ien-wang,* Hung claimed to be not only the ruler of China, but the ruler of mankind. Despite his persistent orders calling for observation of the Ten Commandments, he lived like a Patriarch of the Old Testament, with dozens of concubines and hundreds of servants to cater to every whim. After he took Nanking his power was usurped by ambitious and cunning colleagues. As he disappeared into his harem, he became relatively inactive in public affairs. Feuds developed among his subordinates, which finally brought disintegration to the rebel

---

Chungking, 1944, pp. 49-51; Lin Shan-ch'ing, *T'ai-p'ing t'ien-kuo yeh-shih* (An unofficial history of the t'ai-p'ing t'ien-kuo). Shanghai, 1923, Bk. 10, p. 1.

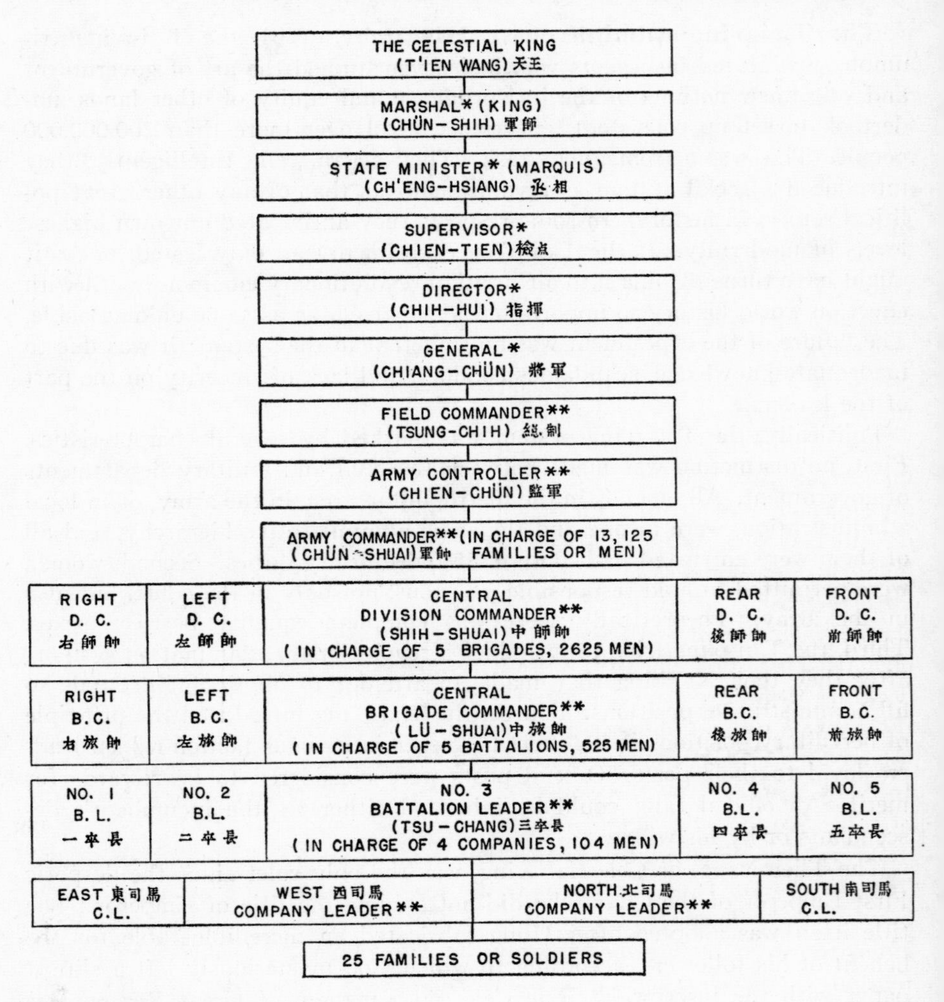

* METROPOLITAN OFFICIALS.
** LOCAL OFFICIALS.

CHART 3—Organization of the T'ai-p'ing Government and Army System

kingdom and the ultimate triumph of Manchu-Chinese forces in the North.[10]

Underlying the basic pattern of the T'ai-p'ing administration was an attempt, curiously modern, to make all farmers into soldiers, for purposes of

[10] Chart 3 shows the T'ai-p'ing administration. Under the *T'ien-wang* were a number of kings *(wang)*—who also assumed the title of marshal *(chün-shih)*—and marquises *(hou)*. In addition there were state ministers *(ch'eng-hsiang)*, supervisors *(chien-tien)*, directors *(chih-hui)*, generals *(chiang-chün)*, field commanders *(tsung-chih)*, army controllers *(chien-chün)*, army commanders *(chün-shuai)*, division commanders *(shih-shuai)*, brigade commanders *(lü-shuai)*, battalion leaders *(tsu-chang)*, and company leaders *(ssŭ-ma)*, making a total of 16 different grades. All officials above the rank of general were metropolitan officials, whereas those below the rank of field commander were local officials.

war, and turning them back into farmers in times of peace. The whole Empire was, in a sense, an army and army reserve system. So thoroughgoing were these arrangements that the local administrative system was arranged on a military basis, and all local officials were also commissioned officers of the army.

For the smallest of local areas, the lowest unit was the family. Each family was responsible for the contribution and maintenance of one soldier in the army organizations. For every 25 families there was a company commander. Whenever the central authorities required active service, the company commander led 25 men from his locality to war; for ordinary peacetime purposes he was the local government official for the communal group of 25 families. During harvest time, the company commander led the 25 families *in toto* to gather the crops.[11]

The administration of 100 families was controlled by a battalion commander, of 500 families by a brigade commander, of 2,500 families by a division commander, and of 12,500 families by an army commander. All disputes between individuals were to be settled by the company commander, but if his decision was not observed, the litigants could appeal step by step until the case reached the Celestial court. When it came to actual practice, the field commander and the army controller were the highest government officials (corresponding to the prefects and the sub-prefects of the Ch'ing), deciding all local matters and imposing the death penalty at will. Although this system did not achieve universal application and stability, it was enforced for at least a few years in some areas under T'ai-p'ing jurisdiction. In many respects, the 25-family group resembled the modern Soviet system of collective farming.[12]

T'ai-p'ing Personnel Practices. In the first stages of their conquest the T'ai-p'ings were badly handicapped by the lack of literate persons in their own service. People who volunteered for so desperate and dangerous an enterprise were likely to be irresponsible desperadoes or uneducated and pretentious fortune-seekers. After the establishment of the capital at Nanking, the T'ai-p'ing leaders attempted to follow the example of other dynastic founders in history: they opened their own examinations to recruit talented men for the new administrative service.

From 1853 to 1862, ten metropolitan examinations were given, one in each year. According to available sources the system went through many changes before it became a fairly well-established system in the last years of the long rebellion. At the beginning the examinations were simple in form and the

[11] "The blessings of the Heavenly Father should be shared by the people of the whole empire, land should be tilled, food should be consumed, clothes should be worn, and money should be spent by all. There must be no inequality among the people and no one shall suffer hunger and cold." *T'ien-ch'ao t'ien-mou chih-tu* (Land system of the Celestial Dynasty).

[12] Lo Erh-kang, *T'ai-p'ing t'ien-kuo shih-kang,* pp. 81-87.

participants were few. Very little is known about these examinations. As the system settled down, the regulations became more definite.[13]

At the beginning of the system the titles given to successful candidates were the same as those given by the Ch'ing. The winner of the highest honor in the metropolitan examination was also given the title of *Chuang-yüan*. Provincial examinations were also given in many provinces. Successful candidates from the provinces were assigned duties in the capital. Stiff qualifications were required of these candidates and most of the participants were very poorly educated. It was said that among the participants there were many dispossessed Buddhist monks and Taoist priests, whose temples and monasteries had been destroyed in the fighting. Most of the actual scholars refused to participate in the examination because they were ashamed of associating with the riffraff who applied. Whereas on the Ch'ing battle line one candidate out of 300 passed the lowest of the state examinations, there is still available the record of a T'ai-p'ing examination in Hupeh where 1,000 poorly qualified participants showed up, 800 of them obtaining degrees.

So low was the standard of the examinations that, instead of being competitive, the system appears as though it may have been an insurgent draft of all the available scholars, good or bad. This view is reinforced by the probability that participation in the examination was made compulsory for certain classes of people. According to a private account of the rebellion the first few examinations were so outrageous a caricature of Chinese culture that many candidates wrote satirical and libelous essays and willingly faced the death penalty in consequence. One of these pro-Manchu orthodox scholars was asked to write a couplet eulogizing the Celestial court as a condition for pardon. Instead of doing his best and writing something nauseously flattering in order to save his life, he wrote: "The whole domain complete with mountains and rivers is 105 square miles" (the area of Nanking); "the entire court, composed of both civil and military officials, is drafted from 36 different low-grade craftsmen." The T'ai-p'ing leaders were so outraged that they had him torn to pieces by five horses.[14]

So far as modern scholarship has been able to ascertain, there was at least

[13] The details of the examination system for both the literary and military offices were defined in *Ch'in-ting shih-chieh t'iao-li.* This document provided that those who wished to take the literary examinations should prepare themselves by becoming well-versed in the Old and New Testaments, and in the Heavenly Decrees of the Celestial Kingdom. Those who wished to take military examinations should be able to demonstrate their capacity to handle the tools of war. In addition, they were required to know the book on military tactics published by orders of the Celestial King. It was also provided that the traditional Confucian canons, the *Four Books,* and *Five Classics* should not be totally prohibited, but the passages that were in conflict with the true precepts of the Heavenly Father, God, should be considered deleted. A bureau for the revision of the Chinese classics was set up. Several editors were appointed. The title, *The Revised Four Books and Five Classics,* was among the titles of books published by Imperial order. Since the revised edition has never been discovered in modern times, its actual publication is an unsettled question to this day. See Wang Chung-ch'i, *T'ai-p'ing t'ien-kuo ke-ming-shih* (History of the T'ai-p'ing revolution), Shanghai, 1933, pp. 120-123.

[14] This popular legend is to be found in Ling Shan-ch'ing, *op. cit.,* Chap. 8, pp. 4-6.

one examination for women, given in 1863. The examiner was the half-sister of the Celestial King. The subject given as text for the examination was taken from the Confucian classics: "Women and persons of mean character are difficult to deal with." Fu Shan-hsiang, a talented woman who repudiated the Confucian dictum in her essay with feminist arguments, later became the secretary of the all-powerful official who bore the title, Eastern King, and played an important part in his life.

The remuneration to kings and marquises was high, and the remainder of the important officials also enjoyed luxurious living. The remuneration of government officials was measured by the amount of meat allotted to them with a concomitant scale of food supplies and luxuries. The process of paying salaries was called the "division of meat," a term which had often been used in the Chinese underworld. From the state ministers downward each grade received five catties of meat less per day than the grade next above. The lower grades were paid meagerly, and their remuneration was not enough for bare subsistence. The lowest grade officials who served in metropolitan areas were anxious to be transferred to the army or to local areas so they could live on the people.

Feudalistic Socialism. Although the T'ai-p'ing organization had these marked patterns of reform, it also fell back on definitely feudal characteristics. It is perfectly plain from the above that the T'ai-p'ing rebels intended, within the limits of their language and education, to encompass what we would call a "socialist revolution." In part of their area a crude form of communism was practiced. Sun Yat-sen, at the end of his life, allowed himself a bold sneer at the Russians in 1924 when he said, "Communism in other countries is still in the stage of discussion, it has not been fully tried out anywhere. But it was applied in China at the time of Hung Hsiu-ch'üan. His economic system was the real thing in communism and not mere theory." [15]

Although socialists, the T'ai-p'ings attempted to make all offices hereditary posts. The socialism becomes an incidental of their total and everlasting mobilization on the basis of the spiritual and military organization for constant readiness. Seen in this light, socialism is not an end in itself, but an attempt to make the communal group the logistic base of the fighting group for a secret empire.

Despite the talk of universal love and equality, the planners of the T'ai-p'ing Empire placed strong emphasis on the creation of a powerful leadership group. The investiture of kings and marquises was definitely feudalistic in character. At the beginning there were below the Celestial King himself only seven kings, each one in command of one of the first seven armies; but as time went on hundreds of kings and marquises were created and all their titles were made hereditary.

[15] *San Min Chu I,* Principle of Nationalism, Lecture IV. Translated by Frank W. Price, Chungking, 1943, p. 97.

The T'ai-p'ing Administrative Failure. The T'ai-p'ings had all the ingredients of a successful revolution at hand—an inspiring ideology, an audacious leader, an oppressed people, an alien ruler against whom they rebelled, and a real program of reform—but they were unable to make the best of their opportunity. Their failure was due partly to lack of capable leadership and partly to their inability to devise an effective administrative system.

The Rebellion began to slow down just as the T'ai-p'ings reached power over the Southern half of China, not so much because of Manchu resistance but because they themselves were unable to manage, to mobilize, and to activate the immense populations and territories they had conquered.

Although individual T'ai-p'ing leaders were brilliant and resourceful, T'ai-p'ing techniques as a whole were not far different from those used by other fanatic mobocrats in the Chinese past, such as the Yellow Turbans of the late Han or the White Lotus who rebelled against the Mongols. Whenever the T'ai-p'ings were unable to control the situation, they used terror. Ferocity became a substitute for efficiency.

In terms of the sociology of revolution, T'ai-p'ing leaders tried to create a new pyramid of society without obtaining an elite capable of carrying out the managerial functions of the new society. The intellectual class had always been the articulate, potent group from which bureaucracies were drawn up after rebellion, but the T'ai-p'ings were too uncouth as revolutionists to create their own literati in time to salvage the regime.

Despite their conscious efforts to win the support of the scholar-gentry, their religious practices and economic policies were too radical to be reconciled with the prevailing Confucian tradition. The T'ai-p'ings suffered final defeat from a native Chinese army, raised and trained by a great Confucian general and administrator and supplemented by foreign adventurers. The general was Tsêng Kuo-fan, whose loyalty to an alien Emperor prevented him from developing sympathy for what looked like, at first, a nationalistic rebellion.

Three generations later the Chinese Nationalists had Chinese Protestant Christians to supply them with a corps of political leadership; a generation after the Nationalists, the Communists had their own Marxist-trained cadres. The T'ai-p'ings failed to draw orthodox scholars to their side. Their administrative system was, therefore, at best a makeshift arrangement incapable of handling the huge volume of governmental paper work.[16]

Most of the T'ai-p'ing leaders devoted little attention to administration

[16] The Loyal King *(Chung-wang)* was a man named Li Tzu-ch'eng, who proved to be the ablest and most farsighted general in the T'ai-p'ing army. When he was captured by Manchu forces he wrote a confession, which can be found in Lo Yung and Shen Tsu-chi, *T'ai-p'ing t'ien-kuo shih-wen-ch'ao* (Anthology of the T'ai-p'ing t'ien-kuo literature), Shanghai, 1934, Vol. I, pp. 60-103. In his confession, he listed "ten mistakes" of the T'ai-p'ings and made ten recommendations to the Manchus. Among the ten, there was the fundamental mistake of not having an effective administrative system. He gave this as the chief cause for the T'ai-p'ing failure.

and government, but concentrated on private enjoyment and personal privileges. In the last stages of the Empire, Hung Hsiu-ch'üan himself relied on his kinsmen, who were unfortunately mediocrities. He made many of his cousins into kings, giving them power over experienced field generals. So obsessed was Hung Hsui-ch'üan by the religion he had invented out of his disappointment and delusions that, as his empire finally crumbled, he asked the Heavenly Father and the Heavenly Elder Brother to tell him what to do, and paid even less attention than before to the practical problems of military strategy and administration of the state. Hung did not fail because he entertained new principles of government, but because he lacked an administrative system to put those principles into practice. If he had succeeded, China might be in fact, as well as in pretense, one of the greatest political and economic powers on earth today.

Finally, it must be remarked that in their separate ways the great T'ai-p'ing Rebellion, and the much smaller Boxer Rebellion of 1900 (described in the following chapter), were different responses of ordinary Chinese to a world which threatened their way of life and their sense of being people, real people with real lives. The T'ai-p'ings tried to meet the Western World with a crude and vulgar adaptation of Christian terms. It was primarily a self-contrived Chinese experiment, and it failed. The Boxers followed and tried to reject the Western World in full. They too failed. But the end of Chinese rebellions brought only the beginning of Chinese revolution and the further, gloomy failure of experiment in Western forms of government. The old stability was gone; instability moved up from the rank of the exception to the position of rule.

CHAPTER SIX

The Old First Republic, 1912-1928

ONE of the most fantastic spectacles in the political history of mankind was the attempt of the Chinese to set up a parliamentary constitutional republic between 1912 and 1928. The Chinese republican revolution of 1911-1912, which set about this immense undertaking, was led by the visionary and genius, Sun Yat-sen. The result was chaos, not freedom. Progress was made, but the progress was a particularly nightmarish kind of anarchy which, in its turn, led inevitably to the invasion of China by foreign powers and to the Nationalist and Communist revolutions. Rarely has a government fitted its people so poorly. Rarely has a nation undertaken a political experiment with so little understanding of what the experiment involved. Chinese history, 1912-1928, is a story of growth, tragedy, disappointment, failure.

The political forms of the old first republic of China were phantoms. It is hard for Americans of the mid-twentieth century to realize that a Chinese of today might look back on China's period of parliamentary democratic government as an age of hypocrisy, humiliation, civil war, chronic disorder, and frustration on an immense scale—yet this is the case. The political institutions are, therefore, not significant in their own right but are tragically and monumentally appropriate as a case history of an immense failure.

The triumph of the *Kuomintang* (Nationalist Party), and after that, the *Kungch'antang* (Communist Party), was possible only because the ideas and the institutions transmitted to China by the heirs of the American and French revolutions and by the proponents of British parliamentarism meant nothing. No one took the Chinese republic very seriously after its first few months. No one lamented it when it fell. No one today advocates reconstituting it.

Failure this complete is indeed an unusual political phenomenon. The republic of China came, was perverted, survived as a parody of itself, and then disappeared under the onslaughts of the Nationalist-Communist coalition in the Great Revolution of 1926-1928.

On paper there was not much wrong with the republic. It was a very fine government, amply supplied with all the documents that a progressive and forward-looking political system required. It had a plethora of constitutions, splendid parliamentary procedure which meant nothing, admirable law codes which were never enforced, and just about everything on paper, and on paper only, that a good twentieth-century republic should possess. The republic did not possess people who understood democratic institutions, a population willing to give allegiance to a cultural form so completely alien, administrators who knew how to administer, or any of the other practical features which make a government a series of consecutive and meaningful operations in the lives of most of the population of any country part of the time and of part of the population all of the time. The first Chinese republic was a foreign office attached to domestic chaos, a bureau of protocol, and not much more.

The First Wave of Manchu Reform. The ephemeral and pitiable Chinese republic was preceded by decades of internal struggle within China. The Ch'ing regime was collapsing as part of the inevitable cycle of Chinese conquest, decline, disorder, and rebellion, a cycle older than the Western states themselves. Foreign aggression and internal dissension brought the Manchu Empire of China to the brink of disintegration in the last part of the nineteenth century. The climax of the crisis was reached when the Sino-Japanese War of 1894-1895 resulted in complete military disaster and utter political humiliation.

With Japanese victory the crisis of Western technology became something terrifying and immediate to the most blindly orthodox of Confucian minds. No cultivated man in China could pretend that the outside world did not exist. The Chinese Boxers attempted to do in a vulgar and ignorant way that which their betters had begun to despair of—the driving of hated "foreign devils" from Chinese soil. The Boxer movement, considered as a great manifestation of political emotion, was an instance of ruinously misplaced patriotism, a patriotism white hot in its devotion but ignorant beyond all belief. The Boxers were crushed by an international army and by those parts of the Manchu court which had given them covert encouragement. The Boxer Rebellion was really the crusade of the common man in China to do something for his own country, since the government did not seem able or willing to do it; when the common man was cut down by the foreign guns and disavowed by the educated government, it took a long time to make him believe again that he himself had a role to play in China's political destiny.

The Boxer movement tried to meet the Western threat with a bitter and total rejection of everything Western, human, intellectual, mechanical, and spiritual. It was anti-Christian, anti-modern, anti-white race, anti-European, anti-American, anti-progressive. The Boxers went down to a speedy and bloody defeat. Prussian cavalry hunted the Boxers like rabbits across the province of Chihli (now called Hopei), and the sloppy Russian troops, half-trained louts with inadequate supplies, had no trouble crushing every vestige of Chinese power in Manchuria.

Homogeneous old China may have been, but under the strain of Manchu decline and the Western and Japanese impacts the homogeneity declined. The agonizing strains of the Sino-Japanese War stimulated to an extreme a group of enlightened scholars around the Manchu Throne who had acquired Western political ideas. These scholars reached the conclusion—a conclusion which was to prove fatal to China over and over again in ensuing decades—that it was the *lack of constitutional government* which made China weak and Japan strong.

Japanese modernization had been visible. The most striking visible sign of modernization had been the obvious process of constitutionalization undertaken by the Meiji Emperor and his advisers. Actually, in Japan constitutionalization had been more striking and visible than real; a number of forces worked toward modernization, as we shall see, other than the simple process of adopting a constitution. The Chinese, being Chinese, were unable to understand that in some respects the Japanese might be better citizens, better subjects, more loyal, more brave, more devoted than themselves, or that Japan, simply because it was smaller and had been better governed and *more* governed, was more amenable to such political changes than China. Factors such as these required a reach of history which we, half a century later, living completely outside the Sino-Japanese world, can readily attain. It was too much to expect of a Chinese bureaucrat or a Manchu noble. They did their best. Their best was wrong.

The first wave of Manchu reform was carried out in three separate stages. The first stage was a futile effort on the part of the young and ambitious Emperor Kuang Hsü to obtain power for himself and to save his empire. In this he was assisted by a serious, talented Confucian scholar named K'ang Yu-wei. In his fleeting ascendancy to power in the summer of 1898 K'ang persuaded the Emperor to issue a number of edicts pertaining to administrative and educational changes. Together this bold experiment—all of it on paper, since there was no time to implement any of the edicts—was known as the Hundred Days of Reform.

K'ang and his associates believed that the introduction of Western learning was fundamental to China's educational and intellectual development. They held that the adoption of the Western administrative system was essential for the revitalization of the mandarinate. Among the reform measures proposed in that brief period was an Imperial command abolishing the eight-legged essay, based upon the Confucian classics, and the introduction into traditional civil service examinations of material pertaining to current events in real everyday life. Another edict proposed the establishment of a great imperial university of Peking, in which the Western arts and sciences were to be taught. Other mandates from the Dragon Throne undertook to abolish a number of meaningless sinecures, thus making the matter of government more clean-cut, to reorganize China's military establishment which had been shamed and degraded by the abjectness of its defeat at the hands of the Japanese, to encourage the development of trade, industry, and communications, and to improve diplomatic relations with foreign countries. Considered as paper measures these reforms were practical and to the point. They were intended to remedy many of the administrative defects and political anachronisms which burdened the tottering dynasty. Even had these succeeded in remaining legally in force, it would have taken an immense effort to translate them from the august classical Chinese phrasing of an Imperial command into the administrative workaday reality of actual change.[1]

The reformers did not even get this much of a chance.

The reactionary group at the Manchu court represented by the Empress Dowager, Yehonala, who was also known under the Chinese name of Tz'ŭ Hsi, undertook a countercoup. Some of the reformers had their heads chopped off. The Emperor was imprisoned in the middle of his palace. (It is popularly believed that, as the Empress Dowager lay dying on the night of the 14th and 15th of November, 1908, she sent word that the young Kuang Hsü should die before herself. The story continues that obedient servants poisoned the imprisoned Emperor and reported to the dying woman that her antagonist had died before her.) Back in 1898 one of the people who made possible the success of the countermeasures undertaken by the reactionary clique of the court was a man whose name was to figure ominously in Chinese history, Yüan Shih-k'ai.

The vested interests supported the reactionaries and therewith supported their own early destruction, because they understood even less than did the young Emperor the depth and danger of the changes all around their world. Once the reformers were out of the way and after the Boxers had tragically demonstrated that the Chinese were incapable of driving the Westerners out by sheer physical violence, the reactionaries themselves undertook the second wave of Manchu reform. The reform movement of the Manchu court was undertaken more as a means of easing the revolutionary spirit abroad in the country than of increasing the strength of the nation, but the reforms were undertaken by men who were insincere and irresolute. The old ruling class was intellectually and psychologically incapable of moving with the time. In comparison with the elegant perfumed ignorance of the court reactionaries in Peking the czarist reactionaries of Petrograd a few years later

[1] For the edicts issued during this period, see Chu Shou-p'êng, *Tung-hua hsü-lu, Kuang Hsü* (Annals and memoirs of the Ch'ing dynasty, Kuang Hsü period), Shanghai, 1909, *chüan* 124-145.

seemed to be relatively progressive characters. Even the most moderate reform was fought with an unreality and capriciousness which, in the light of what has happened in China since then, seems close to insanity.

Manchu Reform, Second Wave. Inadequate as it was, the second wave of Manchu reform did start in 1901. Atrocity, cruelty, deceit, and blind rage had all been tried in the Sino-Japanese War and in the Boxer Rebellion: they had all failed. Foreign garrisons were in Peking and American officers were joining their Japanese and European confreres in looting the palaces, burning the libraries, and buying souvenirs from the Chinese rabble who joined in the looting. Pekingese dogs, long a near-sacred monopoly of the Forbidden City, had suddenly become quaint trophies from a comic opera war. After imposing humiliating terms on the Manchu court and exacting reparations, the international forces withdrew and the Empress Dowager started her own measures of modernization. The first basic reform was the acceptance even within the Manchu system of the foreign nations as equals of China. The old examination system was abolished. Tentative experiments in sending students abroad were followed up with a large-scale dispatch of a considerable number of students to foreign countries, most particularly to Japan, and the further establishment of modern schools.[2]

The Manchu reforms were undertaken in a Never-never Land which could not possibly have survived for long. They were too shallow to affect the basic economic and strategic sources of China's weakness and yet strong enough to add strength to the forces of revolution.

At this time Sun Yat-sen was becoming a major leader among the Chinese outside of China. He covered himself with publicity and notoriety, but he was as elusive as a ghost when the Manchus sent henchmen overseas to kill him.

Manchu Reform, Third Wave. Only as the Empress Dowager began the slow, dogged process of dying—and in dying she was as brave, ignorant, and obstinate as she had been in her long ruthless life, rising to power over all China from an obscure corner of the Manchu harem—did the third wave of the reform movement get under way. In 1906 the central administration was completely reorganized. The traditional six departments inherited from the long-dead glories of the T'ang bureaucracy were reorganized into ten ministries, copied very bluntly from Western administrative systems. By an edict of 1907 the Manchu court convoked provincial assemblies of loyal notables. In 1905 and 1907 the Manchus sent two commissions of high dignitaries abroad to study constitutional development. These commissions were neither intelligent nor imaginative and the best they could suggest was a rather dull copy of the Japanese experience with some cross references to the Prussian model.

As a consequence a set of constitutional principles (*Hsien-fa ta-kang*)

[2] For edicts issued during this period, see *ibid.*, *chüan* 164. A brief summary of the reform movement is given in Vinacke, *op. cit.*, Chap. X.

was promulgated on August 27, 1906, promising full constitutional government to the Chinese Empire by the end of 1917.[3] (Of course by 1917 the Empire was gone.) Many laws, regulations, and codes were enacted in pursuance to the requirements set forth in these principles: few of them were ever put into practice.

With the same frenzy of trying to meet a problem which, seen from our time, was insoluble at the start, the Manchus tried to establish the Central Legislative Council (*Tzŭ-chêng-yüan*) in 1910. The Council was composed of two hundred members, half of whom were elected by the provincial assemblies from among their own members and the other half being appointed by the Emperor. The Council did little to satisfy the rising demand on the part of the educated classes for better government. After the revolution had actually begun in 1911 the Manchu Emperor promulgated the so-called Nineteen Constitutional Articles (*Shih-chiu hsin-t'iao*) of November 2, 1911, embodying fundamental principles of liberal constitutional monarchism.[4]

At their very best the reform movements had a very scant chance of success. The impact of Europeanism hit a Japan which was economically and socially vital, alive, disciplined, patriotic, and fairly well unified. The same impact hit a China too large to be governed effectively and a China which even by Chinese standards was in wretched condition. The Manchu princes and their Chinese advisers who, taken all together, were at their very best intellectual mediocrities, asked of China the same thing which George Catlett Marshall was to ask thirty-seven years later: that China install good government without having the men who could operate good government; that China set up a democracy when no one understood democracy as Americans and British understood it; that out of corruption, humiliation, and defeat the Chinese rid themselves with a single miracle (by processes which neither the Manchu princes acting for the infant Emperor nor Marshall managed to specify) of all their troubles in a single instant; that simply and bluntly China stop being China. The "how" was left unanswered.

The Revolution of 1911-1912. Sun Yat-sen understood by rote and by instinct the sociology underlying Chinese political behavior. He knew that shifts in tenure of political power were most readily launched by dramatic or shocking events which, though minute affairs in themselves, proved themselves socio-psychologically capable of precipitating a species of creative political panic peculiar to China. No Western community has ever gotten so used to its own revolutions as has China, since the Western communities now extant are in most cases the product of a single creative revolution. Sun Yat-sen undertook to precipitate violent and dramatic assassinations and raids in the hope that one of them would catch fire. The incident which did catch fire was unplanned.

[3] See Appendix 2.
[4] For the English text, see *The China Year Book*, London, Tientsin and Shanghai, 1912 edition, pp. xxiii-xxiv.

Some bomb makers at Wuchang, opposite Hankow on the Yangtze River, had already subverted a great part of the Imperial garrison nearby. When the bomb makers were discovered by the czarist police in the Russian extraterritorial settlement at Hankow they threatened to expose their fellow conspirators in the Imperial garrison if their lives were not preserved. Since the soldiers could neither rescue the bomb makers nor ignore the incident, they mutinied in order to save their own lives and the inglorious revolution was precipitated so suddenly that Sun Yat-sen in Denver, Colorado, read about it in the American newspapers. He had been right, medical man that he was, in his prognosis of his patients' behavior. The Chinese, startled by a single incident, bolted into revolution. Within a few weeks the insurrection turned into a nation-wide revolution.

In South China the rebels undertook massacres of the Manchus in the helpless garrison cities, throwing Manchu men, women, and children dead or alive into ditches as enthusiastically as the Germans murdered the Jews at Auschwitz; the Manchu cavalry who had overawed China for three centuries dispersed without a fight. Within four months the Manchu ruling family abdicated the Chinese Throne.

The rebel forces were able to get immediate response from the various existing provincial governments which in insurrectionary hands appointed delegates to hold meetings first in Shanghai and then in Hankow in order to consolidate revolutionary strength and to discuss plans for future government. On December 2, 1911, these delegates offset the attempted Imperial reforms of a month before by issuing a document containing twenty-one articles and entitled *The Organic Law of the Provisional Government* (*Lin-shih chêng-fu tsu-chih ta-kang*). This was the first republican constitution ever devised by Chinese. Briefly the outline provided that a national assembly was to be convened after six months and that the national assembly should decide upon a permanent constitution. The Organic Law outlined an administrative establishment to comprise five ministries of Foreign Affairs, Home Affairs, Finance, Military Affairs, and Communications. By authority from the respective provincial governments a council of representatives to be sent from the provinces was to act as a legislative body. It is significant that the representatives were not to be elected from the provinces: there was no means of holding an election; no one even had the faintest idea of what "electing" meant; therefore the provincial representatives had to be designated *ad hoc* by the revolutionary group in charge of each province. This set a pattern for all the rest of the experiment. The representatives of the revolutionary military governors of the several provinces were to elect a provisional President.

Sun Yat-sen went back to China and was immediately elected provisional President. On January 1, 1912, he swore allegiance to the new republic which he headed. As a good Christian he also prayed and incongruously but naturally went to the tombs of the Ming emperors, the last Chinese emperors of China, to inform the hovering spirits of the illustrious Ming dead that barbarian rule had been erased from China and that once again the men of Han ruled themselves from Nanking. The republican government was officially under way at Nanking.

Unfortunately the Imperial government remained in Peking. A Western people under such circumstances might have fought it out. The two Chinese governments negotiated, the republic attempting to abolish the Empire by fiat and the Empire attempting to authorize the republic as a means of making the republic lose face and of providing a possible re-entry for the ruling dynasty into politics. The Manchu court did not have much spine of its own, but it recalled Yüan Shih-k'ai, who had been the chief military modernizer among the Imperial forces. Yüan Shih-k'ai had control of the only modern army and several hundred pieces of heavy artillery. Himself a schemer, Yüan used his position to double-cross both the Manchus and the republic and to put himself in supreme power. He persuaded the regents for the infant Emperor to issue an Imperial edict ordering the Republicans to set up a republic. He obtained from the Republicans the assurance that the republic would survive if he, Yüan Shih-k'ai, were made the first republican President. The Manchu court tried to establish a sort of Vatican City for itself in the Forbidden City, retaining for the infant Emperor the privileges of a monarch and an annuity of four million Chinese ounces of silver and extraterritorial status within the palace-domain at Peking for the survival of the Imperial house. The new Empress Dowager, who was by no means the equal of her ferocious predecessor, accepted on behalf of her small son and proclaimed the abdication on February 12, 1912.

If Machiavelli had been living in 1912 Sun Yat-sen's behavior would have driven him completely out of his mind. Sun Yat-sen was so filled with enthusiasm for the power of modern ideas and so trustful in the goodness of human nature that he accepted the deceitful deal offered by Yüan and agreed to resign as provisional President, letting Yüan, who hated and mistrusted the republic, take over command. Sun Yat-sen left office on March 10, 1912, and Yüan was sworn in as provisional President.

The Presidency of Yüan Shih-k'ai. The constitutional formula under which Yüan took office as President of the Republic of China had been outlined by the revolutionary Council of Representatives which had drafted a constitution as a means of curbing Yüan. In this they showed the same vainglorious dependence upon the written word which their Manchu predecessors had displayed in the period of Imperial reform. They wrote a Provisional Constitution (*Lin-shih yüeh-fa*),[5] important because it represents the shadowy tie of legality which, feeble though it was, represented the incorporated loyalty to China of the Nationalist part of the revolutionary movement from 1912 all the way through to 1928. Since the revolution had been seized by supporters of Sun Yat-sen, some sincere and recognized

[5] See Appendix 3.

others opportunists and unknown, it was natural for Sun and his friends to feel that the revolution was their act, the government their government, the law their law. Under their various party names and governmental forms the followers of Sun Yat-sen, most commonly known by the party name of Nationalist Party or *Kuomintang,* stayed faithful to this Provisional Constitution of 1912 until they themselves reached final power. It is easy today to pay tribute to the pertinacity of the Chinese Communists who fought for twenty-odd years before they became masters of all China; one should remember that the Nationalists had done the same thing before the Communists and had done it without the support of a world movement such as Communism or the moral and military aid of a great power such as the Soviet Union.

The Provisional Constitution is important because it shows how far the Nationalists themselves went in the period of the first republic. This constitution contained fifty-six articles. It was drafted under a strong democratic impulse incorporating the fundamental theory of popular sovereignty. This constitution vested sovereignty in the whole body of the Chinese people, delegating the power to exercise sovereignty to the National Council, the provisional President, the Cabinet, and the Judiciary. It also provided a Bill of Rights for the people.

The National Council (*Ts'an-i-yüan*) was to be a unicameral body elected by the several provinces of China proper and by the outlying territories. Each member was to have one vote. To all intents and purposes the National Council was to function as a true legislative body possessing the usual powers of enacting laws, voting budgets, electing the provisional President and Vice-President. The provisional President was to execute laws, to command the army and the navy, to appoint and to remove civil and military officials, to declare war, and to conclude treaties with the concurrence of the National Council. The Cabinet was to be composed of a Prime Minister and heads of government departments who were to be selected by the provisional President. A Department of Justice was created to handle criminal and civil cases. Judges were to be appointed by the provisional President and to be guaranteed full independence and security of tenure during good behavior. Finally the Constitution provided that a regular Parliament composed of two houses was to be convened by the provisional President within ten months after its promulgation. Upon the date of the convocation of the Parliament, the National Council was to be automatically dissolved and its powers were then to be exercised by the Parliament.[6]

This document was undoubtedly democratic. In so far as legal formula could help the situation at all this Provisional Constitution probably did as much as could be done. From a technical point of view one of its shortcomings was its omission in clarifying the distribution of powers between the nation as a whole and the provinces and its failure to define the role

[6] Provisional Constitution, Article 53.

and character of provincial governments. The omission led to subsequent arguments concerning unitary versus federal forms of government. Another shortcoming was the compromise between a presidential and a cabinet form of government. The power of the provisional President was restricted by the provision that he could not act in many significant matters without the concurrence of the National Council, but the constitution did not give the National Council any effective political, moral, or legal restraint to apply to the provisional President.

The system was deficient as a cabinet system in that the Cabinet did not have the power to initiate legislation in the National Council. The President and the Premier each had extensive executive powers. A third shortcoming was to be found in the fact that China started off with a straight geographic election of members of the National Council on the basis of high-level provincial autonomy.

Even as a dream this constitution was unwieldy. In terms of the tangible realities of political power in China the constitution had virtually nothing to do with sources of power. Power rested on ideological leadership expressed through education, agitation, indoctrination, and the operation of revolutionary parties, or upon the possession of wealth, or upon the command of armed men, or (least and last) upon the control of the actual persons holding this public office or that. Power certainly did not rest on any recognizable nation-wide political scheme. The Provisional Constitution of China might therefore have been applied to New Zealand or to Italy, but it certainly had nothing to do with the Chinese culture into which it was so suddenly and so prematurely interjected.

The Dictatorship of Yüan Shih-k'ai (1912-1916). Article 53 of the Provisional Constitution provided that a Parliament was to be convened within ten months and that the election and organization laws of the Parliament were to be decided by the National Council. On August 10, 1912, these laws pertaining to the Parliament were promulgated.[7] The Parliament, consisting of a Senate and a House of Representatives, was duly convoked on April 8, 1913. Trouble began almost at once. Instead of working harmoniously with the provisional President, the Parliament from the beginning found out that the Chief Executive was not prepared to accept Parliament procedure. Chinese society had for once moved more rapidly than the political system above it; the national groupings of men had formed into factions which had greater group-coherency than did the brittle governmental forms into which these factions attempted to thrust themselves. The Executive Department of the government was now under the control of the conservative-reactionary group consisting mostly of Northerners, while the Parliament was under the control of the Southern liberal-radical clique, the largest portion of which was the newly reorganized Kuomintang.

A violent political clash was immediately precipitated by President Yüan's

[7] For the English translation, see *The China Year Book,* 1914 edition, p. 464.

negotiating a loan from Western bankers. This was the so-called Reorganization Loan of twenty-five million pounds sterling. In negotiating this loan he acted without the consent of Parliament and the parliamentary-minded Chinese were startled to discover that not only did their own President violate the new Constitution with impunity, but that the Western powers acquiesced in this procedure. They were practical enough, despite their deficiencies in understanding the Western World, to know that no Westerner would trust twenty-five million pounds on the basis of poor or inadequate credit.

At the same time, within China, Yüan strengthened his control over the provinces by supplanting self-appointed or volunteer revolutionary governors with military henchmen of his own. When the Kuomintang realized that it was impossible to cooperate with Yüan, a few of the Kuomintang governors in the southern provinces started a revolt in July, 1913, which they grandiloquently styled the "Second Revolution." This insurrection was easily quelled by Yüan who had both money and troops at his command. The government was beginning to play its true role, a screen for the real power exercised by means of military command or economic property, but not a source of power in itself. Sun Yat-sen was obliged to seek exile in Japan. The provisional President quickly solidified his position in the Parliament by frightening the opposition out of its wits with a few well-selected murders and obtained his own election as President of the Republic for a term of ten years. On this basis he took office as regular President on October 10, 1913.

The Parliament was authorized by the Provisional Constitution to adopt a permanent constitution for the new republic.[8] Accordingly, the Parliament set up a Constitution Drafting Committee composed of thirty members from each chamber. This Committee worked out a draft constitution, known as the Temple of Heaven Draft (*T'ien-t'an ts'ao-an*) of 1913, completed on October 31, 1913.[9] Significant points in this draft were the limitation on the powers exercised by the President and the institution of a Cabinet government. Since this draft was contrary to the wishes of the all-powerful Yüan Shih-k'ai, it was not considered by the Parliament. As a matter of fact, Yüan outlawed the Kuomintang on November 4, 1913, depriving the Parliament of a quorum.

Although Yüan knew little about modern government he realized that a president had to have some sort of a parliament. He accordingly instigated his own governors in the provinces to petition him that Parliament be dissolved and that a new assembly be convened. He thereupon created, in gracious response to their request, his own Constitutional Council (*Yüeh-fa hui-i*) composed of fifty-six members elected proportionately from the provinces and from outlying territories. The newly convened council was of

[8] Provisional Constitution, Art. 54.
[9] For the English text, see *The China Year Book*, 1914 edition, pp. 490-499.

course completely amenable to Yüan's dictation, drafting and promulgating a Constitutional Compact (*Chung-hua min-kuo yüeh-fa*) on May 1, 1914.[10] According to this document the power of the President was further strengthened. All restrictions put on him by the previous constitution were removed. He was given absolute control over the legislature, which he could dissolve at any time with the concurrence of the Council of State. This concurrence was not hard to obtain since the members of the Council were nominated by him and were directly responsible to him.

In his own crude way Yüan was simply fitting the overt pattern of government to the design of authority which he had already obtained covertly through military command and through the possession of money. Thus far he was realistic. Unfortunately he was romantic and out-of-pace with the times, and he attempted to become the sovereign of a monarchy. His taking an absolute role in a nominal republic under a constitutional compact was perhaps tolerable. His aspiration to found a new dynasty was, given the circumstances of China's bewilderment under the Western impact, premature if accepted in conventional terms and incomprehensible if accepted in "modern" terms.

Nevertheless he persisted. Shortly after the promulgation of his constitution, the movement to reconvert China into a monarchy began. He employed all the arts of political warfare to this end—bribery, conspiracy, organization, and a limited publicity campaign.[11] In the autumn of 1915 a series of provincial elections were held according to the proclaimed electoral law of October 8, 1915. Almost one quarter of one per cent of the population voted and votes ran as high as ten Chinese dollars apiece. By December the delegates from the provinces unanimously approved the reestablishment of an empire. After observing the ancient Chinese formula by declining the proffered honor three times, Yüan finally yielded to the insistence of his subordinates and announced that he would accept the overwhelming popular demand that he make himself Emperor. He fixed the date for his own enthronement as January 1, 1916.

Resistance to this program came as much from South China because it was southern as from the Liberals because they were liberal. The pattern of regional struggle began. Yunnan province in the far Southwest broke into open opposition in December, 1915, and the other southern provinces with an increasing degree of military autonomy supported Yunnan. The real pattern of power, which rested on infantry and on provincial treasures more than it did on international recognition or the possession of the City of Peking with its governmental machinery, emerged very plainly. The Peking

[10] For the English text, see *U. S. Foreign Relations, 1914,* pp. 56-60 and *The China Year Book,* 1916 edition, pp. 432-435.

[11] As well as a memorandum written by Dr. Frank J. Goodnow, a former American political adviser, who argued that a monarchical system was better suited to China than was a republic and that it would be easier to form a constitutional government by adopting a monarchy rather than a republic. The text may be found in Stanley K. Hornbeck, *Contemporary Politics in the Far East,* New York, 1916.

regime was militarily unable to suppress southern insurrection. Yüan realized that his dream of creating a new system was doomed. On March 22, 1916, he canceled all his monarchial plans and restored the republic. The reign of a dynasty which was to be called *Hung Hsien* (The Dynasty of Glorious Constitutionalism) lasted less than three months, leaving behind nothing more than some extremely rare proof coins for the delectation of numismatists.

Having tested the machinery of real power and having found, perhaps to their own surprise, that the Peking government did not really matter, the southern rebels were not satisfied. By April, 1916, five provinces south of the Yangtze declared their independence and had gotten away with it. A military government was organized in Kwangtung as a rival to the Peking regime. The danger of civil war was imminent, but it was averted for the time being by Yüan's sudden death—some say from exasperation, others say from poison—on June 6, 1916. Li Yüan-hung, who had served as Vice-President throughout Yüan's administration, succeeded Yüan as the President. He had joined the revolutionaries reluctantly in 1911, had made few enemies, and was neither liked nor disliked. Under his presidency the power of the provinces stood forth plainly and the first republic, except as a legal and diplomatic formula, was dead.

The Politics of Least Resistance, 1916-1928. The diplomatic and political fiction of the supremacy of the Peking government as the *de jure* government of China during the age of the warlords, 1916-1928, is one of the most peculiar political phenomena of the twentieth century. Warlordism was in part a normal Chinese response to a catastrophe, in part the Chinese pattern of allowable disorder which the Chinese, by virtue of the political traditions of their civilization, foresaw and therefore tolerated as the price of interregnum between Imperial houses. In its own cool and savage way the tumult between dynasties had been a popular, democratic force in Chinese history; the plebiscite of banditry and disorder may be an ungainly way of exercising the popular will, but it is one possible way.

No other major civilization embodied so plainly the tradition of *expected political collapse,* with the concomitant expectation of the *re-installation of order.* In other political cultures, the cycle of integration and collapse can often be observed, sometimes on an extremely long-time cycle, sometimes on a short one, but it is rare for a people to expect that their political institutions should dissolve into anarchy and that the anarchy should, after a suitable period of precipitation and crystallization, provide the foundation for a new order. The period 1916-1928 also comprised, in addition to an expected collapse, a real revolution—revolution more profound and more disturbing than anything which the Chinese had previously experienced. The two phenomena canceled each other. Since the disorder was expected by tradition-minded Chinese, it impressed them as the tolerable. Nevertheless, since the disorder could not end, as Yüan himself so obviously expected it would not end in the simple installation of a new monarchy, the chaos in China represented the intolerably oppressive commitment of the lives and fortunes of all Chinese to a future which they could neither foresee nor desire. In a Western description of Far Eastern governments, such as the present book, it is perhaps possible for us to discern in the Chinese people traits of political behavior which, when they appear in our own situations, are too close to us to be seen plainly: factors of fatigue, inertia, and the least political resistance.[12]

It is possible to see in the Chinese experience, therefore, the operation of a political factor which, although perhaps universal, is visible only at long range. No one in China decided in favor of anarchy, in favor of corruption, or in favor of an inadequate central government; at each step of modern China's political tragedy the political alternatives were always more painful, at whatever moment they were considered, than was the immediate situation.

Northern Warlordism. The pattern of provincial warlordism demonstrates this very plainly. Warlordism was not only warlordism; it was a malignant growth of a political factor which, considered by itself, was entirely healthy when contrasted with the top-heavy centralization of the Manchus' regime. That factor was provincial autonomy, combined with the long overdue re-unification of the civil and military powers of government. The Chinese had suffered for a long time under a dual government—the one administrative pattern being military and Manchu, the other being civil and a Manchu-Chinese amalgam. The twofold structure of government represented on the one hand by viceroys and provincial governors, and on the other by Tartar generals, was replaced by the creation of single provincial authorities in which civil and military powers were once again in the same hand. This was a step forward. The over-elaboration of provincial autonomy to inter-provincial power politics and even inter-provincial war was, of course, disastrous.

Yüan himself was initially responsible for the development of warlordism. He set the example for others by utilizing the New Army of Chinese soldiers with Western type training for the advancement of his own personal ambitions. It was Yüan who placed a provincial military commander in charge of every province which he could govern and then proceeded to keep the peace of China by over-awing these provincial military rulers. When he died, the government did not change, but the human relationships which had kept the government steady disappeared as soon as Yüan himself, who had been a figure of respect and terror to his provincial counterparts, was no longer there to keep them in their places.

After Yüan's death his henchmen fought one another. Behind the various warlords, the outside powers struggled with each other and with the Chinese

[12] See George S. Pettee, *The Process of Revolution,* New York, 1938, especially pp. 41-61 and 141-144. Pettee's study is directed exclusively to the Western experience, but it is, within the limits set by the author, as fundamental a statement as anything thus far available.

for the covert control of China. The ensuing decade was characterized by alliances, counteralliances, maneuver, and open fighting betwen military factions. These factions were usually nipped together by personal bonds such as kinship, nativity in a province or smaller locality, or sworn brotherhood. The various military groups had neither fixed principles nor loyalty toward one another, nor a feeling of responsibility toward the country and the people. They could group together to seek a mutual benefit for a short period and could split apart the next day if their separate and individual interests demanded it. The central republic authorities at Peking were like the last of the Chou emperors of long ago, or like some of the Roman popes or emperors at particular times when the Roman imperial or ecclesiastical authority was weak, the puppets of whichever military adventurer controlled the metropolis.

To digress for a moment with a brief glance to the future, the era of warlordism ended with the Northern Expedition (described below). The spirit and effects of warlordism, however, persisted in ensuing periods. Not only were the old warlords permitted to join the rank and file of the Kuomintang revolution and given high military posts, but political leaders of any consequence henceforth were military men or those with close connections with the military. They could scarcely conceive that military power should be subject to civil control. Warlordism cut across the military phase of the Kuomintang revolution and was enhanced by later instability and war pressures. To the fall of the National Government in 1949, military leaders were retained and given responsible positions in both central and local administration. The Communists too came to power mainly through military conquest. The line between warlordism and militarism remained thin indeed. Orderly government remained impossible so long as the political scene was dominated by militarists.

After Li Yüan-hung assumed the presidency following Yüan's death, the Provisional Constitution of 1912 was restored; the original republican parliament, which had been dissolved by Yüan, was reconvened and opened its first session on August 1, 1916. Tuan Ch'i-jui, the leader of the Anhwei Clique, was made the Premier of the new government. The Constitutional Compact adopted under the influence of Yüan was declared illegal; therefore the first task of the reconvened parliament was the drafting of a permanent constitution. The parliament was unable to reach an understanding because of the controversial legal issue of federalism versus centralism. Meanwhile Li had been opposed to the policy of Tuan in throwing China wholeheartedly on the Allied side of World War I.

Li committed a further mistake which led to the only serious monarchial coup attempted in Peking. He called in monarchist warlord Chang Hsün. On Chang Hsün's advice Li dissolved the parliament which he had summoned ten months before. Chang Hsün, after concentrating his troops in the capital city, turned to the task of monarchial restoration. The abdicated

Emperor P'u Yi was restored to his Throne on July 1, 1917, but his restoration lasted only a fortnight. The Anhwei Clique mobilized by the ex-premier successfully defeated and dispersed the monarchists and acquired political power over the City of Peking with the assistance of the military Chihli Clique headed by Fêng Kuo-chang.

Back in power, Tuan refused to reconvene the old parliament a second time and organized a new one according to his own preferences. This parliament, known as the An-fu Parliament, which lasted from August, 1918, to August, 1920, also attempted constitution making. It decided to abandon the Temple of Heaven draft constitution of 1913 and adopted a new version, known as the An-fu Draft, on August 12, 1919.[13] This was similar to the old draft in content. It suffered the same fate. Neither was officially adopted. The temporary alliance between the Anhwei and Chihli cliques did not last long because the two cliques, named for their respective provinces (Chihli being the old name for Hopei) began to compete for power. As far back as the early winter of 1917 the Chihli Clique under the leadership of Ts'ao K'un and Wu P'ei-fu gained the ascendancy and Tuan Ch'i-jui of the Anhwei Clique was forced to resign.

Meanwhile Chang Tso-lin of Manchuria appeared on the intramural Chinese political scene and began his open bid for power. The subsequent history of North China was a turmoil of alliances and counteralliances between these different factions and their warlords, each trying to outwit the others by betrayals and occasional tests of strength.

The Fictitious Republic. Considering its lack of money and near-impotence, the fictitious government of the Republic of China in Peking did very well indeed. On the basis of virtually no domestic power and very undependable sources of income, the cabinet and departments in Peking maintained an entirely admirable diplomatic establishment, an irreproachably strong pretense that China had a government in fact, and a few limited services in such neutral fields as Customs Collections and Postal Communications. It is true that on one occasion the Prime Minister of China escaped alive only because he hid in a basket of laundry, but all in all the Chinese foreign ministers composed notes in flawless English, Chinese legations abroad represented their country with complete *sang-froid,* and spokesmen for China to the community of nations steered China through the difficult times of the Paris Peace Conference, the Versailles Treaty, the Washington Conference, and the preservation of China as a nation in the fictions of international law, if not in the facts as reported by the press of the world.

By June, 1922, Ts'ao K'un of the Chihli Clique aspired to reach the Presidency himself and ousted the then President Hsü Shih-ch'ang. For reasons of legitimacy Ts'ao persuaded Li Yüan-hung to resume the office of President on June 11, 1922, keeping himself as the power behind the Throne. Not satis-

[13] See Pan Wei-tung, *The Chinese Constitution, A Study of Forty Years of Constitution Making in China,* Washington, 1946, Appendix F.

fied with the *de facto* status of ruler of the republic, Ts'ao prevailed upon the members of parliament to elect him President; he was kindhearted enough to do this by bribery instead of terror. He assumed office on October 5, 1923. With Ts'ao in power the parliament hastily adopted a new constitution (*Chung-hua-min-kuo hsien-fa*) which was duly promulgated on October 10, 1923.[14] Although this was the first constitution officially promulgated since the establishment of the republic in 1912 its adoption by a bribed parliament gave the constitution very little credit in the eyes of the public. This constitution was, needless to say, never put into force.

President Ts'ao K'un and his supporter, Wu P'ei-fu, were at odds with the Manchurian warlord, Chang Tso-lin. War between the Chihli and Manchurian forces began in August, 1924. Wu sent his trusted general, Fêng Yü-hsiang, to fight the Manchurian forces. Instead of marching toward the north, Fêng turned his troops toward Peking and set up his own regime in the capital. This treachery led to the defeat of Wu, who was obliged to retire to central China. Fêng imprisoned President Ts'ao and raided the palace of the abdicated Emperor. In order to consolidate his power he reached an understanding with the Manchurian warlords and invited the retired politician, Tuan Ch'i-jui, the old leader of the Anhwei Clique, to become the provisional Chief Executive on November 24, 1924. Tuan was successful for a while in balancing the power of Fêng and Chang. In order to put his government on a legal basis, Tuan called a Rehabilitation Conference in November, 1925. A brand new draft constitution (*Hsien-fa ts'ao-an*) was adopted on December 12, 1925.[15] Like its predecessors, this draft did not have enough time to be put into practice before its sponsors were forced out of office. While Tuan was trying to legalize his government, the inevitable conflict between Chang and Fêng broke out in November, 1925. In April, 1926, the Manchurian forces marched into Peking and forced Tuan to flee to Tientsin. North China was thenceforth dominated by Chang Tso-lin, who set up a puppet "regency cabinet" and appointed himself military dictator (*Ta yüan-shuai*). His regime was overthrown by Kuomintang forces in 1928 and he was murdered a few weeks thereafter.

Shadow Governments of South China. The situation of South China was no less turbulent and discordant than that of the North. The three southwesternmost provinces of Yunnan, Szechuan, and Kweichow were controlled by opportunist local leaders who were neither connected with the Northern militarists nor with Sun Yat-sen's Kuomintang in the Southeast. The Kuomintang organized a military government in Canton in 1918 and invited the Kuomintang members of the old parliament to sit in an extraordinary session. Starting in the spring of 1919, the North and the South negotiated with one another for peace, with the South demanding restoration

[14] For the English text, see Pan, *op. cit.*, Appendix G.
[15] For the English text, see Pan, *op. cit.*, Appendix I.

of the old Provisional Constitution of 1912 and the reconvocation of the parliament of 1913 as a point of departure for legitimacy.

The South was in a poor position to haggle. The internecine strife which characterized North China also plagued the South. Sun Yat-sen governed in Canton by virtue of bargains he had made with the local warlords of the two Kwang provinces (Kwangtung and Kwangsi). When the Kwangsi militarists demanded a larger share of the southern government, Sun Yat-sen as leader of the Kuomintang party resigned as Generalissimo of the Military Government on May 4, 1918, to protest against the split. Thereupon a Directorate of Seven was established in the South with Sun as a member. He resigned and fled in August, 1919. In October, 1920, Sun's followers successfully entered Canton and expelled the Kwangsi militarists. Sun returned to Canton and convened his Rump Parliament, which adopted an *Outline of the Organic Law of the Government of the Chinese Republic* (*Chung-hua-min-kuo chêng-fu tsu-chih ta-kang*) in seven articles.[16] He was elected President on May 5, 1921. The newly organized government was not destined to last very long. The defection of his followers compelled Sun to flee to Shanghai again in August, 1922. This defeat made Sun all the more determined to establish a military base in Canton from which he could unify the country by force. Through a series of political and personal maneuvers, Sun was able to return to Canton where he assumed the title of Generalissimo once more in March, 1923, and was ready to venture into another revolution.

The Resurrection of the Kuomintang. Beneath the disorder of the fictitious republic and warlordism, Northern and Southern, two significant forces were at work—one ideological, one organizational—which were to have a powerful effect on emergent Chinese government. Out of the two decades of conspiracy and the bitter experience of premature revolution, Dr. Sun Yat-sen had begun to rethink a program for China's future. As the most important antecedent political thought of the National Government under the Kuomintang, 1928-1949, Dr. Sun's Three Principles of the People is discussed in the next chapter. Between 1923 and 1927, Sun's program and the second force, the resurrection of the Kuomintang, took an elite of opposition, converted it into an effective party with an army and later a government under its control, with a schedule of promises to fulfill and a second revolution to vindicate.

While Sun Yat-sen was in Shanghai in 1922 he conferred with the Soviet emissary, Abram Adolf Joffe, concerning the future organization and tactics of his party. Sun saw that much of the Leninist party system could be profitably incorporated into his own Kuomintang. After Sun's return to Canton in the spring of 1923 he undertook the drastic process of Leninizing

[16] See Ch'ien Tuan-shêng *et al.*, *Min-kuo chêng-chih shih* (History of the political system of the Chinese republic) Shanghai, 1946, pp. 133-134. For the text of this organic law, see Tung Lin, *Chung-kuo chêng-fu* (The Chinese government), Shanghai, 1941, Vol. I, pp. 286-287.

the Kuomintang so far as party structure and discipline were concerned and sovietizing his South China government, without in either case adopting the communist policies and principles along with the communist organizational and operational doctrine. Meanwhile the Chinese Communist Party which had been organized in July, 1921, declared its adhesion to the Kuomintang; many of its leaders and members joined the Kuomintang as private individuals.

In the autumn of 1923 another Soviet envoy, Michael Borodin arrived. Borodin's strenuous labors reinforced Sun's efforts at reorganization of the Kuomintang. The party became a full-scale modern totalitarian party. Long before Fascism in Italy or National Socialism in Germany, the Kuomintang set up a one-party rule in Canton. On January 20, 1924, the First Party Congress was held in Canton; members of the Chinese Communist Party participated within the Kuomintang structure. The Congress adopted a party statute and issued a manifesto which laid the foundation for the future relationship between the party and the government. In organizational importance, both for the role of the party in the period of China's tutelage, and for continuity of effect on the National Government, 1928-1949, the work of the First Party Congress cannot be overemphasized (as such it is detailed in the next chapter). In the short run, the result was a new engine for propaganda and political power. The new principles of government were modeled after the Soviet structure and were totally different from the loose republican forms of government which Sun had sought to establish throughout the preceding decade. In order to strengthen the military power of the party, a military academy was established at Whampoa in May, 1924, and a young officer, Chiang Kai-shek, who had just been in Moscow studying the organization of the Red Army, was appointed as the commandant.

The ascendancy of Tuan Ch'i-jui as provisional Chief Executive in Peking in 1924 prevented the possibility of a reconciliation between the North and the South. Sun went to Peking in the hope that a merger of the two regimes might result through peaceful negotiation and agreement. However, both the lieutenants in his own party and the Northern militarists were opposed to his plan. His effort at effecting a fusion came to naught, and he died in Peking on March 12, 1925, leaving a last testament urging his followers to complete his unfinished revolutionary task.

After Sun's death his followers reorganized the Generalissimo's headquarters into a formal government known as the Nationalist Government of China on July 1, 1925. The governing council of this government, a committee of sixteen members, was appointed by the Central Executive Committee of the Kuomintang with Wang Ching-wei as its chairman.

The Northern Expedition. The Nationalist Government, after consolidating its bases in Kwangtung and Kwangsi, was ready to venture into the conquest of the whole of China. The Northern Expedition under the military command of Chiang Kai-shek started from Canton in July, 1926. It started despite considerable doubt as to the wisdom of major military action at that time. First, the power position of the South still seemed relatively weak. Second, the new Nationalist Government openly boasted a unity which was not to be found behind the scenes. Conservatives feared the effects of radicals' participation, specifically communist motives, in the government. Finally, the Left began to wonder about the objectives of the military leader of the Expedition, Chiang Kai-shek.[17]

Nevertheless, within three months Nationalist forces had swept to Hankow and in January, 1927, the seat of government was transferred to the area of the three sister cities—Hankow, Hanyang, Wuchang—thus taking the name, the Wuhan Regime. At this point, the inevitable conflict between Communists and Nationalists broke out. The Communists proved unwilling to stop with the establishment of a Nationalist Government, according to Sun's principles, pushing on with the socialist revolution, also according to Sun's principles, as soon as the Nationalists began to slow down.

Wang Ching-wei, who had temporarily left China, returned to Wuhan in March, 1927, and advocated continued collaboration with the Communists. But demonstrations by the Wuhan Regime against foreign concessions in the mid-Yangtze cities alarmed Chiang Kai-shek and the Rightists, who set up a rival Nationalist Government in Nanking in April, 1927. There followed a widespread purge of Leftists in the lower Yangtze. The Rightist cause was aided by raids on Soviet headquarters in Peking by the warlord, Chang Tso-lin, and by leaks concerning the activities of M. N. Roy, an Indian Communist attached to the Wuhan Government. Both made clear Russia's interest in making use of the Chinese revolution for her own purposes. The Wuhan Regime purged itself, came to an end in the autumn of 1927, had a momentary resurrection in Canton, and finally merged with the Nationalist Government, Nanking.

With the remarkable successes of the Nationalists carrying them to the Shanghai-Nanking area, the old warlords of the North were faced with the choice of alliance with the Nationalists or defeat. Fêng Yü-hsiang and Yen Hsi-shan chose alliance and ended up as Army Group commanders, with Li Tsung-jên, under the Commander-in-chief, Chiang Kai-shek. Chang Tso-lin fled Peking and met a mysterious death on his return to the Northeast.[18] Settlement of the military issue with his son, the Young Marshal Chang Hsüeh-liang, was postponed because of his own strength, because of obvious

[17] In August, 1925, the assassination of Liao Chung-k'ai, radical but trusted lieutenant of Sun Yat-sen, shocked Party unity. In Peking, the so-called Western Hills group (named for the place where Dr. Sun's body awaited burial) met to denounce the Leftists and to expel them from the Party. The Second Party Congress, January, 1926, in turn denounced the Western Hills movement, but brushed over the remaining dissension. Shortly after the Congress, Chiang Kai-shek himself moved against various Communists in Canton. For details, see Ch'ien Tuan-shêng, *The Government and Politics of China,* Cambridge, 1950, pp. 91-95.

[18] The mystery has been plausibly explained as, in fact, a product of struggle within the Japanese Army, which shared complicity in the murder. See Paul S. Dull, "The Assassination of Chang Tso-lin," *The Far Eastern Quarterly,* Vol. XI, No. 4 (August, 1952).

Japanese interests in the Northeast, and because Chang voluntarily hoisted the Nationalist flag over his capital at Mukden on December 31, 1928. China was once again reunified, for the first time since the momentary restoration of the Manchus in 1917.

The collapse of the old republic, and especially the Northern Expedition, remarkably cast political shadows of things yet to come. We shall have to return to the effects of the reorganization of the Kuomintang, its brief alliance and split with the Communists, the rise of Chiang Kai-shek, his alliance with *some* warlords, and the semi-independent status of the Northeastern Provinces under the Young Marshal.

Evaluation of the Early Republican Governments. The republican era, 1912-1928, was *pro forma* a period of political experimentation. As Professor C. P. Fitzgerald points out in his study of the Chinese revolution, the only democracy which took actual effect in China after the republic, under either Nationalists or Communists, was the quasi democracy of a one-party government acting *for* the people, not the elected parliamentarism of Western Europe or Japan.[19] The paper constitutions of the early republican period demonstrate that in Chinese society there were many politicians who clearly understood the practical functioning of modern democratic states, but there was lacking in the population many of the cultural prerequisites for the kind of democracy which cannot be legislated into existence.

The major mistake of the early Chinese revolutionaries was their attempt to impose a modern parliamentary democratic government on a loosely confederated chain of provinces. Chinese society, strong in family ties and in personal relations, was not yet ready to accept a mechanistic republican procedure. The masses of the people were unaware of the nominal political changes which went on in Peking other than to realize that the generals had taken over from the Emperor and most people found little in modern politics to interest them. Sun Yat-sen, the most assertive and perceptive of all the revolutionaries, finally comprehended China's political inertia after numerous disappointments. He realized that, for the time at least, the line of least political resistance for most Chinese people consisted in abstention from political activity. He finally decided in 1924 that the consummation of Chinese unification by force of arms had to be followed by a period of political tutelage in which the common people would be trained in the responsibilities of government.

From 1912 to 1928 the Peking regime in the North had gone through many changes and functioned under many constitutions. After the death of Yüan Shih-k'ai, China was virtually divided into two regimes, but the Western governments continued to recognize the Peking regime as the legitimate representative of China and to treat the Southern government as a rival

[19] Charles Patrick Fitzgerald, *Revolution in China,* New York, 1952, especially Chap. 6, "Revolution and Orthodoxy," pp. 143-167. While Professor Fitzgerald provides one of the most carefully thought out descriptions of the Communist rise to power in China, he stresses with too great finality the Chinese cultural ingredients in Chinese Communism.

faction. The organization of the Southern government in its last phases was based on an entirely different principle to be described in the next chapter concerning Nationalist China. In the North there were no less than six constitutions or draft constitutions:

1. The Provisional Constitution of March 11, 1912,
2. The Temple of Heaven Draft Constitution of October 31, 1913,
3. The Constitutional Compact of Yüan Shih-k'ai of May 1, 1914,
4. The Draft Constitution of the An-Fu Parliament of August 12, 1919,
5. The Ts'ao K'un Constitution of October 10, 1923, and
6. The Draft Constitution of Tuan Ch'i-jui of December 12, 1925.

The appearance of so many constitutions can be attributed to the politicians' craze for legitimacy and their desire to have a constitution attributable to themselves. In operational fact, these constitutions and draft constitutions were more or less the same; they were all based on democratic principles and they also aspired to achieve a republican form of government for China.

The issues brought up by these constitutions were not fundamental issues. The solutions presented were never solutions which could be applied in real life. The creation of a political system which could emerge as a functioning and organic part of Chinese society was left to the Nationalists and Communists after the titular republic had passed away. The most profound issues to trouble the Northern constitution makers were subordinate issues, which would have become important only if their daydreams had materialized in fact. These two major issues were, first, a controversy between the Presidential and Cabinet government, and, second, the problem of a federal state as opposed to a unitary state. In dealing with these issues the draft constitutions reflected the petty quarrels of Peking, not the long-range probabilities or preferences of an operating Chinese elite.

The question of Presidential versus Cabinet form of government was, for example, the direct result of contests for power between the nominal Presidents and their even more nominal Cabinet ministers. The Chinese people of the past had been accustomed to personal government, but they were also accustomed to the use of boards; an entirely valid choice existed therefore between singular or plural leadership if—and only if—one makes the invalid assumption that the Chinese people of that period were prepared to understand any constitutional system whatever. In Chinese tradition strong political personalities usually paid little or no respect to formal law. Under the republican form of government most of the intelligentsia expected that there should be a constitution according to which the new government was to function. Seasoned politicians deemed it convenient to amend the constitution to their own liking rather than to break it too flagrantly. Therefore, in the early republican era a strong President, upon coming into office, set up a constitution providing for a Presidential form of government. On the other hand, a warlord behind the scenes or a relatively strong parliament would demand a constitution providing for the Cabinet form of government. Shadowy though the political authority of Peking was, the constitution always followed the *de facto* situation in the metropolis. The situation was never the other way around: never did the balance of power even in the single city of Peking change itself because of a constitutional prescription.

Presidential and Cabinet forms of government existed almost alternately through the republican era. Where the provisional government of Sun Yat-sen in Nanking in 1911-1912 was a Presidential form of government, when Sun resigned the Kuomintang tried to impose a responsible cabinet on his successor, Yüan Shih-k'ai. The Provisional Constitution provided that the provisional President could not act on his own authority without the concurrence of the National Council. Yüan, himself a strong personality, would not tolerate any such arrangement; the result was the creation of Yüan's own Constitutional Compact. The Constitutional Compact provided a strong executive, unmistakably Presidential in form. Actually the President already possessed dictatorial powers with or without the constitution, but such a constitution was a convenience if not a necessity. Li Yüan-hung, who succeeded when Yüan died, was such a weakling as to deserve the nickname of the Buddha, while his Premier, Tuan Ch'i-jui, had strong military support as leader of the Anhwei Clique; therefore the Draft Constitution of the An-fu Parliament of 1919 provided ample power for the Premier. When Tuan himself became provisional Chief Executive, he changed the government into the Presidential form in his 1925 Draft Constitution and dropped the Cabinet form which he himself had previously advocated.[20]

The question of a unitary or federal system of state was, comparably, the result of personal politics in the early republican era. Generally speaking, the provincial authorities wanted a federal system, and the federal government favored a unitary system; in Peking itself, the out-group demanded local autonomy while the in-group advocated centralization, and neither had the slightest chance of doing anything about the basic impotence of government.

The Provisional Constitution of 1912 was silent on the relationship between the central government and the provinces, but since China had been historically a united and centralized state it was within reason to assume that the system was intended to be unitary, as under the old order. During the time of the deliberation of the Temple of Heaven Draft Constitution, the chief object of controversy was the problem of dividing power between

[20] Much the same pattern was to continue into the Nationalist period in which power in the National Government of China tended to attach itself to whatever office Chiang Kai-shek happened to hold. Whenever Chiang was President, the Presidency was a strong office; when he became President of the Executive *Yüan,* the Presidency of the government lapsed back into unimportance. Under the Communists the issue has not arisen because Mao Tse-tung has maintained unchallenged primacy as head of the government, head of the party, and chief of everything else of importance.

the central and provincial governments. The Kuomintang members favored a large measure of local autonomy as a device for checking the autocratic powers of Yüan Shih-k'ai, while the Northern militarists advocated a strong central government. After the death of Yüan Shih-k'ai, the power of government had been divided among the local militarists. These provincial chieftains ruled their territories after the manner of the tyrants of Chinese antiquity, preying upon the provincial treasuries, maintaining large personal armies, and paying only nominal allegiance to the central governments when and if the Peking clique in power happened to be composed of their own friends. In order to establish themselves as *de jure* rulers of their provinces, these militarists became strong supporters of the principle of federalism. From 1920 to 1926 the movement for provincial autonomy progressed uninterruptedly. In Hunan province a draft Provincial Constitution was carried by referendum on December 11, 1921, and formally promulgated on January 1, 1922. The Provincial Constitution provided for the rights of the people including the rights of election, initiative, referendum, and recall. But the province of Hunan made itself virtually independent of the central government. A draft Constitution for Chekiang was published on September 9, 1921, and was tantamount to a declaration of independence from the central government. On January 1, 1926, Chekiang published a draft of the Law for the Self-Government of Chekiang Province. None of these laws was intended to give the ordinary people democratic participation in the provincial government; all of them were designed to ward off interference from the central government. Other provinces, such as Szechuan and Kwangtung, made similar attempts but no change in the methods of government rose from any of them.[21]

By the time Ts'ao K'un reached the Presidency, the demand for provincial autonomy had gained enough momentum for the principle to be incorporated into the Constitution of 1923. Among other things this Constitution provided that public power relating to local affairs was to be exercised according to the several self-government laws of the provinces. This Constitution, like its predecessors, was never put into practice, but the provision shows the political tendencies of the time. The Nationalists put an end to all this. With the triumph of the Northern Expedition, the movement for local juridical autonomy was completely eradicated.

Education Through Chaos. Despite the blunders and mistakes which characterized the early republican era, the period between 1912 and 1928 was not entirely profitless from the standpoint of practical experience. By the process of experimentation and frustration, the Chinese people began to learn that an actual democratic government could not be attained without long struggle, serious study, and personal sacrifice. Furthermore, the political experience of this period showed the Chinese at least two unmistakable facts: first, monarchism was gone forever; second, the Chinese had to move

[21] W. Y. Tsao, *The Constitutional Structure of Modern China,* Melbourne, 1947, pp. 5-6.

from a succession of negative choices, avoidances of painful decision, and over to positive commitment if they were to obtain any kind of serious government.

That monarchism was destroyed was undeniable. The two attempts at monarchial restoration, the first by Yüan Shih-k'ai on behalf of himself, and the other by Chang Hsün on behalf of the boy Emperor, failed tragically. The failure in each case was not so much due to a lack of military power or to a failure of political ingenuity as to popular revulsion and resentment toward the monarchical system. Themselves hypnotized by the success of their own monarchy, the Japanese failed to learn a lesson from modern Chinese history when they established P'u Yi as chief executive and then as Emperor in "Manchukuo." The government, puppet though it was, would have received more popular support without him. One of the basic Chinese arguments on this point concerned the technique of the Ch'ing abdication. When P'u Yi abdicated the Throne in 1911, he did not surrender the *mandate of heaven* to another person but to the entire people, and many Chinese thenceforth argued that once the mandate had passed into the hands of the people it could never again be appropriated by an individual.

The need for positive action became equally clear. As Sun Yat-sen argued, the Chinese people should not be deprived of the benefits of democracy merely because they did not understand its principles. At the time of the revolution of 1911 only a handful of people knew what republicanism or democracy really meant. If the early revolutionaries had waited for the universal diffusion of political knowledge throughout China, they would never have been able to overthrow the Manchu dynasty, and they themselves would have died of old age before daring to undertake the establishment of the republic. They hoped to establish a democratic republic and to teach the new form of government while practicing it; in this they failed. Their failure made the problem of tutelage—the problem of teaching democracy while governing the country effectively—a major point in future Chinese politics. Both Nationalists and Communists came up with answers; the other parties did not.

The political experience of the republican era, although comic and tragic by turns, was a major experience in the formation of political demands among the Chinese who were mature and active by the middle of the twentieth century. Before they had ever seen a real democratic government in action, the modern Chinese had already learned how bad democracy could be at its worst.

CHAPTER
SEVEN

China under the Kuomintang, 1928-1949

The National Government of China which ruled much of China between 1928 and 1949 and which ruled almost all of China for brief periods during 1930-1931, 1937, and 1945-1947, was the first *national* government which China ever possessed. It will be realized, from the earlier chapters, that China-the-civilization had often had an ecumenical government covering the whole world known to the Chinese; not until the coming of the Chinese Nationalists to power can China be said to have developed a government which was domestically as well as internationally a functioning part of the world-wide nation-state system of the twentieth century. Without Nationalist China, Communist China could not have come to exist. Although the Nationalist cause is today a forlorn hope it is still a potentiality—a long-shot in the perennial gamble of Far Eastern history.

Antecedents of the National Government. The National Government of China had two separate genealogies. For diplomatic purposes it was the successor-state to the Republic of China at Peking which in turn was the successor to the Manchu Empire of China.[1] For its own domestic purposes it was the successor of the Nanking Government set up as a secessionist move, a successful one, by Chiang Kai-shek when he broke with his Wuhan colleagues in April, 1927. The Wuhan Government in turn was the successor of the Nationalist Government of China, soviet in form, which had functioned intimately in the early 1920's in Canton, had been consolidated in Canton in June, 1925, and had been transferred to Hankow on January 1, 1927. According to the National Government's own genealogical tree,[2] the

[1] As such it was recognized by the United States, July 25, 1928.

[2] See *Tang-chêng chien-chih t'u-piao* (Outlines of the development of the government and the party), Chungking, 1940, p. xxix, a tentative but never completed archival com-

predecessor-governments to the National Government of China have been those governments established by Sun Yat-sen in Canton, the Wuhan regime, and the Nanking Government first set up by Chiang Kai-shek.

Apart from the historic and international tragedy of the fall of the Nationalists two decades later, a description of the National Government as a functioning government is of major importance in demonstrating the strengths and limitations of an attempt to govern China as though it were a Western nation-state.

Antecedents of the Kuomintang. The Kuomintang, the successor to the *T'ung Mêng Hui,* a revolutionary anti-Manchu secret society, was formally organized as an open political party in the first year of the republic. Although the success of the revolution was due, in large measure, to the effort made by the members of the *T'ung Mêng Hui,* they found that after the establishment of the republic real power was usurped by crafty politicians who had exploited the situation and consolidated themselves in the new government. Hence, the members of the *T'ung Mêng Hui* and other dissident groups and individuals organized the Kuomintang mainly as an opposition party in the government.

The Kuomintang was indeed the handiwork of a single person, Sun Yat-sen, who, up to the time of his death in 1925, had guided its policies and directed its activities almost singlehandedly. Sun Yat-sen, being a man of broad experience and profound education, realized that the evils of the country were not cured by the simple process of the overthrow of the Manchu dynasty. He was deeply impressed by the democratic political machinery of Western countries and the economic prosperity of their people. In addition to the idea of nationalism, which was readily understood and accepted by his contemporary revolutionists, Sun further advocated principles of democracy and people's livelihood (these principles are discussed fully, just below). Only a few of his followers, however, really appreciated the implication of these conceptions.

The statute of the Kuomintang of 1912 included a political platform of five points. These were the maintenance of political unity, development of local self-government, realization of racial assimilation, implementation of Sun's principle of peoples' livelihood, and maintenance of international peace.[3] It is to be noted that the idea of nationalism at that time was mainly directed against the Manchus, not Western foreigners. After the revolution it was the assimilation of racial minorities within the country that became the order of the day.

After the failure of the Second Revolution of 1913, some members of the Kuomintang, realizing that the party, being a coalition of various dissident

---

pilation showing the structure and development of all the Nationalist Governments and all successive stages of Party organization.

[3] Tsou Lu, *Chung-kuo Kuo-min-tang shih* (History of the Kuomintang of China), Shanghai, 1946, p. 62.

groups, could not serve as an effective weapon for the attainment of their political goals, organized the Chinese Revolutionary Party (*Chung-hua ke-ming-tang*) in Tokyo. The platform of the new party differed very little from the old one, but it put a renewed emphasis on the revolutionary strategy which divided the revolutionary process into three stages, namely, the stages of military rule, political tutelage, and constitutional government. However, the name of the party was changed back to that of the Kuomintang of China in 1919 in order to accommodate many old Kuomintang members both in China and abroad.[4]

While Sun was leading the Kuomintang against the Peking Government in the North, he pleaded for help from Western powers, but his appeals fell on deaf ears. Just about this time the newly organized Soviet regime in Russia found itself isolated by a bristling rim of hostility. The Russians believed in Lenin's teaching that socialist Russia could not survive alone in a hostile capitalist world. Rather naturally then, they turned to the East in search of support and sympathy and gave active attention to a chaotic China. It was under such circumstances that Sun came to an agreement with Adolph Joffe, the Soviet Representative in China, in 1923, putting the Kuomintang revolution under the tutelage of Soviet advisers. Although Sun was fundamentally opposed to the dialectics of Marxism, as clearly stated in the Canton-Moscow Entente, he welcomed Soviet aid as a measure of expediency.[5]

After the Sun-Joffe Agreement of 1923 was signed, a host of Soviet advisers, headed by Michael Borodin and General Blücher (known as Galens), came to China and brought with them their newly acquired experience of the Bolshevik Revolution. During 1924 the Kuomintang was completely reorganized on the Soviet model. A military school under Russian auspices at Whampoa gave birth to an army with a completely new outlook and technique. The freshly formed Chinese Communist Party was put to work for the Kuomintang, and its members were admitted into the Kuomintang on an individual basis. At the First Congress of the Kuomintang a Manifesto was issued on January 30, 1924, embodying the so-called Three Policies, namely, "Alliance with Russia," "Admission of the Communists," and "Emphasis on the Agrarian and Labor Policy." These policies doubtless marked the peak influence of Communist tactics on the ideology of the Kuomintang, which rested in turn on the political doctrines of Sun Yat-sen.

The Ideology of Sun Yat-sen: Nationalism. The political ideology of Sun was embodied in a set of sixteen lectures which he gave in 1924 and

[4] *Ibid.*, p. 100.

[5] For ideological aspects of the agreement, see the subsequent discussion of Sun's theories; and Tsui Shu-ch'in, "The Influence of the Canton-Moscow Entente upon Sun Yat-sen's Political Philosophy," *The Chinese Social and Political Science Review*, Peiping, 1934, Vol. XVIII, pp. 177 ff.

which he called "The Three Principles of the People."[6] The Three Principles included *Min-tsu* or People's National-consciousness, *Min-ch'üan* or People's Power, and *Min-shêng* or People's Livelihood. They have been roughly translated as nationalism, democracy, and livelihood. But since definitions of political terms have become so hopelessly mixed up in the fruitless battle of semantics, such translations can convey no exact meaning except misleading conceptions. Hence, it is better to stick to the romanized terms for the principles, *Min-tsu, Min-ch'üan,* and *Min-shêng*.

The principle of *Min-tsu* contained a number of ideas, varying according to different phases of China's political development. It represented an anti-Manchu sentiment before the fall of the monarchy and embraced the doctrine of self-determination by racial minorities within the borders after the revolution. When the principle was formally proclaimed in Sun's lectures in 1924, it definitely acquired a new anti-imperialistic outlook. China was to shake off the imperialistic yokes and to establish a progressive, national state.

Sun Yat-sen preached a peculiar, but vivid, kind of Chinese nationalism. He argued in favor of a racial nationalism now more reminiscent of the *völkisch* theories of Hitler than of the simple nationalism of Americans, Mexicans, Netherlanders, or Swiss. He preached that the Chinese race was in fact the Chinese nation and that the Chinese nation was the only nation comprising an entire race. He argued that this race had to return to its ancient morality and revive its ancient ethical and moral knowledge, and that to this revived traditionalism there should be added little more than a few political skills and physical science from the West.

Sun Yat-sen's entire life was, therefore, a dramatic attempt to revive a long-gone ancient China and to give it modern vitality, modern tools, and modern weapons with which to survive. In order to make nationalism possible he favored, toward the end of his life, the creation of a one-party dictatorship which would replace the lost Dragon Throne. He argued that this party should set in force programs for economic nationalism and political nationalism. He argued that China should be on Japan's side in the struggle of Asia against the whites, while simultaneously pleading that China should join the Soviet Union in the class war of the have-not nations against the oppressing nations.

SunYatsenism: A Limited Democracy. The principle of *Min-ch'üan* was essentially borrowed from Western conceptions of democracy, but reconciled with ancient Chinese political practices. Sun's political utopia could be traced to four separate origins: (1) the Western conception of the

[6] A complete description of the political ideology of Dr. Sun, as applied to the organization of government, can be found in Paul M. A. Linebarger, *The Political Doctrines of Sun Yat-sen,* Baltimore, 1937. The two outstanding translations of Sun Yat-sen's own lectures are those published by Frank Price under the title, *San Min Chu I, The Three Principles of the People,* Chungking, 1943; and by Paschal M. d'Elia, S.J., *The Triple Demism of Sun Yat-Sen,* Wuchang, 1931.

republican form of government; (2) the Swiss doctrine of initiation, referendum, election, and recall; (3) the Soviet idea of democratic centralism; and (4) the Chinese devices of examination and control. All these elements contributed toward the creation of an ideal government which, according to Sun, possessed the technical capacity (*nêng*) to act on behalf of the people who were vested with political power (*ch'üan*) or sovereignty.

Within the framework of a triumphant nationalist ideology, Sun Yat-sen argued that a Chinese democratic theory should accept the natural inequality of men and should recognize the existence of a three-grade series of citizens. The top class of citizens should consist of the real leaders, an elite who could both understand the past and face the future creatively by their capacity to interpret coming events. The second class of citizens should comprise those capable of understanding the leaders and of expressing the wishes of the leaders to the mass of the governed. The third class of citizens should consist of those who could neither understand the world nor even interpret the leaders, but who had the mere capacity of saying whether or not they liked what the leaders offered them.

Instead of the traditional three-way separation of power, Sun's government was to have a five-power division—namely, executive, legislative, judicial, examination, and control. Obviously, the people could not be expected to exercise political power to which they were not accustomed, without previous training; Sun thus ingeniously designed a period of political tutelage in which the Kuomintang, acting as a trustee, would train the people in constitutional government. After a certain prescribed period, the Kuomintang would abdicate its power in favor of elected officials. The assumption was that the period of tutelage would end when the people became politically capable of governing themselves.

Why, asked Dr. Sun, was *Min-ch'üan* important? Democracy was justified in five basic terms. It was an obligation laid upon modern China by the sages of Chinese antiquity; it was a necessary consequence of nationalism, since nationalism was the self-rule of a free people, and democracy the effectuation of that self-rule; it was the government of all characteristically *modern* states; it was the political form best calculated for the obtaining of good administration; and it was, of itself, a force driving men to modernity.

SunYatsenist Theory: Livelihood. The principle of *Min-shêng* was an economic pot-pourri embodying the merits of socialism, collectivism, free enterprise, and humanitarianism. To achieve the goals in this theory, Sun made two concrete proposals: the equalization of land tenure, and the regulation of capital. As practical steps, he advocated that the unearned increment of land value should accrue to the state, and that principal industries and enterprises should be operated by the state.

The term *Min-shêng* is often translated as "People's Livelihood." A more accurate, if more cumbersome translation, is the "economic demism" set forth by the Italian Jesuit scholar, Father Paschal M. d'Elia. Actually neither of these terms conveys to Western minds a reasonable proximation of what Sun Yat-sen thought he was thinking about. One of the collaborators in this book obtained the doctrine of *Min-shêng* at first hand from members of Sun's family, from his own father (who was Sun's adviser), and from that oldest generation of Kuomintang leaders who died off in the 1930's; from these sources, he believes *Min-shêng* to be so peculiarly Chinese an amalgam that it had best be left with its Chinese name and considered untranslatable.

Ideologically, *Min-shêng* can be considered an ecological and demographic extension of basic postulates of nationalism. In order to have a big race survive so as to become the biggest nation in the world, it is necessary that this race have proper economic supplies in the present and proper economic arrangements to carry the present justly and bounteously into the future.

In terms of formal economics, Sun Yat-sen expressed what statesmen today might call the repair of "underdevelopment." The national economic revolution was an indispensable political and cultural concomitant of the Chinese revolution taken as a whole. Secondly, *Min-shêng* implied positive national enrichment, the actual accumulation of both capital and consumer goods in China. Thirdly, *Min-shêng* was a doctrine of economic justice, vague as to its specifically *economic* modes of implementation, but very concrete in its demands for economic justice to all classes of the population, particularly the broad masses.

SunYatsenism after Sun Yat-sen. Even today, both Chinese Nationalists and Chinese Communists put SunYatsenist scriptures to their own uses; both Taipeh and Peking profess to have the monopoly of genuine SunYatsenism. It is noteworthy that neither of the two parties in China now refers to those teachings which have become unfashionable in the world. One teaching, the intense *racialism* of Chinese nationalism, came to be obsolete when Hitler made all racialism seem vulgar and ominous.

Within the Kuomintang proper the first major schism was between the Left wing, who favored rapid constitutionalization, and the Right wing, who favored the consolidation of national power first. In 1930 Wang Chingwei was the leader of the protestants and was generally considered to be a liberal, a democrat, and a reformer. Hu Han-min, an austere but highly ethical conservative, was driven from power because he wanted working democracy to be installed in the early 1930's. During this same period, the various Kuomintang schisms produced a great deal of polemic literature. The main body of SunYatsenism was of course the official government and party line. This line followed the personal career of Chiang Kai-shek, his reaction to the Communists, to the Japanese occupation of Manchuria, to the problems of resistance or appeasement, and similar current political topics. Chiang added a great deal of his own to Sun Yat-sen, but attempted within the limits of his intellectual capacity not to violate the general framework of SunYatsenism.

Unfortunately for the Kuomintang, the organizational aspect of the revolution developed much more rapidly than the ideological. The Kuomintang was much better at obtaining party offices and establishing half-trained cadres than at the difficult job of purging, re-purging, and again purging the party so as to obtain ideologically articulate and fanatically devoted exponents of the party teaching. By the 1940's the Kuomintang party line had become both official and sterile.

Many of the most gifted theorists of the Kuomintang followed Wang Ching-wei into exile, treason, and self-destruction. Such men as Ch'en Kung-po and Chou Fu-hai had written vividly and patiently concerning the content of SunYatsenism; they, along with the internationally famous T'ang Leang-li, joined Wang in his ill-starred attempt at salvaging Chinese nationalism through the establishment of a quisling government at Nanking.

Kuomintang Structure. After the reorganization of 1924 the Kuomintang, equipped with new ideological concepts and military vigor, embarked on the Northern Expedition which enabled it to win a decisive victory over the disorganized warlords. The death of Sun Yat-sen in 1925 gave the Kuomintang new inspiration to drive northward to carry out the bequeathed teachings of its late leader. The military phase of the Kuomintang revolution, described in the previous chapter, brought the party to an open split with the Communists in 1927. The Russians retreated from party ranks, and even severed diplomatic relations with China.

Between the time of the reorganization of 1924 and the reform movement effectuated in 1950, the fundamental framework of the Kuomintang remained on the whole unchanged. Not only had the party structure retained its main features; its leaders, who had been active twenty years before as young revolutionists, occupied the same responsible positions in the party hierarchy.

The foundation structure of the Kuomintang was laid down in 1924 by the First Party Congress when it passed the Constitution of the party. There were four tiers of authority. At the apex of the pyramid, there was the central organization; below that were the provincial organizations, the *hsien* organizations, the district organizations, and the membership. Each level of organization maintained an executive committee and a supervisory committee. These committees were elected directly by party members in the case of district organizations, and indirectly by congresses of party delegates in the case of higher level organizations. The National Party Congress (*Ch'üan-kuo tai-piao ta-hui*) possessed the highest authority and theoretically was supposed to meet every other year according to the Party Constitution. Only five Party Congresses were held in twenty years; the sixth was held in 1945 in Chungking, and the seventh, in Formosa in October,

1952, after the conclusion of the Party Reform Movement, which was inaugurated in 1950.

The National Party Congress was to act through the Central Executive Committee (*Chung-yang chih-hsing wei-yüan-hui*) when not in session, and the latter, through its Standing Committee (*Chung-yang ch'ang-wu wei-yüan-hui*). The Standing Committee, therefore, was the seat of power of the whole Kuomintang hierarchy. Parallel to the Central Executive Committee was the Central Supervisory Committee (*Chung-yang chien-ch'a wei-yüan-hui*), which had control over disciplinary and financial matters. Its membership was usually reserved for party elders.

The post of *Tsung-ts'ai,* or General Director, was created by the Emergency Congress held in Hankow in 1938. To all intent and purpose, it was created to enable Chiang Kai-shek to ascend to the position of party leader formerly held by Sun Yat-sen, who was *Tsung-li,* or the General Manager of the party. Out of consideration for the spirit of reverence to the late leader, the Emergency Party Congress reserved the old title exclusively for him in perpetuity. The *Tsung-ts'ai* possessed absolute veto powers over the decisions of the Central Executive Committee and had the final say in all party matters.

The curious student of comparative government, unfamiliar with Chinese politics, could be expected to raise a quizzical eyebrow. Party congresses, executive and supervisory committees, and a standing committee—are these the organs of a party which *fought* the Communists for years? History, of course, would tell him these were the indelible stamps of Russian organizational collaboration, 1923-1924. At the lowest levels too, the Kuomintang, like other revolutionary parties, was composed of formal members. A Chinese who subscribed to Sun's Principles applied for membership; he was then investigated and made a probationary member for a year; if he did not engage in un-Kuomintang activities, he could then become a full member. Later, applicants joined the *San Min Chu I* Youth Corps (named after Sun's Principles), from which they were graduated into Kuomintang membership. In 1945, there were approximately 3,000,000 members of the Kuomintang, organized into the lowest units of the party, the cell (*ch'ü fên pu*). At some points in the party's history, self-criticism and public confession were reminiscent of evangelist meetings of some American Protestant sects and also amazingly prophetic of later Communist practices.[7]

The link between the party and the government was supplied by the Central Political Council (*Chung-yang chêng-chih wei-yüan-hui*), a subcommittee under the Central Executive Committee. It was the replica of the Politburo of the Russian Communist Party. From its establishment in 1924, the CPC underwent several changes both in its functions and in the size of its membership. But in 1939 it was completely reorganized and adopted the name of the Supreme National Defense Council (*Kuo-fang*

[7] See China Information Committee, *China At War*, Vol. V, No. 3 (October, 1940).

tsui-kao wei-yüan-hui). The Council exercised the party's sovereign powers to give direction to and supervision over the government. Its functions included deliberation on principles of legislation, military policies, fiscal administration, and important appointments. In other words, it was the instrument with which the party controlled the government under the tutelage system. After the War, when the New Constitution was adopted, the Supreme National Defense Council was abolished, and the old Political Council restored; this marked the end of tutelage government. Before the end of tutelage, the system shaped up, as one Chinese authority put it, to "an aristocratic oligarchy." [8]

A description of the operation of the Kuomintang Party headquarters would be redundant at this point, except for the generalization that the Central Executive and Standing committees of the Kuomintang were, for all practical purposes, the final authorities in the party structure. However, their power was somewhat curtailed after the installation of the post of *Tsung-ts'ai*. The Supervisory Committee, corresponding to the Orgburo of Western Communist parties, never functioned with any degree of vitality. The Kuomintang as tutelary party under its own contrivance, the Constitution of 1931, exercised final governmental authority over the National Government of China through its agency, the Central Political Council of the Central Executive Committee, which was superseded by the Supreme National Defense Council across the war years. (Chart on page 154 shows this relationship.)

The administrative matters of the party, at each tier, were handled by a secretary and a host of departments or commissions. In the case of the national organization, there was a secretariat and a number of departments and committees which were responsible to the Central Executive Committee. These departments grew so big that they approximated government departments both in size and in prestige.

A separate yet affiliated organization was the *San Min Chu I* Youth Corps which existed from 1939 to 1947. It was created by the Emergency Party Congress in the hope that an organization of younger people would introduce new spirit into the party and build up party strength. It maintained a separate structure similar to that of its parent body, but its key positions were essentially controlled by influential party members. It was amalgamated into the party in 1947 when it was found that dual existence was neither economical nor advisable.

Outside party structure, but closely related both in purpose and personnel, was the New Life Movement which was inaugurated by Chiang Kai-shek in 1934 in Kiangsi. The movement was intended for economic and ideological reforms in areas devastated by Communist-led agrarian insurrections; it soon spread throughout the country as a national movement. The Industrial

[8] Y. Y. Lu, "How the National Government in Nanking Works," *Chinese Social and Political Science Review*, Vol. XVII (1933), pp. 442-456.

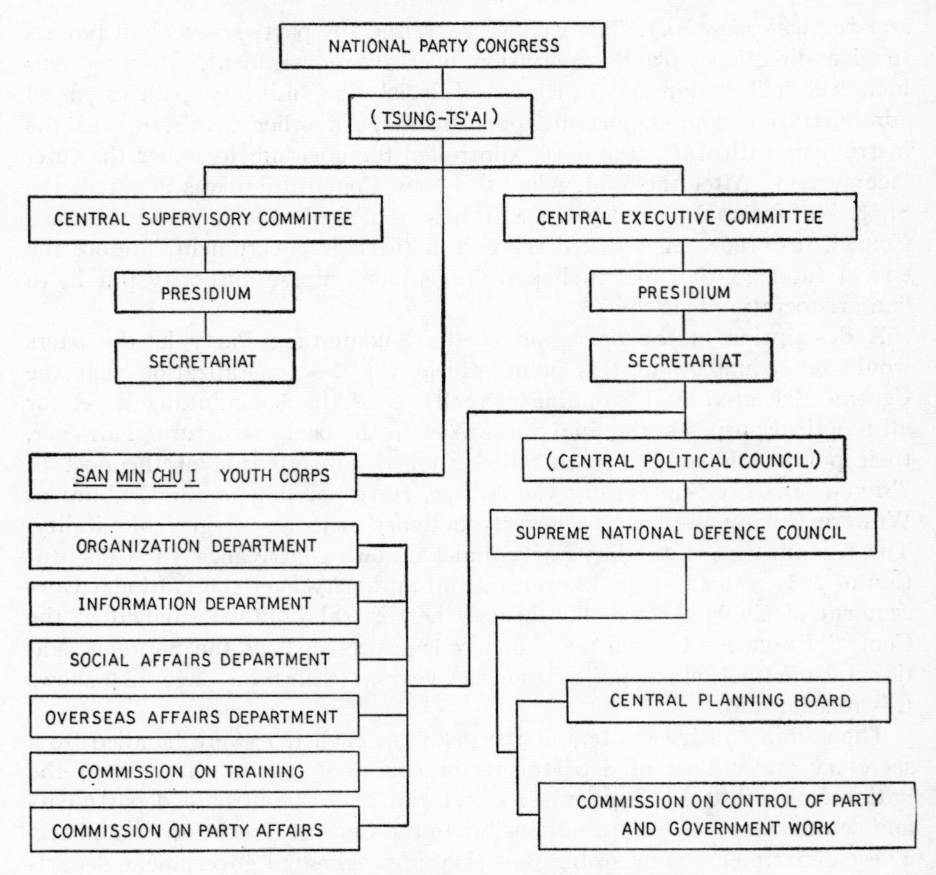

CHART 4—The Organization of the Kuomintang

Cooperative Movement represented another effort of the Kuomintang to promote economic reconstruction in the war years. Although the achievements of these movements, in terms of material gains, were negligible, the social consciousness which they generated among the Chinese people was instrumental in bringing about significant social repercussions.[9]

The Kuomintang in Retrospect. The National Government was a Kuomintang creation. Leadership of the party became leadership of the National Government. Chiang Kai-shek, as chief of state—by whatever name—depended upon the Kuomintang. Thus Chiang, for example, must and will be

[9] Chiang Soong Mei-ling (who is, of course, Mme. Chiang Kai-shek), *China Shall Rise Again,* New York, 1941, gave a full account of New Life enterprises, with emphasis on the role of women. The work of the Industrial Cooperatives (known also as Chinese Industrial Cooperatives—C.I.C.—or Indusco.) was as well known outside China as within, thanks to publicity releases by the American Committee in Aid of Chinese Industrial Cooperatives, New York.

judged as both Party Leader and chief of state (in which role he is described below).

Actually, neither the wartime Kuomintang nor the wartime Communist Party was a mass party. In terms of patronage, procedure, power, and policy, the National Government was a one-party government; but the party was "a conglomeration of innumerable personal leaderships knit together by a common outlook, a common interest in the maintenance of the National Government and formal party power, and a common loyalty to the Party Chief."[10] Once the party came to power, intra-Kuomintang cliques tended to lose their general character as groups and to carve out spheres of influence on the ill-defined boundaries of party and governmental affairs.

Despite repeated injunctions ordered by Chiang that no cliques should be permitted to exist within the party, informal groups and cliques were formed to assert influence and to seek patronage. The most notable among these was the so-called C. C. Clique or the *Erh Ch'en* Clique led by Ch'en Li-fu, Minister of Education, and Ch'en Kuo-fu, head of the Central Political Institute who were shrewd manipulators of party and government personnel. Graduates of the Whampoa Academy who went into politics instead of the army organized themselves into a semi-secret organization known as the Regenerationists, or "Blue Shirts," and were manifest admirers of Fascist political methods. Political police work was handled by Tai Li and a small corps, whose existence was merely whispered. The party also maintained its own system of secret police which worked under the innocent title, Bureau of Investigation and Statistics. The Political Science Group (*Chêng-hsüeh-hsi*) included more mature politicians with Western training, interested in development of political economy, and entrenched in important government positions.

The Kuomintang has played a major role on the Chinese political stage for nearly half a century. As a secret organization, it brought about the downfall of the Manchu dynasty; as a revolutionary party, it unified China by defecting various political factions and numerous military warlords; as the trustee of the tutelage government, it guided the country through the turmoil of a major world war. Prior to the Japanese invasion of 1937, the Kuomintang was at the prime of its prestige and strength and enjoyed a brief period of popularity and prosperity. But years of war and inflation heavily taxed its resources and energy. It became completely bureaucratized and gradually lost its capacity to take any kind of initiative in the struggle with the Communist Party. The Reform Movement of 1950-1952, inaugurated in Formosa after the loss of the mainland, brought some new and younger elements into the party, but it did not rejuvenate the lax and weary organization as it promised. The party lost the vitality and resourcefulness that

[10] Paul M. A. Linebarger, *The China of Chiang K'ai-shek; A Political Study,* Boston, 1943, p. 142. This study, on the whole favorable to the Kuomintang, was a thorough canvass of the Party and National Government in wartime (to 1941), based on official documents and personal interviews.

characterized its early revolutionary days. The system of political tutelage, conceived by Sun Yat-sen as a device for the training of the people for constitutional government, succeeded only in complete bureaucratization of the rank and file of the party. Perhaps the Kuomintang has a lesson to learn from the Confucian maxim that "the trouble with people is their obsession to teach others." Unfortunately, this obsession has been inherited by the Communists today; hence, democratic constitutionalism is farther than ever out of reach of the Chinese people.

Constitutional Basis of Tutelage. When Sun Yat-sen wrote his *Fundamentals of National Reconstruction,*[11] he predicted an early conquest of his opponents. He argued that, after the consummation of the military phase of the revolution, the party should be enabled to train the people in the art of self-government by exercising, for a limited period of time, the full power of sovereignty on behalf of the people. The Kuomintang should assume the role of the tutelary party until the people were ready for constitutional government.

The period of *military conquest* turned out to be longer than he expected. In 1923, before the launching of the Northern Expedition, the organization which directed campaigns was only a military junta which was called the "General Headquarters" with Sun himself assuming the title of Generalissimo. In 1925, the headquarters was reorganized and assumed the formal name of the "Nationalist Government," in Canton, in turn succeeded by the Wuhan regime and the Nanking Government. In October, 1928, the country entered the phase of political tutelage. The period of tutelage, intended to be an intermediate period, lasted twenty years.

The *Fundamentals* had provided that "when a census of any *hsien* shall have been taken, the land therein surveyed, an efficient police force organized, roads built throughout the *hsien,* the people trained in the exercise of their political rights . . . then the *hsien* shall be deemed fit for self-government." In spite of his keen observations and well-intended plans, Sun Yat-sen could not have predicted the Japanese invasion and the World War, which pushed Resistance into the forefront ahead of Reconstruction. It has often been charged that the Kuomintang failed in any serious effort to train the Chinese people in the art of self-government during the war years. The fact remains that the war and preoccupation with Communist plans consumed most of the attention and energies of the party.

The period of constitutionalism, viewed by Sun Yat-sen as the time for the abdication of the Kuomintang in favor of a popularly elected government, was ushered in on December 25, 1946, with the adoption of a new Constitution. (This Constitution was promulgated on January 1, 1947; see below, and Appendix 5.) Popular pressure, the demand of minor parties which were anxious to share in government, and the insistence of the United

[11] *Chien-kuo ta-kang,* an outline program of 25 points, which may be found in Leonard Shih-lien Hsü, *Sun Yat-sen, His Political and Social Ideals,* Los Angeles, 1933.

States pried the Kuomintang out of the position of tutor. A constitutional government was organized in April, 1948. It is one of the ironic tragedies of Far Eastern history that the new Constitution is still in force—but only on the island of Formosa, which had only so recently been returned to Chinese rule.

It is therefore the fate of the present-day Kuomintang to be chiefly identified with the tutelage government of 1928-1948. Furthermore, to understand the present political structure of the National Government on Formosa, it is necessary to study the form of that tutelage government.

The Organic Law of the National Government, promulgated in October, 1928, provided for a presidential and five-*yüan* system of administration. *Yüan,* literally "Boards," marked off the Chinese fivefold (as compared with the American threefold) separation of power. They can be thought of as great branches of the National Government and should be left in the romanized term, *yüan.* In any case, the system was an innovation in Chinese political experience.

According to Dr. Sun, the people were capable of exercising the four *political powers* of initiative, referendum, election, and recall. These were perhaps the most Western elements in all of his theory. They were to provide almost completely un-Chinese powers of the people over administrators, and over laws. Beyond these, the government should be protected against undue interference and should enjoy the five governing powers of administration, legislation, adjudication, examination, and control. The system was obviously an adaptation of the Western tradition of threefold separation of powers, and an adoption of time-honored Chinese practices of examination and supervision.[12]

Even during the period of tutelage, the government apparently could not rule without some sort of fundamental law. A Provisional Constitution (*Yüeh-fa*) was adopted on June 1, 1931, by a national convention of some five hundred delegates. (For text, see Appendix 4.) This Constitution was originally designed for five years of use, but it remained in force until it was superseded by the new Constitution of 1947. By Chinese standards, it was a long-lived document. The Provisional Constitution reaffirmed the political authority of the Kuomintang during the tutelage period. It contained several articles on civil liberties and personal rights. The power of interpretation rested with the Central Executive Committee and on several occasions the constitution was modified by basic ordinances subsequently issued by that organ. This Provisional Constitution was a unique document in that it was admittedly transitory in nature. The preamble of the Constitu-

[12] Linebarger, *Political Doctrines,* cited, especially Chap. VI. The five powers thus would reconcile, Dr. Sun thought, the best features of democracy and dictatorship, of free enterprise and socialism, of the Western World and China. Sun's ideology lives on in the structure of the National Government on Formosa (see the next chapter) and is imbedded in the Constitution of the Republic of Indonesia. Elsewhere it has been superseded by Communism, or by forms of parliamentary democracy.

tion provided that the purpose of this document was to "accelerate the development of constitutional government whereby political power shall be returned to a government elected by the people."

The Center of Gravity. There is no denying that personal politics played an important role in the government under the Kuomintang tutelage. Chinese tradition since time immemorial had sanctioned government by strong men instead of government by law. Therefore, juridical niceties could not explain political phenomena adequately; a government by strong personality could not be held responsible for breach of the law of his own creation.

From the installation of the National Government in 1928, two men held the position of the President of the National Government. The President (*Chu-hsi,* literally, the Chairman) was actually the Chairman of the Council of State (*Kuo-min chêng-fu wei-yüan-hui*). Since he was the highest governmental official in China during the tutelage period, his office was commonly translated as the Presidency of the National Government. Both the President and the State Councilors were elected by the Central Executive Committee of the Kuomintang. The function and character of the Presidency seem to have varied according to the prestige and power of the man who happened to hold that office. When the venerable Lin Sen was President of the National Government he was only a titular head of state. Nevertheless, Mr. Lin was perhaps the ideal man to fill the office of titular head. Like a President of the Third French Republic, he neither reigned nor governed. An old man with a flowing white beard against a bright red face, he habitually wore the blue gown and black jacket of Chinese formal attire, gracefully and with dignity. His clear voice often spoke words of virtue and moderation. As an old revolutionary from the province of Fukien, he was beloved by the people and esteemed by those who wielded actual power over his name. When his term expired in 1936, the authorities found reasons to keep him in office. First came the war and then Lin's death, in the summer of 1943. His passing was not only the death of a person, but of an institution —an institution which had brought to the nation an element of stability and loftiness, inherited from the past, in a period of political turmoil and savage war, the heritage of the present. But when Chiang Kai-shek succeeded him in 1943, Chiang made the position of President a real center of political gravity.

The President presided over the meetings of the Council of State, performing the ceremonial functions of his office. His signature was required on all important government documents. He received foreign diplomats. When Chiang became President of the National Government, he frequently took action independent of the Council of State and often issued orders directly to the several administrations. He was concurrently the Commander-in-Chief of the armed forces. The President of the Executive *Yüan* was nominated by him from among the State Councilors, although the final election was made by the Central Executive Committee of the Kuomintang. What seemed more important was that the President of the Executive *Yüan* was responsible to him for the conduct of the administration of government (the political structure of which is shown, in outline, below).

The Council of State was a body of from 24 to 36 persons whose powers and importance in the general scheme of government waxed and waned in close relationship to the rise and fall of the powers of the President.

In the early years the National Government operated on a commission basis, all governmental decisions being made through Council of State resolutions. Under such a system the Council of State was the most important

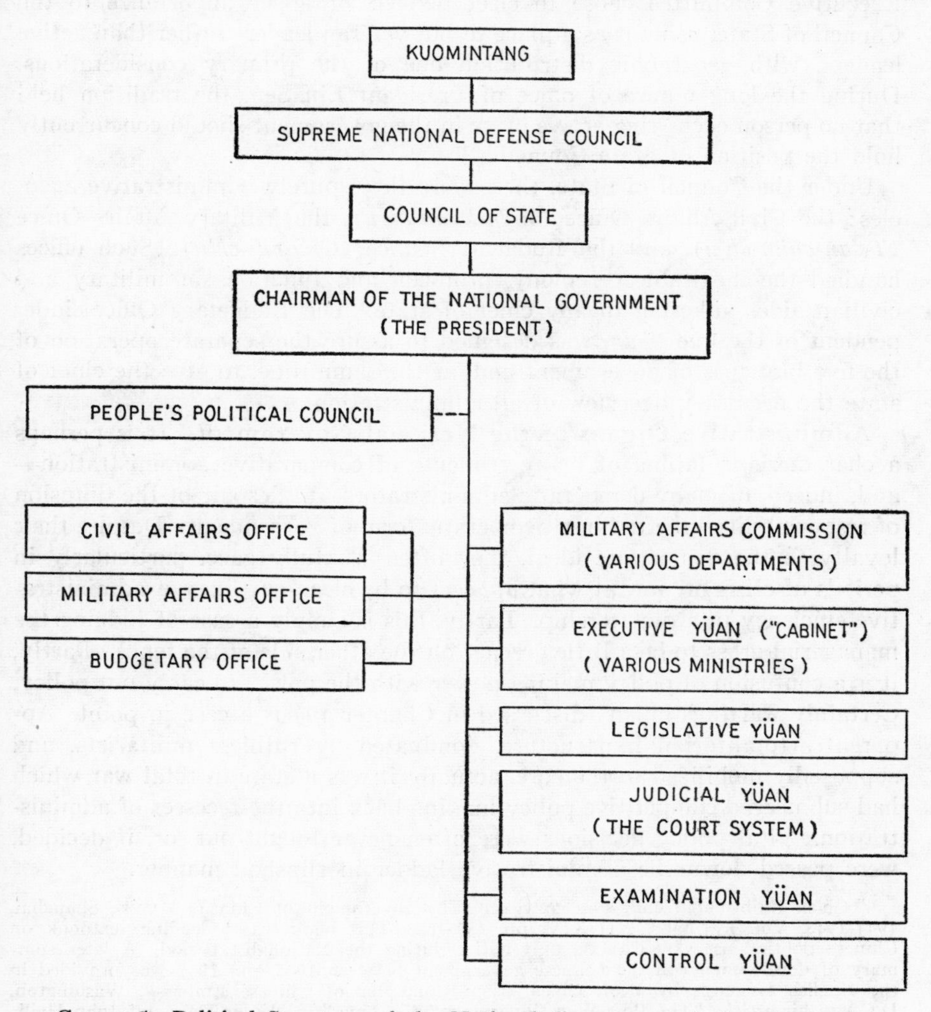

CHART 5—Political Structure of the National Government during the Period Tutelage

organ of the government. Even in those days, however, the Council of State, which was conceived as the policy-forming organ at the highest level, had a powerful competitor in the Central Political Council of the Kuomintang, which acted as the sole link between the party and the government. Both were policy-forming organs but, inasmuch as the theory of political tutelage called for decisions on policy by the party rather than by the government, the Council of State became an organ possessing more prestige than actual power. In fact, the personnel of the two organs, both of them designated by the Central Executive Committee of the Party, was such that the Council of State could not possibly emerge triumphant in the contest. The Central Executive Committee chose to elect persons of lesser importance to the Council of State, using it as a place to put veteran leaders rather than active leaders, with geographic distribution one of the primary considerations. During the long tenure of office of President Lin Sen, the tradition held that no person occupying active office in the government should concurrently hold the position of State Councilor.[13]

Under the Council of State, there were three purely administrative agencies: the Civil Affairs Office (*Wên-kuan-ch'u*), the Military Affairs Office (*Ts'an-chün-ch'u*), and the Budgetary Office (*Chu-chi-ch'u*). Such offices handled the inevitable ceremony, protocol, and functions of military and civilian aides adhering to any chief of state. The Budgetary Office, independent of the five *yüan*, was designed to assure the separate operation of the five branches of government and, at the same time, to give the chief of state the necessary overview of all administration.

Administrative Organs of the National Government. It is perhaps a characteristic failing of many students of comparative administration—and, indeed, of many democratic administrators—to despair of the diffusion of responsibility inherent in a democratic form of government. Despite their loyalty to the democratic ideal, they often wistfully gaze, particularly in periods of crisis or war, at what *appears* to be clean-cut lines of administrative efficiency in a dictatorship. Partly, this is simply a case of judging the managerial grass to be a little greener on the other side of the fence. Partly, it is a confusion of policy-making power with the power to carry out policy. Certainly wartime Japan (discussed in Chapter 19) is a case in point. Apparently totalitarian in structure, dominated by ruthless militarists, and supposedly mobilized to the core, actually it was a state in total war which had submerged competitive policy-making back into the recesses of administration. Vital policy decisions were often never fought out, or, if decided, were passed down the administrative ladder in slipshod manner.

[13] Ch'en Chih-mai, *Chung-kuo chêng-fu* (The government of China), 3 vols., Shanghai, 1944-1945, Vol. I, Chaps. XII-XIV, pp. 131-162. This book was a leading textbook on Chinese politics, used by Chinese universities during the Nationalist period. A later summary of developments in the Chinese government between 1945 and 1947 was provided in the English language by Prof. Ch'en (then Counselor of Chinese Embassy, Washington, D.C.) in his article, "The Post-War Government of China," in Taylor Cole and John Halliwell, editors, *Post-War Governments of the Far East,* Gainesville, Florida, 1947, pp. 503 ff.

Was the National Government a dictatorship? True, the government at Nanking, later at Chungking, was a one-party state. Personal leadership played an important role, as it always had in China. Yet, even policy-making power was never the sole prerogative of Chiang Kai-shek. He remained almost sovereign in technical military matters and, through shrewd balancing of family connections, party control, international prestige, and clique support, he possessed more political influence than did any other individual. True, the power of policy-making did rest with Chiang and perhaps a hundred individuals in the party and government. Some of the ablest had once been warlords; some of the most aggressive had never handled anything more dangerous than an abacus. In any case, how many more than a hundred actually wield policy-formation power around a Roosevelt, a Truman, or an Eisenhower? Chiang's problem, like that of his American contemporaries, was to balance the views of his party, various cliques, and the top administrators of his government.

The state machinery of Nationalist China, resting on a unique, complex constitutional system of five powers, was one of the most elaborate in the modern world, almost as elaborate as wartime Washington. Dr. Kan Nai-kuang, former Deputy Director of the Kuomintang Secretariat, once said, "That the administrative system of China needs reform, is a fact as hard as a piece of iron."[14] He went on, knowledgeable in administrative science as he was, to say that the weak points of Nationalist administration lay in its institutions, its personnel, and its equipment. It would be difficult to say how prophetic were this expert's words. That administrative inefficiency was a factor in the collapse of the National Government, no one can deny. That institutions and personnel played a part, there is little doubt. Beyond that, the Chinese had their own tragicomic difficulties. Chinese administrative jargon, for example, emphasized form rather than substance, and would make the most expert analyst of Washingtonese shudder. Although there were shorthand systems, few administrators cultivated the habit of dictating memoranda or letters. Filing of documents was at best a great confusion, since the Chinese language offered no convenient alphabetic cross-referencing system. Government documents were always impersonal. Of course, the best techniques and equipment in the world will not make or execute good policy. Nevertheless, such shortcomings were indicative of a way of doing things: indeed, if the administrative shoe fits, it may be worn in any country, at any time!

Nationalist administration, in the Western sense, shaped up under the Executive *Yüan* (*Hsing-chêng-yüan*). In terms of policy-making, it was often called in English the "Cabinet," its President, the "Premier." But if one of the main characteristics of the parliamentary form of government is the responsibility of the cabinet to the legislature, then the Executive *Yüan* bore little resemblance to the cabinet of the United Kingdom or to

[14] Dr. Kan's views were summarized in Ch'en, *ibid.*, pp. 74-97.

that of the Third French Republic. The Executive *Yüan* began as an organ subordinate to the party, whose mandate it executed; after 1943, it was responsible to the President of China for the administrative functions it performed. In only two senses was the Executive *Yüan* a cabinet: it was a meeting ground for adjustment of the administrative problems of various departments, and members did share collective responsibility.

The most important person in the Executive *Yüan* was, of course, the President (*Yüan-chang*). He was elected by the Central Executive Committee of the Kuomintang, after 1943, on the nomination of the President of the National Government. The power of both the *Yüan* and its President underwent many changes. At a time when the President of the National Government was merely a figurehead, the Executive *Yüan* and "Premier" tended to develop real executive power; at a time when the President of the National Government exercised strong leadership, the power of the *Yüan* correspondingly diminished.

Under the Executive *Yüan* there was a varying number of Ministries (*Pu*) —like the familiar Ministries of Interior, of Foreign Affairs, Finance, Justice—and also Commissions (*Wei-yüan-hui*) of ministerial rank—like the Natural Resources Commission. Heads of these various subdivisions were members of the Executive *Yüan* Council (*Hsing-chêng-yüan hui-i*), which met regularly every Tuesday to deliberate matters of general administrative policy, as well as those pertaining to individual ministries. Although there was a regulation that decisions should be carried by a majority vote, in practice the judgments of the President of the *Yüan* were usually honored and accepted by his colleagues without much deliberation.

This nonpolicy-making characteristic of the *Yüan* suggests two controversial subjects in modern Chinese politics. During the war, American newspaper readers were entertained by accounts of interdepartmental squabbles, for which the Roosevelt Administration showed positive genius. In China, one seldom heard or read of such things. The point is, there *were* vigorous differences of opinion within the National Government, but there were different techniques of arriving at compromise. For one thing, there were two staff organs attached to the Executive *Yüan,* the Secretariat (*Mi-shu-ch'u*) and the Office of Political Affairs (*Chêng-wu-ch'u*). Both exercised an important influence on administrative matters, since all reports and memoranda from different ministries were studied, screened, and assorted by secretaries and councilors before they came to Council meetings for decision. The Secretariat defined or ironed out areas of dispute, in much the same way as cabinet arguments in the American government have been first delimited by the Budget Bureau or National Security Council, on orders from a strong President, weary of family debate in public. Since the Executive *Yüan* also exercised control over various levels of local government, staff organs acted as a coordinating link among departments as well as between the central administration and municipal governments throughout the country.

Before the fall of the government on the mainland, minor parties, and especially the Communists, urged the transformation of the *Yüan* into a true coalition cabinet. Ministers were to become something other than glorified administrative messenger boys. The legitimate stake of the American government in Chinese democracy was also thus expressed, in part, in what became known as the Marshall Coalition Program. In the narrow sense, this program confused a technical administrative problem with a political demand. It is noteworthy that when the Communists themselves took power, they established a government for all China which was far more centralized than the Kuomintang was ever able or dared to design.

In the scheme of tutelage, the highest policy-making power of the National Government was retained by party organs. Hence, any comparison between the Legislative *Yüan* (*Li-fa-yüan*) with a congress or parliament was inappropriate and even meaningless. The Legislative *Yüan* was neither a representative body nor a policy-determining organ of government. Theoretically, there was a distinction between "legislative principles" and "legislative content." The Central Executive Committee of the Kuomintang was charged with the responsibility for legislative principles, while the Legislative *Yüan* only translated principles into law. Thus in practice, this *Yüan* was merely a law-drafting bureau, such as the Legislative Reference Service is to the American Congress.

Under the Provisional Constitution of 1931, the Legislative *Yüan* consisted of a President, a Vice-President, and from 49 to 99 members. Its officers were nominated by the President of the National Government and appointed by the Central Executive Committee. Choice of membership was, to a certain extent, guided by geographic representation, but most of the members succeeded in getting themselves continuously reappointed. They were not permitted to serve in any concurrent capacity in the government and were also barred from practicing law. Members grouped themselves into five standing committees—on Law, Foreign Affairs, Finance, Economics, and Military Affairs—and *ad hoc* committees—such as the Constitution Drafting Committee. The *Yüan* had a Secretariat and an Office of Compilation and Translation, which completed several valuable works on legislative reference.

Legislative drafting by experts produced some remarkable results: laws were better worded; terminology was rigidly correct; on the other hand, Chinese law became so advanced that it bore little relation to actual conditions in China. This was too bad, for in the zeal to achieve a rule of law, the drafters probably retarded rather than advanced the process of legislation.

Apart from the study of constitutionalism and law-drafting, the *Yüan* found more and more of its work accomplished elsewhere, either by executive decrees of the Executive *Yüan* or by administrative ordinances of the

Supreme National Defense Council. Jurisdiction which remained included: deliberation (1) on laws, (2) the budget, (3) general amnesty, (4) declarations of war, (5) treaties of peace, and (6) "other important matters" (in the field of international relations). Even in these areas the *Yüan* could not act independently, but needed the approval of the Supreme National Defense Council. Occasionally inspired by the Western practice of interpellation, the *Yüan* requested the President of the Executive *Yüan* to appear, mainly to embarrass him rather than to gain information. Then the Legislators gained temporary prominence and even popular acclamation. Nevertheless, the *Yüan* had no legal right to question the executive branch or to compel ministers to reply to questions on political matters.

The elevation of examination and censorial powers to the same level occupied by executive, legislative, and judicial departments of government was justified by deep-rooted Chinese political tradition. For thousands of years under one regime or another, the Chinese government had conducted civil service examinations to select and qualify public officials. It had been a system well-conceived, although at times it had been far from well-conducted. Ancient custom set up an ideal of elaborate and extraordinary precautions to insure complete impartiality of examiners. In other words, regardless of slips in practice, the power to examine was traditionally an independent power, and Dr. Sun thought it should be kept as such. In addition, there had long been a panel of men known as censors, "the eyes and ears of the Son of Heaven."

The Examination *Yüan* (*K'ao-shih-yüan*) and the Control *Yüan* (*Chien-ch'a-yüan*) did not seem as spectacular as the Executive, or as active as even the Legislative *Yüan*. Once again, as in ages past, the traditional ideal outshone the more seamy practices. Yet both *yüan* did have functions to perform under the National Government. The inner organizations of both *yüan* were similar to those of other branches, with a President, a Vice-President, and a Secretariat in each. Under the Examination *Yüan* were an Examination Commission (*K'ao-hsüan wei-yüan-hui*) and a Ministry of Personnel (*Ch'üan-hsü-pu*); under Control, a Ministry of Audit (*Shen-chi-pu*). In one respect, the Control *Yüan* differed from its counterparts in that it had seventeen regional organizations, headed by Control Commissioners (*Chien-ch'a-shih*).

Civil Service: Selection and Control. Ssŭ-Ma Kuang, the great Chinese statesman and historian of the eleventh century, once said, "The most important thing in politics is to get the proper personnel; if all the officials are equal to their posts, everything will be properly run." Under the National Government, these were the responsibilities of the Examination Commission and the Ministry of Personnel. Twenty years of political tutelage, however, did not lead to the recruitment of civil servants through the sole means of examination: recommendation, affiliation with a clique, family connections, personal influence, school and native ties continued to play important roles in the building of the Chinese bureaucracy. Had the National Government taken the traditional ideal more seriously, the collapse of morale in its civil service before the breakdown might not have been so rapid or complete.

When examinations were held, outside scholars in various professional fields were invited *ad hoc* to serve as examiners. There were three kinds of civil service examinations: higher, general, and special. The higher examination qualified comparatively important administrative posts, in which only university graduates were allowed to participate. The general examination was for junior civil posts, in which middle school graduates were qualified to participate. The special examination was held only for special appointments. The first examination took place in 1928; then, during the first four years of World War II, the system was temporarily suspended. Only a small fraction of the civil servants in China was recruited by means of examinations.

The Ministry of Personnel was charged with the duty of confirmation. Chinese law drew a sharp distinction between what were known as "political officials" and "administrative officials." Strictly speaking, only the latter were civil servants, subject to the laws and regulations governing the civil service. The definition of the term "political officials" in Chinese law was totally inadequate. The law merely specified that all officials whose appointments were made by resolution of the Central Political Council of the Kuomintang were "political officials." This category included such officials as the Chairman of the National Government, members of the Council of State, Presidents and Vice-Presidents of the five *yüan,* and other high government officials. These posts were said to belong to the "elected rank" (*hsüan-jên*).

In addition there were other officials who also owed their selection to resolutions of the Central Political Council of the Kuomintang. These included ministers, chairmen of commissions, members of the Legislative and Control *Yüan,* political vice-ministers of ministries, ambassadors, ministers plenipotentiary to foreign countries, members of the Provincial Government Commissions, and sundry other posts of high rank such as the secretaries-general of the various *yüan.* These were all known as political officials. Their appointments were made on political grounds and were not subject to civil service regulations; they were said to be in the "special rank" (*t'e-jên*).

The mass of civil servants were known as administrative officials; their appointments were governed by civil service laws and regulations. They were either initially qualified through civil service examinations or appointed by high government officials and subsequently recognized by the Ministry of Personnel. Broadly speaking, the civil service was divided into three ranks and each rank was subdivided into a number of grades. Putting the three ranks and their various grades together there were altogether 38 different grades. The "invited rank" (*chien-jên*), presumably appointed by a letter of invitation, was reserved for high officials such as vice-ministers and directors of services. The "recommended rank" (*tsien-jên*) occupied the middle echelon of the bureaucratic hierarchy, including section chiefs in the various ministries. The lowest was the "delegated rank" (*wei-jên*), which made up the large bulk of civil service personnel.

The pay of civil servants was fairly good before the war. But across the war years the economic situation deteriorated so fast that the government found itself unable to adjust the remuneration of its employees. Most of the civil servants scarcely had enough to keep themselves and their families alive. Some resorted to irregularities and corrupt practices which consequently demoralized the whole system.[15]

Under the Organic Law, the Control *Yüan* was to be "the highest supervisory organ of the government, obligated to exercise the power of impeachment and auditing in accordance with law." Thus was enshrined in legal language Sun's overemphasized reverence for the old institution of censors, and his absorption of Western writers' criticisms of the manner in which parliaments make use of their impeachment power. As a matter of fact, the Chinese control power was quite different from the Western power to question or to interpellate or to cast a vote of nonconfidence. Likewise, it was entirely different from the American practice of congressional investigation. It might rather be described as a general administrative post-audit, such as the American Comptroller-General exercises, but only in the fiscal field; or, even better, such as an Inspector-General of the United States Army exercises, but only in the military field. In theory, the control power seemed to encompass a conglomeration of functions, possible under the Empire where there was no separation of power and when there was no distinction between ethical and political action. Unofficial observers of the National Government, both Chinese and Westerners, felt the control power contained enormous possibilities and the need for control was great indeed. In practice, such a diffusion of functions was not possible under a modern five-*yüan* government. Party power and wartime executive and military growth relegated the control power to a secondary position. The power to control became strictly nonpolitical in nature, clearly borne out by the fact that cases of impeachment were tried not by the control authorities, nor by the legislature, but by a special tribunal attached to the judicial branch of the National Government. In theory the impeachment power was broad; because it was ill-defined and because it was handled loosely but not fearlessly, the theory was lost and the system did not quite work.[16]

[15] Ch'en, *ibid.*, Vol. II, Chaps. XXXII to XXXIV, pp. 199-243.

[16] The interested reader is invited to consult descriptions of the National Government—under the heading of the control power, for example—descriptions which are often rejected in advance because of some "slant" on the government, read into them at a later, controversial period. Professor Ch'en, thereafter a government official, in the treatise cited above, estimated the role of control as compared with Western functions of impeachment. Professor Linebarger, in his generally favorable *China of Chiang K'ai-shek,* cited, described the value of the control function as well as the wartime eclipse of the Control *Yüan* in favor of ex-

Partiality toward symmetry is almost a national obsession of the Chinese. It was manifest in the orderly arrangement of Imperial palaces and in the planning of the old city of Peking. The other four branches of government were known as *yüan;* the temptation to create a Judicial *Yüan* to round out the fivefold separation of power was irresistible. Although the Judicial *Yüan* was defined as the highest judicial organ of the National Government, its President and Vice-President were customarily included in such high political organs as the State Council and the Supreme National Defense Council. As to the function of adjudication, the *Yüan* was forbidden by law to interfere with the business of law courts, which were more or less independent. In 1943 the Ministry of Justice (*Ssŭ-fa hsing-chêng-pu*), considered more administrative than judicial in character, was transferred to the Executive *Yüan*.

There were three specific functions which fell within the authority of the *Yüan* itself. One was to interpret laws and orders and to alter legal precedents through a conference of heads of divisions and the Chief Justice of the Supreme Court, presided over by the President of the Judicial *Yüan*. Another was the initiation of pardons, reprieves, and restitution of civil rights. A third was to introduce legislative matters concerning the *Yüan* itself. The effectiveness of the Administrative Court (*Hsing-chêng-fa-yüan*) as a protector of individual rights against administrative encroachment was never sufficiently proved. Since the heaviest disciplinary measure which the Commission for Disciplinary Action of Public Officials (*Kung-wu-yüan ch'êng-chieh wei-yüan-hui*) could impose on an impeached official was deprivation of his right to hold office, the value of the Commission was doubtful.

A law of July 1, 1935, planned the establishment of a new system of courts in China, with a Supreme Court, one High Court in each province and special district, and Local Courts. Eventually, there was supposed to be at least one Local Court in each of some 2,000 *hsien* and municipalities. According to 1946 statistics, there were only 500 local courts in existence. Most *hsien* had only a judicial section attached to the district government.

The Military Affairs Commission. To the average Chinese, the five-power constitution and the system of political tutelage conveyed very little meaning. He knew of only three controlling forces which he was obliged to respect: *tang, chêng,* and *chün*—the party, the government, and the military constituted the all-powerful triumvirate. Although militarists had been regarded with suspicion in the traditional Chinese view, the urgency of modern Chinese power politics pushed the military element into a prominent and unique position. It had not been successfully absorbed into the normal

---

ecutive organs. Professor Ch'ien, in the volume already cited, thought the control power sufficiently important to devote a critical chapter to its operation. All three, as political scientists, were able to discuss this and other powers in moderate language, as Chinese contributions to the art of government.

pattern of government, as it had in most Western democracies. The outbreak of war in 1937 further promoted the expansion of the Military Affairs Commission (*Chün-shih wei-yüan-hui*), which had been in existence since 1925, and made of it an agency comparable to a sixth *yüan.*

The Commission consisted of a Chairman—Chiang Kai-shek—and nine members, appointed by the State Council with the approval of the Supreme National Defense Council. In order to facilitate prosecution of the war, there were created a number of subsidiary organs with the rank of ministry, a few branches of confidential character, and a host of lesser offices dealing with all kinds of civil and military affairs. The Ministry of War was under the joint jurisdiction of the Commission and the Executive *Yüan.* Other important establishments under the Commission included the Department of Military Operations, Military Training and Supply Services, the Political Department, the Aeronautical Commission, which did a superb job in organizing China's air power, and the Office of the Naval Commander-in-Chief, concerned mainly in making plans.

One office which received very little publicity and yet possessed a great political influence was the Office of Aides to the Chairman of the Commission (*Shih-ts'ung-shih*). The First Section was the military affairs group, also charged with intelligence and espionage. Second Section concentrated on civil affairs and kept the Chairman advised on matters of administration throughout the country. Third Section dealt with personnel and kept records on all military, as well as civilian and educational, employees. Actually it could recommend or censor appointments to all government offices, since the Chairman of the Commission was concurrently the head of the party and of the government. The Ministry of Personnel of the Examination *Yüan,* entrusted with the duty of confirmation, appeared to be only the adjunct of Third Section.[17]

The Struggle for Local Government. According to Sun Yat-sen's ideas, emphasis was to be placed on the development of *hsien* in order to enable the people to by-pass provincial authorities and to maintain direct connections with the central government. In actual practice, provincial governments continued to occupy a dominant position, and in twenty years of tutelage government showed no signs of withering away. The war practically destroyed vestiges of purely provincial militarism. Provincial Chairmen (*Shêng chu-hsi*), usually civilian, steadily gained in influence but frequently had as military cohorts officials curiously called Pacification Commissioners (*Sui-ching chu-jên*).

To the Chinese, the war beginning in 1937 was not a war between nation-

[17] For a detailed explanation of the relationship between the government and the military, see Linebarger, *The China of Chiang K'ai-shek,* cited, Chap. II; Ho Yao-tsu, "The National Military Council," *The Chinese Year Book, 1938-39,* Shanghai and Honkong, 1939, pp. 361-363; and Evans Fordyce Carlson, *The Chinese Army: Its Organization and Military Efficiency,* New York, 1940. Literature on the war, the struggle of Free China, American participation, and developing friction with the Communists reached monumental proportions by 1945 and would occupy at least a full-page citation.

states; it was a war for whole provinces, often the size of European nations; and it was a war for the creation of government at the provincial level. At one stage (1940) four provinces of China's twenty-eight were under Japanese domination and called Manchukuo; fourteen were wholly under Chinese control or slightly touched by invasion and were referred to as Free China; of these fourteen, four—Sinkiang, Yunnan, Kwangsi, and Fukien—cooperated with the National Government but showed strong traces of autonomy; ten provinces were under dual, or even triple government—by Japanese and pro-Japanese Chinese, by recognized and unrecognized Communist and guerrilla groups, and by constitutional authorities.[18]

At the truly local level, government authority was as always shadowy. China remained rural, but also congested as only a rural Far Eastern area can be. Corruption in public life, squeeze in economic life, and demoralization in family life—familiar Western, urban patterns—were hidden in each single village but summed up to China-wide political decay.

In structural terms, under the Organic Law of 1931 the administration of local affairs was to be organized on two tiers. Provincial government was to serve as liaison between the central and local governments; municipalities and *hsien* were to be the basic units of self-government. Provincial governments were organized on a commission basis, with seven to nine members appointed by the National Government, more or less like the Galveston plan in American municipalities.

There were two types of municipalities: special municipalities under the direct control of the Executive *Yüan,* and ordinary municipalities under the supervision of the provincial authorities. All were organized on the mayor-and-council pattern, with a secretariat, and bureaus of social affairs, public safety, finance, and public works under the mayor.

The birthplace of true democracy was supposed to be the *hsien.* Regardless of theory, the demand for local self-government was so urgent that in 1939, amidst a total war, the National Government saw fit to promulgate a so-called "new *hsien* system." At the end of the tutelage period, however, only a portion of the nation's 2,023 *hsien* had adopted the new system. Each *hsien* had a magistrate who administered local affairs as well as orders of the central and provincial government. Subdistricts under the *hsien* included *hsiang* (village), *chên* (town), *pao* (neighborhood), and *chia* (a group of households).

At all levels, as at the top, the war saw the emergence of representative government in Provincial People's Political Councils (*Shêng ts'an-chêng-hui*), Municipal Advisory Assemblies (*Shih ts'an-i-hui*) in some of the larger municipalities, and representative councils drawn from the subdistricts of areas which adopted the new *hsien* system. But contrary to Sun's own earlier predictions, democracy did not develop from below. Instead, it was

[18] Harold S. Quigley, "Free China," *International Conciliation,* No. 359 (April, 1940) gave a clear definition of these areas.

at the highest level that the first serious experiments in democratic processes were tried.

Democracy from the Top. As a defensive weapon of political consolidation and as a bridge to constitutional government, the People's Political Council (often PPC; in Chinese, *Kuo-min ts'an-chêng-hui*) was created by resolution of the Emergency Session of the Kuomintang Party Congress, held in Hankow, March, 1938. The Congress resolved that "the government should set up an organ for participation by the people in public affairs, to utilize the services of all persons of outstanding virtue and of great wisdom in the formation of state policies."

Establishment of the PPC was a compromise between proposals for a European-type United Front, based on popular elections,[19] and continuation of Kuomintang monopoly of government in the period of tutelage. Thus with all its many weaknesses, the PPC was a first approximation of representative government, one of the few China has ever known. Nevertheless, members were not popularly elected and increasing efforts were made by the Kuomintang to control the Council. For one reason or another, Kuomintang representation increased and proportionately the strength of other parties decreased. At its worst, the PPC became just another consultative organ whose decisions were not binding upon the government. Perhaps most fateful, the Council later served as a model for an *ad hoc* consultative conference of various parties, attempting coalition under the prodding of General George Catlett Marshall.

Certainly the PPC was a colorful, if not accurately representative, body. As first organized in July, 1938, it had two hundred members including seven Communists (one was Mao Tse-tung), a former Prime Minister, a Living Buddha attached to the Panch'an Lama, a Reserve Member of the Executive Committee of the Third International, and the Head of the Mêng Clan, descendants of Mencius.[20] In more mundane terms, the Organic Law of the PPC stipulated that members should be selected from four categories: (1) representatives nominated on a regional basis; (2) representatives from Tibet and Mongolia; (3) representatives from overseas Chinese communities; and (4) representatives from leading cultural and economic

[19] Between the establishment of the National Government and the appearance of the PPC, much political water had flowed under the bridge. China had been caught in the vice of anti-Communist "bandit" campaigns and steady encroachment by the Japanese. The spectacular kidnapping of Chiang Kai-shek at Sian, December, 1936, was the Chinese shot heard round the world, in favor of Resistance and Reconstruction, the slogan of the anti-Japanese United Front. In this sense, the forerunner of the PPC was perhaps the convention of the All-China Federation of National Salvation Unions. Its Manifesto (May, 1936) called for an end to civil war between the Nationalists and Communists, the merger of all parties in an anti-enemy front, freedom for political prisoners, and sanctions against any party which broke the united front agreement. The Chinese Communists, taking their cue from world-wide Soviet tactics, published their own Declaration on Unity (1935) and, after the kidnapping and release of Chiang, their Statement on Unity (1937). Before Lawrence K. Rosinger gained fame in a different context, before Congressional committee investigating the Institute of Pacific Relations, he published *China's Wartime Politics,* Princeton, 1944. This volume is useful for its collection of the documents described.

[20] Linebarger, *China of Chiang K'ai-shek,* cited, pp. 70-71.

organizations. There were no elections. All members were selected by the Kuomintang and their term of office was two years.

The second session of the People's Political Council was held in 1941, but the Communist members stayed away from its meetings in protest against the disbanding of their New Fourth Army. They requested government recognition of the Communist border regime as a prerequisite for their presence, but the request was refused. The third session of the People's Political Council was held in 1944. As a gesture of compromise, the PPC sent a five-man mission to Yenan to sound out Communist reactions but the mission returned without results. The People's Political Council Organic Law was again revised, increasing membership to 290 and adding budgetary and investigatory powers to the Council. The fourth Council session held three plenary meetings, the last in May, 1947. In its nine years of existence, the People's Political Council had held 13 plenary meetings in which something like two thousand resolutions had been adopted.[21]

The scope of Council powers included: (1) for the duration of the war, power to deliberate on all important measures of domestic and foreign policy before they were put into execution, (2) power of proposal to the government, (3) power to hear reports from various branches and to interpellate government officials. In 1944, the Council was given additional powers to make preliminary examination of the national budget and to make investigations.

Although the People's Political Council never could claim that it had successfully laid the foundation of democracy in China, it did, nevertheless, make many concrete and useful suggestions which were adopted by the government. The Council went out of existence when the National Assembly was called, under the New Constitution, on March 29, 1948. Although government under Kuomintang tutelage was often accused of harboring flagrant authoritarian tendencies, this consultative agency—designed to advise and criticize—was tolerated and even cherished for nine years out of a total period of two decades.

The United Front and the Marshall Mission. It must be borne in mind that the tutelage government described above existed under an extraordinarily strenuous period from 1937 to the war's end, when a greater part of the coastal China was under Japanese occupation and the presence of the Communist regime in the North constantly threatened its very existence. Earlier, the Japanese intervention in North China and the popular demand for resistance made it mandatory for the Kuomintang to seek compromise with the Communists in 1937 and to establish the United Front, in which the Communists recognized the seniority of the Kuomintang and the government in return promised to institute immediate democratic reforms. According to these agreements, the Communists were to give up their program of sovietization of the country and the policy of forcible confiscation of land

[21] *China Handbook, 1950*, New York, 1950, p. 139.

and were to accept the Three People's Principles as the code of the land. The Communist Government in the border region was to be incorporated into the National Government and the Red Army to become a part of the National Army. This unique experiment in politics was as much a surprise to persons who knew China as to those who did not. The most surprised among all were perhaps the Japanese who dreaded the idea of a united China in which Communism was tolerated and condoned. They wasted no time; open warfare began with the attack on the Marco Polo Bridge.

There is no doubt that the United Front movement, cemented by a common fear of extinction and the desire for national salvation, was the spearhead of Chinese resistance. Without an understanding based on mutual trust and cooperation, neither party was willing to entertain the idea of putting up resistance to the formidable Japanese war machine.

Toward the end of the war, there were many conflicts and much mutual distrust. The Communist Government in the Shan-Kan-Ning Border Region had never become a part of the National Government administration, and the Eighteenth Group Army had never accepted routine orders from the National Military Affairs Commission.

After V-J Day, a new movement for democratization and unification began. In an effort to strengthen postwar democratic defense, the United States government assumed the responsibility of helping the Chinese put their house in order. The program which it conceived for the achievement of unity, democracy, and peace for China can be summarized under these points:

1. There was to be a coalition government of all parties in which the Communist Party would be represented, competing fairly with the Kuomintang for the support of the people.
2. The two parties would stop the civil war which was raging and would merge their armies into one reorganized national army.
3. The proposed coalition government would end the one-party dictatorship by the Kuomintang and usher in a multi-party system, thereby giving the Chinese people the blessings of political democracy.
4. The new coalition government, founded on a new constitution, would receive economic aid from the United States to give work, food, and clothing to the starving millions.

When General George C. Marshall arrived in China to assume the role of mediator in December, 1945, he came with this blueprint in his pocket, a plan which was unfortunately made in the United States and which did not fit too well into the Chinese scene. With the usual American empirical diligence, he set to work on it, while the Chinese people merely waited to see a miracle performed.

The plan was agreed to by all parties in January, 1946, and for a moment China stood at the door of prosperity and peace. An Executive Headquarters in Peiping was set up to send out truce teams composed of Nationalist,

Communist, and American representatives. These were to guarantee a cease-fire order at all points where military conflict might flare up. But an atmosphere of basic agreement for coalition government was nullified by military elements of both parties. These extremists had never entertained a sincere intention to cooperate with each other and had not hesitated to put the blame on the other party for the breach of truce. In a mixed climate of fighting and negotiation, both parties had espoused peaceful settlement but had used force whenever they felt it to be expedient.

The period from the date of the Japanese surrender to the departure of General Marshall in January, 1947, was an epoch of uneasy peace. After Marshall left, full-scale civil war resumed and military maneuvers took the place of political maneuvers.

Realizing that it was impossible to put the political cart before the military horse, General Marshall conceded that his mission was a failure and put the blame on the extreme elements of both parties. In a statement issued on January 7, 1947, he said that irreconcilable groups within the Kuomintang, interested in the preservation of their own feudal control of China, evidently had no real intention of implementing his plans; on the other hand, dyed-in-the-wool Communists did not hesitate to adopt the most drastic measures to gain their ends, for instance, the destruction of communications in order to wreck the economy of China, thus producing a situation that would facilitate the overthrow or collapse of the government without any regard to the immediate suffering of the people involved. The reason for deadlock, he believed, was the complete, almost overwhelming suspicion with which the Chinese Communist Party and the Kuomintang regarded each other. Salvation, he concluded, lay in the assumption of leadership by liberals and minority parties—a splendid group of men who, as yet, lacked political power to exercise a controlling influence. Successful action on their part, under the leadership of Chiang Kai-shek, would lead to unity through good government.

Suffice it to say that General Marshall's mission was a complete failure. It was doubly tragic inasmuch as it was probably as great an intervention into the politics and government of a friendly foreign state as can be found in the history of the United States in peacetime. One by-product incidental to his mission, however, was the promulgation of the Constitution of 1947, which formally terminated tutelage government by the Kuomintang. This step in a way represented the consummation of twenty years of effort toward constitutionalism and the realization of Sun Yat-sen's vision of constitutional rule.

Constitutionalism as a Continuing Issue. War would seem to provide a poor climate for tinkering with constitutional structure. China, 1931-1945, offered no real exception to this general supposition. Yet fundamental political beliefs, tied closely to survival, respond quickly to the stimulus of war just as do human birth rates. When the first shot of the Pacific War, so far as the Chinese were concerned, was fired in Mukden in September, 1931, the whole country entered a period of sustained alarm. At first there was little energy left for either the government or the populace to devote themselves to the problems of self-government. When the first shock of invasion had passed, many people, including members of the Kuomintang, began to feel that a constitutional government, instead of one-party rule, might be the best means of bringing about consolidation of all forces to deal with the crisis. In the National Emergency Conference, held in April, 1932, at Sian, a resolution was passed that the Kuomintang should wind up its party rule as soon as possible. The Central Executive Committee of the Kuomintang also decided that the Legislative *Yüan* should draw up a draft Constitution and that preparations should be made to hold elections throughout the free provinces for the formation of a National Constituent Assembly.

The subsequent history of the constitutional movement can be divided into three periods. The first started in 1933, with the drafting of a constitution, and continued to the outbreak of total war in 1937. The second period stretched from the beginning of the war until victory in 1945. The third period ran from V-J Day to the inauguration of the Constitution in 1947.

In the first stage, a resolution of the Central Executive Committee of the Kuomintang established a committee of forty-two to begin the task of constitution drafting. It took nearly three years of continuous work and discussion before the Legislative *Yüan* completed the job. The draft was submitted to the Fifth Congress of the Kuomintang, which met in Nanking on November 12, 1935, and was accepted. The congress further decided that a National Assembly should be convoked during 1936 at the latest. The official version of the draft was published in a National Government decree on May 5, 1936, and from the date became popularly known as the "Double-Five Draft Constitution."

Holding a national election in China was no simple matter: primary machinery was defective; there was no census to guide local officials; there was no register of qualified voters in the villages and towns. Hence, there were repeated delays in complying with the decisions of central authorities. The year 1936 passed with no National Constituent Assembly in session. So in February the next year, the Central Executive Committee again fixed a target date, November 12, 1937. But the Marco Polo Bridge attack of July 7, 1937, signaled the outbreak of the big war. Electoral campaigning and preparations for the National Constituent Assembly stopped.

The second period of the constitutional movement was characterized by increasing clamor for a constitution and criticism of the Double-Five Draft. In 1938, the People's Political Council sponsored an Association for the Inauguration of Constitutionalism to make further studies and revisions of the Double-Five Draft Constitution. In 1943, a Preparatory Commission for the Enforcement of Constitutional Rule was appointed by the government.

This commission, composed of 49 members of different political groups, was concurrently a fact-finding and advisory body. Its duty was to solicit, through an extensive, nation-wide campaign, the people's views on the Constitution.

The third period started in January, 1946, with the inauguration of the Political Consultative Conference in Chungking. The Political Consultative Conference, to which all parties, including the Communists, and nonpartisan leaders were invited, was called to exchange views on national affairs, particularly the negotiation with the Communists. It had as one of its aims the discussion of questions concerning the convocation of the National Assembly and it also decided to subject the Double-Five Draft Constitution to revision. The Conference agreed upon a number of basic principles to guide revision, of which the four important ones were: (1) amendment of provisions for laws restricting people's freedom; (2) establishment of a modern, representative, parliamentary government; (3) establishment of a cabinet system; and (4) granting power to the provinces to establish their own constitutions. Corollary to the second and third points were the need for an elected Legislative *Yüan,* with parliamentary powers similar to those of democracies, and the need for an Executive *Yüan* responsible to the legislature.

The Political Consultative Conference set up an examination committee to study the Double-Five Draft comprehensively, in accordance with the principles of revision laid down by the Conference. The committee met several times, but headed into a deadlock when the Communists put forward a proposal calling for the retention of all Conference points without amendment. On the other hand, the Central Executive Committee of the Kuomintang met in March, 1946, and passed a resolution which completely repudiated the principles put forward by the Political Consultative Conference. A compromise agreement was finally reached on principles to be incorporated in the New Constitution. This step led to the decision to convene the National Constituent Assembly (*Kuo-min ta-hui*) without further delay.

The National Constituent Assembly of 1,744 members was convened on November 15, 1946, while the civil war with the Communists went on in full blast. The Communists and members of the Democratic League [22] boycotted the Assembly. On December 25, 1946, the National Assembly adopted the New Constitution and decided that it should be promulgated on New Year's Day, 1947. It also resolved that interim measures for the inauguration of constitutional government should be taken immediately.

[22] In March, 1941, China's splinter parties—hopeless without wealth, guns, or practical political power—formed a left-of-center Federation of Chinese Democratic Parties. With the advent of semi-constitutional government, these parties were revived as the Democratic League *(Min-chu t'ung-mêng)*. One of these parties, called the Chinese National Socialists (later, more appropriately, the Social Democratic Party), was headed by Dr. Carson Chang. He has given us a detailed account of proceedings in the National Constituent Assembly in *The Third Force in China,* New York, 1952.

The Constitution of 1947. The product of the National Assembly is still in force on Formosa. It contains 14 chapters and 175 articles, accepts Sun Yat-sen's ideas of five powers of government, four rights of the electorate, and the Three Principles of the People as its basic philosophy, and incorporates the main points agreed upon by the Political Consultative Conference of 1946. The essential provisions of the New Constitution may be summarized as follows:

Guaranty of Personal Liberties and Rights. The Bill of Rights contains provisions for the guaranty of all personal liberties and rights, including *habeas corpus*. The phrase, "such freedom shall not be restricted except in accordance with law," in earlier drafts is omitted.

The National Assembly. The National Assembly is to be the supreme organ wherein the sovereignty of the people resides. Its functions are those of a Constituent Assembly. It elects the President and Vice-President, amends the Constitution, brings impeachment against the President or Vice-President, and exercises the right of initiative regarding national legislation.

Governmental Structure. The structure of the government retains the five powers but does not clearly reveal whether it is a presidential or cabinet form. The President is elected for six years by the National Assembly. He appoints the President of the Executive *Yüan* with the consent of the Legislative *Yüan*. Generally speaking, the President possesses the power of the chief executive of a strong presidential type of government. The Executive *Yüan* operates on the principle of collective responsibility. Ministers, with or without portfolio, are appointed by the President of the republic through the recommendation of the President of the Executive *Yüan*. The Legislative *Yüan* is bicameral. Its members are elected mainly on the basis of territorial and professional representation for a three-year term, and are both eligible for re-election and subject to recall. The Judicial *Yüan* is responsible for the administration of justice and the interpretation of the Constitution. Its President and judges are appointed by the President of the republic with the consent of the Control *Yüan*. The Examination *Yüan* remains very much the same as it was before. The Control *Yüan* is vested with the power to approve the appointment of certain high officials, in addition to its original powers of impeachment and audit. Its members are elected by provincial assemblies for a term of six years.

Cabinet Responsibility. The Executive *Yüan,* with the consent of the President of the republic, may veto resolutions of the Legislative *Yüan*. But the Legislative *Yüan* can override the veto by a two-thirds vote. The President of the Executive *Yüan* has either to abide by the resolution or to resign.

Local Governments. The powers of both the central and provincial governments are enumerated. The province and the *hsien* are local self-government units. In each unit, there is to be a popular assembly. The provincial governor and the *hsien* magistrate are to be elected by the people. A province may adopt its own self-government law.

National Policies. National policies regarding defense, foreign affairs, national economy, social security, education, and border regions are specifically stated in the Constitution. Observance of treaty obligations and the Charter of the United Nations is expressly provided for.

Method of Amendment and Interpretation. Amendment of the Constitution is made either by the National Assembly alone or by resolution of the Legislative *Yüan* combined with ratification by the Assembly. The power of interpretation resides in the Judicial *Yüan.* Any law, whether national or local, may be declared unconstitutional by the Judicial *Yüan.*[23]

Fundamentally, the Constitution of 1947 is a democratic instrument. There are noticeable shortcomings and contradictions among some of its provisions, many the product of compromises arrived at between parties in the Political Consultative Conference. There was no opportunity to try them out and iron them out on a country-wide scale. There was only time for transition from tutelage to the new Government of 1948, and from the mainland of China to Formosa.

The National Government in Transition. After the Constitution was promulgated on January 1, 1947, the Communists declared that it was illegal because Communist-held areas were not represented in the Assembly. The government went ahead with its plans, because possibility of rapprochement with the Communists appeared to be remote. The period of transition, in which the Kuomintang made preparations to relinquish its position as a tutelage party and to inaugurate constitutional government, involved three steps. First, all laws in conflict with the new Constitution had to be repealed or amended. Second, laws had to be drawn up relating to the organization of the National Assembly and the five *yüan,* and to the election and recall of public officials. Third, elections had to be held for delegates to the Assembly and members of the Legislative and Control *Yüan.*

The government began on April 18, 1947, by making revisions of the Organic Law of the National Government. This move did not signal the formal conclusion of political tutelage, but was designed to allow broad participation of non-Kuomintang personnel in the government, as a preliminary step toward constitutionalism. Membership in the Legislative *Yüan,* in the Control *Yüan,* and in the People's Political Council was expanded in order to accommodate minor parties which had participated in formulating the Constitution. The Central Executive Committee of the Kuomintang voted to abolish the Supreme National Defense Council, to make way for a revived Council of State of 40 members. The Council was composed of 17 Kuomintang members, 4 nonpartisans, 4 each from the Young China Party

[23] For a contemporary, but nonetheless incisive analysis, see Roscoe Pound, "The Chinese Constitution," *New York University Law Quarterly Review,* XXII (April, 1947). For text, see Appendix 5.

and the Social Democrats; 11 vacant seats were reserved for Communists and representatives from the Democratic League. The Council of State promptly appointed a new cabinet which included a number of non-Kuomintang ministers. The Military Affairs Commission was abolished and a new Ministry of National Defense was created in its place. The *San Min Chu I* Youth Corps went out of existence, and a Youth Department was created, strictly within the party organization.

Elections for the National Assembly were held in a three-day period beginning November 21, 1947. Two months later the election of members of the Legislative *Yüan* was conducted in accordance with newly adopted electoral laws.

The new National Assembly was convened on March 29, 1948. On April 19, the Assembly elected Chiang Kai-shek President of the Republic (*Tsung-t'ung*). The new Legislative *Yüan* was convened on May 8 and nominated Wêng Wên-hao, a noted geologist, President of the Executive *Yüan*. He then submitted a list of cabinet members who were promptly approved. Establishment of the new constitutional government brought an end to Kuomintang tutelage, which had lasted for twenty years.

The new government was born amidst a civil war of severe intensity, which soon threatened its very survival. Suffice it to say, it did not have a chance for a fair trial. It was forced off the mainland before its first anniversary. Many of its constitutional provisions have therefore become inoperative and most of its agencies have been reduced to skeleton structure. Hence, any attempt here to make a juridical or political appraisal of the government, in light of its constitutional provisions, would serve no practical purpose. The skeletonal structure of the Government of 1948, so far as it affects the island government, will be described in the next chapter, under the appropriate heading of Government Structure in Formosa. It might be said in advance that, from all indications, *government* in Formosa has made remarkable progress—an approximation of a balanced budget, an earnest attempt at land reform, fairly stabilized commodity prices, and a real effort to achieve democratization. From these achievements, credit cannot be given to the equipment—namely, brief experience with constitutional government during 1948—salvaged from the mainland in 1949. Are the improvements due to a change of system or a change of heart? Can members of elected organs on Formosa really claim delegated authority, when their constituents have come under Communist rule?

The Kuomintang Government in transition, from political tutor of the Chinese through brief abdication in favor of constitutional government to prolonged emergency on Formosa, did show one element of continuity. Throughout, the center of political gravity remained close to Chiang Kai-shek. For better or for worse, judgment on the National Government of the past and estimates of its role in the near future will never depart far from his person, his career, and his thought.

The Political Thought of Chiang Kai-shek. The "Generalissimo" is perhaps best known to Westerners by this widely used but inaccurate title.[24] He is actually a Methodist, like his wife, and in his prime he was a good strategist, a master of Western warfare. Perhaps because of these acquired Western characteristics, the destiny of the National Government, linked to him, is regarded as dim by self-styled Asian neutrals. It is ironic that the traits Westerners do not understand are Chinese; and Chiang Kai-shek is predominantly Chinese.

Chiang Kai-shek's political actions and military accomplishments, together with his failures, have been well known to the world at large. They are the subject of a large shelf of political histories, and it is not necessary to review them in a book essentially on governments. On the other hand, his intellectual contributions have been little noted in the West. It is no accident that his political personality and thought have been more understandable to the Chinese.

Marxists have abstracted occasional parts of his thought in order to distort his thinking and to subject the man himself to ridicule. Most non-Marxists in the Western World have appeared to assume that if Chiang Kai-shek stood for democracy, he stood for something close to the reactionary wing of the Grand Alliance, far to the right of the New Deal President or of the Conservative Prime Minister. When Chiang seems neither a compradore capitalist who serves foreign interests nor a sinister warlord who profiteers for his own good, he bewilders many Westerners. They seem to forget that Chiang was dedicated to Sun Yat-sen's peculiar formulation of democracy, and that Sun undertook a sensitive and serious attempt to find a kind of democracy which would be neither Marxist nor American, but characteristically Chinese.

Chiang differs from Sun in that he foreshortens the historical perspective of Sun's thinking. Sun Yat-sen took all mankind to be his province and was willing to deal with universals. He would have challenged St. Thomas Aquinas, had he had the intellectual opportunity to do so. Not so Chiang.

While Sun went back to the foundations of civilization, the nature of progress, the fundamental character of society, and, doctor that he was, China's political illness, Chiang deals primarily with China of the last one-hundred years. Chiang's chief work was his important *Chung-kuo chih ming-yün* (China's Destiny). It is significant that this book was published in Chungking in 1943, but that the Nationalists themselves delayed publica-

[24] Chiang was the Chairman of the Military Affairs Commission *(Wei-yüan-chang)*, as well as Party Chief *(Tsung-ts'ai)* and most recently, President *(Tsung-t'ung)*. Even Kai-shek is only a Cantonese pronunciation, picked up by the Western press, of the name under which he first became well-known, Chiang Chieh-shih. There is really not a sound biography of Chiang, although glimpses of the man come through in various editions of his speeches. The official biography, something like the story-book life of an American Presidential candidate, was written by the Nationalist public relations expert (now Ambassador to Japan from the Republic of China), Hollington K. Tong, *Chiang Kai-shek: Soldier and Statesman*, Shanghai, 1937. A shrewd but highly critical picture is presented by Theodore H. White and Annalee Jacoby, *Thunder Out of China*, New York, 1946.

tion of an English edition until 1947. The book is a frustrating one for Western readers. To most Americans, it is somewhat bitter in tone.[25]

To understand Chiang's thought, it is necessary to realize that he is not a political philosopher, as was Sun, who dabbled occasionally in action, but a man of action, who turned to creative thinking only when the exigencies of very pressing affairs permitted him to do so. Pragmatically, Chiang's thought at any given year was apt to be a reflection of the jobs he had immediately before him. In the 1920's he was the leader of the revolution. In the 1930's he was the patriotic unifier and the leader of national resistance to Japan. In the 1940's he attempted to become the spokesman of China as a world power.

China's Destiny deals with the Chinese revolution in the light of the oppression of China by the capitalist states. The revolution is seen as Sun Yat-sen saw it. It was first of all a struggle between Chinese and foreigners, both the Manchu foreigners, who operated the old Empire, and the European and American foreigners, who operated the new and oppressive world-wide economic system. The unequal treaties—that is, the old treaty arrangements set up by the British, French, Russians, Americans, and others in the mid-nineteenth century—were the chief targets and enemies of Chiang's kind of nationalism. Only in Chapter Six of *China's Destiny* did he reach points which Americans would regard as pertinent to the future, for as he grew older Chiang Kai-shek turned increasingly toward an austere, careful conservatism of philosophy and personal ethics. His "Problems of Revolution and Reconstruction" sounds extremely Chinese to Western ears and singularly out of tune with the kind of world which Roosevelt and Churchill so confidently foresaw at Teheran and Yalta.

Indeed, Chiang Kai-shek turned more and more to the immense store of ethical knowledgeability which can be found in Chinese literature. He left the contemporary European and American scene behind, or *vice versa* as we would put it. Dexterous secretaries could always provide him with suave generalizations, which made it sound as though Chiang himself supported the kind of democracy which Truman, Adenauer, Churchill, or Eisenhower might advocate. Actually, this kind of ideology stands forth as a mild irrelevancy when it is seen through the eyes of Chiang Kai-shek. If people actually have it, so much the better for them. If they do not have it, they might as well wait awhile. The important problem is somewhere else.

What—in the Chiang who is revealed by his own speeches and writings—stands forth as being truly important for China?

By the late 1930's Chiang had already become preoccupied with the fact that the Communists, whose doctrines he regarded as perverted, nevertheless demonstrated a zeal which his own troops did not always manifest. Later

[25] Three translations are available in English. One is Philip Jaffe, *China's Destiny and Chinese Economic Thought,* Roy Publishers, New York, 1947, with very hostile notes and comments. The official version is Wang Ch'ung-hui (translator), *China's Destiny,* with an introduction by Lin Yutang, The Macmillan Company, New York, 1947. A third is Wang Shêng-chih, (translator), *The Destiny of China by Generalissimo Chiang Kai-shek,* Singapore, n.d. [1946?], published by the author.

he was haunted by the wrongness of Japanese thinking, and yet the concomitant success of Japanese military and economic policies. He sought his political refreshment at the very core of human personality, and attempted to work out codes of personal behavior, which would explain both the practical and the metaphysical aspects of political decisions.

It is no easy task for a busy national leader to work out his own metaphysics during the time of a great war and many civil wars. Chiang may or may not have succeeded, from our viewpoint, but after all it is his viewpoint which counts. Many of his answers are at the borderline between religious writing and practical affairs: this borderline is subject to more serious literary and psychological re-examination by Western students and writers in the 1950's than it was in the 1930's.

Chiang is more Asian than Nehru or Yoshida, strangely more truly Asian than many of the political leaders of Asia. Chiang still concentrates on problems of personal incorruptibility. He quotes Chinese ethical essayists, particularly the nineteenth century General Tsêng Kuo-fan, whose brilliant personality contributed so much to the Chinese civilian volunteers, who finally rallied for the salvation of the Empire against the heterodox T'ai-p'ing rebels. Such an outlook is perhaps at once Chiang's strength and his weakness, and is responsible for his successes as well as his failures.

The Nationalist Collapse. One thing is certain. Chiang Kai-shek's outlook alone cannot explain the massive collapse of Nationalist China in 1949. Nor can the shortcomings of the Kuomintang, as a party, alone explain the fall of the mainland. After all, Western liberals and conservatives alike regularly admitted that in the inter-War period and in the crucible of World War II resistance, Czechoslovakia constituted a genuine bright spot in the otherwise gloomy story of the failure of democracy on the continent of Europe. Nevertheless, Czechoslovakia too eventually fell before the tides of authoritarianism.

Nor, fortunately, can one readily prove that the fall of the Nationalists was the product of brilliant tactics and the undeviating adherence of Soviet statesmen to a closed system of thought. The impression grows that there are, in their pattern of operations too, elements of the contingent and of the accidental.[26]

Chiang Kai-shek and the Kuomintang were the latest victims, Mao Tse-tung and the Chinese Communists and the Soviet Union, the hard-working but also fortunate tenants of a revolution within Chinese revolutions. Before them, the T'ai-p'ing rebels, the Boxers and the reformer-intellectuals of the Hundred Days had tried to claim the inheritance. Even Dr. Sun, who first came close to describing the process and, as a professional revolutionary, succeeded in formulating channels for its use, never succeeded in converting revolutionary energy into political power.

[26] This is one of the conclusions of a significant book, by Max Beloff, *Soviet Policy in the Far East, 1944-1951,* London, New York, and Toronto, 1953.

It would be a brave man who would, at this point, try to assess the whole picture of the Nationalist collapse. It would be a brave and unwise political scientist who would attribute the whole course of a society in revolution to political factors. Revolution marks the formal abdication of government, and a forceful moratoria on politics in the ordinary sense too; revolutionaries do not fit into any discipline.

It is hoped that the preceding analysis of National Government may offer some explanations of one corner of the canvas. There was an inherent weakness in the political theory behind the National Government to begin with. No matter how good the tutor, Democracy is *learned* in a democratic atmosphere. No matter how good the tutor, he cannot *learn* his pupils. This is not only ungrammatical; it is logically impossible. Americans particularly tend to be suspicious of political tutelage by an elite. Yet, faced with the same dilemma that Sun and Chiang faced, in the same East Asian area, Americans optimistically substituted the tutelage of the victors, in order to *democratize* the Japanese people, for the more familiar if authoritarian Imperial Japanese Government.

Both the Americans in postwar Japan and the Kuomintang in Nationalist China, must, of course, be held responsible for the manner in which they exercised the power of the podium. The Kuomintang operated as China's teacher so long that, when the time for competition came, it had forgotten how to act as just one other political party. As has been pointed out, there were specific charges of government by personal leadership, by clique, and by corrupt administration. There was also overconfidence.

On the government-to-government level, in the cruel neighborhood of nation-states, the Soviet Union must be held responsible for one more broken promise in a growing list of broken promises. The shortcomings of the domestic Chinese government and the naïveté of that government and its friends in believing the promise cannot obscure the breach. In the Soong-Molotov Agreement of August 14, 1945, the late Soviet ally promised to "render China moral support and assistance with military equipment and other material resources, this support and assistance *to be given fully to the National Government as the Central Government of China.*" The italics were added, after the surrender of Japan, by Russian actions in Manchuria.

Many years will pass before American historians can render a final judgment on the share which United States policy contributed to the fall of the Kuomintang and the disappearance of the National Government of China from the mainland Chinese scene. Somewhat more impatient than historians, Democrats and Republicans alike have argued as though decisions made on the banks of the Potomac had nothing to do, or had everything to do, with the fate of Nationalist China.

It seems possible that as the years pass the importance of the American contribution to the collapse of Nationalist China will increase in its apparent size. No one, conservative or liberal, ever questioned the assumption that vigorous American intervention would have strengthened the Nationalist Government in 1947, 1948, or 1949. American disagreements concerning the fall of China to Communism have arisen over the moot questions: How much aid? How much intervention? How high a price? What kind of support? To whom?[27]

Meanwhile the issues must be left to diplomacy for international purposes and to partisan debate for the ascertainment of future policies. There are some subjects with which scholarship, *qua* scholarship, cannot and should not cope; the immediate past involving facts, most of them clouded with hidden documents and official secrets, impugning and espousing men recently or still living, such as Generals Hurley and Wedemeyer, Stilwell and Marshall, cannot be handled with the intellectual techniques which are valid in describing or assessing the historical roles or political philosophies of the long dead and the far away.[28] A decade, a generation, or a century from now, other Americans may decide the nature of the American contribution to the Chinese Nationalist disaster.

Meanwhile, for Americans and Chinese alike, there is now the more pressing problem of the two Chinas. For there are, of course, both the National Government of China, on Formosa, and the Communist People's Republic, on the mainland. The ideological gap between them is even broader than the Formosan Straits.

[27] One of the contributors to this volume brought up the point that the United States was in no position to measure what it had been doing in China. See Paul M. A. Linebarger, "Outside Pressures on China, 1945-1950," in *Report on China* (H. Arthur Steiner, Ed.), Vol. 277 (September, 1951) of *The Annals of the American Academy of Political and Social Science,* Philadelphia. Another of the contributing authors, admittedly the least expert in Chinese affairs, registers what amounts to a dissent to the main emphasis in the paragraph of the text of this book, above. Without entering the morass of conflicting detail, he feels that "vigorous American intervention," beyond the political intervention of mediation, would have meant sizable military commitment. This was impossible (from an American public's view, enamored by rapid demobilization) and even undesirable (in light of worldwide American commitments). Thus in the continuity of Chinese revolutionary experience, American policy played only a peripheral role.

[28] After Nationalist China fell, one side of the American case was presented by the State Department White Paper on China, officially entitled *United States Relations with China with Special Reference to the Period 1944-1949.* Department of State Publication 3572, Far Eastern Series 30, Division of Publications, Office of Public Affairs, Washington, D. C., released August, 1949. Three years later part of the other side of the case was presented in the McCarran Subcommittee hearings concerning the Institute of Pacific Relations, printed under the general rubric, *Institute of Pacific Relations* (officially denominated *Hearings Before the Subcommittee to Investigate the Administration of the Internal Security Act and other Security Laws of the Committee on the Judiciary, United States Senate, Eighty-second Congress, First Session, on the Institute of Pacific Relations).* Both documents show a tendency to move away from the worrisome complex of reasons for the collapse, within China, and even from the broad issue of policy alternatives before the United States as a whole. Meanwhile, after the pages of this text were written, it was an encouraging sign to see the job of scholarship begun. One of the first dispassionate attempts to begin the telling, and effectively too, is Herbert Feis, *The China Tangle: The American Effort in China from Pearl Harbor to the Marshall Mission,* Princeton, 1953. It is no disadvantage that Dr. Feis was in the Department of State when the fateful events transpired; his former official connections made it possible to interview personally many of those who played in the drama. It is significant that he was not directly responsible for China policy. It is fortunate that Dr. Feis writes with only the motive of intellectual curiosity, whether it be on the Spanish story, oil in the Middle East, the road to Pearl Harbor, or the rough road in China thereafter.

CHAPTER
EIGHT

The National Government of China on Formosa

SIDE by side with the immense mainland Chinese government of the Communists, the National Government of China survived in Formosa—an island which had been Japanese territory for fifty years[1] and which was under a common regime with the rest of China only during the four years, 1945-1949, in the entire twentieth century. (Formosa, the name originally given the island by the Portuguese, has now been generally accepted by the Western World.) Nationalist China is therefore both at home and in exile: to the degree that Taiwan can be considered a portion of China, the National Government still maintains a small, rich, but full segment of the Chinese home territory as "Free China"; to the degree that Taiwan is outside China, the Chinese Nationalists have gone into exile.

On two basic points Chiang Kai-Shek and Mao Tse-tung agree. First, China and Formosa are the same political entity. Second, China, including Formosa, should have only one government. From this point on they disagree, Mao holding that his government is the only government of China, whereas Chiang maintains that before Chinese morality and the comity of nations his regime should be the representative of all China. There are therefore two Chinas in fact and, at the time of writing, there is no immediate prospect that either China will swallow up the other; indeed, there is a fair presumption that the two may survive for years or decades into the future. A peace is more than often a hodgepodge of expedients left over from the last war, awaiting settlement by the next war. Unfortunately the people who look to a "next war" often forget that that war in turn will leave compromises and expedients in its turn.

Viewed affirmatively, it is a great blessing to all Chinese, whether Com-

[1] See pp. 80, 420.

munists or Nationalists, that their country should, if under Communism, have a selected portion of its territory left under non-Communist government for the sake of experimentation and contrast. This way China obtains the benefit of competing and contrasting political experiments, dual representation in the family of nations, and concurrent membership in both the Moscow and Washington groups of nations. No matter what happens in the world one of these two Chinas will emerge among the victors. Although this point of view may be rational, it is not palatable to most of the Chinese at the present time. Chinese Nationalists regret their own downfall and plan a return to power. Chinese Communists demand a free hand in Formosa.

The Flight of the Mainland Nationalists. As the nationalist currency, armies, government, and morale all collapsed together, President Chiang Kai-shek announced his own "withdrawal" from the presidency and went to Hangchow on January 21, 1949. Vice-President Li Tsung-jên took over as "acting president." Subsequent events proved that Chiang's "withdrawal" made it possible for him to return to power, and that Li had never achieved more than the "acting presidency."

This was not the first time that Chiang voluntarily went into retirement as a measure of political strategy with a view to coming back stronger than before. The circumstances of his retirement were obvious. The Chinese Communist Party had demanded peace negotiations on the basis of an eight-point program. Since one of these points required the arrest and prosecution of persons designated as "war criminals" by the Communists—a list comprising almost every influential Nationalist leader or prominent pro-Nationalist sympathizer—it was difficult for Chiang to submit to a Communist arrest, as a pre-condition for a peace to be "negotiated" entirely on Communist terms. Both Peking and Tientsin had fallen into Communist hands.

The Nationalists had proposed that both sides cease fire first and then appoint delegates for peace negotiations; the Communists, adopting in 1949 the position which they were to describe as American atrociousness and perfidy in 1951-52, demanded that peace negotiations be conducted first with a cease fire following later. There was not much hope that peace with the Communists could be obtained on any terms short of a complete Communist victory, but the negotiations had to be attempted. For this, it was necessary for Chiang to step aside. Li took over promptly.

On January 24, Li ordered the abolition of martial law throughout the country, the release of political prisoners, and the end of secret political activities. At the same time the Central Political Council of the Kuomintang decided to evacuate the National Government organization from Nanking to Canton. The long flight of the Nationalists had begun. Unlike the long march of the Communists fifteen years before, the Nationalists' flight was neither purposeful nor orderly. Amid wild turmoil and extreme demoralization some generals salvaged the best of their troops in order to fight on, while others ignominiously abandoned their men and loaded expensive American automobiles instead of Nationalist refugees on the evacuation ships. The ignominy of the Nationalist flight was reported with brutal clarity by the world press, while the pitiable heroism of some Nationalist leaders and soldiers in staying on to the bitter end was overlooked as obstinacy or stupidity. While Chiang was in Hangchow, he almost fell into the trap of one of his trusted lieutenants. He had appointed General Ch'en I chairman of the Chekiang Provincial Government after Ch'en had done miserably in Formosa. He had trusted Ch'en, as he had trusted so many other people, much too long. Ch'en repaid Chiang's loyalty with treason. He plotted to have Chiang kidnapped and to defect to the Communist side. His plot was discovered. Ch'en was arrested, taken to Formosa, tried, and put to death. If Chiang had any idea of living comfortably in retirement, the Ch'en plot must have given him grounds for disquiet. Actually his withdrawal from official duties enabled him to devote more time to the evacuation of the government itself and to the planning of a last stand against the Communists.

On March 15, 1949, the Legislative *Yüan* adopted a resolution to simplify the governmental machinery, leaving the Executive *Yüan* with only eight ministries and two commissions. On April 29 the Executive *Yüan* announced that all governmental departments had been evacuated to Canton, bringing with them only a limited number of government functionaries whose services were considered indispensable. From Canton part of the government departments went to Chungking, hoping to make the great southwestern area of China once more a stronghold for Nationalist resistance, as it had been during the period of the anti-Japanese war. Before the Nationalists could stabilize their regime in Chungking the Communist armies won sweeping victories on the mainland. According to Western sources Chiang Kai-shek was almost out of his mind with grief and rage as he attempted to make the outnumbered and demoralized Nationalist units turn and fight at Chungking; his personal staff almost had to drag him into an airplane in order to avoid Communist capture. The fall of Szechuan province left only one really secure retreat, Formosa.

Theoretically Chiang's retirement from the Presidency did not release him from the duties of acting as *Tsung-ts'ai* of the Kuomintang. In practical terms he had never relinquished control of political and military affairs during his "withdrawal." Acting president Li was reported to have raged, wept, and sulked before he became both genuinely and diplomatically ill and came to the United States for treatment. Almost disregarding Li, Chiang established his own office as Party Chief of the Kuomintang in Taipeh, Taiwan, on August 1, 1949. It was as *Tsung-ts'ai,* not as President, that Chiang went to the Philippines to confer with President Quirino and to Korea to confer with President Rhee. Not until February 28, 1950, when acting president Li refused to return to Formosa from his voluntary exile and new-found security in New York did Chiang resume the office of Presidency.[2]

Kuomintang Reform from Formosa. The first thing which the Kuomintang strove to do after its retreat to Formosa was to undertake a thorough reform of the party itself. The loosening of its organization, lack of discipline, and loss of revolutionary spirit were quite evident; they had contributed to its failure in the struggle with the highly organized and disciplined Communist Party. For years the Kuomintang had been torn by unauthorized actions. It was an obvious step to attempt the recreation of some kind of real party unity.

In order to carry out basic party reform Chiang acted in his role of Party Chief of the Kuomintang and appointed two committees on July 26, 1950, the Supervisory Committee and the Reform Committee.[3]

The Supervisory Committee consisted of twenty-five members selected from among veteran party leaders. Its function was to supervise the execution of the reform plan.

The Reform Committee also consisted of twenty-five members, but only sixteen of them were appointed, leaving the rest to be chosen later from among party leaders representing women, overseas Chinese, and frontier races or tribes. The members appointed were mostly middle-aged men of experience in various fields. The function of the Reform Committee was to carry out a basic plan of reform. The plan of reform itself was to be the work of the Committee. The Committee was given very wide powers. During the unspecified period of reform the regular Central Executive Committee and Supervisory Committee of the Party were suspended; all their powers were transferred to the Reform Committee.

The Reform Committee was to work according to the reform plan and was to organize all the provincial and other local branches of the party. The Reform Committee had four subcommittees dealing with finance, planning, discipline, and training affairs. It was announced that, when the reform work of the whole party was accomplished, a Party Congress (*Ch'üan-kuo tai-piao ta-hui*) would be called.

Kuomintang party congresses were not a common feature of the Nationalist political system between 1924 and 1952. Only six had been held, plus an emergency party congress at Hankow in 1938 and a bogus party congress made up of the followers of Wang Ching-wei when that unfortunate gentleman elected himself quisling president of China. The Seventh National Party Congress was held on October 10, 1952, in Taipeh. The meeting marked the end of the twenty-seven-month Kuomintang Reform Movement. The Congress elected thirty-two members to the Central Executive Committee to take the place of the Central Reform Committee. In addi-

[2] Chiang was re-elected *Tsung-ts'ai* in Taipeh, the latest occasion being the seventh plenary session of the party, October 19, 1952. See subsequent text.

[3] *Chinese News Service,* NN-L-2, New York, August 15, 1950.

tion, the Congress named forty-eight party elders and others as advisers. The session was attended by two hundred party delegates representing various provinces and municipalities on the mainland and overseas Chinese party members. Obviously, only delegates representing overseas Chinese were elected. Of the 52 delegates, 32 came from Asia, 18 from North and South America, one from Europe, two from Africa, and two from Australia.[4]

The obligations of the Reform Committee were well described by Ts'ui Shu-ch'in, himself a member of the Committee, and a political scientist, in the following terms:

> Realizing that it has made many blunders in the past, the Party now decides to change its way in doing things. In particular, it will encourage all its members to study the history of the Party and the revolutionary principles, to participate in Party activities and observe Party discipline, to try to inspire confidence of the masses of the people in the Party by merging with them and making them understand and support the principles and policies of the Party, to increase administrative efficiency, and to eliminate all factional prejudices so that a comradely spirit of cooperation can be developed. . . .
>
> During the period of tutelage, the Kuomintang assumed the sole responsibility for the governing of the country. Having entered the constitutional period, it has to play a somewhat different role. Though it still is the largest party in free China, yet it cannot control the government in such a way as it used to. It can only play the role of an ordinary political party. In view of this, the reform has to provide for the regulation of the relations between the party and the government. The central, provincial and local parties will decide upon the policies for the central, provincial and local government respectively, and entrust their execution to the members of the people's assemblies elected and the government officials appointed with the support of the party. This does not mean that the party has the right to interfere directly with the official duties of these party members. They are merely required to see that the people's assemblies legislate according to the policies of the party or that the governments adopt them as their official policies.[5]

Legislation and Representation. In point of practical politics as opposed to legal theory, the Nationalists had a double problem of representation as soon as they established themselves on Formosa. They had, during their twenty years of power on the mainland, often been criticized for failure to install representative government. Much of the defection of the independents and intellectuals to the Communists had been expedited because of a feeling that the Kuomintang represented no one but itself. Even when this was not the case there was enough bitterness left in the long-standing

[4] *Chinese News Service,* NN-L2-45, New York, November 4, 1952.

[5] "Reform of the Kuomintang," *Modern China Monthly,* Taipeh, No. 1 (October, 1950), pp. 24-26.

criticism to make any easy remedy impossible. The Nationalists had to try to provide representation for something more than a handful of Nationalist bureaucrats and military officers, if they were ever to win the respect of China and to draw to themselves on Formosa the moral allegiance of the Chinese people. At the same time it was necessary for them to provide a reasonable local representative system so that the Taiwanese, the actual Chinese families domiciled for generations or centuries on the island, would not feel themselves excluded from the government which had settled itself amid them without so much as a by-your-leave.

In the turmoil of evacuation and torment of political choice, a great many of the mainland members of the Legislative *Yüan* remained behind. The elected legislators of 1948 were supposed to serve a term of three years ending in April, 1951. Fortunately, the National Assembly had granted the President emergency powers on April 18, 1948, and the tenure of the elected legislators on Formosa was finally prolonged by presidential fiat in 1950.

Subsequent events were to demonstrate that this was in fact a turn for the better. Taiwan is a very beautiful island comparable to Hawaii. While it was a part of the Japanese Empire, it regularly contributed a rich surplus of foodstuffs to the Japanese economy. The Nationalists had very badly abused the island when they first took over from the Japanese, and the bitterness of the local Taiwanese against the mainland refugees was extremely sharp. In the light of subsequent experience it is possible to look back to 1950 and to appreciate the fact that the Nationalists made a real change in their own fortunes by housecleaning within their own political structure. From September, 1950, onward, conditions had been steadily improved. Expenses for the armed forces had been cut. Excessive military units had been disbanded. The President of the Executive *Yüan,* Ch'en Ch'êng, reported in 1950 that 82 units of the government had been abolished or amalgamated. The entire executive establishment of the National Government had been cut to 874 persons, one ninth of the original staff. A budgetary balance was also sought through an increase in production and in rationalization of the tax system. Starting in 1950 the Nationalists escaped the disastrous pattern of inflation which had contributed so much to their ruin on the mainland. Ch'en Ch'êng said, "In the last six months the government neither relied on the printing press nor on the introduction of new taxes to meet its financial needs." [6]

Government Structure on Formosa. The National Government on Formosa claims legitimacy within the framework of the Constitution promulgated on January 1, 1947; its structure is an emergency model of the Government of 1948 (see pages 177-178); its operations are confined by the territory under its control.

The position of the President, under the system established in 1948, was quite different from that of the Chairman of the old National Government.

[6] *Chinese News Service,* NI-L-6, New York, October 11, 1950.

His actions were not subject to the restraints of the party. Only in a limited sense was he made responsible to the Legislative *Yüan*. Aside from the usual powers pertaining to the chief executive of a state, he was given rather wide emergency powers which were provided by the Constitution. The National Assembly on April 18, 1948, one day before it elected the President, voted emergency power to the President-to-be for the duration of the struggle against the Communist rebellion.

The Organic Law of the President's Office was adopted by the Legislative *Yüan* on March 25, 1948. The President's Office was organized along the same lines as the former Office of Aides to the Chairman of the Military Affairs Commission. As a matter of fact, a great part of the personnel of the old establishment was transferred to the new organization. The President's Office was composed of a Chief of Staff's Office and a Secretary General's Office. Under the latter were six bureaus dealing with secretarial functions, confidential matters, military matters, protocol, archives, and general affairs. (See Chart 6.)

The Executive *Yüan* differed from the old *Yüan* in that, to a certain extent, it was made responsible to the Legislative *Yüan*. Not only was the appointment of the President of the Executive *Yüan* subject to the approval of the Legislative *Yüan*, but he was obliged to submit to legislative interpellation.

The new Legislative *Yüan* was also entirely different from its predecessor. Its members were elected instead of appointed. Unlike leaders of the old organ, the President and Vice-President were elected from among its members. Instead of being a law-drafting bureau, which the old *Yüan* could be properly called, the new Legislative *Yüan* was to initiate legislation, review the national budget, interpellate ministers, make independent investigations, and, in general, exercise genuine control over the bureaucracy.[7]

The Control *Yüan* was also retooled as a representative body. Its members were to be elected by provincial and municipal assemblies for a period of six years. Its President and Vice-President were also to be elected from among its members. According to the new Constitution, the Control *Yüan* was to exercise powers of consent, impeachment, censure, and audit.

The Examination *Yüan* was given a President, a Vice-President, and nineteen Examination Commissioners, each with a six-year term of office.

The Judicial *Yüan* was to be composed of a Council of Grand Justices, a Supreme Court, an Administrative Court, and a Disciplinary Commission. The Council of Grand Justices, a newly created organ, was to have seventeen members appointed by the President of the Republic with the consent of the Control *Yüan*. The Grand Justices were vested with the power to interpret the Constitution and to unify the interpretation of laws and decrees.

To say the least, both the Constitution of 1947 and the Government of

[7] See George E. Taylor, "A New Look at Formosa," *The Atlantic Monthly*, Vol. 191, No. 4 (April, 1953).

1948 are now largely in hibernation. It soon became apparent that having a full-fledged five-*yüan* government on Formosa is a luxury, more than the economy of the island can bear. Most of the central government agencies try very hard to create a semblance of dignified activity. Nevertheless, to speak of freedom of domicile as a civil right or of relations between central and local governments as a real problem, at the moment is to indulge in academic discussion. The Republic is still in a state of emergency, which calls for extraordinary measures.

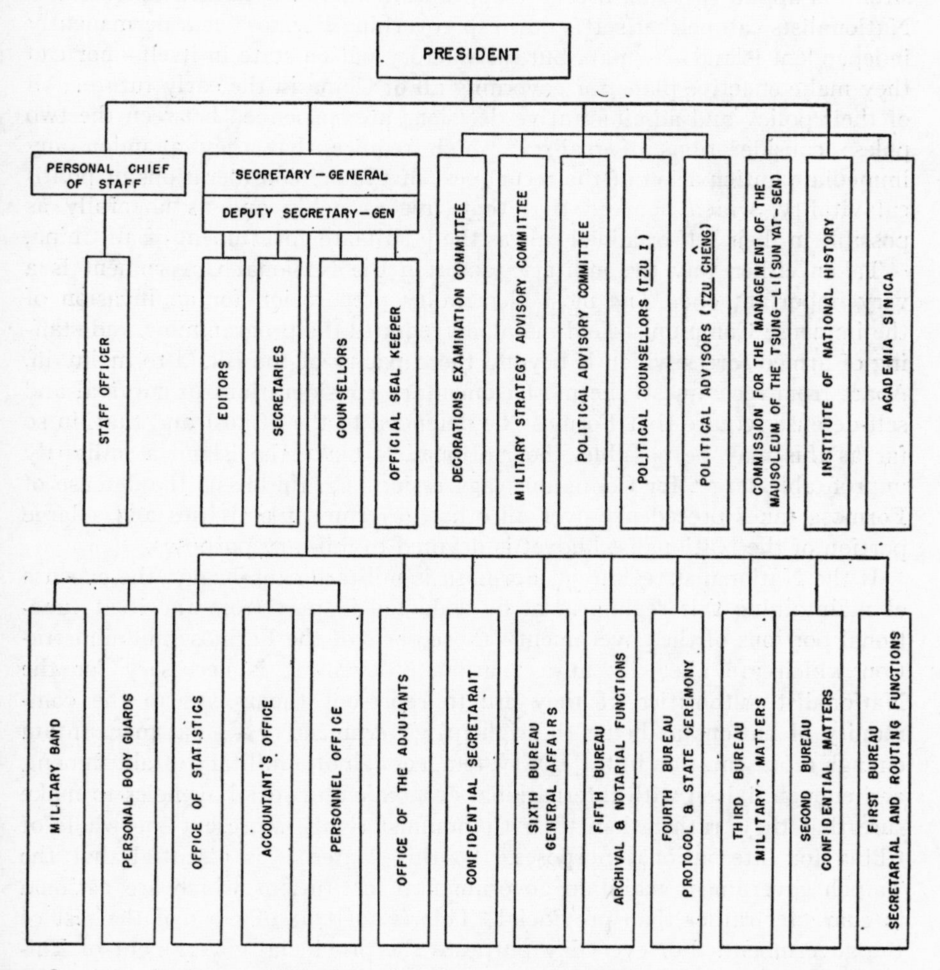

Source: A chart published in the Chinese Central Daily News (Chung Yang Jih Pao) March 26, 1948. Nanking.

Note: The organic law of the office of the president was adopted by the Legislative Yüan on March 25, 1948.

CHART 6—Organization of the Office of the President

Policy and Administration in Formosa. The Nationalists are at a disadvantage in contrast to their Communist antagonists in the matter of what can be called a "sense of permanence" permeating their institutions of government. The Chinese People's Republic on the mainland may not consider the unification of China complete until the Nationalist remnant on Formosa is subdued and destroyed, but the Communists need not be restrained by considerations of temporariness or short-range uncertainty merely because they possess only the mainland and not the island; the converse of this situation applies with unfortunate appropriateness to the Nationalists. The Nationalists can neither settle down to governing Formosa as a permanently independent island—a small, but satisfactory nation-state in itself—nor can they make effective plans for governing all of China in the early future. All of their policy and administrative decisions are suspended between the two poles: considerations of realism, which require that they abandon any immediate anticipation of the reconquest of China; considerations of political vitality, which demand that they live as nobly and as hopefully as possible in their self-ordained rule as the legitimate government of all China.

Taken either way the military factor in the National Government is a very important one. The most elementary preparation for an invasion of the immense Communist-held mainland requires the programming and staffing of armed forces which is beyond the capacity of the island to maintain. Apart from reconquest, the most elementary considerations of survival and self-defense require that Formosa be defended to the utmost and that, in so far as this may be possible, the Nationalists make the island a militarily unprofitable target for Communist aggression. On this basis the defense of Formosa takes precedence over all other government activities and a large portion of the Nationalist budget is devoted to military purposes.

If the Nationalist regime on Formosa is militarily top-heavy, the expense of maintaining this regime must be deducted in part from the least functional portions of the government—those parts of the Formosan administration which are allegedly at a "national" level. It is necessary for the Nationalist authorities, if they are to represent themselves to the community of nations as being the rightful government of China, to maintain enough representation in the UN system, enough of a military establishment, and enough liaison with international economic and social agencies to make sure that they, rather than their Communist rivals, represent the whole of China for international purposes. To this degree it is essential that the Taipeh government maintain governmental institutions which are national in character rather than provincial. This is not true of most of the rest of the government. For everyday purposes the provincial government of Taiwan can meet almost every reasonable governmental need posed by the island's population, whether aborigines, settled Chinese, or newcomers. In the years since 1949 the National Government of China has been trimmed down very sharply so that it is for many purposes a skeleton organization ready to be reactivated if the Nationalists ever return by force of arms to the mainland.

The simplified structure of the Chinese government in Taiwan is shown in Chart 7. Many of the old mainland offices such as the Tibetan and Mon-

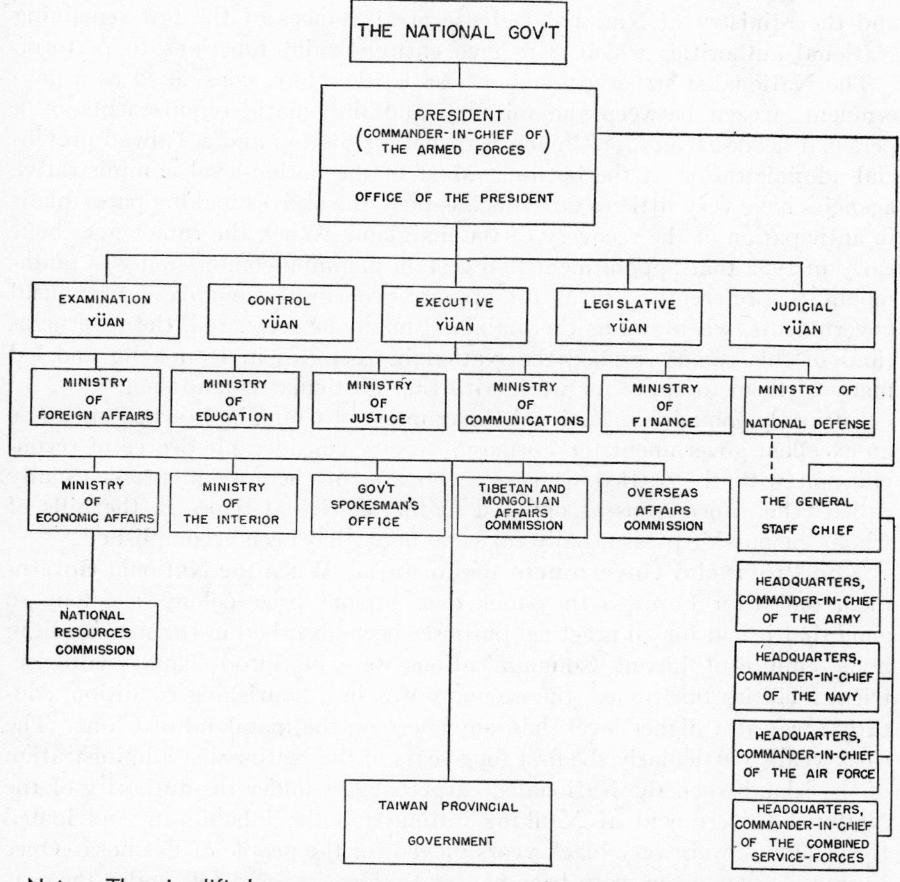

Note: The simplified government structure was based on a resolution adopted by the emergency session of the Legislative Yüan held in Canton on March 15, 1949.
The fundamental organization remained the same, but many comparatively less important activities and commissions were abolished.

CHART 7—Simplified Structure of the Chinese Government of Taiwan

golian Affairs Commission have nothing to do on the island itself, except to maintain a handful of anti-Communist refugees and to dabble with espionage or subversion whenever these are not too expensive. Other agencies such as the Ministry of Education, the Ministry of Communication, the Ministry of the Interior, and the like can continue to exist and function by duplicating the corresponding facilities of the Taiwan provincial government. Only a very few of the organs of the National Government of China have specifically applicable functions to perform which are neither well-suited to the Taiwan provincial government, nor vestigial because of the removal of the Nationalist authorities from the mainland. The Ministry of Foreign Affairs and the Ministry of National Defense are instances of the few remaining National authorities which still have entirely valid functions to perform.

The Nationalist structure on Formosa is, therefore, considered as a government, frozen between the military and diplomatic requirements of a personal headquarters for Chiang Kai-shek at the top and a Taiwan provincial administration at the bottom. Most of the nation-level administrative agencies have very little to do. Officials busy themselves making paper plans in anticipation of the recovery of the mainland. When the rumor got about early in 1952 that appointment to a certain planning commission was tantamount to preferential status for appointment in the mainland provincial governments, when and as the mainland might be recovered, the reverberations of this rumor reached the Nationalist émigrés in Hongkong and led many of them to apply for work with that particular commission.[8]

Curiously enough the National Government of China had turned out to be an excellent government for Formosa. A very considerable degree of reconciliation with the settled Chinese—who are, in the foreign press, usually called "the" Formosans as opposed to the aboriginal tribes in the hills of whom the outside press usually takes no note—has been accomplished.

The Provincial Government of Formosa. When the National Government took over Formosa they took over Japan's prize colony, a colony so good that it had for all practical purposes been absorbed in the metropolitan home empire of Japan. Communications were in tiptop shape, hydroelectrical facilities functioned, the economy was in a flourishing condition, education was at a higher level than anywhere on the mainland of China. The early years, particularly the first four years of the Nationalist administration of the island when the Nationalist carpetbaggers under the authority of the National Government at Nanking intimidated the inhabitants and looted the economy, were very black years indeed for the people of Formosa. Once Formosa became the main base of the Nationalists and fell under the personal scrutiny of Chiang Kai-shek and his immediate aides, conditions began to improve. There is no doubt that a very genuine increase in the welfare and security of the island has been made since 1949.

One of the most marked areas of improvement is in the field of local administration. The Nationalists accommodated themselves to the local environment by making possible a very substantial degree of self-rule on the part of the *hsien* (counties) and *shih* (municipalities). In April, 1950, the Executive *Yüan* approved a set of general rules for *hsien* and municipal

[8] Pu Shao-fu, "On the Bank of the Tan-shui River," *Hsin Wen T'ien Ti (Newsdom)*, Hongkong, No. 167, pp. 4-6.

self-government, specifying that the program be carried out within a specific time in different parts of the island. In August, 1950, the Executive *Yüan* approved the Program for the Readjustment of the *Hsien* and Municipal Governments of Taiwan; this administrative act divided the province into 16 *hsien* and 5 municipalities, replacing a previous pattern of 5 *hsien* and 9 municipalities. Through this readjustment the area, population, and wealth of each subordinate administrative unit has been brought closer to a common and uniform standard, thus facilitating the realization of self-rule. (Chart 8 shows the organization of provincial Taiwan.)

For the enforcement of city or county self-government, the city or county

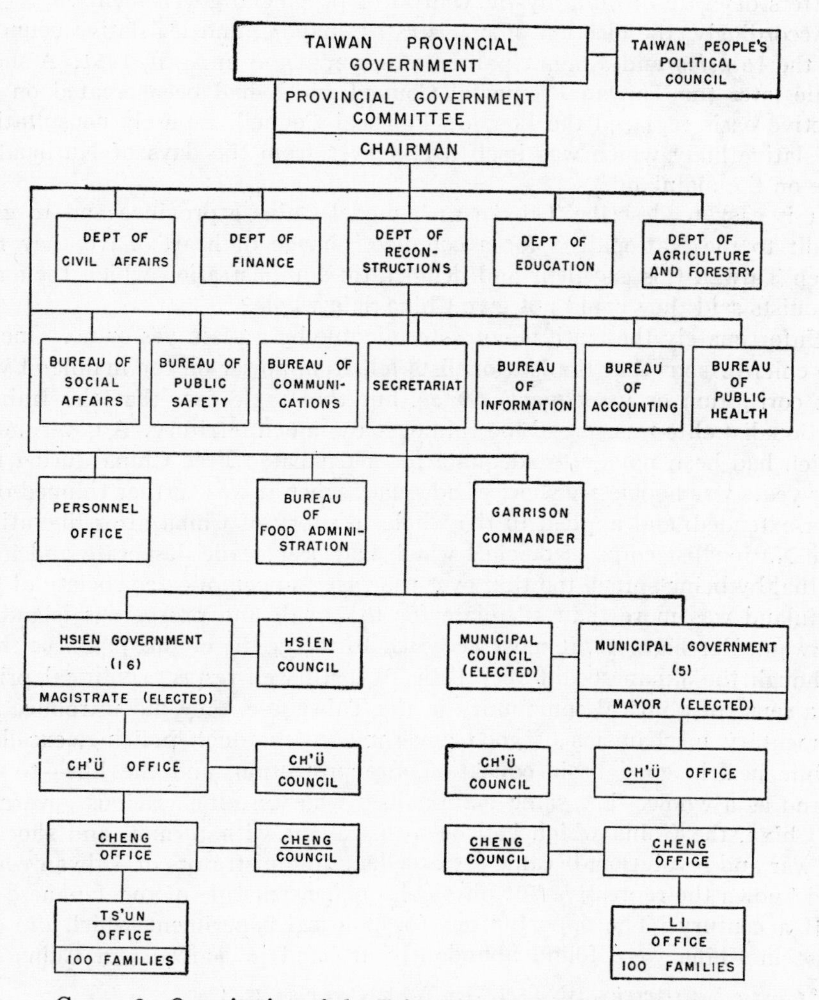

CHART 8—Organization of the Taiwan Provincial Government 1950

convened its own assembly and enacted a self-government law. Considerable latitude was allowed for this law so long as the enactment did not contervene the national constitution or the provincial self-government law of Taiwan. In most cities and counties a popularly elected council had moved into full exercise of the legislative power. The constitution stipulates that the people in the city or county shall, in accordance with law, exercise the rights of initiative and referendum in matters pertaining to city or county self-government, as well as the rights of election and recall of the magistrate and other self-government officers. The city or county is also provided with an elected mayor or magistrate to whom is given the executive authority in enforcing the local self-government as well as the routine administration matters delegated to him by the central or provincial governments.

Accordingly, the election of magistrates, mayors, and legislative councils for the 16 *hsien* and 5 municipalities was completed in April, 1951. A short while later the Taiwan Provincial Council which had been created on an elective basis replaced the People's Political Council, a purely consultative legislative body which was itself a hangover from the days of Nationalist rule on the mainland.[9]

It is easy to describe Taiwan as a model Chinese province and to give credit to the Nationalists for a complete change of heart: have they not given Taiwan this excellent and democratic administration which their antagonists said they could not give China as a whole?

Unfortunately the truth is not determinable by a plain yes or no. One of the chief reasons that the Nationalists fell from power on the mainland was not corruption or inadequacy *per se,* but the tragic fact that the trained Nationalist elite was spread too thin over too much territory. A government which had been not quite adequate for a truncated Free China during the war years was hopelessly short of adequacy when it was further thinned out, over-extended, and applied to the whole territory of China after liberation. The Nationalist corps of officials which had been made desperate and ineffectual by being spread too thin over the vast and complicated society of the mainland was more than adequate for the small and prosperous island of Taiwan. Furthermore, it must be noted to the credit of the Japanese that, although the Japanese did very little to instill self-respect, political pride, or a sense of political community in the Taiwanese, they did introduce the elementary mechanisms of good government—thorough policing, excellent public health, good basic education, fire protection, and the like—to the island as a whole. The same Nationalists who were inefficacious governors of China, the China which had been distraught with turmoil and shocked by war and revolution, became the excellent administrators of Taiwan which had known the repressive but physically beneficent rule of the Japanese for half a century. The opportunities for political experiment which did not exist in China were found abundantly at hand in Taiwan: in China the

[9] *Chinese News Service,* NN-L-21, New York, December 27, 1950.

Nationalists could not be both humane and experimental, since experiment required authority, authority demanded power, power required the use of arbitrariness and even of terror upon occasion, and the Nationalists were too good, in the wishy-washy sense of the term "good," to lead a revolution. The Nationalists had become Neckers when they should have been Marats, but on Taiwan the season for Neckers or Lafayettes had not yet passed and the term for Marats and Robespierres had not yet arrived.

The Nationalists' political success on Taiwan is therefore no proof that they would have had a comparable success had they remained in power in mainland China. Neither is it a disproof. It is instead a political experience of a wholly noncomparable and different order indeed. The Formosan reforms of the Nationalists went through because the Nationalists were able to concentrate their talented officials and because the people of Taiwan had been rendered humble and docile by a full half-century of very drastic Japanese benevolence—a Japanese administration which did their bodies good at the price of their political souls, a kind of colonialism which encouraged health and literacy, but savagely refused countenance to the most elementary pretentions toward irredentism or independence.[10]

Land Reform in Formosa. In 1952 the National Government of China in Formosa finally asked a grandiose hypothetical question: What should the Nationalists do about the Communist land distribution on the mainland when and if the Nationalists took power on the mainland again? Should the Nationalists attempt to restore all the old landlords to their previous titles? Should they instead confirm the titles conferred by the Communists, who from the Nationalist point of view were bandits or rebels? The solution was ethically admirable although not very relevant to the immediate course of affairs. The Nationalists decided to leave all new landholders who had been put in possession of land by virtue of Communist ownership titles undisturbed in their new situation, but to compensate the landlords out of public funds without cost to the tenants.

It was not possible for the Nationalists to reach any such simple solution in Formosa. Even fifty years of Japanese colonialism had not modified the landlord and tenant relationship. Formosa was little better than the rest of

[10] It is worth noting that the people of the ancient kingdom of Liuchiu, now called Okinawa and administered by the United States as a U.N. strategic trust territory, have shown the same kind of amiable submission to their American conquerors that the people of Formosa have shown to their Nationalist conquerors. The Chinese part of the Formosan population, itself an overwhelming majority, attempted some mild remonstrance against the worst malpractices of National rule. This was in the period when the National Government was still in Nanking and remonstrance was met with massacre and police terrorism of an unpleasant kind. Once the ebullience of liberation had passed the Formosans have been as submissive as the Okinawans. It would be easy for American liberals or Chinese Communists to shed crocodile tears over the oppression of the Formosans by the Nationalists, just as it would be easy for the Moscow radio to sympathize with the Okinawans whose small but proud and self-sufficient kingdom has become nothing more than an American airbase complete with suburbs. A dispassionate observer would not be apt to detect much political *Weltschmerz* in either of these areas as long as the process of government remained fairly dependable.

South China in the matter of the exaction of an undue share of the produce of the land by landlords. Under the traditional tenancy system, which was not very different from the land tenure arrangements of the province of Fukien, many tenant farmers paid more than 50 per cent of their total harvest to their landlords. This was done not by virtue of any island-wide standard procedure. These arrangements were reached by virtue of individual leases and contracts. In the negotiation of such leases and contracts the tenant was often at a disadvantage, since the landlord could pick that time of year at which the tenant was most destitute. In some cases land rents went as high as 70 per cent of the gross produce of the land. Furthermore, the tenant farmers did not enjoy security even within the framework of their tenancy, since the land owners could repossess land at any time on demand. Security deposits demanded by the landlords were sometimes twice the yearly rental. These and comparable practices made the livelihood of the Taiwanese farmer both difficult and precarious.

The Nationalists faced this situation as soon as the National Government moved to the island. Chiang and his chief lieutenants realized that if they were ever to stand a chance of recouping power on the mainland it would be necessary for them to make the Nationalist zone on the island a showcase of economic and political democracy, and that it was up to them to effect an equitable solution of the Taiwanese land problem before Communist agents began stirring up the local peasants and before Communist mainland propaganda derided them as oppressors who could not even repair the malpractices of a small island.

As early as April, 1950, the provincial government of Taiwan adopted a series of regulations governing the reduction of land rental to the maximum rate of 37.5 per cent of the total yield of the land. This in the time-honored Chinese practice was put into immediate legal effect. In practice the method of administration determined whether this reform was to remedy the lot of the Formosan peasant or not. The Nationalists gave every appearance of intending to administer this law seriously and wisely.

In enforcing the "37.5 per cent maximum" rental system the authorities specifically provided that land rent was not to exceed the prescribed maximum percentage of crop yields. Original contract rentals exceeding the limit were to be reduced to the specified ceiling; rates lower than the maximum were frozen at the contract level. The amount of regular crop harvested in each crop period was to be decided by special local committees for the promotion of the new land rental reduction measure. Furthermore, the reform prescribed that land contracts be fixed for a period of three to six years so the tenants could enjoy security. All leases were to be recontracted in accordance with the new regulations.

Besides reducing high rentals, the land reform measures cut the amount of security deposits. These were restricted to a maximum of one-fourth of the total annual rental. The traditional "iron rent" (wherein tenants paid up no matter what happened, even accepting the risks of famine, typhoon, crop disease, or other failure) was abolished, along with special rentals on such separate items as pigs or poultry. Rent prepayment was forbidden.

This rural phase of land reform, concentrating on the reduction of land rental to a maximum of 37½% of the main annual crop yield, was followed in 1951 by the sale of public lands to tenant farmers in 1951. Terms were easy.

In 1953, the land-to-the-tiller program was inaugurated. Excess arable land was purchased from the owners and resold to tenants on ten-year installments.

Results were discernible in hard economics, not just morale. The crop output increased; so did farm capital. By 1956 the provincial government ventured to make census-taking and urban land measures the most importhat fiscal measures for 1956-1957.[11] The essence of this program was implementation, at long last, of some of the Henry George doctrines incorporated as the single-tax features of the Sunyatsenist teachings.

(Western observers sometimes argue that reforms on Formosa would of themselves constitute a psychological force against Communism in China. In so doing, they underestimate the screen of distortion which the Communist regime has set up. Reforms help Formosa's standing with the outside world.)

Labor Insurance. The steps taken by the National Government toward improving the welfare of labor on the island of Formosa are elementary by American standards, but revolutionary by Chinese standards. The number of skilled workers involved was only up in the 300,000's for the entire province, but the Nationalists, acutely self-conscious in view of their special role in promoting their kind of revolution as against the revolution of the Communists, have done everything which they, as Chinese and as Nationalists, were able to contrive to improve the livelihood and health of the workers on the island. Mediation and arbitration facilities for the avoidance of labor disputes were set up in fact. All public and private enterprises and factories employing 20 or more workers fell under the jurisdiction of special labor insurance regulations promulgated by the provincial government. The insurance provisions cover such contingencies as injury, disability, the birth of children, the death of the insured, and old age retirement. The premium for each such insurance policy was 3 per cent of the worker's monthly wage.

[11] The *Chinese News Service,* New York, NN-LVI-27, July 3, 1956, top page, outlines this program as stated by the provincial governor, C. K. Yen. A vehemently pro-Chiang but first-hand account of Taiwanese reform is to be found in Geraldine Fitch, *Formosa Beachhead,* Chicago, 1953, especially at pp. 195–210. The urban land reform program preserved private ownership for use, but struck at ownership for speculation by imposing 30% to 90% assessments on increments in land value. Sun Yat-sen's cherished little tax trick was imposed at last; an owner assessing his own property more than 20% below the government's estimate will find that he has given the government an irrevocable option on the land at his stated price. The actual tax on urban land, as opposed to the tax on unearned increment, was kept within moderate limits—between 1.5% and 6.5%. Nationalist China has always been a socialist country on paper. In Taiwan the economic socialism is probably more comprehensive than it is in Britain under the Labor government. A model ex-colony almost invites experimentation.

The worker himself paid only one fifth of the premium, three fifths being contributed by the employer and the remaining one fifth out of undistributed public funds. The worker's share is therefore *pro rata* lower than in Britain or America.[12]

The Survival Factor in Formosa. While the Nationalists have been able to carry out in Formosa many of the reforms which they planned but were unable to execute while holding authority on the mainland, their long-run survival as a competitive government in the Chinese theme depends first upon their capacity to retain some degree of external military protection and external diplomatic recognition from the anti-Communist powers, and in the liability of the island economy itself. Even the American Seventh Fleet would not be much protection to Chiang and to his associates if Formosa were to go hopelessly bankrupt with the result that scattered peasant insurrections, general strikes, and major Communist infiltration threw Taiwan into an uproar.

The question of the Nationalist survival is therefore a double-barreled problem:

First, can the Nationalists affiliate themselves with the anti-Communist defense system and remain valuable enough in that defense system to warrant their retention in the face of Peking's hostility?

Secondly, can the Nationalists make the island of Formosa prosper sufficiently to afford a real contrast to the economic conditions developed under Communist control on the mainland?

For each of these questions, the base period 1945-1949 was extremely unpromising. The Nationalists had little either in political purpose or in administrative performance which compelled the outside powers to come to their aid. The Japanese, ably engulfed in the problems of the occupation, were unable to do anything whatever about Mao's rise to power. Even the well-wishers of the Nationalists sometimes doubted whether the Nationalist political experiment could continue in the years 1945-1949 in the face of chronic and irremedial inflation, sustained military defeats, and economic programs insanely out of touch with the country's current requirements. In their last year of control in the city of Shanghai, the Nationalists succeeded in estranging the most conservative members of the British and American capitalist business community, since even in the shadow of defeat the Nationalists insisted on chauvinistic and impractical economic regulations, which strangled the little business that survived the turmoil of foreign occupation and domestic war.

The Nationalists' economic failure may have been the result of overextension into the vast areas of China liberated from Japanese occupation in 1945, complicated by the pitiless economic warfare of the Communists. No matter what the extenuations were, the economic failure was real—and it was bitter.

[12] A dispassionate account of the Nationalist rule in Formosa is given in F. W. Riggs, *Formosa under Chinese Nationalist Rule,* New York, 1952.

The Nationalists were hated before they fell, hated because they failed to offer security or hope to peasants, workers, merchants, or intellectuals. The number of people who felt assured in their livelihoods as a result of the Nationalist political control dwindled in the last Nationalist years on the mainland to a tiny handful of the Nationalist inner circle. Only those members of the middle class or of the skilled working class who had themselves suffered the penalties of living under Communist rule preferred the Nationalists with all their faults, as of 1949 and 1950.

In contrast, the Nationalists offered a much more promising record for the base period 1950-1956. The excruciating faults—both of commission and omission—which characterized their regime in its last months on the mainland have been in great part eradicated in Taiwan. Corruption, which even on the mainland was badly exaggerated, had dwindled to the vanishing point. (Parenthetically, it may be noted that corruption was an important demerit of the Nationalists at the end of their mainland period, not because corruption *per se* occurred on an immense scale or was damaging to the Chinese economy, but because the economy as a whole was so wretched, so demoralized, so insecure, so capriciously unjust that the Nationalist corruption stood forth as a glaring fault.) The endless succession of inflated currencies, first the national dollars, and the so-called Customs units, then the new gold dollars themselves, all of them inflating with nightmarish speed and insecurity, have disappeared into the limbo of lost fiat money; there is no Nationalist Chinese currency as such. The only money which the Nationalists use is a modest and relatively stable provincial currency for the province of Taiwan. This currency has inflated much less than has the Japanese *yen* and actually bears comparison with the Okinawan *yen* issued by the American authorities on the adjacent Okinawa island.

The Nationalist efforts to restore the island economy were successful in general—almost as successful as their efforts to restore the mainland economy had been unsuccessful. Very intelligently, the Nationalists met the need for the foodstuffs for the additional population by effecting a double production of wheat only in their occupation of the island. The unbalanced economy, although persistent, is not as serious when measured in terms of the United States dollar. Sugar, rice, pineapples and pineapple products, tea, and camphor have been among the major exports of Formosa. Imports into the island have come chiefly from Japan through bilateral trade agreements and from the United States under economic and military aid. Formosa is, therefore, a perilous outpost of constitutional democracy—perilous and not altogether representative. The orderliness and welfare of its people depend as much upon their Japanese colonial tutelage as upon the benefits brought them by the good features of the Nationalist regime. No matter how much the self-government may develop, the military exigencies of a small island threatened by immensely superior mainland Chinese Communist armies requires the sustained application of intense police methods. Travel into the island and out of it is made under the most elaborate guarantees. The Nationalists realize that with one Communist coup everything would be lost. They are resolved that no Communist coup shall take place. The repression of unpopular opinion is at a wartime level. It is much easier for exiled anti-Communist Chinese to be demonstrative, opinionated, articulate, and politically active in British Hongkong or British Singapore than in Formosa.

The prestige of the National Government on Formosa goes up with every military and diplomatic reverse suffered by the Communists at Peking or in the field in Korea. In 1952 and 1953, the Nationalists made major efforts long overdue to recapture the effective leadership of the overseas Chinese world.[13] It was from overseas China that the Nationalist revolution first entered China under the leadership of Sun Yat-sen and the leverage of Overseas China upon China proper is not, even in the middle of the twentieth century, to be discounted.

Under the Constitution of 1947, Chiang Kai-shek's term of office as the President of the Republic expired in 1954. The First National Assembly, which had elected him in 1948, was reconvened as far as possible in February, 1954. It effectively represented most if not all of non-Communist China. The second session of the reconvened assembly, under the provisional chairmanship of Dr. Hu Shih, duly elected Chiang as President for a second term of six years, impeached and removed Vice President Li Tsung-jên when Li refused to come home from New York, and elected General Chên Chêng to be the new Vice President. Meanwhile, the Nationalist émigrés and the long-domiciled Chinese of Formosa achieved reasonably amicable relationships. Defections from Nationalist China to the Red mainland were few and largely unimportant. Only as the seat of Nationalist power could Taipei be a world capital. From being inhabitants of a Japanese colonial backwater, the Formosans became something close to a power in their own right through the National Government. The armed services and the peasants were well fed. Tragedy and humiliation seemed to have been passed. Almost all of Formosa's worries lay to the outside.

Survival in Formosa is not a question; the Nationalists have made it into an accomplished fact. The larger question of Kuomintang leadership remains. National Government and Kuomintang can return to power over all China by virtue of a future global war—if the Kuomintang endures until that war arrives, if that war does occur, if the anti-Communist powers of a future global war desire to use the Kuomintang, if the people of China show any interest in Kuomintang leadership at that remote time, and if the Kuomintang is not denied access to power by heresiarch Chinese Communist leaders who (quite conceivably defecting to the anti-Communist powers

[13] The Overseas Chinese Affairs Conference, attended by 260 delegates representing 12,500,000 overseas Chinese, was held in Taipeh on October 20, 1952. The meeting pledged, among other things, to tighten economic boycott against the Communists and, in cooperation with the governments under which these overseas Chinese communities live, to resist Communist inroads. *Chinese News Service,* NN-LII-45, November 4, 1952.

early in a future global war) might offer the invaders of China better bargains in quislings than could the Kuomintang. This is one apparent course of the Nationalists—a precarious one.

The alternatives are arduous. If the Nationalists are not to come to power as a result of some foreign invasion of China they must make power in China by themselves. To make power in China by themselves they must exploit the three factors of strength which will remain to them.

First, they possess the only non-Communist Chinese revolutionary ideology of any importance. For better or for worse, they are the heirs of Sun-Yatsenism, inheritors of the Republican and Nationalist revolutions, the spokesmen for a militant and independent China in which Confucianism will be more than an obsolete memory.

Secondly, given the world strategic balance of power between Moscow and its satellites, and the group of states affiliated with the North Atlantic powers, or the implicit American-Japanese alliance, most of the Chinese outside China live in the non-Communist countries, not in Communist countries. Potentially it should be easier for the Nationalists to inspire, to recruit, to lead, and to train these dynamic overseas communities than for the Communists to manipulate these communities through the double curtain imposed by Communist and anti-Communist administrative authorities. Overseas China is there waiting to be taken; if the Nationalists do not seize the leadership of Overseas China they are surely beyond hope, but if they do seize it they have taken at least one step forward toward survival.

Third and finally, the Nationalists have before them the revolutionary ferment of China itself. In Formosa they possess a larger base than the Communists had in 1935. They have connections with every Chinese province, every major Chinese city. They themselves came to power by way of revolution and they lost power when revolution was carried out against them. There is no comfortable, legal, and easy road back. A Nationalist return to power must, by any analysis, be a return through the process of revolution itself. This involves establishment of Nationalist guerrilla territories inside Communist China, the increasing liberation of areas from Communist control, the organization of passive resistance against the Communists, the development and exploitation of a dynamic revolutionary situation against the regime of Mao Tse-tung. No greater task has ever faced a government with liberal and democratic pretentions.

If the Nationalists return to power in China without running alongside China's invaders in a future global war, *if they take China by virtue of their own efforts,* the Kuomintang leadership will have achieved a vindication unparalleled in modern history. The odds against such a success are tremendous, but the odds are no greater than they were against the Communists in the bleak days of the middle 1930's. Formosa is either a failing stronghold in the slow long defeat of the democracies of Asia, or it is a base for resolute, purposeful anti-Communist operations which, over the years, must meet spectacular success or complete ruin. It is barely conceivable to imagine that Formosa will be neither and that two Chinas over the indefinite future will co-exist for generations or centuries. Given the degree of unfriendliness between the Washington group of nations and the Moscow group of nations, it is difficult to anticipate that so sensitive a specter of the Moscow-Washington frontier could be left undisturbed.

The Nationalist View of the Future. Whichever of the grim alternatives develops—the uneasy coexistence of two Chinas or the recapture of the mainland by Nationalist efforts or reconquest in a future global war—the immediate tasks of the government on Formosa are clear. The Nationalists must hold the defensive island beachhead. No matter what their fears, they must appear confident.

To the non-Communist Chinese world which will listen, the Nationalists stress that they and they alone speak freely for China. Dr. Tingfu F. Tsiang, chief Chinese delegate to the United Nations, put it this way:

> The map of mainland China has changed color. The people on the mainland have not changed color. They are Chinese and wish to remain Chinese and not puppets of Soviet Russia. Diplomats, who spend their lives writing treaties, conventions, protocols, have thought they can write off China. The Chinese people refuse to be written off by any diplomatic pen.

Specifically, Dr. Tsiang has little patience for the formula of *de facto* recognition. "Some people say that the communist conquest of mainland China is an accomplished fact and therefore the world might as well accept it," he added. "It is not an accomplished fact." [14]

Mainland China remained the key to Taiwan's destiny. The Nationalists knew that their own previous revolutions in 1911 and 1926 had been consummated only after years of failure. Chinese themselves, they knew that the wiles of ancient Sun Tzŭ, the first great artist of war, and the demonic patience of Mao's "protracted strategy" could not save Communism from ruin once Communist leaders began a succession of choices both irreversible and unfortunate. They did not intend to wait for Communist ruin to come of its own accord. They themselves had to help bring about the downfall of the Reds. On May 20, 1954, at the opening of his second term, Chiang pledged:

> . . . On the basis of the powers vested in me by the Constitution, I am going to discharge my duties as a public servant by striving for our people's deliverance, the suppression of the Communist revolt, and the rejuvenation of the nation.
>
> . . . The so-called "agrarian reform movement" under the Communist bandits and their successive "Five Anti" movements against the industrial and commercial circles are designed to effect complete

[14] Speech delivered by Dr. Tingfu F. Tsiang, West Orange, New Jersey, June 18, 1953, and reproduced in *Free China Review,* August, 1953, pp. 50-51.

> control over the people's livelihood and to deprive the people of their last vestiges of freedom. . . . Our land-to-the-tiller policy and that of affording protection to industrial and commercial enterprises should not only be carried out in free areas but are to be implemented as quickly as possible on the recovered mainland.[15]

More than a year later, he sounded the Chinese war-cry of limitless patience and interminable self-reliance—a theme no different from the Communist appeal from remote Yenan. From Communist despair had come Communist triumph. A Nationalist change could come only from deep self-confidence, and not from foreign aid:

> First, we must hold in our own hands the key to success in our national revolution. To permit ourselves to be swayed by the world situation and to rely on external assistance would be tantamount to submission to that *status quo* which our revolutionary efforts aim to change. . . .
>
> Secondly, we should understand the relationship between our revolution and other nations. China is one of the countries receiving American aid. The United States is helping us in such a positive way that the volume of aid now being extended is at a peak never reached before during the last fifteen years.
>
> Thirdly, let us first examine the objective factor insuring the success of our counter-attack, that is, the internal crisis of the Peiping puppet regime inherent in its own nature. . . . Behind the Iron Curtain, according to the Communists' own estimates, there were 364,604 cases of "anti-revolutionaries" and "economic saboteurs" from January last to May this year [1955]. Does this not mean that almost every minute, indeed every second, someone was hitting the Communists somewhere on the mainland? This is not only a sign of the people's indignation but also a manifestation of the deepening of a national sense of moral justice.
>
> Now let us look at the subjective factor, namely, growth in the military strength of free China as a bastion against Communism and Russian aggression. Our strength is based not only on our armed forces but also on the more intangible assets of national spirit nurtured throughout our history.
>
> We do not fight the Communists with military weapons alone. . . . The whole Chinese mainland will be the battlefield in which we fight the Communists. Every Chinese patriot will be a fighter in our counter-attack.[16]

The Nationalist appeals may be based on hope, but what revolution was not admixed with hope? If the Chinese Communists are among the toughest and smartest Communists on earth, the Nationalists, one must remember, are the most experienced anti-Communists upon the earth and not under it. Have they not fought Communism for thirty-odd years?

[15] The Chinese News Service, NI-LIV-4, May 20, 1954.
[16] The same, NI-LV-5, October 10, 1955. Slightly edited and abridged.

CHAPTER NINE

Communist China: the People's Republic

DURING their long and industrious struggle with the Kuomintang, the Chinese Communists learned that revolution is a grim business. Bitter experience taught them that the possession of a government was a luxury rather than an asset. The earlier history of the Communist struggle for power in China can be divided into two phases. From 1921 to 1927, the formative years, the Chinese Communist Party participated in the regeneration of the revolution and in the Northern Expedition of the Kuomintang, with which it joined in a short-lived coalition. The alliance abruptly ended in 1927. From 1927 to 1937, the Communists prematurely set up governments which they then had to abandon. The later history of the Chinese Communists saw government used as a means to power, not as an end in itself. The final proclamation of a Communist-controlled government was delayed until Chinese Communist power had permeated all of the mainland provinces by military and party method.

The Formative Years of the Chinese Communist Party. The stage for the introduction of Marxism-Leninism-Stalinism into China was set by the Student Movement of 1919 when a group of intellectuals started a series of demonstrations against the decision of the Versailles Conference which conceded to Japan the former German rights in the province of Shantung. The Student Movement led to a general awakening of national consciousness and a popular demand for political and social reform.

It was against this background that the Chinese Communist Party came into being. A young professor and popular literary figure, Ch'en Tu-hsiu, organized the Institute of Marxism in 1920. In the same year, Lenin sent to China his secretary, Marin, as his representative to help in the organization of the Chinese Communist Party; its First National Congress was held in Shanghai in 1921. Meanwhile, Chinese students in Europe also organized

Communist branch organizations in various countries. For instance, Chou En-lai was one of the founders of a branch in Paris and Chu Têh took part in the organization of the Berlin branch.

Ch'en Tu-hsiu was elected General Secretary of the party by the First Congress. When the Second Congress was held in 1922 in Canton, a resolution was passed to the effect that the Chinese Communist Party should join the Third International and serve as the latter's Chinese branch.

The most important problem of the party at that time, however, was to decide what should be its relationship with the Kuomintang. In conformity with Lenin's teaching that the Communist movement in colonial and semi-colonial countries should merge with the main streams of national liberation movements, the Third International ordered the Chinese Communist Party to join the Kuomintang. Starting from the end of 1922, Chinese Communists began to join the Kuomintang while secretly maintaining their membership in the Communist Party.

A host of Soviet advisers went to China to render assistance on revolutionary tactics. Adolf Joffe, representing the Soviet government, was sent to deal concurrently with the Peking Government and the Kuomintang. He was succeeded by Leo Karakhan, who obtained official recognition of the Soviet government from the Peking Government in 1924. Later, as has been described, Michael Borodin and General Blücher (Galens) were sent to Canton to help in the reorganization of the Kuomintang and the training of the army. Throughout this period, the Soviet government maintained formal and correct diplomatic relations with Peking, while the Third International actively participated in the activities of the Kuomintang-Communist entente.

After the reorganization of the Kuomintang, its First Party Congress held in January, 1924, endorsed the admission of the Chinese Communists to the Kuomintang, on condition that they accept Kuomintang principles. A number of Communists held important posts in the Kuomintang organization. T'an P'ing-shan became head of the Kuomintang Board of Organization; Lin Tsu-han was head of the Board of Farmers; and Mao Tse-tung was on the Central Executive Committee of the Kuomintang. The Communists within the Kuomintang organized and directed a number of anti-British and anti-foreign strikes and boycotts which drew nation-wide attention. In the meantime, a new army was organized under the direction of Russian advisers headed by General Blücher, and a number of civilian organizations were also created as auxiliary groups to help in the revolutionary effort.

During the period of the Northern Expedition, which swept like wildfire from South and Central China, the Kuomintang concentrated on discrediting the power and influence of foreign imperialists and native warlords, while the Communists specialized in infiltration of urban and rural areas to organize impoverished workers and peasants in order to create popular unrest. By the end of 1926 the Northern Expedition Army had won a succession of quick victories and reached the Yangtze, and the Kuomintang Government was moved to Hankow.

The relationship between members of the Kuomintang and those of the Communist Party began to show signs of strain. The Kuomintang realized that Communists, with a flair for mass organization, were quickly turning a nationalist and democratic revolution into a gigantic class struggle which was not altogether the original Kuomintang objective. They also realized that government leadership would gradually pass into the hands of the Communists unless something could be done quickly. Chiang Kai-shek decided to make a break with the Leftist Wuhan Government and moved his headquarters to Nanchang. It was not until Chiang's forces occupied Shanghai, however, and he was assured the financial support of the banking circles of that great metropolis that he felt competent to liberate himself from dependence upon Soviet help and to take steps to purge the rank and file of the Kuomintang of all Communist elements.

Before the fall of the Wuhan regime, Leftist Kuomintang leaders also had a split with their Communist colleagues. An Indian representative of the Third International, M. N. Roy, confided to Hankow leaders a Soviet plot to oust the Kuomintang from power. At a meeting of the Kuomintang Central Executive Committee held in Hankow on July 15, 1927, a resolution was passed to expel all Communist members from the Kuomintang and to declare the Communist Party an illegal party.

Meanwhile, the Peking Government severed diplomatic relations with the Soviet Union, following a dramatic raid on the Soviet Embassy in Peking on April 6, 1927. It was conclusively proved that Soviet diplomatic officials were actively supporting the Chinese Communists and that Marshal Fêng Yü-hsiang, a Northern warlord, was being given financial aid by the Soviet government.

When the new National Government of the Kuomintang was established in Nanking in 1928, many of the leaders shifted their loyalty to the new government. A large number of the Communist leaders were either killed or imprisoned; the rest went underground. In August, 1927, a revolutionary regime was established by certain Communists in Kiangsi. There followed a series of bloody and unsuccessful uprisings in a number of cities in Central and South China. Failure of the Canton Commune, December, 1927, finally convinced even a stubborn, always correct Comintern that the first wave of Chinese revolution had passed by and over the Communists. Next came the inevitable discrediting and purge of elements, who had not correctly predicted the unpredictable, and the appearance of new leadership elements, who had not bothered to predict. The period between 1927 and 1931 was characterized by frequent shifts of party line and party leadership, which always followed tactical failures in the Communist movement.

Nevertheless, the Chinese Communists learned several lessons in the years of formation, both from their failures and from their successes. Urged on by the new Stalinist line, they had hoped to control and even to capture the Kuomintang, with its powerful, indigenous, revolutionary heritage. At no time, however, did they ever control the military power of the Kuomintang. The Red Army was eventually to fill this gap.

On the other hand, in the formative years the Communist Party maintained intimate contact with Moscow and learned thoroughly Leninist concepts of party organization. Marxism-Leninism had made vast inroads among the Chinese intelligentsia. And the Communists had acquired wide and practical experience in mass leadership. Marxism-Leninism-Stalinism still had to be adjusted to the peculiar Chinese scene. Mao Tse-tung was eventually to fill this gap.[1]

The Chinese Soviet Republic. The "People's Republic of China" is an organization different from the old "Chinese Soviet Republic." The Chinese Soviet Republic (*Chung-hua su-wei-ai kung-ho-kuo*) was a precarious and short-lived organization, set up in 1931 and abandoned by the Communists themselves, somewhat informally, in 1937. The People's Republic of China (*Chung-hua jên-min kung-ho-kuo*) is the powerful, relatively stable Communist government of all mainland China, formally proclaimed in 1949 and still in power at the present time.

The Chinese Soviet Republic represented a remarkable comeback, a resurrection from the failures of coalition, the failures of the Canton Commune of December, 1927, and the subsequent twistings and turnings of the party line and party leadership. Actually, the first Chinese Soviet Government had been proclaimed at Haifeng near Canton in November, 1927, and had survived the fall of the Commune. But it was not until November, 1931, the fourth anniversary of the Canton Commune, that the Soviet Republic of China was established in Juichin, Kiangsi. (The detailed organization of the Soviet government is shown in Chart 9, page 210.)[2]

The First All-China Soviet Congress, which proclaimed the Constitution

[1] A brilliant account of the formative years, based on Russian and Chinese sources and pointing up the success of Mao in absorbing the lessons of these years, is Benjamin I. Schwartz, *Chinese Communism and the Rise of Mao,* Cambridge, Mass., 1951, especially Chap. V, "An Appraisal of Key Trends." An equally brilliant but somewhat biased account —the account of a Trotskyist, with a plague on both the Kuomintang and Communist houses—may be found in Harold Isaacs, *The Tragedy of the Chinese Revolution* (Rev. edition), Stanford, 1951. For a recent review, see "Report Submitted by Brig. Gen. P. E. Peabody," in *Hearings* on the I.P.R., cited, Part 7A, Appendix II. For a view from the other, Chinese side, see Tsou Lu, *Chung-kuo Kuo-min-tang shih-kao* (Draft History of the Kuomintang), Chungking, 1944.

[2] For a graphic description of the early fighting in South China, see Gustav Amann, *Bauernkrieg in China,* Heidelberg, 1939, which corresponds rather closely to the Communist sources. See also J. Johanson and O. Taube, *Rate-China Documente der Chinesischen Revolution,* Moscow, 1934, especially pp. 166-167. As to the area of the Chinese Soviet Republic in 1931 and 1932, the description in Victor Yakhontoff, *The Chinese Soviets,* New York, 1934, is based on superficial gleanings from the Russian-language press. Fortunately, many of the basic documents of this, earlier, and later periods are now available in English, in Conrad Brandt, Benjamin Schwartz, and John K. Fairbank, *A Documentary History of Chinese Communism,* Cambridge, Mass., 1952. See especially Section IV, which includes the Constitution of the Soviet Republic, November, 1931, and Land Law of the Soviet Republic, November, 1931.

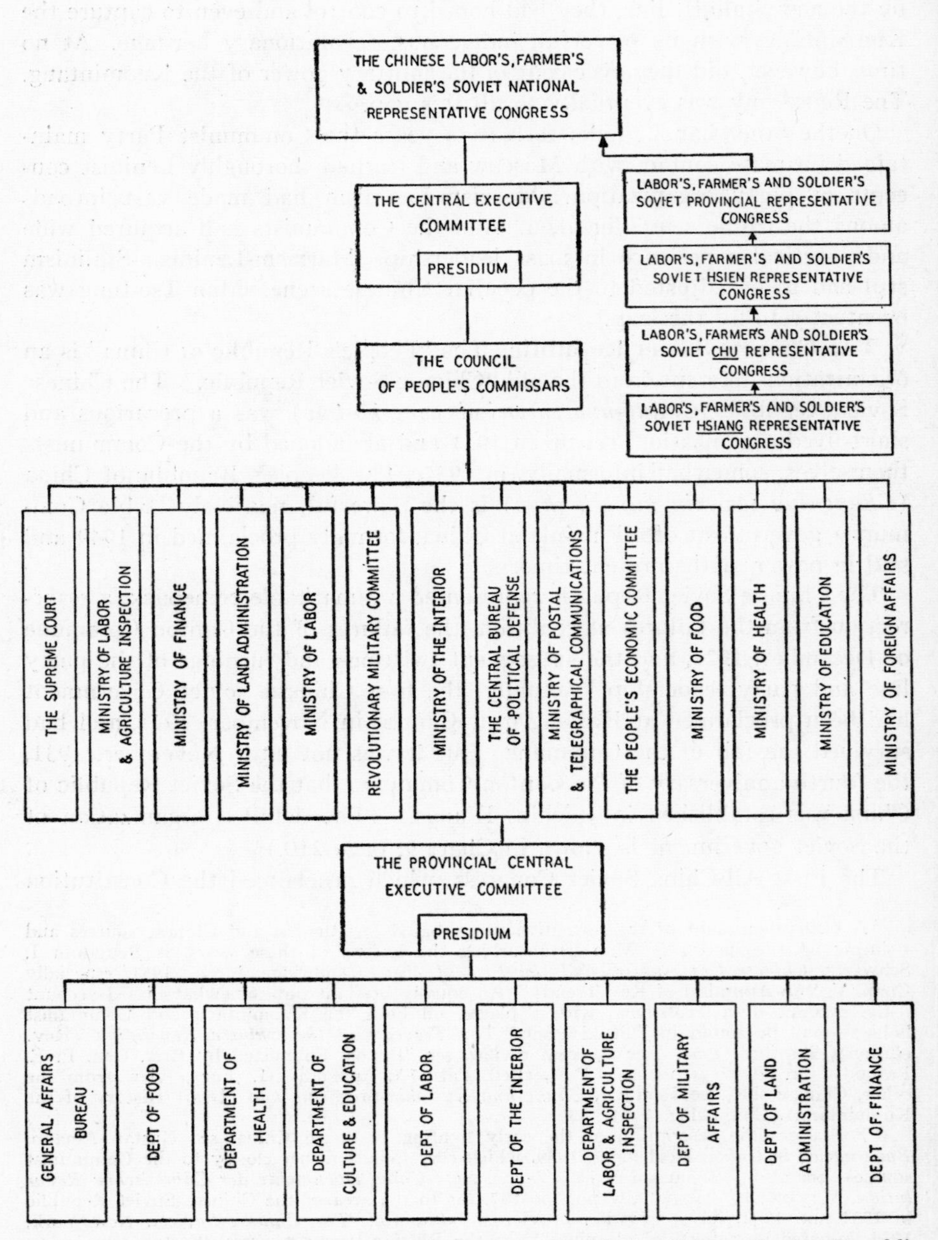

CHART 9—Organization of the Central Government of the Chinese Soviet Republic (Established on Nov. 7, 1931 in Kiangsi)

of the new government, was called in December, 1931. Mao Tse-tung was elected Chairman of the Council of People's Commissars of the Central Soviet Government and Chu Têh, the Commander-in-Chief of the Army. Realizing that the overwhelming majority of the Chinese were peasants and that the strength of the industrial proletariat was rather limited, Mao advocated a moderate policy of land reform, which tolerated small landownership. In this sense, he seemed to discredit the previous Comintern policy of urban uprisings and direct action.

The Nationalists embarked on their long campaign to suppress the Communists by military force. Several difficult campaigns were carried out before they finally succeeded in forcing the Communists to take up the long and epic trek to Yenan, a small city in mountainous North China. After the outbreak of the Sino-Japanese War in 1937, the Chinese Communists voluntarily abolished their central Soviet Government and nominally incorporated their army into the National military establishment, as the Eighth Route Army.

In the early years of the Chinese Soviet struggle against the National Government of China the Communists placed an unnecessary premium on maintaining a government which even the USSR did not recognize. They sought prestige in the issuance of bank notes and the minting of coins. The area of their Fourth Army was held in the face of tragic odds in order to maintain a political base which was extensively costly in terms of the prestige or leadership it offered the Communists for future operations.

The Chinese Communists were weary and face-to-face with defeat by 1936, but they were not altogether ready to give up. For one thing, the structure of international relationships—Russo-Japanese, Sino-Japanese, and Sino-Russian—came to their rescue and had tremendous impact, particularly on the domestic situation. A united front agreement among the Kuomintang, the Communists, and minor groups became mandatory, thus giving the Communists the breather they so desperately needed. The Japanese attack levered Kuomintang power off its base of prematurely modern, coastal China and made it possible for the Communists, as "patriotic" anti-Japanese guerrillas, to infiltrate large areas behind enemy lines. Thus the critical point in Communist survival lay not only in their resoluteness in fighting immense odds in the twenties and in the thirties, when they laid the foundation for their slow climb to power in the 1940's; it lay also in their willingness to learn from the social situation itself in the critical period between the fall of their South China positions and the reconstitution of their movement as a patriotic, anti-Japanese guerrilla-based system in the years 1937-1945.

Period of Retrenchment and Reconstitution. The Chinese Communist Party in 1936 and 1937 showed itself to be the most adaptable Communist Party on earth. In order to survive, it abandoned almost all the cut-and-dried dogmas of seizing political power and displaying the conspicuous but meretricious insignia of authority. The Communists made a decision (and there seems to be little doubt at this time that it was the genius of Mao Tse-tung which did the deciding) to go after real power in terms of practical support and working military and party organization, while relinquishing evident power in terms of a capacity to issue bank notes, to fly grandiose flags, or to establish hollow titles. The Communists even flew the Kuomintang flag if that was the price of toleration and survival. They made their main army into the titularly Nationalist Eighth Route Army, although they set up their southern forces under the purely Communist nomenclature of the New Fourth Army.

From 1937 to the proclamation of the People's Republic in 1949, the Chinese Communists were severe and shrewd in their use of semantics. They referred to governmental actions very carefully. They let the Nationalists keep all the titles and the labels: all they wanted was real power, power expressed in terms of acres of farm land, companies and battalions of armed able-bodied men, party organizations controlling entire communities. In terms of administrative procedure the Communist Party took over the governmental functions which Communists had previously attempted to carry out with the administrative device of the Chinese Soviet Republic. The party without benefit of a government in front of it promulgated laws and decrees for the Communist-controlled areas, decided upon policies which were governmental in character, and sent envoys—carefully calling them logistic representatives of the Eighth Route Army (later the Eighteenth Group Army)—to Chungking and to San Francisco. When the Communists maintained local governments they improvised them as guerrilla territories and were careful to avoid an open breach with the existing provincial pattern imposed by the Kuomintang authorities. The stability of the Nationalist-Communist border between the two different parts of China was attested for many years by the existence of customs stations on each side of the frontier. Thus, for a period of ten long years, the Communists had managed, governed, and developed an area larger than the territory of a medium-sized European state. They had governed this nation-sized countryside without benefit of a central government. By the 1940's they had become as careful in avoiding the premature responsibilities of government as they had been reckless in their earlier years.

In their fight with the Nationalists, the Communists became seasoned strategists, hardened realists. Continuous struggle made them realize that what really mattered in revolutionary struggle was ideological, political, and economic control, not just the apparatus of government. Revolution, in Mao's now-famous aphorism, is not an invitation to a picnic. The picnic comes only when the grim struggle was over. After twenty-six years of severe and continuous fighting, after the loss of millions of friends and the killing of millions of enemies, the Chinese Communists came into final and substantial power. It is characteristic that they should proclaim a People's Republic, not a Soviet Republic, and that they should proclaim it in the confirmative old capital of Peking. The Chinese Communist Government has been a solemn, self-assured, and powerful government, careful and deliberate from the day of its initiation on October 1, 1949. The leader of this government is one of its most seasoned strategists, one of its most hardened realists, one of its most solemn and self-assured spokesmen.

Mao Tse-tung and the New Democracy. When Mao Tse-tung is described as the leader of a Communist China, which is at the same time passionately nationalist, Western observers are often tempted to believe that Mao is the exponent of some peculiarly Chinese aspect of Chinese civilization. The reverse is the case. He is far more Western in his thinking than is Chiang Kai-shek.[3]

As a literary and philosophical artist, as well as an accomplished leader, Mao has done superlatively well with the bad intellectual material given him by his environment. He does not know how out-of-date and trivial much of the content of Marxism has become, because he cannot stand outside Marxism long enough to see that most of what Marx believed and Lenin later taught has now become poor economics, mistaken sociology, discarded philosophy, and wretched politics. Nevertheless, Mao has dealt with his materials creatively, shrewdly, and with great individual insight. His chief work, *On New Democracy,* is the most important and unusual Marxist book of our time. It is a successful attempt to push Marxism forward in the Chinese scene and to transform it into a political philosophy and a set of social and economic theories, which will in fact work in the context of the Chinese revolution.[4]

Mao's logic may be mid-Victorian; his economics may be a hundred years out of date when viewed from the America of Dwight Eisenhower; his sociology and psychology may be little more than bold hunches or glittering improvisations supporting an old-fashioned, but tough European revolutionary doctrine. Nevertheless, Mao's thought is, by Western standards, solid.

Reasoning in the European fashion is not a common experience offered by Chinese literature. Most Chinese political peroration, even in modern times, is argument by example, by analogy, by the imaginative elicitation

[3] For the contrast, see pp. 179-181.

[4] Mao's principal writings on ideology and policy include the following: *Chung-kuo kê-ming yü Chung-kuo Kung-ch'an-tang* (The Chinese revolution and the Chinese Communist Party), November 15, 1939, an English translation of which is to be found in *China Digest,* Vol. 5, Nos. 9-10; *Hsin min-chu chu-i lun* (On new democracy), January 19, 1940, English translations of which were published by the *Chinese News Service,* New York, 1947, and by New Century Publishers, New York, 1945; *Lun lien-ho chêng-fu* (On coalition government), April 24, 1945, an English text of which may be found in *Fight for a New China,* New York, 1945, p. 40; *Mu-ch'ien hsing-shih ho wo-men ti jên-wu* (The present situation and our tasks), December 25, 1947; *Lun jên-min min-chu chuan-chêng* (On the people's democratic dictatorship), July 15, 1949, an English translation of which is available in mimeographed form published by The Committee for a Democratic Far Eastern Policy, New York, under the title, "The Dictatorship of People's Democracy." Extracts from "On New Democracy," "On Coalition Government," and the text of "On the People's Democratic Dictatorship," in English, may be found in Brandt, Schwartz, and Fairbank, cited, Sections V and VII.

of parallels which will stir sympathy or indignation. Cold intellectual conviction in the Western sense is rarely sought outside of Communist circles; even among the Communists, few Chinese can reason in as consummately Western a fashion as can Mao Tse-tung.

On New Democracy develops the idea that there must be two stages in the process of the Communist revolution in China. This idea is in conformity with nineteenth-century Marxism, which believed that there should be first a revolution marking the transformation from feudalism to capitalist democracy and then a revolution marking the transformation from capitalism to socialism. Mao accepts this theory as applied to China, but he further recommends that the two stages can be blended into a continuous process when revolutionary conditions are suitable. Mao holds that the two-stage revolution can be conducted by a coalition of all progressive classes, excluding imperialist, feudal, and bureaucratic elements among the people. The coalition is necessary only in the pre-socialist stage, which is to be succeeded by gradual shifts to socialist dictatorship. Thus he carefully avoids the necessity of violent break from the old social order, lessens opposition, and very effectively allays fears from outside China. This does not mean, however, that violence is not necessary in the Chinese Communist revolution; it means that violence can be largely postponed until after the attainment of power. Another central thesis of the essay, *On New Democracy,* is that, in international politics, China must follow the leadership of the Soviet Union and take the hand of friendship offered by the international proletariat. This last dogma at least temporarily rectifies any possible reformist tendencies (that is, from Soviet dogma) involved in the former two. The fundamental technique of Mao Tse-tung is, therefore, aimed at attaining political power by collaborating with non-Communists, without compromising Communist objectives.

Mao's main preoccupation is to avoid both reformism and leftism, as denounced in Soviet dogma. *On New Democracy* represents not only a blueprint whereby the Chinese Communists can seize power, but also a revised version of Marxism especially fitted to the contemporary development of China.

In the field of practical politics, *On New Democracy* frankly envisages a system of government which is ingeniously called "Democratic Dictatorship." According to orthodox Marxism, all governments represent the dictatorship of a class; therefore, dictatorship is a synonym for government and there is no use pretending it is not. But it is democratic, Mao claims, because it is a dictatorship of a coalition of classes and also because it has an elective, representative body. In establishing the new Communist Government of 1949, Mao gave practical expression to the political ideology contained in his work, *On New Democracy.* Mao's ladder to power was a tough, tested Chinese Communist Party.

Communist Party Structure. The Chinese Communist Party, which today claims a membership of five to six million and controls a bulk of humanity larger than any single homogeneous population in the world, is perhaps the strongest political party outside the Soviet Union. The organization of this party follows that of the Communist Party of the Soviet Union. There is the usual hierarchy of party cells and district, *hsien*, provincial, regional, and central organizations, which correspond respectively with administrative counterparts in the government. The supreme party organ is the National Party Congress. As in the Soviet Union, however, the real authority of the party is vested in the Central Executive Committee, composed of 42 members and 30 reserve members. Under the Central Executive Committee are the Central Political Bureau and the various central departments in charge of organization, publicity, training, and youth, farmers' and workers' movements.

The Central Political Bureau (or Politburo, *Chung-yang chêng-chih-chü*), the equivalent of the Soviet Politburo, is the real policy-determining organ, of which Mao Tse-tung is the Chairman. It dispatches representatives to all administrative areas and army units. It also controls the secret service and the New Democracy Youth Corps.

The fundamental principle governing the operation of Party functions is the familiar Communist doctrine of "democratic centralism." [5] According to party theorists, a distinction must be made between party policy and party administration. Members of the party are expected unconditionally to obey the party line; lower party organs must carry out resolutions of higher party organs without question. But any member, in principle, is permitted to discuss policy as it is made on each level at least until a decision is reached; even more theoretically, each member is permitted to criticize the manner in which the party line is administered. Actually, as any distinction between matters pertaining to basic policy and those pertaining to administration is difficult and dangerous to make, only minor and irrelevant matters are open for discussion and criticism.

The following simplified chart of the Chinese Communist Party shows local-central relationships and important Party organs:

Constitutional Status of the Central People's Government. During the war years the Chinese Communists had followed a so-called three-thirds system.[6] This was, in brief, an attempt to keep Communist power in an apparent minority while retaining command of all the real organs of political

[5] For the inclusion of this doctrine in government practice, see pp. 220-224. For documents and critical commentaries on Party organization and documents, see Brandt, Schwartz, and Fairbank, *op. cit.*, especially Sect. VI, P. "The Indoctrination of Party Personnel" and U. "Constitution of the Chinese Communist Party, June 11, 1945."

[6] The three-thirds system was a means of governing enforced by the Chinese Communists in the "liberated areas," before their military victory in 1949. Under this system, the Communists voluntarily limited their participation in all administrations or representative organizations to one third of the total membership; the other two thirds were occupied by the representatives of the "progressive elements" and the "middle class." But in actual practice, only those who were sympathetic with the Communists got elected or appointed. This self-imposed limitation was a whitewash, put up for the sake of a democratic front.

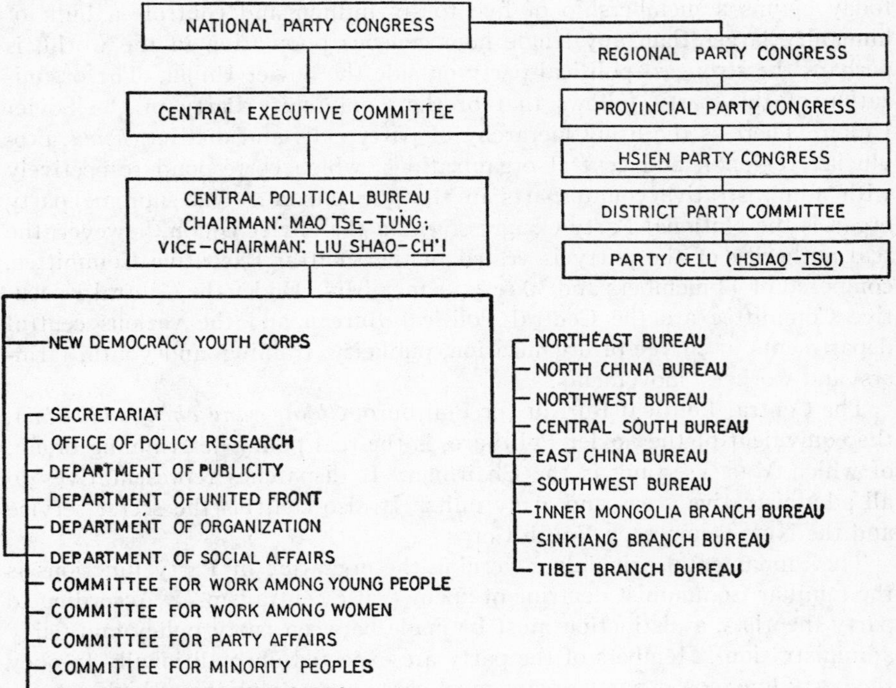

CHART 10—Simplified Structure of the Chinese Communist Party

and economic authority. The People's Republic, which the Communists sought to establish, was, in their view, to be under the firm "leadership" (in Communist parlance, this means control) of the Communist Party itself, but comprising a coalition of all "democratic" (meaning not anti-Communist) parties and groups. The Communist leadership was extremely careful to keep up this appearance of a modified democracy, to make the party one of several parties, and to establish a coalition government for the people's democracy.

In the spring of 1948 the Central Committee of the Chinese Communist Party decided to call a People's Political Consultative Conference in order to promulgate a new constitution and to establish a formal government as soon as the Chinese Communist forces, which bore the collective title of the People's Liberation Army, had won a clean-cut victory over the mainland considered as an entirety.[7]

The People's Political Consultative Conference (*Jên-min chêng-chih hsieh-shang hui-i*) was convened on September 21, 1949, when the military

[7] By far the best book on the Chinese Communist army is Lt. Col. Robert B. Riggs, U.S.A., *Red China's Fighting Hordes*, Harrisburg, 1951. His description of the Nationalist defeat, pp. 265 ff., is the most articulate to be found.

conquest was in its final stages. Even its name was borrowed from its Nationalist predecessor, preceded only with the word "People's" (see page 175). This group was a quasi-constituent *ad hoc* organization composed of 662 hand-picked delegates from 45 representative units, including political parties, regional governments, field armies, social and occupational associations, and individual notables such as the renegade Kuomintang generals, social leaders, scholars, and stage actors.[8] During its busy twelve-day session the People's Political Consultative Conference adopted an *Organic Law* (*Tsu-chih fa*) making itself a quasi-legislative body, pending the convocation of an All China People's Congress, made a declaration on fundamental policy for the forthcoming government in the form of the Common Program (*Kung-t'ung kang-ling*), and also adopted the *Organic Law of the Central People's Government* (*Chung-yang jên-min chêng-fu tsu-chih fa*), upon which the new regime was to be based.[9]

Besides these law-making activities the People's Political Consultative Conference also approved the design of the new national flag of China—a red flag with one large yellow star and four small yellow stars. The large star represented the Chinese Communist Party and the four small stars, the four classes of people in New China—the working class, peasantry, petty bourgeoisie, and national capitalists. The red background of course proclaimed the government's ideological affiliations. The conference also adopted the famous militant Guerrilla Song of war days as the national anthem.[10]

The *Common Program* of the People's Political Consultative Conference set forth the principles underlying the economic, cultural, military, and foreign policies of the new regime. It defined the duties and obligations of the people and explicitly excluded the feudal landlords, bureaucratic capitalists, reactionaries, and counterrevolutionaries from enjoying civil and political rights. It is the manifestation of principles embodied in Mao's

[8] For the list of names of these delegates and their party or group affiliations, see *Jên-min shou-ts'ê*, 1950 (People's year book, 1950), *Ta Kung Pao*, Hongkong.

[9] See Appendix 6. *The Organic Law of the People's Political Consultative Conference, the Common Program of the People's Political Consultative Conference,* and *the Organic Law of the People's Central Government,* now known as the Magna Charta of the People's Republic, are the most important documents of the new regime. Their texts are to be found in all Chinese reference books on political studies, for instance, *Jên-min shou-ts'ê,* 1951 (People's year book, 1951), *Ta Kung Pao,* Hongkong. English translations of the two Organic Laws are published in *China Digest,* Hongkong, Vol. 7, No. 2 (October 19, 1949), and of the Common Program in *China Digest,* Supplement to Vol. 7, No. 1, pp. 3-9.

[10] For complete documentation of the proceedings of the People's Political Consultative Conference, September 21 to October 1, 1949, see *Jên-min shou-ts'ê, 1951,* cited; also *Chung-hua jên-min kung-ho-kuo k'ai-kuo wen-hsien* (Documents on the establishment of the Chinese People's Republic), Hongkong, 1949. An extremely useful collection of documents, translated into English, is contained in H. Arthur Steiner, *Chinese Communism in Action,* Los Angeles (U.C.L.A. Student Store), 1953 (mimeograph). Vol. I, Chaps. I-III, covers "Insights into the Chinese Mind," "Basic Constitutional and Governmental Structure" (19. The Organic Law of the CPPCC; 20. Membership of the First Plenary Session of the CPPCC), and "The Chinese Communist Party," Vol. II, Chaps. IV-IX, covers such topics as administration, elections, law, police, propaganda, and non-Communist parties. Vol. III was due to appear late in December, 1953.

classic treatise, *On New Democracy*. Fundamentally Marxist in outlook, the *Common Program* recognized the exigencies of local Chinese requirements. Furthermore, the *Common Program* did not introduce anything new other than principles enumerated in an earlier "Minimum Program" of the Chinese Communist Party, the realization of which was declared to be a first real step toward ultimate socialism.

The working principles of this modest but deadly serious Chinese Communist approach had already been hammered into a hard core of doctrine. The minimum program of the Chinese Communist Party represented an interim step in the revolutionary process. A tactical moderation was recognized; special attention was paid to the necessities imposed by China's peculiar requirements arising from the preferences of the Chinese people in the light of their social and economic development. The Chinese Communist Party, which ideologically recognized nothing beyond the dialectical and historical materialism of Marx, Engels, Lenin, and Stalin, showed consummative skill in adapting its dogma to the local scene. Nothing of the ultimate purpose was abandoned. The minimum program led inevitably back to the maximum program, the actual accomplishment of socialism and communism.[11] In accepting the *Common Program* the Chinese Communist Party did not modify its original ideological content, but sought and won the plebiscitary assent of all groups which could be drawn into a common front with the Communists.

In combination, the *Organic Law* and the *Common Program* formed the basic law of the land for mainland China until 1954, when the new constitution was proclaimed. The *Organic Law* opens, "The People's Republic of China is a state of the People's Democratic Dictatorship led by the working class, based on the alliance of workers and peasants, and rallying all democratic classes and various nationalities within the country." The use of the term "People's Democratic Dictatorship" involves two ideological implications. First, it implies that the new government is not a dictatorship of the proletariat, in the traditional Leninist style, but a coalition government comparable to the people's democracies of Eastern Europe. The Chinese made this into a very special Chinese justification.[12] Secondly, the use

[11] For further development of this theme, see an address by Liu Shao-ch'i, Vice-Chairman of the Central People's Government, in the People's Political Consultative Conference on September 21, 1949, "China Enters the Era of People's Democracy," *China Digest*, Vol. 7, No. 1, pp. 6-7.

[12] Cf. an article published in *Chin Pu Jih Pao* (Progress Daily) which reads in part:

". . . Lenin has stated that the basic issue of a revolution lies in the question of political power, in other words, who is to rule whom, or who is to impose a dictatorship over whom. A proletariat dictatorship, then, is the rule by the proletariat over the bourgeoisie, and the mission of such a dictatorship is the wiping out of the bourgeoisie . . .

". . . However, in China, the people's democratic government today is a dictatorship enforced jointly by four elements—the proletariat, the peasantry, the petit bourgeoisie and the national capitalist on three foes, imperialists, feudalists and bureaucratic capitalists. It is not a dictatorship imposed by the proletariat on the bourgeoisie.

"For the mission of the Chinese revolution today is the expulsion from China of imperialism, the annihilation of feudal influences, and the wiping out of only a portion of the bour-

of the term implies that the state is necessarily an instrument of the new ruling classes, whereby the new ruling classes govern the ruled classes.

The *Organic Law* not only conferred leadership upon the working class and the peasantry; it also recognized the potential usefulness of other "democratic classes," which for Chinese purposes include the petit bourgeoisie and the new national capitalists. This appears to be a distinctive departure from orthodox Marxism. Nevertheless, the Chinese Communists had learned a great deal from twenty-six years of struggle. Not the least of their skills was a capacity to manage their own unwieldy philosophy.

The Chinese Communists were able to adjust Communist doctrine to the postwar Stalinist situation and specifically to China without compromising Communist objectives. They did nothing in China that was not done in Poland and Czechoslovakia and in Hungary and in Rumania. They differed from Russia with Russia's consent. They were even able to go back into Russian Soviet history to obtain precedents. It was Lenin himself who laid down the rule in his famous *Left Wing Communism and Infantile Disorder* —that Communists should not isolate themselves from reform movements, that they should take part in them, but that while participating they should keep their own character as Communists and sacrifice none of their own particular ultimate objectives.

The conveniences of collaborating with non-Communists helped the Chinese Communists to surmount the difficulties that had brought themselves to ruin in the 1930's when they tried to govern prematurely, and that had led to the destruction of the Kuomintang when the Kuomintang leaders tried to run China all by themselves. The Chinese Communists skillfully adapted the postwar Communist doctrine on people's democracies for their own country. Their own tragedy, following the extreme leftist experience of the Chinese Soviet Republic, warned them against the premature rejection of potentially friendly elements in the population.

The Chinese Communist Party procedures of 1949 called for a sharp break in the pattern of class power to get rid of the anti-revolutionary forces, this to be followed by the establishment of a new democratic society representing the combined dictatorship of all "democratic" classes and by a gradual shifting of power to the proletariat and the ultimate abolition of all classes.[13]

---

geoisie—the bureaucratic capitalists. It is as yet not the time for the obliteration of all capitalism and the bourgeoisie. In the task of the restoration and development of production, the national capitalists today still have a decisively progressive role to perform. Accordingly, it seems incorrect to say that the people's democratic dictatorship in China is 'materially' or 'basically' a proletariat dictatorship."—*Kuan-yü jên-min min-chu chuan-chêng ti chi-tien i-chien* (Some views on the "people's democratic dictatorship"), by Yang Fu, *Chin Pu Jih Pao* (Progress Daily, Tientsin, October 5, 1949).

[13] One of the most brilliant available epitomies on the ideological character of the Chinese Communist movement is to be found in the basic report on China by the Bolton Subcommittee. See the Report of the Subcommittee No. 5 of the Committee on Foreign Affairs, House of Representatives, on the *Strategy and Tactics of World Communism, Supplement III(C): Communism in China,* 81st Congress, 1st Session, House Document No. 153—Part 3 (Washington, 1949), pp. 24-28.

On the basis of a multi-class policy, the Chinese Communists allowed the participation in power of social classes other than the proletariat during the transitional period of their "New Democracy." The inclusion of the so-called national capitalists and the petit bourgeoisie is of particular interest. The national capitalists were described as those native industrialists and business executives who were in actual possession of production facilities, in basic sympathy with the socialistic principles of the government, and whose cooperation was—from a technological point of view—urgently needed in the current stage of economic reconstruction. The petit bourgeoisie included the intellectuals, government employees, handicraftsmen, practitioners of the professions, and small tradesmen. The great majority of this class, said the Communists, are exploited parties and only a very few of them are themselves exploiters. However, the consciousness of these petit bourgeoisie is different from that of the proletariat. Since they are small producers, they are not used to the collective life. The Communists hoped that mild treatment of these people would lead them to the revolutionary path.

Pragmatically, the term "people's democratic dictatorship" implies that the state power belongs to the alliance of four classes of "people" who exercise a dictatorial rule over the "reactionary" elements who are not "people," but "nationals." Reactionary elements, as described by the Peking authorities, are persons who cannot be assimilated into the revolutionary camp. Such people have to be re-educated or destroyed if their interests, their heritage, or their inclinations make them unassimilable.

In this cool and fantastic constitutional distinction between "people" and "nationals," the Chinese Communists assign to the category of "nationals" bureaucratic capitalists, war criminals, feudal landlords, imperialist lackeys, and other reactionaries. Commenting on the *Common Program* Chou En-lai, Premier and Foreign Minister of the People's Government, remarked:

> There is a difference between "people" and "nationals." "People" include the working class, the peasantry, the petit bourgeoisie, the national capitalists, and certain other patriotic democratic elements. The remaining reactionary elements are not within the category of "people," but are "nationals" of China. For the time being they cannot enjoy the rights of the "people," but they have to observe the obligations of "nationals."

Democratic Centralism. The second article of the *Organic Law* defines the political system of the new regime as following the already described Communist pattern of "democratic centralism." In theory and in terms of administration, popularly elected people's congresses at various levels are to be established: these in turn would select the personnel of their respective governing councils to be called people's governments. Once the personnel of a people's government had been selected, the formal appointment and approval of these selections would be required from the people's government of a higher level, and the people's government on the lower level was to be required to obey that higher level. The election of people's congresses, no matter how contrived the election may be, was required as a manifestation of democracy. Obedience by a lower level people's government to a higher level people's government was called an expression of centralism. The reconciliation of these two principles was called democratic centralism.[14]

The Communist leaders themselves said that the aim of democracy is to facilitate the full realization of the will of the people. This must be understood of course in the light of Communist doctrine: the will of the people is not what the actual living people themselves happen to want, but what the Communist Party experts think that the people ought to want if they know what is, in Communist terms, good for them. Similarly, the purpose of centralism is to have that will carried out fully and effectively. This, too, is a familiar part of Communist doctrine in the West and is not peculiar to China.

The first few years of authority exerted by the People's Republic showed no serious modification of the process of centralization by the principles, Communist or other, of a recognizable democracy. As the new regime consolidated its position, centralization triumphed over democratization. One obvious consequence of "democratic centralism" had been foreshadowed by the *Organic Law:* the separation of powers was totally denied.

Communist state authority took clear form under the *Organic Law.* The supreme power of the state was vested in the Central People's Government Council *(Chung-yang jên-min chêng-fu wei-yüan-hui)* composed of a Chairman and six Vice-Chairmen of the Central People's Government, together with fifty-six Council Members elected by the first session of the People's Political Consultative Conference. When the Council itself was not in session, its powers were delegated to a State Administration Council *(Chêng-wu yüan)* of twenty members; this was the nearest approach to a cabinet in the Western sense.

Meeting twice a month, the Government Council enacted and interpreted laws, promulgated decrees, determined state policies, made treaties, dealt with questions of war and peace, approved the governmental budgets, and appointed the members of the Administration Council. In short, the Government Council at Peking had an authority not unlike that of its imperial predecessors: it was executive, legislature, and supreme court for many purposes, since the final interpretation of organic law lay in its own hands.

The lesser body, the State Administration Council was responsible to the Government Council and accountable to it; when the Government Council was not in session, the State Administration Council reported to the Chair-

[14] A philosophical discussion of the theory of democratic centralism is to be found in an article written by Chang Chih-jang, Vice Chief Justice of the People's Supreme Court and formerly Professor of Law, National Peking University, entitled, "A Tentative Analysis of the Organic Law of the Central People's Government," in *China Digest,* Vol. VIII, No. 3.

man—Mao Tse-tung, of course—of the Central People's Government. Under the Council there were four committees: the Committee on Political and Legal Affairs, the Committee on Finance and Economics, the Committee on Culture and Education, and the Committee of People's Supervision. The first three committees each directed the work of an enumerated group of ministries falling in their respective fields; the last one, a control organ such as both Chinese and Soviet practice had long demonstrated, supervised the faithful discharge of duties on the part of government organs and on occasion investigated named individuals.

The State Administration Council is peculiar in that it was, for its time, the largest high-level administrative body in the entire history of China. No fewer than thirty ministries, commissions, boards, and separate administrations had been set up under its authority. The new organization is noteworthy in placing heavy emphasis on economic affairs. Aside from a Ministry of Trade, there were Ministries of Heavy Industries, of Textiles, of Food Industries, and of Light Industries.[15]

The State Administration Council was made up of a *Tsung-li* (usually translated as "Premier") a number of Deputy Premiers, and Council Members who might or might not hold concurrent posts as ministers or commission chairmen. Not all ministers and commission chairmen were *ex officio* members of the State Administration Council; those without specific personal membership in the council were not entitled to attend its meetings. This was another departure from cabinet analogy. Membership was individual, and the changes of role gave outside observers some clues as to what was happening in the personal politics of the ruling group.

In the central structure of the People's Government, directly under the Government Council and on the same footing as the State Administration Council, there were the following high organs: the People's Revolutionary Military Council, which had over-all control and commanded the entire armed forces; the People's Supreme Court, highest judicial organ in the land, but not superior to the State Administration Council, even in legal matters; and the Prosecutor General's Office, carrying the responsibility of observing that the laws were strictly followed by all government organs as well as by individual Chinese everywhere, whether "people" or "nation-

[15] The Central People's Government Council decided in its seventeenth meeting on August 7, 1952, to make several changes in its administrative setup. The Ministry of Trade has been split up into the Ministry of Foreign Trade and the Ministry of Commerce. Five more ministries have been created; these are: the Ministries of Primary Machine Industries, Secondary Machine Industries, Building Industries, Geology, and Food. The last one was created to take the place of the original Ministry of Food Industries which was abolished in December, 1950. Among the ministries abolished at the same time were the Ministry of Trade, Central Bureau of Information, and Central Bureau of the Press. In its nineteenth meeting held on November 15, 1952, the Central People's Government Council decided to add four more organizations in the Central Government; these are: National Planning Commission, National Physical Education Commission, Ministry of Higher Education, and the Committee for the Elimination of Illiteracy. All these newly created agencies are under the direct control of the State Administraton Council. See *Ta Kung Pao*, Shanghai, August 12, 1952, and *Ta Kung Pao*, Hongkong, November 17, 1952.

als," and of instituting prosecution whenever infractions were found (see Chart 11).

Constitutional Preparations. In early 1953 the Communist government announced that in order to install regular government on a permanent Communist basis, an All-China People's Congress *(Ch'üan-kuo tai-piao tai-hui)* would be called as soon as the necessary preparations were completed.

One of these preparations was the taking of a national census. The number of Chinese was stated to be over six hundred million.

The other preparation consisted of regrouping villages for administrative and electoral purposes, so that local congresses could be held in tiers made up from groups of villages, towns, counties, muncipalities (where applicable) and provinces. At each level of this electoral hierarchy there was an election committee designated to appoint official lists of candidates.

According to the National Election Law promulgated on March 1, 1953, cities of more than 500,000 population obtained one representative's seat in the proposed National Congress for each 100,000 of population, and provinces were generally awarded seats on the basis of one seat for each 800,000 of population. Most members of the Congress were elected by provincial or municipal congresses. In addition, 150 seats were allocated to the non-Han minorities within China, now called "national minorities," and 30 seats were allocated to the Chinese overseas. Under the election law all citizens over eighteen years of age were granted the vote, with the obvious exception of elements of the landlord class and of counterrevolutionaries.

Elections were actually held in the early months of 1954. Congresses were held on the pyramidal basis first popularized in the Soviet Union. *Hsiang* and township congresses elected delegates to *hsien* congresses, which in their turn elected delegates to provincial congresses. The provincial congresses, together with a number of municipal congresses, elected delegates to the First All-China's People's Congress.

This congress became the legal and political cornerstone of the new regime.

The First All-China People's Congress met on September 15, 1954, and adjourned on September 28. In its thirteen days it adopted the new constitution and otherwise replaced the provisional governmental instruments of the People's Political Consultative Conference, itself now superseded, with more permanent instruments of government.

The tempo of Chinese Communist government-building has been the most deliberate of any totalitarian regime. Previous dictatorships in other parts of the world have been set up with dramatic haste; both the appearance and reality of urgency have driven them to power. The five-year delay, 1949-1954, of the Chinese Communists in "finishing" their government was itself attestation of their understanding one important pattern in the thinking of modern Chinese. After many ephemeral Chinese governments, here at last was a government seemingly built for the ages.

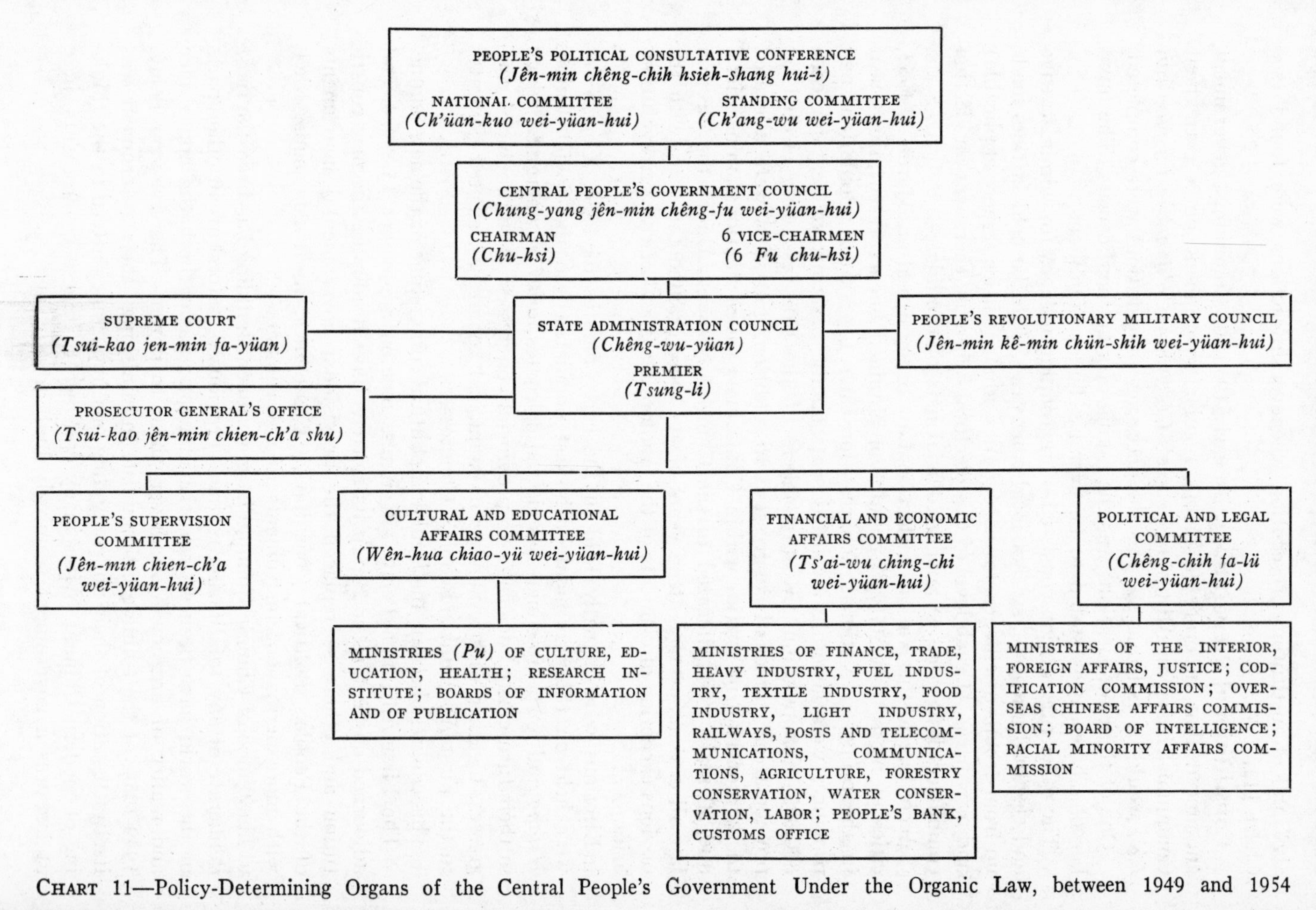

CHART 11—Policy-Determining Organs of the Central People's Government Under the Organic Law, between 1949 and 1954

The new permanent constitution had been openly in the making for a year and a half. From the spring of 1953 onward, a committee had been working on drafts. In March, 1954, Mao Tse-tung, acting on behalf of the Chinese Communist Party, submitted a so-called "Preliminary Draft" to the committee, which, after several meetings, discovered that his draft was exactly what it had been seeking all along.

Subsequently, this draft was relayed downward to various public and semipublic groups throughout the country for "public discussion." This followed the common Communist practice, more effective for its emotional effect than for its legal consequences, of inviting mass approbation for a *fait accompli* of the regime.

The Congress adopted the new Constitution on September 20, 1954, and also adopted its own organic law, as well as organic laws for the State Council, the People's Courts, the People's Procuratorate, and the various levels of People's Congresses. The Congress also elected its own Standing Committee and designated, in new form, the leading members of the government. All this was accomplished within the framework of the new Constitution.[16]

The Constitution of 1954. The constitution consists of a preamble and 4 chapters comprising 106 articles. In comparison with the Nationalist constitution of 1947, it is a short document; the Nationalist constitution had 14 chapters with 175 articles. The new Communist constitution, like its Soviet archetype of 1936, covers general principles, the state structure, fundamental rights and duties of citizens, and the national capital, emblem, and flags.

The preamble declares itself to be an advance over the *Common Program* of 1949, though it is obviously based on the *Common Program.* The *Common Program* had characterized China as a "new democracy" with the immediate tasks of fulfilling the revolution against imperialism, against feudalism, and against bureaucratic capitalism, while the Constitution sets forth that these goals have been fulfilled and that the Chinese are on the road of achieving a socialist state. The preamble also declares that the various parties will continue to perform their functions and that the mutual assistance and friendly relations between the various nationalities within China is to be maintained. (In this respect the Communists of 1954 reverted to the Republican principles of 1912, since the old first republic started with a five-striped banner—one stripe each for the Chinese, Mongols, Manchus, Tibetans, and Moslems—and preached, but did not practice, a racial congruence which the Nationalists downgraded or neglected. The Communist doctrine on "national minorities" owed more to Stalinism proper than to any Chinese precedent, but the precedent was nevertheless extant.)

[16] See Franklin Houn, "The Draft Constitution of Communist China," *Pacific Affairs,* Vol. XXVII, No. 4 (December 1954), pp. 319-336.

More important, perhaps, is the preamble's direct statement of friendship between the Chinese, the Soviet Union, and the "people's democracies"—surely, in all of modern history, one of the strangest locations for a foreign policy plank. This is the only foreign policy pronouncement in the Constitution, except for a passing reference to China's struggle against imperialism.

Chapter I is a mature, seasoned recapitulation of the Maoist rhetoric. It would be sheer nonsense to take the provisions literally; practice and principle differ as much as they did in the USSR under Stalin. Even though it is rhetoric, it is important rhetoric, since the Constitution enshrines the verbal symbols by which Mao and his paladins came to power. "Democratic centralism" is reaffirmed. The People's Republic of China is declared to be a democratic state led by the working class and based upon the alliance of workers and peasants. All authority of the Republic belongs to the "people"—exclusive of economically counterrevolutionary elements who may (Article 19) become citizens only after rehabilitation—who exercise that authority through the All-China People's Congress and the local congresses (*hui-i,* "meetings," "councils," almost literally "soviets") at all levels. The Chinese People's Republic is therewith, constitutionally speaking, closer to the Soviet model than most of the "parliamentary" democracies of East Europe, but it in neither in name nor formal structure a soviet state like the old "Chinese Soviet Republic" (see above, pp. 209-211).

The remaining articles in Chapter I deal mainly with the economic and social structure of the state. The Constitution recognizes four categories of property ownership: state ownership, cooperative ownership, ownership by individual working people, and capitalist ownership. State ownership of property is declared the predominant economic form and is to enjoy priority in development, while the other three categories are at present permitted to exist side by side with state ownership. Additional provisions declare that the state will protect the ownership of land and other forms of property by peasants, but will encourage them to form voluntary cooperatives for production, distribution, and credit. The state will even protect the capitalists' ownership of production materials and other properties, but will at the same time follow the line of utilizing, restricting, and reforming the capitalist economy in such a manner as to bring about its gradual disappearance. Work is declared to be the honorable duty of every able-bodied citizen, and the state encourages the initiative and creative activity of citizens in their work.[17]

[17] Had this constitution been written fifty years ago as an Utopian dream, it would certainly have won the plaudits of liberals and intellectuals in many countries for its clarity, spirit, and humaneness. The harsh reality of life under a Communist government cannot be shown to derive from the humane principles, warmly espoused, which a constitution such as this sets forth. Political students and historians of some later epoch than ours may find out, with the wisdom of retrospect, why a fatal strain of persecution, secrecy, and cruelty pervades every Communist regime. Many hostile explanations have, of course, already been offered from the anti-Communist camp, but they have all been hostile. The nearest thing to a humane assessment of China's failure to humanize Communism is to be found in

Chapter II of the Constitution outlines the state structure. Few really major changes in government organization resulted from adoption of the new constitution, though there was extensive renaming and some reallocation of functions. The document registered the changes and developments in the government over a period of five years.[18] Outstanding among the changes—perhaps the only deeply significant one—was the erasure of the Great Administrative Areas as government units. This was done to remove even the potential of military separatism. (The details of the new government structure are given below, pages 230 ff. and Chartiz.)

The Chinese Communist bill of rights is incorporated in Chapter III of the 1954 Constitution. It enumerates practically all fundamental rights and privileges enjoyed by the people of democratic states. All citizens are declared equal before the law. The right to vote and to be elected is guaranteed all persons over eighteen years of age, without reference to (intra-Chinese) nationality, race, sex, profession, social background, religion, degree of education, or length of residence, except for insane persons and individuals deprived of political rights. The freedoms of religious belief, of the person, of speech, of the press, of association, of assembly, and of other forms of private and public behavior are also guaranteed. The Constitution goes on to protect the right of the citizen to work, to rest, to be educated, to obtain old-age assistance, to be supported during sickness and disability. The Constitution asseverates the freedom of citizens to engage in scientific research, literary and artistic creation, and other cultural activities. The Constitution declares that women shall have the same rights as men in the economic, political, cultural, social, and domestic spheres, and it declares that the state protects marriage, the family, the mother, and the child. Citizens are also awarded the rights of petition and of seeking indemnity from the state or from official persons for damages resulting from the wrong-

---

Michael Lindsay [Lord Lindsay of Birker], *China and the Cold War: A Study in International Politics,* Melbourne, 1955. Lindsay lived among the Chinese Communists in the Yenan period; he then admired them and loved them as friends. In this book he undertakes the real intellectual adventure of trying to find out why the Communists who were likable as revolutionaries became detestable as rulers. More books like this are needed before the world discovers whether the paranoid public mind is an *inevitable* concomitant of Communist over-thinking of human rationality detached from honored values or is merely an unfortunate symptom which has been displayed by every major Communist government thus far. The Chinese Communist Constitution gives few hints of the mistrust for their own common people, amounting almost to hatred, shown by many of the Communist rulers. (P.M.A.L.)

[18] The best summary of Communist China in these five years is undoubtedly Richard L. Walker's *China Under Communism: The First Five Years,* New Haven, 1955. Walker loves the Chinese people and sometimes excoriates the Communist regime. For readers who wish their facts in more sober guise, W. W. Rostow and others, in *The Prospects for Communist China,* Cambridge (Massachusetts) and New York, 1955, present much the same time span in a brilliantly understated synopsis of most of the things which Western scholars know that they know about Communist China. A French Catholic work by Jean Monsterleet, S.J., *L'Empire de Mao Tse-toung,* Paris, 1954, rounds out one's choice of viewpoints. Additional material is temptingly listed but not translated in John K. Fairbank's and Masataka Banno's stimulating voyage of intellectual discovery, *Japanese Studies of Modern China,* Rutland (Vermont) and Tokyo, 1955.

ful or irregular discharge of official duties. Finally, there are provisions for the protection of overseas Chinese rights and interests and for the granting of asylum to foreign persons who may be persecuted for having supported a just cause.

These elaborate provisions concerning the rights of citizens are themselves free from any qualifying phrases, but they must be read in the general context of the principles underlying the 1954 Constitution—principles which deny the enjoyment of these or any other rights to persons designated as traitors or counterrevolutionaries. Article 19 ominously and sweepingly declares:

> The People's Republic of China safeguards the people's democratic system, protects the security and rights of its citizens, suppresses all kinds of treasonable and counterrevolutionary activities, and punishes all traitors and counterrevolutionaries.
>
> The State, in accordance with law, deprives feudal landlords and bureaucratic capitalists of political rights for a specified period; at the same time it provides them with a way to live, in order to enable them to reform themselves by work into citizens who earn their livelihood by their own labor.

Since anyone at all can easily and arbitrarily be declared a traitor or counterrevolutionary—even Communists of long standing are not immune—by police initiative before an ignorant and untrained group of citizens sitting as a court, merely because he is accused of being out of sympathy with the existing political system, these rights and freedoms can be enjoyed on paper only by those who are in complete agreement with the present regime, and enjoyed in fact only in some far-off Utopian day when the Chinese economy may have enough money left over from forced industrialization to take care of its needy individual citizens.

Chapter IV quaintly and pedantically reaffirms existing fact by declaring the flag to be red, the state emblem to be "the Tien An Gate under the light of five stars," and the capital to be Peking.

A second look at the new constitution immediately reveals that its major theme is the *acceleration of socialization* in People's China. What might have been an easygoing socialist peasants' republic, led by revolutionary intellectuals, is erased forever; an industrialized state-capitalist system, committed to enrichment of the collective nation whatever the expense to the peasants and workers who compose it, is decreed. Meiji Japan, not socialist Ceylon, is the model.

By its own fiat, the whole power of the Chinese state is committed to the elimination of exploitation and the establishment of a "socialist" society through the process of socialist industrialization and transformation.

Another important feature of the new constitution is the exaltation of the position of the Chairman (President) of the People's Republic. He is the center of political gravity and the real locus of power. Not only does he possess the powers usually wielded by the titular head of the state, as in the USSR, but he is also actual commander in chief of the military forces of the People's Republic (Article 41: "The Chairman of the People's Republic of China commands the armed forces of the country, and is Chairman of the Council of National Defense.") It is evident that the Communists are moving in the general direction of preventing tuchünism or satrapy. The abolition of five of the six vice-chairmanships (or vice-presidencies) under Mao not only pointed up the importance of Chairman Mao himself; it also ejected from supreme public office such "non-Communist" running mates of the Communists as the much-discussed Mme. Sun Yat-sen.

Further peculiar to the new Constitution is the extraordinary position occupied by the judiciary. At every level of government the people's courts *(jên-min fa-yüan)* are directly responsible to the people's congresses (literally, "council of people's delegates," *jên-min tai-piao ta-hui)*, not to the next higher level of courts except for specified cases. This is reminiscent of other regimes in which legalism has had to be curbed by declaring the judicial system a political instrument of the class war or the racial health, not an apolitical umpire above the policy decisions of the rulers.[19]

The power of the new Constitution comes from its consolidation of a Red government which can afford, as no other Red government before it, the luxury of immense ceremony and the application of glacial deliberateness. Autonomy yields to centralization; even "democratism," Communist though it is, yields to state power. The Chinese 1954 Constitution is as beautiful a document as the Soviet 1936 Constitution; like its Russian counterpart, it is remote indeed from workaday reality.

The Permanent Communist Government. The appearance of this new "constitutional" Communist government has been overshadowed in the world's press by such relatively minor issues (minor in comparison with the whole fate of China) as the seating of a Peking delegation in lieu of a Taipei delegation in the United Nations, or diplomatic relations between Washington and Peking, or the local military threats in Vietnam and Laos. Actually, the economic and military success or failure of Communist China will depend, to a high degree indeed, on the Communists being able to *govern.* Everywhere in the world, and nowhere more than in China, the first task of government is the effective routine performance of duties and

[19] At this point one may point out that the USSR had made sharp swings back to "socialist legality" in 1955 and 1956. The return to law, however limited and partial it may be, is a symptom of the revulsion against excessive personal authority which Stalinism engendered. No one can predict how far the Soviet Union will swing in the general direction of decency before the popular response to partial freedom frightens the oligarchs—as increasing liberty has frightened all alert oligarchs since the beginning of politics—into a resumption of intimidation, cruelty, and repression. What can be said with a considerable degree of assurance is that the People's China and Kruschchev's Russia were in 1956 going in momentarily opposite directions. China was becoming more Stalinist, following the impetus of the 1954 Constitution, while Russia was becoming less so. (P.M.A.L.)

services which government owes the people. To many Chinese, Communism is obligated not only to deliver a socialist order and world peace: it must guarantee them modernity as well.

The transition from a local semirebellion in 1943 to China-wide ascendancy in 1949 was purchased by the use of what Mao calls "protracted strategy," an adaptation of the traditional Chinese uses of deliberateness and deception in warfare to the purposes of modern Communism. Sun Tzŭ and Karl Marx coincide more fruitfully than either could have dreamed. The temporary and almost ramshackle little local governments by which the Communists worked their way to power were superseded, at the moment of power, by Military and Political Committees *(Chün-chêng wei-yüan-hui)*, of Great Administrative Areas *(Ta Hsing-chêng Ch'ü)*, organizations with a Jacobin austerity. These were replaced in 1953 by the new administrative organ of an Administrative Committee *(Hsing-chêng wei-yüan-hui)* for each area.[20] In 1954 this whole structure was wiped out. The Constitution of 1954 followed.

Government under the new Constitution is shown in Chart 12. The powers of the *Chu-hsi* (Chairman or President) have been very substantially increased; the organs at the top of the state have been simplified. Five vice-presidents were lopped off. The People's Government emerges as a Chinese improvement on the government of the USSR.

The All-China People's Congress[21] meets annually for a short period; it serves as the supreme organ of state power. It is easy for outsiders to see in this only a sham parliament, but the fact remains that if totalitarian states are to endure at all, they must have facilities for settling crises or deaths in their leadership. (Hitler's posthumously published conversations showed a concern with his successors which Mao may think but may not voice today.)[22] The Congress, convened by its own standing committee, has elected the major officials, "decided" on the national economic plan presented by Mao and other leaders, and has enacted law.

The Standing Committee, in general, carries out those functions which had been maintained—during the two decades of Kuomintang rule—by the Central Executive Committee of the Kuomintang (see pp. 153-154). It is executive and administrative as well as legislative. It may interpret laws, annul orders and decisions of the new State Council *(Kuo-wu yüan)*, and

[20] For a careful study of the emergence of the Communist government, see the detailed description and analysis given in S. B. Thomas's illuminating *Government and Administration of Communist China,* New York, revised edition, 1955. An interesting companion work, showing a different Chinese Communism at work in the larval stage, is Gene Z. Hanrahan, *The Communist Struggle in Malaya,* New York, 1954.

[21] The term "National People's Congress" is often used in the official English-language broadcasts from Peking; but the term "national" is so firmly attached to the Nationalist phrase *kuo-min* ("nation-people") that the authors have used the more literal translation of "All-China" in rendering the Communist phrase "whole-nation" or *ch'üan-kuo.*

[22] Dr. Henry Picker (transcriber), *Hitlers Tischgespräche im Führerhauptquartier 1941-1942,* Bonn, 1951, pp. 222-223. In the intimacy of the dinner table the megalomaniac Hitler finally confided to his intimates that there was one real use for his *Ja*-voting Reichstag.

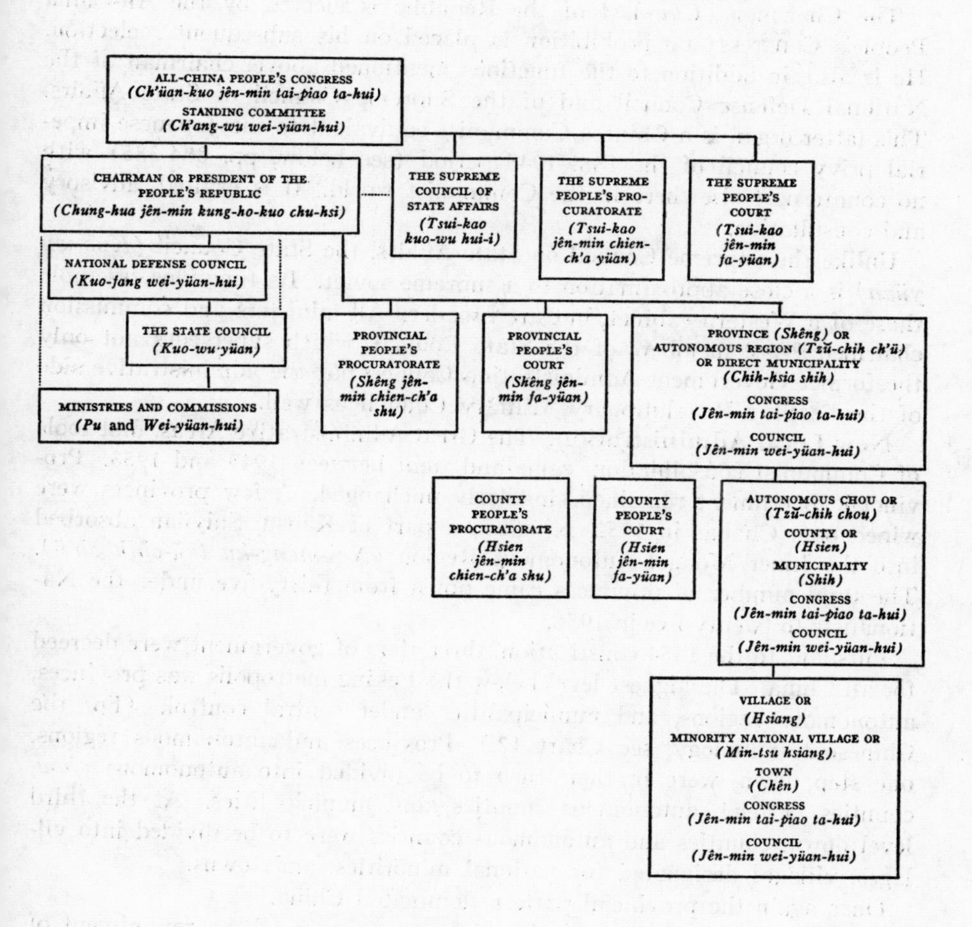

CHART 12—New Policy-Determining Organs of the Central and Local Chinese People's Governments After the Constitution of 1954

supervise the work of government organs. It misses the parallel with the presidium of the Supreme Soviet of the Soviet Union in that its chairman is not titular head of the government, but is subordinate to the *Chu-hsi.*

The Chairman *(Chu-hsi)* of the Republic is elected by the All-China People's Congress; no prohibition is placed on his subsequent reelection. He is also, in addition to the functions mentioned above, chairman of the National Defense Council and of the Supreme Council of State Affairs. This latter organ is a Chinese Communist equivalent to the Japanese imperial privy council of the 1889-1945 period (see below, pp. 384-385) with no counterpart elsewhere in the Communist world. It is exalted, advisory and consultative.

Unlike the Supreme Council on State Affairs, the State Council *(Kuo-wu yüan)* is a close approximation to a supreme soviet. Its functions resemble those of a Western cabinet, but are broader. All ministers and commission chairmen [23] are members of the State Council, which supersedes not only the former Government Administration Council but the administrative side of the People's Revolutionary Military Council as well.

New Local Administration. The Great Administrative Areas, first tools of Communist consolidation, came and went between 1949 and 1953. Provincial government remained singularly unchanged. A few provinces were wiped out: Chahar in 1952, Ninghsia a part of Kansu, Suiyüan absorbed into the Inner Mongol Autonomous Region *(Nei-mêng-ku tzŭ-chih ch'ü).* The total number of provinces came down from thirty-five under the Nationalists to twenty-five in 1956.

Pursuant to the 1954 constitution, three tiers of government were decreed for all China. The highest level below the Peking metropolis was provinces, autonomous regions, and municipalities under central control. (For the Chinese terminology, see Chart 12.) Provinces and autonomous regions, one step down, were in their turn to be divided into autonomous *chou,* counties *(hsien),* autonomous counties, and municipalities. At the third level down, counties and autonomous counties were to be divided into villages, villages designated for national minorities, and towns.

Once again the provincial pattern dominated China.

The new Peking outline was in this respect, as in others, reminiscent of a return to imperial practices along with Communism.

The Chinese Communists themselves use the word "congress" in designating the new elected bodies of each level, but the Chinese term *Jên-min tai-piao ta-hui* is closer to "soviet of people's delegates" than it is to any use of the word "congress" made in everyday American or British English.

[23] A Hongkong dispatch of May 12, 1956, indicated a broadening of the Communist list of ministries to cope with the heavy industrialization plans. Ten new ministries and two commissions were added, according to the New York *Times,* among them a National Economic Commission, a National Technological Industry Commission, and ministries of metallurgical industry, of power equipment, of city construction, of food, of land reclamation, and of marine products.

Communist Civil Service Practices. It is not without importance that the Communist breakthrough in China's long deadlock between liberty and progress was accomplished in part by the brilliant selection of "cadres." In their language, a *cadre* is a model man from whom others can learn through copying what he *is* and what he *does,* not by learning out of a book what he thinks he thinks.[24] Much of the success of the Communists can be attributed to their personal policy. Their policy discipline is more rigid than the discipline of the old Prussian army. The selective and promotional devices are as practical and brilliant as any to be found anywhere in the world. They have learned to use man's nature for their own ideals, understanding things which Confucians and Christians have long known, but applying old doctrines anew: "Whence can wee take a better argument, a clearer demonstration, that all the *Greatnes* of this world, is built upon *opinion* of others, and hath in itself no *reall being,* nor power of subsistence, than from the *heart of man?* It is always in *action,* and *action,* still busie, still pretending to doe all, to furnish all the powers, and faculties with all that they have; But if an enemy dare rise up against it, it is the soonest endangered, the soonest defeated to any part."[25] So wrote John Donne in 1623, and Mao, who never heard of him, applies it.

Heart and essence of all Communist personnel teaching is the *leadership* of the entire revolution by the Communists, but no *monopoly* by them of the right to support the revolution.

Thus, the Communists do not have to resort to the legal fixture of a "period of tutelage" employed by the Kuomintang (see pages 156-158) in order to exercise the powers of sovereignty. They simply assume that the leadership belongs to themselves by virtue of their philosophy and talents, and consolidate the "people's power" in their own hands. Practical leadership of the Communist Party is achieved by several familiar and characteristic devices: (1) appointment of trustworthy party members to important government posts, and all policy-determining organs; (2) employment of enthusiastic and young trained staff workers (called cadres, *kan pu*) in various governmental and social fields; and (3) provision of opportunities for socially esteemed personalities who are willing to denounce their past to support the Communist policy.

Obviously, key positions in the government are held by leading personalities of the Communist Party, despite the claim of government through a united front. The Chairman of the Communist Party concurrently holds the position of Chairman of the People's Central Government. Important

[24] The Nationalists tried to get into this and Chiang wrote a forgotten but brilliant essay, "A Philosophy of Action," in an attempt to find values amid the turmoil of revolutionary life. The essay may be found in Paul M. A. Linebarger, *The China of Chiang K'ai-shek,* cited, pp. 373-388.

[25] John Donne, *Complete Poetry and Selected Prose. Nonesuch edition,* London and New York, 1949, p. 525, Devotion XI.

ministries, such as the Ministry of Foreign Affairs, of Finance, of Heavy Industry, are headed by leading Communists, and in ministries headed by non-Communists, Communist vice-ministers are usually assigned. The overlapping of personnel in various levels of local governments and the local party headquarters is even more evident. In order to assure a "correct" trend in public opinion, the Communists always make sure that they have comfortable pluralities in all people's conferences. However, after two decades of Kuomintang tutelage, this party-to-government relationship is automatically accepted by the Chinese people without much sense of novelty.

For better or for worse, Sun Yat-sen himself preached freedom through subordination to discipline and to dogma. Sun Yat-sen said to Judge Paul Linebarger in 1922 that he himself had to obey his own principles. He admitted that freedom had to follow obedience by commenting:

> First of all, [we need] subordination and loyalty to our party so that we can put into action our three principles. How can China ever be free if we do not subordinate ourselves individually to the collective spirit of nationalism? How can China ever become a modern democracy, if the individuals of the local units, and those local units themselves in turn, do not subordinate themselves to the purpose of the Party so that the Party can apply our doctrines efficiently? And if we do not subordinate these nationalistic and democratic Party aims to the purpose of *min-shêng,* how can we ever banish poverty and misery in China and give to every Chinese man, woman and child their just share of happiness in the same measure as enjoyed by the most favored Nationals of the globe, thereby bringing about better conditions for humanity the world over and laying the foundations of a new planet with an economic life which will do away with much of the human unhappiness of today?
>
> We shall perform this service to humanity and the whole world first through the nucleus of our Party, making China free, and through the nucleus of a free China we shall help in the uplift of the whole world. And how wonderful it is to think that this seeming miracle may come about merely from self-subordination to the Party and through guidance of its doctrines.[26]

[26] Paul M. W. Linebarger, *A Commentary on the San Min Chu I,* typescript copy, unpublished, written in 1933 in Washington, D. C., p. 6 of section entitled "The Kuomintang Part in the Three Principles." The Nationalists felt themselves to be entirely orthodox in establishing freedom through repression and liberty by the denial of dissidence. The Paul Linebarger who contributes to this book is a son of the Paul M. W. Linebarger who was one of the few Americans to be a Kuomintang revolutionary and government official during the thirty years, 1906-1936. Much of the material concerning the one-party rule of the Kuomintang was derived by this author at close secondhand through his father from Sun Yat-sen. Sun himself appears to have been emotionally disappointed and intellectually surprised by the almost complete failure of tolerated multi-party government under the old first republic and to have been much more comfortable in his role of revolutionary leader once he had, with the help of Joffe, Borodin, and other Communist advisers, relieved himself of any obligation to respect the views of his adversaries. His views were far more *voelkisch,* in the German sense of that term, than democratic. Both the Kuomintang and the Communists agree in denying the admissibility of an intellectual opposition to themselves. In this they reflect a Chinese dread of intellectual freedom which has been characteristic

One-party rule is nothing new to the Chinese. The Kuomintang, in adopting the Leninist pattern of one-party rule, was in a sense importing a European concept, but in another sense it was merely giving modern content to the age-old doctrines of Confucianist ideological control.

Cadres and Communists. The strength of the Communist Party really lies in the selfless and efficient services rendered by the staff workers, the *kan pu* or cadres. Cadres are usually young enthusiastic party members, sometimes even nonmembers who are especially designated by the party to take the lead in various governmental or party activities. The qualities required of every cadre are loyalty, obedience, initiative, and ability in organizing the masses. A man of thirty is usually regarded as being too old to become a good cadre.

Back in the days of the war against Japan, the Communists established at Yenan a number of schools for the training of cadres, such as the Central Party School, the Military Institute, the Yenan Resist Japan University, the Lu Hsün University. Admission to these institutes was restricted to promising young candidates, either Communists or close sympathizers, who showed high aptitude for profiting by training in professional, political, ideological, or cultural fields. The formal education was only part of their training. The final processing they obtained through these facilities came through "learning from the masses." In simple terms this meant field work. Among the cadres those who came from the peasant and worker classes had to take the courses on cultural matters, and those with good intellectual backgrounds were required to live among the peasantry to learn the language of the common people and to think in terms of their everyday living. Only after thorough training for one or two years were the cadres sent forth to do real work in the field.

These cadres contributed a great deal in the military campaigns against the National Government. They took over a great part of the noncombatant work of the non-Communist army, such as propaganda, mass organizations, provisional land reform, and the "take-over process." An immense force of the so-called Southbound Working Group was organized by the cadres who were in the latter stages of the Nationalist-Communist civil war, incorporated into the political departments of the People's Liberation Army. At the time that the Nationalists finally fell, the Communists had enough trained young people on hand to incorporate 150,000 of them into the land program of the "newly liberated areas" alone.

Without cadres, the Communists would have had difficulty in taking and holding power. The party was simply not big enough to manage the compli-

---

of Chinese civilization in most of its phases. To assume that the Chinese Communists' application of one-party rule is, therefore, in any sense "un-Chinese" would be a dangerous assumption indeed. After Chinese Communism is some day historied, its provision of "correct" orthodox answers may be one of the features which its successor system will most zealously attempt to copy. It could almost be said that the Chinese are willing to have democracy if they do not have to have freedom as the price for it.

cated political, economic, and social situation after the Communist conquest. Since then, the Chinese Communist Party has increased its membership sharply. In 1937 there were only about 40,000 members. In 1945, the figure jumped to about 1,210,000. In 1952 there were about 5,000,000 members. A conservative estimate would put membership today at between five and six million. Not all Communists can become cadres and not all cadres are necessarily Communists. The cadres are the young probationary workers who do the actual work of the party for the Communist government among the population. A cadre showing exceptional qualities is always invited to become a party member. Conversely a party member who does not have the energy to get out and work efficiently and vigorously would not be a cadre.

Rapid expansion of the Communist Party led inevitably to the infiltration of the Party by opportunists and fortune-seekers. The Communists have from time to time purged their party through a process which they call the "rectification movement" (*chêng-fêng yün-tung*). The first rectification movement was inaugurated in 1942 and directed chiefly against Communists of the higher echelon who exhibited "subjective or individualistic tendencies." The second rectification movement was carried out in 1947-1948 and was directed against the cadres employed in land reform, weeding out the ones who showed leniency toward landlords or maintained relations with the condemned classes of the population. A third rectification movement was inaugurated in April, 1950. Each rectification movement called for reciprocal criticism and for public self-criticism.[27]

In actual practice this means that every cadre and Communist Party member must be prepared to enumerate his own faults upon demand. He should not only confess his faults; he should also be sure to make himself acquainted with the latest utterances of Mao or Liu so as to demonstrate his capacity to remedy his personal defects in accordance with the latest confessionals issued by the top party spokesmen.

The Communist Capitalists. After the beginning of their "take-over" of power, the Chinese Communists made a very serious effort to acquire support from as many native Chinese capitalists as they could. As of 1948-1949, it appeared quite possible that the Communists would win power only to lose it—win it by political vitality and military dash, but lose it by economic mismanagement. The Communists saw this danger too. They met it by the extraordinary audacious device of recruiting all the industrial leaders they could possibly obtain. The area of Shanghai was critical.

Right after the Communists took Shanghai they invited many well-known Chinese capitalists to participate in the People's Political Consultative Conference. Men such as Jung Te-shêng, the owner of a chain of cotton and flour mills, and Chou Ts'ang-po, a public utilities magnate, were given very

[27] "*Chung-kung chung-yang chüeh-ting ch'üan-tang chêng-fêng*" (The Central Executive Committee of the Chinese Communist Party decides to start the rectification movement within the Party), in *Hsin Hua Yüeh Pao* (New China Monthly), Vol. II, No. 3 (August 11, 1950).

cordial invitations. The Communists even persuaded Chinese capitalists who had fled to British Hongkong to come back to Shanghai to assist in the reconstruction and management of the city. Liu Hung-shêng, the famous manufacturer of woolen goods and matches, was invited to return. When he got back he was asked to make a public statement of his conversion to socialism. He visited Peking, was allowed an audience with Mao Tse-tung, attended numerous conferences, made public speeches, returned to Shanghai, and so far as the outsiders can tell, is operating his factories as before—with a Communist Party member at his elbow. As a member of the All Circles Conference of Shanghai, Liu acted on the all-powerful Labor Disputes Conciliation Board and the Price Evaluation Board. He suffered no personal material loss or inconvenience. In his own factory, however, he was not the boss he used to be. He had to deal with a management committee composed of representatives from both the managerial staff and the factory workers; the committee, not he, decided the policies of production and management. The workers' union made decisions on employment and working conditions. The products of his factory were sold to the government; the raw materials were supplied by the government; Liu had to comply with all of the regulations issued by the government. The price of his product was fixed by the government. In short, although he seemed to be managing his own factory, he had been converted from capitalist into one unit of Communist economic managerial personnel.

Liu is not alone.

Liu is typical of the so-called national capitalists whose status was represented by a small star on the Communist flag and who was offered the opportunity, according to the *Common Program,* of remaining a "capitalist" in a socialist state. Theoretically, the private property of these capitalists remained intact. In fact, it became an integrant in the Communist state economic account. In their personal lives, the majority of the national capitalists enjoyed the same amount of material comfort, until the necessities of the Korean War caused most of them to "volunteer" to give up a very substantial proportion of their personal possessions. Although they could not enjoy the management of mobile capital, they still had a measure of security and a comfortable living provided they paid for their new status with abject docility and complete obedience. The Communists retain the capitalists—on conditions.

Landlords, as a class, however, were never asked to survive, although some did. Often they were dispossessed without mercy or question. Even when they fled their possessions and attempted to disguise themselves as common laborers and seek employment, they were hunted down and identified by their soft hands and educated ways of talking. The suicide of landlords and the employment of their womenfolk as maids or prostitutes no longer make news. The capitalists were retained because they had skills that might contribute toward the modernization of China. The former owning classes on the land were often discarded as incorrigible and irremedial. Estimates of the numbers of deaths involved are almost completely unreliable, but it seems probable that executions or suicides have run into the millions. Since landlords, however, are usually among the most unpopular human beings in any society, the tortuous treatment of landlords was more a spontaneous movement of an angry populace than a fixed policy of the Communist Government. In fact, Chinese Communist policy toward landlords and rich peasants has varied from region to region. In some areas, rich peasants enjoyed quite lenient treatment.[28]

Intellectuals and Independents. When the Communists first came to power in 1949, their original policy was one of leniency toward intellectuals, professionally trained persons, and the lower grades of former Kuomintang administrators. In this manner they secured the cooperation and services of a large body of trained people without whom the country could not have been run. In the joint proclamation of Mao Tse-tung and Chu Têh issued on April 25, 1949, as an incidental to the Communist capture of Nanking, they promised that, apart from the incorrigible war criminals and counterrevolutionary elements, personal immunity would be offered to both high ranking and low ranking officials of the former Kuomintang Government. These officials of municipal, provincial, or national organs of government were enjoined to stay at their posts but cautioned to avoid counterrevolutionary activities. As a result of this proclamation about 95 per cent of the Nationalist employees of the municipal government of Shanghai stayed on the job after the Communist capture of the city.[29]

Tenure was by no means comfortable. The Communist Party was frank to point out that these people were needed for a take-over period, and the necessity of keeping the former officials and intellectuals was a passing necessity, not a basic point in revolutionary doctrine. Continued survival required participation in self-criticism meetings and study groups. Frequent interrogation by the young Communist cadres was usual. The Communists set up re-education processes and re-indoctrination facilities for all these formerly skilled people. Each person going through such facilities had to review his own past activities and had to explain in concrete personal terms just how wrong his own thinking had been. Persons who were incapable of condemning themselves vividly and of expressing gratitude for their Communist salvation have disappeared.

With really famous public characters the Communists adopted a more lenient and civilized method. So eager were the Communists to give an impression of continuity that they even took in the leaders of society in the society-page sense of the term. Persons who are famous have been given

[28] The earlier desperate struggle between landlords and peasants and the resultant bloodshed and destruction are vividly described in Jack Beldon's journalistic account, *China Shakes the World,* New York, 1949.

[29] Report of Mayor Ch'en I, English translation in *China Digest,* Vol. 6, pp. 8-9 (September 21, 1950).

honorary positions in the government or have been allowed to retain their original positions in their respective professions. From time to time they are required to write articles eulogizing the policies of the new government. These people are considered to have been won over and a reasonable degree of comfort has been assured them.

The material rewards for orthodoxy under the Communist regime are very substantial. A professor who follows the Communist line can obtain three times as much gross income as a junior Communist official. Since virtually all public and educational posts are controlled by the government, since private enterprise in any field, profit or nonprofit, has been almost entirely obliterated, Chinese intellectuals can survive only by making an individual adjustment with the new Communist authorities.

As a result the Chinese newspapers have been filled for years with confession-type essays in the form of "general reviews," indicating the progress made by individual Chinese. These essays are written in a stereotyped form. Each essay begins with the writer denouncing his own past of bureaucratic connections, reactionary practices, and individualistic inclinations. If the writer has lived in America he is expected to denounce the filthy degradation of his mind and emotions which had been brought about by contact with the shameless filth of so-called American civilization. The Chinese Communists have been particularly bitter about the United States, possibly because they dread the long-standing sentimental, religious, and intellectual connections between the United States and China. The essays then go on to explain the individual's progress toward socialistic enlightenment, the joy and clarity with which he has accepted revolutionary ideas. It is common to conclude with a stirring sense of personal loyalty toward the incomparable leader Mao Tse-tung.[30]

Criticism and self-criticism, on the part of these intellectuals, involves not only self-degradation and self-repudiation, but also includes attacks on one's friends and relatives who may have stayed outside the Communist following. Mr. Huang Chia-têh, former publisher of a popular magazine, had to express his grief and guilt at having translated garbage from American magazines.[31]

Hu Ssŭ-tu had to denounce his father, Hu Shih, as a reactionary and as intellectual public enemy number one; since Hu Shih is the greatest philosopher of modern China and the advocate of the written vernacular language, which the Chinese Communist leaders themselves use, the irony is pathetic.

[30] A particularly interesting volume entitled *Fei-ch'ü chiao-shou tzŭ-wo chien-t'ao ti wên-chang* (Self-criticism essays of professors in the Communist occupied area), edited and published by the Kuomintang Reform Committee, Formosa, 1952, contains essays written by such prominent professors as Ku Chieh-kang, Mao I-shêng, Ou Yüan-huai, Liang Ssŭ-ch'êng, Kao I-han, and others.

[31] Huang Chia-têh, *"Ts'ung chien-ch'a pien-chi hsi-fêng tsa-chih têng shih-chien chung ch'eh-ti ch'ing-suan wo ti fan-tung ti mai-pan ssŭ-hsiang"* (I liquidate thoroughly my reactionary comprador thought by a self-appraisal of my editing of the West Wind Magazine), in *Chieh Fang Jih Pao* (The Liberation Daily), Shanghai, July 16, 1952. See also *Ta Kung Pao,* Shanghai, September 6, 1950, for the famous denunciation by Hu Ssŭ-tu of his father, Hu Shih.

As a consequence, the intellectual climate of Communist China is appallingly dull. Chinese magazines and books even in wartime retained variety, lightness, and humor. In the long years of Kuomintang rule there was never a year in which vociferous complaint of Kuomintang oppressiveness failed to reach the outside world. At the present time, no one complains about Communist China from within the country. Everything is perfect except for those defects ordered to exist by the latest ukase of the Communist authorities. It is perhaps safe to say that, in the years 1949-1953, the Chinese Communists performed the equivalent of a prefrontal lobotomy on the intellectuals of all Chinese civilization that they controlled. The magazines and books continued to be published. Only the content was missing.

The Agrarian Reformers At Work. Of all the political issues of China outstanding during the period of Nationalist control, land reform was the most important and controversial. The Communists exploited the issue extensively, using it as one of their major propaganda fronts.

To the tiller belongs the land was not only a Communist policy. Advocated by Sun Yat-sen, it had been a theoretical principle of Nationalist policy as well. As early as 1930 the National Government passed laws providing for a 25 per cent reduction in all land rents, prohibiting land rents amounting to more than three eighths of the gross value of the crops, and guaranteeing security of tenure to all peasants. However, owing to administrative inefficiency and undue emphasis on legal technicalities, the National Government never put its own laws into actual practice. If it had it might be in existence on the mainland today.

The Communists, on the other hand, carried out land reform with excessive vigor and brutality in their early period of the Chinese Soviet Republic. When they started again in the Northwest and North, they operated on a much more tolerant and intelligent basis for land reform.

From 1931 to 1934 the slogan was, "Landlords Get No Land, Rich Peasants Get Poor Land." During the war of resistance against Japan the Communists masked their land policy by doing little more than to administer in fact those general policies which the Nationalists had enacted on paper. They even sold irredeemable paper-money bonds to the landlords and let the landlords clip coupons in order to buy more irredeemable bonds as a means of keeping the landlords healthy. After V-J Day the Communist land policy changed back to forcible confiscation and free distribution of land. They did this as an emergency measure to win the influence of peasants. The Communist Party directive putting this into effect was dated May 4, 1946. In September, 1947, the Communists convoked their own National Land Conference and, after long deliberations, proclaimed their own *Outline of the Land Reform.*[32]

[32] Text of the *Outline of the Land Reform,* 1947, can be found in *I-chiu-ssŭ-ch'i-nien i-lai Chung-kuo Kung-ch'an-tang chung-yao wên-hsien-chi* (Important documents of the Chinese Communist Party since 1947), Hongkong, 1949, pp. 11-14; English translation in *Chinese Press Survey,* Vol. III, No. 3 (March 21, 1949).

The *Outline of the Land Reform,* 1947, provided that all land held by landlords should be confiscated and that all "excessive" land held by rich peasants should be requisitioned. Excessive land was defined as land which could not be cultivated by the owner himself with the assistance of his family. Land possessed by family guilds, temples, schools, and public organizations was also subject to confiscation. Land so obtained should be distributed among the poor peasants through the peasants association; the peasants association was to be composed of middle peasants, poor peasants, and farm hands. The change was therefore a struggle against landlords and rich peasants.

Critical to the entire Communist land policy, therefore, has been the definition of economic classes in the agrarian population. In 1947 the Communists put out two important documents as guides to this difficult topic: *How to Determine Agrarian Classes* and *Decisions on Certain Problems Concerning Land Reform.*[33] It is significant that these documents were reissues of two proclamations of the old Chinese Soviet Republic in 1933, in its most drastic, doctrinaire days. According to these documents, the entire agrarian population was divided into five classes:

1. The landlord class composed of those persons who possessed a large amount of land, but did no manual work themselves and whose livelihood depended entirely upon rent through exploitation and usury.
2. The rich peasants who were exactly similar to the landlords except that they participated in the work on the farm and rented only a part of their land to poor peasants.
3. The middle peasants who owned their own land, draft animals, and farm implements, but did not exploit other peasants.
4. The poor peasants who owned little land and some farm implements, but who had to sell at least a part of their land to others.
5. Hired hands who owned no land and whose livelihood depended entirely upon the sale of their labor.

In actual operation the established policy was to strengthen the poor peasants and farm hands, to neutralize middle peasants, and to liquidate landlords and rich peasants. During their struggle with the Kuomintang, the Communists demanded large support from the poor peasants and farm hands in order to obtain both recruits and grain. To get the support of the poorest classes in Chinese society a great deal of land had to be confiscated from landlords and from rich peasants for the purpose of redistribution.

From September, 1947, when the land law became effective to the end of 1949 when the Communists reached final power, bitter struggles were carried out in the plains of North China with countless brutal murders and

[33] For the texts, see Jen Pi-shih, *"T'u-ti kai-kê chung ti chi-ko wên-t'i"* (Certain questions concerning the land reform movement) in *Important Documents,* cited in footnote 32, pp. 32-55.

much meaningless destruction. Social relationships were disrupted and actual farm output was curtailed. The productivity of the land was sacrificed to the social revolution by devices such as "settling of accounts" (in which poor peasants and tenants were encouraged to claim repayment for anything which they thought they had overpaid in previous regimes) and "mass accusation movements" (catharses of hate in which the Communists used social psychology with pitiless skill to create village unity by inventing and destroying live human scapegoats, usually landlords, whose deaths drained off the common people's resentments and left the community ready to proceed with new collective tasks).

The bitterest challenge of all, *collectivization of the land,* threatened the Chinese people more and more in 1955 and 1956. There were signs that the Communists relented their pace in some respects, but the goal of actual land socialism became more distinct. If this is carried through, it will be at the expense of human suffering unparalleled since prehistoric times, and unless intelligently timed, it could crack the military-political foundations of the People's Government.

Minor Political Parties. At the outset of rule in 1949 the Communists worked hard to set up a facade of multiparty government which would justify the democratic pretensions of the regime. The vice-chairmen of the People's Government were non-Communists—kidnaped warlords, society ladies, or tempestuous liberals, trapped at last—who lent a flavor of popular-frontism to the government as a whole.

By the middle 1950's this had changed. The vice-chairmen lapsed into obscurity at home or were sent touring Asia to beguile innocent neutralists who, not knowing China, might confuse fastidious drawing-room manners with military nonaggression. The first session of the People's Political Consultative Conference started in 1949 with 142 minor-party representatives as against a mere 18 Communists. By 1956 the minor-party elements were still in the showcases, but they had been carefully screened away from the actual chambers of power. Non-Communist elements were once tolerated on condition that they support Communism utterly and without reserve. This is no longer enough: they must support Communism in the precise manner which the Communists require.

Minor parties survive, at least in name.[34] The Communists employ them in a curious experiment, a kind of political vivisection, whereby the members of the newly degraded classes, not tolerated in the Communist Party itself, can join pro-Communist parties suitable to their previous stations in

[34] For detailed information concerning these parties and groups, see *"Chi-ko min-chu tang-p'ai ti ta-kai"* (Notes on a few democratic parties and groups), *Chieh Fang Jih Pao* (The Liberation Daily), June 30, 1949; *Jên-min shou-ts'ê, 1950,* cited, Section B; Allan B. Cole, "The United Front in New China," and A. Doak Barnett, "Mass Political Organizations in Communist China," in H. Arthur Steiner (editor) *Report on China* in *The Annals,* cited. S. B. Thomas, work cited, pages 45-51, outlines these parties dispassionately, while Richard Walker, work cited in passing brief mentions, relegates these parties to the obscurity which their impotence makes appropriate for them.

life. Merchants should join one party, ex-Kuomintangites another, intellectuals a third. This ordering of Chinese life by social caste is new to China and imparts a strangely Hindu flavor to mainland China. While Nehru abolishes the old untouchables, Mao creates new ones. The parties are therefore not mere propaganda weapons. They are police devices, man-made purgatories wherein opponents of the regime can survive at the price of servility and can strive for sustained recognition as actual members of the "people."

The minor political parties have begun to lose touch with their pre-1949 forms and programs. One of the authors of this book believes, on the basis of some years' acquaintance with the late General Fêng Yü-hsiang, that Fêng intended a real coalition of minor parties at Peking when he headed back to China from the United States, only to die (presumably murdered) on a Soviet ship in the Black Sea; this dream, if it ever did exist as a political plan, was vain. The minor parties had elegant hopes and immense ambitions, but no power and little real leadership, even in Nationalist days; under the Communists they have become not only phantoms but compliant phantoms as well. They still possess immense value for political warfare[35] among the overseas Chinese and the Asian-African nations, but they have little other serious value remaining.

The Revolutionary Committee of the Kuomintang is the coterie once clustered around Dr. Eugene Chen, the Trinidad Chinese mestizo who was a world figure as foreign minister of the Wuhan Government (see above, p. 139) and a celebrated Hongkong refugee for decades thereafter; now it centers about Mme. Sun Yat-sen, the junior widow of the Nationalist leader. *The Democratic League* is the leftover of a once important association of minor groups which sought but did not obtain power in the period of Nationalist-Communist deadlock following World War II. The Third Party *(Ti-san Tang)* was a well-meant attempt to reconcile Communists and Nationalists by maintaining a party outside of both; it was led by the zealous Chang Po-chün. *The Chih-kung Party* is an odd overseas organization, claiming descent from the *Hung-mên-hui* (an anti-Manchu secret society of the Ch'ing period) but now shot through with Scottish-rite masonry; it exists on a world-wide basis with separate anti-Mao and anti-Chiang organizations. *The Democratic Reconstruction Association* was at once time a high-principled group of practical reformers seeking a real democracy within the Kuomintang framework; now it is approved by the Communists as a party suitable for merchants. *The People's Salvation*

[35] Political warfare is, in this context, the use of persons or organizations to accomplish overt or covert ends of national policy which cannot be reached with conventional diplomacy; it is distinguished from psychological warfare in that psychological warfare, in the narrow sense, relies on media of communication, and only on communication, whereas political warfare depends on the use of a personality or group of personalities. In this field the Peking government has already made rich use of the minor party personalities in dealing with Pakistan, India, the Chinese of Hongkong, and other targets.

Association was a patriotic and reformist anti-Japanese party in the 1930's; voluntarily dissolved in recent years, it remains only as a political memory. A member is on the Communist Supreme Court.[36]

Autonomous Regions for Non-Chinese Nationalities. Though the Kuomintang had had a Mongolian and Tibetan Affairs Commission, there had been little interest in the "non-Han" or aboriginal peoples, most of them primitive tribesmen, scattered about the Chinese interior. Central and South China were particularly rich in such enclaves.

Under the *Common Program* the Communists made a serious beginning on this problem, probably under the direct stimulus of Stalin's emphasis on his nationalities policy.

Under the 1954 Constitution, Section 5 of Article 4, these submerged nationalities were granted a special constitutional status for the first time. Autonomous fractions of various kinds and sizes were specified.

Progress was rapid. As early as October, 1953, no fewer than fifty national autonomous areas of the county level and above had been established. Inner Mongolia and Tibet were so large as to constitute obvious problems; in addition to these there were such units as the Autonomous Region of the Chuang People in Western Kwangsi, the Autonomous Region of the Tai People (first cousins to the Thai of Siam) in Yünnan, the Autonomous Region of the Koreans in the Yenpien area of Kirin province, and others. In this, the Communist forestalled a Nationalist movement to use the "insurrection from the hills."

Mongolian irredentism was placated before the People's Government was set up; inside Communist territory, on May 5, 1947, there was established the Inner Mongolian Autonomous Region *(Nei-mêng-ku tzŭ-chih ch'ü)*. In November, 1952, the province of Chahar was added to this Region, and in March, 1954, the province of Suiyüan. This represented a Chinese retreat from the settlement-advancing policies of the Nationalists, in which the entire administrative momentum was in favor of creating Chinese governmental and economic units out of Mongol tribal land.

The case of Tibet was even more striking, amounting almost to the conquest of a foreign country. Tibet had been the least governed of China's remaining dependencies, and at the time of the Communist-Nationalist switchover, the Tibetan authorities held firmly to their separateness. The Chinese Communists were ready from the beginning to convert an old and shadowy suzerainty over Tibet into sovereignty of the most direct and tangible kind. In January, 1950, they announced that the liberation of Tibet was on their immediate program. They used half-Tibetan or Tibetan-Chinese border troops to fight in the high altitudes, along with Chinese regulars, and launched their invasion in October, 1950.

[36] Readers with a taste for the tragic and picturesque can contrast the report on these parties in Linebarger, *The China of Chiang K'ai-shek,* cited, pp. 175-182, with the calm, up-to-date account in S. B. Thomas, work cited, pp. 45-51.

Tibetan politics, centering in the Lamaist ecclesiastical structure, was understood and used by the Communists from the beginning. They had the cooperation of one of the chief leaders of Tibet, the Panchen Lama, and after conquest they secured the assent of the other, the Dalai Lama. The Dalai Lama had fled, but returned after negotiation.

Peace was decreed by an agreement signed on May 23, 1951, which significantly made Tibet an integral part of the People's Republic of China. (At this time, Indian diplomacy threw away a great many safeguards for the autonomy and integrity of Tibet which had previous been won from China by the British rulers of India and which Nehru's administration had inherited. There may have been psychological rewards for this abandonment of India's frontier interests, but there were no tangible ones.)

The agreement specified that the Tibetans were "to return to the Chinese motherland." Called *The Agreement on Measures for the Peaceful Liberation of Tibet,* it contained seventeen articles. The Tibetans agreed to drive out imperialist aggressors. Tibet was granted national regional autonomous status under the unified leadership to the Central People's Government. In return, the Chinese promised not to alter the political system in Tibet nor to change the status, functions, and powers of the Dalai Lama and the Panchen Lama. The incumbents of various ecclesiastical and lay Tibetan offices were to continue to hold their respective ranks. The Peking government agreed not to compel local reform, which was left to be carried out by the Lhasa government "of its own accord," but the external affairs of Tibet were to be handled henceforth exclusively by the Chinese Central People's Government. Tibetan troops were absorbed into the People's Liberation Army, and Chinese soldiers appeared on the frontiers of India, Nepal, Bhutan, and Sikkim. A Military and Administrative Committee, following the Communist political fashion of that particular time, was to be established as the supreme national government organ for Tibet.

The proposed Military and Administrative Committee was finally established in May, 1952. It followed, by a safe margin, the creation of the Military District of Tibet of the People's Liberation Army on February 10, 1952. In the spring of 1956 a Tibetan Autonomous Region Preparatory Committee was set up, but the advance to full Region status was not at once proclaimed.

This Chinese policy should not be confused with the development of national republics in the Soviet Union. Russia and its affiliated Soviet countries are federal; China is unitary. The comparison should more properly be made between the autonomous *rayons* and *oblasts* within the Russian Soviet Federated Socialist Republic and their Chinese counterparts than between Tibet and the Ukraine, or Inner Mongolia and Byelorussia. As a matter of fact, the two Mongolias provide the sharpest contrast to be found on almost any Communist-to-Communist frontier. Mongolia proper is legally as independent of the USSR as Cuba is of the United States—

completely. Inner Mongolia is a creation of the Chinese People's Republic, with no international standing, no separate currency, military, or other appurtenances of sovereignty.

Sinkiang or Chinese Turkestan is another problem. In the Nationalist days a Soviet-supported East Turkestan Republic established since 1944 had constantly harassed the Chinese administration. When the Kuomintang provincial authorities surrendered to the Communists in 1949, the Turkestan movement was dissolved.

A "coalition government" came into existence. At first the Communists moved carefully. Communists and ex-Kuomintang and local East Turkestan leaders all participated. The predominant personality came to be the commanding officer of the Sinkiang Military District of the People's Liberation Army, a certain Wang Chên, who was also the head of the Sinkiang Subbureau of the headquarters of the Chinese Communist Party.

No general plan for the over-all autonomy was set forth. The establishment of Sino-Soviet joint enterprises on a major scale from 1950 onward complicated the picture.

After 1953 a few localities occupied by compact minorities had achieved a certain measure of regional autonomy. Five autonomous *chou* were already in existence at the time of the adoption of the new Constitution in 1954. On October 1, 1955, the establishment of the Sinkiang Uighur Autonomous Region was formally announced. Sinkiang is under the direct administrative scrutiny of the Central People's Government in Peking.

In the Southwest of China the Communists appear to have enjoyed the effort of winning over the backward, primitive tribesmen of the aboriginal tribes. Dictators and colonial rulers often enjoy their more primitive subjects after struggling with the adult guile and masked resistance of their more advanced subjects. The Peking leaders seem to be no exception in this respect. The Lolos have been given a Latin alphabet (which, incidentally, had been given them by Protestant missionaries more than a generation ago) and the other primitive tribes are brought to Peking for international festivals of folk art, folk dance, local costumes, and primitive music. A Mao Tse-tung or a Po I-po, standing beside an open-mouthed East German visitor straight out of Leipzig, can feel that Chinese Communism is truly the directing force of a vast and variegated empire. He may forget that he could have done better on prewar Nanking Road in Shanghai, on which—if one stood still enough for a few minutes at any one spot—almost every known variety of human being would pass by.

The Chinese Communist nationalities policy is evidence of one more major development imported from the West—this time by way of Communist thinking and example.

The Administration of Justice. The participation of minor parties in the People's Government might lead an outside observer to consider that the Chinese People's Republic differs in significant respects from the Chinese Soviet Republic. An examination of the Communist judicial system and of Communist legal methods would quickly dispel the illusion of Western-type constitutional democracy and confirm the impression of rigorous Communist discipline and of the characteristically dogmatic Marxist approach to problems of law and justice.

Article 17 of the *Common Program* provided: "All laws, decrees, and juridical systems of the reactionary Kuomintang government designed for the oppression of the people shall be abrogated. Laws and decrees designed for the protection of the people shall be promulgated and a people's juridical system shall be established." Accordingly, the Nationalist legal code was officially declared to be an intimate employed by the landlords and bureaucrats to oppress the common people and to protect the interest of the reactionary classes. At this point the Chinese legal situation began to sound like the first voyage of Gulliver, since the Communists abolished the Nationalists' legal code before they set up their own. Consequently China had no legal rules and would not have them until a Codification Commission of eighteen members headed by Ch'en Shao-yü mapped up new laws.

For the interim period legal decisions had to be based on the judges' sense of justice and on fundamental Communist principles. Chinese Communists have been much less troubled by law than have Russian Communists. The Chinese Communists have no A. Y. Vishinsky. In the older Communist guerrilla zones which were designated the first liberated areas, the Chinese Communists used people's courts as effective instruments of Communist control. People's courts consisted of informal crowds led by party agitators. The crowds served as plaintiffs, prosecutor, judge, and executioner. Sometimes people were not killed but were merely required to make humiliating public confessions or to sign over all their property. These methods would not work in the city.

When the Chinese took the major cities they had to create Communist courts under military fiats. Appointment to the courts came through military channels of the army. No law was provided. In the case of the Shanghai People's Court, the court was not established until August 11, 1949, three months after the Communist capture of the city. Naturally enough a backlog of criminal and civil cases accumulated. Nevertheless this pattern was followed by other urban districts.

The Shanghai People's Court was set up in six divisions: the Mediation Commission, the Judication Commission, the Commission for Jails, the Jurisprudence Research Office, the Forensic Medicine Division, and the Secretariat. In lieu of law the Shanghai Military Control Commission promulgated as guidance for the people's court the *Provisional Regulations for the Handling of Civil and Criminal Cases,* of which the second article reads: "Cases shall be decided according to factual circumstances and based on the outlines, laws, decrees, regulations, and decisions promulgated by the People's Government and the People's Liberation Army and the fundamental policy of the New Democracy." [37]

Pending the codification and final promulgation of people's legal codes,

[37] *Ta Kung Pao,* Shanghai, August 12, 1949.

the judges of such courts have to decide cases according to sundry laws and decrees issued by the Communist government and army from time to time, the latest speeches of Mao or Liu, and whatever interpretation they dare to give to the Communist Party documents concerning the Communist Party dogma of the New Democracy.

With the promulgation of the *Organic Law* of the Central People's Government, a People's Supreme Court, a People's Procurator General's Office, a Codification Commission, and a Ministry of Justice were established; except for these organs the *Organic Law* was silent concerning the structure of the juridical system.

Presumably the Codification Commission was assigned the function of drafting the Communist legal codes and the Ministry of Justice, the task of establishing a future juridical system. The first important new law to be proclaimed was the Marriage Law of April 30, 1950,[38] which was promulgated by the Central People's Government Council. The urgency for its promulgation can be explained by the fact that the Chinese Communists were undertaking a fundamental change in Chinese family relations as a means of breaking away from China's ancient tradition, which they regarded as feudal. This was soon followed by a security law called a *Directive for the Suppression of Counterrevolutionary Activities,* promulgated on July 23, 1950.[39] This empowered the people's courts and local people's tribunals to pass death sentences on reactionary bandits, counterrevolutionaries, saboteurs, and Kuomintang agents. With this the people's courts took over some of the work which had up to then been covered by the military tribunals only.

A special court system was set up for land reform. The Central People's Government established Special People's Tribunals as a branch of the people's courts to police the land reform in the *hsien.* Under regulations promulgated on July 20, 1950,[40] each tribunal was to comprise one chief judge, one deputy judge, several other judges. The chief judge and half of the other judges were to be selected from a panel of local people's courts; the remainder of the judges were to be selected by people's representative conferences or groups. These tribunals were authorized to sit in final judgment on matters of class status and were empowered to pass sentence up to and including death on recalcitrants who opposed the land reform or who disturbed the revolutionary order by discussing land reform adversely. Armed with the power to "arrest, try, and sentence," these courts could legally impose the following penalties: death, imprisonment, confiscation of property, hard labor, public apology and repentance, or acquittal. All sentences were, in theory, legally subject to review by the provincial people's government; death sentences had to be approved by the chairman of the provincial

[38] *Ta Kung Pao,* Shanghai, May 1, 1950.
[39] *Ta Kung Pao,* Shanghai, July 25, 1950.
[40] *Ta Kung Pao,* Shanghai, July 21, 1950.

government. No appeal was permitted in the cases of those who were found guilty as bandits, spies, or counterrevolutionaries. The inclusion of the representatives of people's organizations and groups as judges was reminiscent of the earlier Communist "mass trials," but the endeavor to settle land reform disputes by an established court with some semblance of procedure seemed to indicate an attempt, mentioned earlier, of the Communists to slow down their own headlong rural revolution of 1950 and to restore productivity to the countryside.

The new Constitution establishes a hierarchy of People's Courts *(Jên-min fa-yüan)* at levels corresponding to the territorial administrative structure. Highest is the Supreme People's Court *(Tsui-kao jên-min fa-yüan)*, responsible to the All-China People's Congress and its Standing Committee. Presidents of People's Courts are elected by People's Congresses of their respective levels for four-year terms. A system of People's Assessors monitors judicial proceedings. The constitution also provides procurators at appropriate levels to exercise the "control" power (like the Russian *Orgburo* or the Nationalist Control *Yüan)* to supervise government officials. With the exception of the Supreme People's Procuratorate *(Tsui-kao jên-min chien-ch'a-yüan)*, which is responsible to the All-China People's Congress, the new Constitution provides an exception to the local concentration of power in making local procuratorial offices independent of other local facilities. This is reminiscent of the independence of the censorate under the old imperial Chinese system (see pp. 52, 57) and is entirely compatible with the needs of a modern police state.

Meanwhile codification was apparently being carried on by the commission in Peking. According to the Communist press, the new legal system was to stress mediation for civil cases and education in lieu of punishment in criminal cases. It seems evident that the future Chinese legal codes will be modeled on the Soviet pattern. The most severe punishments will be reserved for the political opponents of the regime. In paper form, if not in fact, a very enlightened body of laws will be adopted for the protection of private rights, including the right to work, the right to freedom of movement, the right to association, and so on. Under both Russian and Chinese legal practice, security cases—that is, cases involving persons suspected of opposing the government—can always be tried by special police or military facilities without notification or public record. Given the immense changes which the regime has undertaken to bring about, and the amount of resistance which the wily and recalcitrant Chinese people have offered to so many governments before the Communists, it seems unlikely that the Communists will want to throw away any tool of repression at the present stage of development. Though law will not become primary, its auxiliary function will be useful.

Communist Foreign Policy. The Chinese Communists in their Yenan days successfully convinced some foreign observers that they were agrarian reformers, not real Communists. The agrarian reform theory was very popular in the Western press for a while until the Communists achieved success on the mainland in 1949. Thereafter the agrarian reform theory was replaced by another theory. This time some experts believed that the Chinese Communists would certainly become Far Eastern Titoists within a certain period of time. However, the Titoist theory, which represented a kind of wishful thinking on the part of foreign observers, was shattered by the Chinese entrance into the Korean War in late 1950.

The Chinese Communists perhaps encouraged the agrarian reform theory, but they have repudiated the Titoist theory openly and scornfully. The former idea was encouraged because it helped to gain sympathy for the Chinese Communists when sympathy was desperately needed; whereas the latter idea was repudiated because, so far at least, it has not been among the intentions of the Communists at all. In either case, the Chinese Communists have remained faithful Communists throughout.

A study of the utterances of the Chinese Communist leaders will show that the agrarian reformer theory was a wishful myth. Wang Chia-hsiang, the Chinese Communist Ambassador in Moscow, frankly pointed out, while he was in Yenan, that the Chinese Communists would never abandon their ideals and the theories of Marxism-Leninism and that the program of the Chinese Communist revolution consisted of two parts: the minimum program of national democratic revolution and the maximum program of socialist revolution. There is no higher authority on the true notion of Chinese Communism than the words of Mao Tse-tung himself. In his essay, *On New Democracy,* Mao observed in 1941:

> China's revolution is part of the world revolution. But the Chinese revolution must pass through two stages: first, the change of our colonial, semi-colonial and semi-feudal society into an independent democratic society; second, the establishment of a socialist society. The first is our present goal, a new bourgeois-democratic revolution. But do not confuse this with the bourgeois-democratic revolution in capitalist countries. Although the objective of the first stage of our revolution is the destruction of feudalism and imperialism and the development of capitalism, it is certainly not the establishment of a capitalist society dictated by the bourgeoisie. On the contrary, our objective is to establish a New Democracy based on an alliance of several revolutionary classes, but led wholly or partially by the proletariat. After the accomplishment of this first stage, the revolution will be developed into the second stage—the establishment of a socialist society in China.

Therefore, the fundamental policy of the Chinese Communist Party laid down by its leaders, long before the agrarian reform theory became a vogue, was precisely (1) to seek alliance with the Soviet Union and (2) to achieve the final goal of Communism by all expedient means. Strategic considerations have demanded variations in the party line, but the fundamental goals of the Chinese Communist Party have remained constant.

It is against this background that the foreign policy of the Chinese Communist Party is formulated. In fact, there is not the slightest inkling that the Chinese Communists may turn Titoist. The basis of the Chinese Communist foreign policy is characterized by the now famous clause of Mao: "You lean to one side." In a speech delivered on July 1, 1949, Mao outlined the Chinese Communist Party's objective in the outside world as follows:

> . . . This is to ally with the Soviet Union, to ally with the new democratic countries, and to ally with the proletariat and masses of the people in other countries to form an international united front. "You lean to one side." Precisely so. The 40 years' experiences of Sun Yat-sen and the 28 years' experiences of the Communist Party have made us firmly believe that in order to win and consolidate victory, we must lean to one side. The experiences of 40 years and 28 years show that, without exception, the Chinese people either lean to the side of imperialism or the side of socialism. To sit on the fence is impossible; a third road does not exist. . . . Not only in China but also in the world without exception, one either leans to the side of imperialism or the side of socialism. Neutrality is a camouflage and a third road does not exist.

For the time being at least, the Chinese Communist policy of "leaning to one side" has paid dividends. Already, the Treaty of Friendship, Alliance and Mutual Aid signed on February 4, 1950, between the Soviet Union and the Chinese Communist government has brought the two countries closer together both militarily and economically. An agreement for the extension of a long-term loan, the equivalent of three hundred million dollars, by the Soviet Union to the Chinese Communist government was signed on February 14, 1950. Seldom has a treaty been put into service so fully. Chinese participation in the Korean War could not have been undertaken had it not been for Soviet aid in the form of military equipment and moral support.

The Chinese Communist View of the Future. After the signing of the armistice, the Chinese Communist government has concentrated its effort on economic development of the country. The Chinese Communists have outlined their immediate tasks in economic reconstruction which are made possible by Soviet aid. These four tasks are: (1) to develop China's economy systematically by using the enterprises newly built or renovated, with Soviet aid as a nucleus and following the principle of the proportional development of the national economy; (2) to strengthen capital reconstruction work, especially geological surveying and prospecting; (3) to make preparations for enterprises covered by Soviet aid; (4) to learn more from Soviet experience and to train construction personnel. An even closer cooperation between the Soviet Union and China, especially in the economic field, can be safely predicted at the time of writing.

One point then, often misunderstood by Western observers, is used to plot the future,[41] according to the Chinese Communists. It involves the minimal program of a "people's democracy" and the maximal objective of socialism. Chou En-lai, speaking frankly of the need to watch private economic activity with care, put it this way:

> Only such a course for the Chinese economy can lead to the transition from the New Democracy to Socialism. Otherwise, if private economic affairs are allowed to develop freely without guidance and control, then the transition of the Chinese economy will not be along the line of the New Democracy but along lines of Capitalism, it will not be along lines of Socialism but back to the economy of dependence and imperialist-colonial status. It must be one way or the other. There is no middle way.[42]

The Battle of Ideologies in Modern China. In one sense, the survey of Chinese governments in this book has been given over to an exposition of the hypothesis that Chinese politics have been primarily a reflex of ideological dynamics, with armies, economics, and governments playing secondary and tertiary roles. Political struggle in China depends not only on what men profess to believe, in order to justify the power they hold, but even more emphatically on *the search for sharable belief*. Chinese political competition is actuated not merely by competition for places of power within an agreed society, but by attempts to create new societies. In this struggle two sets of operations are involved, the first ideological and the second organizational.

The ideological struggle consists of the presentation of successive beliefs and attempted reconciliation of the old world of Chinese cultural experience with the modern world of national and international power politics. The two chief systems of belief which have gained currency in modern China have, of course, been the nationalism of Sun Yat-sen and the particular Marxism expressed under the rubric of "the people's democracy" of Mao Tse-tung.

Naturally, no ideology would get very far unless it had organizational implementation. Thus, in modern China there has also been a struggle for government. In other words, for beliefs to take effect they must not only be believed, but men must band together in order to train others in the beliefs, to spread the beliefs by teaching revolution or by warfare, and to suppress other contradictory beliefs by persuasion, by legal prohibition, or by armed forces.

This ideological-organizational interaction is difficult to comprehend when it is viewed from the vantage point of a secure and stable political society such as the United States. From America, Chinese politics seem almost

[41] To compare the Nationalist view, see pp. 204-205.

[42] Chou En-lai, "The Course of the Chinese Economy," Report to the Thirty-fourth Standing Committee Meeting, January 5, 1952 (*New China News Agency*, January 7, 1952).

volcanic in their depth and fury. The Chinese have not easily agreed on a government and then discussed their problems in relation to the government. They do not even agree on a society, or upon the nature of the world in which all nations live, and then discuss politics against the background of this common world-view. At the forefront of every Chinese political and administrative question there comes the biggest question of all, "Who are we Chinese and what are we doing?"

In Chapter Seven, the latter day impact of the West on China, in the form of American policy toward the National Government, was discussed as a topic for a long-range historical research. Now that we know something more as to who the Chinese Communists are, at least, the reconciliation of Nationalists and Communists undertaken by American mediation in the years 1947 and 1948 appears as one of the boldest political experiments on record. It was bold even though both Nationalists and Communists paid lip service to political reconciliation, even though there were ample grounds for assuming that neither party regarded reconciliation as being feasible. Men were asked to get together on such matters as taxation, local police powers, democratic representation, and the like, when in fact they could not agree on who they were, whither the world was going, or what human life meant. The creation of an amalgamated organization out of the medieval Papacy and Caliphate, at the time of the crusades, could not have posed more difficulties than did the attempted reconciliation of Nationalists and Communists in China; nevertheless the attempt was made. At least medieval Christians and Moslems agreed in worshiping one Supreme God; the Kuomintang and the Chinese Communist Party did not have so much as a single god in common.[43]

[43] The Communists promise to approach democracy sometimes; the Nationalists occasionally swing away from it. The great Communist purges, like the "Three Anti Movement" (anti-corruption, anti-waste, anti-bureaucratism) of December, 1951, or the "Five Anti Movement" (anti-bribery, anti-tax-evasion, anti-fraud, anti-theft of state property, anti-betrayal of state economic secrets) of February, 1952, have by 1956 been followed by a slightly less nightmarish atmosphere, but there is little prospect of the slightest modicum of true democracy in Communism, while none of the Nationalist tendencies toward dictatorship in the period 1949-1956 have become more than rudimentary tendencies.

PART
TWO

The Government and Politics of Japan

A NOTE ON CHINESE AND JAPANESE NAMES

Chinese and Japanese personal names are given in the conventional form, with the family name preceding the given name, *except* where Chinese or Japanese authors have had their works published in English. In such cases, bibliographic citations follow the order of names as given on the title pages and are often listed according to Western usage.

Chinese and Japanese place names—as well as other Chinese and Japanese words—follow (in Chinese) the Wade-Giles and (in Japanese) the Hepburn systems of transliteration, *except* for a few Chinese place names which have become more commonly familiar in Chinese Postal system spellings.

CHAPTER TEN

The Cultural and Physical Background of Japanese Government

CHINA, Japan, and the United States can, in many ways, be thought of as a political triangle. America and Japan share many characteristics—modernity, constitutionality, patriotism, stability—which are not characteristic of China. America and China share many characteristics which are not characteristic of Japan: disrespect toward government, democracy in everyday social affairs, the secular spirit, and economic stratification combined with loose social equality are among the most prominent of these. Japan and China, in their turn, share features not enjoyed by the United States—such as the Confucian morality, the Buddhist heritage, doctrines of nonrational common sense, and the systematization of prestige factors in everyday life.

Such a triangular concept leads to a more wholesome appreciation of Japanese features than does the popular attempt to lump China and Japan together as Orientals or the equally popular identification of America and Japan as up-to-date countries in contrast with backward China. Even in the language structure the position is in many respects triangular. The movement of the English language itself is away from complicated inflection toward the simple, uninflected forms used in Chinese. In this respect the Chinese and English languages can be called very loosely similar. English and Japanese are closer to each other than to Chinese in their capacity to conjugate verbs. Chinese and Japanese are more like each other than English in their use of ideographs.

What does this signify in terms of American understanding of Japan?

Most simply it means that the stereotypes which Americans have learned to apply to China cannot be applied to Japan, and the Japanese national character and politics will be best understood if Americans attempt to obtain a direct, calm, reasonable, first-hand sense of the fitness of things within a Japanese context. Even the most mysterious Japanese characteristics become understandable when placed against reasonable or persuasive explanations. The character of the Japanese individually and collectively is quite possibly not as complex or as contradictory as the character of Americans. The physical background of Japan explains many of its differences from China. The cultural background explains even more. Before present-day Japanese government can be understood, it is necessary to review and to assume particular Japanese features which in some respects entitle Japan, more nearly than any other nation now extant, to be considered unique.

The Emperor Myth. The most celebrated characteristic of Japanese politics in our time has been, in ideological terms at least, the Emperor myth. This myth has a variety of interpretations. Two groups of interpretations are particularly important: those entertained by foreigners, and those entertained by Japanese. Even within these groups there is no unanimity to be found. Americans, who ten years ago regarded the Japanese Imperial tradition as an ugly or superstitious foundation for militarism, have, in many cases, by now accepted the Japanese Throne, ringed with constitutional safeguards, as a quaint and useful adjunct to the democratization of Japan. Russians whose propaganda identified the Japanese Emperor with both feudalism and fascism have been given no reason to revise their estimate. If it was a mistake ten years ago to identify the Japanese Emperor with Adolf Hitler, it is perhaps a mistake today to identify him with the late King George VI. The position of the Japanese Emperor is unique. He is the only descendant of a Stone Age monarch to hold political office in the modern world by direct descent from his neolithic forebears (or so some Japanese claim) and he rules the country which, with the possible exception of India and its national religion of Hinduism, comes closer to possessing an authentically national cult than any Western state has possessed since the displacement of the Roman state religion by Christianity. Siamese kings may share his religious position, but not the myth of his unimpeachable genealogy. Monarchs elsewhere lack in fact the continuity possessed by the Japanese Imperial office, continuity which is exaggerated in the reverence paid the Emperor by Japanese public opinion and tradition.

This sense of continuity is derived from the history of Japan itself. Japanese history has always been specifically dominated in good times and bad by a feeling for family solidarity and by a patriotic principle symbolized by the Emperor, whatever his political role may have been at the time.

Irrespective of the point of departure, whether established facts as Western authorities concede them or romantic legends transmitted by Japanese tradition, the Japanese political story leaves a strong impression of historical continuity. In some respects this continuity is to be likened to the integrity of a great symphony or of a masterly painting. Its internal consistency is artistic more than logical. The appeal which it makes to the emotions is the appeal of a great work of art. It is therefore closer to the institutional characteristics of religion than to those usually associated in the American mind with government.

Constitutionally since May 3, 1947, the Emperor has been "the symbol of the State and of the unity of the people, deriving his position from the will of the people with whom resides sovereign power." With the first part of this description almost all Japanese are in hearty agreement today. The second part, like most of the new constitution, is a foreign concept concerning which many Japanese entertain doubt. So precise a location of sovereignty is not necessarily a juridical fault, but it is to Japanese ways of thinking perhaps unnecessary. Despite the new streamlined constitution the Japanese title for the Emperor is still *Tennō* (literally, Sovereign of Heaven).

It is also true that the Emperor on January 1, 1946, formally renounced the belief that the Throne was wrapped in divine sanction. Doubtless, few sophisticated Japanese believed him to be a god in any case. Nevertheless, it is equally true, in the words of the Imperial Rescript: "The ties between us and our people have always stood upon mutual trust and affection. They do not depend upon mere legends and myths." This Rescript was entirely in harmony with the trust and affection evoked by the present Emperor's grandfather, the Emperor Meiji (1868-1912). Trustful affection was so powerful a factor that, on one of the historically rare occasions when a Japanese Emperor decided something for himself, the present ruler, Hirohito, was able to tip the scales of war and peace in favor of the civil and military —especially naval—circles who desired to end World War II. When he spoke to a Conference of Imperial Advisers on August 14, 1945, Hirohito is reported to have said: "I cannot bear any longer to see the people of this country suffer from the war. Bearing the unbearable to my ancestors and the people I wish to take the course which I have already chosen before." He followed this with surrender on September 2 in the twentieth year of his own reign. His surrender command was the political counterpart of the atomic bomb. America very literally won the war because the Emperor's authority was enough to put into effect the results our nation sought in the bombing of Hiroshima and Nagasaki. It is picturesquely paradoxical to consider that the newest weapon in man's history took effect only when it was implemented by one of the oldest of living human institutions.

Even in the process of surrender, however, the Japanese Emperor assured his people that "The national polity [*kokutai*] has been protected" along with the "eternity of the divine country."[1]

[1] The Emperor's words, quoted from his remarks on August 14, appeared in the *Mainichi Shimbun,* August 14, 1945; the best Japanese description of the Emperor's dramatic decision is given in Genji Okubo, *The Problems of the Emperor System in Postwar Japan,* Tokyo, 1948 (Pacific Studies Series), Chap. I. For the January 1, 1946, Imperial Rescript, see Appendix 25, Department of State, *The Occupation of Japan: Policy and Progress* (Publication 2671, Far Eastern Series 17), Washington, 1946, pp. 133-135. The new Constitution was published in English in the Department of State, *The Constitution of Japan* (Publication 2836, Far Eastern Series 22), Washington, 1947. It should be pointed out that the most

Before the war against America the eternity of Japan seemed even more assured. February 11, 1940, was a very special *Kigensetsu* (Day of the Founding of the Empire). To the Japanese the year marked the 2600th anniversary of the establishment of their Empire in 660 B.C. by Japan's first "historical" Emperor, Jimmu *Tennō*. The Japanese position can be made plain by quoting an extract of the comments made by a Japanese historian, Akiyama Kenzō, for the education of foreigners in Japan:

> And when we consider Japanese history in retrospect and realize that this empire has occupied the same geographical position, has been inhabited by the same people and has been ruled over by the same dynasty for so long a time, in spite of the vast historical changes that have taken place, and still continues to grow and flourish, then we can understand something of the joy that is to be found in every Japanese heart today.[2]

Fifty years before, Japan had faced and surmounted a crisis almost as severe as the tragedy of 1945. The Japanese had faced destruction and had escaped—as China did not—from the impact of the Western economic, political, and cultural system on their traditional national entity. On February 11, 1889, the Japanese celebrated their first great step toward survival in the modern world—translation of Asian policy to modern form—by the adoption of their first Imperial Constitution. On that occasion the constitution was presented as a gracious gift to his subjects by the Meiji Emperor, and its first article intoned, "The Empire of Japan shall be reigned over and governed by a line of Emperors unbroken for ages eternal."

The appeal of 1889 for continuation in the modern world of a traditional institution was effective in 1945. The phrase "reigned over and governed" should not be taken too literally because the Japanese Throne had had vicissitudes of power and misfortune which interrupted its capacity for government even though the nominal continuity remained undisturbed. Nineteen forty-five and 1889 in turn look back to A.D. 700 when the Japanese began to respond to the greatest cultural threat in their world at that time.

Thus, three hundred years before William of Normandy set foot on English soil, when the East Roman Empire was still under Leo III, the Japanese first accepted as proper for themselves a role of political behavior which applies today: in times of supreme crisis turn again to the Emperor. The legends, of course, go back far before A.D. 700. The men who collected the legends had a political motive. Thirteen hundred and more years ago they

common name for the Emperor is *Tennō,* that used in the new Constitution. *Mikado,* although useful enough as a theme for Gilbert and Sullivan, is obsolete in foreign and Japanese literature alike.

[2] Kenzō Akiyama, *The History of Nippon,* Tokyo, 1941, p. 45. This book was originally a series of lectures to foreign residents of Tokyo, given under the auspices of the *Kokusai Bunka Shinkōkai* (Society for International Cultural Relations). Chapter III, "The Principles of the Japanese State," stresses the continuity of Japanese political life.

activated the political machinery which turned propaganda into belief and belief into tradition, the tradition of the Japanese *Tennō.* Their political objective and the materials they used are to be found in the *Nihon shoki* (or *Nihongi,* Chronicles of Japan) and the earlier *Kojiki* (Record of Ancient Matters).[3] These books survive today, although attempts to interpret them encounter difficulties. Even with these materials, however, at the very beginning of Japan there is to be found the interpenetration of economic, political, and spiritual affairs which remains characteristic of Japan today.

The Indigenous Cult. From the beginning to the present the Japanese national cult has existed. Repeated efforts have been made across the centuries to give it precise form. Even with the help of modern anthropology it is impossible to assign clear and rigid beliefs to this cult at any phase of its development. Inoue Tetsujiro, Professor of Philosophy at Tokyo Imperial University, wrote that before the introduction of Buddhism and Confucianism there was no philosophy in Japan. There was instead *the Japanese spirit,* much like Confucianism, already in practice and thenceforth authorized by the imported precepts of the Chinese teacher. Japanese primitive animism survived more vigorously than did the supernatural elements in early Chinese moral philosophy. Whereas the Chinese classics explained the supernatural down to a level of matter-of-fact reverence, the *Nihongi* and *Kojiki* undertook the contrary course of exalting the divine factors in moral philosophy. This *Japanese spirit,* multifarious and many-faceted, can be called *Shintō* and can be identified with the modern national cult of Japan —despite its original framework of Chinese language, its mimicry of Chinese thought, and its successive exegeses across the centuries.[4]

[3] The first Japanese book, the *Kojiki* (Record of ancient matters), was completed in 712. This was two centuries after the official adoption of Chinese script. Thus our earliest description of prehistoric Japan was filtered through a foreign language and distilled by means of foreign ideas. Similarly the *Nihon shoki* (Chronicles of Japan) was completed in 720 and was composed almost wholly in Chinese. For myth and legend, there is little to choose between the two; in terms of history, the *Nihon shoki* is superior. A convenient Japanese edition of the earlier work is Iwanami Bunko (Series No. 13), *Kojiki,* Tōkyō, 1932; the Yasumaru version, rendered into English, was edited by Basil Hall Chamberlain, *Translation of Ko-ji-ki or "Records of Ancient Matters"* (Notes by W. G. Aston), Kobe, 1932 (2nd edition). The parallel Japanese edition of the latter work is Iwanami Bunko (Series No. 204-206), *Nihon shoki,* Tōkyō, 1932; the English translation is by William George Aston, *Nihongi; Chronicles of Japan from the Earliest Times to A.D. 697,* London, 1896 (2 vols.). An excellent bibliographic history of the two books is given in the introduction to Vol. I of *Nihongi,* Aston translation.

[4] "The Japanese Spirit" was the phrase used by Professor Inoue in his Foreword to Robert C. Armstrong, *Light from the East; Studies in Japanese Confucianism,* Toronto, 1914. Sometimes indigenous Japanese religion is identified with *shintō* (神道, literally the Way of the Gods). Yet the term itself was first used in the *Nihon shoki* (720 A.D.), when Japanese and Chinese scholars had already associated together for three hundred years. It is equally important to distinguish *shintō* from ancestor worship, with which the former is often loosely identified. Ancestor worship, as practiced in Japan, is a cult definitely imported from China. See also Okakura Yoshisaburo, *The Japanese Spirit,* New York, 1905. For more objective views of these early politico-religious ideas, see Professor Kumitake Kumi's "Japanese Religious Beliefs: Shintō-Kami," Chap. II, pp. 22 ff. and Count Ōkuma's "Culture and Education in Old Japan," Chap. VII, pp. 113, 119 of Ōkuma Shigenobu, *Fifty years of new Japan (Kaikoku gojūnenshi),* London, 1910 (2 vols.); also John F. Embree, *The Japanese Nation; A Social Survey,* New York, 1945, p. 165; and

Serious historical flaws exist in the accounts presented by the *Nihongi* and *Kojiki*. At base they are probably no more historical than *Beowulf* and the Arthurian Cycle. Yet they are invaluable for an understanding of the basic society of Japan. Like their counterparts in other mythological systems they explain the origins of heaven and earth, the beginnings of man, and the moral necessity for human death. Few Japanese have read these works in their original language, just as few Americans have read their own Bible in Hebrew, Aramaic, and Greek. But just as Americans know their Bible at second or third hand, the Japanese know their own canonical stories through the retelling. To Japanese eyes the Old Testament includes a lot of preposterous nonsense, such as the account of the Garden of Eden, Lot's wife turning to salt, Jonah in the whale's belly, and the story of Noah. Undoubtedly Japanese wonder how it is that Americans capable of building B-29 airplanes can believe legends such as these.

The American feels amused when he encounters the early stories from the *Nihongi* and *Kojiki*. The legends from these books introduce the important deities (*kami*, starting with the August Sun Goddess, Amaterasu Ōmikami), the imperial regalia (mirror, jewels, sword), and the first Japanese to change down from divine form to human (Jimmu *Tennō*).[5]

Significant in the legend of Japan's beginning are the factors of divine ancestry for the Emperor, the hallowing of the land (present-day Japan, starting with the Inland Sea area) by his sacred presence, and identification of the people with their myriads of *kami* of superhuman ancestors. Whatever else the legend does, it reinforces in the Japanese the disposition, sought by many other nations in their respective ways, to think of themselves as divine.

When Jimmu *Tennō* celebrated his victorious campaign into Central Japan and witnessed the construction of the first Imperial palace at Kashihara in Yamato (present-day Honshu), he issued this significant edict:

> Thereafter the capital may be extended so as to embrace the whole land and under the heaven [*hakkō*] as far as the *Tennō's* rule extends may be formed so as to compose a single household [*ichi-u*]. Will this not be well?

This was the origin of *Hakkō Ichi-u* (Under the Heaven—One Household), originally applied only to the Japanese national family but destined to become the flaming slogan for *Dai Tōa Kyōei Ken* (the Greater East Asia Co-

George B. Sansom, *Japan; A Short Cultural History*, New York, 1943, pp. 55 ff., especially Note 1. Sir George Sansom's magistral cultural history is still the best either as an authoritative analysis for experts or as delightful reading for the student just introduced to things Japanese.

[5] In the modern, technical sense of sociology, of course, *kami* turns out to be almost anyone or anything that inspired awe. An interesting, short summary of the legends is presented in J. F. Embree, *The Japanese*, Washington, 1943 (Smithsonian Institution War Background Studies), pp. 1-8. For an excerpt, see Appendix 7.

Prosperity Sphere). Again, in ascending the Throne, Jimmu *Tennō* merely carried out the divine directive given by Amaterasu Ōmikami:

> The Land of Luxuriant Crops (*Ashihara-no-chi-i-ho-aki-no-mi-zuko-no-kuni*) is the region which my descendants shall be lords of. Do thou, my August Grandchild, proceed thither and govern it. Go! and may prosperity attend thy dynasty, and may it, like heaven and earth, endure forever.[6]

This divine imprecation should have been chosen to symbolize the foundation of Imperial authority, not the initial conquest of Yamato by the first Emperor. In legend this was a reconquest by which a Japanese neolithic ruler reassumed authority. Japanese scholars of repute point out that the Imperial house exists as a principal family of Japan quite apart from its mythical status as the ruling family. As *the* family it needs no surname. For example, the term *Ōyake* (Great House) was formerly used in the sense of Imperial court or Emperor and today is in common employment with the meanings "public" or "government."[7]

Down to the present the Japanese continue the intra-family cult of the Imperial house along with the Japan-wide acceptance of the Emperor as ruler. This behavior, entirely compatible with the Chinese Imperial tradition, combines religious and political principles. The character 政, *matsurigoto,* is used by the Japanese for the concept expressed in English as *government* and is derived from *matsuri* (to venerate) and *goto* (administration).

Every year the Japanese open the New Year with the ceremony of *Goyō-hajime* or Beginning-of-affairs-of-state on January 4. The ceremony concerns the affairs of the temple of the first ancestor and thus initiates the business of government with matters pertaining very modestly and practically to a problem of worship.[8]

Collateral to the claim of divine ancestry, there are implications in the *Nihon shoki* and *Kojiki* legends supporting subordinate national moral principles: benevolence, mutual affection, the people's welfare, the veneration of ancestors. The Way of the Emperor, *Kōdō,* embodies not merely the divinity of Japan, but more particularly its unity and its sense of almost familial sympathy. Sober Japanese as late as 1940 were impressed on the occasion of their twenty-sixth centennial with the successful continuity of their nation as

[6] Translations from Kenzō Akiyama, *op. cit.,* p. 51.

[7] Professor Hozumi Nobushige, formerly of the Law Faculty, Tokyo Imperial University, explained the patriarchal concept as follows: "The Nation is considered as forming one vast family, the Imperial house standing at its head as the principal family. . . . It is for the same reason, again, that the Imperial house has no clan or family name." *Ancestor-Worship and Japanese Law,* Tokyo, 1913, p. 103. For an excellent, short analysis, see Seigo Takahashi, *A Study of the Origin of the Japanese State,* New York, 1917 (a Ph.D. dissertation).

[8] Hozumi, *op. cit.,* p. 34. For a brilliant exposition of the impact of Japanese language on political thought, see Robert Karl Reischauer, *Japan, Government-Politics,* New York, 1939, Chap. I. Unfortunately now out of print, this is still the best one-volume survey of pre-World War II Japanese politics.

much as with its claim to supernatural origin. They had survived together, emperors and many generations of men, committed across the centuries to mutual loyalty and to the well-being of the entire Japanese people.

Modern Meanings of the Japanese Mythology. Every great body of myth in the world has two sets of explanations. In the first place, if the myth is still valid and possesses emotional appeal for a large group of people, it has a living spiritual significance which may or may not coincide with its historical origin. The figure of Jesus as understood by American revivalists bears very little resemblance to the historic character in the two Jewish kingdoms of the first century after Christ. Nevertheless the Jesus believed in by American revivalists or evangelical preachers is, in twentieth century terms, a more important figure in American culture than the Jesus understood by scholars. This second version of any myth, the actual historical meaning, is of great significance to historians and to persons who want to undertake a study of the origins of human belief; it is not necessarily important to the understanding of the living belief.

Meanings of the historical origins of Japanese mythology must therefore be undertaken with reserve and with the express understanding that these explanations are of academic value, but of little practical effect in the life of the ordinary Japanese today.

How did the Japanese national cult develop? What are the origins of the Japanese canonical stories?

Professor R. K. Reischauer has explained that the central core of Japanese mythology consists of tales told by mountain people and developed by some tribe residing in Yamato. A second, more primitive cycle of mythology concerns the stories told by seafaring peoples, probably residents in northern Kyushu. A third group is closely related to the myths of various peoples in the South Seas and the East Indies; this group seems to be the most primitive. A fourth group centers around Izumo (present-day western Honshu). Finally, Jimmu *Tennō* and his expedition into Yamato constitute the central theme for a different group of myths. In these legends and in the explanation of their use can be found the clues to many of the peculiarities of Japanese political thought.

One explanation, mostly fiction, is that the legends attempt to justify the Emperor's position by means of a one-tribe theory. Yet the Imperial family who could have used such a theory, and would have, had it existed, has never claimed this particular fiction. In contrast, the theory of Imperial clan predominance and succession has a long tradition dating back to the *Kojiki* and *Nihon shoki* and has been reiterated in every important decree recorded since the seventh century. Another historical hypothesis selecting its data chiefly from the myth cycle of the Yamato expedition states that the legends justify war and conquest in their simplest and crudest forms. This theory is valid only to the extent that comparable tales in the Old Testament are also valid, and is of use in supporting the once popular, by now obsolete, theory that states, governments, economic systems, and religions all developed by a process which was at some point in early history a consequence of conquest. Sociologically it would be dangerous to press either of these theories to an extreme.[9]

However it may have developed, the patriarchal theory became fundamental to Japanese ideology representing the prevailing sentiment of the nation, supporting and supported by the institution of the Imperial house. Final systematic formulation and inculcation of this theory belong to the modern epoch. In the form of the Japanese political religion, *Shintō,* it became the most notable ideological characteristic of pre-surrender Japan. Even under the Constitution of 1947 the patriarchal theory is accepted implicitly; its tenets are the unspoken assumptions which appear in almost all debates among Japanese students of law and political science.

Two dominant Japanese definitions of the state (post-World War I) both accepted the unspoken patriarchal assumptions, even though the first identified the state as an association of men who seek welfare and common advantage in their combination of effort; and the second called the state a person or persons possessing sovereignty.[10]

Despite surrender, occupation, a new constitution, a re-evaluated Emperor, and *Demokurashi,* the Japanese show no tendency outside of Communist circles to challenge the familist and patriarchal assumptions which they have made for so long about their own government.

Even after the war well-informed Japanese still are inclined to build their political assumptions around the concept, *Tenjō mukyū no kōi* (the Throne, eternal as heaven and earth). Such Japanese still assume that the Imperial family arose at the very edge of history from the nation family (*minzoku*).

This continuity has been maintained through the Emperor and national myth complex; there has been a practical de-emphasis upon the idea of divinely granted Imperial prerogatives. So far as the official record is concerned, specific divine claims have been virtually eliminated since the Re-

[9] Professor R. K. Reischauer outlined the origins of the legends in his valuable two-volume reference work, *Early Japanese History (c. 40 B.C.—1167),* Princeton, 1936, Vol. I, p. 6; for brilliant interpretative studies, see the late Professor Asakawa Kanichi, *The Early Institutional Life of Japan,* Tokyo, 1903, especially pp. 26-31; and Carl W. Bishop, "The Historical Geography of Early Japan," *Geographical Review,* XIII (1923), pp. 40-63. The so-called War-and-Conquest Theory is, of course, a part of Marxist theory. Its most vigorous exposition was in the *Manifesto of the Communist Party,* London, 1888 (authorized English translation). But the theory has been shared by many non-Marxists too, for example, Oppenheimer, Jenks, and Treitschke. Frederick Schuman mentions it in his recently revised text, *International Politics,* New York, 1949, but cites a modern critique by Robert MacIver, *The Web of Government,* New York, 1947, pp. 12-38. Dr. Takahashi, whose dissertation has been mentioned, concluded that the Japanese State—as distinct from the Japanese Nation, ethnologically defined—originated in the Yamato conquest. He thus followed the historical view summed up by his teacher, Charles A. Beard: "The real origin of the state, in Western Europe, at least, is to be found in conquest. . . ." (*Politics,* pp. 17-18.)

[10] A distinguished constitutional lawyer, the late Dr. Minobe Tatsukichi, argued the first view in *Kempō kōwa* (Lectures on the Japanese Constitution), Tōkyō, 1918, pp. 2-22. For the second view, see Professor Nesugi, *Kempō kōgi* (A discussion of the Japanese Constitution), Tōkyō, 1918, pp. 77-208. For a summary in English, see Takahashi, *op. cit.,* Introduction, pp. 9-14.

script of January 1, 1946. On the one hand, there are the arguments of Japanese scholars such as Professor Takagi Yasaka who says that ". . . if a fair study of our history be made no one will admit the need for complete abolition of the Emperor system . . . because of recent militarism." This may be compared with the minority view of Sir William Webb, who wanted to accept at least the *present* Japanese Emperor's moral responsibility with judicial literalness and therefore wished to try him as a war criminal.[11]

The Japanese of today is singularly uninterested in justifying the origins of his national mythology in the light of post-surrender and especially post-treaty conditions. The mythology has existed for a long time. Its tenets lie outside of logic or proof. Since the Japanese take their own cultural state of affairs for granted, it is difficult for the outsider to extract for them theories which would be articulate and acceptable by Western standards. The Japanese are much more apt to reach common intellectual terms with the West when they talk about their physical setting and its problems than when they try to elucidate the hypothetical, logical foundations or origins of their most private moral feelings.

Physical Structure of the Home Empire. The home islands of Japan, comprising the four principal islands of Hokkaido, Honshu, Shikoku, and Kyushu, are a major arc intersected at Hokkaido by the arc of the Kuril Islands, at Kyushu by the arc of the Ryukyu Islands, and at Honshu by the arc of the Bonin Islands. Each intersection is marked by masses of irregular highlands with associated clusters of volcanos.

This topography makes for a country very rich in scenery and natural beauty, but poor in terms of strategic or industrial resources. The instability of the land itself imposes special conditions on Japanese industrial and military construction. With more than 500 volcanos within the country and an average of 1,500 earthquakes per year, the Japanese land itself is as insecure as any major land mass on earth. Tokyo, for example, averages one earthquake every three days.

[11] Benevolent rule *(jinsei)* was the element Prince Itō Hirobumi stressed in his *Commentaries on the Constitution of the Empire of Japan* (standard English translation by Itō Myoji), Tokyo, 1889; a recent Japanese edition is *Teikoku kempō kōshitsu tempan gige,* Tōkyō, 1935; see Chap. I, "Kempō Gikai." A moderate, orthodox view by a leading political theorist in postwar Japan is Takagi Yasaka, in the Japanese equivalent of our *Annals* of the American Academy of Political and Social Science, *"Kempō kaisei sōan ni taisuru shiken"* (On the draft of the Japanese Constitution), *Kokka gakkai zasshi* (Journal of the Association of Political and Social Science), Vol. LX, No. 5 (May, 1946), pp. 1-21. Professor Takagi is the retired Chief Librarian of Tokyo (formerly Imperial) University, Professor of Constitutional Law, and an outstanding Japanese authority on American politics and law. In an interview with the author of this section, in the Library of Congress, Washington, 1949, Professor Takagi left two distinct impressions: first, he recognized the responsibility of all Japanese for the military adventures of the last decade; second, this responsibility could have been met under a differently applied Meiji Constitution, thus avoiding adjustment to an essentially un-Japanese organic law. In a second interview in the ultra-modern Reader's Digest Building, Tokyo, summer of 1952, Dr. Takagi said he had no reason to change his mind. At that time, the rearmament question and "unconstitutionality" were the topics. On November 12, 1948, Sir William Webb, presiding justice in the International Military Tribunal, Tokyo, read sentences on Japanese war criminals and, in a separate opinion, denounced the Emperor as "the real leader" in war crimes.

Physical structure, in turn, controls the characteristics of Japanese soil, which obviously has its influence on the economic and political nature of the people. Five rock types, igneous and therefore resistant to erosion, constitute almost two thirds of the area. Alluvium and diluvium, characterized by slopes of 15 degrees or less, constitute the other third. In terms of everyday life, most of Japan is rugged hill or mountain country, and only about 16 per cent of its total area can be cultivated.

Japan is small only in contrast with China. The homeland is larger than the United Kingdom or Italy. In terms of latitude and climate Japan has about the same spread as the Atlantic Coast of the United States, with Hokkaido comparable to Maine, the Inland Sea area comparable to the Carolinas, and Kyushu analogous to Georgia.

The insularity of Japan is a major cultural feature as well as a geographic one. The startling parallels between Japanese and British history, which can be found by any reader with a taste for picturesque chronology, are to be attributed to the fact that they are both island kingdoms. Japan's national character, so extraordinary for East Asia, although it would be a commonplace for a European state, is explicable in terms of the clean-cut geographic boundaries provided by nature. The first successful invasion of Japan—aside from that by the Japanese themselves—was the peaceful invasion of General MacArthur following Japan's surrender. It is natural for a nation of this type to have a strong seafaring and naval tradition. One of the most uncertain factors of the world's history for the next few decades is the probable future role of Japanese shipping wealth and naval power.[12]

The People. Instead of making poetic claims of divine origin, postwar textbook histories tell Japanese school children that "our race too is one among these peoples [of the world] and exhibits certain individual anthropological characteristics."[13] The pre-history of Japan can be represented in terms of three early cultural levels, of which the first is neolithic, characterized by total absence of metal and the presence of pottery not turned on a wheel. Prehistoric shell heaps bespeak a predominance of fish in the diet.

[12] Professor George Etsujiro Uyehara was among the first modern Japanese writers to link the Japanese Nation, its isolation, and its political mind: *The Political Development of Japan, 1867-1909*, London, 1910, Chap. I, pp. 6-9; see also Nyuzekan Hasegawa, "Our Civilization and the Sea," *Contemporary Japan*, February, 1942 (this journal, published by the Foreign Affairs Association of Japan—and in English straight through the war—is the equivalent of our *Foreign Affairs*, perhaps more officially inspired). For other brief surveys of the effects of geography on history, see E. O. Reischauer, *Japan—Past and Present*, New York, 1947, Chap. I; or almost any issue of *The Japan Year Book*, also published by the Foreign Affairs Association of Japan (in the 1946-48 edition, Chaps. I, II on geography and population); or for the tourist, Tourist Industry Division, Ministry of Transportation, *Japan, the Official Guide* (Revised), Tokyo, 1952. The standard one-volume geography of Japan is Glenn Trewartha, *A Regional and Cultural Geography of Japan*, Madison, Wis., 1945.

[13] Japan. Mombu Shō (Ministry of Education), *Nihon no rekishi* (History of Japan), Tōkyō: Chūtō Gakkō Kyoka-shō Kabushiki Kaisha, Shōwa 21 (1946), 2 vols., Vol. I, p. 1. Chapter 1 describes the primitive culture *(Jōmon and Yayoi)*; Chap. 2 deals with the development of Yamato Government, establishment of national unity, and appearance of family and tribal groups *(sho kokka)*.

A second less distinct culture is symbolized by bronze vestiges. Although a preponderance of archeological evidence suggests that the bronze culture came from central and eastern rather than southern Asia, the presence of a decided Malayan element is of interest, even though the people now known as Malays did not come to prominence until a thousand years after the settling of the Japanese in their present islands. The stock of these people appears to be Ural-Altaic. The dominant physical type is Mongoloid, broad-skulled, prognathic, yellow-skinned, straight-haired, with the epicanthic fold in Mongol form in the upper eyelid. This stock appears to have been supplemented by successive small-scale immigration from northeast Asia. Evidence of the Malay contribution is visible anthropologically, but is not measurable as yet.

The third Japanese culture is represented by remains found in sepulchral chambers. An iron culture, it had strong links with Korea. Traditionally this culture is surrounded by its link to the Yamato area. It is from this Yamato group, who probably came into Kyushu between 1000 and 500 B.C., that Japanese consider themselves to be descended today.[14]

This Yamato culture provides us with some of the earliest evidence concerning Japanese political and social organization. The term *rice castle* (*inaki*) meant a fortified granary guarding not only the provisions of the garrison, but symbolizing also the political power which accompanies the possession of wealth. Rice was already the staple food, a form of currency, and a medium of taxation. By tradition the *Nihongi* attributes irrigation, a prime requisite of such a rice culture, to the Emperor Suinin (A.D. 6). The first recorded offense calling for capital punishment was the destruction of fields and the disruption of rice streams. Chinese notices do little to expand our knowledge of Japan in this earliest phase other than to call the Japanese dwarfs and to mention that Japan had not attained political unity.

For modern purposes it is perhaps most significant that the Imperial claim to authority, as shadowy as the rest of proto-Japan, seems to have existed from the very beginning.

At the very edge of history the Imperial clan was, of course, only one among many clans located throughout the country. There were Imperial clans tracing their ancestry back to some sovereign, deity clans claiming descent from canonized personages, and foreign clans descended from Chinese or Korean immigrants, but the Imperial clan established a monopoly from the beginning on the office of *Tennō* and established even in the earliest of Japanese books the ideology of the authority of the Emperor.

Early Clan Economics. The period from 40 B.C. to A.D. 645 in Japan has

[14] Although archeological evidence makes this culture appear indigenous, there are strong Korean evidences: for example, from remote times, the sword, mirror, and curved jewels (Imperial regalia) are all associated with Korea. Still the most complete survey of archeological evidence is Neil Gordon Munro, *Prehistoric Japan,* Yokohama, 1908; somewhat shorter is his "Primitive Culture in Japan," *Transactions of the Asiatic Society of Japan* (cited hereafter as *TASJ*), Vol. XXXIV, Part II (1906). An even shorter summary is to be found in Sansom, *op. cit.,* Chap. I.

been called the Age of Clans and Hereditary Titles. The land was occupied by innumerable clans. As in the case of modern Greece or the medieval Scottish Highlands, the topography made self-contained units inevitable. Each clan was governed by a clan chief who claimed the patronage of a clan deity, and each household under its master was a part of a clan. The economics of this system rested on the clan system of household economy (called by modern Japanese the *shizoku seido*). The guiding principle of the *shizoku* was the assumption of cosanguinity since the community called *shizoku* required the hypothesis of actual blood relationship. Although the facts of genealogy often made it difficult to affiliate strangers with such groups, elaborate fictions were devised to maintain the nominal integrity of the group. (To this day the quasi-clan, the quasi-group, and the quasi-family are significant elements in Japanese life.) [15]

Shizoku land was not subject to sale. There is thus visible a tradition, which persists to the present time, contrary to individual land ownership. The diffusion of rights over the land rather than the concentration of all title to each specific tract has been the characteristic of Japanese cadastral practices from the very beginning.

An economy such as the *shizoku* system already had accompaniments which did not fit the narrow limits of a cosanguine structure. Guilds (*be* or *tomo*) coexisted with the clan. These included social or ritualistic groups, groups created to commemorate events in Imperial clan history, and groups of workers forming a specialized caste. During the winter of 1952-53, one of the authors visited a modern site—Bizen-chō, Okayama Prefecture—a direct descendant of one of the earliest guild groupings. Indeed, the village itself is called *Imbe* (from Imu-*be*) and still produces pottery by the name which links its potter-families to the edge of Japanese history.

Units of local government also appeared from the *sato* (village), *mura* (township), *kōri* (roughly a township), up to the *kuni* (equivalent to a modern province but using the ideograph employed by the Chinese for country).[16]

Clan economics pressed forward rapidly. At its first known historical level

[15] The clan itself offers a clue to the primitive origins of the highly important and modern neighborhood association *(tonarigumi)*, which has great tenacity and antiquity (a similar grouping was highly developed in the China of T'ang). First reference to the system in Japan is found in the *Nihon shoki*, begun in 652. See General Headquarters, SCAP, Civil Information and Education Section, Analysis and Research Division, *A Preliminary Study of the Neighborhood Associations of Japan*, Tokyo, 23 January 1948 (mimeographed), pp. 1-2.

[16] It has already been pointed out that worship and government were closely associated in ancient times. Similarly, the guild seems to have had a religious basis in Japan (as it did in Europe). There is some evidence that the guilds *(be)* were even branches of primitive government. W. G. Aston, translator of the *Nihongi*, gives a complete description of guilds in work cited, Vol. I, pp. 42-43, Notes 5, 7. For an authoritative definition of the *shizoku:* Honjō Eijirō, *Nihon shakai-keizai shi* (Japanese socio-economic history), Tōkyō, 1928, *"Shizoku seido,"* pp. 32-35 (Professor Honjō is one of Japan's outstanding economic historians; his *Social and Economic History of Japan*, Kyoto, 1935, may prove useful to the student of Japanese politics who would like to keep one eye on parallel economic developments).

it was already beyond mere hunting and fishing. The agricultural system expanded technologically and became complex in terms of property relationships. Cultivators began to suffer decreasing yields under the law of diminishing returns. Population growth outran the rate at which land was put into cultivation. The net effect was the sharp increase in the value of land itself and the incapacity of loose household systems to maintain effective control and operation of land in the face of a land shortage and in the face of inequalities of wealth resulting from inequalities in the accumulation of rice.

Private clan ownership resulted in the concentration of great wealth which, in turn, placed strong political influence in the hands of *Ōmi*—literally, the Great Persons. Wealth led to preferment; ordinary clan chieftains fell into line behind powerful families which had obtained recognition through appointment of Imperial ministers for their most promising men. Professor Asakawa Kanichi comments on this situation that had come into existence by the seventh century in the following terms:

> The fundamental difficulty of the pre-Reform Japan arose from the sharp contradiction the one against the other between the powers claimed by the Emperor and the actual quasi-tribal organization of the State. . . . The Emperor alone in theory owned land and people, and was identical with the State, but this authority was normally exercised only through the heads of the clan and group and the local servants. If these magnates grew formidable, they would successfully dispute the powers of the Emperor. This state of things, it will be noted, constitutes in general the meanings of restricting the royal power in a tribal nation. Japan could be no exception to the rule.[17]

The Chinese Model for Reform. This early Japan turned to China when searching for a model of civilized life. It is easy today for Americans who have seen both countries to dismiss China as backward, corrupt, sprawling, while praising Japan as progressive, well organized, and compact. It is nevertheless important for the understanding of the two countries to remember that Japan in the seventh century turned with immense admiration toward China and that there were excellent reasons for this admiration. The Chinese, as noted previously, had already developed a form of government which combined the highest requisites of virtue, practicality, and beauty. In the seventh century the two countries differed in that China accepted the principle of rebellion and the installation of new secular dynasties, whereas Japan was already committed to hereditary succession. The

[17] Asakawa, *op. cit.*, p. 135. For an excellent survey of the economic background of the Taika Reforms (645-654)—replacement for the *shizoku* system—see Yunoki Shigezō, "Taika kaishin" (Taika reforms), *Nihon keizaishi jiten* (Encyclopedia of Japanese economic history), Vol. V, pp. 960-961. Professor Honjō has pointed out that from the beginning, the rise and fall of clan control roughly paralleled economic concentration. The early Soga Clan, for example, supervised *imikura, uchikura* and *ōkura,* all early government treasuries. Honjō (English translation), *op. cit.*, pp. 2-6.

Chinese and Japanese also differed in this early period in that Japan 1300 years ago was already concerned with the future, whereas China was concerned with the past. The Japanese of the twentieth century are the remote descendants of men who escaped the *shizoku* system by copying a foreign model. No matter how imperfect their knowledge of history, they know that their nation has gone through travail and change before; they know that good changes came of imitating the foreigners. What the Japanese know, the Chinese do not. In this there lies one of the most important political distinctions between the two cultural positions.

CHAPTER
ELEVEN

The Japanese Model of a Chinese Empire

THERE are few instances in history in which relatively primitive peoples have vaulted to a high level of cultural development by borrowing from a foreign civilization. These cultural adoptions have, in most cases, been motivated by the threat of strategic power; the primitive peoples have moved forward only when they were faced with the challenge of outside attack. Yet there are exceptions to this rule. Ireland in the time of the first great Celtic Christian surge of creativeness and civilization was under no immediate pressure from the Mediterranean. The transplantations of early Hindu culture in the South Seas area are remarkable for their nonviolence, but in this case the credit must be divided between the Hindu merchants and missionaries who spread their arts and faith and the intelligent peoples of the area who desired the gift of such cultural treasures. The Japanese case in the seventh century after Christ is almost unique in that the effort was overwhelmingly a Japanese effort, with only minor Chinese or Korean contributions, and in the added factor that the creation in Japan of a Chinese Empire, Japanese model, was erected without the stimulus of a Chinese preponderance of power.

Japan's Ancient Korean Possessions. From an unspecified point in the second or third century down to a tremendous naval crisis in the seventh century, the primitive Japanese state and its subordinate tribal units had maintained various forms of political, economic and territorial control in Korea. An empress whose name sounds peculiarly apt to Westerners, the Empress Jingō (A.D. 201–270) is credited with leading some of the most effective Japanese campaigns to Korean soil.

Korea itself was divided at the time into three kingdoms. In the north, reaching well into present-day Manchuria, there was the great kingdom of Koguru. On the east coast, facing the Sea of Japan, there lay the kingdom of Silla, whose identity still persists in the modern Arabic name for Korea, *A-shila*. On the south and west coasts there was the kingdom of Pakché. These three kingdoms played a cruel but real-life miniature of the man-devouring game of an international balance of power. The Japanese played into the situation by supporting one or the other of the contestants, usually the kingdom of Pakché. Strong Chinese support was thrown by the Sui and T'ang Emperors to Silla on the basis of the ancient Chinese adage, "Oppose the near: befriend the far," so as to crush China's immediate enemies by alliances with barbaric nations on the far side of the enemy's frontier. Chinese influence poured richly into Korea with the adoption of Chinese ideographic script and the progressive introduction of Chinese political institutions. The Japanese participants in these Korean wars, fighting at the side of their Korean allies or maintaining themselves directly, as they did in the small bridgehead of Mimana, near present-day Pusan, could not help being first-hand witnesses of the effect of Chinese culture on a non-Chinese state. By A.D. 622 the Japanese had abandoned their own direct Korean interests, and in a naval battle which occurred in A.D. 622 the Chinese and pro-Chinese Koreans destroyed Pakché and destroyed Japanese naval power in Korean waters.[1]

Japan's contacts with China were therefore framed against the intimacy that nations achieve with one another through fighting—the curiosity that intelligent men have always shown about their enemies, the romance that surrounds a remote or threatening adversary, the significance that attaches itself to an encounter with alien power.

The security of Japan itself, one must emphasize, was not in question. No Korean or Chinese force threatened Japan. But the Japanese imagination was quickened by Korean adventures, and the Japanese defeat in Korea, progressive as it was, must have forced some Japanese to realize that their claims to primacy among nations (inherent in the character of their religion) was a vain pretense against the cultural splendor and the strategic power of the immensely larger Chinese Empire.[2]

The Confucian Irradiation. As noted in Chapter Four, the world sys-

[1] The standard if somewhat uncritical treatment in English of this early interpenetration, from the Japanese viewpoint, is Yoshi S. Kuno, *Japanese Expansion on the Asiatic Continent; A Study in the History of Japan with Special Reference to her International Relations with China, Korea, and Russia,* Berkeley, California, 1937 (3 vols.). In Vol. I, Appendix 13, p. 234, Professor Kuno concludes from the documents that after the seventh century, Japan abandoned her claims to Korea and stayed out of the peninsula—with the exception of the sixteenth-century adventures of Hideyoshi—until the nineteenth century.

[2] An interesting extrapolation from history can be made on the basis of Japan's participation in foreign wars. The suggestion can be made that the Japanese, more than any other nationality, know how to give up once they have been beaten in war. After their defeats in Korea the Japanese left the peninsula alone for more than nine hundred years. Defeated once again after the tragic, ferocious campaigns of Hideyoshi, the Japanese stayed out of Korea completely until 1875. If either of these defeats is to be taken as a precedent, the imaginative assumption can be made that following the defeat in 1945 Japan will not attack America again before A.D. 2220 at the earliest or A.D. 2845 at the latest. The illustration may be extreme, but the cultural response which prompts it is a well-established datum of Japanese behavior.

tem of pre-modern China was based upon the strategic and economic assumption of the unbalance of power. Chinese foreign policy was based upon a distinction between nations capable of being nurtured by Chinese morality, which were therewith entitled to become the moral tributaries of China, and nations not within the reach of China's civilizing influence which were treated without honor and without respect as irredeemable barbarians. In the interests of securing their frontiers the Chinese, therefore, employed, across the milleniums, the double policy of Sinifying the nearer nations and at the same time of making alliances whenever expedient with the outer neighbors of those nations so as to grip the states along their borders in a vise, one side of which would be Chinese power and the other Chinese intrigue.

Chinese imperialism was an economic force in so far as the direct annexation of territory was concerned. Across the centuries China was slowly growing. The area south of the Yangtze was occupied by Chinese from the Han dynasty onward. The Siamese were not expelled from the present-day province of Yunnan until the thirteenth century. Once beyond the limits of Chinese settlement-cultivation, however, the Chinese displayed singularly little interest in obtaining mercantile or military footholds. They ran an immense chain of garrisons across the deserts of Central Asia to secure their silk routes to the west. But they did not bother with Formosa until relatively modern times. And the Chinese government left the Philippines and Borneo out of official count centuries after Chinese merchants had been domiciled in those islands.

The introduction of Chinese culture into Japan was, therefore, something which was out of immediate concern to the Japanese, but only remotely and theoretically interesting to the Chinese. Had Japan been immediately contiguous to China, it is likely that Imperial Chinese armies would have overrun Japan, forcing the Japanese into a condition of morality and subservience. Had the Japanese been immediately contiguous to a border state of China's, it is possible that Chinese envoys would have cajoled Japanese chieftains or the Japanese Emperor into waging war against a common enemy.

The oceanic position of Japan was such as to prohibit both these alternatives. Japan simply was too far away.

Korea therefore served as the prime intermediary between mainland culture and the Japanese. The haunting echoes of Athenian civilization, which finally reached Japan in the form of a few artistic motives and certain forms in music, reached Japan through Korea. The shocking impact of the good side of Hindu civilization, which appeared in the electrifying form of a benevolent and mature metaphysics to a world of men who had never tasted metaphysics before, also came through Korea. Most of the Chinese pattern first came through Korea.

The Japanese went to meet their destiny when they meddled in Korea;

their destiny came to meet them, not in the form of Hindu saints proceeding directly from India, or of Chinese sages intent upon expounding Confucianism to the unenlightened, but in the more modest form of the governments of one borrower to another. The Korean kings seeking to entice Japanese aid to their particular causes and to draw Japanese man power into the blood bath of a long-divided Korea boasted to their Japanese neighbors of the benefits of the higher standard of Chinese culture. Both Confucian political-ethical ideas and Buddhist religious concepts were relayed into Japan by Koreans seeking the favor of the Japanese and trying to obtain that favor by giving the Japanese cultural gifts. In A.D. 522 the King of Pakché sent Japan an image of the Buddha and the opportunity to accept the Buddhist faith. Other envoys from Pakché brought the Confucian classics and sent congratulatory tutors to teach the Japanese heir apparent.

While Buddhism rushed swiftly from Korea to fill the philosophic vacuum left open by the absence of indigenous metaphysics and Japanese culture, Confucianism came to Japan more smoothly and more easily. Chinese ideas, although alien to Japan in many important respects, were far from inapplicable to the Japanese situation. The Confucian precepts fitted the Japanese view of their own world and must have seemed progressive in character rather than merely alien.

The Confucian Concepts in Japan. Basic Confucian concepts, epitomized previously in their original Chinese form, can now be restated as the Japanese understood them so as to show the welcome familiarity with which the Japanese in the seventh century turned to the Chinese model.

Confucianism underlined the Japanese belief, for example, *that the community is more important than the individual.* In fact, the individual cannot be said to exist except in his social contacts. The five Confucian relationships (ruler and subject, husband and wife, parent and child, elder-brother and younger-brother, friend and friend) gave meaning to human existence. The Chinese extended the context of the community to a humanism denoting civilized mankind, themselves. The Japanese extended this to the more modest limits of the Japanese family-nation.[3]

The Confucian idea, *that the Emperor is the font of benevolent government,* is a lay extension of the idea of ideological control. The Japanese

[3] Thus much later the traditional Japanese regarded as anathema the capitalist emphasis upon rugged *individual* initiative, or the communist formula of *class* struggle, or the democratic reliance upon *party* loyalty. Two illustrations drawn from modern Japanese writings, in different fields, demonstrate the inheritance. Professor Koizumi Shinzō, economist and chancellor of Keio University, wrote in a basic economics text the truly *individual* "economic man" is a Robinson Crusoe who exists only in the imaginations of Daniel Defoe and of Ricardo! (*Keizai hen,* [Volume on economics], Tōkyō, 1938, p. 11). Ozaki Yukio, dean of Japanese parliamentarians and leader of political liberalism in Japan, always stressed that political *parties* transplanted in Japan partook of the nature of personal factions. Relations between leader and members resembled those between a feudal lord and his liegemen. Because parties in the 1920's and 1930's were identified in the Japanese mind as divisive factions, they became discredited. (K. K. Kawakami, Editor, *What Japan Thinks,* New York, 1921, Chap. IV: Ozaki Yukio, "Japan's Defective Constitutional Government," pp. 63-78.) See also R. K. Reischauer, *Japan, Government-Politics,* cited, p. 24.

never quite mastered the sophisticated Chinese techniques of controlling morality by teaching the rules of good behavior and by personifying good behavior in a nonhereditary class of scholar-bureaucrats. The Japanese left the Confucian phrases alone, accepting them without the context of secularism with which the Chinese had already begun to invest them. The Japanese transvalued the Chinese idea of the Emperor by the simple process of accepting literally what the Chinese meant figuratively, and of turning to their own religious beliefs for justification of the Imperial status. It is natural, therefore, that the Japanese also came to believe

that religion, ethics, and politics are one in a cultural unity. It may seem incomprehensible today, in the eyes of the Westerner unfamiliar with Japan, that a true Japanese can be a Shintoist, a Confucianist, and Buddhist or Christian all at the same time. To the Japanese the answer is simple: Shintō tells him where he came from, Confucianism tells him how to act while he is here, and Buddhism assures him where he will next go. To the Japanese there is no necessity for separating religion from politics, since government can be moral or government can be immoral, but it cannot, by any stretch of the imagination, be amoral. Lastly, Shintō and Confucianism both taught the Japanese

that all men are by nature created unequal. According to the Shintō hierarchy this inequality was based on pedigree, as it was in some of the more naïve manifestations of aristocracy in Europe. Confucianism contradicts this in essence by denying the hereditary superiority of noble blood. Confucianism accepts this in fact by recognizing that superiority and inferiority are the consequences of personal virtue,[4] which emphasizes inequality as a fact and at the same time prescribes the one channel—personal cultivation—through which inferior status can be changed to superior. It was possible, therefore, for the Japanese to take the facts of Confucian life and, by omitting some of the *rationale,* to accommodate them to circumstances like their own.

Buddhism, it must be noted, underwent the same transvaluations as Confucianism. By the time Buddhism was well established in Japan, ingenious Japanese had managed to argue that the Supreme Buddha manifested himself in the Emperor of Japan by virtue of the fact that the Supreme Buddha had already showed up in Japan in the form of Amaterasu Ōmikami (the Sun Goddess). This ludicrous Japanification of Gautama can be compared with the religious lunacy of Jayavaran VII, who decreed that his own "inmost me" was the guiding principle to which all absolutes of the universe

[4] The virtue referred to here is, of course, the Confucian idea *têh.* This corresponds, so far as European idea is concerned, more closely to the Italian Renaissance idea of *virtu* than to the modern English "virtue" which is unfortunately surrounded with narrow connotations of a purely negative chastity, abstemiousness, and refusal of bad behavior. The Italian *virtu,* like the Chinese *têh,* asks the more basic question, "What is a man good for? What is *his* special capacity for being himself? What are the factors by which he can achieve and display his own individual and particular merits? How best can a real life individual human existence be exhibited and fulfilled?"

were appended, or the convenient discovery by Joseph Smith in upstate New York that Jesus Christ had had an American incarnation.

Buddhism affected Japanese civilization very profoundly, in that it provided the Japanese with spiritual values hitherto unknown in that part of the world. The Buddhist impact on the spirit of government was profound; its effects on the frame of government were negligible. Buddhism had the result concomitant with its spiritual consolations of reconciling men to the inequalities and inequities of an existence in a feudal and Imperial Japan. So far as it became an established religion, Buddhism developed into an instrument of government, but although Buddhism brought its Three Treasures (Buddha, *dharma,* or the law, and *sangha,* or the priesthood) and although it touched Japanese belief, moral behavior, ritual, family customs, architecture, sculpture, industrial arts, economic behavior, and practical politics, it contributed less than Confucianism did to the structure or the technical processes of government.[5]

The First Great Japanizer, Shōtoku Taishi. A Japanese prince, born to the name Umayado (which literally means "the door of the stables" and which may be a remote echo of the Tale of the Manger), came to be known as the Sage Prince (Shōtoku Taishi). Born in A.D. 573 he was selected, according to Japanese history books, by the Empress Suikō to be Regent of the Empire at the age of twenty. At the very outset of his official career he devoted his efforts to the study and propagation of Buddhism. Later he established twelve grades of court rank, abolished hereditary office-holding, and tried to open the way for men of ability to get into government careers. He himself compiled traditional narratives, rearranged the mass of data on the annals of the Imperial house and clans, and attempted to arouse an understanding of the need for a working state in Japan.[6]

Shōtoku Taishi's fame rests chiefly upon his *Kempō Jūshichijō,* usually translated into Western languages with the somewhat grandiose term, "the Constitution of 17 Articles."

[5] Even though the Nara Era (A.D. 710-793) has been dubbed the period of "Government by Buddhist Prayers." Furthermore, the practice of *inkyo*—retirement—seems to be an exception to the above generalization. *Inkyo* was frequently the habit of an Emperor, a member of the court, or later, a head of a house. Even today, in Amerikamura, *issei* and *nisei* returnees to Japan are said to have engaged in *inkyo,* preparing for death. A few citations will lead the interested reader into further discussion of the effects of religion on political thought: for Confucianism, see R. C. Armstrong, *op. cit.;* for Buddhism, A. K. Reischauer, *Studies in Japanese Buddhism,* New York, 1925; Kawada Shiro and Okamoto Ichirō, *Nihon no keizai to bukkyō* (The Japanese economy and Buddhism), Tōkyō, 1912 (especially Chap. I, which treats of general conditions before the arrival of Buddhism). The best short treatment, in English, of all these influences is contained in R. K. Reischauer, *Japan, Government-Politics,* cited, Chap. I.

[6] Mombu Shō, *Nihon no rekishi,* cited, Chap. 3, Part 1. The Prince (A.D. 573-621) was born under the name Umayado; after the issuance of his famous code in 604, he won a third name: Toyosato Mimi no Miko (Great King of the Law). For his life, the Iwanami Bunko edition (in Japanese) of the *Nihon shoki,* cited, Book XXII, pp. 89-90, is matched by Aston's translation (into English), *op. cit.,* Chap. II, Book XXII, "Suikō," pp. 122-123. The most exhaustive study of the life and work of the Prince is by Herman Bohner, *Shōtoku Taishi,* Tokyo, 1940, (in German), which contains translations of two important early texts on the life of Shōtoku Taishi.

Actually, as Professor Asakawa has pointed out, the prince's code "is no constitution or law in the modern sense, for it defines no state institution, contains no positive legislation, and has no word of punishment or enforcement." The code is a group of moral maxims, either Buddhistic or Chinese in principle. There is no clear concept of a particular political structure that would be peculiar to the Japanese Empire, as became so apparent in the later reforms of A.D. 645. The idea *state* occurs in three Articles, but the expression is borrowed Chinese and is not clear in the contemporaneous Japanese sense. The Constitution refers to the Japanese Emperor in several forms, any of which could be applied to the sovereign of a non-Japanese country. Its chief emphasis is upon *officials,* not clan heads, and distinctions between superior and inferior officials in the bureaucratic sense. The prince was obviously working with Chinese ideas.

The direction of his motives was, however, plain. His concern was the selection from Chinese materials of governing ideas and procedures that could be fitted to the Japanese scene. If, from the viewpoint of Japan he was a Sinicizer, he was more particularly a Japanizer, so far as the materials themselves were concerned. His intent, like that of the great performers who came after him, was not to make Japan Chinese, but to make the best features of Chinese life Japanese. It is this characteristic direction, this absorption inward, which makes significant not only the reforms of the seventh century, but the tremendous changes of the nineteenth and those which may be undertaken in the twentieth. Each time that Japan has ingested major factors from a foreign culture the stress—as, naturally enough, seen by the foreigners—has been upon the Japanese Sinifying themselves or Europeanizing themselves or Americanizing themselves. Seen the other way around, in terms of what intelligent, ambitious, purposeful Japanese themselves thought that they were doing, the direction should more properly be considered as that of a leader or a prevailing group Japanizing Chinese culture, Japanizing European industrialism, Japanizing American democracy. Shōtoku Taishi may have been naïve in particulars. The significance of his work lies in what he left out and in the zeal, apparent even across the centuries, which he showed in trying to select aspects of higher foreign civilization that might take hold in Japan and therewith contribute to the character of his country.

The text of this Constitution can be epitomized briefly. Article I begins with the Chinese character for harmony and decries factionalism. Article II commends the Three Treasures of Buddhism. Article III admonishes the Japanese in measured Chinese phrases to obey their Emperor:

> When you receive the Imperial commands, fail not scrupulously to obey them. The Lord is Heaven, the Vassal is Earth. Heaven overspreads and Earth upbears.

Articles IV through VIII show the Chinese influence, with IV exhorting ministers to be decorous, V and VI warning against flatterers and sycophants, and VII prescribing, "Let every man have his own charge, and let not the spheres of duty be confused." Article VIII admonishes officials to begin public business early in the morning and to retire late.

Articles IX, X, and XI enjoin hard work and good faith, praise the reward of merit, and admonish against anger while asking for the punishment of derelictions.

Article XII directly contradicts the semi-tribal hierarchy which then existed by stating that the provincial authorities and local governors should not, on their own accounts, levy exactions upon the people, since ". . . in a country there are not two lords; the people have not two masters."

Articles XIII through XVI are general exhortations to ministers and officials. Article XVII concludes with the warnings, "Decisions on important matters should not be made by one person alone. They should be discussed with many." The text of the Articles themselves was written in straight Chinese which had been adopted *in toto* as the hieratic language of Japan.[7] In content the Articles synthesized Shintō, Confucianism, Buddhism, and Chinese legalism. Economically Shōtoku Taishi assumed that an increase in wealth to the Imperial family was a gain so absolute that it did not need embellishment. Politically the Constitution represented a new view of the state with a stronger ruler and weaker clans. Legally it presented neither substantive nor procedural law, but escaped juristic questions by attempting to regulate through morals.

The prince died young in A.D. 621 after succeeding in his last great task, the establishment of official relations directly with China. The family of the Sui Emperor had impressed Japan so much that an embassy was sent arriving in time to accredit itself to the immeasurably greater and more vital T'ang court which had, in the interim, superseded the Sui.

The T'ang Exemplar in Japan. The T'ang Exemplar provided the model for both the Taika (A.D. 646) and the Taihō (A.D. 702) reforms. Like the Constitution of Prince Shōtoku, the Taika reform was a blueprint. Placing the cornerstones for the state, it set a pattern which was supposed to endure for many years. The cornerstones were: the *nationalization* of land, the *centralization* of administration, the *registration* of subjects, and the *taxation* of produce. The Taihō reform more modestly, more practically, and more effectively provided detailed specifications in administrative and judicial codes.

[7] Texts of the "Constitution" in English are contained in Aston, *op. cit.*, Chap. II, pp. 128-132; in Arthur L. Sadler, *A Short History of Japan*, Sydney and London, 1946, Appendix IV, pp. 327-329; and in Joseph H. Longford, *The Story of Old Japan*, New York, 1910, Appendix IV, pp. 371-374. Even earliest Japanese editions carried interlinear, phonetic *kana* to represent the then-current "Chinese" reading of the characters; modern editions add *kana to* represent modern *on* (Chinese) or *kun* (Japanese) readings. Obviously the Japanese started early on the road to linguistic confusion! Modern readings in *kana*, with a running commentary, are presented by Igarashi Iukō, *Kempō jūshichijō jōsetsu* (Introduction to the Constitution of 17 Articles), Tōkyō, 1943. For a brief analysis, see also Asakawa, *op. cit.*, pp. 253-256.

Seventh-century Japan was replete with unresolved contradictions. The Imperial clan had, with the progress of arts and settlement, become a government, but it had not yet found ways in which to make itself effective in governmental form. Weakness and negligence prevailed at the level of the court. Local government was ridden with irregularities and laxity of control. From the *Nihon shoki* it would appear that many Japanese considered all their fundamental institutions to have reached a point of danger. The source of danger was the clan nobles who, on the one hand, poached on the political preserves of the Emperor and, on the other, oppressed the people with forced labor, high taxes, and even with dispossession.

In a quarrel over the introduction of Buddhism at the Japanese court, one of the clans—the Nakatomi—had withdrawn before the encroachment of another, the Soga. The Soga, originally supporting Shōtoku Taishi and therefore pro-Chinese, was nevertheless planning to usurp the Imperial power. Thoroughgoing reform had to wait until the Imperial clan finished its fight with the Soga clan. The Soga fell in A.D. 645, and the first phase of the reform was proclaimed in June of that year from the council hall of the Imperial palace. There had scarcely been time enough to clean the floor since a Soga leader had been murdered in the same room just seven days before.

From outside the Imperial clan itself the second great Japanizer, Nakatomi Kamatari—better known by his later name, Fujiwara Kamatari, founder of the great Fujiwara clan—stood forth as the chieftain of a new pro-Imperial coalition. Under his leadership the Soga defeat was consummated. Strongholds of the Soga clan were razed. The Empress, put in power by Soga influence, was compelled to abdicate and her brother, the Emperor Kōtoku, was enthroned.[8]

The Second Great Japanizer, Fujiwara Kamatari. Power behind the Throne remained in the hands of Fujiwara Kamatari, who, from the onset, had the help of two Japanese who had studied in China itself and upon whom there were conveyed the titles of Learned Men of the Realm (literally "National doctors"). Kamatari himself was a Confucian who had learned his Confucianism second-hand in Japan. The Emperor Kōtoku was a Buddhist who took Buddhism so seriously as to be neglectful of the primeval beliefs upon which his own power and personality rested. The drive behind the reforms was the personality of Kamatari, and the new clan which he founded remained a living force in Japanese politics for centuries after his death.

[8] As Sir George Sansom has pointed out, procedures prior to the reforms were characteristic of peculiar Japanese political development then and now. Kamatari, a Confucian, represented the influence on Japanese thought of Chinese concepts of emperorship. The dispute with Soga represented the dominance of clan politics. The new Emperor was a Buddhist, contemptuous of native religion upon which his own prestige rested. The abdication of the Empress was the first of a long series of manipulated surrenders of the throne. The advisory function of great ministers was an early example of government from behind the screen. G. B. Sansom, *op. cit.,* p. 94.

At the very outset of his reign the Emperor Kōtoku promulgated Japan's first reign period, entitling it *Taika,* the era of "Great Reform." Indeed the hands of the reformers touched everything in the state system. At the blueprint level everything was altered, from the new departmental system in the central government to the smallest subdivision of local administration, from the specifications for grades in the bureaucracy to commands concerning the equal division of land, taxation, and military obligations in the provinces. (A chronology, Appendix 8, pages 582-583, gives the major steps toward reform and illustrates the extent to which the reformers planned renovation.)

Actually the decrees of A.D. 645 were addressed only to the eastern provinces in the vicinity of the capital. At a later date special agents were sent to all provinces under Japanese control to collect weapons and to take the census. In any case the reformers had to move slowly. For some sixty years the problem of reform caused a great deal of political unrest among the upper classes who were dubious about their status and rewards under the new system.

In the first month of the second year of Taika, A.D. 646, the Emperor issued the *Kaishin no Mikotonori* (the Imperial Reform Edict). This comprised four brief articles which would, if enforced, have completely altered the political and economic structure of Japan. The measures can be summarized as follows:

1. *nationalization* and the clan-controlled guilds according to the precept of "public land, public citizens" (*kōdo-kōmin*);
2. *centralization* of government in a county and province system (*gunken*) and liquidation of the clan system of political economy;
3. *registration* of population by family (*koseki*) and allotment of land according to the precept of "mouth-share-field"; and
4. *taxation* of land, labor, and produce in a fixed ratio for the direct benefit of the Imperial court.

Through these four brief articles the Japanese were to be introduced to a new system of land tenure, a new system of administration in local government, and a new system of taxation. To this degree the Taika represented a revolution from above; the purpose of the four articles was as much a redistribution of economic power as it was a shift of political authority from the clans to the central government.[9]

As results can be judged, the reforms were not as radical as their texts implied. In historic fact the political objectives were not achieved until

[9] Mombu Shō, *Nihon no rekishi,* cited, Chap. 3, especially Part 2; Tazaki Masayoshi, "*Taika kaishin shakaijō keizaijō oyobi ni shisōjō no igi*" (The social, economic, and philosophic meaning of the Taika reforms) in Kobe Shōgyō Daigaku, *Kokumin keizai zasshi* (Kobe University of Commerce, National Economic Journal), Vol. XVII, No. 3 (September, 1914). The best analysis in English is that of Asakawa, *op. cit.,* pp. 260-270, from which most of the chronology (Appendix 8) is taken. Sansom, *op. cit.,* pp. 95-106, is a clear, brief summary of both Taika and Taihō.

adoption of the supplementary Taihō code in A.D. 702, and even then enforcement remained difficult. Nevertheless the Taika decrees represent convulsive political change in its first impact. They stand for the Japanization of the Chinese model of government.

From the beginning a T'ang model democracy began to take shape. Its first members appointed at the outset in A.D. 645 were three ministers and two learned men acting as counselors on law and institutions. The three ministers were the Great Minister of the Left (*Sadaijin*), the Great Minister of the Right (*Udaijin*), and the Great Minister of the Center (*Naidaijin*). The Great Minister of the Center was, of course, Fujiwara Kamatari himself.

Beneath these major officers the important officers of state were called *Daibu*. In A.D. 699 they were organized into eight departments and numerous offices.

Their ranks, in close imitation of the Chinese model, were denoted by cap colors prescribed by law in A.D. 647 and revised in A.D. 649.

The Emperor Kōtoku died after a ten-year reign, but the power of Kamatari endured. The Crown Prince, Naka-no-Ōye, assumed the throne under the reign title of Tenchi *Tennō*. The most enthusiastic reformer of all, he concentrated all his efforts on reorganizing the central government, moving his capital to Ōmi-no-kuni, and there he presided over the formulation of the Ōmi Laws. These were the first civil and penal codes of Japan. Kamatari was given the new family name Fujiwara for his outstanding service to the reformation.

When Fujiwara Kamatari died in A.D. 669 and Tenchi *Tennō* died in A.D. 671, the new emperor, a younger brother of the Emperor Kōtoku, reigning under the style of Temmu *Tennō,* led the wave of reaction. Involuntarily he consummated the great purposes of Kamatari and his emperors. By reacting within the framework of the reform he helped finish the Japanizing of the Chinese models. The Ōmi codes were revised and promulgated at last in A.D. 702 as the Civil and Penal Codes of the Great Treasure (*Taihō*), consisting of six volumes of law (*ritsu*) and eleven volumes of orders (*ryō*).

Far more particular than the Constitution of Shōtoku Taishi or the Taika decrees, the Taihō code reduced the reform to applicable and livable institutions and procedures. By modern standards the code is a hybrid of constitutional law, penal law, military law, and the law of public ceremony. The administrative system set up in these codes was, of course, mongrel; in time it had to be revised. To this day, however, some features of the Japanese government can be traced back in almost unmodified form to their origins in the Taihō codes. The ordinances themselves provided regulations for the organization of the state and the management of the administration. (Chart 12 presents a simplified outline of this bureaucracy.) Legally, sovereignty rested in the person of the *Tennō* (Emperor) at the apex. It is decisive that the reforms were brought about in the names of successive emperors, although not necessarily by their personal acts. The basic political principles of the reforms were a mixture of Chinese and Japanese, Chinese as to the organization of the bureaucracy, and Japanese in the peculiar theory of sacred sovereignty. By the reforms the Imperial succession Japanized the Chinese model so successfully as to make it a prop to the older form of the empire. The new government went further. It used the devices of the T'ang Exemplar to maintain peculiarly Japanese spiritual features, wholly alien to the T'ang outlook on life, as props for morality and government.

The central government itself was composed of a Department of Religion (*Jingikan*) and the Great Council of State (*Dajōkan*). The *Jingikan* was comparable neither to the Division of Ministers (*Shang-shu-shêng*) nor to the Court of Sacrificial Worship (*T'ai-ch'ang-ssŭ*) of the T'ang. The *Dajōkan* was comparable to the great councils which had long, under one style

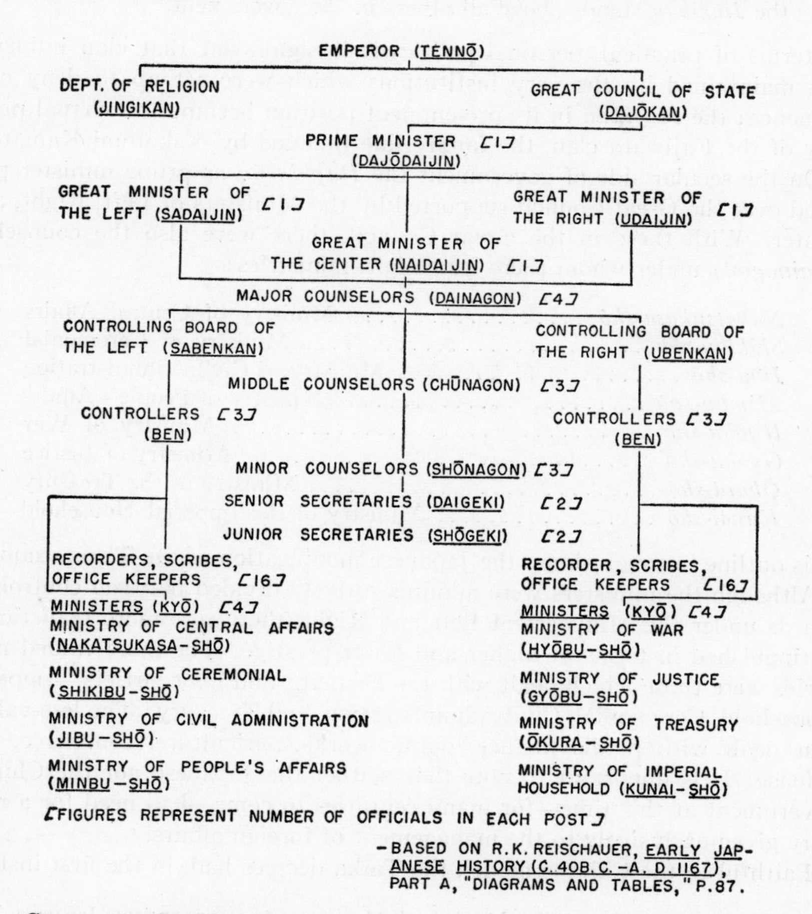

CHART 12—Organization of the Japanese Government from the Taika to the Kamakura Era (Courtesy of Princeton University Press)

or the other, been a feature of Chinese government, but the *Jingikan*, extending into the religious field, boldly asserted the Japanese character of Chinese government from the first instant it was installed in Japan. Not only was the Department of Religion a feature of government itself, claiming jurisdiction over the national cults, religious ceremonies, and shrines throughout the land; it was also the senior-most department of government. A modern Japanese commentator explains this by saying,

> If a state has its origin in military prowess, which is essentially human, then by human agencies also a state may by overthrown. To insure against such vicissitudes a throne must be based upon something superior to man's potentialities. Divine authority alone fulfills that definition, and it is because the throne of Japan had a superhuman foundation that its existence is perennial. Therefore the *Jingikan* stands above all others in the government.[10]

In terms of practical, personal politics it is significant that clan influence was maintained by the very institutions which were set up to deny clan influence: the *Jingikan* in its pre-eminent position became the virtual property of the Fujiwara clan, the family line founded by Nakatomi Kamatari.

On the secular side of government the *Dajōdaijin* as prime minister presided over the Great Council supported by the Ministers of Left, Right, and Center. With these in the Great Council, there were also the counselors (*Dainagon*) under whom there were eight ministries:

Nakatsukasa-shō .... Ministry of Central Affairs
Shikibu-shō .... Ministry of Ceremonial
Jibu-shō .... Ministry of Civil Administration
Mimbu-shō .... Ministry of People's Affairs
Hyōbu-shō .... Ministry of War
Gyōbu-shō .... Ministry of Justice
Ōkura-shō .... Ministry of the Treasury
Kunai-shō .... Ministry of the Imperial Household

This outline in rough shows the Japanese modification of the T'ang example.

Although the ministers were administratively divided between controlling boards under the Ministers of Left and Right, they were more realistically distinguished in terms of higher and lower prestige. The more-valued ministries were those which dealt with the Emperor and his courtiers—Imperial Household, Ceremonial, Civil Administration, and Treasury. The less-valued four dealt with public finance, public works, agriculture, commerce, and defense. It is important to note that neither the Japanese nor the Chinese government at this time—for many centuries to come—had need for a ministry given exclusively to the management of foreign affairs.

Faithful to the Chinese model, the Taika decrees had, in the first instant,

[10] Ariga Nagao, *Nihon kodai hō shakugi* (A commentary on ancient Japanese law), Tōkyō, 1908, pp. 29-30.

already defined an Inner Country (*Kinai*), a sort of metropolitan area given special status in China and faithfully reproduced in Japan. The only important modern Western nation to have a comparable special metropolitan zone is, of course, the United States with its nonself-governing District of Columbia. The eastern part of the Empire, including the Inner Country, was divided into eight circuits (*dō*), which were further subdivided into provinces (*kuni*), counties (*gun*), townships (*mura*), and villages (*sato*). The Japanese term for the province, *kuni,* uses the same ideograph as the Chinese character *kuo,* which to the Chinese means realm, kingdom, or country. The scattered topography of Japan and the tradition of clan independence made it easy for the Japanese to think of their newly reformed Empire as a composite of many little realms. Within each province, the provincial governor had the following functions: census-taking, registration of cultivated lands, the investigation of claims presented by local chieftains, levying new taxes, appointing county officials, collecting arms, and encouraging agriculture.

As early as A.D. 646 the status of the village had been stabilized with the decree: "Let every 50 houses be reckoned a *sato* and in every *sato* let there be one elder who shall be charged with the superintendence of the houses and the people, the direction of the sowing of crops and the cultivation of mulberry trees, the prevention and examination of offences and the enforcement of the payment of taxes and of forced labor."[11] Down on Kyushu Island a special governor-general (*Dadaifu*) was set up to take charge of administration, foreign relations, and western coastal defense on a local basis.

Militarily speaking, the reforms were ineffectual. Specified guards, surviving from pre-reform times and supposedly distinct from clan warriors, were left in existence. In the first theoretical stages of reform, soldiers were to be mustered universally among the people by voluntary enlistment. By A.D. 689 one fourth of all able-bodied men in each *kuni* were under obligation to serve. The Taihō code extended the service to one third. It is probable that when actual recruitment took place it continued as before on the basis of clans and groups.

Japanization of Chinese Land Tenure. There is a very important transition from Taika to Taihō codes which indicates the practical retreat beaten by the Japanese from the high and formalistic of the Chinese model down to the practical manipulation of things as they actually stood in Japan.

[11] From Aston's translation of the *Nihongi,* cited, Chap. II, p. 208, with alterations. See also Mombu Shō, *Nihon no rekishi,* cited, Chap. 3, Part 3. Out of the Taika Reforms and the Taihō code emerged an administrative system which was the theoretical basis of government until the nineteenth century, and which has been the subject of a wealth of commentary. For detailed legal aspects, the advanced student should consult the classic by Dr. Miura Shūkō, *Hōseishi no kenkyū* (Essays on Japanese legal institutions), Tōkyō, 1925, especially Part I, pp. 1-3, for the effects of Chinese on Japanese law; and pp. 7-8 for a brief history of the Taihō code and subsequent commentaries. From the administrative point of view, Sir George Sansom's careful working notes constitute a valuable outline of administration in the eighth century: "Early Japanese Law and Administration," *TASJ,* 2d Series, Vol. IX (1932), 74-109 (see chart, p. 73); Vol. XI (1934). R. K. Reischauer, *Early Japanese History,* cited, Vol. A, p. 87, presents a chart of the central government from which Chart 12 in this book is adapted.

The Taika code undertook an implementation of the Chinese theory of land tenure, always imperfect when it came to actual execution in China itself, upon the principles of land nationalization and of equal distribution. The Chinese kept in their laws what they rarely saw in practice: the preservation of land as the working capital of the whole people. Time and again revolutionists or reformers attempted to clear the land of debt and to assign it to families on a basis of its actual usability; generation after generation the unequal talents of the Chinese led to the accumulation of more land by some than by others. The Taika code took the Chinese model, not the Chinese fact.

The Taihō code was more practical in admitting exceptions. Japanese tradition was and is aristocratic when it comes to the matter of landholding. The Taihō code legitimized those Japanese features which the Taika code had not swept aside, and in so doing it warped the foundation of the Japanese economic structure so that, in course of time, the entire system departed very far from its formal Chinese model.

Briefly the Taihō code divided all land into two types, official and private. Private ownership did not mean, as it often does in the West, virtually untrammeled private enjoyment of the produce of the land. Both public and private land in Japan could be further subdivided into taxable, nontaxable, or rent land. Private land was private only on the basis of an almost endless subdivision of particular styles of titles, each of which had legal and economic burdens peculiar to the style.[12]

The social effects of this land system were to translate the actual social system of Japan into the terms of agricultural economics. Land became an award which could be given as a consequence of social prestige or political power. Property followed high position, not high position property. The social connections of the high courtiers became factors which could be translated fairly readily into exemptions from taxation, grants of private land, and other economic privileges. A modern Japanese economist goes so far as to state that the legal currency of Japan in the Taihō period was based on "the noble standard." [13] He meant thereby that aristocratic status was the determinant of wealth, and that within a system of movable statuses the Japanese found their most important economic market place. Property was not exchanged for property. Quite the contrary, property was the result of position; position, the result of merit or intrigue, social connections, or Imperial favor.

[12] For example, ***kubunden*** (the "mouth-share-field"); ***iden,*** "titles" to which were transferred to officers at the court; ***chokushiden,*** land granted by order of the Emperor; ***shokuden*** ("actual-service land"); ***shiden*** ("merit land"); ***yakuden*** ("ricefield instead"); ***handen,*** an allotment from the Government; and many others.

[13] Yunoki S., *"Taika kaishin"* ("Taika reforms"), *Nihon Keizai Jiten,* cited, Vol. V, p. 961; in this and in later sections commenting on the growth and significance of parallel economic institutions and ideology, the author has drawn upon his earlier, unpublished dissertation: A. W. Burks, *Economics in Japanese Thought,* Washington, School of Advanced International Studies, 1948 (typescript).

Survival of the T'ang Model. The last major step taken by the Japanese in this first period of political centralization was to decide upon a site and to build a great capital city. The Japanese tried several locations before picking the most famous and enduring of them.

Not until A.D. 710 was Japan's first real capital, the city of Nara, completed. Nara gave its name to an era (710–793) which symbolized the first flowering of Sino-Japanese culture. Like a Chinese capital, Nara was symmetrically laid out. Its architecture was Chinese, as was its religion; laws, ordinances, and public documents were written in Chinese. The city and the process, both of them were remarkable. A foreign culture, not imposed by force, but drawn in from outside and embodied in a magnificent city, dominated the main island of Japan.

In A.D. 784 the government moved from Nara to Nagaoka. In one sense the removal seems almost inexplicable, since Nara had been built at the expenditure of immense treasure and effort. The immediate practical reason may have been the reappearance of strong clan pressure on the Imperial court. Finally, in A.D. 793 the court moved to the most enduring capital of the ancient empire, Heiankyō, which today is known as Kyoto, and which was spared, along with Nara, the visits of American B-29 bombers because of its antiquity and beauty.

Heiankyō too gave its name to an era, the Heian period (A.D. 794-1191) and came to symbolize a way of life. In its time it must have been one of the largest cities in the world, with some estimates placing its population as high as 500,000. At the capital the aristocratic life was an almost perfect fusion of the Chinese model with the Japanese materials. T'ang ceremonials, ritual, and etiquette were slavishly followed. Buddhism bolstered the screen of formalism. The increasing seclusion of the court, however, made it almost impossible for even the most self-willed ruler to realize and to attack the increasingly urgent problems of the political economy.[14]

These changes, which resulted from the Taika and Taihō codes and their aftermath represented a peculiarly reverse revolution. Like so many things Japanese, it was accomplished from the top down. Change was effected in detail as much as *en gros*. The Japanese had moved from the confines of an increasingly cultivated tribalism to the framework of a civilized state.

The capital and the Empire, although they dominated Japan, did not become the whole body of Japan. Like some of our modern motion-picture characters, they bore a relation to reality that was purely coincidental. The

[14] Captain Frank Brinkley, in Vol. I, pp. 133-134 of *Japan; Its History, Arts and Literature*, Boston and Tokyo, 1901, gives a brilliant and amusing description of the ancient Nara capital; similarly, a description of Kyoto, p. 253, note 36. Chapters V-VII are, indeed, a fascinating account of the architecture, clothing, customs, and literature of these periods. Although now somewhat outdated, Captain Brinkley's volumes (I-VIII of J. B. Millet's Oriental Series) still constitute an amazingly reliable description by one who first viewed Japanese life after the opening of the country. E. O. Reischauer, *Japan, Past and Present*, cited, offers a brief description and a plan of ancient Heiankyō, superimposed on modern Kyoto.

model of the ancient Chinese Empire in Japan was, in some respects, a tremendous humbug. The *shizoku* tradition was not dead. The clan life went on with undiminished vitality. It had been made unofficial and therefore—according to the book—did not exist, but it was to reappear, a few centuries later, stronger than ever and more resistantly Japanese than before. The Japanized version of the Chinese Empire was a world built up around poetry, ideals, and official decrees. Its chief beneficiaries were the *literati,* the worthies, and the courtiers.

Japanese scholars have recognized this fact. The late Dr. Miura Shūkō, a famous legal historian at Kyoto Imperial University, expressed his doubts as to the breakdown of the guild system of handicraft production in the Taika period. Dr. Kume Kumitake pointed to the lack of realized land reform. Professor Asakawa has surveyed the most important surviving institutions, nobility by birth, and its effects. Most vital, the elaborate Chinese system of education and examination for merit was made to answer the interests of the nobility. The guiding principle of the reformers in regard to the nobility was, on the one hand, to consider the nobles individual subjects of the state, and, on the other hand, to convert them into upper layers of state officers, therewith annexing their personal influence to the new system.[15]

This omission of the two working foundations for the Chinese system—the nonaristocratic tenure of land and the nonhereditary selection of scholar bureaucrats—meant that, in course of time, the Japanese aristocracy would hammer the Chinese model into the form of its social life.

The interaction of social and economic with the political effects of the reform period is significant. Since Japan, like China, was at base an agrarian state, the application of Chinese doctrines of cadastral reform hastened the economic collapse of the old tribal land system. The land capital developed a *dilettante* society widely separated from life on the land. The grant of wealth to nobility and the shift of wealth with court influence or favor meant that the provisional system had to be twisted this way and that, meant that the peasantry had to undergo extortions to help their unstable superiors, and meant that taxes would be increasingly evaded by the strong and thrust upon the weak.

The vital weakness was a lack of adjustment in apportioning income between the producers and the state. The nonproductive population began to increase, but with the advance of civilization so did the claims of the producers. The share of the Imperial household grew smaller and that of landholders larger. An expansion of tax-free estates and the re-emergence of hereditary chieftains set up a rival to the central government itself; in succeeding centuries this was to topple the Japanese version of the Chinese Empire.

[15] Miura S., *"Taika kaishin ron,"* (Discussion of the Taika reforms), Vol. VII, No. 1 (January, 1896), and Kume K., *"Taika kaishin no ronzu,"* Vol. III, No. 32 (July, 1892), both in Tōkyō Teikoku Daigaku, *Shigaku zasshi* (Tokyo Imperial University, Journal of History); K. Asakawa, *op. cit.,* pp. 321-322.

CHAPTER
TWELVE

The Florescence of Japanese Dual Government

IF GOVERNMENT on the T'ang model is considered the first government of a truly civilized and literate Japan, the long period of shogunal government can be considered the second major governmental form. For almost a thousand years the Japanese moved onward, constant in change, developing from within their own resources of imagination, intellect, scholarship, and tradition a special kind of government peculiar to themselves alone. More than any other civilized people on earth they developed dualism.

Dualism is a political tradition that sets up one government for the purpose of reigning, while leaving the practice of ruling to another. In Europe an analogy can be found in the coexistence of the mayors of the palace and the kings of the French monarchy of the late Merovingian period, or in the coexistence of the Holy Roman Emperor with the Pope in those times when both stood forth as secular rulers. No European dualism attained the completeness reached in Japan.

The source of Japanese dualism can perhaps be found in a psychological characteristic, true of all human beings, which leads any anxious or greedy person to desire things in duplicate. In its most innocent form, this desire is manifested by the possession of an ordinary set of table silver for everyday use and a choice set preserved for special occasions which may never arise. In American life the untouchable and unusable parlor, where no one ever went except for funerals, disasters, or the reception of the local preacher, is a characteristic of the psychological need to keep something so good that it cannot be used.

No matter how one approaches it, Japanese character has its own particular and rather admirable strain of compulsiveness. A typically Japanese obsession, cleanliness, is one Japanese characteristic of this strain. Another characteristic is an emphasis on political perfection—a kind of political perfection unattainable by any government that might be set up by mere human beings to regulate day-to-day life on this earth. Instead of transferring their perfect government to the precincts of eternity, the Japanese reconciled a profound need for governmental perfection with an equally profound need for tactical authority. They set up one government so beautifully, so (literally speaking) immaculately, that it could not possibly govern; hence, it could fulfill the Japanese emotional need for a government forever beyond the contaminating touch of dishonor, mundane controversy, partisan struggle, or defeat. Side by side with this government, the Japanese in various forms and at various times have established brutal, practical, hard-headed governments which needed only the amount of honor for everyday life and which dedicated themselves to the immediate task of ruling over the problems, epochs, and generations for which they were established.

On the other hand, the source of Japanese dualism may well have been—as it was in the days of Soga—a pure power struggle. In this sense, excessive concern for the doctrine of Imperial divinity—as it was felt later during the Shōwa Restoration—may well have been the effect rather than the cause of dualism. In any case, the Imperial cult acted as a perfect screen for indirection in Japanese politics.

The Age of Civil Dictators. The fissioning of the Japanese corporate personality, setting the immaculate reigning instruments to one side and the practical governing instruments to the other, took place within the structure of the Japanized model of the Chinese Empire itself. This particular brand of dualism first became apparent in the years from the seventh to the twelfth centuries, when certain subtle changes occurred in the administrative structure copied from the T'ang. Concurrently, social and economic developments provided the bases for an eventual feudalism wholly assimilated to the Japanese national character.

The Japanese, even when adopting the Chinese model most zealously, had not installed a mere facsimile of the T'ang prototype. Even in the great days of the Taika and the Taihō reforms, the central government was a half-fictitious rendering which did not deeply affect provincial Japan. Even in the innermost circles of the Sinifiers, fundamental assumptions at variance with Chinese political practice were allowed to remain simply because they were so deeply Japanese. For example, the aristocratic emphasis on gentilitial ties, inherited from primitive Japan, proved stronger than the relatively more democratic emphasis upon rule by virtue of merit, imported from Confucian China. Never did the Japanese accept the Chinese doctrine that the Emperor himself was subject to the requirements of ideological conformity and that his subjects had the right to rebel when he lost the Mandate of Heaven. For Japan there could be but one embodiment of virtue, one descendant of the Sun Goddess, one unbroken line of *Tennō*. In Japanese eyes China could have many dynasties, all of them secular and therefore mortal; Japan had the one, spiritual and therefore immortal.

But how could the sacred and immaculate Emperor exercise sovereignty? How could he rule without incurring demerit? Who, century after century, could absorb all blame for mistakes and leave all credit to the Imperial family, to whom credit divinely belonged? The Chinese answer was not enough.

The Chinese, of course, had mitigated the monarchic features of their administration by means of a bureaucratic system based on merit. In theory and, to a great extent, in practice, anyone could aspire to Imperial appointment by meeting high educational requirements through the examination system.

Government-by-merit never became the rule in Japan. A hierarchical emphasis on genealogy permitted only members of a closed social caste to take examinations for a governmental post. In the first few centuries after the adoption of the Chinese model of empire, all important Japanese posts became hereditary and fell into the tight grip of an aristocratic civilian bureaucracy. This trend is illustrated by the dominance of the Fujiwara family and by the superficial evidence of the control exercised over all Japan through the office of a hereditary civilian dictator called *Kampaku*.

The term *Kampaku* literally means Regent.

Yet the Regency was no mere transitional institution comparable to its European counterparts. As in Europe the post originally provided for men who would control the government during the minority of an Emperor. In fact the Regent soon outstripped the Prime Minister (*Dajōdaijin*) and became a Civil Dictator. As Civil Dictator the *Kampaku* was theoretically a mouthpiece of the sovereign to whom he reported on matters of state, but, from the tenth century on, the post was always held by a member of the Fujiwara family and became the first regularized system of dual monarchy in Japan.

The *Kampaku* thus represented the persistence of clan control, the reemergence of the *shizoku* principle in practical Japanese politics, and dominance through family solidarity rather than through considerations of individual merit.

As Sir George Sansom has pointed out, analogies in other countries—mayors of the palace, king-makers—are easy to find; but the translation of family solidarity into political dualism is peculiarly Japanese. Before the installation of the T'ang model, the Soga clan had claimed and won paramountcy on a relatively noninstitutionalized basis. In the period after the Age of Civil Dictators, here under consideration, the Fujiwara were succeeded by Taira and Minamoto control. In the Tokugawa period dualism was carried to its peak. Even in modern times Prince Saionji, the last of the *Genrō* (Elder Statesmen), and Prince Konoe (Konoye), the last Japanese prime minister of *Kuge* (Noble) rank, were actual family descendants of Civil Dictators from a thousand years past, as well as their political heirs.

General MacArthur, whether he knew it or not, was consummately Japanese when he established for the purposes of the Occupation a government parallel to the established government of Japan; he too, perhaps not realizing it at first, fitted the pattern of two governments in one realm.[1]

The development of the *Kampaku* was matched by comparable distortions of other T'ang-inspired institutions. A Fujiwara-dominated Bureau of Archivists (*Kuraudo-dokoro*) had moved by the end of the ninth century outside its original jurisdiction over confidential court papers, and had acquired such real legislative and executive power as to render doubtful the juridical authority of the Great Council of State (*Dajōkan*) and of the Ministry of Central Affairs (*Nakatsukasa-shō*).

Dualism marched more rapidly in the country where the T'ang reforms had never penetrated very deeply than in the capital. The provinces were linked to the capital through two administrative posts. The great codes of the seventh century had provided *mikoto mochi* (provincial governors), who in theory represented all departments of the capital. In fact, early incumbents were only titular absentee officials who counted for little in practical local affairs. *Gunshi* (district governors) were appointed by the Imperial court on the recommendation of the provincial governors; they, as resident deputies, exercised actual control. The district official was usually a local noble who, in turn, held his post by hereditary succession. He had the local political know-how, the working influence, and the connections of family and friendship. Thus, the duties of the provincial governors were supervisory and administrative, becoming in time nominal; those of the district governors were executive and judicial, and remained real.

Structurally only one other change of great importance occurred in the few centuries after the Taika and Taihō reforms. The barbarian Ainu, then known as *Emishi* and inhabiting the northeast of the mainland of Honshu, were a constant military challenge. Strategically they were no more dangerous to the existence of Japan than were the American Indians to the United States of Presidents Washington and Adams; but, like the American Indians, they were a nuisance of very real proportions. In A.D. 784 a *Seitō-shōgun* (General for subduing the east) was appointed; after a short lapse the commission was reinaugurated with the title *Sei-i Tai-shōgun* (Barbarian-subduing Generalissimo). The post became important only later when the title became the style of *de facto* military dictators.

The effects of the campaigns against the Ainu in the East and North cannot, however, be measured in mere terms of the creation of new posts. Japan's frontier and resultant sectionalism (as Frederick Jackson Turner might have put it) constituted a steady drain on Imperial finances and man power, as the Japanese, roughly from the seventh to the tenth centuries, continued the old process of conquest and assimilation of the islands' aborig-

[1] For the earlier parallels, see Sansom, *op. cit.*, pp. 206-207; for later echoes, R. K. Reischauer, *Japan; Government-Politics*, cited, p. 46.

ines. Successive campaigns led inevitably to the decline of the prestige of court nobles and an opportunity for the rise of new leaders in the East. This period saw also the beginnings of a hereditary, privileged class of soldiers, which later characterized feudal Japan.[2]

None of the administrative or military alterations—Civil Dictator, Bureau of Archivists, Barbarian-subduing Generalissimo—was more than a mere shift in the center of gravity of the governmental machine. The shift was not decisive, but it was symptomatic of profound social and economic changes in Nara and Heian Japan.

Final political change followed economic change.

The economic change, equally gradual, was more far-reaching. When the Japanese fashioned their political economy after the T'ang model, they accepted the fictitious blueprint of equal division of the land. Even at the beginning, only a small proportion of the available land was so divided. Collapse of the land system, the underpinning, led to collapse of central control, the superstructure. Economic changes thus brought political and legal changes; economic changes also, inevitably though indirectly, brought ideological changes—the kind of chain-phenomena which Karl Marx a thousand years later might have called "forms of social consciousness."

Had Marx been able to read Japanese, for example, he would have been provided by the examples of Nara and Heian Japan with remarkably demonstrative instances of the economic determination of both political institutions and of ideology. The closeness of the correlations would almost certainly have delighted him. (See page 327, footnote 6.) Only in our own times have Japanese historians and economists been deeply affected by the intellectual invasion of Marxism. Writers such as Kawakami Hajime applied Marxian dogma to early Japanese history with considerable dialectical success.[3]

The Japanese departure from the ideal of equal division of landholdings was a progressive one. This is evident from historical records. Even the Taihō codes, as already described, had permitted exception of certain private lands. In A.D. 711 an Imperial ordinance disapproved the behavior of nobles and of territorial gentry who were appropriating large tracts of tax-free land to the detriment of court income and of the small, taxable farmer. In A.D. 713 another order was aimed at parallel practices by Buddhist monasteries. At the capital, however, the government itself continued to grant to temples tracts of tax-free land in return for prayers uttered in wholesale quantities on behalf of Imperial ancestors.

The pressure was thus cumulative. As land moved from taxable jurisdictions to nontaxable ones, the weight on the remaining taxable land increased and so, too, did the pressure to move the remaining land over to a tax-free status. By A.D. 743 a law permitted land to be held privately in perpetuity;

[2] Sansom, *op. cit.*, pp. 196-203.

[3] See, for example, Kawakami Hajime, "On Marx's Forms of Social Consciousness," *Kyoto University Economic Review*, Vol. I, No. 1 (July 1926).

this was the first outright admission of the end of the Taika program of land nationalization.

Buddhism and Feudalism. In the transition to political decentralization, Buddhism was among the first and most vital influences. Among the three systems of thought then extant in Japan—Shintō, Confucianism, Buddhism—it was Buddhism which made the most spectacular gains as a popular belief in the Nara era. Buddhism enjoyed the practical advantage of sound institutional economics out in the countryside. Confucianism remained bound up with the court. While Confucianism remained the hobby of elegant courtiers, practical Buddhist clerical officers managed their monastic and temple economies far from the center of fashion. In so doing they contributed some of the earliest elements to Japanese feudal practices.

Buddhism never worked expressly against the interests of the court. On the contrary, some scholars have referred to the Nara political epoch as "Government by Buddhist Prayers." At the capital the great Tōdaiji Temple became the religious headquarters of Buddhism as a concurrent state religion; out in the provinces government-protected temples (*gokoku-ji* or *kokubun-ji*) were established by an Imperial order in A.D. 741 as branch temples in the chief centers of local governments. The economic history of Japan offers detailed data on the economic interests of these temples. Buddhist temples controlled land, fiefs, slaves, and workers; the temple authorities had the organizational ability to manage their holdings effectively. Many priests had been to China and had a better knowledge of practical affairs than did contemporary soldiers or nobles. Buddhist clerical officials became engineers, land reclamationists, capitalists, and loan sharks.[4]

It is patent that, although the Buddhist religion brought Japan great spiritual and material benefits, the Buddhist institutional structure also brought grave evils. The strong institutional entrenchment of the church and its rapid rise to wealth were accompanied by abuses. Church organs were forever entangled in court politics, seeking worldly profits, milking the laity, and ultimately outranking all other classes in economic strength. Church holdings of tax-free land were large and widespread. Buddhists established the manor as an economic unit, became Japan's first manorial lords, and finally provided a counterweight to the political influence of the court itself. As they became rich, the temples formed military units with their own fixed garrisons and thereby accelerated the adoption of garrisons by other local magnates. Buddhism became a state within a state.

[4] The standard economic history of Japan in English is the unfortunately cumbersome three-volume translation, Takekoshi Yosaburō, *Economic Aspects of the History of the Civilization of Japan,* Tokyo, 1930. Used judiciously, this work offers a wealth of data: for example, Vol. I, pp. 81-90, describes holdings of typical Buddhist temples. Kawada and Okamoto, *Nihon no keizai to bukkyō,* cited, Chap. 2, deals with the economic effects of the arrival of Buddhism; Chap. 3, economic results in the Nara Era. To digress to the modern, postwar era, it is of interest to note that in rural Japan today, there are often attached to the ancient *kokubun-ji* nursery schools for pre-school children. The program of establishing such nursery schools received impetus and encouragement under the Occupation.

The lay nobility learned rapidly from the Buddhists. Provincial governorships fell more and more into the hands of absentee courtiers. Family influence in the provinces began to assert itself against the crumbling bureaucracy. From the end of the eighth to the end of the twelfth centuries the capital degenerated into a system of aristocratic (*kizoku*) politics; the provinces saw a regeneration of clan-family (*shizoku*) politics. Prompted and paced by Buddhist innovations, the tax-free estates developed so rapidly that their appearance is the characteristic feature of Heian history. These tax-free estates were the *shōen*.

The Shōen Grant. Literally, *shō-* means a country home; *-en,* well-managed grounds. A *shōen,* thus, was a rural tract of land or a manorial estate. Somewhat like the *villa rustica* of Rome, it represented land, the produce from which was divided between cultivators and landlord. Professor Asakawa, the outstanding authority on Japanese feudalism, described the *shōen* as requiring three features:

> *a tract of land* newly brought under cultivation (as the chief requisite of the grant);
> *under patronage* of a person or institution of influence;
> with the enjoyment of, claim to, or aspiration toward *fiscal immunity.*

The earliest *shōen* holders were, of course, the Buddhist temples. Once the Buddhists started the landslide away from taxable to tax-free status, two new processes accelerated the change from one category to the other. Members of the Imperial family and court officials sought and obtained private tax-free holdings. Beyond this there were arbitrary appropriations of unreclaimed lands by private persons who thereupon put in for *shōen* status.

The process of establishing *shōen* was made possible by two techniques: first was *commendation,* whereby the taxable owner surrendered title to his land to the holder of a tax-free estate; the second was the reverse, *benefice,* whereby the commendee made a grant or lease down to the cultivator. In either case the cultivator retained possession in a limited feudal sense and received protection from the commendee, who might in turn find it politic to commend title to the land upward through the administrative pyramid to an influential person near the apex of society. Both techniques were undertaken to avoid the heavy load of taxation imposed on the diminishing taxable land by the central government. Many extensive scholarly explorations of these aspects of Japanese economic history have been carried out by both Japanese and Western scholars of our time.[5]

[5] There is no attempt here further to duplicate this exhaustive research into feudal institutions. Standard treatment of the *shōen* in Japanese may be found in Honjō Eijirō, *Nihon shakai-keizai shi,* cited, Chap. 4, "*Shōen seido no jidai*" (The era of the *Shōen* system), Part I, pp. 136 ff. In English, R. K. Reischauer has contributed a useful, short article containing a wealth of definitions: "The Japanese *Shōen,* or Manor: Some Useful Terminology," *Journal of the American Oriental Society,* Vol. LVII, No. 1 (March, 1937), pp. 78-83. The minimum characteristics as defined by Professor Asakawa are to be found

Social changes marched alongside political and economic shifts of power. The seventh-century reforms theoretically gave the lower ranks of free people—pre-reform clansmen, peasants, and guild members—specified allotments of land. In turn they helped to support the state by taxes paid in commodities or with labor. With the coming of the *shōen* system the right to land *use* became the peasant's; the rights of *taxation* and *administration*, the lord's. Lords who seized widespread holdings were precursors of later Tokugawa feudal magnates (*daimyō*). The patent became as much the archetypal Japanese community as it was in Norman England. At one and the same time the *shōen* was a political and economic unit, a social group, headed by a landlord as represented through his deputy or bailiff and inhabited by peasants with or without resident merchants. Manorial headquarters grew until they produced the familiar castle-towns of Tokugawa Japan.

Beginnings of a Military Caste. One more element hastened the coming of decentralized feudalism. Although the precise origins of Japanese military caste are not known, the choice of historical probabilities is one that intrigues Japanese historians. Chivalric militarism with its accompanying romantic and honorific ideology is an important enough Japanese datum to merit detailed scrutiny. The exact beginnings were so modest that they have defied precise pinpointing.

At the time of the Chinese-model reforms, military posts of the capital were purely honorary or else established on an *ad hoc* basis to deal with short-lived Ainu crises. The holders of Imperial military commissions were largely ineffective. As the *shōen* process cancerously ate away the court's sources of revenue, the central government became less capable of maintaining law and order in the provinces. Economic atrophy led to military feebleness.

Buddhist temples were the first to organize their own small bands of soldiers to maintain a law and order which the government could not give them. Then, as large landholders spread their economic and political power over whole provinces, they translated that power into military force. Furnishing their own police and soldiers, they established a new military class (the *bushi*, later to be known as *samurai*). The justification in everyday terms for the existence of this class was a low level of public order and the presence of rich economic bases, the manors.

The interleaving of this new class of warriors between peasants below and lords above is illustrated negatively by the appearance of *rōnin* (literally, "wave men"). *Rōnin* were human flotsam washed up during economic storms. With no lord to protect them and no manor which they could call

---

in "Some Aspects of Japanese Feudal Institutions," *TASJ*, Vol. XLVI (August, 1918), p. 83. Professor Asakawa's most exhaustive study of feudal structure consists of a collection of source documents, translations, and notes: *The Documents of Iriki, Illustrative of the Development of the Feudal Institutions of Japan*, New Haven, 1929 (The Shibuya family settled in Iriki, subject of the documents, in 1247, during the later Kamakura Era).

home, they were as imperiled as are the "stateless persons" of our own time. Apparently this term was first applied to a garrison of unattached soldiers stationed in the north of Japan about the beginning of the ninth century.[6]

Upward Fall of the Empire. Against the forces of *shōen* and *bushi* the old Empire scarcely had a chance. When its time came to lapse from power, the court could not fall downward into disrespect or oblivion, since its origin was identified with the claims for a divine national origin. Contrariwise, the court, as it were, fell upward when its time came to fall. Instead of going downward, the way a Chinese dynasty might have done, it was translated completely out of real life and into a dreaming-and-playing world where it could remain honored and neglected for centuries.

In the decade A.D. 830-840 Imperial rule reached its zenith of power, but the benefactions conveyed by Imperial authority itself doomed the Imperial family. By the tenth century the capital had fallen to the practical control of the Fujiwara clan and the great temples, whereas the countryside was under the immediate control of the Buddhist temples and other *shōen* holders, all of them equally contemptuous of court orders. In one last pathetic attempt to maintain Imperial prestige the Emperor Shirakawa attempted in A.D. 1073 to seize actual control of the state machinery over and above his vestigial, sacerdotal functions. His effort failed.

While the Empire faded, so too did the Civil Dictatorship, which had so long maintained the Fujiwara.

With poetic justice the Fujiwara were overwhelmed by the system which they themselves did so much to establish. Temples which this clan had endowed in centuries past turned against the heirs of their sponsors. And the power of the land was decisive. The Fujiwara, with historic shortsightedness, withdrew the profits from their estates and poured them down the rat-hole of court politics. While the Fujiwara maintained their control over the atrophying capital, two frugal provincial clans constructed strong military systems in the countryside, Taira becoming predominant in the south and Minamoto in the north. As Imperial power faded in the capital itself, the court turned to the outer lords and invited their forces into the capital to preserve order. Taira came first, only to become bewildered and entrapped in the maze of the court's intrigue. Minamoto followed, establishing order, but avoiding commitment to local politics.

No matter what the court did each successive step reduced the Imperial power. Each remedy for dualism strengthened and perpetuated dualism. The T'ang model had promoted an Imperial plan into the status of a real monarchy, but it ended with dyarchy. The central bureaucracy had turned into a pattern of hereditary privileges. Land nationalization was wasted away at the expense of feudal tenure. The shining Chinese civilian codes, grandiose and unamended, were superseded by summary military rule and a practical body of local precedent.

[6] Sansom, *op. cit.*, p. 201.

The fall of the Empire occurred as the consequence of a struggle between outer clans. Minamoto, having vanquished Taira, consolidated its power—*outside the capital.* The Empire never fell downward. It was left hollow, useless, and beautiful, to reign without ruling. The final change came when a great Minamoto leader by the name of Yoritomo established a new separate capital at Kamakura.

An analogy in American terms can be found by imagining that America may some day become the victim of overwhelming attack by enemies who command fissionable and radiological weapons. Suppose that in such an America the constitutional government disappears and is replaced by a Theater Headquarters, which, with frugal and harsh military practicality, saves what is left of the country and restores much of it. Imagine then that by authority of such a Continental Theater Command state governments and a national government were once again permitted to come into being with the express understanding that they did not interfere in the process of military production, military man power control, military education, military news dissemination, and military administration. Suppose that decorative governors, legislatures, and supreme courts in the states found that the key word "military" covered all the important affairs of life and that they, along with an impotent President and Congress, had nothing to do but to proclaim holidays, arrange for parades, revise the words of the national anthem, and establish the colors to be used on automobile license plates for each successive year, everything else—by sheer military necessity—having to be left for an indefinite period in the hands of the military. Such an America would be much like the Japan which Yoritomo established. The court continued in Kyoto, the ancient Heiankyō, but power moved to the austere little city of Kamakura.

The Kamakura Dictatorship. The establishment by Minamoto Yoritomo of a dual government at Kamakura led to complete emergence of a system called *hōken seido* (the feudal system). The Kamakura era (A.D. 1185-1338) was the youth of this system; the Tokugawa period (A.D. 1603-1867), its maturity. "Feudal system" in this special sense is to be distinguished from the earliest *shizoku* system of planned political economy—from the system of nationalization, planned under Taika and Taihō—and from its immediate precursor, the *shōen* manorial holdings. Furthermore, Japanese economic historians make another distinction: since there were important differences between early Kamakura practices and later Tokugawa developments, the former is known as decentralized feudalism and the latter as centralized feudalism.[7]

[7] See Honjō, *Nihon shakai-keizai shi,* cited, especially Chap. V, Part I, pp. 195-197, "*Hōken no igi*" (The meaning of feudalism); to Professor Honjō, territorial and personal relationships form the essential ingredients of the feudal system. During and after Kamakura not only the warrior class became feudal, but also the society as a whole. By the Tokugawa Era even the commercial class became dominated by the master-servant relationship. Professor Asakawa ("Some Aspects . . .", cited, pp. 78-79) defined feudalism—of a Japanese

When Yoritomo took power he left behind in Kyoto only two aspects of real government—ceremony and foreign affairs. He and his successors exercised a veto on Japan's contacts with foreign countries, except for the notorious instance of Ashikaga Yoshimitsu (A.D. 1367-1395) who let himself be invested directly as "King of Japan" by the Ming Emperor of China. The shōguns were careful to leave moral authority for diplomacy with the titular emperor, retaining only a veto for themselves. It was in 1185 that the separate shogunal government was set up in Kamakura. In 1192 *de facto* control became *de jure* when Yoritomo received the commission which he coveted of *Sei-i Tai-shōgun.*

Shōgun rule was not outright military monarchy. The Minamoto were in no position to take over the properties or fiefs of the other great clans and temples. The government was much more on the order of a military federation wherein Yoritomo as chief of the predominant outside clan established a rule applicable to all of the countryside of Japan, displacing the complex Imperial bureaucracy by the simple process of taking over its work without modifying its legal title. Yoritomo led Japan to himself by establishing governmental facilities, badly needed by the various feudal lords and temples, but not provided by the powerless capital. He acquired a predominance of military power without attempting to monopolize all military force in Japan. He had his own troops in power to present as a threat; as an inducement he offered practical, useful military justice. It was possible for lesser or greater lords to come to him for the settlement of disputes and to get an answer without going through the tedious, corrupt, and unfamiliar intricacies of Kyoto administration. Yoritomo's councilors started with the facts and built the first Shintō government from Japanese facts, not from Chinese theories. The Kamakura system was simple, austere, befitting an army headquarters or *Bakufu* (literally, "Tent Government").

At first the Kamakura dictatorship had only three central organs of control: a military tribunal, an administrative board, and a judicial body. Each was extraordinarily simple in contrast to the complex bureaucracy of the court. Each accepted existing Japanese practices as the norm. The *Samurai-dokoro,* which dealt with complaints of the military class, was modeled on a body originated by the Fujiwara. The *Man-dokoro,* a civil policy board and hereditary civil service, was a replica of smaller bodies which landowners had found useful in the administration of manors. The *Monchū-jo,* a court of final appeal, headed up private manorial courts which had been found necessary since the transformation of tracts into tax-free and autonomous status.

---

or Western variety—as having the following characteristics: (i) *a ruling class* consisting of groups of fighting men, chained together by links of loyalty; supported by (ii) *a division of classes* coinciding with private, but relative tenures of land; whereby (iii) private tenures of land condition the exercise of *public rights and obligations,* ". . . that is, in government, in finance, in military affairs, and in the administration of justice there should be a complete confusion or coalescence of the public and the private" (p. 79). He divided Japanese feudalism into these three stages: (i) 1185-1338; (ii) 1336-1600; (iii) 1600-1868.

The Kamakura regime sought success by freezing the contemporary Japanese system of landholdings. Even when he tried to rationalize the land system, Yoritomo moved gradually. At the beginning of his rule he received reluctant approval from the court to establish military governors loyal to him, *Shugo* (literally, Protectors), in as many provinces as he could. Imperial commission came more rapidly when he posted a thousand cavalrymen in the capital as persuaders. Wherever he dared he appointed *Jitō* (Stewards) in public and private domain. Each steward controlled a number of armed men, collected taxes, and took a commanding position in the *shōen.* Although stewards were the key to the whole system in the beginning, military governors outstripped them in later development of the shogunal system and became the autonomous feudal lords, *daimyō.* When Yoritomo obtained permission to send out his own local officers, he also won the right to levy a universal "military" tax. This tax cut across the ruinous pattern of tax-free exemptions, although at first he did not dare tax manors which belonged to temples or those actually in possession of members of the Imperial family. (A later shōgun, Hōjō Yasutoki, used an abortive Imperial uprising, which he suppressed, as a pretext for extending his own *Shugo* and *Jitō,* together with their tax-collecting powers, over the whole of Japan.) [8]

Minamoto Yoritomo died at the end of the twelfth century. He had built his shogunal machine so well that it ran on for a hundred years. When his heirs proved themselves inadequate, a new family, the Hōjō, established the hereditary office of *Shikken* (Regent) to rule in the place of the Minamoto. The Hōjō were of Taira stock which had been displaced by the Minamoto. For a while this meant three-level government instead of two, since a hereditary regent ruled for a hereditary military dictator, who ruled for a hereditary emperor. Even at Kyoto complications continued. Powerless though the court was, emperors often found it more convenient to reign when they escaped the constriction of ceremony by abdicating and then exercising their function through their titular successors. In the thirteenth century, Japan reached a degree of complication, almost unimaginable to a Westerner, of delegations and sub-delegations of individual responsibility. At one and the same time an abdicated emperor could really reign on behalf of the titular emperor, while nominal power was held by delegation from an atrophied civilian bureaucracy to a hereditary military bureaucracy on behalf of a nominal military dictator, for whom there acted an advisory council under the chairmanship of a hereditary regent.

Intricate though it was, the system worked. The Hōjō regents brought to its climax the historical momentum set in motion by the daring of Yoritomo. The regents often showed impartiality, efficiency, and courage. Under them the Kamakura system attained its maturity in legal form.

[8] Takekoshi, *op. cit.,* Vol. I, Chap. XIII, "The shugo system . . ." is relatively clear, compared with other involved sections of his volumes. Takekoshi used the phrase "Military Republic" to describe the Kamakura Administration.

Law Codes and Land Registers. Decentralized feudalism flowered in various ethical, religious, institutional, and legal forms. In a surprising, but fortuitous, parallel to the flowering of Anglo-Norman law which was occurring at the same time in an island kingdom at the other end of Eurasia, the Kamakura administrative council in A.D. 1232 adopted a set of laws known as the *Jōei Shikimoku* or *Go Seibai Shikimoku.* Designed to solidify the *status quo,* the Code was worked out within the first fifty years of the *Bakufu.* It came close to paralleling the development of the common law of England. Its chief field of interest consisted of the regulation of land tenure and rights—questions which a feudal, agricultural economy needed to keep settled and clear.

The Code is written in Chinese, not Japanese, but the style—as befitted a military headquarters—is clumsy and unpolished. A council of eleven men wrote the draft, and it was then submitted to the Regent for approval, being proclaimed in the first year of the *Jōei* reign period. Under the title, *The Institute of Judicature,* it has been translated into English by John Carey Hall.[9]

Fifty-one articles in length, the Code, like the constitution of Shōtoku Taishi, is as much a handbook of morals as a legal compendium. It exhorts to loyalty and commends filial piety. Only toward the end does it deal with concrete problems of legal procedure. Article I requires that Shintō shrines and festivals be maintained. Article II requires that Buddhist temples be kept in repair and that Buddhist services be performed. Article IX conveys wide discretionary powers upon officials who must deal with rebellious plots. Article XXXIII deals with robbery, larceny, and arson. Article XXXIV treats adultery. Article L describes the responsibilities and punishments of outsiders who may interfere in brawls. Such a code, it is apparent, reflects little of the Confucian reliance upon ideal behavior. Practical and feudal, the Code is a reflection of Japan as it then existed.

Politically the Code adjusted relationships between the new government

[9] After the death of Yoritomo, government officials sponsored a Japanese translation, called the *Jōkan seiyo,* of a compilation of records and anecdotes of famous Chinese statesmen. Thus, despite the pragmatic characteristic of summary codes of this era, for standards of moral conduct, they leaned heavily upon imported concepts of Chinese propriety. Surprisingly, the famous *Jōei* Code was not printed until Tokugawa times and then was often used as an elementary manual of Chinese ideographs. This code, together with the whole of statute law of old Japan (seventh century to close of Tokugawa), has been compiled in one volume of less than a thousand pages: Hagino Yoshiyuki, Editor, and others, *Nihon kōdai hōten* (Legal records of old Japan), Tōkyō, 1892. Of the collection edited by Hagino, two fifths of the volume holds all the Imperial Laws (seventh-twelfth centuries); three fifths is devoted to law of the feudal areas. Excerpts cited below follow the standard English translation by John Carey Hall, "Japanese Feudal Law: The Institutes of Judicature: Being a Translation of the *'Go Seibai Shikimoku';* The Magisterial Code of the Hojo Power-Holders (A.D. 1232)," *TASJ,* Vol. XXXIV, Part I (1906), pp. 1-44, although the text in Hagino was used for slight alterations. For an extended discussion by a Japanese legalist, see Miura, *Hōseishi no kenkyū,* cited, Vol. I, Part I, sections 8, 9, 10, dealing with the military system and its legal development, pp. 26-37. For economic aspects of the code, see Terao Kōji, *"Go seibai shikimoku," Nihon keizai jiten,* cited, Vol. III, p. 562.

in the Kantō plain and the ancient Imperial government in the capital. Article XXXVII, for example, reads as follows:

> Of vassals of the Kantō applying to Kyoto for side offices [*hō-bōkan;* in modern Japanese *daikan,* deputy] and for the superintendentships of estates.
>
> This practice was strictly forbidden in the time of the Minamoto House. Of late years, however, some persons, following the bent of their own ambitions, have not only disregarded the prohibition, but have entered into competition with others seeking to obtain the same appointment. Henceforth anyone found indulging in such ill-regulated ambition shall be punished by the forfeiture of the whole of his fief.

The effect of this prohibition was to impose drastic punishment upon any tradition-minded dreamer who might try to use the sacred, but suspended, prerogatives of the Empire to undermine the *Bakufu.* Of course, very few of the warriors governed by the Code understood its specific language, and no attempt was made to legislate in language understandable to common folk. The affairs of ordinary people were left to the judgment and honor of the feudal lords. The purpose of the *Jōei* Code was to benefit the ruling and exploiting class; but it is to the credit of that class and its leaders that they were intelligent enough to perceive in the land and its cultivators the basis of their own prosperity.

As originated, the *Jōei* Code was a military house law. To a large extent, therefore, it was based on militarism. Professor Terao Kōji of Kyoto Imperial University has shown, however, that the Code leaned toward legalism (*hōji-shūgi*) as much as upon military principles (*buke-shūgi*). Its remote predecessor, the Taihō Code, had been a systematic body of jurisprudence; this was the practical summation of a half century's experience in a young feudal system. The Taihō Code had represented the Chinese Empire, Japanese in form, expressed through an elegant literary aristocracy; the *Jōei* Code represented the florescence of Japanese feudalism expressed through a military-landed nobility of the countryside. The new code in its practicality and realism progressed from the moral laxity of the Heian period and the vain strictness of the Minamoto.[10]

Since the *Jōei* consisted of a bare fifty-one simple articles, it was early recognized that the Code could not possibly cover all legal tangles. Japanese law did not develop at this point the subtle branching shown by English procedure in the departure of equity from law. Instead there was a forthright need for Amendment Laws (*Tsuika-hō*). There followed, for example, the *Kenchō Shikimoku* which lent its name to an era (A.D. 1249–1255). In general, however, the *Jōei* remained the foundation. The Muromachi

[10] Terao, *ibid.,* p. 562.

Bakufu and the Tokugawa *Bakufu* followed it. Not until the Japanization of the Western state were the successor codes to the *Jōei* swept aside.

Along with the *Jōei* Code the Japanese produced a land register comparable to the Domesday Book. This was the *Nihonkoku taidenbun* (Land record of Japanese Empire). In the five hundred years since adoption of the Taihō Code, manorial freeholds had been overgrown with a jungle of conflicting rights. The *shōen* and the *shiki*—the manor and the various specific legal rights—were the subject matter of much of the *Jōei* Code, in so far as the Code sought to clarify title and thus to secure the individual and the enjoyment of his property. Professor Chitoshi Yanaga of Yale University has expressed it penetratingly for Westerners by saying that the Code was Japan's first crude expression of individualism in terms of property rights. The door was not open far enough to let a Western-type sense of proprietorship into Japan; an essentially familistic feudal landholding system remained. But for the first time there was a distinct legal demarcation between public and private rights.[11]

The Confucian ideal of nothing private, nothing public, which subsumed all individual rights and privileges into a general roster of the common good, could lead to serious maladjustments of justice in any well-stratified class society such as existed in Japan at that time. The Japanese paralleled medieval England part of the way, but they did not leave for themselves that singular release of individual spirit and private adventure which juridical and economic individualism has activated in some nations and in some fortunate times.

Feudalism and Religion. The new clean-cut military government of the Shōgun marked a change in the temple of all Japanese life. Not only did the Japanese clarify economic relationships which had been muddied and confused, but they found themselves venturing forward with genuine religious innovations which had a deeply inspiring effect on subsequent generations of Japanese. Japanese Buddhism flowered in this stimulating feudal environment.

One of the first of the new Buddhist sects, for example, was the Jōdo or Pure Land, founded in the late twelfth century. Men and women in all

[11] The term *shiki* (literally, office or function, as distinguished from the *shiki*— in *Jōei shikimoku,* meaning a procedure or enforcement) will serve to demonstrate the difference in tradition between the Japanese and Western legal ideas of property. Although the words "manor" and "ownership" have been used loosely, it must always be kept in mind that the Japanese manor differed considerably from its European counterpart. Each *shōen* became a complex of *shiki:* the latter came to mean rights, sometimes income, and later, the land itself. Since the *shiki* could be computed in terms of units of produce, it took on the character of currency in an age when money economy had not yet been established, and thus a medium of exchange. Nevertheless, the strongest *shiki*—the right of cultivation—always resided in the peasant. Such popular customs in landholding under public and private control—indivisible tracts and divisible *shiki*—enabled the new warriors and peasants to squat upon the land. For the *shiki* meaning procedure, see Sansom, "Early Japanese Law," *loc. cit.,* Vol. IX, pp. 67-68; for *shiki* discussed here, Asakawa, "Some Aspects," *loc. cit.,* Vol. XLVI, p. 84; and for an unimprovable summary of effects, Asakawa, *Documents,* cited, "Summary of Points," p. 71, and corresponding documents.

stages of life—courtiers, the warrior class at Kamakura, clerics from other sects, even emperors and the lowliest fishermen—flocked to this unorthodox and popular free church. Jōdo Shinshū, or True Sect of Jōdo, extended religion to the poorest classes and reduced doctrine to the simplest points. Within ten minutes' walk of Kyoto's brand new railroad station, even today, the American GI or tourist can see the great Honganji Temples, monuments to the popularization of Buddhism seven centuries ago. Another sect, Hokke, or the Lotus Sect, was protestant, popular, militant, and nationalistic.

The great Nichiren (A.D. 1222-1282) is often and justly compared by modern Japanese to the Martin Luther of Germany. Nationalist and religious both, his spirit is exemplified in the title of his chief work: *Risshō ankoku ron* (A treatise on the establishment of righteousness and the safety of the country). He preached particularly to the new military class of *samurai* and to their masters. He was as much concerned with the salvation of Japan in this world as he was with the preservation of souls in the next. With him the impenetrable exultation of historical Indian Buddhism was transformed into an aggressive everyday piety not unlike the ethical spirit of early German Protestantism.

Along with the Lotus Sect the *Zen* Sect of Buddhism had a pervasive influence on Japanese political thought. Already developed in China and Korea, it offered a salvation through grace not unlike the basic teachings of John Wesley. Then Buddhism offered the untutored soldiers of the Hōjō and Ashikaga periods the kind of salvation which they could understand and could obtain. Then priests did not hold themselves aloof from worldly affairs; one monk made a rudimentary collection of diplomatic documents, while others drafted the dispatches between the shogunal court of Japan and the Ming court of China.[12]

The Florescence of Chivalry. Horseless chivalry is, of course, a *contradicto in adjecto* in Western language terms. Under the stimulus of *Zen* teachings the Japanese converted the actual class relationships of soldier to lord and soldier to peasant into an ethical code with spiritual overtones. In their own way they achieved that ennoblement of the everyday which has been characteristic of every chivalric period in man's history. What started as a code for a class became the doctrine for a caste and finally the myth for a nation. Although the word *bushidō* is of more recent origin, the psychological and spiritual initiation of a morality based on austerity, honor, self-abnegation had its beginnings at this time.[13]

[12] By 1400, the famous Five Monasteries School of *Zen* had transferred its attention to secular philosophy, historical research, and a revival of Chinese studies. These groups thus provided a direct bridge to orthodox Neo-Confucian doctrines of Tokugawa Japan. For a brief, readable biography of Nichiren in English, see Anesaki Masaharu, *Nichiren the Buddhist Prophet,* Cambridge, 1916. In his most spectacular prediction, Nichiren foretold dire disasters—especially foreign invasion—if rulers did not suppress false teachings (the Mongol invasion attempts occurred in 1274 and 1281!).

[13] An excellent object lesson in the need to examine the past, in order to understand the

During the later Muromachi period (A.D. 1339-1573) a certain Takeda Shingen put down all the basic fashions of contemporary ethics. From Confucianism he drew benevolence, decorum, loyalty, and filial piety. From Buddhism he drew faith. From Japan itself he demanded courage, honor, and frugality. During the Pacific phase of World War II American troops were often mowed down by machine-gun fire directed at them by Japanese soldiers who were themselves starving. In a later historical context these Japanese peasant boys were trying to live up to the ethical ideas established by the ancestors of their own nobility. The Japanese phrase, "*Bushi wa shoku wa nedo taka yoji . . .*" says that the *bushi* (soldier) may not eat, but he holds a toothpick in his mouth. It makes abstinence a virtue instead of a necessity and offers a moral good in the place of a military requirement.

In straightforward political thinking, works such as the *Jikkinsho* (Ten Precepts, about A.D. 1252) present us a philosophy of statecraft. In this work as in other contemporary writings there originated much of the widespread contempt for money and commerce which was held *pro forma* by the *samurai* class until our own times.

Climactic to the development of this chivalric feudalism was the *Jinnō shōtōki* (True genealogy of the Divine Sovereigns), written in A.D. 1339 by Kitabatake Chikafusa. In characteristic Japanese syncretic form Kitabatake sought to teach young emperors by encouraging Buddhism, furthering Confucianism, and assimilating Taoism all at the same time. His book is important because in some respects he was the first Japanese who attempted to apply philosophical principles to everyday politics. Heterodox in one minor respect, he departed from the pattern of other feudal writings by emphasizing the legitimacy of Imperial rule and justifying the righteousness of the old Fujiwara Regency. Kitabatake was the first writer to stress Japan's uniqueness as the Land of the Heavenly Beings, the first to use for Japan the honorific name Great Japan (*Dai Nihon*), the first to attribute to supernatural interference the origin of the Sacred Windstorms (*Kamikaze*) which wrecked the Mongol fleets. The opening sentence of the *Jinnō shōtōki* reads, "*Dai Nihon wa shinkoku nari . . .*" (Japan is the Land of Heavenly Beings . . .).[14]

Already in this florescent period of Japanese feudalism there were laid the foundations of the modern Japanese half-sacred, half-secular empire.

---

present, is Mr. E. Herbert Norman's short study of Japanese militarism: *Soldier and Peasant in Japan: The Origins of Conscription,* New York, 1943. Mention might also be made of two excellent unpublished studies, which explore aspects of the same problem: M. Frederick Nelson, "The Samurai of Japan: Class, Caste, and Myth," *Far Eastern Papers,* 1938-39, Duke University (typescript), 1939; and Nathan Weiss, "The Origin of Japanese Peasant Unrest and Its Contribution to Military Totalitarianism in Japan (1930-36)," Rutgers University (M.A. thesis, typescript), 1949.

[14] A complete translation, with introduction and notes, was made by Hermann Bohner, *Jinno-shoto-ki; Buch von der Wahren Gott-Kaiser-Herschafts-Linie,* Tokyo, 1935. A. L. Sadler, *op. cit.,* gives a partial translation into English in Appendix V, pp. 333-334. For a brief essay on the *Jinnō shōtōki,* see W. G. Aston, *History of Japanese Literature,* New York, 1899, pp. 164-169.

Although Kitabatake Chikafusa lived in the period in which Buddhism flourished most richly, he was willing to accept the ancient indigenous legends and perpetuated Shintō. He looked back to the origins of Japan to justify the uniquely divine character of his own country. He himself said flatly of Japan, "For the Imperial Ancestor founded it in the beginning and the line of the Sun Goddess has been carried on ever since. There is nothing of this kind in any other country. It is solely confined to our country. . . ." Work such as his refutes the twentieth-century supposition, often badly exaggerated on the Allied side during World War II, that Japanese Shintō was a mock religion, artificially revived in the nineteenth century for the purpose of creating a modern military state. Shintō was revived, it is true; but the revival was the revival of a real, although overshadowed, religion, not of a mock religion.

Internal Wars and Feudal Turmoil. Japanese history is as diverting and instructive as the history of any nation of Europe. For Westerners, particularly, Japanese history can serve as an admirable intellectual corrective to generalizations which they might draw from the history of the European states, considered by themselves. In contrast to the history of India, of Java, of Siam, China, or Korea, Japanese history was poured into the sharp geographic and cultural limits of a nationality not much less confined than the nationalities of Europe. Its cycles and events bear a dreamlike resemblance to the epochs and happenings of our own past. In the patterns common to Japanese history and to West European history there can perhaps be found much that is basically true of all human nature under given economic and geographic stimuli. Unfortunately, it is impracticable to unroll the scrolls of Japanese romance and to tell the thrilling stories of Japan's saints and conquerors, rebels and unifiers, patriots and blackguards.

It can only be said that, although the Hōjō dominance started well, internal pressures dragged it down. The *Bakufu* had brought peace to Japan and, with peace, had drawn down upon Japan the Asian disaster peculiar to times of peace: overpopulation. Feudalism could not cope with overpopulation any better than do modern capitalism or communism. Feudal civil wars and attempted redistributions of power were the result. Crises in the cadastral cycle—the overload of land property by an excess of human beings—was aggravated by the greatest danger to Japan to occur until the days centuries later prior to the surrender closing the Pacific war. The Mongols attacked twice, using immense international armies and international faiths in A.D. 1274 and A.D. 1281. After these attacks failed, a senile Kublai Khan went to his death befuddled and beguiled by the falsified plans for a third, successful invasion of Japan which his realistic and indulgent staff officers dreamed up out of whole cloth for his eyes alone. Although the Mongols were repelled, the two actual invasions and the threat of a third made demands upon the feudal economy which the Japanese fiscal system could not stand. Like Great Britain in 1945, Japan stood forth victorious, but bankrupt.

In these sorry times an Emperor of the junior line attempted to restore the Japanese model of Chinese empire by destroying the Kamakura *Bakufu* which supported the Imperial candidate of the senior line. Kamakura itself was captured and burned in A.D. 1333. Kyoto became momentarily the seat of government, Imperial in form. When the Ashikaga clan re-established shogunal government two years later, shōguns and emperors ruled and reigned from the same city—the emperors from the palace and the shōguns from their own quarters elsewhere in town. Muromachi, the shogunal street in Kyoto, gives its name to the Muromachi era (A.D. 1339-1573). The Ashikaga ruled a declining world. Japan lay in a state of near anarchy. The resilience of Hōjō authority gave way to extreme realism and suspicion. Individualism—to contemporary Japanese a horrendous phenomenon—became rampant. From 1450 on, central government control was virtually erased. The shōguns did not have much more power than the emperors. The Japanese had more than a hundred years of civil war, their own Time of Troubles, the *Sengoku Jidai.*

The Three Inward Napoleons. Japan was conquered from within by the efforts of three remarkable men, no blood kin to one another, who at the end of the sixteenth century erased a lawful anarchy and set up a state which compared favorably with any nation of the European Renaissance. These three great unifiers were Oda Nobunaga, Toyotomi Hideyoshi, and Tokugawa Ieyasu.

They did not build on a hopeless basis. Even during the dark period of civil war, transportation, communication, and trade had continued to improve. Localized manifestations of unity appeared in the near-sovereign authority of the larger feudal lords. The anarchy itself served the purpose of circulating the elites of Japan. Superfluous civil aristocrats and archaic court nobles (*kuge*) were eliminated from the scene. Many of the newer military barons were wiped out. In a time of uncertainties, economic wealth began to seem more practical than local reputation, and in the accumulation of wealth merchant guilds won their appointed place in the Japanese world. Indeed, one city, Sakai (near present-day Osaka) used mercenary troops to win its independence of all feudal overlordship, becoming a virtual republic of Sakai. This lonely cultural manifestation of one Hanseatic city all by itself was not paralleled elsewhere in Japan. For a while, merchants governed themselves by means of a city council chosen from among the wealthiest. A monied class had become a permanent fixture in Japanese life, although many centuries were to pass before a *bourgeoisie* could exist proudly and legitimately in its own light.[15]

[15] Professor Takekoshi has pointed out the similarity between the Japanese *Za* (Merchant Guild) of Ashikaga days and the Hanseatic League. See Takekoshi Y., *Nihon keizai shi* (Economic aspects of the civilization of Japan), Tōkyō, 1934 (12 vols.), Vol. II, Chap. VIII:

By the 1540's the Portuguese first arrived. They were soon followed by the Spaniards, the Dutch, and the English. For a hundred years Japan was in contact with Europe. Japanese noblemen swaggered around the streets of Nagasaki with large, floppy Portuguese hats and long European capes. A few Japanese visited Rome. Japanese-built ships sailed to Peru. Japanese naval power threatened the Philippines. A Japanese invasion slaughtered and terrorized the Koreans, leading to such a terrible decline of Korean wealth and culture that five hundred years later the marks of that invasion are still evident. The story of Japan's first contact with the West is important culturally, religiously, and historically, but it has very little to do with the process of government itself in Japan. One of the effects of the Western contact was to frighten the Japanese into insulation of their nation against foreign ideas. Another earlier effect was to upset the military functional priority of different social classes, attained through an unbalance of weapons which came about with the introduction of Portuguese firearms.

In a sense the European intrigues were an extension to a larger scale of the domestic disunity and quarrels which the Japanese had known for generations before the Europeans arrived. When Spaniard denounced Portuguese, when Catholic decried Protestant, when Englishman hinted dark things of Hollander, the Japanese were quite correct in supposing that the outside world was as turbulent as themselves. The political influences of the Westerners departed, but the smooth-bore musket did not.

Fired by the matchlock principle—a piece of glowing punk moved by the trigger instead of a piece of flint—the Portuguese smooth-bore muskets revolutionized the role of the individual soldier within Japan. Each farmer became a potential musketeer. Isolated small-scale feudal fortifications became militarily worthless. The old-fashioned baron who relied on chivalric expert swordsmen of the old *bushi* class had to give way to the modern baron who used rank-and-file light troops, *ashigaru*. The consequences of European contact were therefore twofold, although wholly compatible with trends which had been appearing from within Japan. First, the stratification of a knightly class was broken down, as it was to a great degree in the European Renaissance, by the reappearance of peasant-class effectives for combat use. Second, the small-scale lord had to yield to the larger combine capable of providing the long-term economic assurance required for the maintenance of standing armies, however small.

A Western contact served as a strategic threat and intellectual stimulus and a concurrent precipitant of the forces favoring national unity in Japan. The Minamoto experience was to be repeated. The lords of the countryside were to be re-confederated. Among the lords of the countryside there were a new group, the Sudden Lords (*Niwaka-daimyō*). War reached its climax

---

"Ashikaga jidai no kokunaiteki hansa dōmei" (Internal Hanseatic League in the Ashikaga epoch); the English translation, *op. cit.*, Vol. I, Chap. XVIII.

in peace, but it was a peace of a military kind, the well-policed paradise of isolated Japan.

The three successive Napoleonic characters who unified Japan have been described by Japanese verses which tell what each, in his turn, does about a cuckoo that refused to sing. Oda Nobunaga is represented as saying, "I'll kill the cuckoo if it won't sing." Toyotomi Hideyoshi, more the diplomatist, is represented as saying, "I'll wheedle the cuckoo into singing." And Tokugawa Ieyasu can be freely translated as expressing the attitude, "I will damn well wait until the cuckoo does sing."

Oda Nobunaga started out as a *daimyō* whose power was centered in three provinces around the modern city of Nagoya. He seized Kyoto in 1568. In the course of his rise to power he was quite pro-Christian for one of the most un-Christian reasons in history: he liked Christians because he hated the Buddhists. Since the Christian missionaries irritated the powerful vested Buddhist interests to an inexpressible degree, Nobunaga regarded Christianity as an opportune practical joke which he could play on his religious antagonists. Himself a man of adroit and startling violence, he bore no sign that the Sermon on the Mount meant anything whatever to him personally. It took him a ten years' siege to capture the great temple fortification of the Buddhist Pure Land Sect in Osaka. His career finished suddenly when he was murdered by a vassal in 1582.

Toyotomi Hideyoshi, who had been Nobunaga's ablest general, took power next. More diplomatic than his predecessor, he was also more grandiose in his ambitions. He published his intention of conquering the whole world and announced a plan which his unfortunate successors attempted with disastrous results 350 years later. In Japan he established a military government at Osaka, revitalized the archaic posts of Prime Minister and Civil Dictator by assuming them himself, and conquered or overawed all of Japan. Then he proposed to conquer Korea in order to conquer Manchuria, in order to conquer China, in order to conquer India, so that he could then rule over the whole world. Japanese armies fought through many Korean winters, and Chinese help to the Koreans was as tardy and catastrophic in meeting Hideyoshi in the 1590's as it was in meeting the United Nations forces centuries later. Hideyoshi died furious, sick, and brokenhearted on September 18, 1598. Japanese troops withdrew from Korea, and after an interval of domestic politicking the last great consolidator took over.

Tokugawa Ieyasu more wisely concentrated on the political unification of Japan itself. By 1600 he had defeated all pretenders. It took him fifteen years to wipe out the last of Hideyoshi's family in another siege of Osaka. He did not live to see the end of the remaining influence which might rival his in Japan: it was left to a successor to wipe out the last Japanese Catholic rebellion at Shimabara in 1637-38, when 37,000 people were killed after they had fought uselessly and valiantly for months while screaming for the Virgin Mary or Saint James to save them and while waiting in vain for the sails of European ships which might bring them Christian gunpowder and the hope of Christian victory. Tokugawa Ieyasu moved the capital to Edo (Yedo), now called Tokyo, and immediately moved to establish complete control for himself and his clan over Japan. He relegated the Emperor and the court to a well-budgeted and powerless round of ceremony in Kyoto. Thus a tradition as old as Japanese political life continued. *Shizoku* control had existed a thousand years before it was climaxed by the Soga. It had been retained in another form by the genius of the Fujiwara. Held briefly by the Taira, put into shogunal form by the Minamoto, and held weakly by the Ashikaga, now the Tokugawa plan concentrated on the main business of keeping itself at the top of Japan forever.

Seldom in the history of the world has a country been governed by three military geniuses, one succeeding the other. Quite correctly did later Japanese say, "Oda Nobunaga was a genius at Creation, Toyotomi Hideyoshi was a genius at Administration, but Tokugawa Ieyasu was a genius at Magnificence."[16] The freezing of this magnificence into political form is the story of isolated Japan.

[16] Ardath W. Burks, brief articles on Nobunaga and Ieyasu; and Paul S. Dull, on Hideyoshi, in *Collier's Encyclopedia,* New York, 1950, Vol. 14, p. 656; 11, p. 287; 10, p. 42.

CHAPTER THIRTEEN

The Well-Policed Paradise of Isolated Japan

NATIONS or individuals in the history of mankind from time to time achieve an almost perfect rendering of a given dramatic and esthetic role—a real-life performance so consistent, so true to itself, so compelling as a work of art, that it lives on in the minds of posterity as being superb for its kind.

By such limited standards of *effective emphasis*, Tokugawa Japan is one of the great political creations of mankind. Nowhere else in history, it would seem, has a civilized nation made so complete an effort to attain law, order, and peace as did the Japan which *The Mikado* and *Madame Butterfly*, themselves naïve, present as a quaint and trivial little country. Yet in that Japan some of the fundamental values in which all modern men believe were carried to their logical extreme and then beyond it. With fierce and purposeful resolution the Tokugawa leaders selected certain aspects of human life for practical development and carried them through to their uttermost. Seeking ideals with strategic security beyond the wildest dreams of our present-day Joint Chiefs of Staff, the Japanese realized those dreams so perfectly that they stood still militarily while the world went on. Dreading intrigue and espionage from abroad, the Japanese set up a quarantine beside which the Iron Curtain is a rusty sieve and enforced that quarantine for more than two hundred years, accepting—as most of us do in our more stupid moments, and as the stupidest among us do all the time—the foolish assumption that life within one nation is all that a civilized man requires. The Japanese set out to be Japanese and nothing else but; they fulfilled the ideals of nationality and nationalism so perfectly that at the end they had to cosmopolitanize themselves on an unprecedented scale in order to catch up with the rest of mankind.

The real-life superlatives of Tokugawa Japan are so extreme, so startling, that it would be hard to exaggerate them with mere words. The Japanese passion for perfection reached its peak in many fields. They carried through an experiment in autarchy which could, if it were better understood, provide a precedent for all mankind. On this experiment the judgment of history must still stay suspended. Judging by Japan's share in the modern world, the astonishing thing about Tokugawa Japan's near-perfect isolation, perfect international peace, and near-complete quarantine is not that the Japanese accomplished so much, but that, relative to the history of India, Turkey, or China over the same period, they accomplished so little.

Although conceived in perfection, Tokugawa Japan was not, of course, perfect. Like American Normalcy of the 1920's, it was an "onion" of prosperity, successive layers of which could be and were eventually peeled off.

The Origins of Isolation. Tokugawa Ieyasu was himself born and nurtured in a Japan filled with chaos and uncertainty. He had seen the sneering Nobunaga welcoming Christians to vex the Buddhists; he had noted that the Christians, preaching the brotherhood of man, promptly conspired for one another's humiliation or assassination. Ieyasu came to believe in security, a "security" not much different from the phantasmal security exemplified in our use of the term "National Security Council." Instead of seeking the psychological security which can be preached for India—a security which relied on the spirit and mind alone and was therefore to be impenetrable by the instruments of this world—Ieyasu attempted to create the kind of purely physical, practical security of which so many Americans, high and low, dream of today in vain. He did not see life, individually or internationally, as an inescapable succession of adventures and uncertainties which could be met confidently and courageously, with each triumph over difficulty a reward in itself and an experience in living for a man or for a country. Instead he did for Japan on the national scale what maniacs so often do for themselves today on the individual level. He removed his people completely from the community of nations and sought security in isolation. Nowhere else on earth has a political purpose been carried through more completely than in Tokugawa Japan.

Tokugawa Neo-Confucianism. Obsessed from the start with the ideal of political stability, Tokugawa Ieyasu used military hegemony to attempt the creation of a social order more secure than any previously done. As just noted, he and his heirs came closer to fulfilling this idea than has any other modern dynasty or republic. When he first stabilized Japan, he found at hand a new standard of ideological orthodoxy. He used a combination of feudal common sense from the Japanese countryside, combining a synthesis of the *Jōei* Code and early feudal ethical works with the stimulation of Japanese Neo-Confucianism. Tokugawa Japan did not introduce a foreign model; it resynthesized elements which had been extant in Japan.

The most revealing clue to the political methods of the early Tokugawa is contained in the work of Honda Masanobu who wrote *Honsa roku*

(Basic guide). Honda was interested in the techniques of government and neglected the philosophy. He did not think it was possible to govern through benevolence alone. Military force and intrigue were necessary to establish power; constant vigilance was needed to maintain it. Honda's work was the first bible of the Tokugawa administrators and he was in a very real sense a braintruster to the new regime. His contribution was not enough.

Tokugawa ruling thought soon turned from such pragmatic bases. Its fundamental characteristics soon revealed great weaknesses. Propounded largely by government spokesmen, official policy and thought became deeply concerned with the moral welfare of the subjects of the Tokugawa shōguns. Only spasmodically did political writing or debate lapse into discussion of practical political realities or economic necessities. The reason for this moralistic trend can be found in the resurgence of Confucianism. In this time a majority of the Japanese writers on social, political, and economic problems had turned back to the Chinese classics. The Shogunate encouraged this, giving special preference to scholars proficient in the Confucian materials. Confucian scholars assisted in the drafting of laws and the formulating of ethical principles upon which the administrative structure was based. To understand the paradox of a Japanese nationalism refreshing itself with Confucian Chinese intellectual instruments, it is necessary to review what had happened to Chinese thought in Japan.

Japanese Confucianism had already played many roles.

The first importation of Chinese learning had preceded the Taika Reform. Confucianism flourished in the early period when Chinese culture was being Japanized. With the advent of feudalism, Buddhism had come into its own. Even in the Tokugawa era, Buddhism was strong as a living religion among the people. The educated classes turned in this period, however, to Confucianism. It is quite Japanese for the upper classes to have appropriated a better philosophy for themselves without making any attempt to interrupt the superstitions of their inferiors. From the viewpoint of the new rulers Buddhism was appropriate to the common people; its phrases made good moral discipline. But the Tokugawa elite felt that something more sophisticated was needed for the process of government.

Just as the T'ang exemplar had served the seventh-century Japanese administrative structure, Sung Neo-Confucianism became the bulwark of Tokugawa social policy. The official philosophy and authorized system of education came to be based on the philosophy of Chu Hsi, known in Japan as Shushi, whose commentary under its Japanese title of *Shisho shinchū* (New exegesis on the four classics) acquired canonical status. Chu Hsi himself, who lived between A.D. 1130-1200, was a major Chinese philosopher, essayist, and official. Such was his brilliance that, although his writings were stale with the passage of centuries, they were capable of convulsing Japan. In his own lifetime he had claimed that his doctrine was Confucian, although it might at the same time be considered a new system of thought. The Japanese accepted his claim.

Thus Confucianism in a new guise once again led Japanese upper-class thought.

Originally the teachings of the Confucian classics had been a comparatively simple code of ethics based on an implicit but profound set of workable sociological assumptions. (See Chapter Two, "The Confucian Ideology.") Neo-Confucianism added a metaphysical system, responding to the challenge of the Indian metaphysics in Buddhism and the native Chinese metaphysics developed by Taoism in response to Buddhism. In Chu Hsi's writing, the Confucian social doctrines were interlocked with a complicated causative, cosmic system. The law of nature became moral law in a more complex way than Confucius or his immediate exponents had ever envisioned.

Chu Hsi believed in self-culture. Man, he said, is innately disposed to right conduct, just as all nature is driven by beneficent principles, but man, to comprehend virtue, must study the laws of the whole universe. Only thus will he discover that relations among natural phenomena are matched by relations among individuals.[1]

From China, Neo-Confucianism first spread to Korea and in turn to Japan, where it became known as *Shushigaku-ha* (The School of Chu Hsi). The first effective exponent of *Shushigaku-ha* in Japan was Fujiwara Seika (A.D. 1561-1619). Tokugawa Ieyasu was his outstanding follower. His intellectual heir was Hayashi Razan (A.D. 1583-1687), who is called the father of Neo-Confucianism in Japan. He became counselor to the Tokugawa *Bakufu* and during his assignment had control of the whole educational system. Although other schools of philosophy were studied, no rival body of doctrines possessed as much influence. Neo-Confucianism was not shaken until Western thought came in during the 1850's.

Encompassing Tokugawa political theory, Neo-Confucianism justified the Tokugawa *rationale* when it was applied in policy. Its effects can be traced in a succession of philosophers. Hayashi was succeeded by Kinoshita Jūnan, one of whose pupils was Arai Hakuseki. And Arai was Japan's first, perhaps Japan's greatest, master of the science of political economy. He and his colleagues represented the prevailing orthodoxy.

Why did this particular system triumph in Japan? First, Buddhist com-

[1] The transfer of Chu Hsi's concepts into Western semantics is almost an impossible task: for example, some scholars assert he tends toward materialism; others, that he leaned toward theism. The standard Japanese work on Neo-Confucianism is Inoue Tetsujirō, *Nihon shushi gakuha no tetsugaku* (The Chu Hsi school of philosophy in Japan), Tōkyō, 1906; the preface deals with development of the school in China; Chaps. 1, 2, pp. 11-113, summarize Fujiwara's life, writings, and disciples; Hayashi's work and succeeding scholars. For a more brief summary, Iwanami Shoten Zōhan, *Tetsugaku jiten* (Iwanami Publishers, Encyclopedia of philosophy, rev. edition), Tōkyō, 1922, *"Shushigaku,"* (The doctrine of Chu Hsi), p. 459. For a brief, general summary in English of Tokugawa philosophic climate, see James Murdoch, *A History of Japan,* London, 1926 (3 vols.), Vol. III, Chap. 3, "Chinese Philosophy as an Instrument of Government"; also Armstrong, *op. cit.,* pp. 29-31.

petition had evoked the Neo-Confucian response from simple Confucianism and Buddhism in Japan and had thus paved the way for its Chinese metaphysical rival. Second, the Japanese were more interested in practical ethics than in remote speculation. Although Chu Hsi offered an interestingly complex cosmology, it was his ethical concepts which fired the Japanese imagination. They happened to suit the Tokugawa book almost perfectly because their central point was loyalty. Furthermore, there was an emphasis upon learning, but learning was kept under control because great store was set on orthodoxy. The patience and fears of the Tokugawa responded to the attunements of Chu Hsi's system. Rarely elsewhere have society and ideology matched so perfectly as did the express policy of the Tokugawa, seeking security, and the philosophy of Chu Hsi, which went so far as to define *evil* itself as *confusion*.

In short, Chu Hsi and his Japanese disciples did little more than recommend virtues which had already been seized with frenzied yearning by the Tokugawa. Heretofore Confucian morality had been dogmatic. Now it was sophisticated and systematized far beyond the imagination of Confucius himself. The stars in their heavens were shown to support the isolation and the security of the Tokugawa shōguns.

Centralized Feudalism. The Tokugawa era (A.D. 1603-1867), like the Taika epoch of the seventh century, was a significant transition period in the political history of Japan. It becomes understandable only in context. In theory Japan had been centralized under the Japanized model of Chinese Empire of the seventh century. In practical terms central control was first achieved—then only temporarily—by the Minamoto family, who in turn delegated administration to the remarkable Hōjō Regents. Even at this time central control was diffused through complex federated feudal structures. This limited centralism collapsed in the chaos of Muromachi. When Ieyasu founded a shogunal dynasty and inaugurated an epoch by establishing his new capital at Edo, he seized more widespread control than had any previous shōgun. Indeed some Japanese scholars like Fukuda Tokuzō and Asakawa Kanichi have denied that a state so centralized could properly be described as feudal. One point, of course, is clear from the beginning: Tokugawa centralization obviously made possible the quick conversion from the *Bakufu* to national government under the Meiji.

It is revealing to adopt the terminology of the Japanese socio-economic historian, Professor Honjō Eijirō, who contrasts the early phase of *decentralized feudalism* with the late phase of *centralized feudalism*. This distinction points up the contrast between the Japanese and European experiences with loosely comparable feudal systems.

Seventeenth-century Europe moved from the feudal system over to national governments under the crown; the Japanese of the same century once again delegated power to a central feudal overlord. Furthermore the political relationships between the surviving *daimyō* and the *Shōgun* were of a feudal character. The local control of each *daimyō* depended upon vassalage and their armed retainers were, through subinfeudation, at the disposal of the *Shōgun.* Moreover, early Tokugawa political power derived exclusively from control over agricultural produce (rice) and the producer (the peasant). Despite the obvious difference from European feudalism, in which direct feudal title to the land determined power, the Tokugawa society can accurately be called feudal.[2]

This distinction between stages of Japanese feudalism helps to explain the particular meaning of the Tokugawa transition: *Fundamental economic changes—from lawful chaos to centralized feudalism, and from centralized feudalism to a mercantile but semi-feudal economy—occurred throughout the Tokugawa epoch, not just at the end.* The impact of the West thus falls into perspective as the occasion for revolutionary change, rather than the cause.

From a purely Japanese standpoint the closed and policed perfection of an isolated Japan represents perhaps the peak of a thoroughly Japanese and Japanized culture. Tokugawa society was based on narrow laws, caste privileges, and moralistic principles, but in practice the Japanese achieved tremendous urbanity and a superb style of their own. No contemporaneous European community was more civilized or more polished. Demonstration of this is afforded by the reactions of the Europeans themselves who were startled and delighted by the Japan which they first met after 1853.

History has often imposed on rulers results contrary to the policies which they think they are fulfilling. It is certainly one of the supreme paradoxes of history that the Tokugawa regime, militarist and suspicious, achieved the world's greatest record of sustained peace, while a modernized Japan, overtly seeking peace, has been embroiled in a hundred years of increasingly catastrophic war. The Tokugawa motif, like so many other great artistic performances, was splendid in a manner quite contrary to the intentions of its creators.

The *Bakufu* as a Command Post. The Tokugawa administration was, like the early *Bakufu,* an extension into peace of the pattern found useful by headquarters commands in time of war.

In theory, of course, all military commands like to think of themselves as instruments of policy rather than policy creators. The Tokugawa *Shōgun,* for example, never attempted to seize the Imperial Throne itself. The fiction of final Imperial authority flowed on. Yet the Emperor's prerogatives were

[2] For a complete discussion of the degree of Tokugawa centralization, on the one hand, and feudalism, on the other, see: E. Herbert Norman, *Japan's Emergence as a Modern State; Political and Economic Problems of the Meiji Period,* New York, 1940, p. 12, fn. 1 (a summary of Fukuda's and Asakawa's views). Mr. Norman, one of the most careful students of Japan's emergence, has contributed here a classic, which refers mainly to the late Tokugawa and Meiji Eras. See also G. B. Sansom, *The Western World and Japan,* New York, 1950, Chap. 9, "The Tokugawa Regime," especially p. 182. For the difference between centralized and decentralized feudalism, see p. 298, fn. 7, and Honjō Eijirō, *Kinsei hōken shakai no kenkyū* (Research in recent feudal society), Tōkyō, 1930, Chap. 1, especially pp. 9 ff.

purely *pro forma:* appointments (at the direction of the *Shōgun*), enjoyment of adequate revenue for the court (assigned by the *Shōgun*), and knowledge of policies (addressed in properly humble language to the Throne by the *Shōgun*). Ceremonial and religious duties were also carried out by the Throne. The *Shōgun* maintained a subheadquarters in Kyoto; a suitable garrison made sure that all shogunal recommendations were underlined by a readiness of armed force. Finally no *daimyō* dared approach the court except through shogunal channels.

The refined circle of civil aristocrats, *kuge,* whose ancestors had swaggered across Japan a thousand years before in the Fujiwara times, were reduced to impotence and sometimes to starvation. One famous *kuge,* behind the screen of immunity against shogunal police, was so poor that he allowed his house to be used as a gambling resort in order to support his family. Wrapped up in the memory of past glories, the *kuge* were nevertheless a potential source of long-range trouble for the Tokugawa Shogunate. Their contacts with the *daimyō* were therefore severely restricted.

Actual Tokugawa power centered at Edo, which was at one and the same time the military headquarters and the shogunal court of the Tokugawa. With the title of *Sei-i Tai-shōgun,* successive Tokugawa rulers acted as commanders-in-chief of their feudal armies. The reality of the Tokugawa monarchy was more accurately reflected in the illegal *Taikun,* from which our modern word "tycoon" is derived. When the *Shōgun* happened to be a minor, one of his councilors acted as *Tairō* (Regent).

Tokugawa Administration. At first glance the central administration seemed simple. Policy was decided by the *Shōgun,* the Emperor's delegate, and head of the Tokugawa ruling house. But just as the affairs of a Japanese family are nominally regulated by the head of the house, but in effect by a family council, so frequently government was run not by the *Shōgun* himself but—with typical indirection—by his councilors.

Four or five or six councilors made up the all-powerful *Gorōju* (Council of State). These men served for life and, in practice, filled vacancies on their council as a matter of hereditary privilege. They advised the *Shōgun,* controlled Imperial affairs and the *daimyō,* and supervised the entire national administration. They also appointed chiefs of bureaus in Edo.

Below the council was the junior council, made up of two to six *Wakadoshiyori* (Young Elders). This group controlled the lesser feudal lords and supervised the Edo officials below the rank of bureau chiefs. Thus the staffs of the bureaus of police, military affairs, education, and finance were directed by the Young Elders. The lords and the feudal hierarchy were called *daimyō* (literally, great names) or *hatamoto* (bannermen). Of course, only lords loyal to the Tokugawa could be appointed to the central councils.[3]

[3] For detailed descriptions, from various points of view, of Tokugawa administration, see the following: Murdoch, *op. cit.,* Vol. III, Chap. 1, "The Social and Political Structure," pp. 1-61, the views of a historian; Harold S. Quigley, *Japanese Government and Politics,* New York, 1932, Chap. 1. "The Political System Prior to the Meiji Era," especially pp.

On the map of Japan, the Tokugawa territorial administration resembled a huge checkerboard. First of all, the *Shōgun* retained certain provinces, including key cities—Edo, Kyoto, Osaka, Sakai, and Nagasaki—under his direct control. Officers for these areas were appointed from among the three branches of the Tokugawa family, the Owari, Kii, and the Mito, who thus administered approximately one fourth of Japan. The remaining three fourths of Japan were split up among various *daimyō*. Those *daimyō* whose ancestors had been in league with the Tokugawa clan from the beginning were listed as *fudai daimyō* (dependable lords). Numbering 176, they were favored and granted governmental appointments. Those whose ancestors had submitted only after the critical battle of Sekigahara (A.D. 1600), 86 in number, were designated *tozama daimyō* (outside lords) and excluded from the central government, while being allowed relative autonomy in local affairs. Such families were often the wealthiest among *daimyō:* Mori of Choshu, Shimazu of Satsuma, Date of Sendai, and Maeda of Kaga.

Each *daimyō* exercised virtually complete political control over his own *han,* a fief or clan. The *han* was neither a tight-knit family unit, like the Scottish clan, nor a loose pre-feudal unit, like the ancient Japanese *shizoku. Han* simply designated the territory and peoples under the political control of a *daimyō,* who drew rice revenues from them. His title rested on legal rights obtained or legitimized by his ancestors.

Checks and balances were used by the Tokugawa to play vassals off against one another. One minor aspect of this system was to have consequences, wholly unforeseen at the beginning, in the field of Japanese economics; this was the requirement of hostages. Under the *sankin kōtai,* perfected in A.D. 1634, all lords resided alternately in their domains and in Edo. When they went back to their fiefs, they had to leave their wives at the capital as guarantees for the husbands' good behavior. The Tokugawa police were alert for some of the most remarkable and romantic contraband in the world: *deonna irideppō* ("outbound women, inbound guns"). In this phrase there was epitomized the dangerous materials with which *daimyō* might trifle if they began to plan sedition. Each lord would try to get his wife or wives out of the capital and firearms into the capital for a *coup d'état* or into his fief for a rebellion.

Naturally enough the Tokugawa officials kept a sharp eye peeled. Travel between fiefs was discouraged. Castles and moats could be built or even repaired only by direct permission from Edo. Even marriages between one daimiate and another had to have *Bakufu* approval.

Espionage and Police. One of Japan's own historians has referred to the Tokugawa as the world's first absolute police state. Tokugawa espionage was organized on a scale perhaps unknown in any other feudal state. Its

---

6-18, the view of a distinguished political scientist; and Norman, *op. cit.,* Chap. II, "The Background of the Meiji Restoration," especially pp. 11-35, a social and economic survey of the decay of feudalism.

effects linger into our own time. The *ōmetsuke* (great inspectors) were called the "eyes and ears of the *Shōgun*"; they watched and listened for any *daimyō* disaffection. *Metsuke,* inspectors, scrutinized the lesser lords, *samurai,* and their people. Originally the inspectors resembled archaic Chinese censors; later they were distinguished judicial officers; finally they were espionage administrators. During the time of the eighth Tokugawa *Shōgun,* Yoshimune (A.D. 1716-1745), an elaborate system was instituted under the crafty Muragaki Sadayu. Even the office of chief detective became hereditary under the whimsical cover name, Head of the Park Guards.

The Tokugawa administrators used considerable inventiveness in devising new methods of policing people. One intriguing device was the petition box, placed within reach of the general public at the principal court of justice. Anyone could drop in a suggestion Special officials under the watchful eye of a *metsuke* transported the box to the *Gorōju.* Thence, still locked, the box was taken first to the Business Chamber of the Tokugawa. There the *Shōgun* himself took possession of it. All alone he drew from his bosom a brocade bag in which he kept the key to the petition box. He opened the box himself, read its contents, submitted some items directly to administrative officials, put others aside for further investigation by his spies, and destroyed the ones he wanted to keep to himself.

Tokugawa Local Government. Local government swung between two poles: shogunal control and local feudal custom. Here as always hereditary despotism was softened by Japanese common sense.

Each daimiate, no matter how small, was a miniature replica of the Tokugawa government. Each had its own bureaus of treasury, justice, censorate, military affairs, census, coinage, and public works. Each domain was divided into districts and towns, governed by magistrates of the *hatamoto* class. Magistrates were appointed by the *Shōgun* on nomination of the *daimyō,* with due respect to local sentiment. The magistrates were of two ranks, *gundai* and *daikan,* determined by the greater or lesser productivity of rice of the various districts. Like Chinese *hsien* magistrates, Japanese local officials saw that revenues were up to quota and that public order was maintained. Major towns, under direct Tokugawa control, often had two magistrates (*bugyō*) who were judicial as well as administrative officials.

Ordinary districts were made up of villages. Down at the bottom of the structure the villages often retained a surprising degree of independence. The village headman was often chosen by the larger landholders; his office was, under conditions of good behavior, practically hereditary. There was a village assembly made up of landholders and of the heads of the five-family groups into which villages were subdivided. Roughly, as in China, village officials acted as go-betweens, representing the mass of the people from below to the *daimyō* and the *Shōgun* above.

Neighborhood associations, as mentioned above, run back to the prehistoric period of Japan. By the time of the Taihō Code (A.D. 701), formal organization of the five-family group (*goningumi*) provided local channels for police, economic, and mutual aid functions. The technique was abandoned during the Kamakura era, but revived in the lawless Muromachi epoch for the sake of local protection. By the time of the *Shōgun* Iemitsu in the early seventeenth century the five-family group was used to enforce the proscription of Christianity. Later in the Tokugawa period the most minute requirements of the feudal regulations were enforced through these instruments of social control. The regulations put into effect by means of the *goningumi* fell into six categories:

maintenance of public peace and order;
control of religious observances and ritual;
security, for payment of taxes;
encouragement of diligence and economy;
mutual aid and support;
moral education and individual betterment.[4]

Feudal Law Enforcement. From the Hōjō foundations of Japanese law down into the Tokugawa, Japanese administrators held tenaciously to the concept that knowledge of the law was the concern only of administrators. This is at sharp variance with the legal theory of the West, where a knowledge of the law is in many instances a prerequisite for the proper determination of a case at law. Ignorance of the law was in Japan not merely "no excuse"—more than that, it was a requirement of proper behavior on the part of the layman. Instruction of the general public was limited to the general principles expressed in ethical terms of right and wrong. This doctrine was based on the familiar Japanized Confucian concept, *"Tami wo shite yorashimu-beshi shirashimu-bekarazu"* ("Make the people obey; never let them know").

In a spirit closely approaching Chinese experience the archaic Taihō Code had embodied comprehensive rules for the explicit guidance of ruler and ruled alike. These rules applied to the whole nation. With the coming of feudalism, each fief tended to legislate independently for its own people. Uniformity arose only from the uniformity of linguistic, customary, and social background. Legislative principle, if not detailed, was fairly uniform everywhere; the Tokugawa was able to compile house laws into general codification without serious clashes. Such famous feudal judicial relics as

[4] Quigley, *op. cit.*, pp. 10-13, provides a brief summary of Tokugawa local government. See also Asakawa, K., "Notes on Village Government in Japan after 1600," *Journal* of the American Oriental Society, Vol. 30-31 (1910/11); A. Lloyd, "Notes on Japanese Village Life," *TASJ,* Vol. XXXIII, part 2 (December, 1905); and SCAP, CI & E, *A Preliminary Survey of Neighborhood Associations,* cited, p. 14. Such studies only limn the legalistic outlines of Tokugawa local government and do not go far to describe how the *han,* basic unit in feudal control, actually ticked. Teamed up with field research in contemporary problems, American and Japanese historians are filling the gap. For example, Dr. John Whitney Hall has completed a year's intensive study and collection of documents on Bizen-han (Okayama) at the University of Michigan Center for Japanese Studies, Japan. See his "Materials for the Study of Local History in Japan: Pre-Meiji Records," *Occasional Papers,* Center for Japanese Studies, Ann Arbor, No. 3 (1952).

the "Twenty-one Statutes" and the *Jōei Shikimoku* of the Hōjō, the "House Laws" of Takeda, and the "Seventeen Precepts" of Asakura, could be reconciled.

In the reign of the enlightened eighth Tokugawa *Shōgun,* Yoshimune, the assumption was made that an obedience to laws could not honorably be expected from persons ignorant of the provisions of law. From this period onward, each law, it was prescribed, was to be read to the people, explained to them in lay terms by the magistrates, and posted conspicuously on public notice boards.

Tokugawa justice, along with *Bakufu* administration, was the extension of martial law in time of peace. Hideyoshi's Sword Hunt had fixed a rigid division of classes, separating soldier from peasant. Then Tokugawa Ieyasu's Law of the Military Houses (*Buke Hatto*), promulgated in 1615, set the tone of loyalty and obedience. This was the fundamental characteristic of Tokugawa justice. Like the Taihō and Jōei Codes of earlier times, the military house law was not so much a codification of legal definitions, standards, and procedures, as a collection of exhortations, injunctions, and moral maxims, supported by frequent reference to Chinese and Japanese classics.

Such regulations laid the foundation for successive orders which attempted to regulate the popular morals in the most minute detail. Sumptuary regulation was thus a prominent characteristic of Tokugawa law. A third and highly conservative feature is illustrated in the *Osadame-gaki Hyakkajō* (Edict of a Hundred Articles), which announced that a law in force for fifty years could not be amended, no matter how unworkable it may have become. The Tokugawa regime treated its own laws as basic and unamendable. Apart from the Military House Law and Hundred Articles, there were special laws for the Imperial court, for the Shogunate, for the immediate administration, as well as a special category of "Orders Posted in Edo." This last dealt with specific offenses, such as commerce in forbidden drugs, falsification, and adultery. Above and around all written regulations there were the continuing force of moral authority, semi-legal in effect, of local custom, Japanese historical precedent, and the ethical teachings of Confucianism, Buddhism, and Shintō.

Indeed, Tokugawa administrators concentrated so much on setting a moral tone for society that they scarcely saw the need for a code of criminal procedure. In this respect Tokugawa justice was advanced and backward at one and the same time. Americans today will regard grading the punishment of an offense according to the rank of the offender as an exceptional procedure, yet the Tokugawa rulers made the entirely valid sociological assumption that guilt varies directly with the degree of a man's education and his station in life. There was, of course, practical expediency as well as legal philosophy to support this view: offenses committed by *samurai* were regarded as crimes against the state, more portentous of ill results than crimes committed by foreigners or mere traitors.

Barbarously stringent measures were taken against theft. Death was the penalty for stealing anything whatever. Yet a peculiar discrimination was allowed in favor of pickpockets. For them punitive tattooing was considered sufficient. Although exaggerated in Western writings, Tokugawa torture must have been formidable in its time—perhaps as bad as contemporary British or French tortures of the late seventeenth century, possibly even worse. The law required that the accused must confess before final determination of guilt; through this requirement torture became almost inevitable. In actual practice administrators sought for external evidence, resorting to torture only if they failed in the procurement of outside data.

Administratively the Tokugawa judicial system was very simple. Resort to the courts was itself a socially suspect act and was therefore rare. The overwhelming majority of disputes were settled within villages by the arbitration of headmen or elders. This was in accord with long-established Sino-Japanese precedent of settling all possible issues through ideological control exerted by means of social institutions less formal and less strict than legal procedure. Even district magistrates often referred cases back to the locality for arbitration, although they had the option of referring the matter to a higher court. When appeals were made, they went up to the High Court at Edo, the *Hyōjōsho,* which also acted as a court of first instance for cases involving different domains. Occasionally cases originating in central Japan were delegated by the High Court in Osaka or Kyoto. In all matters the *Hyōjōsho* was supervised by the Council of State. In important matters the *Shōgun* himself might attend.[5]

The Lunatic Economy. The combination of a state highly civilized in arts and manufactures (taking the latter term in its etymological sense) with a political economic policy of rigid autarchy produced some very remarkable economic developments. The progress of Tokugawa Japan was amazing, yet all this progress was made within the same geographic limits and without recourse to foreign trade. The result was an economy which was as brilliant as it was unstable. Dependence on rice as a basic commodity led to a fantastic swing of markets and prices, at their worst exceeding the wildest fluctuations of the stock or commodity exchanges in Western states. Since the people of the Tokugawa period knew no other economic system, their extraordinary accomplishments in the face of self-imposed difficulties struck them as being entirely normal and reasonable. This naturally raises the suspicion, in the mind of any intelligent twentieth-century observer, that posterity may regard us as unwitting economic freaks in much the way that we find ourselves looking at the Tokugawa. The economic development was

[5] A standard Japanese summary of feudal law is Hagino Y., Editor, *Nihon kōdai hōten,* cited; see also Miura S., *Hōseishi no kenkyū,* cited; Ikebe Yoshikata, *Nihon hōseishi* (History of the Japanese legal system), Tōkyō, 1912, a masterful treatment of the history of Japanese law by a professor of law, Kyōto Imperial University. The most complete survey in English was written by the indefatigable John Henry Wigmore, "Materials for the Study of Private Law in Old Japan," especially Part I, introduction, *TASJ,* Vol. XX (1892), supplement.

so out of line with the previous social heritage of Japan that it drove the Japanese into systematic thinking about problems of systematic economics.

Tokugawa writing was the first, significantly, to begin use of the modern Japanese compound designating the study of political economy, *keizaigaku*. This compound was derived from *kei-koku* (or *keisei*), statecraft, from *sai-min* (salvation of the people), and *-gaku* (study).[6]

Such an economic approach began and ended with the concept of welfare, set against a context of moralizing, and relying heavily upon government as the universal provider or controller of welfare. Japanese economic thinking in this period was not set up as a separate and compartmentalized specialty in its own right. It is important to note that all writings on public affairs, even though they were of a moralistic nature, showed a scholarly concern with the problems of political economy. Since most of the writers were themselves Neo-Confucians, they inevitably tended to emphasize the importance of agricultural pursuits.

[6] The autochthonous crisis in the Tokugawa system, significantly economic in nature, together with orthodox and unorthodox views of the political economy, is discussed in its proper perspective in the next chapter. There it is placed alongside Western pressure which provided the occasion for collapse of the Shogunate. Tokugawa economic writings were edited in 1927 by Professor Takimoto Seiichi and incorporated in the massive 55-volume *Nihon keizai taiten* (Collection of Japanese economic writings). This vast reservoir of primary materials has, in turn, served as a foundation for secondary interpretation, in Japanese. Burks dissertation, in English, already cited. Some of the more important writings were compiled by Neil Skene Smith, *An Introduction to Some Japanese Economic Writings of the 18th Century,* London, 1935; and "Materials on Japanese Social and Economic History," *TASJ,* 2d series, Vol. XIV (1937).

CHAPTER FOURTEEN

The Coming of the Sea-Borne States

DYNAMIC though Japanese history was in the period before Western contacts, the world of Christendom was even more dynamic. While Japan moved from one kind of feudalism to another, developing meanwhile one of the world's most perfect examples of the police state, the nation-states of Europe sprang from the rich ruins of medieval Christendom and, for the first time in human history, made the "world" of their power politics co-terminus with the planet Earth.

The greatest change in all Japanese history came, as it has come sooner or later to every single Asian country, from the outside. Even in the mid-twentieth century it is still true that the West European peoples, together with their American, South African, and Australian offsprings, and their East European rivals, are the most dynamic of the human race. From the sixteenth century onward, change in Asia has been colored by the fact that the Western World first remotely and then proximately set the standards for change, if not for forward movement.[1]

It would be an oversimplification to suggest that the native dynamism of Japanese history has disappeared, or to allow the inference that the only forces making for change in Japanese society are forces from the outside. Great though the Western impact may have been, and greater still the extraordinarily creative fusion of Japanese national character and the stimuli provided from the West, it would be an exaggeration to make the *major* factor into the *exclusive* one. It is wise therefore to preface any recitation of changes provided by the Western impact within Japanese government by a statement of what was happening to Tokugawa Japan at the very time that this impact took place.

[1] A mature, reflective study of this central problem of intercultural penetration—with Japan chosen as the principal illustration—is offered by Sir George Sansom in his recent *The Western World and Japan*, cited.

The Year of Crisis. The year A.D. 1868 is identified as the climactic year in the process of Japan's governmental adjustment to the arrival of the sea-borne states—states whose power was based neither on walls, nor infantry, nor mounted raiders, but on naval forces which were easily capable of operating in the open waters anywhere on earth.

Down to 1868 Japan underwent a period of strain, challenge, trial, and preparation; after 1868 the Japanese raced toward modernization, accepting as a concomitant the inevitable Westernization of the organization of their armed forces, of some of their law, and of much of their government.

It was on March 14, 1868, that the *Tennō* called together the princes and high officials to the *Shishinden,* or Inner Shrine of the Imperial Palace, and took a strange new oath before his ancestral gods. This Imperial Oath provided the foundation for a new regime. The Emperor concluded:

> To accomplish this unprecedented reformation, We go before the people, and proclaim the fundamental national principles even in the presence of the gods of heaven and earth, to establish the way for the public welfare. Ye, Our Subjects, shall be united all together, according to these principles.[2]

Traditionalism and innovation were characteristically mixed in the oath. Once again the Japanese people had met internal difficulties and an external challenge by the response of turning toward unity and asserting their independence. Once again it was the name of the Emperor and the presence of Japanese deities which called for a supreme dedication of effort on the basis of what the Japanese conceived to be *fundamental national principles.* With this oath the Japanese put behind them the long-postponed crisis of the Shogunate, internally, and met the challenge by insistent states of the West, externally. This time they themselves had set about the business of making their own country into a nation-state.

Creation of a nation-state is no mere process of Westernization. Western scholars during this process first greeted it with indiscriminate admiration, later with equally indiscriminate denunciation, and now with an inquisitive eye on those features of pre-Meiji Japanese life, which made the Meiji modernization possible.[3]

In the adjustment the most striking feature was, despite the collapse of the Shogunate after a near-millenium of power, the historic compromise

[2] Texts of the final *Gokajō no goseimon* (Charter oath of five articles) and preceding drafts, are contained in Fujii Jintarō and Moriya Hidesuke, *Sōgō Nihon shi taikei: Meiji jidai shi* (Synthesis of the history of Japan: the Meiji era), Tōkyō, 1934, pp. 213-216. This citation follows an official translation to be found conveniently in *The Japan Year Book, 1946-48,* cited, p. 70. For further discussion of the Charter Oath, see Chapter Fifteen, p. 350.

[3] Meiji is, of course, a *nengō* or reign title for the years 1867-1912. Norman's *Japan's Emergence as a Modern State,* cited, is the most brilliant treatment in English, although admittedly only a reconnaissance study. It concentrates on the period from the late Tokugawa to consolidation under the Meiji Constitution, 1889. Norman carries his analysis topically, rather than chronologically, up to the Treaty of Portsmouth, 1905.

between merchant and feudal elements inherited from the previous regime. The former feudal leaders and their chivalric ideology marched straight through the transition period. In terms of class adjustment there was a transfer of power from the upper-class *samurai* to lower-class *samurai*. The modernized product bore a striking similarity to the "clan government" of ancient Japan; its by-product was modern Japanese bureaucracy.

Economically the Meiji transformation furnished Japan with "the forcing house for the nurture of capitalistic economy." The international economic policy of Meiji Japan was a combination of Hideyoshi's mercantilism and Friedrich List's *nationale System der politischen Ökonomie*. Thus, a Japanese economist, Dr. Nagai, called the Meiji period the last of the mercantilist epochs; Dr. Moulton of the Brookings Institution regards this as the first time a national economy was subjected to planning.[4]

Demographically the change-over marked a swift transition from a Japan with a high birth rate and a high death rate, resulting in a stable population, to a Japan with a diminishing death rate and an increase in births and in infant survivals. The population curve swerved upward very sharply. The transformed economy was called upon to bear the burden of the additional population.

The agricultural base of this changing population pyramid remained overburdened by excessive rents, parceling of holdings, and primitive techniques of cultivation. The results were a surplus population, a high proportion of female labor, a narrow home market, and an army of peasant conscripts. Politically, peasant character galvanized that peculiar feature of Japanese cultural personality which so often puzzled later observers: at one and the same time it was revolutionary and reactionary.

It is important to recognize that to the Japanese themselves the division between the Tokugawa and Meiji eras is not as sharp as it appeared to Westerners. Although Japanese historians agree that political and economic unification was the great accomplishment of the Meiji Restoration, they often point out that there had been an irregular growth of central authority from within Japanese feudalism. Modern Japanese trying to render into words the unconscious elements of their national self-awareness explained it in terms of a *racial state* (*minzoku kokka*) inherited from indescribable antiquity.

Racialism is no better a foundation than Marxism.[5] The Japanese mod-

[4] For a review of the *samurai* victory, see Honjō, *Kinsei hōken shakai no kenkyū*, cited, Chap. 10, section 2, pp. 133-136; for the alliance between *samurai* and *chōnin* (literally "townsmen"; merchant class): Horie Yasuzo, "An Outline of the Rise of Modern Capitalism in Japan," *Kyoto University Economic Review*, Vol. XI, No. 1 (July, 1930), pp. 99-101; and by the same author, "The Economic Significance of the Meiji Restoration," *ibid.*, Vol. XII, No. 2 (December, 1937), p. 81. An excellent Western-language survey of these forces is Alexandre Halot, "Le Japon economique pendant l'ere de Meidji," *Bulletin Trimestriel de l'Association des Licencies de l'Universite de Liege*, Liege, April, 1910. Norman, *op. cit.*, made reference to Doctors Nagai and Moulton, p. 109, fn. 13.

[5] Nothing could seem more remote from the Japanese explanation than the Marxist formula, which attempts to explain the Meiji Restoration as a "revolution of bourgeois, cap-

ernization is singularly important in that it hit both the Japanese and the Westerners at a time when their societies were, relative to their respective past, well governed, in the process of speedy enrichment, and filled with curiosity and hope for the future.

The Autochthonous Crisis. Modernization was speeded by the collapse of the Tokugawa system from which it sprang. The fall of the Shogunate cannot be blamed on Western blows alone. It was also proportionate to the failure of Tokugawa policies, judged as they may be by wholly Japanese standards. Agrarian unrest and natural calamities had accentuated the critical position of Tokugawa Japan just before the arrival of Commodore Perry. It was a blessing in disguise for Japan that an internal crisis forced change at the very time that a new international challenge demanded a redefinition of Japan's national entity and position among nations.

Of the corrosive influences, the economic one was of primary significance.[6] Peasants were heavily oppressed by the *samurai,* who in their turn were exploited by a rising and uneasy merchant class. As the *samurai* and their *daimyō* sought to transfer burdens of debt to the already overloaded peasants, the old agricultural economy broke down and was replaced, on a wholly intra-Japanese basis, by a mercantile economy. Implicit in the growth of any mercantile economy is money. The Tokugawa economic

---

italist Japan." In a laborious work whose title, translated from the Russian through Japanese and rendered in English, reads *The Growth of Japanese Capitalism,* a Soviet writer named Svetlov explained: "Tokugawa Japan can be viewed as a nation in the last stages of feudalism. That is, it had the beginnings of capitalistic production methods with manufacturers, domestic industry, and the development of commercial capitalism. It was, so to speak, like France before 1789 or, better, like Russia before 1861. It was, however, *of a strictly Japanese variety* and must be distinguished from the European model with which it corresponds, in numerous and individual characteristics." This analysis is of interest, first, because it admits Japanese *uniqueness;* and second, because it admits the continuity from the Tokugawa within historical determinism. On the other hand, the Marxist fails when he dogmatically attempts to apply a class struggle formula to the emerging society in Meiji Japan. For the rise of capitalistic enterprises occurred first in *feudal* clans; the *bourgeoisie,* who might be expected to lay siege to the feudal castle, had long since sneaked in the back gate; change was rapid, if not *revolutionary,* but it was partially imported and wholly controlled by *autocrats* at the top; *masses* shared little in the shifting balance of power. For this Marxist view, see the original Russian work by V. Svetlov, *Proiskhozhdenie Kapitalisticheskoi Iaponii,* Moscow, 1931, p. 125; the quotation is from a Revised Japanese Edition (Hayakawa Jirō, trans.) and was translated into English by the author of this section from Hattori Yukifusa *"Bakumatsu henkakki no ideorogii ni tsuite"* (Concerning the ideology of the revolutionary period at the close of the *Bakufu*), *Kaizō* (Reconstruction), Vol. XVI, No. 1 (January, 1934), pp. 208-215.

If the Marxist interpretation falls short, neither is it useful to evolve a theory that Japan skipped into proto-fascism (Freda Utley, *Japan's Feet of Clay,* New York, 1937, p. 221, refers to the *samurai* as counter-revolutionaries). It is safer to follow Mr. Norman, leaving aside for the moment such terms as "revolution" and "counter-revolution" and conclude that the purpose, at least, if not the effect of the Meiji Restoration was anti-feudal. See Norman, *op. cit.,* p. 43, fn. 82.

[6] It should be quite clear that one need not adopt a Marxist view to understand the internal, and chiefly economic, forces which first laid the basis for a transformation from Tokugawa to Meiji Japan. Many Japanese and some Western writers slip easily into such general terms as "the internal crisis of feudalism" or "contradictions in the Tokugawa economy." Such phrases imply an inexorable, deterministic force but do not adequately describe the complexity of factors at work. This point is thoroughly discussed by Sansom, *The Western World,* cited, pp. 223-233.

decline was marked by the penetration of the old economy by money values and, even more significantly, the failure of the Tokugawa leaders to understand or even to perceive the function of money in their changing society. For both the central Shogunate and the various daimiates, expenditures outran revenues. The *sankin kōtai,* the hostage system described in the preceding chapter, tended to increase the poverty of the nobility. Chronic deficits were met with debased currency and forced loans. While the country went bankrupt beneath them, the Tokugawa leaders devoted themselves to rule by ethical theory.

Economic changes were paralleled by social changes. Political disaffection grew. Peasants finding life unrewarding either could rise in unmotivated and pointless protest-revolts or could abandon their holdings and flee into the towns. Decreasing acreages under cultivation led to lower production. Agrarian weaknesses, which are almost mechanically obvious today, were expressed in chronic moral and psychological unrest; the Japanese of the nineteenth century mistook the symptom for the disease and attempted to resettle ground and to cultivate neglected fields by means of ethical or moral leadership; sages such as Ninomiya Sontoku (1787-1856) enjoyed a high vogue in the last years of this doomed period for their admirable but useless moral attack on an agronomic situation. Even among those peasants who revolted there was no articulate demand for the destruction of the feudal system, only a plaintive and desperate unrest which reiterated that the old, familiar world was all wrong.[7]

In sharp contrast, merchants and pre-modern industrialists gained immensely at this time. The volume of domestic trade revealed by rice and commodity indexes rose considerably. An autogenous but sophisticated capitalism manufactured a large proportion of the commodities. The rise of rural industry transferred wealth from the military feudal classes to new merchant-*entrepreneurs*. The extension of monopolies, particularly among the outer clans of the Southwest, shifted the management of economic and political affairs into the hands of the lower *samurai.*

Loss of ground by the upper *samurai* to merchants and to lower *samurai*

[7] Peasant resentment against their role as the feet of clay for the Tokugawa body politic took both passive and active forms. Infanticide (*mabiki,* literally "thinning out") was the most dramatic reaction but abortion seems to have been the main passive technique to combat overpopulation. Far more serious were active expressions of dissatisfaction: *tsuchi ikki* (uprisings from the soil), *hyakushō ikki* (peasant uprisings), and rice riots, in the form of *uchikowashi* (wrecking agitations). Tokugawa peasant problems, population pressure, and riots have called forth an extensive literature. A standard treatment in Japanese in Honjō, *Kinsei hōken shakai no kenkyū,* cited, Chap. 5, pp. 60 ff.; Chap. 7, pp. 84 ff. deals with the problem of population. The most thorough treatment in English is, of course, Hugh Borton, *Peasant Uprisings in Japan of the Tokugawa Period* (reprint from *TASJ,* Vol. XVI, 1938); in a note, p. 20, the author summarizes two Japanese views concerning the uprisings: Professor Ono believed they led to the overthrow of the Tokugawa; Professor Kokusho believed they contributed to the downfall of the *Bakufu* but held no motives to transform society. Professor Borton, after an extensive study of the uprisings, concluded that they were merely symptomatic: ". . . They were not so much a revolutionary movement as a continual protest against economic distress in which the peasants found themselves."

threatened the entire Tokugawa class structure. Dr. Kada Tetsuji, a Japanese student of social changes, has emphasized the dilemma of the warrior who agonizably sought to manage his personal affairs across the contradiction of a victorious money economy and a traditional economy-in-kind, based on rice. Thus, "the development of the town-money economy was the most important reason for the internal collapse of the feudal system." [8]

Such economic maladjustment and social unrest provided one basis for inarticulate political movements developed against the Tokugawa. There was a gradual collapse of central authority and a rising denunciation of exclusion, which, contradictorily, but understandably, included denunciation of belated shogunal attempts to end exclusion. The opposition to the Tokugawa amounted to a spontaneously formed league of disaffected *kuge, tozama,* and merchants. Another front of the anti-Tokugawa opposition arose from ideological currents. The revival of pure Shintō led to criticism of things Chinese and glorification of the indigenous cult. Various centers of scholarship showed obliquely that the *Shōgun* was a usurper and the Emperor the only rightful ruler.

What has been neglected in the histories of Japan's transformation is the contribution and ideological effect of the wealthier rural classes in the century preceding 1868. Money lenders, pawnship operators, merchants, and small industrialists soon provided the personnel pool for local administrative officials. These men were literate, maintained ties with scholars, met economic frustration shrewdly, opposed the growth of state monopoly, and resisted forced loans. In countless ways they actively contributed to the undertow: they often financed the growing class of *rōnin,* the masterless *samurai,* and at the end even helped in the purchase of arms to be used against Tokugawa. Although largely overlooked in historical accounts, these men were the precursors of post-Meiji oppositionists who first broke out the standards of democratic rights.[9]

Precipitation of the crisis came with the arrival of Commodore Matthew Calbraith Perry, USN.

Perry's expedition, far from stirring up a torpid but happy society, precipitated a crisis long in the growing between two general types of political-economic thought, both of them Japanese.

The first type was the responsive thinkers, largely unaffected by Western ideas, who offered either Chinese or native answers to the Tokugawa dilemma.

[8] Kada Tetsuji, *Meiji shoki shakai-keizai shisō shi* (History of socio-economic thought in the early stages of the Meiji era), Tōkyō, 1937, pp. 23-27; and Part I, Chap. 3, "Contradictions in the Feudal System," pp. 100 ff. A more recent survey of newer Japanese literature on the subject is contained in John Whitney Hall, "The Tokugawa Bakufu and the Merchant Class," *Occasional Papers* of the Center for Japanese Studies, No. 1 (1951), Ann Arbor, University of Michigan Press, pp. 26-33.

[9] It is most fortunate that Dr Nobutaka Ike (now with the Hoover Library, Stanford) followed the path marked out by Norman's study and closed the gap in his excellent volume, *The Beginnings of Political Democracy in Japan,* Baltimore, 1950; see especially Chap. II, pp. 18-23.

The second type resulted from the seepage of Western ideas past the Tokugawa ideological blockade. Neither of these types had a monopoly on unorthodoxy. The native unorthodox thinkers made possible in great part that reconciliation of the Japanese intellect with Western civilization which caused Japan, so obviously much more than any other nation-state, to adjust itself to a world governed by the practices of Western nations.

Orthodoxy and Unorthodoxy in Tokugawa Thinking. Even in the closed world of the Tokugawa there were varieties of Japanese thought. Officially the *Bakufu* endorsed and encouraged the Neo-Confucianism of Chu Hsi. State policy rested on the insistence that a knowledge of faith revealed moral law. As a corollary, wise men were expected to instruct the people, whereupon good government would depend upon the wisdom and judiciousness of the ruler and the loyal obedience of the ruled. This doctrine, furthering the support of autocracy, proved a useful adjunct to centralized feudalism.

A pre-eminent adviser to the Shogunate was Arai Hakuseki (A.D. 1675-1725). He was a philosopher, scholar, and statesman, possibly the greatest of the Tokugawa period. His advice was sought on such subjects as law, the Imperial Family, currency, social legislation, superstition, and foreign relations. In meeting the challenge of the money economy he suggested that (1) the quantity of gold and silver coins be returned to a sound base; (2) the government be parsimonious in dealing with coinage; (3) the interests of the people not be sacrificed; (4) properly trained administrators be appointed for financial policy; and (5) the government struggle to retain popular confidence.

Ogyū Sorai (A.D. 1665-1728) was an ardent Sinophile and classical purist who rejected the age-old reinterpretations of Confucius and Mencius and who, economically speaking, attempted to meet the effects of a rising money economy by lopping off the head of that economy with sumptuary legislation. Other Japanese thinkers such as Miura Baien (A.D. 1723-1789) and Dazai Shundai (A.D. 1680-1747), both moralists and economists, tried to meet the challenge in ethical terms.[10]

Opposition to the extreme orthodoxy of Chu Hsi was also founded on a revival of the Confucianism of Wang Yang-ming, known in Japan as *Ōyōmei*. More pragmatic and experimental in outlook, Wang Yang-ming prepared his Japanese disciples, centuries after his own death, for as strange an intellectual victory as the Westernization of Japan.[11]

[10] Nomura Kanetarō, *Edo jidai no keiseika* (Edo period statesmen), Tōkyō, 1942, is a convenient selection of essays on outstanding political economists. Arai Hakuseki, incidentally, is the only Japanese political economist, early or modern, on whom an article is written in the *Encyclopedia of Social Sciences* (Vol. II, p. 49).

[11] A few of the earliest Western observers realized this fact. William Elliot Griffis said, in an address delivered in Kirkpatrick Chapel, Rutgers College, June 16, 1885: "Let us note the forces that finally upheaved the old state of things; for these were mostly intellectual, from within and not from without. The schoolmaster and the student preceded the revolutionist and the soldier." Most of the students of Dutch at Nagasaki, whom Griffis knew,

Many of the Japanese students of Chinese philosophy were at the same time Japanese classicists, like Nakae Tōjū (A.D. 1608-1648), founder of the *Ōyōmei* School. There was also the so-called Mito School, founded by Tokugawa Mitsukuni (A.D. 1628-1700). It is an irony of history that the downfall of the Tokugawa was thus aided by the scholarship of one branch of the family. Mitsukuni's *Dai Nihon shi* (History of Japan) was not printed until 1851, but his work did stimulate others who became interested in the relative position of the Emperor and the *Shōgun*. Kamo Mabuchi (A.D. 1697-1769), for example, studied the *Kojiki* and the *Nihon shoki* and succeeded in arousing the patriotism of the scholar class even though his work did not reach the masses. Motoori Norinaga (A.D. 1730-1801) is best known for his participation in the revival of pure Shintō. His *Kojiki-den* (Commentaries on the *Kojiki*) contributed to the sanctions of nationalism by giving the ancient texts the authority of scriptures. His ideas greatly influenced the modern Japanese theory of the state. Motoori also set down penetrating observations on wealth and poverty: what he advocated would today be defined in terms of state socialism. Perhaps most effective was Rai Sanyō (A.D. 1780-1832), who wrote *Nihon gaishi* (Private record of Japanese history). Rai carefully discussed only pre-Tokugawa matters but criticized the Ashikaga Shogunate (thus, by implication, the Tokugawa) and exalted the Throne.[12]

In the realm of political economy, some of the critics of the Tokugawa regime were truly remarkable in their constructive purposes and brilliance. They would rank with the more famous orthodox Tokugawa thinkers, save for the fact that their ideas were generations in advance of their time.

One of the ablest administrators of the era was a Confucian scholar, Kumazawa Banzan (A.D. 1619-1691). As head secretary to the *daimyō* of Okayama, Kumazawa was largely responsible for his lord's reputation as a good governor. Kumazawa's political ideas were contained in *Daigaku wakumon* (Certain public questions in light of "The Great Learning"). Kumazawa saw economic maladjustments—exclusion of foreign trade, extravagant expenditure, and decline of agriculture—as the root of all social problems including disaffection among *samurai,* agrarian unrest, and unemployment. The measures he proposed would do justice to a modern political

were first students of *Ōyōmei,* philosophy. See *The Rutgers Graduates in Japan,* Rutgers College, New Brunswick, N. J., 1916, pp. 7, 9. In a stimulating interview with the author of this section, in Japan, 1952, Professor Nomura Kanetarō—one of Japan's outstanding students of social thought—stressed the invasion and growth of *rationalism* as the intellectual leaven which made Japan's transformation possible. See also Inoue, *Nihon shushigakuha no tetsugaku,* cited, Chap. 2, pp. 49-113.

[12] Motoori's part in the revival of Shintō attempted to purge it of Buddhistic elements, preparing the way for an even greater concentration of Emperor deification. Under the Meiji regime this trend was so intensified as to lead some scholars erroneously to conclude that it was an entirely new aspect of Japanese thought. See Reischauer, *Japan: Government-Politics,* cited, p. 59, fn. 2; also Ernest Satow, *The Revival of Pure Shintau* (reprint from *TASJ,* Vol. III, 1883, Appendix). Hugh Borton, "A Survey of Japanese Historiography," *American Historical Review,* Vol. XLIII (October, 1937, and July, 1938) provides a convenient summary of this spectrum of historical analysis.

party platform. Among others, he suggested (1) a reform of the media of exchange; (2) encouragement of agriculture, industry, and commerce; (3) protection of forests and flood control; (4) relief for the unemployed; (5) reform of taxation; and (6) simplification of family and social customs. His ideas were considered so revolutionary that he was put under house arrest for the last five years of his life.

Honda Toshiaki (or Honda Rimei, A.D. 1744-1821) followed in the tradition set by Kumazawa. One of the most advanced Tokugawa thinkers, he became interested in mathematics, astronomy, navigation, politics, and economics. Earnestly applying scientific method, he found himself opposed to the tenets of Asiatic thought; like the National scholars, he found himself opposed to Confucianism. His *Keisei hisaku* (A secret book of statesmanship) provides an interesting Oriental counterpart to the Malthusian analysis. Honda discussed government control of the merchant marine, foreign trade, colonization, and industry; in short, he proposed the equivalent of state socialism. In *Seiiki monogatari* (Tales of western lands), he advocated the colonization of Karafuto (Sakhalin) and even Kamchatka. His belief in international interdependence led him to criticize the *Bakufu* for its refusal to trade with Russia.[13] In 1792, another patriotic scholar, Rin Shihei (or Hayashi Shihei), published *Kaikoku heidan* (Essay on the military problems of a maritime state).

Still within the general framework of Japanese thought, Andō Shōeki was born about 1700 in the area of the present Akita prefecture and studied European medicine under official clan sponsorship. Such study was permitted by a partial lifting of the ban on Western learning adopted by the *Shōgun* Yoshimune. Andō planned to go abroad, but was stopped by the rigorous exclusion edicts. His chief work, *Shizen shineido,* was published in Kyoto in 1753. Andō's *Shizen shineido* is physiocratic in outlook as its title, in English "The way of nature and labor," indicates.[14] Andō, like physiocrats in other civilizations, regarded the farmers as the producing class and dismissed *samurai* and loafers alike as nonproducing idlers who were "the lice of the nation."

Even more strikingly, Andō was an egalitarian. He is unique in the history of Japanese political thought in that he developed his egalitarianism from

[13] A translation of Kumazawa's *Daigaku wakumon* is given by Galen M. Fisher in *TASJ,* 2d series, Vol. XVI (May, 1938), pp. 259-356; Honda's *Seiiki monogatari* is included in the *Nihon keizai taiten,* cited, Vol. XX, pp. 211-286.

[14] E. Herbert Norman, "Andō Shōeki and the Anatomy of Japanese Feudalism," *TASJ,* 3d series, Vol. II (December, 1949), 2 vols. Vol. 2 of Norman's study is a supplementary text of passages quoted in Vol. 1 from Andō's treatises: *Shizen shineido* (The way of nature and labor) and *Tōdō shiden* (A true account of the supreme way). In Vol. 1, Chaps. 4 and 5 bring together Andō's most revealing passages on Tokugawa classes, comments on Andō's style, and a summary of his amazing attack on feudal society (in the form of satirical dialogues among animals). Chap. 6 deals with Andō's hopes, his program for reform, and his utopia. Mr. Norman's work is perhaps the most significant revelation of new material available since, and made possible by, surrender and liberation of Japanese thought.

local materials. At his most extreme he wrote, "To rule is in itself an extreme injustice."

In practical terms he advocated the transformation of *daimyō* officials, the establishment of a single sovereign over the single sovereignty, the liquidation of the merchants and bureaucrats into cultivators themselves, the allocation of small plots of cultivable ground to the unemployed, and the replacement of a money economy with barter. Andō represents the high-water mark of the native literature of progress.

The Pro-Western Thinkers. The great Arai Hakuseki was among the orthodox Japanese who condemned the ideological blockade of the Tokugawa because it affronted intellectual integrity and freedom for purely scholastic thought.[15] Despite the rigidity of the ban, two channels for Western thought remained open. One was the contact with the Dutch at Nagasaki where Tokugawa officials, attempting to use Nagasaki as a peephole on the outside world, could not help being affected by the learning which they acquired in attempting to do their job skillfully.

As early as the Genroku era (A.D. 1688-1703) Nishikawa Joken wrote a book, the title for which may be rendered as *Polyhistorical Description of the Commerce of China and the Barbarian Countries*. Arai Hakuseki himself wrote two books dealing with foreign matters.[16]

The other source of Western learning consisted of European materials relayed by means of Chinese translations; these became common toward the middle of the nineteenth century.

The direct Dutch impact on Japanese thinking was felt chiefly in two narrowly specialized fields in which the Japanese admitted themselves to be the inferiors of the Europeans: medicine, particularly surgery; and positional warfare, with special reference to artillery and fortification. Under the restricted license on Western books which came into effect by order of the *Shōgun* Yoshimune in 1720 and the personal contact which he allowed after 1744 between Dutchmen at Nagasaki and Japanese desirous of studying European science, a veritable school of Dutch thought (*Rangakusha*) became a factor in Tokugawa thinking.[17] Among the *Rangakusha* there

[15] Arai Hakuseki was officially assigned the job (which he doubtless relished) of questioning a "man from Rome," who was almost certainly Pére Sidotti. See the Rev. W. B. Wright, "The Capture and Captivity of Pere Giovanni Batista Sidotti in Japan from 1709 to 1715," *TASJ,* Vol. IX, Part II (August, 1881), pp 156-172.

[16] A few titles will illustrate the trend from simple geography and medicine over into politics: Arai Hakuseki, *Sairan Igen* (Foreign topography) and *Seiyō kibun* (Notes on Western things), late eighteenth century; Kukichi Shoko, *Taisei yochi zusetsu* (Explanatory diagrams of the Western world, 1789); Yoshiyo Sen, *Anyakuria jin seijōshi* (On the character of the English, 1825); Aoji Rinso's translation of a Dutch geography, about 1827, went so far as to describe the British Parliament; of the Chinese studies, Wei Yüan's *Hai-kuo t'u-chih* (Illustrated record of the maritime nations, 1844) was reprinted in Japan and was widely read. These works, and others, are cited by Asai Kiyoshi, *Meiji rikken shiso ni okeru Eikoku gikai seidō no eikyō* (The influence of the British parliamentary system on Meiji constitutional thought), Tōkyō, 1939, cited by Ike, *op. cit.*, pp. 26-27.

[17] See Mitsukuri, K., "The Early Study of Dutch in Japan," *TASJ,* Vol. V (February, 1877), pp. 207-216; C. R. Boxer, "Notes on Early European Influence on Japan (1542-1853), *TASJ,* Vol. VIII, 2d series (December, 1931), pp. 67-94; Sansom, *The Western World,*

were two schools, named after districts in the city of Edo (modern Tokyo). The Shitamachi School studied only medicine; the Yamanote School studied all branches of Western learning.

Characteristic of this latter, broader school are the lives of Watanabe Noboru and Takano Nagahide.

Watanabe, born in 1794, formed an illicit club which criticized Chinese studies and sought to spread Western learning. He was tried in 1839, disgraced, and committed suicide in 1840. In 1870 the Japanese government, characteristically enough, got around to pardoning him. Takano, ten years younger, studied medicine and Dutch in Edo and attempted to understand the British Empire through the double screen of remoteness and misconception. He did so under the impression that Britain was the most powerful country in the world. In order to circularize his thoughts he wrote a book called *The Dream,* for which he was arrested in 1839 and sentenced to life imprisonment. He escaped during a fire at the prison, lived a few years in hiding, and committed suicide when the police caught up with him.[18]

The Long Twilight of the Tokugawa. King William II of Holland wrote a letter dated February 15, 1844, to the Tokugawa *Shōgun* advising him to open the country. The basic theme of King William's letter was:

> "This, All-powerful Emperor, is our friendly advice: ameliorate the laws against the foreigners, lest happy Japan be destroyed by war. We give Your Majesty this advice with honest intentions, free from political self-interest."[19]

The chronology of the opening of Japan is itself an intricate and complicated series of steps. In general terms it will suffice to say that Western ships made contact with Japanese shores and sought relations with the Japanese authorities at increasingly frequent intervals from the early eighteenth century down to the actual time of opening. Before the Perry mission in 1853 the Japanese had almost forty years of sustained warnings that sooner or later the foreign powers would employ measures too harsh for the Toku-

cited, traces in detail the careers of Takashima Shūhan (1798-1866), who devoted his life to the study of Western military science, and of Sakuma Shōzan (1811-1864), who became impressed by the advances made in gunnery and tactics by leading Western powers (Chap. 11, pp. 248-253).

[18] The *Yume monogatari* (The dream), circulated widely, became so well known that crude imitations of the book began to appear (*Zoku yume monogatari,* or "Popularized dream," for example). A life of Takano was prepared for private circulation by Osada Kenjiro; its appendices contain Takano's most famous work, parts of which have been translated by D. C. Greene, "Osada's Life of Takano Nagahide," *TASJ,* Vol. XLI, Part III (August, 1913). An interesting sketch of Watanabe is given by Miss Ballard in "The Life of Watanabe Noboru," *TASJ,* Vol. XXXII, Part I (May, 1905).

[19] William's letter was directed to the eleventh *Shōgun* Ieyoshi but the reply emanated from the *Bakufu.* The friendly advice was ignored because, as *Bakufu* officials pointed out, such a course would contravene ancestral law. Dr. Nitobe Inazo referred to this correspondence in his *Intercourse Between the United States and Japan,* Baltimore, 1891, p. 2; Watanabe Shujiro, *Sekai ni okeru Nihonjin* (The Japanese in the world), Tōkyō, 1897, pp. 26 ff. contains the Japanese text and comments; see also D. C. Greene, "Correspondence between William II of Holland and the Shogun of Japan, A.D. 1844," *TASJ,* Vol. XXXIV (June, 1907), pp. 99-132.

gawa regime to refute their existence by the simple process of closing its collective political eyes. The long and tragic twilight of Tokugawa power is known in Japanese history as *Bakumatsu*.[20]

The Pandora's Box of Commodore Perry. Commodore Matthew Calbraith Perry was appointed in March, 1852, to open relations with Japan. He took command of a naval force which had gone through organizational and readiness stages under another officer. His instructions were pacific, but forceful. Even while the ships were being readied in United States harbors, the Kingdom of the Netherlands was urgently warning the *Bakufu* of what the Americans planned.

On July 8, 1853, Perry anchored in Tokyo Bay with four ships—ships which impressed the Japanese as being immense, unnaturally black in color, and terrifying in their potentous hints of steam mobility and artillery power. Perry, diplomatically enough, remained only ten days, leaving a letter from the President of the United States to the Emperor of Japan.

In addressing the "Emperor" the Americans themselves were none too sure as to the recipient of the letter. They, like most of the Western nations who now and then concern themselves with the remote, quaint political institutions of Japan, heard rumors of a weak Emperor, meaning the *Shōgun,* whose power was in some remote way limited by an even weaker ecclesiastical Emperor or pseudo-pope in another city of Japan. Perry stayed away once he lifted anchor until February 13, 1854: when he returned he returned for results. The Japanese had neither the physical force nor the moral power to persuade him to leave. On March 31, 1854, there was signed between the Japanese shogunal government and the government of the United States the Treaty of Kanagawa, which opened Japan at the point of an American naval gun. Once Japan had made a concession to the United States, concessions to other Western powers followed in rapid succession. The British obtained a treaty in October; Russia and Holland, within the years immediately following.[21]

The Pandora's box opened by Commodore Perry will never be closed again. The effects of Japan's opening are unchangeable so far as Japanese domestic institutions and politics are concerned. Even in the realm of world affairs the arrival of Japan as a great power is a factor which, once initiated, has played its own forceful and independent role for a century. It is an irony that the two greatest strategic crises of modern Japanese civilization—

[20] The chronology of early contacts with the West is a familiar story, told in several standard diplomatic histories. For a survey of these events from a Japanese point of view, particularly the impact upon Japanese opinion, see Kada, *Meiji shoki shakai-keizai shisō shi,* cited, p. 28, and Part I, Chap. 4; Count Soeshima, "Japan's Foreign Relations," an essay in Ōkuma, ed., *Fifty Years of New Japan,* cited, Vol. I, Chap. 4. Sansom's *The Western World,* cited, Chap. 12, pp. 275-281, gives an amusing account of the Perry mission.

[21] A recent and fresh reinterpretation of this early diplomatic intercourse, with emphasis on American interests, is contained in L. Ethan Ellis, *A Short History of American Diplomacy,* New York, 1951, especially Chap. 15, "The Far East: Japan." See also Arthur Clarence Walworth, *Black Ships Off Japan; the Story of Commodore Perry's Expedition,* New York, 1946.

the opening of Japan by the ships of Commodore Perry and the surrender of Japan to General of the Army MacArthur on the *Missouri*—should have occurred on the decks of United States naval craft.

To describe the ramifications in world politics of the Perry visit would require dropping the subject of Japanese domestic political development and pursuing the forces released by Perry to their outermost peripheries. From the Amazon valley to the cold pole of Asiatic Siberia, from the Polish underground in East Prussia to the birth of Indonesia in Java, Japan's far-flung role attested to the violence with which Japan did open, once the lid was taken off by Perry.

The Anti-Tokugawa Resurgence. Immediate in its effect on inward Japanese affairs was the possibility that any kind of a disturbance would precipitate in Japanese life a loose coalition of the forces opposed either to Tokugawa as a family or to the *Bakufu* as an institution.

In the uproar attending Japan's acceptance of Perry's demands three parties became active in the confused politics attendant upon problems of unprecedented diplomacy, complicated by the issue of shogunal succession. The first and most active political force was the League of Outward *Daimyō*—the so-called *tozama daimyō*—who needed nothing more than a crisis, any kind of a crisis, to spring into action against their hereditary antagonists. Within the *tozama han,* and even among other clans, the balance of power gradually swung over to the younger *samurai.* These, in turn, linked up with *kuge,* who had waited for almost a thousand years to be restored to real power, and other opportunistic pro-Imperialists to form a second group. The third element in this loose and shifting coalition consisted of the immense merchant houses which had grown as far as they could within the limits of the *Bakufu* system and which looked beyond the existing regime toward some greater and more elastic system which would permit the full flowering of their acquisitive and mercantile talents.[22]

The addition of the Perry mission brought the Japanese domestic situation to critical mass. The uproar in Japanese life precipitated by the Perry visit and the resulting treaties was far out of proportion to the modification of the policy of exclusion. The sensitive balance of forces within Japanese social and economic strata was undone just enough for each to flare into violent activity.

The issues of the shogunal succession, although an important part of political history, are not necessarily reflected in significant changes of the constitutional or governmental structure of Japan. The rivalry between two separate Tokugawa claimants to the position of feeble *Shōgun* Iyeyoshi, who died at the worst possible time in 1853, itself did a great deal to confuse the political scene and to hide behind a screen of personal politics the major

[22] Details of various phases of the movement are given in W. W. McLaren, *A Political History of Japan During the Meiji Era, 1867-1912,* London and New York, 1916, Chap. I; and in Murdoch, *op. cit.,* Vol. III, Chap. XVIII, "The Fall of the Bakufu."

social and institutional issues which had to be fought out by the Japanese.[23]

Even in its immediate response to the Perry demands the *Bakufu* hierarchy committed two serious political mistakes. It requested the advice of the Emperor, thus for its own part conjuring up the ghost of its ancient rival and bringing into question the fundamental legitimacies of its authority as a government. The *Bakufu* also sought the advice of the *daimyō;* with such a confession of weakness it allowed the *daimyō* to vociferate over questions which had been kept secret or unmentionable by the Edo authorities for generations past.[24]

The Advice of the Clans. Of the unsettling groups capable of organization and action, the outward clans were most nearly ready. The southern *tozama* were alert and sharp in seizing the opportunity afforded by internal crisis, external pressure, and the impact of new Western learning. These clans in particular were the ones marked by the highest pre-1853 development of commercial and industrial activities—the ones where a rudimentary, but radical Japanese capitalism had sunk its deepest roots. Their immediate objectives were both practical and violent: they desired to accumulate specie in order to initiate the manufacture of arms and at the same time sought to shift themselves from the economic bases of feudal daimiates to a working alliance with merchant capitalism.

Just how and by whom the League of *Tozama* was effected is the central thread in the formation of the new constitutional entities of Japan. The coalition succeeded because of the rich contribution of personal talent and group enthusiasm made by members of four outstanding clans, clans which rewarded themselves with pre-eminent roles in Japanese history for the ensuing ninety years. These were Satsuma, Chōshū, Hizen, and Tosa. From Satsuma one leader, Saigō Takamori, and from Chōshū another, Kido Takayoshi, helped set up the superficial arrangements. Even their individual personalities are insufficient to explain just how each clan in turn fell under the leadership of lower *samurai* and how the two clans assumed the effective super-heading of the anti-Tokugawa cause. Kido seems to have been motivated by an antiquarian, but authentic loyalty to the Imperial cause; Saigō seems to have struggled for the military power and pre-eminence of his own clan, Satsuma.

From the very beginning the clan revolt and the reappearance of the legitimacies were inextricably commingled. Satsuma started as a moderate

[23] For various phases of Tokugawa politics, during the last days of the regime, see Honjō Eijirō, *Bakumatsu no shinseisaku* (New policies at the end of the Bakufu), Tōkyō, 1935; and also the English translation of his social and economic history, *op. cit.*, Chap. XI, "The Men of the Day," pp. 317-319.

[24] After the appearance of the U.S. warships, a considerable number of *daimyō* maintained that it was no longer possible for the Shogunate to adhere to a policy of exclusion. Some advocated outright acceptance of the American overtures; some proposed a limited trade; some advocated preparation for war, and then cutting off of all trade. All these views swelled chauvinism, contributed to pro-Emperor propaganda, and created opportunities for anti-Tokugawa politics. See Honjō Eijirō, "The Views of the Various Hans on the Opening of the Country," *Kyoto University Economic Review*, Vol. XI, No. 1 (July, 1936), pp. 16-31.

clan, and as late as 1861 its *daimyō* proposed a *modus vivendi* based upon a coalition of court and Shogunate and the over-all reform of *Bakufu* administration. Extremists, represented by the Chōshū clan, combined demands for the expulsion of foreigners, the condemnation of the *Bakufu,* and the restoration of the long-dormant empire.

Even within the Chōshū clan the clansmen divided into factions. The *Zokurontō* (Party of the Vulgar View) clashed with the radicals of the *Kaimeitō* (Party of the Enlightened View). With typical Japanese volatility the *Zokurontō* led in power until the practicality of expelling foreigners was put to the test by trying out American and European naval bombardments. As soon as the conservatives realized that it was impractical to expel foreigners who could stand a safe distance offshore with their war vessels and burn Japan piecemeal, they relinquished power to the radicals. Among the Chōshū radicals one particular young *samurai* modified the threefold program, demanding instead the restoration of Imperial power, the condemnation of the *Bakufu,* and friendly relations with foreigners instead of the expulsion of the barbarians. Under the name of Prince Itō Hirobumi he was to play a major role in Japanese history after the *Bakufu* was finally set aside.

Enlightenment Through Reaction. The struggle between the anti-Tokugawa insurgents and the rapidly declining *Bakufu* authorities was waged by a combination that was brilliant and efficacious on the rebel side of warfare and conspiracy. Chōshū and Satsuma conspired in Kyoto itself until they were finally expelled by the shogunal police. They got in touch with Emperor Kōmei, making him party to a scheme for an "abduction," an entirely voluntary arrangement on his part. In the campaigns of 1864-75 lordless *rōnin* filled the fighting ranks of the southern clans and demonstrated that the *samurai* as a class no longer possessed a monopoly of fighting power within Japan. All these conspiracies and troubles, progressive in their net effect in that they expedited the change from feudalism to capitalism, were undertaken in terms of the loyalty-symbols of a conservatism so reactionary as to be romantic, almost antiquarian in tone.

Kuge nobles who had survived in poverty-stricken and elegant desuetude for seven centuries saw a chance to bring themselves and their class back to real power. Traditionally attached to the inactive, impotent Imperial court as liaison officers, they found the taste of real politics stimulating in the extreme and plunged rapidly into the conspiratorial business.

Had the *daimyō* of the insurgent clans managed to control their own kind, it is possible that Japan might have appeared on the threshold of the modern world as a loose federation of satrapies, not too different from the republican China in the period of the *Tuchüns.* The pre-eminence of the younger *samurai* developed so strongly that, when the *Bakufu* fell, the *daimyō* fell with it, and the clans emerged as the cement of a new and centralized Imperial state.

So meticulously had the Japanese preserved the formalities of their government across the centuries that the Imperial Throne still had an ideologically appealing position, even though it had not been used as a tool of government (save for the abortive Daigo restoration of 1333-1335) since 1192. Nevertheless, from the domestic point of view the Imperial tradition guaranteed success of the anti-*Bakufu* movement. Anti-foreignism helped the Imperial cause until the naval demonstrations of 1863 convinced even the restorationists that exclusion was not physically practicable in terms of the availability of combat forces. Once the Imperial restorationist group turned toward a policy of intercourse, it was inevitable that, whoever won in Japan, the national pattern would accept the presence of the sea-borne nations and would attempt intercourse on a large scale with the Western world.

As a third major element, parallel to the rebel *daimyō* and to the court, the merchant groups began to play a part. Foreign trade did not begin in earnest until 1858, but when it did the fantastic Japanese price of gold led to a violent monetary upheaval in Japan. Everywhere else in the world gold was fifteen or sixteen times the value of silver; in Japan it was five times the value of silver. At any Japanese seaport a fortune was to be had for the asking by anyone who arrived with a sufficient amount of bulk silver to exchange for gold bullion at a two-hundred-per-cent profit. The net effect was to stimulate the export of raw materials, expedite a sharp rise in all domestic prices, and import manufactures prepared by Western machinery at a price which drove Japanese handicraft industries into ruin.[25]

Those Japanese economic groups which tried to follow a business-as-usual policy faced uncertainty or ruin. Bold or enterprising men, alert to the possibilities of the new situation, had unprecedented possibilities to get rich quickly. The official guilds which had been given special privilege and monopolistic positions by the *Bakufu* found their position challenged by the *entrepreneurs* of the modernizing groups. Sometimes the clans themselves went directly into business. Satsuma undertook a new monopoly of sugar production. Tosa attempted to control the manufacture of paper. New rural merchants and industrialists adopted modern techniques and new market situations to make fortunes.

The modernizing movement which had started out as picturesquely traditionalist became forceful, capitalist, and practical when the great urban mercantile and financial houses threw the weight of their funds in favor of change. Such houses as Mitsui, Ono, Shimada, and Konoike joined the anti-*Bakufu* movement.[26]

[25] The economic effects of the opening of Japan to trade, with attendant political results, are discussed in Ike, *op. cit.*, pp. 14-23, and in Norman, *Japan's Emergence*, cited, pp. 61-70.

[26] See Mitsui Gomei Kaisha, *The House of Mitsui; A Record of Three Centuries*, Tokyo, 1933, p. 15; and Honjō Eijirō, *Social and Economic History*, cited, Chap. 12, "The Importance of *Goyōkin* or Forced Loans in the Meiji Restoration."

The Last Policies of the *Bakufu*. Even while the foundations of its power melted away the *Bakufu* tried to deal with the foreign diplomatic situation. In 1855 it established a foreign-language school (*Yōgakusho*), later to become Tokyo Imperial University.

In 1860 the Tokugawa authorities dispatched a mission to the United States to exchange ratifications of the 1858 treaty. This was an unprecedented action, since Japanese had been strictly forbidden to travel abroad. Shimmi Masaoki, *Kami* of Buzen, led the mission, which included Fukuzawa Yukichi, a young *samurai* interpreter. The mission visited Congress, where the members tried to make sense out of the speech-making and verbal fireworks. The Japanese mission, complete with kimonos and swords, followed the news concerning the Republican National Convention which met in Chicago to nominate a lean, youngish lawyer, Lincoln, for the Presidency. To the Americans of the time the passing of the picturesque Japanese must have seemed a light and silly episode, interrupting the drama of our own great national tragedy of disunion. In 1861 the Tokugawa authorities dispatched envoys to Europe. In 1863 another group was sent to England and France. In 1865 an economic mission was sent to England and France to study plans for the establishment of Japanese shipyards and ironworks.

At the same time that the Tokugawa were sending young and energetic men abroad the Chōshū and Satsuma clans were sending their own people with shogunal permission. The Japanese travelers may have looked trivial or quaint to the Westerners, but as soon as they returned to Japan they plunged into practical affairs and seized all the political and economic leadership which they could.

For a while the *Bakufu* had what amounted to an alliance with the French Empire of Napoleon III. Léon Roches was the French Minister in Edo; he associated on terms of extreme cordiality with the shogunal authorities, while the British consorted with the anti-*Bakufu* elements. While the Ch'ing dynasty in China underwent the supreme torment of a mass rebellion led by Hung Hsiu-ch'üan, "the younger brother of Jesus Christ," the Japanese factions made a maximum use of French and British help without ever violating their downright loyalty to Japan. If either side had brought in the British or French as combatants in domestic fighting, Japan might have gone the way of Burma or Indochina.[27]

Attempts at reform made the anti-*Bakufu* elements uneasy: they dreaded the possibility that the Tokugawa might recoup prestige and power by a vigorous and progressive policy. Ii Naosuke, Senior Minister of the *Bakufu*,

[27] It is often forgotten what valuable services France rendered the *Bakufu*, and to Japan as well. Roches drew up detailed schemes for Cabinet reorganization, reform of taxation, establishment of corporations, and increments to military strength; the French participated in founding the Yokosuka Iron Works, trade centers at Hyogo and Osaka, and made a large loan through the Société Générale and French Mail Steamship Company. See "Léon Roches and Administrative Reform in the Closing Years of the Tokugawa Regime," *Kyoto University Economic Review*, Vol. X, No. 1 (July, 1935), pp. 35-54, where Professor Honjō tells this interesting story.

brought on himself the frenzied hatred of the Imperialists when he signed the treaty of 1858 without awaiting Imperial sanction. He added to their fury when he arbitrarily selected his own cousin as the shogunal successor. In doing this he slighted an influential group, including the *daimyō* of Mito, Echizen, Owari, and Satsuma. He even locked up two of the *daimyō*. This so-called Purge of Ansei led to Ii's assassination in 1860, but the *Shōgun* whose appointment he had tried to forestall, Keiki, became the fifteenth and last of his line.

At the same time that the shogunal succession changed, so too did the Imperial. One of the most famous emperors in Japanese history stepped forth upon the scene:

The fifteen-year-old Emperor Mutsuhito, who was to reign as the Meiji *Tennō,* took the Throne in February, 1867, and immediately reversed the anti-foreign policies of his predecessor.

The year 1867 was one of continuous political uproar in Japan. Mutsuhito came to power in February. In November, Keiki surrendered not only his own personal authority, but the entire power of the *Bakufu* as well. The centuries of dual government came to an end. The Japanese people found themselves nakedly and precariously governed by that Imperial institution which they had revered for centuries and had tried to keep so perfect that it would not be sullied with the dross of everyday living. The adherents of the *Bakufu* made a last play for survival by expressing the hope that the Imperial government when inaugurated as a *de facto* government would rely upon the support and advice of all the clans.[28] In order to insure their being heard, they too plunged into Westernization. By October, 1867, Gotō Shōjirō had tried to make up a compromise acceptable to all parties when he drafted a memorial to the *Shōgun* and suggested three major steps:

first, return of administration to the Imperial court;
second, centering of the organization and laws of the new government in a legislature (*gisei-sho*), to be divided into upper and lower houses;
third, representation to include all classes all the way from *kuge* down to mere commoners.

In the very month in which the *Bakufu* finally fell, one Nishi Amane presented two drafts of a proposed constitution to the Throne proposing a curiously functional confederation for the Empire of Japan, whereby the *Shōgun* under his more vulgar title of "Tycoon" (*Taikun*) was to become the presiding officer of an upper house, amalgamating Shogunate and Empire. Such plans showed that the Tokugawa no less than the Imperial family tried to maintain their power by reconciling themselves to change.

The end came anyhow.

[28] Ike, *op. cit.,* Chap. III, pp. 30-34, covers these early schemes suggested by the Comte de Montblanc, Yokoi Shōnan (both during the Bunkyu era, 1861-1863); by Ōkubo Ichio, a Tokugawa official (1862); and by Akamatsu Kosaburo of Ueda (1861).

In the autumn of 1867 the great outer lords forwarded a joint letter to the *Shōgun* demanding his resignation from office. By this time the Satsuma and Chōshū clans had reconciled their differences in tactics and, under the leadership of Saigō and Kido, had drawn up a secret agreement to work toward the complete overthrow of the *Bakufu*. They were backed by Owari and Echizen whose *daimyō* had been locked up in the attempted coup of the Lord Ii. Only Yamanouchi, the Lord of Tosa, still sought some kind of compromise. But the *Shōgun* was all tired out. The *Bakufu* replied to the ultimatum with compliance. In a note dated November 3, 1867, the *Shōgun* acquiesced in the demand for his personal resignation and the dismantling of his government.[29] On November 12, his resignation was accepted. Two hundred sixty-five years of Tokugawa rule and almost eight centuries of shogunal government came to an end. The Japanese opened 1868 with a double mission: the reactivation of a government which had been kept on a stand-by basis for centuries, and the re-creation of their national entity in a form sufficiently Western to insure Japan's survival in a world dominated by the machine-supported military and naval power of the West.

[29] W. W. McLaren, *Japanese Government Documents, 1867-89* (reprint from *TASJ*, Vol. XLII, Part I, 1914, pp. 1-2). Hereafter this document will be referred to as *JGD*.

CHAPTER
FIFTEEN

The Japanese Model of Europe

CONSTRUCTION of a Japanese model of Europe was one of the most spectacular surprises of the nineteenth century. While the process itself was occurring, it attracted a great deal of attention from the outside world and was interpreted as being a factor of major importance in foreign and perhaps in world politics. The Western peoples of that time found it supremely easy to accept the simple dogma of their own absolute superiority to all other civilizations, and they were therefore able to explain Japan's adaptation of a Western state form in the primitive positive statement that the Japanese were trying to catch up with civilization.

To us of the twentieth century Japan's adaptation must necessarily appear to be a more intricate process. We do not have the naïve confidence in our own superiority enjoyed by our great-grandfathers. We do not accept history as a continual straight line from backwardness to progress, nor even as a spiral in which we represent the unqualified best produced by the human race. It is possible for people in the mid-twentieth century, even from the advantage of the Western World, to review the change from Shogunate to modern empire without being circumscribed by the assumption that the *Shōgun's* government was *in esse* quaint and backward and that the European style of government was progressive and modern.

Furthermore, present-day observers have the advantage of knowing what happened when the Japanese did make "progress." We realize, as our forefathers did not, that the progress led not only to horse cars in the streets of Tokyo, but to torpedo warplanes in the Hawaiian skies. Far more than our predecessors we understand the prices which nations must pay for change of any kind. By bitter experience we have learned to dread the momentum of mechanical and technological change which is not geared to a corresponding degree of spiritual or ideological development. Many of us are dismayed by the coexistence of the nation-state and atomic weapons;

dismayed or not we understand that the nation-state cannot be willed away by the hopeful expectations of well-meaning men; neither can atomic weapons be wiped out of existence because of a belief that the world would be better off without them. Perhaps it can be said that we are to so sensitive a degree the victims of our own civilization that we have learned to discriminate. Discriminating, we can afford to look back at the Japanese acceptance of the European empire in a critical frame of mind and can permit ourselves the intellectual refinement of asking what the Japanese got out of it.

Japanization as Repetition. Western observers of the mid-twentieth century can afford to take into account the elementary but overwhelming fact that what occurred in Japan in the years 1868-89 was far more a *Japanization* of European influences than a *Westernization* of Japan. The assumption was made very widely that political institutions were such profound determinatives to national existence that the mere change of the most overt political mechanism in Japan automatically transformed Japanese culture beneath it. Not until the period of Japanese militarism did most Westerners begin to understand that what had happened in Japan was far less a transformation of the Japanese social and public motives and behavior than a shallow Japanization of a few of the most obvious political instruments.

Like any other insight, this evaluation of the Meiji transformation as a Japanizing process applied to Western forms, rather than a Westernizing process applied to Japanese substance, can be overstressed. The most striking feature about the Meiji epoch to anyone contemplating the spectacle of Japan in defeat and occupation is the repetitiveness of fundamental Japanese politico-cultural processes. To paraphrase the late Gertrude Stein, one can say that, in Japan, what happened in 645 happened in 1868 happened in 1945. . . . The events and the controversies change; the social responses and the deeply ingrained cultural patterns remain.

The Meiji Restoration is strikingly important, viewed from the past, as a repetition of the Taika reforms of 645; viewed from the present, the Meiji Restoration is important as a precursor to the reconstitution of Japan after 1945. In contrast with the chaos and uncertainty which has overtaken so much of the rest of the world, what has become most striking of all is not that Japan should have changed, but that Japan should have remained so continuously Japanese despite the convulsiveness of the changes.

Contemporaneous Interpretations. Even among the leaders of the Restoration movement there were two quite different views as to its meaning. To conservatives it was a Revival of the Ancient Regime (*Ōsei Fukko*); to radicals, it was the Meiji Renovation (*Meiji Ishin*). Sometimes the two factors were almost perfectly blended. The dismantlement of the Tokugawa Shogunate was, for instance, both a restoration of antiquity and a step toward modernism. On other occasions the two interpretations broke apart and their proponents struggled for dominance. Both trends were plainly visible in the new attitude toward foreign relations. Both were apparent in the character of Japan's new leadership, in the settlement of the fate of the Tokugawa, in the sweeping aside of feudal institutions left over from the *Bakufu,* and in the creation of new governmental machinery.

Even the conservatives could not turn the clock all the way back to the years before A.D. 1192. The Imperialist faction gave up its bitter anti-foreignism, partly because the old Kōmei Emperor died and the new Meiji Emperor took over, partly because even the most rabid Imperialist could not explain how the foreign nations could be wiped out of real life existence. The anti-foreign propping which the supporters of the Throne had used to embarrass the *Shōgun* was discarded. The new government inherited the treaties signed in behalf of Japan by the Tokugawa and discreetly took the advice of the resident French and British ministers, abandoning anti-foreign activities.

The exclusionists had revived the dormant tradition of Japan as a divine land; those who had argued for intercourse saw Japan's destiny fitted into the world at large. Those who had become aware of conditions abroad emphasized the argument that the country had to be opened in order to avoid war; at the same time, the majority of those who stood for exclusion also wished to avoid war. Both earnestly desired to preserve Japan's independence. Thus, the early national consciousness of Meiji leaders inherited from the exclusionists doctrines of conservatism (*hoshuron*) verging on chauvinism (*taigai-kōkyoron*) and from the anti-exclusionists a doctrine of cultural progress and enlightenment (*bummei-kaika*). The blend of these policies enriched the character of modern Japanese nationalism. The Japanese writer, Kada Tetsuji, concluded, "In this point is found the unique characteristic of Japanese social thought." [1]

The Self-Dismantling Feudalism. The Japanese model of Europe involved the dismantling of the special kind of centralized feudalism established under the centuries of the Tokugawa. In practical but paradoxical terms, that meant that the clans which took over were responsible for the abolition of clans as such. In Japan it was young *samurai,* partly feudal, partly anti-feudal, who dismantled feudalism in order to establish a new and more powerful method for the exploitation of political, economic, and social power—in the interest of their nation, of themselves as individuals, and of that part of their class which could adapt itself to the new circumstances. The important feature of this change is that some feudal leaders managed to create a new kind of power while they knocked away the scaffolding of their old feudal privileges; it is almost as though a fraction of the first two Estates had led the French Revolution, possessing enough intelligence and imaginativeness to assure their physical and party-political control of the revolutionary Republic, or as if the Southern slave owners

[1] Kada, *Meiji shoki shakai-keizai shisō shi,* cited, p. 31.

had become seriously divided, some taking the lead in abolition so as to use the funds from compensated enfranchisement to change themselves from the owners of Negro man power to being the proprietors of natural resources and capital goods.

Persons from the clans controlled the new regime, but they left the legal and, to a considerable degree, the social cohesion of the old clans behind them. Indeed it is often said that the pre-eminence of the Chōshū and Satsuma clans in the new government was so great that they erected what amounted to a new Shogunate. The first decade of the Meiji was dominated by Satsuma with Saigō Takamori and Ōkubo Toshimichi in control; during the next ten years leadership centered in the Chōshū, which furnished Kido Takayoshi, Itō Hirobumi, Inoue Kaoru, and Yamagata Aritomo. Hizen was represented by Ōkuma Shigenobu. In the military services Chōshū soon gained control of the new army, and Satsuma that of the navy. Much of the ensuing politics of the Meiji era was thereafter marked by a struggle on the part of outsiders to rid the government of domination by the Sat-Chō combination.

Who were the outsiders? The outsiders were other lords, particularly those drawn from the *kuge* nobility, who made it possible for the leading Outer Clans to organize a new government. Since no clan was powerful enough to assume the position vacated by the Tokugawa or to defy the tradition of unbroken Imperial rule, authority was once again returned to the Emperor. The particular personal talents of the Meiji Emperor speeded up this return. As time went on the area from which government personnel were drawn steadily widened, but the role of the oligarchy remained disproportionately high.

The oligarchy, most authoritatively explained for American readers by Professor Reischauer, was drawn from the *kuge,* to a limited extent from former *Bakufu* leaders, and from *samurai* of the Satsuma, Chōshū, Hizen, and Tosa clans. The whole upper class of Japan can be estimated as not more than 7 per cent of the total population; the oligarchy, as identified by Reischauer, was only a small fraction of that upper class.[2] In terms of personal rather than institutional succession, the oligarchy persisted down to the surrender of Japan in 1945.

Imperial Restoration. In January, 1868, the young Emperor issued his Restoration Rescript. All offices of the Tokugawa regime were abolished; a provisional machinery of government was set up. Immediately following promulgation of the Rescript a conference was held in the Imperial palace in Kyoto to decide the method of disposing the Tokugawa family.[3] Moderates represented by Yamanouchi Lord of Tosa approved the abolition of the Shogunate, but felt that the former *Shōgun* should personally participate

[2] Reischauer, *Japan: Government-Politics,* cited, p. 64, fn. 6.

[3] A dramatic description of this conference is presented in Chap. I, "Coup d'Etat," of Ike, *op. cit.*, pp. 3-6.

in the conference and in the provisional government. But the balance of power had shifted to the Sat-Chō forces who were represented at the conference by a court noble, Iwakura Tomomi. The conference decided to force the former *Shōgun* to resign his court position and to surrender his fiefs to the Throne. This drastic procedure helped precipitate a rather unsystematic civil war which dragged on for eighteen months until the Tokugawa forces were completely worsted by the new armies of the provisional government under Satsuma and Chōshū leadership.

In the field of domestic administration the provisional regime faced an urgent need to choose between a *hōken* system of centralized feudalism and a *gunken* system of national prefectures and counties. The idea of some kind of federation of clan areas persisted in plans considered as late as the second year of Meiji, but the majority of the new leaders set about uprooting the old political forms. Their first moves included the retrocession of fiefs (*hanseki-hōkan*) and the immediate substitution of prefectural for clan administration (*haihan-chiken*).

Thus, the daimiates a thousand years in the growing died in a month.

The moves to abolish fiefs forever were partly motivated by financial reasons: the new government needed the direct revenue which had been collected by the various *daimyō*. Abolition was also inspired by the political assumption, retrospectively quite properly made, that independent daimiates could also provide the political bases for revolt. The first steps of conversion were engineered by Iwakura and Ōkubo, who convinced first the *daimyō* of Satsuma; by Kido, who persuaded Chōshū; and then by Ōkubo and Kido, who talked the *daimyō* of Tosa into petitioning the Throne in 1869 to accept their holdings. It is obvious that the four Sat-Chō-Hi-To lords relinquished their power in its old form only in anticipation of acquiring even more power in the new government; it is nevertheless a tribute to their intelligence that they understood the opportunity.

Actual planning of the conversion was not done by the *daimyō* as principals, but by *samurai* loyal to them, acting as agents; these *samurai* immediately rewarded themselves for their own statesmanship in effecting the change. High positions in the new government were found for Itagaki Taisuke of Tosa, Saigō Takamori of Satsuma, and Ōkuma Shigenobu of Hizen.

In practical economic terms, the *daimyō* received from the new government an annual pension of one tenth their nominal income, while being relieved of the need to support their retainers; they were also allowed to shift their debts to the new government. For most of them this amounted to the wiping out of complicated old balance sheets and the prescription of clean-cut new assets instead.

The Modern Nobility. At the same time the titles *kuge* and *daimyō* were abolished, both court nobles and feudal lords were transformed into *kazoku* (peers; literally, "flowering families"). Clan *samurai* were given the class name *shizoku* (gentry). As early as 1871 intermarriage between these upper classes and the common people (*heimin*) was permitted.

At first the transition seemed to be one of hollow titles, since former *daimyō* were appointed governors of new prefectures. The personal feudal relationship of lord and governed carried on. In 1871 the Emperor was coached to summon the ex-*daimyō* of the remaining seventy-six fiefs and to proclaim the direct control of the national government over the new prefectures. Even this reform did not uproot the feudal nobility; indeed, it gave to the more enterprising members of that nobility the opportunity to escape limitations on their ambitions which had hitherto been set by geographical frontiers of their respective daimiates. Many of them soon appeared in high government office. By 1884 *kazoku* had become a real peerage. After 1889 substantial constitutional power was assigned to them in the new constitutional House of Peers.

The Japanese nobility acquiescing in their own dispossession put their new opportunities to good use. Since the old world was bankrupt they bought bargain shares of stock in the new. Many of them bought government lands which were offered for sale at fantastically cheap prices. Others became stockholders and industrialists in the new money-based economy. In the case of the new national banks, for example, as of 1880 peers and gentry held 32 million out of 42 million *yen* total valuation of stock—76 per cent of the entire issue.[4]

The Fate of the *Samurai*. While the nobility accepted the change-over in good grace, the ordinary *samurai* did not fare nearly so well. A few outstanding individuals moved into capitalist enterprises or into government careers; some of them became important contributors to the creation of a new Japan. Most of the *samurai* found their nominal incomes the same as their actual ones. They were bewildered and discontented. Particularly outrageous to them was the promulgation of conscription laws which extended the precious privilege of carrying weapons to all able-bodied men.[5]

Nothing makes members of a social stratum more embittered than the necessity of sharing their own uncertain privileges with the members of strata below them. Relative privilege, like relative deprivation, can keep a

[4] Donald H. Shively, "The Rehabilitation of the Japanese Peerage, 1884," an unpublished paper read before the Far Eastern Association, April 14, 1950, Ann Arbor, Mich. Norman, *op. cit.*, p. 100, gives a breakdown, by social classes, of shareholders in the National Banks in 1880.

[5] On March 8, 1874, a missionary-educator wrote a letter to his colleague, William Elliot Griffis, describing conditions in Fukui, in north-central Japan: "Merchants & Farmers all look as happy as can be, taxes are easy for them they say now and they can save coin while the samurai look as sour as can be, all have different minds, some want the old feudal system in Fukui, ⅔ or so, the other ⅓ don't know what they want I fear. Everybody carries a sword now and slowly are becoming uncivilized in appearance as ever, some run the thing into the ground, and carry two." E. H. Mudgett to W. E. Griffis, Fukui, March, 8, 1874, from the Griffis Papers, Folio No. 32, Rutgers University Library, New Brunswick, New Jersey. Chitoshi Yanaga, *Japan Since Perry,* New York, 1949, especially Chaps. 3 and 4, provides a detailed history of these problems; a map on p. 64 locates various rebellions and disturbances between 1874 and 1886.

class contented for a long time as long as the familiar patterns which provide social and emotional security are not breached. In the case of the *samurai,* the foundations of their class were broken downward and they were not given commissioned status *en masse* in the new army, nor otherwise transferred to a new privileged position.

Samurai discontent underlay the rebellion of 1874-77 and numerous other disturbances, 1881-86. Politically there was a growing division of opinion over the course on which Japan should develop. This division had become apparent in 1871-72 during the agitation for a punitive expedition against Korea. Those in the government who took the long view—men like Kido, Iwakura, and Ōkubo—thought that Japan would progress faster by internal reconstruction and industrialization along Western lines, rather than by policies of international adventure. Cliques outside the government argued for forceful expansion, starting with Korea.

Although the government circumvented the Korea question, it yielded to demands for a Formosan expedition in 1874. This limited military release did not draw off the energy of growing *samurai* discontent. The government had broken faith with the *samurai* when it proclaimed the compulsory commutation of *samurai* pensions in August, 1876. The *samurai,* deprived of their old status and cheated out of the meager pension which had been offered them instead, gave last expression to their class status in supporting the Satsuma rebellion of 1877. When this was smashed the *samurai* were largely liquidated as a class (in the original sociological sense of that term). In rural areas, of course, *samurai* tended to retain prestige and remained something more than a multitude of individuals with pleasant genealogical memories.

Unchanged Peasantry. Significantly, the class to change least in this period was the peasantry. The masters of Japan may have changed roles, but the agricultural majority, never less than 75 per cent of the total population, faced the same old grind.[6]

Agriculture had been the root of Japanese economic life under the Tokugawa. Despite the industrialization undertaken during the Meiji regime, agriculture remained the chief occupation in Japan. Indeed, agriculture still is the chief support of a majority of Japanese. The transformations which appeared to take place in Japan were more adaptations by Japan of external institutions than shifts involving the entire adult population.

Legal emancipation brought two important results. Economically, the right of mobility made it possible for the peasants to shift about and for some of them to become factory workers. Politically, the privilege of bearing arms made it possible for peasant youths to become conscript soldiers.

[6] Ishii Ryoichi, *Population Pressure and Economic Life in Japan,* London, 1937, pp. 77-81, offers an estimate of the proportion of farmers in the total population. Opposition to the Government from the Right and from the Left was described by the (later purged) Soviet authors, O. Tanin and E. Yohan, *Militarism and Fascism in Japan,* New York, 1934, Chap. 1, pp. 25-35.

Although inevitably some peasants made their individual ways upward in the new society, the peasantry as a whole did not face substantial change in its economic or political position.

Against this, however, must be placed the factor of sociological change. The Japanese peasantry participated with the rest of Japan in the opening up of the country, in the advent of railroads and other modern methods of communication and transportation, in the use of modern currency and postal facilities, and in the modernization of education which extended literacy to them on a scale not equaled by any other Asiatic working class.

Stimulated by change and promise, disappointed by the meagerness of tangible reward, peasant unrest generated two contradictory ideological forces. Some peasant spokesmen became revolutionary anti-feudal and sought further abolition of ancient privileges. Other spokesmen were blindly reactionary, opposing innovations which threatened the security offered in its own way by their familiar poverty.

Government Under the Charter Oath. The Charter Oath of Five Articles (*Gokajō no Goseimon*) of 1868 is a brief homiletic document reminiscent of the initial proclamation of Shōtoku Taishi. Its provisions, general in outlook and moral in tone, certainly did not prescribe particular organs of government.

For the interim practical administration was moved from the centuries-old capital at Edo to the even more ancient pseudo-capital of Kyoto, and placed under a provisional administration—the so-called "Three Offices."

This provisional government set up in January, 1868, was more significant in personnel than in organization. The *Sanshoku* consisted of a Supreme Head (*Sōsai*) who was a prince of the Imperial family and two sets of counselors (*Gijō* and *Sanyo*) who were headed by *kuge*. Under the three offices, counselorships were divided equally among *kuge, daimyō,* and *samurai* to the exclusion of the Tokugawa. In theory the Imperial family and the court nobles dominated the new government. In actuality, the real leaders were content to work behind the screen. Outer clansmen were in a position of real leadership except for the representatives of Chōshū, who were technically in disgrace for the conspiracy to "kidnap" the Kōmei Emperor in 1864.

In February, 1868, while hostilities in the field continued between the Tokugawa and the new government, an administrative reorganization was begun. The *Gijō* branch was revamped. The provisional government, marching toward a European form, responded to an ancient stimulus and established the seven departments of the *T'ang* model of empire. To this there was added a board of counselors. In theory this gave the newly born government an executive (*Sōsai*), an administrative facility (*Gijō*), and an advisory body (the *Sanyo*).[7] Chart 13 presents an outline of successive

[7] As the Preamble to what was supposed to be Japan's first modern constitution later put it: "These arrangements, made during a time of civil commotion, were necessarily hur-

administrative reforms between January, 1868, and the formation of a modern cabinet, 1885.

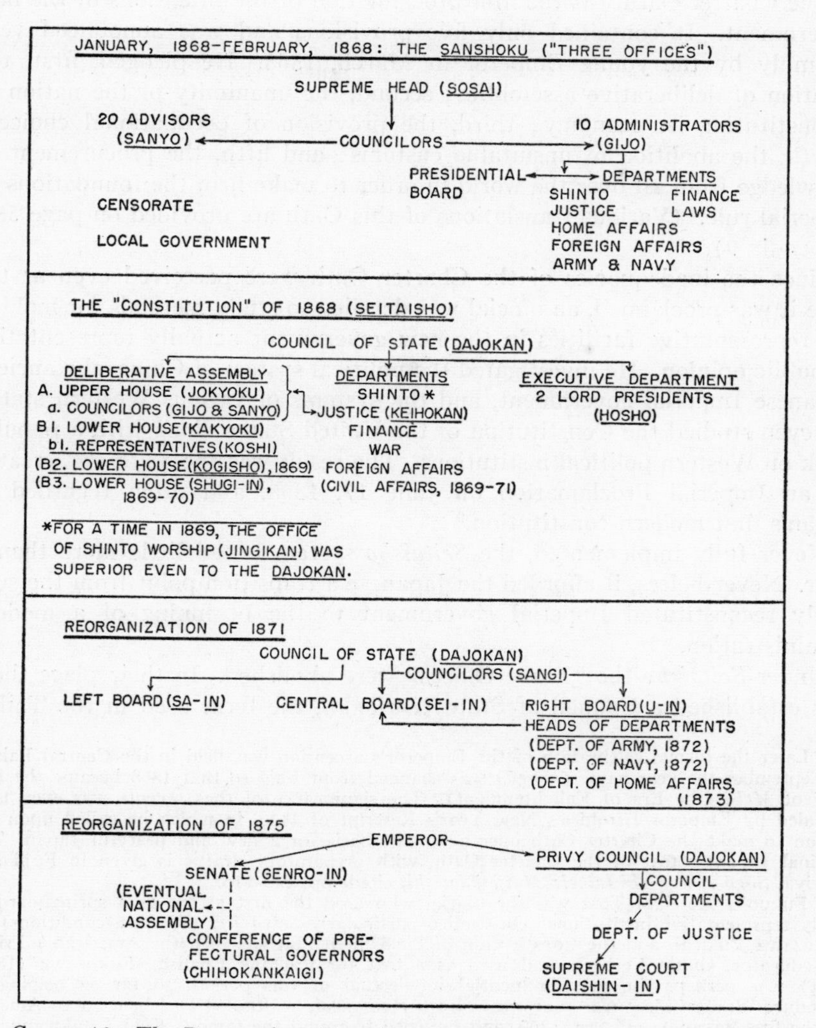

CHART 13—The Restoration: Experiment in Political Forms. Evolution of Central Administrative Structure: Jan., 1868-1885

Along with the reactivation of the Empire after a thousand years' dormancy, the new leaders experimented with the idea of a deliberative assembly. In part, such an assembly had the appeal of being foreign and modern. Internally it obtained the support of Tosa clansmen who wanted to share

ried and imperfect." (*JGD*, cited, p. 7.) The original orders governing former feudal territories are to be found on p. 10; for the structure of the "Three Offices," pp. 4-6.

power with the Sat-Chō forces. The government proper was trying to accommodate Tokugawa remnants and to obtain wide support.

The Charter Oath was the first proclamation of the intentions of the new government. It contained only five provisions and was announced very solemnly by the young Emperor in March, 1868. He pledged, first, the creation of deliberative assemblies; second, the unanimity of the nation in reconstituting its economy; third, the provision of occupational choices; fourth, the abolition of unsuitable customs; and fifth, the procurement of knowledge from all over the world in order to make firm the foundations of Imperial rule. (Various translations of this Oath are provided on page 584, Appendix 9).[8]

Since the inadequacies of the Charter Oath were perceived even at the time it was proclaimed, an official was detailed to study methods for making the representative facilities in the new government actually representative of public opinion. He investigated the political system of China, the ancient Japanese Imperial government, and the systems of various Western states. He even studied the Constitution of the United States along with a popular book on Western political institutions. The result was the *Seitaisho,* created by an Imperial Proclamation on June 17, 1868, and often regarded as Japan's first modern constitution.[9]

Never fully implemented, the *Seitaisho* system lasted little more than a year. Nevertheless, it afforded the Japanese a transition point from the suddenly reconstituted Imperial government to the beginning of a modern administration.

Under *Seitaisho* the "Three Offices" were abolished. In their place there was established a Council of State (*Dajōkan,* the term used in the Taika-

[8] Later the formal celebration of the Emperor's ascension was held in the Central Palace. In September the year-name *(nengō)* was changed from *Keiō* so that 1868 became the first year of *Meiji* (the Era of Enlightenment). The significance of these events was even later revealed by Emperor Hirohito's New Year's Rescript of 1946, in which he called upon the nation to make the Charter Oath once again the basis for a new and peaceful Japan. The original Japanese text of the Charter Oath, with preparatory drafts, is given in Fujii and Moriya, *Sōgō Nihon shi taikei: Meiji jidai shi,* cited, pp. 213-216.

[9] Fukuoka Kōtei of Tosa was the official who used the first article as a springboard to study representative institutions. He studied particularly *Seiyō jijō* (Western conditions) by Fukuzawa Yukichi, and the Constitution of the United States, which the American missionary-educator, Guido Verbeck, had used as a text for teaching English. Fukuzawa (1835-1901) was perhaps the most influential intellectual of this period, so far as helping to introduce Western ideas was concerned. Born a *samurai,* he studied Dutch, went to America on the first Japanese mission, 1860, and returned to found the famous Keiō Gijuku, nucleus of modern Keiō University. His most famous publication was *Seiyō jijō* (1866). It is significant that Fukuzawa's works, subject to criticism during Japan's period of thought control, have enjoyed a post-World War II renaissance. W. E. Griffis, biographer of Verbeck, wrote that the two documents in English used most by the educator were the New Testament and the American Constitution. Both Soyejima Taneomi and Ōkuma Shigenobu (Hizen) were his pupils. *Verbeck of Japan; A Citizen of No Country,* New York, 1900, pp. 124-125. For an authoritative essay by Fukuoka on the origins of the *Gokajō no Goseimon* and the *Seitaisho,* see *Kokka gakkai, kokka gakkai soritsu mansanjūnen kinen Meiji kensei keizai shiron* (Association of political and social science, essays on the constitutional and economic history of the Meiji era commemorating the thirtieth anniversary of the establishment of the association), Tōkyō, 1919. For the *Seitaisho* Proclamation, see *JGD,* pp. 7-15.

Taihō structure). The *Dajōkan* included legislative, executive, and judicial authority. Provision was made under this system for a two-house legislature; the limit of authority of the lower house is made apparent by the provision that it could not legislate but was to be permitted to *discuss* subjects when ordered to do so by the upper house. The upper house, composed of the former *Gijō* and *Sanyo* counselors, was safely in the hands of the reconstituted nobility. The lower house never really materialized.[10] Clan delegates (*kōshi*) met during the summer of 1868 on a provisional basis, but their meeting was abolished nominally *ad interim,* but actually forever, in the autumn of the same year. A committee of the *kōshi* came up with regulations for a new deliberative assembly, the *Kōgisho.*

The *Kōgisho* was one of the most remarkable parliaments ever assembled. It met only briefly in the two years, 1869-70, changing its name in its second session to National Assembly (*Shūgi-in*). Since no one in Japan understood parliamentary debate, the *Kōgisho* members had to figure out parliamentarianism from the ground up. They did get so far as to organize committees like a true legislature and to establish forty-six procedural regulations. The oddity of the *Kōgisho* consisted chiefly of the source of its membership. The representatives were the delegates of 276 feudal clans.

The *Seitaisho* system was set aside in August, 1869, in favor of a transitional device consisting of two outstanding offices (the *Dajōkan,* or Council of State; and the *Jingikan,* or Office of *Shintō* Worship) and six functional departments. This was a direct copy of the model of A.D. 701.[11]

Direct Imperial Government. Successive experiments in premature representative forms ended with the abolition of feudalism. From 1871 onward the government was firmly in control of the nobles who had promoted the restoration. As counselors (*Sangi*) they completely dominated the upper chamber and the administrative departments. With archaic Chinese terminology the government was called by the name of "Boards"—the upper chamber being the "Central Board" (*Sei-in*), the administrative departments collectively, a "Right Board" (*U-in*), and a lower chamber, the "Left Board" (*Sa-in,* successor to the *Shūgi-in*). The lower body was not even representa-

[10] The interlocking directorate is illustrated by a summary of personnel in the new government (June 11, 1868—August 15, 1869): a total of 21 men were appointed *Gijō*—9 Court Nobles (including Iwakura Tomomi and Sanjō Saneyoshi) and 12 territorial nobles (*daimyō* of family representatives from Satsuma, Chōshū, Tosa, Hizen, Echizen, Aki, Awa, Owari, Bizen, Kumamoto, Inaba, Uwajima); a total of 22 were appointed *Sanyo*—3 Court Nobles, the heir to the Kumamoto fief, the *daimyō* of Hizen and of Aki, and 16 lower *samurai* (5 Satsuma, 2 Chōshū, 4 Tosa, 3 Hizen, 1 Kumamoto, and 1 Echizen). Professor Robert A. Wilson of the University of California at Los Angeles concluded: "Thus, in contrast to the theory expressed in the Seitaisho, the Deliberative Assembly and the Executive Department were, in reality, one organ of government exercising policy-making and executing powers." "The Seitaisho: A Constitutional Experiment," *Far Eastern Quarterly,* Vol. XI, No. 3 (May, 1952), p. 301.

[11] Prince Sanjō Saneyoshi later admitted that the reorganization in the summer of 1869 was faithfully copied from the *Taihō* Code of 701 (for the original structure, see p. 283); *JGD,* p. 91.

tive of the clans and was much more a committee for research into constitutions than a legislature.

Modern Ministries. In 1872 separate departments of the army and the navy were created in anticipation of the universal conscription ordinance of 1873. Garrisons had already been established in the key cities. Two outstanding leaders, Yamagata Aritomo and Saigō Takamori, had been sent to Europe to study methods of military organization.

A new department of Home Affairs was created in 1873. Under the direction of Ōkubo Toshimichi the department vastly improved internal administration and public finances, established model enterprises and other facilities to increase national income. Probably most important, so far as the economy was concerned, was the briefly established (1870-1885) *Kōbushō,* or Department of Industry. Acting as central coordinating agency in the process of industrialization from above, the *Kōbushō* handled technological education; supervised all mining enterprises; constructed and maintained railroads, telegraph lines, and lighthouses; built and repaired naval and mercantile ships; engaged in light metals and machine construction; and undertook land and sea surveys.[12]

In the 1870's and 1880's the other government departments moved rapidly forward from their shell of ancient Chinese nomenclature to the kernel of European-type administration as the requisite personnel underwent modern education and as the Japanese increasingly learned how to do things in a modern fashion.

Senate and Court. In 1875 a conference of Japanese leaders was held to reconsider the position of the government and to obtain unity between the different restorationist factions. The Imperial Rescript of April 14, 1875, resulted.[13] The *Dajōkan* was retained, but there was added a *Genrō-in,* a sort of senate, with its membership entirely appointed. This body was authorized only to consider whatever the council of state placed before it. Membership was restricted to (1) nobles, (2) persons then or formerly first- and second-class bureaucrats, (3) persons who had rendered meritorious service to the state, and (4) persons of political or legal knowledge and experience. With a few additions, these criteria later became the qualifications for the House of Peers.

The other innovation was a Supreme Court or *Daishin-in,* which succeeded in providing a focal point for the rapid transformation of the legal system.

Both these institutions remained until the proclamation of the Meiji Constitution.

[12] Norman, cited, p. 129, fn. 65.

[13] The conference was held in Osaka in January, 1875. The Rescript began: "It is Our desire not to restrict Ourselves to the maintenance of the five principles which We swore to preserve, but to go still further and enlarge the circle of domestic reforms. With this in view We now establish the *Genrō-in* to enact laws for the Empire, and the *Daishin-in* to consolidate the judicial authority of the courts." *JGD,* pp. 41-42.

Intellectual Movements and Political Groups. Once the Meiji experiment had been launched, there was little disagreement among educated and intelligent Japanese as to the basic policies for the country to follow. All groups agreed in seeking as a final objective the combination of the rich country and the strong defense (*fukoku kyōhei*). Successive schools of thought differed only in the timing and degree of modernization and improvisation which they recommended.[14] One group accepted the ideas of British utilitarianism, stimulated by the translation of John Stuart Mill's *On Liberty* (translated in 1871). Another group followed an American Protestant and capitalist outlook. A third group became enthusiastic exponents of French theories of popular sovereignty, notably of Rousseau's *Social Contract* (translated in 1877). Other Japanese introduced ideas of socialism, although it was an American missionary, the Reverend Dwight Whitney Learned, who was probably the first man to lecture on socialism in Japan.[15]

In counteracting the effect of such heady doctrines, the senate (*Genrō-in*) went so far as to have the works of Edmund Burke translated as a palliative to the effects of too much Rousseau.

A practical stimulus to the swift development of constitutional progress was provided by the goad of the unequal treaties—treaties originally signed by the Tokugawa regime with all the Western powers. These treaties, comparable to the unequal treaties which the same powers had signed with China, removed all Western citizens from Japanese jurisdiction, gave Japanese approval to the operation of Western courts in Japanese territory, and transferred the control of special Western municipalities within Japanese ports to foreign governments. The test for all progress came to be Japan's capacity to develop a government capable of meeting the standards expected by the outside powers, thus providing Japan with a justification for asking the abolition of the unequal treaties.

While Saigō Takamori was drifting toward outright rebellion, Itagaki Taisuke taught constitutional politics to Japan by playing the game of poli-

[14] All the schools of thought had several things in common in addition to an agreement on the need for *fukoku kyōhei:* all agreed on the need for rapid transformation, technological, if not cultural; each rested on its own body of foreign thought. Indeed, the first decade of Meiji has often been called the Age of Translation. It would be impossible to list all works translated. Yoshino Sakuzō, ed., *Meiji bunka zenshū* (Meiji cultural collection), Tōkyō, 1928-30, 24 vols., is the basic source for materials on all aspects of early Meiji culture; Vol. VIII on politics includes translations of works by Mill, Hobbes, Rousseau, and other Western thinkers; a chronological list of political treatises and translations (1867-1894) is added in an appendix. For briefer analyses, see Kada, *Meiji shoki shakai-keizai shisō shi,* cited, Part VII ("Major literature"), pp. 875 ff.; Professor Honjō contributed an essay on Europeanized thought before and after the Restoration in *Keizai ronsō* (Economic review), Vol. L, No. 5 (May, 1940). In English, Ike, *op. cit.,* Chap. X, "Intellectual Currents," pp. 111-123, covers the same ground.

[15] When a Japanese student, Kimura Takeshi, later named Dr. Learned a "hidden benefactor to Japanese socialism," he stirred up an academic hornets' nest: *"Nihon shakaishūgi shijō no kakureta onjin: Dōshisha no Raneddo shi"* (A hidden benefactor in the history of Japanese socialism: Mr. Learned of Doshisha), *Shakai mondai kōza* (Studies in social problems), Vol. III, pp. 127-131. For a post-World War II discussion of this point, see the autobiography of the old war-horse socialist: *Abe Isoo jijoden, shakaishūgisha to naru made* (Autobiography of Abe Isoo, until becoming a socialist), Tōkyō, 1947.

tics very skillfully indeed. He had founded the Patriotic Public Party in Tokyo, disbanded it under government oppression in 1874, memorialized the government in the same year for the creation of representative facilities,[16] re-established the party once in Tosa and once in Osaka under different names, and disbanded it when he was himself taken into the government in 1875. (Some of the names under which the party is mentioned in historical accounts are *Aikoku Kōtō, Risshisha, Aikokusha.*) Itagaki's manipulations thoroughly aroused public opinion, and by 1879 his group was able to petition the Emperor for the opening of a national assembly.[17] A genealogical chart of Japan's pre-World War II political parties will be found on page 357.

The governmental concessions for representative government were more modest. In 1875 a Conference of Prefectural Governments (*Chihōkankaigi*) was convoked to give advice on matters of local interest. In 1878 a narrow electorate, based on property qualifications, was permitted to vote for prefectural assemblies (*Fu-Ken Kai*). In 1880 the privilege to elect assemblies was extended to cities, towns, and villages. Just to be on the safe side, the Meiji bureaucracy simultaneously centralized its police system and proclaimed laws regulating the use of the press, the holding of meetings, and the censorship of speeches.

The Beginning of Parties. The year 1881 was a year of upsets in the development of Japanese political parties. The bureaucracy exposed itself to public opinion when a swindle was uncovered in the Hokkaido Colonization Office. Ōkuma so bitterly attacked the scandal that he became *persona non grata* with the other councilors and, like Itagaki, turned to the formation of political parties.[18] Itagaki established Japan's first modern party, the Liberal Party (*Jiyūtō*) at an organizational meeting in Tokyo on October 18, 1881. Ōkuma followed him with the establishment of the Constitu-

[16] Itagaki's memorial argued, in brief, for: (1) reform of the government—specifically, the establishment of a "council-chamber"—to check the arbitrary will of the bureaucracy and to return power to the Throne and people where it belonged; (2) recognition of the principle, "no representation, no taxation"; (3) broader participation in the government by the people, as a means of providing the "culture and intelligence" which, it was claimed by the bureaucrats, the people lacked; (4) unification of government and people, through a Council-chamber, to make the state strong; (5) wise imitation of foreign "contrivances" of government (including a parliament), with suitable adaptations. A translation of the text is given in *JGD,* pp. 426-433; for Katō's reply, *ibid.,* pp. 433-439.

[17] The memorial of 1879 was preceded by a *Risshisha* proclamation of 1877; see *JGD,* pp. 457-480. For growth and change in the liberal movement, see Nakayama Yasumasa, Editor, *Shimbun hūsei Meiji hennen shi* (A chronological Meiji history compiled from the newspapers), Tōkyō, 1935, Vol. VI, cited by Ike, *op. cit.,* who summarizes the details in Chaps. VI and VII.

[18] Although eventually forced from the government, Ōkuma effected cancellation of the Hokkaido property sale and, more significantly, forced from the government a promise to convoke an Assembly by 1890, in the Imperial Rescript for the Establishment of a Diet, October 12, 1881. With this concession came a stern warning: "We perceive that the tendency of Our people is to advance too rapidly, and without that thought and consideration which alone can make progress enduring, and We warn Our Subjects, high and low, to be mindful of Our will, and that those who may advocate sudden and violent changes, thus disturbing the peace of Our realm, will fall under Our displeasure." *JGD,* pp. 86-87.

tional Progressive Party (*Rikken Kaishintō,* or more commonly *Kaishintō*) on March 14, 1882. An embryonic socialist party was formed in the same year. The government officials, seeing what was happening, went into the party business themselves, founding the Constitutional Imperial Party (*Rikken Teiseitō*) also in 1882.[19]

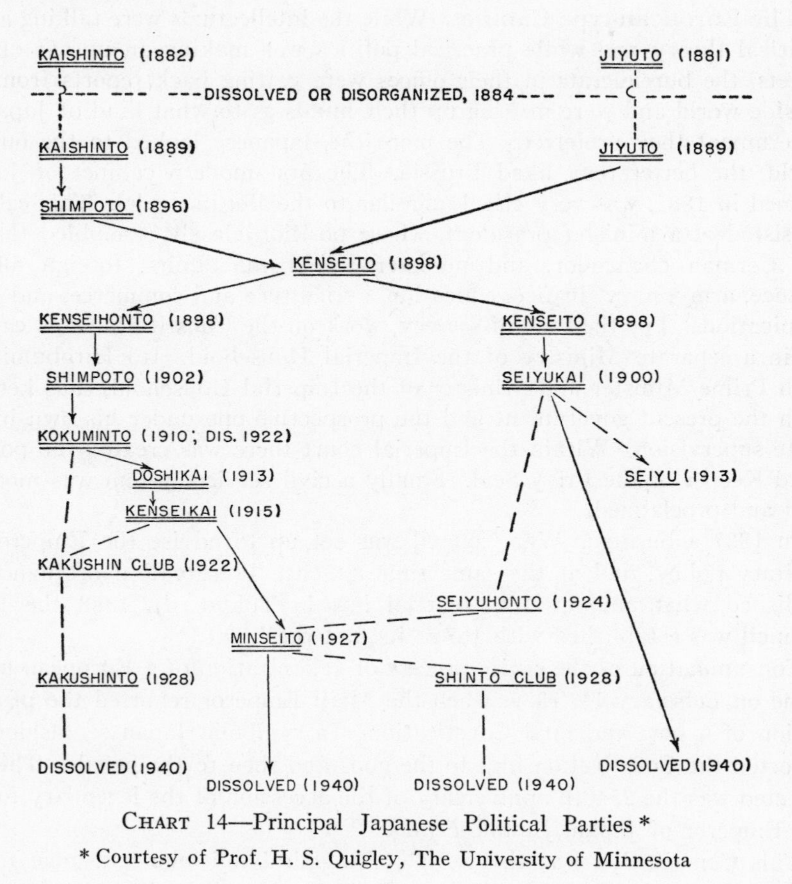

CHART 14—Principal Japanese Political Parties *

* Courtesy of Prof. H. S. Quigley, The University of Minnesota

These parties were loosely representative of potential economic groupings. The Liberal Party drew strength from rural landlords. The Progressive Party was backed by the larger financial interests. A group of the Liberals broke off to found a so-called Rickshaw Party, but they, like the Socialists, were politically ineffectual. The government's Imperial Party was supported chiefly by the bureaucracy.

[19] For details in the history of these early parties, the monograph by Osatake Takeki, *Seitō no hattatsu* (The development of political parties), Tōkyō, 1935, although short and now in the category of a rare book, is invaluable. Ōkuma himself contributed to the essay, "The History of Political Parties in Japan," in *Fifty Years,* cited, Vol. I, pp. 150 ff. The best brief survey in English is Ike, *op. cit.,* Chaps. VIII and IX.

The party politics for the rest of the 1880's was lively, stimulating, confused, and hopelessly unrealistic. By 1885 the parties which had such promising beginnings were without exception in a condition of suppression or collapse. The government had moved more closely to the Prussian model and had ordered their dissolution.

The European-type Cabinet. While the intellectuals were talking about political theory and while practical politics was making an uproar on the streets, the bureaucrats in their offices were getting back reports from the outside world and were making up their minds as to what kind of Japanese government they preferred. The more the Japanese looked to the outside world, the better they liked Prussia. The first modern cabinet of Japan, formed in 1885, was very closely similar to the Berlin model. This cabinet consisted of a minister president, whose position closely resembled that of the German chancellor, and ministers for home affairs, foreign affairs, finance, army, navy, justice, education, agriculture and commerce, and communications. For the sake of secrecy, work on the Constitution was carried on in a separate Ministry of the Imperial Household. Itō Hirobumi was both Prime Minister and Minister of the Imperial Household, thus keeping both the present government and the prospective one under his own immediate supervision. Within the Imperial court there was created the post of Lord Keeper of the Privy Seal. Finally a civil service system was modernized and proclaimed.

In 1887 a Supreme War Council was set up to advise the Emperor on military policy, and at the same time a Peace Preservation ordinance established what amounted to martial law in Tokyo. In 1888 the Privy Council was established with Itō as its first president.[20]

Consummation of the entire process of Japanization of a European model came on February 11, 1889, when the Meiji Emperor reported the promulgation of a new and final Constitution. In symbolic Japanese fashion, he reported the Constitution first to the gods and then to the people. The day selected was the 2549th anniversary of the accession of the legendary founding Emperor of Japan, Jimmu *Tennō*.

This Constitution was the work of Itō Hirobumi who had gone to the United States in 1870 and had studied the American Constitution after obtaining a copy of it quite ceremoniously from Secretary of State Hamilton Fish. In 1882 Itō had headed another mission abroad to study constitutions. He spent most of his time in Germany and interviewed Bismarck. Itō was assisted by three other Japanese scholars and by a German lecturer at Tokyo Imperial University, Professor Hermann Roessler. Between May and December, 1888, the newly constituted Privy Council deliberated secretly

[20] And "with statesmen of tried calibre named as its members." *Japan Year Book, 1946-48,* cited, p. 73 (with a survey of the establishment of all these institutions). For further details, see *JGD,* pp. 32, 88-90, 97, 102-104, 127; and McLaren, *Political History,* cited, Chap. VIII.

over the drafts of the Constitution, with the Meiji Emperor himself taking part in the discussions.[21]

The new Constitution opened a distinct phase in Japanese political history, which will be considered in the chapters that follow. In retrospect it is perhaps too much to expect that the Meiji transformation should have effected a genuine Westernization of Japan. Perhaps one miracle at a time is enough. It is remarkable that the Japanese feudal leaders succeeded in modernizing enough of their technology and their administration to make their country the only Asian great power. The forms were Western in appearance, but the dynamics of development were, for both good and evil, Japanese.

[21] When the Constitution was finally promulgated, it was done in the Emperor's name. His Imperial Rescript read, in part: "Having, by virtue of the glories of Our Ancestors, ascended the Throne in lineal succession unbroken for ages eternal. . . . The rights of sovereignty of the State, We have inherited from Our Ancestors, and We shall bequeath them to Our descendants. Neither We nor they shall in future fail to wield them, in accordance with the provision of the Constitution hereby granted." Professor Harold S. Quigley gives an interesting and authoritative account of the drafting, based on personal interviews with Viscount Kaneko Kentarō, one of the three men most intimately associated with Itō, in *op. cit.,* Chap. III. Itō Myoji, trans., produced the authoritative analysis in English of Itō Hirobumi, *Commentaries on the Constitution of the Empire of Japan,* which will be referred to below. Dr. Hermann Roessler was appointed consultant to the Committee for the Drafting of the Constitution in March, 1884, when the work of drafting was begun. See Suzuki Yasuzō, *Kempō no rekishiteki kenkyū* (Historical studies on the constitution), Tōkyō, 1935; and *"Nihon kempō seitei ni taisuru Heruman Resureru no Kiyo"* (The contributions of Hermann Roessler to the establishment of the Japanese constitution), *Meiji bunka kenkyū* (Studies in Meiji culture), No. 5 (May, 1935). Reflective students of the Japanese political scene have wondered if the eventual constitutional pattern of Meiji Japan was not suprisingly like the structure which would have been produced, even without reference to foreign models and without the brief and abortive challenge by opposition parties. Such students would include Sir George Sansom, who discusses this point in his *The Western World,* cited, Chap. 13, p. 358; and Dr. Ike, "Democracy vs. Absolutism in Meiji Japan," unpublished paper read before the American Historical Association, Chicago, December 20, 1950.

CHAPTER
SIXTEEN

The Meiji Constitution

WITH the adoption of Europe as a model and with the acceptance of the role of a great power as the most civilized and progressive role for Japan to play, the leaders of the Restoration erected an acceptable façade of modern-looking and apparently Westernized government at the front of Japanese society. The bulk of the society remained Japanese in culture, tradition, and language—not to speak of such details as administrative habits, modes of legal thought, and day-by-day ideas of what specific governmental duties might involve.

Japan and Western Nationhood. The Japanese model of European government in Japan, the Europe grafted upon the pre-national Japanese nation, was not a sham. It was authentic, as authentic as the T'ang Exemplar had been in another age.

Constitutionally the most extraordinary singularity about modern Japan is Japan's peculiarly facile adoption of the nation-state as a mode of political existence. Japan had never been a real member of the Confucian family of nations, nor had Japan ever been a satrapy within the confines of the Chinese Empire proper.[1] Japan had been a nation *sans le savoir*. At the time that the nation-state was hammered out across centuries of bitter Western political experience, appearing at last as a proud artifact of the European peoples, Japan was naturally, and without conscious intent on the part of the Japanese, a close, although unwitting, equivalent of the European nation-state. All the other nations of East Asia had to lose their respective Asian political consciousnesses before they could become "nations" in the modern world—the Chinese had to cease thinking of their country as a universal empire, the Korean and Annamites had to cease considering their countries

[1] The concept of "Confucian family of nations" is best presented by the thoughtful work of the late M. Frederick Nelson, *Korea and the Old Orders in Eastern Asia,* Baton Rogue, 1945, while the concepts of ecumenical empire and satrapy are most cogently applied to the Far Eastern scene in an unpublished work on province and acumen in China by Professor Robert Hosack, of the University of Idaho.

in turn as the forever-subordinate tributaries of the Chinese universal state, and so on. The Japanese, who had never claimed universal empire for themselves, except for ceremonial metaphor and the megalomania of Hideyoshi, and who had also refused an honorable but subordinate status in the universal empire of China (save for the unfortunate lapse of the Ashikaga *Shōgun* Yoshimitsu), thus found it easy to adapt to a political system posited upon the idea of a number of countries, each unique, each independent, and each juridically answerable only to itself.

In a very practical sense Japan did not have to become a modern nation. Japan already was the equivalent of a modern nation, without knowing it, before either modernity or nationhood were recognizable factors in Western civilization. Once the "modern nation," intricate phenomenon though it was, appeared in the Far East, the Japanese had only to look at it to see in it the explicit political expression of what they implicitly and increasingly were becoming. The change therefore involved in the acceptance of the model of Europe as a political form suitable for Japanese domestic use was much less of a strain than the Japanese attempt twelve centuries earlier to thrust the model of a Chinese universal empire within the narrow insular limits of Japan.

The actual Meiji Constitution is thus an especially attractive political work to contemplate. It represents the happiest adaptation of an admirable Western political institution by an especially apt non-Western culture. The Constitution is meaningless if one takes it in a literal Western sense, as involving the regrouping of the basic forces in Japanese constitutional life, or as requiring a change in the public or private characters of the Japanese. If it is understood in its happiest sense, however, as an effective and artistically persuasive Japanese adaptation of an important Western political phenomenon, adopted partly for the sake of internal convenience and partly as the dramatic but effective gesture of a people who were prepared to meet the Westerner on his own cultural ground, it is an extraordinarily good constitution—better than its predecessors, since it had no real predecessors, and better than its successors, because its only successor has been the unfortunate document produced under the ægis of the American Occupation and described in Chapter 20, under the deserved nickname of the MacArthur Constitution. At its best, the Meiji Constitution is a stable and beautiful blend of juridical mirage with social reality; at its worst, it never departs from the facts of everyday life as closely or deceptively as does the notorious Soviet Constitution of 1936.

Surviving Preconditions to Constitutionality. The writing, promulgation, and acceptance of a written constitution was effective in nineteenth-century Japan because the grafting took—the attached organ adhered, the additional social factor found its living place within the forces which made up Japanese motivation and understanding. To do this it was much more important for the Constitution to be confluent with Japanese reality than for it to be fashionable in terms of textural attractiveness in Western year-books. In sharp contrast to China (see Chapter Six), where endless successions of constitutions, each more beautiful and more unreal than its predecessor, were adopted until the harsh fiat of a permanent communist emergency put an end to middle-class constitution-making, the Japanese worked out in the Meiji Constitution a document which included almost every phase of Japanese national life. This Constitution had to bear a loyalty, sometimes expressed but more often unspoken, to the other predominant factors in Japanese political existence, each of which survived from its own stratum of history.

By far the oldest of these factors is the tradition of unbroken Imperial rule, which rested on the idea of tribal theocracy. The next layer up was bureaucracy on the grand T'ang model as adopted and adapted by the Japanese of the Taika and succeeding periods, converting the Chinese gentry and civil service state into a bureaucratic civil aristocracy with strong familial features. From their long experience under shogunal government the Japanese inherited the ideas of political dualism and of military power coexisting with civil power and superior to it. From the forty years of turmoil which followed the visit of Commodore Perry, the Japanese had obtained much practical experience in the acceptance of a "rally of the people," not too much unlike De Gaulle's proposal for France, operated in fact by an oligarchy of selfish but reasonable patriots.

Delineation of the Japanese Constitution through the technique of direct paragraph-by-paragraph or clause-by-clause comparison with similar Western techniques would obviously be self-deception if not utter nonsense. Not only did the several institutional strata of Japanese government survive in real life: the ideological residua of each preceding period competed for attention in the fashions of Japanese thinking. Japanese theory of the government of men changed very little. To the Japanese in the Meiji period as well as to Japanese today), government is most readily explained by reference to the institution of a patriarchal family. An individual's obligations to society are more important than his rights. Men are obviously unequal; government by superior men is obviously better than government by miscellaneous men or by law, which erroneously assumes men to be equal. Politics and ethics are indistinguishable if not synonymous. Good government springs from the benevolence of the *Tennō* and from good administrators who hold that benevolence in trust. Thus go the truisms of Japanese politics.

Government in Japan has obviously had an evolution unique in that it combined both extreme isolation and rich intercultural penetration. The Japanese have not only borrowed effectively; they have produced fundamental, although peculiar, assumptions in the field of political theory. The Japan which accepted "constitutional government" after 1889 was the same Japan which had existed before 1889, and the Meiji Constitution must under no circumstances be compared with the American Constitution of 1789 or with the French Constitution of 1790.

Japanese Loyalties and the Political Frame. The Meiji Constitution is significant, therefore, in that its flourishes are as important as its substance, since the flourishes represent the basic spiritual, ethical, and political beliefs which almost all Japanese, irrespective of class or section, accepted in the first part of the twentieth century. More or less specifically, they believed that the Emperor held sovereignty as an inheritance from his divine ancestors, that he reigned as father of the Japanese family-nation, and that since modernity had come upon the Eastern world he would obviously exercise sovereignty according to the most advanced available principles of constitutionalism.[2] The fundamental principle of Japanese government was awkwardly, but quite accurately, called theocratical-patriarchal constitutionalism by Baron Hozumi Nobushige. Strange-sounding though the term may be to Westerners, it is accurate, although unwieldy.

What can one make of the impact of truly believed and honestly accepted Western ideas concerning government on the Meiji Constitution?

This question is a serious one. Perhaps it can be answered only by the anthropologists or the social psychologists. Political science has few standards for distinguishing between what people say they think and what impartial observers can assume they *do* think. Pending further and deeper examination of Japanese semantics and the writing of more histories of modern thought within Japan, it is possible only to make the following layman's observation: although the Japanese at the time of the adoption of the Meiji Constitution and in the decades which have followed have made almost incessant reference to Western political thought, there is very little evidence that the content behind that thought has ever been accepted by them. Whenever European theory became a working part of the Japanese universe of discourse, it became acclimatized in the process. Whether visible to the Westerner or not, the long-enduring Japanese assumptions loomed up behind the Meiji Constitution.

The Organic Law of the Empire. As Fujii Shunichi put it, "Law is a

[2] It can be argued, paradoxically but seriously, that Japan is in no serious danger of accepting communism in the 1950's or 1960's, because communism is by now too familiar a political phenomenon to be regarded by the Japanese as the last word in political fashions. When the Russian revolution first broke out there was a tremendous wave of emotional, artistic, and intellectual response from the younger members of the Japanese intelligentsia. They welcomed the Bolshevik triumph, not because of its beliefs or practices, but because it was so irresistibly brand-new. The appeal of German Fascism in the 1930's and early 1940's can be explained, in part, on the same basis. Hitler looked like "the wave of the future," even to Americans who should have known better. To the Japanese, always somewhat gullible in seeking the Western fashion in politics or economics, the novelties of national socialism proved almost irresistible. In the 1950's Japan's stability is in part insured by the transparently obvious fact that no one anywhere in the world has any particularly fresh or appealing ideas on the subject of government. Almost all the ideological competitors are middle-aged, if not antique. It is impossible for the Japanese to look at Poland, Argentina, or the Union of South Africa with breathless amazement, saying to themselves, "There unquestionably do we observe the most up-to-date and most inexpressibly modern government on earth!"

regulation or rule showing what ought to be with regard to the will of the people or of a regal person." Thus to Fujii, law is effective when it is in harmony with the general purpose of a community, and an agglomeration of men becomes a community when it possesses a sense of loyalty to a common authority and a devotion to common purpose. To him, as to other Japanese commentators, constitutional law is a means of reflecting fundamental principles of political behavior. Appropriately therefore the constitution of the nation-state thus locates sovereignty and allocates the exercise of authority. In certain Western countries constitutionalism has come to have another context, namely, the guarantee of freedoms and rights. A constitution may go so far as to outline the form of government, for example, according to the doctrine of separation of powers. In any case a constitution, above all, may be considered "a historical product of the development of a country." [3]

In Japan, Meiji constitutional structure was a product of a 2,000-year tradition, which may be summed up in the word *shiroshimesu,* "reigned over and governed" by the *Tennō.* The organic law of the Empire—actually a complex of documents—can be quickly characterized. The Meiji Constitution itself was granted by the *Tennō,* and thus could be amended only on his initiative. The Imperial family had to have complete autonomy, so that a separate Imperial House Law was equally binding on the citizens, but was not subject to their consideration. There was a sort of separation of powers, but strictly within limits of the doctrine of Imperial Centralism and quite unlike that found in the West. These principles were plainly set out in the Constitution and the House Law, in the ordinances and statutes made in pursuance thereof. No international agreement could take precedence over the constitutional structure.

Although the Imperial Constitution (*Teikoku Kempō*) was the keystone in this structure, it was but one part of the mass of laws, rescripts, customs, and traditions which made up *the Constitution of the Japanese State.* The Japanese Constitution, developed around the *Tennō,* was thus somewhat similar to the unwritten British Constitution built around the time-honored parliament. The Meiji Constitution consisted of seven chapters, seventy-six articles, and contained only three original Japanese provisions: The Pre-

[3] This summary of the role of law is drawn from the representative and authoritative treatise (in English) by Fujii Shunichi, *The Essentials of Japanese Constitutional Law,* Tokyo, 1940, pp. 63 ff. All commentaries, in both Japanese and English, return eventually to the basic source: Itō Hirobumi, *Teikoku kempō kōshitsu tempan gige,* cited, an article-by-article analysis of the Constitution and Imperial House Law by Prince Itō; the sections on the Constitution were translated by Itō Myoji, *op. cit.* Texts on constitutional law are quite numerous, since the discipline has been exceedingly popular among Japanese political scientists: Hozumi Yatsuka, *Kempō teiyō* (Manual of constitutional law), Tōkyō, 7th edition, 1940, is representative of the older, semi-mystical school; Minobe Tatsukichi, *Kempō kōwa,* cited, is a typical product of Japan's best-known, modern constitutional lawyer, who died shortly after the beginning of the Occupation. For a useful comparison of the old and the new, see Harold S. Quigley, "Japan's Constitutions: 1890 and 1947," *American Political Science Review,* Vol. 41, 1947, pp. 865 ff.

amble (Article I), the article concerning war and national emergency (Article XXXI), and the article concerning the Japanese budget (Article LXXI). Of the remainder, nine were copied from various foreign sources; forty-six were modeled directly after the Prussian Constitution; eighteen were attributed to other German origins. In the eyes of many Japanese, even today, all these provisions erected at least a façade of constitutionalism, if not liberalism. With the exception of the constitutions of German monarchies, however, the Meiji Constitution was the most autocratic constitution in the world. Since it was never legally revised, at least until 1946, it became the Grand Code of the Parliamentary Empire.

In its emphasis upon the unbroken line of sacred and inviolable *Tennō* (Articles I, III), the Meiji Constitution was legally unique. The fundamental characteristic of centralization was limited in only two respects. In the Imperial Oath promulgating the Constitution was a clue to the objective sought, the subjects' welfare according to the tradition of benevolent rule. And although the Emperor *was supposed* to exercise authority "according to the provisions of the present Constitution" (Article IV), he was the Head of the Empire, combining in himself all sovereignty. Nevertheless, inadequate government was never the fault of the *Tennō*. Responsibility was assigned in the Preamble: "Our Ministers of State, on Our behalf, shall be held responsible for the carrying out of the present Constitution. . . ."

Despite the seeming rigidity of Imperial Centralism, below the Emperor there was a distribution, if not separation, of powers. Thus legislation was passed with the consent of the Imperial Diet (Article V); laws and ordinances were promulgated and executed on the advice and countersignature of Ministers of State (Articles VI, LV); and the judicature was exercised, in the Emperor's name, by courts of law (Article LVII). The Constitution, being autocratic, favored the executive. Nevertheless, although hampered by the lack of a true check-and-balance device, the Diet steadily gained as a vehicle for popular control. Since there was no concept of judicial review, the courts were completely overshadowed.

Presumably, interpretation of the Constitution was the prerogative solely of the Imperial grantor. Actually, at the lower levels the law was interpreted by each organ concerned. Where conflict was irreconcilable, there were always "the watchdogs of the Constitution," the Privy Councilors, who deliberated "on important matters of state, when they have been consulted by the Emperor" (Article LVI). During the history of the Constitution, there was only one instance when it was necessary to go to such a high level. In 1892, an issue between the two houses concerning their budgetary powers was referred to the Emperor, who called upon the Privy Council for advice. When he accepted its recommendation, a precedent of interpretation was established.

Amendment is always assigned a vital role in constitutional machinery, although very often it is not the chief method of alteration (the American experience offers a good example). Under the Meiji Constitution (Chapter VII, Article LXIII), amendment could be accomplished only on Imperial (meaning Ministerial) Order; a two-thirds majority (with a two-thirds quorum) of both houses had to approve. This provision was the subject of considerable discussion by constitutional lawyers. There was unanimity among legal experts that the sole power of initiating amendments rested with the Emperor. With regard to the question whether and to what extent the Diet had the power to modify an amendment project, or to enact additional provisions, at least two major schools of thought appeared. The orthodox theorists denied such power completely. However, Professor Minobe Tatsukichi and his students, who went so far as to expound the dangerous thought that sovereignty was vested in the Emperor *and* the Diet, regarded revision as a function of the legislature and modification of an amendment as part of the right of approval. In any case, until the Occupation no amendment project was ever forthcoming.[4]

Because of the difficulty of amendment, the Constitution lost in relative importance; parallel laws and ordinances took up the legal slack. Moreover, the Japanese Constitution was rendered flexible by more subtle changes. The *Genrō,* for example, was an extra-constitutional advisory body of Elder Statesmen, which derived sanction only from custom and usage (as did the President's Cabinet in the United States). Again, the fundamental separation of civil and military administration—both owing allegiance to the *Tennō*—was not written into the Constitution, but was recognized before and after its promulgation. This separation was destined to play a far more vital role than the rigid provisions of a religious and sanctified document, in which such dualism was not mentioned.

The Meiji Constitution was promulgated, as we have seen, partially in response to the demand for more representative government. And as Professor Fujii pointed out, many modern constitutions have as their context, if not their very objective, the guarantee of fundamental rights. An examination of the 1889 Constitution in these lights, and particularly Prince Itō's authoritative commentaries on the role of the Diet and the status of civil rights, is most revealing.

Under the Constitution (Chapter III), the Diet had no real share in the sovereign power: it could *deliberate* on laws, but not *determine* legislation.

[4] The entire question of amendment became something more than an academic exercise, of course, with the adoption of the *Shin Kempō* (New Constitution), in 1946. The problem of maintaining legal continuity, involving basic changes in the fundamental polity *(kokutai)* and modifications by the Diet, was exhaustively treated by Alfred Oppler, Chief, Courts and Law Division, in a memorandum to his Chief, Government Section, on August 25, 1946. See "Powers of the Diet with regard to Constitutional Amendments under the Meiji Constitution," Appendix C:15, *Political Reorientation of Japan; September 1945 to September 1948,* Report of Government Section, Supreme Commander for the Allied Powers, Washington, 1949, pp. 662-666. See also pp. 473 of the present text. Appendix C:1 presents texts of the Meiji Constitution; The Imperial House Law; Ordinances for the Privy Council, Cabinet, House of Peers; and Law of the Houses. For texts of the Meiji Constitution and Imperial House Law, see Appendixes 10 and 11.

Yet Prince Itō believed the Constitution by no means limited the Diet out of existence. For it was designed to "represent the public opinion of the country." The lower house (Article XXV) was based on election districts only for convenience; each incumbent was to speak for the state as a whole. The House of Peers was not designed to be simply a conservative influence blocking the representatives, or so Itō opined. It existed to realize the *organic* character of the state, an indispensable theoretical basis for a representative system! Thus the peers were to serve to maintain equilibrium among political forces, to check political parties, and to bar irresponsible discussion. Furthermore, the Diet was assigned definite duties. Therefore, Itō explained, a just balance—not a separation—of powers is achieved between executive and legislature.

In its summary of Rights and Duties of Subjects (Chapter II), the Meiji Constitution appeared to be among the most modern of constitutions. It paid lip-service to all the familiar civil rights. "But," said Itō, "liberty exists solely in a community in which order prevails." It is no surprise, then, to find *duties* favored over rights; and each *right* granted, "except in the cases provided for in the law." A few samples, with appropriate comments by Itō, will illustrate the point.

> Taxes are paid for maintenance of the State, regardless of services (Article XXI). ("The State has the right to impose taxes, and the subjects have the duty of paying them.")
>
> Japanese subjects are amenable to service in the Army or Navy (Article XX). ("The spirit of loyalty, like the sentiment of honor, has come down to us from our ancestors. . . .")
>
> Independent courts of justice (Article XXIV) are ("fathers in control of justice.")
>
> Rights of inviolability of the house and letters (Articles XXV, XXVI), freedom of conscience (Article XXVIII), and liberty of speech, writing, publication, and assembly (Article XXIX) are necessary to political development; the only restriction is that subject may place himself ("outside the pale of the law of the Empire.")
>
> The right of petition (Article XXX) ("is granted to the people out of the Emperor's most gracious and benevolent consideration . . . ; ") they must show the proper respect.
>
> In an emergency, particularly in war, the sovereign right of the Emperor is supreme (Article XXXI). ("It must be remembered that the ultimate aim of a state is to maintain its existence.") [5]

The law of the Constitution of 1889 made quite clear that it was to be regarded as only one of several enactments, rather than the basic organic law. Existing laws, regulations, and ordinances continued in force, so long as they did not conflict with the Meiji Constitution (Article LXXVI). Moreover, the Constitution spoke (Article II) of succession to the Throne and also (Article XVII) of Regency, both to be decided by Imperial House

[5] Itō Myoji, trans., Itō H., *Commentaries,* cited, pp. 38-68.

Law (*Kōshitsu Tempan*). The latter was also promulgated by Imperial Edict in 1889. It consisted of twelve chapters, sixty-two articles, and constituted an inner constitution, confined to the Imperial family. The Imperial House Law governed succession, ascension, coronation, regency, and the business of the Imperial family. This Law was given complete independence since (Article LXXIV of the Constitution) modifications did not have to receive the approval of the Diet. On the other hand, no provisions of the House Law could modify the Meiji Constitution. Changes in the Law were effected on the advice of the Imperial Family Council, the Privy Council, and the Imperial Household Minister.

Ranking practically alongside the Constitution and House Law were Imperial Ordinances (*Meirei*), by which the executive exercised inherent power of legislation. This power, granted in the Constitution itself (Articles VIII, IX), was greater than that of any constitutionally controlled state at the time. Ordinances were of three general types:

1. *Prerogative ordinances,* such as those governing the Imperial house, establishing the House of Peers, and regulating the business of the Privy Council. They lay outside the scope of the Diet.
2. *Administrative ordinances,* passed by the executive to preserve the general welfare. The Diet had no control over such ordinances.
3. *Emergency ordinances,* which had to be approved by the Privy Council. These had to be submitted to the subsequent meeting of the Diet, if they were to remain in effect, but a Diet disapproval was not retroactive.

All ordinances, of course, bore the countersignature of a Minister of State, since the Emperor never acted without advice.

Statutes (*hōritsu*), pursuant to the Constitution, House Law, and prerogative ordinances, were passed by both Houses. They were subject to an absolute Imperial veto. Treaties and international agreements were ratified by the Emperor, on the consent of the Privy Council. Thus the Constitution and Imperial House Law, together with parallel ordinances, were superior to treaties, which were in turn superior to statutes and ordinances.

Shintō, the Emperor, and Imperial Advisers. Many serious Japanese writers have expressed the belief that the ideal sociological development of a people is from a family into a group, into a race, into a city-state, and lastly, into a nation-state—the entire cycle evolving through blood relationship. They realized, of course, that the Japanese were not a homogenous race; subjects included Ainus, Koreans, and Chinese elements, which had all been assimilated. But these had been assimilated without force. And they too basked in the parental love of all Japanese by the *Tennō*.

> The Imperial Family is to the nation what a tree trunk is to the branches and to the leaves.[6]

[6] S. Fujii, *op. cit.*, p. 95.

Imperial Centralism, so little understood in the West, was buttressed by a faith in the national polity (*kokutai*) and was based on a type of ancestor-worship, as though Japan were a racially pure family-state. Shintō-ism thus became a worship by and of the reigning Emperor, for all Emperors. This was the concept of "Sacred Imperial Rule."

A fundamental distinction between orthodox Japanese and classical Chinese theory concerning the Throne should be noted here. The Chinese had believed Heaven ruled them, through the Emperor as agent. The Japanese concept was of a living God; this concept led in turn to a passion for hereditary succession. Always the relation between the distinct, individual sovereign and his subjects was, however, a patriarchal one. Thus, most Japanese thought they had a sociologically perfect system. But there were difficulties, even so.

One difficulty arose from the historic nature of the Meiji Restoration, which was of a dual nature. By restoring the Emperor in name and in fact, there followed a grand reversion to ancient tradition. We have already noted the almost slavish imitation of the eighth-century Taihō Code, during the period 1868-89. Once again the *Jingikan,* the bureau of Shintō worship, took precedence over the *Dajōkan,* highest council of state. For a time, the re-establishment of Shintō also meant the disestablishment of Buddhism. The latter dug in and barely survived the anti-Buddhist outbreaks of 1868-70.

By the 1880's a reaction had set in: for the Restoration also meant modernization. In 1882 differentiation was made between Shintō shrines that were supported by the state and Shintō temples used for religious worship. The 1889 Constitution, with an eye on foreign countries, granted freedom of religion. Henceforth, the Home Ministry regulated the state shrines, to which all non-Shintoists had to pay homage, and also the temples, where the faithful could practice sectarian Shintō. Politically, the distinction was of little importance. The masses continued to view shrine attendance as a necessity of religious worship. Shintō fostered nationalism, paying tribute to the military heroes of Japan. High on the list of the reigning Emperor's duties were a regular visit to the Shrine of the Sun Goddess at Ise and, by later Emperors, to the Meiji Shrine in Tokyo. In sum, Shintō fostered the ideology of the absolutist state.

But the state *did not necessarily have to be absolutist,* even under the Meiji Constitution. Absolutism arose from the tradition of unbroken lineage, a powerful bulwark because of ancestor worship; from the rigid family system in Japan: and specifically, from worship of the Imperial family. Absolutism was further inculcated by patriots who surrounded the Emperor with mythology and pseudo-science. Absolutism was reinforced deliberately by the conservative school of political theory, which held that the *Tennō* wielded power without check; he had promulgated the Constitution of his own free will, and not in response to popular demand. The leading defenders of this view were Itō himself and his disciples, conservative students of constitutional law. They began their case with his *Commentaries,* and rested it mainly on the first three articles of the Meiji Constitution.

The Emperor's picture, it is true, could not appear on Japanese stamps. And all took the precaution not to look upon Him from an elevated position. His baggage bore no name: "His August Presence" was enough to quiet bystanders. Nevertheless, there were doubts. Parallel with the doubts arose a progressive view. Well-educated people, including some students of constitutional law at Tokyo *Teidai* (the Imperial University), did not hold to the mythology of divine descent.

Historically, claimed the progressives, absolute rule was ended by the Kamakura Shogunate in 1192. No one really disputed the fact that later, real power lay in the hands of the Tokugawa *Shōgun;* nor that this power passed during the Restoration not directly to the Emperor, but to nobles, lower *samurai,* and the bureaucrats. Finally, the Constitution established the *Tennō* as *supreme representative* of the nation, but with his power constitutionally limited.

It would be more scientific, the progressives argued, to examine the entire Meiji Constitution. The first chapter, for example, carefully defined the Emperor's powers. Why should this be done if they were not limited? Again, the right of legislation lay with the Diet; a refusal by the Emperor to use his veto denied absolutism. Article XLV, concerning the duties, advice, and responsibility of ministers, definitely vested vast administrative powers in their hands. Around this vague article experts disputed bitterly, bureaucrats answering with the absolutist view in order to maintain undemocratic rule.

Eventually, the issue came to a head over the location of sovereignty. The conservative met the progressive head-on in the Uesugi-Minobe debates, beginning in 1912. Both Uesugi Shinkichi (a disciple of the conservative Professor Hozumi Yatsuka) and Minobe Tatsukichi (with his followers, Sasaki and Ichimura) were students in the law school, Tokyo *Teidai.* According to Uesugi, the national polity revolved around three basic assumptions: (1) the Emperor is a divine, absolute sovereign; (2) government is a public act of the Emperor; and (3) the Emperor is to be identified completely with the state. Minobe expounded the doctrine that the *Tennō* is an organ of the state, like the Diet, the Cabinet, or the Privy Council. Although the citizen enjoys no right of revolution, still the Emperor on his part may not violate the Constitution. Minobe explained:

> The right of sovereignty does not belong to the Emperor alone, but is a right that exists for the welfare and interests of the entire state.

The issue was even more clearly revealed when Japanese plenipotentiaries, like other nations' ambassadors, signed the Kellogg Pact (of Paris, 1928), "in the names of their respective peoples" (Article I). Within Japan, the Privy Council became aroused; the opposition party condemned the government on the floor of the House; and the Diet, meeting in January, 1929, was consumed with debate. Japan's foremost liberal (and post-World War II visitor to the United States), Ozaki Yukio, joined old Count Itō Myoji, member of the Privy Council, in a denunciation of the offending clause. The Cabinet ought to go into sackcloth and ashes and await the punishment of the *Tennō,* in whose name the treaty should have been signed! Finally, the Privy Council advised ratification with a reservation stating that the phrase, "viewed in the light of the provisions of the Imperial Constitution, is understood to be inapplicable insofar as Japan is concerned." [7]

Constitutionally, at least, the issue of the role of the *Tennō* under the parliamentary empire was finally resolved in the famous "national polity" controversy of 1935. Widespread attacks on what were regarded in Japan as liberal theories reached a peak in the mid-1930's. Although Dr. Minobe's contributions to the state had by then been recognized by his appointment to the House of Peers, there was incessant criticism of his lectures and treatises. Finally a Diet member filed a formal charge of *lèse majesté.* Political parties joined the military in bringing pressure on the Cabinet and Premier to resolve the question once and for all. Eventually the Cabinet was forced to release a statement: sovereignty resided in the Emperor; the whole idea of the state as locus of sovereignty could no longer be suffered. Dr. Minobe resigned from the House of Peers. Thus closed the discussion over the Organic Theory of the State (*Kikan Setsu*).

The orthodox theory that the Emperor was in no way an organ of the state, but *was* the state, offered little more than a baffling generalization as an answer to the query: Who, then, actually exercised the sovereignty under Japanese organic law? Of course, had Japan produced emperors with the personal stature of Charles V or of Frederick the Great, or even of the Meiji *Tennō,* the absolutist language might have made sense.

In fact there is danger, in describing the theoretical assignment of sovereignty to the Emperor, of forgetting that all this power was assigned to a *man.* The man who played the role of a living god, and who, in theory, exercised the sovereignty of the state, could have been—indeed, he was occasionally—of great importance. But it is difficult to see the outlines of the man through the intricate institutional screen.

The outlines of Mutsuhito the man (1852-1912; Emperor 1867-1912), for example, are very dim. We do know that he ascended the Throne at the age of fifteen and that, as Japanese emperors go, he was influential. He softened

[7] Professor Quigley, *op. cit.,* pp. 70-71, has given us a description of the Pact controversy including Ozaki's role; for a different type of analysis, Takeuchi Tatsuji, *War and Diplomacy in the Japanese Empire,* New York, 1935, pp. 262-274. The opposing views of sovereignty may be found in Uesugi Shinkichi, *Kokutai kempō oyobi kensei* (National polity, the constitution, and constitutional government), Tōkyō, 1916; Minobe's views were set forth in, among other treatises already cited, *Saikin kempō ron* (Recent constitutional theory), Tōkyō, 1927, pp. 60-61, and summarized by Kenneth Colegrove, "The Japanese Emperor," *American Political Science Review,* Vol. XXVI, Nos. 4 and 5 (August and October, 1932), pp. 642-659, 828-845. An excellent summary of progressive views is contained in Iwasaki Uichi, *The Working Forces in Japanese Politics,* New York, 1921, Chap. II, pp. 24-31.

the anti-foreign prejudices inherited from his father. He took an eager and interested part in drafting the Constitution of 1889. We are told he took a great share in shaping the changes that took place during his eventful reign, and many times his strong character swayed the Cabinet. Beyond these few facts, there are only institutional remains.

Out on the Yamate "Belt Line," just southwest of Yoyogi Station, is the Meiji Jingu Shrine, dedicated to the memory of the Emperor and his consort. One of the Japanese holy-of-holies, the shrine is visited by millions every year. The main edifices were in pure Shintō style (they were burned in the air raid of 1945), characterized by dignified simplicity. The *torii,* or entrance gate, is made of *hinoki* wood, 1,700 years old. It stands thirty-nine feet seven inches in height. In the *Homotsu-den* (Treasure House) are exhibited many articles actually used by the *Tennō.* A carriage, which was drawn by six horses, is the one used by the Emperor at the time of promulgation of the Constitution. On November 3, birthday of the Emperor, athletic games are held in the stadium, Outer Garden. Each Emperor's reign begins an era, the name of which identifies the Emperor after death. The *Meiji* (Enlightened) now identifies an era and a shrine, not a man.

The less said of Yoshihito (1879-1926; Emperor 1912-1926), the better. With the only son of the Meiji Emperor, Imperial rule continued unbroken but it was slightly bent. It is kinder to think of *Taishō* (Great Righteousness) also as an era.

Of the greatest interest to us, of course, is the present Emperor. The then Crown Prince, Hirohito, assumed the reins of government for his invalid father in 1921. A Regency was thus established for the first time under the Constitution and Imperial House Law. In 1927 Hirohito opened the *Shōwa* (Radiant Peace) era. Of the "Shōwa Restoration," which came a few years after; of how the Americans brought radiance, and later peace, to his realm; of the role of the Emperor in the surrender and Occupation, we shall speak later. By 1946, admittedly without divinity and struggling to appear an ordinary mortal, Hirohito nevertheless had become rapidly submerged in an era. What is forgotten is that his accession in 1927 was heralded as the appearance of the most modern-minded of Japanese rulers.

The young Emperor was interested in politics, modern languages, and science. Personally, he gave every indication that he was in touch with the modern world. Deeply interested in British civilization, Hirohito as Crown Prince had often been compared with the Prince of Wales, in his unconventionality and in his desire to mingle with common folk. Indeed, he visited England and was escorted on his tour by Edward, who returned the visit. Like Edward, he broke tradition when he married, by choosing a wife outside the *kuge* families; unlike Edward, he has not as yet relinquished his Throne. He came to power when the extension of franchise gave promise of more representative government. It was openly rumored that the approach of democracy did not displease the Emperor. That democracy did not arrive immediately perhaps is a commentary on his impotence, as a man.[8]

No, the Emperor as a man falls far short of an answer to the question: Who actually exercised the sovereignty of Japan? Despite the orthodox theory, *the Emperor is the state* became far less important than *the Emperor never acts without advice.* This meant that the doctrine of absolutism, plus the long tradition of loyalty to the Throne, rendered the Emperor above revolt. The *Tennō* became a perfect shield against an irate public, whose only recourse was to insist upon a change of advisers. That brings us to the further and by all odds more frustrating question: *Who* gave the Emperor advice?

The importance of this last question is illustrated by a brief review of specific powers assigned to the Emperor. The orthodox view held that legislative powers were exercised by the Emperor *through* the Diet. Progressives argued that legislative powers were, in reality, divided between the Emperor *and* the Diet. According to the Constitution, such powers were actually limited to three: (1) convening, opening, and proroguing the Diet; (2) initiating and sanctioning statutes; and (3) issuing Imperial ordinances. The last, claimed the progressives, were merely methods of getting the will of the Diet. The "dangerous thoughts" rules of the 1920's illustrated the technique. At one point, it was claimed in the House of Representatives that the Diet, constitutional lawyers, the press, and even the Privy Council differed as to the scope of an emergency which would require arbitrary rule. Even without ordinances, however, the power of legislative initiation gave the Emperor (or his advisors) enormous influence.

The more important concentration came in the realm of executive powers. The Emperor's authority here may be summed up as including: (1) appointments and general administrative control; (2) pardons and judicial administration; (3) control over the organization, mission, and operations of both the army and navy; (4) declaration of war; (5) conclusion of peace, the treaty power; and (6) declaration of martial law. The appointive power was unlimited, and no one was assigned the constitutional right of confirmation. Thus, the Japanese civil service was directed by Imperial ordinance, not parliamentary statute. Professor Minobe tried to assert the doctrine of collective administrative responsibility, but his view was in the minority. The conservative theorists tried to make each minister individually responsible to the Emperor. In actuality, this theory proved impractical. The question of war or peace was withdrawn entirely from Dietary control. Only a qualified limitation was accepted in the treaty-making power: agreements were to be referred to the Privy Council for advice. Control over the army and navy was important because conscription required military training of

[8] An interesting, contemporary sketch of the young Emperor was given by J. I. Bryan in "Japan's New Emperor," *Contemporary Review,* Vol. 131, No. 23 (March, 1927), pp. 344 ff.

all able-bodied men and because peculiar administrative rules were developed by ordinance (these are discussed subsequently). The distinctive role of the Emperor in military affairs, however, deserves special mention.

Indeed, the Emperor's constitutional role in relation to the services perpetuated the feudal tradition of dualism in politics. For there was a separation of functions, even with regard to the Emperor's military personality. His power of supreme command, exercised as Generalissimo, was not the same as his power over military organization, vested in the Head of State. Thus the Emperor alone was responsible for national defense plans and direction of the army and navy. In the words of Itō, this was the *Tennō* operating "within the camp curtains." Organization of the services—decided on the basis of economic, political, and diplomatic factors—was also the function of the *Tennō,* "within the Cabinet." Actually, as we shall see, liaison between the "two Emperors" was maintained by appointing active officers to the positions of Minister of War and Minister of Navy.

Dr. Minobe discussed the position of the Emperor in "the Cabinet and in the Camp" in issues of *Asahi,* at the time of the signature of the London Naval Treaty of 1930. Obviously, under Article XIII of the Constitution, the treaty-power belonged to the Emperor (in Cabinet); estimates as to the size and organization of the naval forces also belonged to him (but seriously affected his role in Camp). A treaty, made by the Cabinet and ratified by the Emperor (on advice of the Privy Council) was presumably binding on the services. It was for this reason that Baron Wakatsuki, an ex-premier, served as chief delegate to the London parley, assisted of course by the Navy Minister. Nevertheless, the Cabinet victory was a costly one: signature of the treaty was one signal which set off the militarist attempt to restore the Emperor "in Camp" at the expense of the Emperor "in Cabinet." [9]

We now turn from the legislative and executive powers conducted in the Emperor's name to the extremely complex and ill-defined organization of government through which these powers were carried out. It is a familiar technique to refer to an absolutist state as pyramidal in form, all authority building toward the top. But such a description implies relatively smooth progress from a broad base up through clear channels of power to the peak. Actually the Japanese government, as defined by law, was only the slimmest kind of skeleton—a sort of jungle gym—and gave no hint of the manner of operation or of the elasticity of detailed organization. There was no clear distribution of powers or division of responsibility. Even the term "centralized executive" is misleading. On the one hand, a national bureaucracy controlled *all* phases of the execution and administration of laws. On the other, the national government to a large degree and lower echelons to a

[9] It seems a pity further to complicate an already involved fiction, but it should be noted that even the services differed as to the extent of their Emperor-centered power. For instance, the navy allowed a civilian to work *pro tem* in the Minister's place, whereas the army never accepted such a principle. See Anonymous (Minobe Tatsukichi), "The Cabinet and Camp," *The Japan Weekly Chronicle,* May 15, 1930, pp. 503-505.

relatively less degree actually handled none of the normal functions of government. The Constitution which might be expected to define those functions, was mere window-dressing. Several important institutions were entirely extra-constitutional. All operations of government were administered by clique and counter-clique; they were often carried out by semi-private and even private organizations subsidized by the government and frequently officered by government officials. The National Diet was only a device for giving the appearance of a parliamentary regime.

Constitutionality and Political Reality. The Meiji Constitution is therefore a poor constitution if it is compared with those long American state constitutions so popular in the nineteenth century which attempted to describe almost every function of government and almost every contingency of politics. It was not a prescription for all political behavior in Japan. The Meiji Constitution was a modern garment of Japanese government, designed to give the Imperial government a pleasant appearance before the world and designed to reconcile the Japanese in their role of modern nation-state with the Japanese as they saw themselves in everyday social habits and popular beliefs.

It is not at all impossible that the Meiji Constitution will some day be reconsidered and that within its broad and generous limits a democratic Japanese government will move forward to the future. The propriety of the MacArthur Constitution is discussed subsequently. The vitality of the Meiji Constitution can be affirmed here. It can ever be said that the Japanese of 1889 did not need a constitution very much. Even more than the British, they were a people both cohesive and traditionalist to whom the application of a written constitution was inevitably the statement of authority after the fact of its appearance, and not the creation of a new authority by legitimate contractual means. A Japanese can no more contract to be a Japanese than he can contract to be a human being, whereas all Americans implicitly, if not explicitly, are heirs to the great doctrine of John Locke that the citizens of free nations are the makers or inheritors of primal contracts upon which the authority of all government must depend.

CHAPTER SEVENTEEN

Government under the Meiji Constitution

PICTURESQUELY, but in authentic Japanese spirit, Chart 15 shows the political structure of pre-1945 Japan against a diagram in the shape of a chrysanthemum. It is thoroughly appropriate to think of the parliamentary government of the Meiji era as a series of concentric inner circles rather than as a frame of rigidly linked boxes, similar to the diagrams prepared for United States official use by the Bureau of the Budget and the Government Printing Office. The limits between official and unofficial, between juridical and customary, between pressures and authorities, were never demarcated as sharply in Japan as in America or other Western nations. The social origin and political epicenters of major factions cut like spokes from the masses of the people toward the very heart of sovereignty.

The Immense Cliques *(Batsu)*. The Chinese character which is read in Chinese as *fa* and pronounced *batsu* in Japanese means "clique, grange, group, faction." In Japan there were four of these, of which one, the aristocratic, withered away in the early twentieth century, and another, the military, crashed to ruin in the year 1945. The financiers as one group and the bureaucracy as another remained; perhaps they have been joined by a new faction, that of the professional labor organizers and careerists in labor politics, but labor has yet to obtain recognition as one of the immense *batsu* of Japan.

The Japanese terms are themselves so common in Western newspaper and textbook usage that they are worthy of note. The clique of the aristocracy was called the *mombatsu.* The clique of financiers was called the *zaibatsu.* The clique of the career military and naval officials was called the *gumbatsu.* And the clique of the indestructible civil service was called the *kambatsu.* It should be noted immediately, of course, that the cliques themselves were by no means so monolithic as the separate terms would indicate. The familial system in society, wholesale adoptions and complex interconnections, and, above all, diffusion and indirection in Japanese politics and the financial

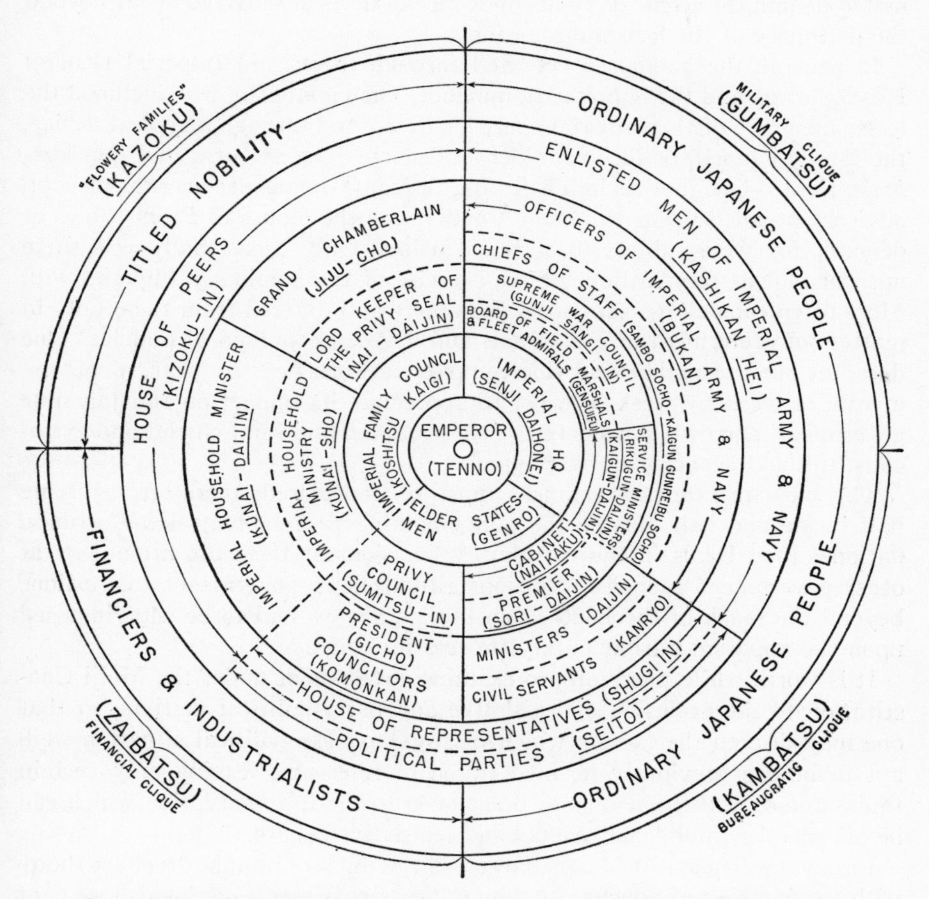

CHART 15—Circles of Influence: The Parliamentary Empire (1890-1931)

world meant that individuals moved rather easily from one clique to another. Any one policy, too, might be the joint product of several cliques or subcliques.

These grand cliques make an appropriate preface to the discussion of parliamentary government in Japan. Japanese parliamentarianism from 1889 to 1945 was a continuous shifting of balance between the influence of pre-parliamentary and nonparliamentary institutions and the forces of public opinion, as well as those of legislative action, set into motion by the creation of a parliament. In most of these years the balance was overwhelmingly weighted against those persons who relied on parliamentary status or parliamentary principles alone. The practical politics of Japan went on by means of unending negotiations between different cliques. Most of the time what the Japanese Imperial Diet did was a reflection of deals already consummated behind the scene, or an acquiescence in decisions arrived at far beyond the periphery of the legislators' vision.

In general, the *gumbatsu* operated through the Grand Imperial General Headquarters and the Supreme Command. The *mombatsu,* who included the lesser members of the Imperial court itself, worked through a typical device, the family council, or through elder statesmen. The *zaibatsu* and the *kambatsu* rivaled one another in infiltrating the same organs of government—top advisory organs such as the Privy Council and the House of Peers. Sines of demarcation were subject to shift or fusion. Only occasionally was there open or violent competition for the exercise of the nominally Imperial will. More often each clique supported the others and differed from them only in matters of preferment of individuals and degree or method of policies. One does not need to understand this complex network year by year, month by month, or week by week in order to appreciate its impact on the Japanese government narrowly considered. Constitutional and semi-official and extra-constitutional agencies all overlapped.

The parliamentary government must be considered, therefore, as lying half inside and half outside the policy-making process central to Japanese national life. Deals in the tea houses, decisions at the club, arguments at other government agencies, decisions ritualized in government institutions beyond the reach of the Diet—such factors always had to be superimposed upon the apparent parliamentary process in Japan.

It is worth while, therefore, to examine government under the Meiji Constitution to the exclusion of legislative and party-political matters, so that one may discern the factors which in any Japanese political situation were apt to be the previously decided frame of reference, leaving only certain topics and only these at certain times open to the full ventilation which can be afforded by public controversy and legislative debate.

In any government it is possible to draw artificial lines and to effect therewith a separation of powers. In Japan it was possible to distinguish sorts of government—on the one hand, the continuing, centuries-old political and administrative momentum of the central government framed against a background of concerted, but competitive cliques, and, on the other hand, the artificialities of parliamentary institutions striving to take a real share in political power and sometimes doing so.

The Imperial Conference *(Gozen Kaigi).* Most important of the institutions of the modernized central government was the Imperial conference. The holding of a conference was exclusively a prerogative of the Throne. This illustrates one essentially Japanese aspect of policy formulation in that, as a matter of fact, all decisions on major policy were "reached" in the presence of the Emperor. The "reaching" rarely involved controversy in the

Imperial presence; most often it was the ceremonial expression of concurrence arrived at before the conference met. This was not always the case. In a few historic instances disagreement carried through, all the way to the Imperial presence, and the disagreeing parties openly appealed to the authority and the personal intervention of the Emperor for a finalization of decision. Once he gave it, the Emperor's sanction conveyed full authority to the predominant clique or combination of cliques and to the policy arrived at on that particular occasion.

Attendance at such conferences varied both in number and in interest represented. In the middle and later Meiji period, the Imperial Princes, high-ranking Military Officers, the Elder Statesmen, the Lord Keeper of the Privy Seal, the Premier, and various Ministers of State were present at important conferences.

In theory neither the constitution nor law authorized the existence of such conferences and the decisions of Imperial conferences were from a Western juridical point of view null even before they were reached. In Japanese eyes, however, the nature of the conference, the fact that the policy was a major one, the further fact that the Emperor was present, the overwhelming fact that the Emperor himself participated in the decision—all this made the effect of Imperial conferences greater perhaps than the decision of any other instrumentality of government. It is significant that the final Japanese decision to surrender after the dropping of the second atomic bomb was reached at a truncated and unhappy Imperial conference, but an Imperial conference nonetheless.

The Imperial Council *(Kōshitsu Kaigi).* In the development of the Western monarchies there is to be observed the slow process of the articulation of governmental organs from the original nucleus of a kingly court. In their respective and quite dissimilar ways, the English and Prussian kingships gradually detached from the personal establishment of the king the central facilities of a government national and finally imperial in form. In Europe this took centuries. In Japan this was accomplished in two generations.

Government under the Meiji Constitution involved, therefore, not only the creation of a modern government for a nation-state, but required the *subtraction* of the national organs of government from an Imperial court in which those organs were theoretically a component part. The Japanese inevitably added to the complication of the process because the court itself had been in disuse for almost a thousand years and because the Japanese were copying governmental patterns from a civilization very different from their own.

In a sociological sense, it was necessary to deduct the larger institution from the smaller—to subtract from the theoretical supremacy of the Emperor and his court the large, ponderous machinery needed to govern a great power. The lesser part remaining at the top was still of importance in the national life of Japan. Comprising a government within the government, it took care of the affairs of the Imperial family itself.

With the advent of 1889 the legal distinction between the affairs of the Imperial household and those of the nation was set up and the Imperial Household Law proclaimed concurrently with the Meiji Constitution. The Imperial Household Law governed the affairs of the Imperial family and authorized the Imperial Family Council.

In membership the Council comprised all male members of the family and the senior male representatives of eleven princely households. *Ex officio* the Lord Keeper of the Privy Seal, the President of the Privy Council, the Imperial Household Minister, the Minister of State for Justice, and the Chief Justice also took part in Council meetings and offered advice.

When the deliberations concerned the Imperial family only, the sole countersignature required was that of the Imperial Household Minister; when the deliberations affected national law, the Prime Minister as well lent his signature to the ordinance. The Council was aided by a number of agencies: the Imperial Economic Council, the Board of Deliberation (with a Bureau of Peerage and Court Honors), a Board of Deliberation (Royal Houses), and an Imperial Governor.

This complex hierarchy was actually needed. The Imperial family was not only a force in politics and an agency of government; it was also a pillar of the national economy. The members of the family constituted the innermost circle of the aristocratic interests. Their wealth made up a substantial proportion of the total working capital of Japan. (On October 13, 1947, fifty-one princes met for the last time under the new postwar Imperial House Law. With the exception of the brothers of the Emperor himself, all the princes renounced their Imperial prestige and became commoners.) [1]

Even the Imperial family proper, quite apart from its circumjacent princely households, was a major economic force. The wealth of the Em-

[1] The following table shows the value of their pre-surrender property, the postwar property tax, and the lump allowances granted by the government:

(Unit: 1,000 yen)

	Property	*Property Tax*	*Allowance Granted*
Higashi-Fushimi	1,915	1,202	1,500
Fushimi	7,920	6,098	4,648
Yamashima [a]	1,543	923	0 [a]
Kaya	1,740	1,071	8,295
Kuni	7,048	5,252	8,393
Kuni (Kyoto)	188	34	1,050
Asaka	10,679	8,443	3,997
Nashimoto	3,686	2,565	1,050
Higashi-Kuni	3,320	2,264	6,647
Kita-Shiraka	4,838	6,528	5,399
Takeda	6,221	4,654	5,446
Kanin	5,681	4,195	1,050

[a] The Yamashima family received no allowance, as the incumbent prince was an army officer and had no family. *Japan Year Book, 1946-48,* cited, p. 6.

peror, apart from his income on the national civil list, ran over one billion yen at a time when the yen was as stable as the dollar and exchangeable at two yen for one dollar. The line between his private and public wealth was very hard to draw, but it was possible to argue with considerable cogency in the 1930's that the richest man in the world in terms of personal revenue potentially available to himself was probably the Japanese Emperor.

In terms of the long range of Japanese history it is quite significant that the Imperial Family Conference and the related agencies did succeed in staying well above the limits of public obloquy or reproach. There were no serious scandals involving any of the three emperors under whom Japan traversed the first eighty-five years of modern national existence. The mental shortcomings of the Meiji Emperor successor, the Taishō Emperor, constituted a deplorable illness, but not a national disgrace. Japan never had a Duke of Windsor, much less an Aga Khan. This may in part account for the almost unimpaired vitality of the Imperial prestige at the time it was most needed—the year of surrender.

***Genrō* and *Jūshin*.** The most interesting, yet amorphous, advisory organ was the group of elder statesmen called *Genrō*. The *Genrō* represented the historical culmination of the trend toward indirection in Japanese politics and diffusion of responsibility. It represented the family approach; the elders were counterparts in national life of village elders. The *Genrō* was a collective aristocratic dictatorship, like the *Kampaku* of Heian Japan. Save for the fact it was largely civilian, it resembled the Hōjō Council of Regents. Some called it the Shogunate-in-Commission. *Genrō* came to describe the role of various distinguished statesmen who exercised more power than any group in Japan between 1898 and 1918.[2]

The *Genrō* were entirely extra-constitutional; unwritten constitutional law, however, gave the institution tremendous power. Elder Statesmen often held the premiership and dominated the Privy Council, the Army, and the Navy. No Premier was selected without *Genrō* approval after 1892 and until the death of the last Elder Statesman. The Imperial will on all vital domestic legislation and on all treaties was expressed through the institution. And yet the *Genrō* was not a governmental agency as such. By the term, specific statesmen—once politicians—were meant, a second generation of clan *samurai* and *kuge* nobility. They became, as their ancestors had been in the Restoration, the real power behind the Throne. The original group consisted of Itō Hirobumi (assassinated 1909), Yamagata Aritomo (died 1922), Inoue Kaoru (died 1915), Ōyama Iwao (died 1916), and Matsukata

[2] Literally the characters for *Genrō* mean "Senior" or "Elder." In 1875, the word was applied to a Senate *(Genrō-in)*. Toward the end of the Meiji, however, transcending the Taishō and into the Shōwa era, a special meaning became attached to the word. Iwasaki, *op. cit.*, p. 38, states that the term was first used in its later political sense in 1900. For a Japanese definition, see *Dai hyakka jiten* (Encyclopedic dictionary), Tōkyō, 1932, Vol. VIII, pp. 573-574.

Masayoshi (died 1924). Later additions were Katsura Tarō (died 1913) and Saionji Kimmochi, the only court noble.

Saionji, the last of the *Genrō,* let it be known that he desired that the *Genrō* should disappear with his death. By 1924 the choice of Premier, for example, was preceded by interviews with the President of the Privy Council, the Imperial Household Minister, Lord Keeper of the Privy Seal, and surviving *Genrō.* Saionji died in 1940 but already a body of Senior Statesmen (*Jūshin*)—also extra-constitutional and vague in membership—took over the functions of the *Genrō.* This group included former Premiers, Lord Keeper of the Privy Seal, Imperial Household Minister, and President of the Privy Council. With certain "inner cabinet" officials, this group became the inner advisory circle.

Imperial Headquarters *(Senji Daihonei).* In time of war and in emergency, all high military officials were concentrated in the Imperial Headquarters. On many a Western movie screen the symbol of this organ became Hirohito on his white horse. The Emperor did indeed conduct meetings of the supreme command, just as he alone called Imperial conferences. Headquarters included the Chiefs of Staff, the Ministers of War and Navy, Imperial Princes assigned field commands, and selected officers. There was also a Chief Aide-de-Camp, a sort of personal Chief of Staff (like Admiral Leahy, adviser to President Roosevelt). In handling his exclusive war powers, the Emperor was also advised by the Board of Field Marshals and Fleet Admirals (*Gensuifu*). Members of this Board (in the military sphere) corresponded to the *Genrō* (in state affairs). Of course, the Board could be perpetuated only through war, as none but Imperial Princes could achieve Board rank in peacetime. In fact, military policy was formulated by a Supreme War Council, which will be described later.

The Executive: Civil Offices. In theory, as has been explained, all power inhered in and emanated from the Emperor. In practice, these powers were exercised by advisers. Thus, in the broadest sense, all Imperial advisers could be regarded collectively as the Japanese executive. In the narrower sense, the executive included civil and military advisers and administrators, next removed from the inner circle which had direct access to the Imperial will. Here, too, positions were traditionally monopolized by members or representatives of four groups: the aristocrats, militarists, bureaucrats, and financier industrialists. Only in the most exact sense, the executive comprised specific agencies of government: Lord Keeper of the Privy Seal and Imperial Household Minister in family affairs; Privy Council, in constituent and foreign affairs; Cabinet, in administrative affairs; and Supreme Command, in military affairs.

If the precise character of the Japanese executive is illusive, at least the nature and powers of executive organs can be described. While the executive was responsible to the Emperor for the policies it formulated, he in turn bore no responsibility for its acts. Still, in theory it was his sanction that gave all measures effect. Japanese politics was characterized, in consequence, not by any line of responsibility among individuals or groups but rather by a sharing of responsibility. The result was unstable equilibrium maintained by compromise; from such a compromise, in varying degrees, groups monopolizing the positions of power derived advantages. Because no legal power over appointments was vested in the Diet, because the Constitution favored the executive over the legislature, and because of unfavorable historical development, evolution in the direction of establishing a responsibility of the executive to the Diet was arrested by the 1930's.

The actual powers and functions of the executive, where they were defined, were set down in the Constitution and in prior laws and ordinances remaining in force. Many of these were directly related to the Imperial prerogative and have been analyzed. Let us review them briefly: management of Imperial family affairs, introduction of amendments to constitutional law, exercise of the supreme command, declaration of war, conclusion of peace and negotiation of treaties, determination of the administrative structure, appointment and dismissal of civil and military officials, power to prorogue and dissolve the Diet, and ultimate sanctioning of all laws.

In addition to the powers which the executive alone exercised, there were others of a legislative nature: the advantage which government bills enjoyed in the Diet, the final veto, and extensive ordinance power. A firm control of the purse, furthermore, was exercised by the executive through its ability to enforce the budget of the preceding year should the Diet refuse to vote the proposed schedule. It was further strengthened by the possession of emergency financial ordinance power, as well as the inability of the Diet to reduce fixed expenditures. Enjoying a privileged position and armed with these powers, the offices described below constituted one of the most powerful executives in the world.[3]

Imperial family affairs, prerogative of the Emperor and his Council, were actually administered by the Lord Keeper of the Privy Seal (*Nai-daijin*) and the Imperial Household Minister (*Kunai-daijin*). The position of Lord Keeper was created in 1884; the Imperial Household Ministry was established, along with the Cabinet, in 1885. The former was officially responsible for advice on family and state affairs, for handling petitions transmitted by subjects, and for affixing the Imperial Seal to all ordinances and laws. In fact, the Lord Keeper became the Emperor's highest personal adviser. The latter was not a Minister of State at all, since he did not belong to the

[3] For convenience Appendix 12 presents in outline form the organization and powers of the executive offices, civilian and military. This outline and parts of the following description are based on the very excellent study by the Department of State, Interim Research and Intelligence Service, Research and Analysis Branch, *The Japanese Executive: Structure and Functions* (R & A No. 3404), October 18, 1945, Restricted (Declassified); SCAP, *Political Reorientation*, cited, Vol. I, pp. 120-123, gives a brief survey of the pre-surrender organization. The official gazette of Japan and the basic source for all aspects of governmental activities is the Naikaku Insatsukyoku (Cabinet Printing Office), *Kampō* (Official Gazette), Tōkyō, 1883—; all laws, ordinances, and administrative regulations became effective only upon promulgation in the *Kampō*.

Cabinet. He was responsible for advice on family affairs and on conferring ranks and titles, as well as for supervision of the Imperial Household Ministry (*Kunaishō*). Both these officials were appointed by the Emperor customarily, though not necessarily, for life. Both advised the Emperor on appointment of a Premier. Both controlled access to the Imperial will since they made all appointments for audiences.[4] Since the Ministry and post of Lord Keeper were not subject to Cabinet control, the holders came to be regarded as quasi-*Genrō* and, later, as full-fledged *Jūshin*.

The Privy Council *(Sumitsu-in)*. The Privy Council had been established to act as a constituent body, advising the Emperor on Japanese organic law. The ordinance creating and regulating the Council, the *Sumitsu-in Kansei* (Privy Council Ordinance of 1888), thus pre-dated the Meiji Constitution itself. Article LVI of the Constitution, which the Privy Council had approved, specifically provided: "The Privy Councilors shall, in accordance with the provisions for the organization of the Privy Council, deliberate on important matters of state when they have been consulted by the Emperor."[5]

The Council consisted of a president (*Gichō*), appointed by the Emperor for life; a vice-president (*Fuku Gichō*), and twenty-five councilors (*Komonkan*). All members of the Cabinet were *ex officio* members of the Council. The President controlled meetings of the Council, introduced matters for discussion, voted in case of a tie, announced decisions, appointed committees, and signed all Council documents. The work of the Council was aided by a secretary general (*Shoki-kanchō*) and performed in committees. In 1930 the average age of councilors was seventy-three years. Among its members only seven had held Cabinet posts, and four were drawn from the army and navy. There were three professors *emeriti* and four former university presidents.

It may seem strange to say so, but the Privy Council might well have disappointed Itō Hirobumi had he been able to return to see it at work, for he had intended it to be strictly advisory: "It shall not interfere with the executive." Itō certainly did not mean to have it control the ministries. It was thus planned as an organ on the same plane as the Cabinet and the Diet.

[4] Premier Tanaka was criticized, in 1929, for presenting Cabinet proposals to the Emperor without the presence of the Imperial Household Minister. Influence tended to move back and forth between the Minister, or the Grand Chamberlain *(Jijūcho)*, and the Lord Keeper. Usually a move from the Ministry to Lord Keeper was considered a promotion. Count Makino, for example, became Lord Keeper after having held offices as Minister of Education, Minister of Foreign Affairs, Minister of Agriculture and Commerce, and Imperial Household Minister. When Prince Katsura became Lord Keeper, he was looked on as a sort of revived *Shōgun*. See Quigley, *Japanese Government*, cited, p. 73, fn. 98.

[5] Six specific powers were assigned to the Council by ordinance: (1) matters under jurisdiction according to provisions of the Imperial House Law; (2) drafts of laws and ordinances supplementary to the Constitution, on which doubtful points were raised; (3) Proclamations under Articles XIV (siege), as well as VII and LXX (ordinances); (4) international treaties and agreements; (5) amendment of the organization and rules of conduct of the Privy Council; and (6) matters especially submitted for advice. A translation of the text of the *Sumitsu-in kansei* is given in *JGD*, pp. 127-132; also in SCAP, *Political Reorientation*, cited, Vol. II, Appendix C:1, pp. 593-596.

In theory, the primary distinction between the Privy Council and the Cabinet was that the former was to act only on request. Although the Constitution somewhat vaguely made such a stipulation, the previous Imperial Ordinance had required that all matters under the Council's jurisdiction be submitted to it. Its entrenched position was further guaranteed by its power to veto amendments of the structure and functions of the Council itself. It gradually took on policy-formulating functions, particularly in the realm of foreign affairs. It thus furnished another example of a body exercising both executive and legislative functions. Of the semi-advisory, semi-administrative organs, it was probably the most powerful and important single agency of the government. No formal action, whether law, ordinance, rescript, or appointment, could be undertaken without its concurrence. It became an unshakable institution of conservative statesmen and the bulwark of autocracy.

Could the Council amend drafts submitted to it? The same familiar arguments arose here as over the constitutional position of the Emperor. Minobe argued that a draft or treaty had a definite content which the Council could not alter. Furthermore, the Council was never designed to be a court of constitutional controversy like the Supreme Court of the United States. Hozumi argued that it could alter projects. Constitutional logic favored Minobe; practice favored Hozumi. As a matter of fact, the Council rendered only one formal interpretation and used more subtle methods of blocking "unconstitutional" action.

In legislative matters, a special committee of inquiry was appointed in the Council. Before it Cabinet officials were interpellated. Very often the Council was referred to as a "third house."

In executive affairs, the Council's most important role developed into advising on the selection of the Premier. By custom, the President as senior statesman often pre-empted the job of giving advice. Another important function came to be supervision of foreign affairs. In the early period of the parliamentary Empire, the Council saw eye to eye with the Cabinet. After all, cabinet ministers sat on the Privy Council. Imperial ordinances had referred to the Council as the Emperor's supreme counsel, and constitutional doctrine had forbidden the Cabinet's going over the Council's head to the Emperor. Such a move would have forced the Emperor to choose between the organs.

In the later 1920's, however, the Privy Council was indirectly assaulted by party cabinets, anxious to extend the spoils of patronage. Nevertheless, advice by the Privy Council contrary to the Cabinet's policy continued to be regarded as Imperial disapproval.[6]

[6] A few examples of Council obstruction may be cited here. The Wakatsuki government fell in 1927 when the Council refused to approve an ordinance granting relief to the Bank of Taiwan. After the intervention at Tsinan-fu, 1929, the Cabinet put through a Sino-Japanese arrangement in the form of an executive agreement, to avoid Council scrutiny. The Council was on the reactionary side in the famous "Kellogg Pact" dispute and again,

The Cabinet ***(Naikaku).*** The battleground of the aristocrats, militarists, financier-industrialists, and bureaucrats was the Cabinet. Despite the entrenchment of each group in the important organs already mentioned, the Cabinet soon became the most important political body in the state and the Premier the most powerful single figure. This was true for several reasons.

First, the Cabinet was the top administrative agency of the state. Consequently, control of the Cabinet was necessary to any clique or group of advisers which desired to enforce its policy.

Second, the Premier (*Sōri-daijin*) was the chief link between the inner circle surrounding the Emperor and the legal government. He and his ministers (*Daijin*) were *ex officio* members of the Privy Council. The Cabinet was primarily responsible to the Emperor (which meant to the complex of inner advisers); it was only secondarily responsible to the Diet (which meant to the majority party and to the people). At first, the theory was that each minister was responsible individually to the Emperor. Later, the Cabinet operated as a unit under the Premier; even later, civilian ministers were not effectively responsible even to the Premier. The major exception, discussed below, was the privileged positions of the Ministers of War and of Navy. The courts, directly under the Cabinet, were little more than instruments of state power. In other words, the Premier and his Cabinet became the chief link between the *seen* executive agencies and the *unseen* organs behind the Imperial screen.

Finally, the Diet—at least the lower house—was secondary to the Cabinet. The Premier exercised considerable authority over the House of Representatives and became the chief liaison between the Diet and the Cabinet.

Actually, the Japanese Cabinet, like its American counterpart, was an organ partly justified under constitutional law and partly born out of usage. A Cabinet as such was not mentioned in the Meiji Constitution; Article LV simply stated: "The representative Ministers of State shall give their advice to the Emperor, and be responsible for it." The term "Ministers of State" nevertheless referred definitely to a Cabinet, since such a system had been established in 1885, before the Constitution, and since existing enactments not in conflict with the Constitution remained in force.[7]

The Cabinet too changed with usage. As the administration of Japanese

in the argument over signature of the London Naval Treaty, the Council badgered the government. Proposals for a reform of the Privy Council were heard about this time; see, for example, a symposium published in the Tōkyō *Asahi Shimbun,* October 13-16, 1930, which advocated: (1) revision in terms of Council membership; (2) in procedure; (3) restriction of ordinance power; (4) creation of a stronger Cabinet; and (5) even abolition of the Council. Kenneth C. Colegrove, "The Japanese Privy Council," *American Political Science Review,* Vol. XV, Nos. 3 and 4 (August and November, 1931); H. S. Quigley, "The Privy Council vs. the Cabinet in Japan," *Foreign Affairs,* Vol. IX (April, 1931). After the early 1930's the Privy Council became less active and less important politically. The center of gravity for influence had shifted elsewhere.

[7] The Imperial Rescript on Functions of the Cabinet is printed in *JGD,* pp. 232-233; and is an appendix to the Meiji Constitution in SCAP, *Political Reorientation,* cited, Appendix C:1, p. 596.

government became more far-reaching, the organization of the Cabinet became more complex. Fortunately we now have several on-the-spot studies of the Cabinet, among which is one made by Professor John M. Maki (now of the University of Washington) for Government Section, SCAP. Professor Maki wrote:

> In Japan the term "Cabinet" has two distinct meanings. The first is a collective term to designate all Ministers of State and the Prime Minister. In this sense the terms "Cabinet" and "Cabinet Council" are interchangeable. The second meaning designates the executive agencies of the Prime Minister, comprising special executive offices directly responsible to the Prime Minister and entirely apart from the ministries and the Cabinet Council.
>
> The Cabinet Council (*Kakugi*) is composed of all the heads of ministries, Ministers of State without Portfolio, the Chief of the Bureau of Legislation, and the Chief Secretary of the Cabinet. The Cabinet Council must pass on the following: draft of laws; the draft budget; treaties with foreign countries and important international agreements; imperial ordinances concerning law enforcement and administrative rules and regulations; jurisdictional disputes among the various ministries; public petitions forwarded by the Diet or from the Emperor; disbursements not provided for in the budget; and the appointment, award of honors to and treatment of first-class officials. The Cabinet as an executive agency of the Prime Minister likewise has important Government functions. However, these functions are, generally speaking, more administrative than policy-making.
>
> . . .
>
> In more prosaic language, the Cabinet in one of its capacities can be regarded as a general administrative "housekeeping" unit of the government as a whole and in another sense it can be regarded as one of the supreme consultative organs for the Emperor. As a "housekeeping" unit it is simply a government body which can be considered in the same light as a ministry; as a consultative body it is the Cabinet Council.[8]

Because of the diffusion of executive responsibility and because of the various political cross-currents centered upon the Cabinet, the selection of a Japanese Premier was always a fascinating test of strength. The Japanese

[8] SCAP, *Political Reorientation,* Vol. II, Appendix D:1, "Study of the Cabinet," by John M. Maki, pp. 684-694. The Cabinet Secretariat *(Naikaku Kambō),* responsible to both the Cabinet Council and Premier, was the key administrative organ and was composed of sections: general affairs, personnel, accounts, legislation, etc. The Chief Secretary *(Shoki Kanchō* occupied a position similar to that of a parliamentary vice-minister in Western governments, with functions similar to those of a vice-minister. Two civilian agencies played important roles in administration, although not properly part of the executive or Cabinet. The Board of Audit *(Kaikei Kensa-in)* was responsible for verifying and confirming accounts of government and reporting on them to the Diet (Article LXXII of the Constitution). The Court of Administrative Litigation *(Gyōsei Saibansho)* heard complaints against administrative acts. There was no appeal from its decisions. The court compiled and indexed its cases: Gyōsei Saibansho, *Gyōsei Saibansho hanketsuroku* (Compendium of decisions of the Court of Administrative Litigation), Tōkyō, monthly.

and even the Western press, filled with the latest rumors, would wait expectantly while hidden forces tugged behind the screen. The Emperor, upon the recommendation of the Elder Statesmen (later, of the *Jūshin*), would command some prominent political figure to form a Cabinet. It should be noted that the *Genrō* (or *Jūshin*) *did not choose the Premier*. As those primarily responsible for the rise and development of modern Japanese government, the Elder Statesmen offered only the most weighty advice. Indeed, in the early days the *Genrō* made sure of their control, by selecting one of their members or at least a henchman, as their nominee. From the first meeting of the Diet in 1890 until June, 1898, the premiership was passed back and forth among clansmen become politicians, soon to become Elder Statesmen.[9]

Later, during the so-called "Period of Normal Government" (*Kensei no Jōdō*)—from the end of World War I to the Manchurian Incident of 1931—the recommendation of the *Genrō* was not primary in the selection of a Premier. Following Saionji's advice, the head of the majority party of the lower House more or less automatically assumed the post. (Such party governments are discussed below, along with the development of political parties.) Cabinets could be overthrown in various ways. Either of the service ministers could withdraw and, if no successor was chosen, the Cabinet would fall. An aroused House of Peers or an irate Privy Council could render all action null and void. With the growth of party organization, the House of Representatives could impeach the Cabinet or pass a vote of no confidence. Even though legally the Premier did not have to possess a majority of the House, the Cabinet would resign. Actually the Premier usually had the Emperor dissolve the House before it had a chance to challenge the government.

The Executive: Military Offices. The unique position of the services under the Meiji Constitution justifies treatment of the Supreme Command as a distinct executive agency. One of the reasons why military affairs were completely separate and outside civil government was the feudal tradition of dualism, which became recognized under constitutional law and by usage. This dualism was symbolized by the separate functions of the *Tennō* "in Cabinet" and the *Tennō* "in Camp."

Another reason for military independence was a group of ordinances, originally drafted by Prince Yamagata and issued between 1894 and 1904, by which the portfolios of the war and navy ministers could be held only by generals or lieutenant generals and admirals or vice-admirals, respectively. Both service ministers insisted upon individual responsibility, despite the growth in custom of collective responsibility of civilian Cabinet components.

[9] In other words, from 1890 to 1898: Itō (Chōshū), Matsukata (Satsuma), and Yamagata (Chōshū); from 1898 to 1918, semi-party cabinets appeared but only because the *Genrō* and their lieges—men like Ōkuma (Hizen), Itō, Saionji *(kuge)*, Katsura, (Chōshū), and Yamamoto (Satsuma)—found it convenient to have the backing of the majority party in the lower house. Professor Reischauer, *Japan: Government-Politics*, cited, presents an unimprovable survey of this period in Part 2, Chap. 5, "The Elder Statesmen *(Genrō)* in Power (1889-1918)," pp. 107-132.

A third reason was that both ministers, as well as the two chiefs of staff, could report directly to the Emperor on matters concerning the Supreme Command function.[10] Thus the ministers themselves had a dual status. They were, it is true, members of the Cabinet reporting on general affairs through the Premier; but they were also members of the Supreme Command reporting directly and independently of their colleagues in the Cabinet. It is obvious, with such a clear channel to the Throne, no Cabinet could be formed without them.

Finally, there was a dualism in the operations of the services themselves. Whereas the ministers advised on organization and administration of the services, the chiefs of staff at the very least shared the command function. Itō had written: "A general staff office has been established for His Imperial Majesty's personal and general direction of the army and navy." From this some concluded that the execution of the Supreme Command was performed not through the ministers at all, but through the chiefs of staff.[11]

Since the Imperial Headquarters was activated only during an emergency and since the *Gensuifu* was perpetuated only through war, peacetime execution of military affairs was actually handled by the Supreme War Council (*Gunji Sangi-in*). Established by Imperial Ordinance in 1903, the Supreme War Council was another example of a semi-advisory, semi-executive agency. It resembled, in the military sphere, the operations of the Privy Council in civil affairs. Field marshals and field admirals were included, of course, as well as chiefs of staff, the service ministers, and other high-ranking army and navy officers. The senior officer present always presided. Deliberations covered the whole range of military policy, administrative problems, and tactical organization, as well as many matters not strictly in the realm of military affairs. As a result, the Council assumed an importance far above what might be expected even of a high military board. Army and navy members frequently met separately to discuss matters concerning only one of the services.

Army and Navy Brass. The "Big Three"[12] of the Army were the Chief of the General Staff (*Sambō Sochō*), the Minister of War (*Rikugun-daijin*),

[10] Paragraph VII of the Imperial Rescript on Functions of the Cabinet read: "With the exception of military or naval affairs of grave importance which, having been reported directly to the Sovereign by the Chief of Staff, may have been submitted by His Majesty for the consideration of the Cabinet, the Ministers of State for War and Navy shall report to the Minister President." SCAP, *Political Reorientation,* cited, Vol. II, Appendix C:1, p. 596.

[11] See, for example, Nakano Tomio, *The Ordinance Power of the Japanese Emperor,* Baltimore, 1923, pp. 154-156. One of the most thoughtful volumes treating the role of the Meiji military is Takeuchi, *op. cit.,* especially Chaps. 2-5, pp. 14-48. Takeuchi's work stresses control of foreign policy, with emphasis on procedure. Many American language officers during World War II, including the author, learned their primary military history, organization, and terminology through two semi-popular surveys: Hirata Shinsaku, *Rikugun tokuhon* (Army reader), Tōkyō, 1932; same author, *Kaigun tokuhon* (Navy reader), Tōkyō, 1933. For more authoritative references to organization, budget, and laws affecting military affairs: Kokusai Gunji Kenkyūkai, *Gunji nenkan* (International Military Research Institute, Military affairs yearbook), Tōkyō, annually.

[12] The expressions *"san chō kan"* and *"sanchōkan kaigi"* were frequently seen in newspapers and heard in radio news announcements in Japan; the more formal name: *Chūō Tōkatsu Kikan* (Central Control Board).

and the Inspector General of Military Education (*Kyōiku Sōkan*). The "Big Two" of the Navy were the Chief of the Naval Staff (*Kaigun Gunreibu Sochō*) and the Minister of the Navy (*Kaigun-daijin*). All but the Inspector General had the right of direct access to the Emperor.

Because the Army was fearful that a Minister of War, serving in the Cabinet as he must with mere bureaucrats and politicians, might be infected by a civilian outlook, the vital field of military training was withdrawn from ministerial control and entrusted to a special Inspectorate General of Military Education (*Kyōiku Sōkambu*). The Inspector was appointed directly by the Emperor, on recommendation of the Army members of the Supreme War Council. He was in charge of all Army schools (except the War College, aviation schools, and certain special schools under jurisdiction of the Ministry), training, education of all officers and men, and coordination of military education.

All Japanese were, of course, considered children of the father-Emperor. But Japanese servicemen were looked upon as favorite children, bound to the *Tennō* in the additional intimate relationship of soldier and sailors to the Commander in Chief. This unique position of the military arose partly from the fact that Japan's first modern conscription law was enacted in 1872, enforced in 1873, and revised in 1883, long before the establishment of a constitution.[13] Thus, the services, and particularly the officers of higher military administration, felt superior to the rank and file of Japanese subjects.

As a matter of fact, the services were set apart legally, too. The Constitution denied them the vote. And an Imperial Ordinance of 1882 warned that servicemen were not to involve themselves or interest themselves in politics. But the militarist clique (*gumbatsu*), on the inner circle of Imperial advisers and astride the administrative structure, were very much in politics. Their activities, particularly in the sphere of military education, will be described later. Suffice it to say here that they too developed semi-private and even private channels of ideological control in order to achieve support for their policies. These were the militaristic organizations and secret societies which glorified the new *samurai,* rationalized war, laid great stress on loyalty to the *Tennō,* and developed a fascistic economic outlook.

The Bureaucracy *(Kambatsu).* Of all the elite groups under the Meiji Constitution, the bureaucrats (*kanryō*) were perhaps the most ubiquitous and insidious. The *Kambatsu* (literally "Official Clique") was both a formalized organ of government—staffing the ministries and entire civil service—and also a semi-independent force—set apart from the Japanese people at large and armed with tremendous power.

[13] The Imperial Rescript accompanying the Act of 1873 read in part: "The military system of the West is thorough and detailed, for it is the result of studies and tests of centuries. But the difference of government and geographic conditions warns us against indiscriminate adoption of the Western system." See Gotaro Ogawa, *The Conscription System in Japan,* New York, 1921, p. 4.

As part of the governmental hierarchy, the bureaucracy was responsible only to those who spoke in the name of the *Tennō*. Its interests were parallel to those of the aristocratic inner circle; indeed its personnel were often drawn from the aristocracy. Theoretically, it was controlled by the Cabinet. It could have come in conflict with the *Gumbatsu,* save for the fact that military affairs were separate from civilian administration. Sometimes there was a threat, particularly in eras of increasing economic control, that the bureaucracy would clash with the *Zaibatsu.* More often the *Zaibatsu* were awarded government contracts and bounties, public land, and special favors. With the rise of political party power in the 1920's, the bureaucracy was forced to defend its privileged position against the onslaught of patronage. It is a tribute to its staying-power to say that of all the pre-World War II groups and cliques—the aristocracy, the militarists, the *Zaibatsu,* and the bureaucracy—the bureaucracy was the last to change under the Occupation, if it changed at all.

The bureaucracy has had high morale, a long tradition, and the administration itself as weapons of defense. Its ethics and legalism have deep roots in the Sino-Japanese tradition of the scholar-statesman, in the Japan-imitated standards of T'ang bureaucratic magnificence, and in the modern dictatorship by an educated elite. In truth, the *kanryō* thought of themselves as the guardians of national polity. Appointed by a divine Emperor, they occupied vital posts in the Imperial Household Ministry and in the courts, in addition to holding membership in the House of Peers and even in the Privy Council. Consolidated just below the inner circle of advisers and executive, the great mass of *kanryō* consisted of chiefs of divisions, bureaus, and sections in the various ministries. They also served as government delegates in the Diet, since ministers or their representatives were privileged at any time "to take seats and speak in either house." The *kanryō* not only looked down on the Diet but knew the techniques for keeping the people's representatives in their places. *Kanryō* moved easily into and out of political parties; they bought protection against encroachment by appeasing political bosses and floor leaders in the lower house. Bureaucrats were in an enviable position to beat down popular movements by declaring them destructive of the polity and therefore subversive. The police, direct agents of the bureaucracy, enforced every law, rescript, ordinance, regulation, and administrative order.

Indoctrination in bureaucratic legalism began in the universities. More accurately, it began in *a* university, for all hopeful bureaucrats competed for admission to the Law Faculty, Tokyo Imperial University. Tokyo *Teidai* enjoyed the highest prestige of any institution in the Far East, and therefore it attracted the most promising young Japanese. It prepared more than three fourths of those who finally entered the administrative service.[14]

[14] The course of studies in the Law Faculty was, as American students would put it, rugged: it lasted three years; the legal emphasis was very heavy. Of 14 required courses,

Once in the permanent civil service, a *kanryō* tended to move up from section chief to bureau, and from bureau chief to division. Eventually, he found himself in the Minister's Secretariat, at the policy-making level, and later he might even become an assistant to the Premier. Along the way were opportunities to become rich, as a director of a semi-governmental agency, a government bank, or a monopoly. The dream, of course, was ultimately to enter the House of Peers and a life devoted to higher politics. A very few fortunate ones were ushered into the Privy Council where Imperial Rescripts, ordinances, and bills were discussed.

For the permanent civil servant, such a pathway to paradise was mapped out up through a hierarchy of fourteen grades, four ranks. The *kanryō* began as

1. *Hannin,* or routine functionary in the classified service; appointed by a superior officer. The junior official moved through Grades IV-I.

When the bureaucrat became a secretary of bureau or chief of section, he was called a "higher official" (*kōtōkan*) and his certificate of appointment bore the Privy Seal. Higher officials were divided into

2. *Sōnin,* an official appointed by a Minister with His Majesty's approval, Grades IX-III; and
3. *Chokunin* (ordinary), an official appointed by the Emperor on the advice of the Premier, Grades II-I.

Ordinary *chokunin* officials included vice-ministers, procurators, judges, directors of bureaus, and prefectural governors. Actually, the term *chokunin* also included the highest rank:

4. *Shinnin,* an official appointed directly by the Emperor.

These appointees attended at the Throne and received patents signed by the Emperor. They included the Premier, Ministers, Privy Councilors, Governors-General, and Ambassadors. In 1927, the three lower ranks numbered about 150,000 members, with an additional 280,000 in the unclassified serv-

---

9 dealt with law; among 10 electives, 5 were legal in nature. Only one course, science of administration (a third-year elective), treated administrative problems in a practical, rather than a legal manner. Another effective tool of this institution was the higher civil service examination, through which the faculty opened or closed the door to all higher careers in government.

There was actually no social science of public administration in pre-World War II Japan. The monthly *Kokka gakkai zasshi,* cited, was published at Tokyo *Teidai* and occasionally carried articles on administration. Professor Rōyama Masamichi, having studied in the U. S. and England, contributed the only real texts in the field. Although he retired in 1938, he has begun a new career in post-treaty Japanese political science. In contrast, the field of administrative law was almost as popular as constitutional law. Professor Oda Yorozu (Kyoto *Teidai*)—later, a member of the Permanent Court of International Justice—was outstanding in this field. His *Principes de droit administratif du Japon,* Paris, 1928, was published in Japan as *Nihon gyōsei genri* (Principles of Japanese administrative law), Tōkyō, 1934.

ice. The total of 430,000 was exclusive of personnel in the Imperial Household Ministry.

What was the relationship between this bureaucratic army and the public? It should be remembered that the Japanese were not novices in administration. In fact, they boasted an administrative tradition based on centuries of experience. Unlike our Federal government of the 1890's or backward state governments today—both performing only a minimum of administrative functions—the Japanese were used to the regulation of political, economic, and intellectual life. But Japanese culture dictated quite different norms for administration. The state was a political family with each member assigned status. The basic criteria were to preserve custom and to avoid any challenge to tradition according to the social values that governed their society; *kanryō* were and are subtle artists in human relationships.

On the other hand, in terms of modern administrative science, the Japanese government left much to be desired, both in philosophy and in procedure. In Oriental terms administration provided the *kanryō* with a detailed and intricate ritual, the mysteries of which only the legal priesthood could understand. The language, as well as documentary phrasing, as in China, separated the *kanryō* from the public, the military, the aristocracy, and the financial clique. In Western terms, the Prussian system with its *Rechtsstaat* ideal became the model. Legalism assumed that every act had to be authorized in advance by statute or by regulation. The corollary was an intricate and formal set of rules designed to cover every administrative situation. Regardless of pragmatic necessity or social demand, the cautious *kanryō* interpreted the absence of specific rule as full justification for failure to act. Regardless of common sense, he followed regulations "out the window."

One result of legality was that Japanese administration became completely overgrown with a jungle of unappraised, unamended procedures. Rules were seldom written. No agency had anything resembling a manual of procedure. Regulations were held in the heads of lower-grade officials who seldom had any conception of government-wide programming. Higher officials trained legally seldom remained in a post long enough to affect operations.

Legal philosophy and the regulatory morass obviously affected administrative organization. The distinction between Line (policy-making) and Staff (housekeeping) functions, common in most modern governments, was nonexistent in Japan. Line officials continued to perform, without help, functions which had long since become highly developed staff specialities elsewhere. There was no central agency for personnel administration. All personnel policy matters were handled by the Cabinet Bureau of Legislation (*Hōsei-kyoku*), which occupied a strategic position in the machinery of government and included some of the leading lights of the Japanese bureaucracy. It was no accident that the Higher Civil Service Examination Committee was assigned to this bureau. Most ministries adopted the pattern of the Cabinet Secretariat, whose sections performed only routine duties in personnel administration, accounting, and record control. The Budget Bureau (*Shukei-kyoku*) belonged to the Ministry of Finance, as in England, and did not prescribe techniques for expenditure analysis. Once the budget was adopted by the Diet, the Bureau's work was complete! In other words, the Cabinet and individual ministries administered the budget. No one allocated funds periodically. No central purchasing agency existed. Nothing was accomplished in organizational or procedural analysis.[15]

In organization also, every ministry tended to follow the same pattern as that of the Cabinet. Immediately below the Minister (*Daijin*) were a permanent Vice-Minister (*Gimu Jikan*), a Parliamentary Vice-Minister (*Seimu Jikan*), and a Parliamentary Counselor (*Sanyokan*). The last two posts were not established until 1924, when it was found necessary to provide sinecures for disappointed party hacks. Both offices provided Diet contact and liaison. The Minister's Secretariat (*Daijin Kambō*), like the superior Cabinet Secretariat, had charge of departmental personnel records, pay, and other administrative matters. Operational organization was subdivided into boards (*-shoku*), divisions (*-bu*), bureaus (*-kyoku*), and sections (*-ka*), in that order. Usually, however, the bureau was the top administrative unit. Ministries averaged about six bureaus. Ministers without Portfolio (*Kokumu-daijin*) were added and subtracted; within each ministry, as in the case of the Cabinet itself, boards and committees were tacked on to fill an advisory role but remained in semi-autonomous status.

Ministries. Consisting at first of a minister-president and nine ministries, membership of the Cabinet was increased to thirteen by 1929. The original portfolios included: Foreign Affairs, War, Navy, Finance, Education, Agriculture and Commerce, Justice, and Home Affairs. A Ministry of Railways was added in 1918. In April, 1925, Agriculture and Commerce was divided into Agriculture and Forestry, and Commerce and Industry. For two years in the late nineteenth century, a Colonization Bureau was located in the Cabinet Secretariat. Its revival under the title Ministry of Overseas Affairs occurred in 1929.

Undoubtedly the ministry with greatest prestige, at least among the civilian departments, was the Ministry of Foreign Affairs (*Gaimushō*). The Higher Civilian Service Examination Committee had a special diplomatic division directed by the Vice-Minister for Foreign Affairs. Candidates took stiff written examinations in compulsory (law, economics, language) and optional (philosophy, political science, history, law, and economics) subjects, as well as oral examinations in international public law, a foreign language,

[15] When the Occupation began, only one member of SCAP, Government Section, was engaged in the study of Japanese administration. Lieutenant Milton J. Esman, AUS, a Princeton Ph.D. and former U. S. Civil Service Commission analyst, has since given us his impressions gained from a study of Japanese administrative techniques. The above description draws heavily on his "Japanese Administration—a Comparative View," *Public Administration Review,* Vol. VII, No. 2 (Spring, 1947), pp. 100-112.

and two subjects chosen from the writtens. The result was that the *Gaimushō* usually took the cream of the *kanryō*. The Ministry itself, before its wartime expansion, consisted of area-policy bureaus: East Asiatic, Asiatic and European, and American; and functional bureaus: Commerce, Treaty, and Intelligence. Between the wars it directed Japan's nine embassies, eighteen legations, a small permanent delegation to the League of Nations, and over one hundred consulates.[16]

The Ministry of Overseas Affairs (*Takumushō*) was a symbol in government of growing Japanese colonial interests. The Ministry had bureaus of superintendence, industry, and colonial affairs; it handled emigration and settlement abroad, in addition to colonial administration. Departmental regulations included Chōsen (Korea), Karafuto (Sakhalin), the Kwantung Leased Territory, and the Mandates.

Because of military autonomy, the War Ministry (*Rikugunshō*) and the Navy Ministry (*Kaigunshō*) enjoyed special status. Administrative organs for the Army and for the Navy, the service ministries also served as liaison with the Diet. The War Ministry, for example, contained as major bureaus: personnel, war plans, military affairs, mobilization plans, ordnance, intendance, medical, and judicial. The General Staff (*Sambō Hombu*) and the Naval Staff Board (*Kaigun Gunreibu*) enjoyed independent status. The organization of the Army General Staff, shown in the accompanying table,[17] may be taken as representative.

The Ministry of Finance (*Ōkurashō*) administered the financial affairs of the government. Military finance and all business relating to the Imperial household were outside the scope of its operations. Four bureaus—accounts, taxation, finance, and banking—collaborated in preparing the draft budget, which was discussed and revised by the end of August for the following fiscal year (April 1 to March 31). As submitted to the Diet, it consisted of four parts:

1. *General Account* presented principal revenue and expenditure;
2. *Special Account* covered income and expenditure also authorized by law, related to overseas projects, government railroads and monopolies;
3. *Supplementary Expenditures* covered deficiencies resultant from the execution of laws and contracts;
4. *Continuing Expenditures* were for public works involving several years' capital investment.

The National Treasury Section (*Kokkoka*) handled actual income and expenditures and was independent of the authorizing agencies, as was the

[16] During World War I and immediately thereafter, the Japanese experimented with an Advisory Council on Foreign Affairs *(Gaikō Chōsakai)*. It was rumored that its abolition, in September, 1922, was a result of Privy Council pressure. Later, Premier Tanaka (1927-1929) sought to establish a similar body. Takeuchi, *op. cit.*, pp. 43-48. The pattern of an inner cabinet was followed in World War II.

[17] *Heigo* (Military Dictionary), "Organization of the Japanese Army," Section 3: The General Staff, Washington: Mimeographed Language Materials, n.d., pp. 6-9.

OFFICE	JAPANESE TITLE	APPOINTMENT	MISSION
Army General Staff	*Sambō Hombu*	.....	1. Preparation of war plans 2. Direction of large-scale maneuvers 3. Movement of troops 4. Compilation of field service regulations 5. Preparation of maps and military history 6. Supervision of War College (*Rikugun Daigakkō*)
Chief of General Staff	*Sambō Sōchō*	(General or Lieutenant General, active) by Emperor	Represents Emperor in matters concerning supreme command
Vice Chief of Staff	*Sambō Jichō*	(General or Lieutenant General, active) by Chief of Staff	Assists Chief of Staff
General Affairs Section	*Sōmubu*	.....	Staff administration
1st Section	*Dai Ichibu-Sakusen*	.....	Operations
2d Section	*Dai Nibu-Jōhō*	.....	Intelligence
3rd Section	*Dai Sambu-Unyukōtsū*	.....	Transportation
4th Section	*Dai Yombu-Senshi, Hei-yōchishi*	.....	War History, Military Geography
Land Survey Bureau	*Rikuchi Sokuryobu*	.....	Military Surveys
Army War College	*Rikugun Daigakkō*	.....	Staff Training

Mint (*Zōhei-kyoku*). The Monopoly Bureau (*Sembai-kyoku*), which controlled the tobacco, salt, and camphor monopolies, was also under the jurisdiction of the Finance Ministry.

Next to the Home Ministry in terms of exercising direct influence on the people of Japan was the Ministry of Education (*Mombushō*). Centralization of control over the entire educational system in this Ministry made it the most important organ for the indoctrination of all Japanese, both youths and adults. Its bureaus supervised all schools, both public and private, special schools, technical institutes, and most scientific research. The educational philosophy of the Ministry stemmed directly from the Charter Oath, the Meiji Constitution, and especially the Imperial Rescript on Education (1890). The latter glorified Japanism to the disfavor of Western currents of learning. It stressed:

> *the fundamental character of the Empire,* united in virtue, loyalty, filial piety, and benevolence;
> *the pursuit of knowledge* and the cultivation of the arts for the development of "intellectual faculties and perfect moral powers";
> *the advancement of public good* and the promotion of common interests, through respect for the Constitution and observation of laws;
> *the needs of the state,* to which subjects should offer themselves courageously "to guard and maintain the prosperity of Our Imperial Throne coeval with heaven and earth."[18]

The functions of the other ministries, except for two, were obvious from their titles. Of all the ministries, the Ministry of Agriculture and Forestry (*Nōrinshō*) with its bureaus supervising agriculture, stock-breeding, forestry, fisheries, and sericulture, has been the least altered to date. In contrast, the Ministry of Commerce and Industry (*Shōkōshō*) went through several reorganizations in periods of mobilization and war. The Ministry of Communications (*Teishinshō*), through its postal, telegraph and telephone bureaus, supervised the government-operated communication facilities. The Ministry of Railways (*Tetsudōshō*) controlled the building and operation of government-owned rail lines which in 1929 accounted for two thirds of Japanese rail milage; it also indirectly supervised private railways. The Ministries of Justice and Home Affairs deserve special attention.

All courts, procurators, and prisons were under the jurisdiction of the Justice Ministry (*Shihōshō*); the judicature was thus merely an administrative creature of the executive. The Ministry was divided into three bureaus: (1) Civil Affairs, handling courts, lawyers, bankruptcy, arbitration, and the civil courts; (2) Criminal Affairs, handling prosecution and trial; (3) Penal Administration, handling prisons, paroles, and juvenile affairs. The bare skeleton of the Ministry, however, gives no hint of the extent of its control.

[18] SCAP, *Political Reorientation,* cited, Vol. II, Appendix B:9a, p. 584, gives the "Imperial Rescript on Education."

Its far-reaching jurisdiction can better be understood after a summary of Japanese legal evolution and a description of the court system.

The Law and the Courts. Japanese law was derived from several venerable traditions, the deepest of which was the principle of conciliation. The tendency to settle disputes by compromise, prominent also in Chinese justice, was a result of Confucian philosophy. It partly accounted for the small number of Japanese judges and the surprisingly few litigations even in modern Japan. A rudimentary national judicial system, hammered out of local custom, first appeared under the Tokugawa with its *Hyōjōsho* or Supreme Court.[19] Yet law, by and large, remained local house law, consisting of restrictions and regulations addressed to officials and rarely publicized. Finally, after the Restoration, the Japanese felt the need to develop a truly national system of law to adjust to the needs of capitalism and to reassure the Western powers, who were reluctant to relinquish extraterritoriality so long as unfamiliar patterns of law continued in force in Japan. Modern Japanese law then was parallel to the Meiji Constitution itself and was rooted in basic codes—civil, commercial, criminal, procedural—heavily drawn from Continental European principles.

To say, however, that modern Japanese law is a product of the innate trait of imitation would be too simple. In the first place, adoption of foreign legal systems is a familiar occurrence in universal legal history. Furthermore, although modeled after Continental principles, Japanese law was careful to exclude any foreign influence which might undermine deep-seated customs and traditions, particularly the all-powerful family system. Finally, the survival of old attitudes in the administration of justice frequently led to strange results in application of imported law. Japan is, even after Meiji modernization, a massive example of the difficulty of superimposing legal structure on a nation which has not gone through the political and social revolution from whence the law has been derived.

In the last two decades of the nineteenth century, Japanese legal circles took equal interest in common and civil law. But it was decided to adopt the Continental system, particularly the German pattern. This too was probably the result of Count Itō's studies in Germany and the presence of German jurists in Japan at the time of the Restoration. Gradually, a large portion of the sum total of law and sub-legislation was codified. The Codes were six in number: constitutional law, civil law, criminal law, commercial

[19] See p. 322, especially fn. 5. SCAP, *Political Reorientation,* cited, Vol. I, pp. 188-192, presents an interesting survey of the pre-surrender legal and judicial system, based largely on John H. Wigmore, *A Panorama of the World's Legal Systems,* Washington, 1928, Chap. 8. Of great value to the student interested in pursuing any phase of Japanese law—or for that matter any phase of recent Japanese government—is Robert E. Ward, *Guide to Japanese Reference and Research Materials in the Field of Political Science,* Ann Arbor, 1950 (Center for Japanese Studies, Bibliographical Series, No. 1). Professor Ward offers a well-selected list of Japanese-language legal reference works, collections of laws, interpretations of the Six Codes, legal indices, judicial decisions and commentaries. See Part XIII, pp. 64-70.

law, the law of civil procedure, and the law of criminal procedure. Collectively these came to be known as the Six Codes (*Roppō*).[20]

Japan also followed the Continental system in dividing the judicature into ordinary courts and an administrative court, the Court of Administrative Litigation (*Gyōsei Saibansho*). In 1928 Japan had 340 courts: 281 local, 51 district, 7 of appeal, and a Supreme Court. These were organized as shown in Chart 16.

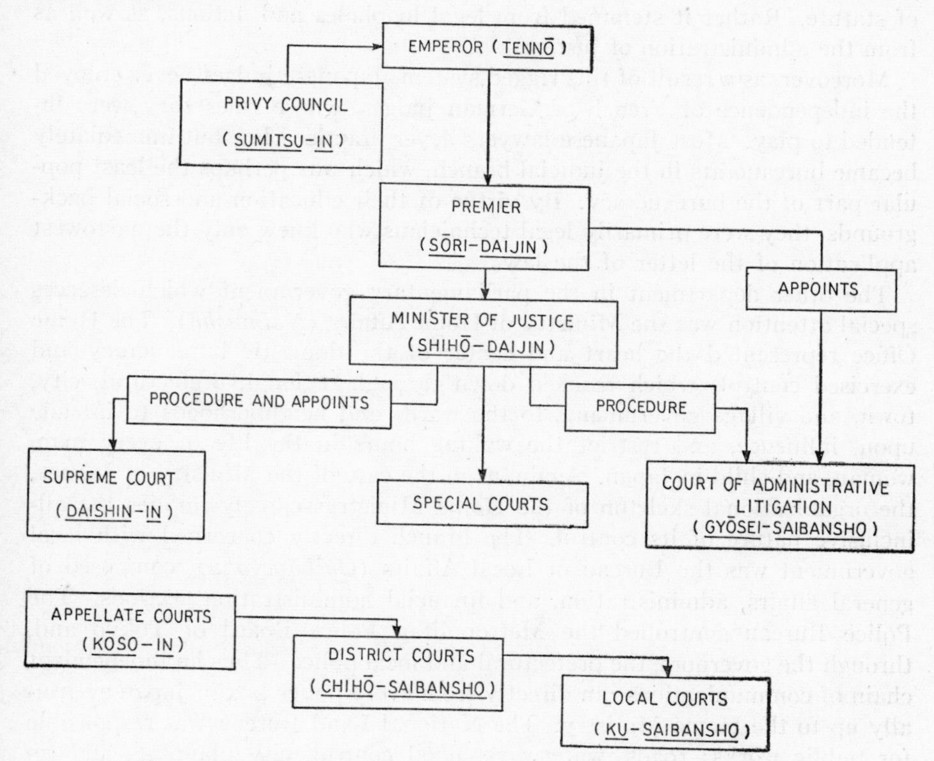

CHART 16—The Court System Under the Meiji Constitution

This judicial organization, under the jurisdiction of the Ministry of Justice, was constitutionally recognized as within the Imperial prerogative under Article IV of the Constitution. Itō wrote: "The judicature is combined in the sovereign power of the Emperor as part of His executive

[20] The Civil Code, adopted in 1898 after three decades of study, was a good example of the fusion of old and new: its first three books dealt with juristic persons, property, and obligations (adaptations of French and German civil codes); the last two dealt with domestic relations, family law, and inheritance (codifications of Japanese tribal customs). The Commercial Code combined German, French, common law, and indigenous Japanese practices. The Criminal Code (1882) was largely of Continental European origin; its distinctive feature was provision for special punishment for *lèse majesté*. The other codes were elaborate arrangements for court organization and procedure. The basic law of Constitution of Courts of Justice (1890) is presented in *JGD*, cited, pp. 625-655.

power." The Constitution further provided that the organization of courts would be determined by law. Since authoritarian Cabinets had little difficulty in causing the Diet to enact whatever statutes were demanded, the Diet as well as the courts lacked initiative and independence. Protection and surveillance commissions, under the direct supervision of the Ministry of Justice, were especially effective against persons convicted under peace preservation laws. The worst abuse of civil liberties was thus not a result of statute. Rather it stemmed from legal loopholes and fictions, as well as from the administration of justice.

Moreover, as a result of this rigged system, Japanese judges never enjoyed the independence of French or German judges, whose roles they were intended to play. Most Japanese lawyers never practiced law but immediately became bureaucrats in the judicial branch, which was perhaps the least popular part of the bureaucracy. By virtue of their education and social backgrounds, they were primarily legal technicians who knew only the narrowest application of the letter of the law.

The other department in the parliamentary government which deserves special attention was the Ministry of Home Affairs (*Naimushō*). The Home Office represented the heart and center of the domestic bureaucracy and exercised controls which reached down through regional, prefectural, city, town, and village governments to the wards and neighborhoods to intrude upon, influence, and restrict the waking hours in the life of every man, woman, and child in Japan. Again, as in the case of the Ministry of Justice, the organizational skeleton of the Home Ministry scarcely implies the all-inclusive nature of its control. The branch directly concerned with local government was the Bureau of Local Affairs (*Chihō-kyoku*), composed of general affairs, administration, and financial administration sections. The Police Bureau controlled the Metropolitan Police Board of Tokyo and, through the governors, the prefectural and local police. Thus an independent chain of communications ran directly from every police box in Japan eventually up to the Home Ministry. The National Land Bureau was responsible for public works: roads, waterways, flood control, city planning, and rehabilitation. The Bureau of Shrines administered State *Shintō,* maintaining a close tie-in with the state. Shrines numbered over 100,000 in the late 1920's and were served by more than 15,000 priests—all members of the civil service! Indeed, chief priests held *sōnin* rank (appointed by the Premier, on recommendation of the Home Ministry); subordinate priests held *hannin* rank (appointed by prefectural governors).

Local Government. Prior to the Meiji Restoration, Japan was divided into 86 *kuni* (provinces), arranged in 9 administrative regions or circuits (*dō*). Although *kuni* were no longer recognized politically after the Restoration, they were frequently employed for indicating locations, as are the popularly used geographical regions (*chiri chihō*) even today.[21] An outline

[21] The old nine circuits (*dō: Gokinai, Tōkaidō, Tōsandō, Hokuridō, Sanindō, Sanyōdō,*

of local government structure, after the Restoration, is shown in Chart 17.

Thus, all of Japan was divided into either urban or rural prefectures; and every spot in Japan was located in either a city or in a town or township. The Ryukyus (*Nansei Shotō*) constituted a *ken;* the Bonins (*Ogasawara*) formed part of Tōkyō-*fu*. There were, in addition, territorial administrations (*chō*) of Hokkaidō and Karafuto. The Kuriles were administered as part of Hokkaidō.

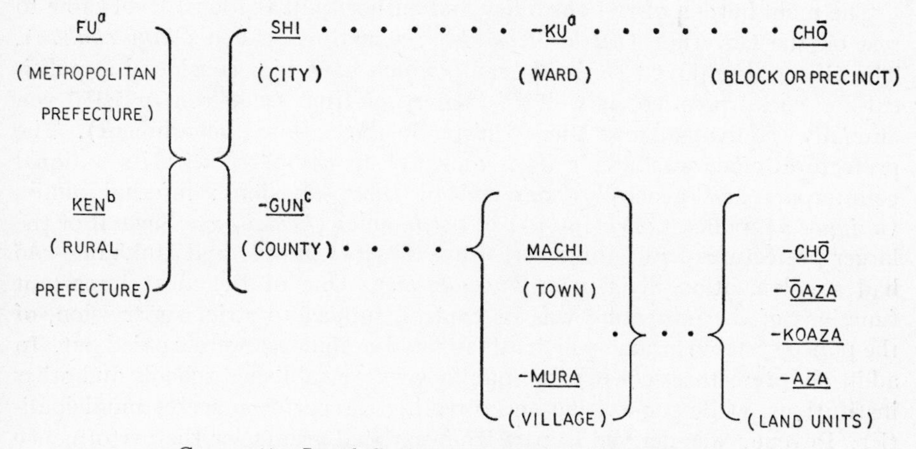

CHART 17—Local Government After the Restoration

[a] There were three *Fu* prefectures: Tōkyō, Ōsaka, Kyōto, containing Tōkyō *Shi,* Ōsaka *Shi,* Kyōto *Shi,* respectively (Tōkyō became a *To,* Capital Prefecture, in 1943).
[b] There were 43 *Ken* prefectures.
[c]-Gun soon came to have no political significance, but continued as a part of postal addresses.

A few general features of local administration can be sketched in immediately. Prefectural officials were members of the national civil service. Nevertheless, these men tended to be supporters of the government in power and to go out of office with it. Despite the semi-political nature of their appointment, however, such officials generally had considerable administrative experience (if not training). Unlike the prefectures, the municipalities were corporate entities and enjoyed a certain amount of autonomy within

Nankaidō, Saikaidō, Hokkaidō) must be distinguished from geographical regions *(chiri chihō: Ōu, Kantō, Chūbu, Kinki, Chūgoku, Shikoku, Kyūshū, Hokkaidō, and Karafuto);* and both must be distinguished from the later, wartime administrative regions *(chihō gyōsei,* established in 1943) and even later superintendencies-general (*sōkan-fu,* established in 1945). Japanese place names were a real secret weapon for the Japanese in World War II, as many language officers came to realize from experience. Standing operating procedure to discover the proper character readings for a place name became: (1) consult Beattie's Gazeteer, to make sure readings were not there; (2) consult Keigansha Gyōsei Kenkyūbu (Government Research Bureau), *Teikoku gyōsei kukaku benran* (Handbook of Japanese administrative districts), Tōkyō, 1901—; (3) consult *one* Japanese, preferably a resident of the area. *Two* would most surely produce different "official" readings for the characters. The chart on local government is based on U. S. Pacific Fleet, Pacific Ocean Areas, *Japanese Place Names Arranged by Character,* August 7, 1945, Restricted (Declassified), Appendix I, "Political Organization of Japan," p. 333.

limitations of national and prefectural supervision. As time went on, this autonomy was increasingly limited. Municipal officials, with the exception of mayors, were not members of the civil service. Their tenure was, curiously, fairly secure.[22] At all levels of local government arrangements were made for representative boards, popularly elected. Decisions of such bodies could be overruled by the local executive, and they could be dissolved on order of the Home Ministry.

The main burden of responsibility and authority at the local level came to rest on the Governor (*Fu-* or *Ken-chiji;* sometimes called *Chihō-chōkan*). The Governor enjoyed *chokunin* rank, which gave him considerable political and social prestige, as well as a salary of from 4,650 yen to 5,350 yen annually (equivalent to a Vice-Minister in the national government). The prefectural office was simple in organization as compared with its national counterpart and generally consisted of three divisions: internal affairs (*naimu-bu*), police (*keisatsu-bu*), and economics (*keizai-bu*). Several of the larger prefectures had public works divisions (*kōmu-bu*) and Hokkaidō-*chō* had a colonization division (*takushoku-bu*). One of the most important functions of the prefecture was its control, subject to strict supervision, of the police system through which all laws and ordinances were carried out. In addition, prefectures constructed public works, established schools and other institutions, while supervising and directing the performance of municipalities. Revenue was derived in part from national grants for the performance of duties, salary, police, and court expenses; and in part from taxation, both surtax on national taxes and independent prefectural legislation. In some prefectures branch administrations (*shichō*) performed the functions of prefectural offices in islands or areas difficult of access.

The functions of prefectural representative assemblies (*Fu-* or *Ken-kai*) were insignificant. These consisted of bodies of from twenty to forty unsalaried members, elected by qualified male voters. They met once a year, usually only during the month of November. Seven to ten members were selected by the assembly to meet in prefectural council (*Fu-* or *Ken-sanjikan*), which met under the chairmanship of the Governor and acted in the absence of the assembly.

Tōkyō-*shi,* despite its predominant position politically and economically, was, until 1943, under the jurisdiction of prefectural (Tōkyō-*fu*) authorities. Although it occupied only 26 per cent of the prefectural area, it elected 103 out of 113 members of the *Fu-kai,* contained 92 per cent of the prefectural population, and paid 97 per cent of the taxes. This was a remarkable growth

[22] To be officially designated a city *(shi)* by national authorities, a municipality had to achieve a population of 30,000 (raised to 50,000 in April, 1943; lowered again to 30,000 in 1947). The municipality could enact regulations in conformity with national and prefectural laws; but its legislative power was severely hampered in that it enjoyed no police power and therefore could not enforce its own regulations. City assemblies *(shi-kai),* elected by male voters, in turn selected councils *(shi-sanjikai),* the mayors, and township heads. Thus, although the mayor, with prefectural support, might overrule his assembly, still he depended upon it for his own re-election.

for the old city of Edo which had been threatened with decadence after the fall of the *Shōgun.* Even in its older, prosperous days under the Tokugawa, Edo's population exceeded a million. Later the *Tennō* made it his "East Capital" (*Tōkyō*). Up until 1932 the political city occupied only about 85 square kilometers and had a population of two million. The inclusion acts of 1932 and 1936 enormously increased the city area and population until it included in the early 1940's 577 square kilometers and a population of 6.8 million. It thus ranked fifth among cities of the world in area and among the first three in population. As a result of the three-day fire, following the earthquake of September 1, 1923, nearly half of the city was destroyed. Through hard work, Tokyo was completely rebuilt between 1923 and 1930.[23]

At the lowest level, wards (*ku*) were administrative subdivisions of Tokyo and the other five major cities. In Tokyo each ward had a chief (*ku-chō*) appointed by the mayor, an elected assembly (*ku-kai*), and a number of paid officials. The smallest township unit was a *buraku* (hamlet), developed by natural evolution from the original socio-economic units of rural Japan. Some existed in rural outskirts of towns. The most interesting feature of local administration, at least in light of later wartime developments, was the *buraku-kai* (hamlet-association) and the *chōnai-kai* (block-association). The use of neighborhood associations, with great antiquity and tenacity in Japanese history, was politically abandoned after 1868; such groups began to reappear near the end of the Meiji and were re-established legally only in the fifteenth year of Shōwa (1940).[24]

[23] Only to be destroyed again by man-made bomb quakes and fire in 1944-45. This time the destruction was even greater. After the war, the United States Strategic Bombing Survey estimated that Tokyo alone received 14,000 tons of fragmentary, H. E., and incendiary bombs. The population of 6,578,000 in 1944 dropped to 2,777,000; 93,000 were killed, 73,000 injured, 2,900,000 dehoused, 57 square miles of the city were destroyed, and 728,000 buildings destroyed. Urban Areas Division, *The Effects of Air Attack on Japanese Urban Economy (Summary Report),* Washington, March, 1947, Table 30, p. 42. Before the war, Tokyo was the center for local government research. The Tokyo Institute for Municipal Research was founded in 1922 by Viscount Gotō Shimpei, assisted by the late Charles A. Beard. It had its own publication, *Toshi Mondai* (Problems of Tokyo), Tōkyō, May, 1925, monthly. See also *The Tokyo Institute for Municipal Research and Its Work,* Hibiya Park, Tokyo, 1948.

[24] SCAP, *Political Reorientation,* cited, Vol. I, pp. 266-278, presents a useful summary of "organic legislation" for local government: (1) Law concerning Organization of Urban and Rural Prefectures (147 articles, 4 provisions), No. 35, May 17, 1890; (2) Law concerning Organization of Cities (181 articles, 6 provisions), No. 1, April 25, 1888; (3) Law concerning the Organization of Towns and Villages (161 articles), April 4, 1911; (4) Law concerning Hokkaido, No. 2, March 28, 1911; (5) various enforcement ordinances. The above summary of local government follows the complete study, made toward the end of the war, by the Office of Strategic Services, Research & Analysis Branch, *Local Government in Japan* (R. & A. No. 2760), Washington, July 31, 1945, mimeographed, Confidential (Declassified January 21, 1947), xii, 115 pp. Chart 20 of wartime local government, p. 435, is based on this study.

CHAPTER EIGHTEEN

Parliamentary Japan

THE weighty bureaucracy, starting with the Emperor and reaching down to the smallest hamlet, provided the framework for two other modern Japans to coexist in the period between 1889 and 1945. One was a parliamentary Japan, complete with the apparatus of a national legislative body, a responsible cabinet, and several political parties. Often taken both by Japanese and foreigners for *the* government of Japan, parliamentary Japan enjoyed at best a precarious grip on the political controls of the empire.

Militarist Japan existed alongside the parliamentary system. Its innermost redoubts in the Japanese system were the vitally important military agencies at the heart of the Imperial government itself. Militarist Japan, like parliamentary Japan, reached beyond the limits of the strictly governmental and had its own quasi-private organizations, its own economic supporters, its own commitments for domestic triumph and a world-wide role.

The three Japans were one—bureaucratic, militarist, and parliamentary. They were both irreconcilable and inseparable. To describe Japan's course toward World War II as the inward conquest of a parliamentary state by a totalitarian group is therefore an exaggeration on a grand scale. The parliamentary state had never existed without the concurrent support and coexistence of the bureaucratic and militarist elements, all of which made up a characteristic Japanese polity.

The Parliament of Parliamentary Japan. The heart of parliamentary Japan was the Imperial Diet. Theoretically a truly parliamentary empire should center around a central legislative body. Such a central legislative body should have, at the least, the following features:

1. Universal suffrage.
2. Responsibility to the electorate.
3. Freedom from executive domination.
4. Plenary legislative authority, including a decisive voice in the handling of public monies.

The Japanese parliament between 1889 and 1945 had no one of these characteristics in full and yet possessed at least a shadow of each of them.

Weak in constitutional and statutory powers and increasingly discredited by ineffectiveness and even venality, the Diet became completely subservient to bureaucratic ministers. The Constitution, instead of creating a true legislative organ, provided simply for a *Gikai* (literally "Talking-club"; officially, "Diet" after the Prussian model). In its very first meeting there were portents of things to come, as is shown in the following description by a Japanese professor:

> On the 29th of November of the 23d year of Meiji [1890], under the personal attendance of the Meiji *Tennō,* the opening ceremonies for the first Diet were held. On December 6th, Cabinet Premier Yamagata Aritomo presented a speech in the House of Representatives. Premier Yamagata related how, as all know, our country lagged behind world progress during the 300-year rule of Tokugawa; and how this lag was taken up from the Restoration to date. Then, in explaining the proposed budget for the following year, he pointed out that the expenditures for the Army and Navy occupied a large part of the yearly appropriations. For the sake of national independence, however, the maintenance of *the line of sovereignty* [*shuken sen*] was vital first of all; the protection of *the line of interests* [*rieki sen*] was also necessary. The former, he said, reached to the boundaries of the nation; the latter he called spheres intimately connected with the fate of our sovereignty. For this reason, expenditures for the Army and Navy had come to occupy an important place in the budget.[1]

In practice, no provision was made in the budget for a contingent fund to serve the houses themselves! Once a budget was adopted—Diet committees had *twenty-one days* to examine and report on the budget—the houses were forgotten.

Indeed, it is easy to forget the Diet in describing government under the Meiji Constitution. Familiar powers which in England or the United States have been exercised by elected representatives of the people were denied the Japanese Diet and were assigned to the Emperor (which meant, assigned to the appointed officials of the bureaucracy). Even in the meager powers exercised, it was impossible for Diet members to match the *kanryō,* who held an effective monopoly of all pertinent data. Without a library, drafting services, qualified assistants, power of subpoena, and authority to investigate, Diet committees could not legislate intelligently. Members were accorded treatment equal to their status in the government. Although they were

[1] Professor Oka Y., "*Dai ichi gikai ni kansuru jakkan no kōsatsu,*" (On the first session of the Imperial Diet), *Kokka Gakkai Zasshi,* cited, Vol. LX, No. 2 (February, 1946), pp. 1-16. Verbatim records of proceedings in both houses from 1890 to 1928 are conveniently reproduced in *Dai Nihon Teikoku Gikaishi Kankōkai* (Society for the Publication of the Records of the Imperial Diet), *Dai Nihon Teikoku Gikaishi* (Records of the Imperial Japanese Diet), Tōkyō, 1926-1930, 18 vols., a source much handier than the special supplements to the *Kampō* or English translation, *Official Gazette.*

given *sōnin* rank, they lacked the privileges and immunities of even lower-class *kanryō*. Diet members had no offices of their own, no clerks of their own, no franking privileges. Their salary (3,000 yen to 5,800 yen) was approximately half that of a vice-minister. Until 1936 they did not even have a Diet building! They tended to be obsequious even to the Chief Clerk of the House, a bureaucrat of *chokonin* rank, whose perquisites included an official residence, an automobile, and life tenure!

Forgotten were the Charter Oath, which had promised an "assembly widely convoked"; the *Kōgisho,* prototype of a more representative lower house; and the promise of the Imperial Rescript of 1881, which forecast a true parliament. In order to make sure that a popularly elected lower house could never usurp executive power, Itō and the founding fathers framed the Imperial Law of the Houses, the Ordinance concerning the House of Peers, the Election Law of the House of Representatives, and the Law of Finance. As a law, the first statute could be amended only with the approval of *both* houses; as an ordinance, the regulation for the House of Peers needed only the approval of the Peers to amend its provisions.[2]

In these enactments Itō showed his contempt for Western doctrines of representative government. In his *Commentaries,* he explained that ideas of division of legislative power between the sovereign and people arose out of a complete misconception of the principle of unified sovereignty.

> The use of the Diet is to enable the head of the state to perform his function and to keep the state in a well-disciplined, strong and healthy condition. The legislative power is ultimately under the control of the Emperor, while the duty of the Diet is to give advice and consent. Thus between the Emperor and the Diet, a distinction is to be strongly maintained as to their respective positions.

The Diet was convoked, prorogued, and closed, and the House of Representatives was dissolved on Imperial order. The Constitution limited the annual sessions to three months, "so as to avoid the endless dilation of deliberations," as Itō put it. A bill passed by both houses did not become law until the Emperor sanctioned it. Although both houses were authorized to initiate legislation, they were admonished by Itō to leave the framing of the law to "the skill and experience of the commissioners of government."

The organic laws actually left the Diet only six functions: (1) consent to every law; (2) initiation of bills, but more often vote on government bills; (3) representations to the executive; (4) addresses to the Emperor; (5)

[2] It will be recognized, too, that Itō and Associates took precautions against any future constitutional amendments resultant from pressure of public opinion. Article LXXIII provided that amendments submitted to the Diet needed two-thirds vote of a two-thirds quorum of *both* houses. And the Preamble made it clear that only the Emperor (read executive) "shall assume the initiative right." The Imperial Ordinance concerning the House of Peers and the Law of the Houses of the Diet are given as Appendices K and L to the Meiji Constitution in SCAP, *Political Reorientation,* cited, Vol. II, Appendix C:1, pp. 596-602. See also Itō, *Commentaries,* cited, pp. 9-10.

receipt of petitions from subjects; and (6) regulations for management of the houses. In short, the Diet was empowered to talk.

Moreover, the Law of the Houses curbed the Diet effectively by: closing Diet deliberations upon government demand; excluding the public from committee hearings; denying the right of subpoena or investigation; disallowing interim committees, except by government consent, as well as real standing committees; giving precedence to government bills; prohibition of remarks disrespectful of the Imperial house or insulting to the government or to the Diet. Finally, the House Laws themselves made sure that the Diet would be subordinate to the executive. The opening ceremony, presided over by the Emperor, was held in the Peers' chamber. Expenses of both houses were arbitrarily fixed by the Finance Ministry. Diet bills were presented to the Emperor by a State Minister. The schedule of Diet committees and joint committee meetings was arranged to suit ministers concerned with the legislation at hand.

Even with such limitations, the Diet could have been an important branch had it held even one string on the public purse. But the Constitution and the Law of Finance removed public monies from popular control. The bulk of the budget consisted of "fixed expenditures" which could be neither rejected nor reduced; the government had a "continuing expenditure fund," with a "reserve fund" for deficiencies; when the Diet was not in session, the government could take "all necessary financial measures" by means of Imperial ordinances. And if for any reason the Diet failed to vote the budget, the government could carry out the previous year's schedule.

While Itō could find no real reason for establishing a Lower House, he was sure of the need for the House of Peers (*Kizoku-in*), which would represent the "prudence, experience, and perseverance of the people, by assembling together men who have rendered signal service to the state, men of erudition and men of great wealth." The *Kizoku-in* in composition thus resembled the *Genrō-in,* the senate which preceded the establishment of the Diet. It purported to represent "interests" rather than areas; in essence it was a perpetuation of feudalism. The House of Peers was "reformed" in 1925, but with the result that the representation of the plutocracy was *increased,* while the number of members appointed for service to the state was *decreased.* Imperial appointees could never exceed in number the noble members.

Membership of the House of Peers, originally set at 292, was increased by approximately 100 over the years and averaged about 400 members. There were six classes of Peers.[3] Princes of the blood (who never exercised their right), princes, and marquises sat by hereditary right. Imperial appointees for erudition and merit also sat for life. Counts, viscounts, barons, taxpayers,

[3] The 58th Session (1930) of the House of Peers, for example, was composed of: (1) princes of the blood, 16; (2) princes and marquises, 43; (3) counts, viscounts, and barons, 148; (4) Imperial appointees: (a) selected for state service or experience, 121; (b) representatives of highest taxpayers, 64; (c) representatives of the Imperial Academy, 4.

and Academy members sat for seven years. Members were seated by the President (*Kizoku-in Gichō*), who followed a most complex protocol. Work was accomplished by five "standing" committees, which had to be reconstituted each session: budget, discipline, petitions, accounts, and qualifications. Before starting to work, each member bowed slightly to the curtained, recessed, and slightly raised chamber where the Emperor opened each session of the Diet.

The House of Representatives (*Shūgi-in*) was composed of members elected entirely by the people—that is, by part of the people. Under its first regulations, the number of representatives totaled 300; this was increased to 381 under the law of 1900, and to 464 in 1919. Under the Electoral Law of 1925, the membership reached 466. Members sat for four years. Despite the overwhelming agrarian nature of the country, farmers by vocation occupied only 9.5 per cent of the seats after the elections of 1928, while businessmen held the largest number, 22.2 per cent of the lower house. In great contrast with the membership of the House of Representatives in the United States, only 15.6 per cent of the Japanese Representatives were lawyers.[4] Members of the House sat in three sections, the major party occupying the center, the opposition on the left, and small-party members and independents on the right. The President (or Speaker, *Shūgi-in Gichō*), chosen by the majority, was an instrument rather than a powerful leader of party. The House too worked through "standing" committees, with titles similar to those of the upper house except that the lower house had no committee on qualifications.

Despite the severe restrictions on the Diet as a whole, the House of Representatives became the preserve of the politicians, those whose tenure depended on the vote of the electorate. From there they attempted to invade the lower ranks of the bureaucracy, with the spoils system. While popular movements had sprung up occasionally (for example, the democratic movement from 1874-84), it was not until after the grant of universal manhood suffrage in 1925 that mass parties, as such, could engage successfully in campaigning.

Elections. Applied for the first time in the general elections of 1928, the Electoral Act of 1925 determined the vote for the members of the House of Representatives. Laws of 1889 and 1900 had all more or less restricted the suffrage by imposing tax qualifications. Chiefly because financial qualifications were lowered and eventually abolished, the national electorate jumped from a half million in 1890 to almost a million in 1900, and from about 3 million in 1919 to 12.5 million in 1925. Nevertheless, the term "universal suffrage," often applied to the electorate by liberals in Japan, was a mis-

[4] These figures are from H. S. Quigley, *Japanese Government,* cited, Chap. 10, "The Diet: Organization and Procedure," pp. 160-181. See also K. C. Colegrove, "Powers and Functions of the Japanese Diet," *American Political Science Review,* Vols. XXVII and XXVIII (December, 1933, and February, 1934).

nomer because women were not enfranchised until the amendment of election laws in 1945.[5]

There were no primaries and no nominating conventions in Japanese elections. As a result "official" candidates, designated by party managers, were often matched against disaffected "independents." Japan never arrived at a satisfactory districting system under the parliamentary Empire. The Law of 1925 provided multi-member districts, with members per district varying between three and five. One Japanese writer likened candidates' chances as about the same as those in a lottery. Illegal and corrupt practices, the open use of prefectural governors and police by the Government, and outright force and violence were quite common.

Rise of Party Government. Japan's first true political parties, the *Jiyūtō* (Liberal Party) and *Kaishintō* (Progressive Party), had in the early 1880's stirred up enough fuss to force the clan oligarchs to fulfill the vague promise to adopt a constitutional form of government. Then in 1884 the two parties were dissolved in the face of severe government oppression. That party tradition was not completely rooted out, however, is shown in the result of the first elections under the Constitution and in the make-up of the first Diet. The *Kaishintō* placed 46 members in the House and the *Jiyūtō,* 17, as a result of the elections of July 1, 1890. Since no party controlled a working majority, various mergers were effected (a typical Japanese procedure), and House members sat down to business with the following allegiances:

Jiyūtō	130
Kaishintō	41
Taisei-kai (Great Achievement Party)	79
"National Liberals," neutrals, etc.	52
	302

Thus the party blocs of "opposition" counted 171 of the 302 members. Although both Itagaki and Ōkuma occasionally surrendered party posts when appointed to government office, they were the true leaders of the parties. At first, fighting members of the anti-government forces entered deliberately upon wrecking the Constitution and the institutions created under it.

From the original party lines, a bewildering network of sidelines were first drawn off and then drawn back to the original groups. With both groups *Constitutionalism,* always the slogan of the minority party, was regularly abandoned in an opportunistic fashion, when the party won the majority. This was especially true in the early history of the Diet from 1890 to June, 1898, the period when the Premier and Cabinet were dominated by the

[5] Statistics presented by the Cabinet Secretariat to SCAP in April, 1948, clearly revealed the slow, uphill battle for the extension of the suffrage. See Appendix 13 below. See also H. S. Quigley, "The New Japanese Electoral Law," *American Political Science Review,* Vol. XX (1926), pp. 392-395. Since official election statistics were difficult to obtain outside Japan, political scientists came to rely on the studies and analyses of the Asahi Shimbunsha (Asahi Newspaper Company), based on Naimushō statistics, e.g., *Fusen Sōsenkyo taikan* (General survey of the universal-suffrage general election), Tōkyō, 1928.

Genrō. It remained true from 1898 to 1917 in the era of semi-party (meaning *Genrō*-controlled) cabinets. Even after 1917 members of the House were organized into informal and shifting factions, based on personal leadership rather than on principles or political programs. Parties, regardless of name, tended to form two main House subdivisions, pro-government and anti-government. Yet the identity of the two original parties was somehow preserved through the following years, even into the Occupation. The *Jiyūtō* eventually became the *Seiyūkai,* while one branch of the *Kaishintō* became the *Minseitō.* Space permits only a summary of the genealogical evolution of these two main "bourgeoisie" parties.[6]

Despite the fact anti-government forces outnumbered government supporters, the bureaucratic Yamagata Cabinet (December, 1889-May, 1891) succeeded in carrying through its measures without dissolving the Diet. Nevertheless, tactical defeats of government budget proposals and "liberal" legislation alarmed the oligarchy and demonstrated the unpleasant reality of the new House of Representatives. Shortly after the first session, Yamagata resigned. The government, insisting on aloofness from the House majority, tried as a first technique outright bullying. Premier Matsukata (May, 1891-August, 1892) dissolved the House and called a special election for February 15, 1892. The Home Ministry set the pattern by bringing strong pressure to bear on local governors, trampling on civil rights, and instigating police violence. Clashes during the voting killed 25 and injured 388 persons. Nevertheless, independent clan rule was doomed: anti-government factions won 163 seats against 137 for the bureaucratic supporters. In the 3d Diet Session the opposition dared even to adopt a vote of "no confidence" in the Cabinet, which calmly refused to resign. The lines of battle were clearly drawn as the majority parties presented a united front in the first four sessions.

By the 5th Session (1893-1894), disunity in the party ranks began to appear. For one thing, Prince Itō, one of Japan's most resourceful statesmen, once again became Premier (August, 1892-September, 1896). For another, the *Jiyūtō* had become tempted by the government, Itō having made an "arrangement" with Itagaki. The latter was appointed Minister of Home Affairs under Itō in 1896. During the 7th, 8th, and 9th Sessions party politics were taboo (because of the Sino-Japanese War) or soft-pedaled (since Itō controlled a peacetime majority). Before Japan's representative Diet was six years old, there thus arose an amalgam of old clan (the Chōshū of Itō) and the new party (the *Jiyūtō* of Itagaki) politics.

[6] Japanese political scientists often distinguished between two classes of parties, "bourgeoisie" and "proletarian." The pre-War major parties were of the former variety. Curiously, parties of the extreme Right as well as of the Left were regarded in the latter category. Genealogical charts of both types are presented on pages 357 and 415. Professor Ward's *Japanese Materials,* cited, arranges selected Japanese literature on parties under similar headings: Sections XX, XXI, pp. 86-91; he himself has contributed an authoritative analysis of the period following that discussed in this chapter; Robert E. Ward, *Electoral Record of Japanese Political Parties, 1928-1937,* Berkeley, California (Ph.D. dissertation), 1948. Yutaka Matsumura, Editor, *Political Handbook of Japan,* Tokyo, 1949, pp. 4-19, gives a brief but convenient review of party history up to the Occupation.

Of course, this left out Ōkuma, who promptly formed a bloc in opposition to the Chōshū-*Jiyūtō* combine. His new *Shimpotō* (Progressive Party) was born in March, 1896. Its principles were those of the old Progressives, plus opposition to party collaboration with clan cabinets. Presumably the liberals and progressives now became bitter rivals. But not really on matters of principle, for Ōkuma himself in September, 1896, accepted the portfolio of Foreign Affairs from the Satsuma *Genrō,* Matsukata, who resucceeded Itō!

Occasionally the Liberals and Progressives, through the haze of rivalry, grasped the fact that clansmen and bureaucrats were their real enemies. Both parties, having been embraced and then ignored by the government, accordingly on June 21, 1898, dissolved themselves simultaneously. The following day at Shintomi Theater in Tokyo they amalgamated in a new party called the *Kenseikai* (or *Kenseitō,* the Constitutional Party). Their two points of agreement were opposition to the bureaucracy and the principle of responsibility of the government to the lower house. What true party cooperation could have meant was revealed by the alarm shown by the Elder Statesmen and the bureaucrats. They held an urgent meeting in the presence of the Emperor to discuss countermeasures. Yamagata stoutly opposed party cabinets and even urged suspension of the Constitution. Itō, who assumed premiership for a brief period (January-June, 1898), resigned and offered the return of all his titles. No clansman dared face the *Shūgi-in* where the party combine controlled five sixths of the membership. Suddenly (June 30, 1898) Ōkuma and Itagaki found themselves heads of Japan's first party cabinet. Ōkuma took the premiership and foreign affairs portfolio; Itagaki, that of home affairs; every post, save those of War and Navy, were filled by party men. The shock of responsibility was too great. The brief excursion into party control failed miserably. The Cabinet resigned October 31, 1898, without even facing the Diet.

The *Kenseikai* fell apart from the centrifugal force of its own incongruous elements. There were squabbles over assignment of cabinet posts and a general election was fought between the factions as though they were openly divided. In October the Liberals left the party and took the name *Kenseikai* with them. The Progressives assumed the title *Kenseihontō* (True Constitutional Party). Clan and bureaucratic rule was restored, General Yamagata receiving the support of the Liberals. They in turn received one cabinet post and finally broke with the government.

In September, 1900, a union of the old political methods and the new was given public recognition. The Liberals now turned to Prince Itō and his Chōshū colleague and *Genrō,* Count Inoue Kaoru, to found the *Rikken Seiyūkai* (literally, Society for Political Friends of Constitutional Government; *Seiyūkai* for short). Thus was born one of Japan's two major pre-World War II parties. Itō's objective, ideal constitutional government with a conservative flavor, was clear. The party's platform was as vague as the platforms of its Liberal predecessors: (1) observance of the Constitution; (2) prosperity; (3) pleasant foreign relations; and (4) local self-government. Most significant was the disaffection of Ozaki Yukio (member of the Diet since its very first session and liberal war-horse) from the Progressives over to the *Seiyūkai.*

Despite its auspicious status and its continuous history until 1940, the first adventure of *Seiyūkai* into government was short-lived. Hard-pressed by the House of Peers on the right and the party on the left, Itō's cabinet lasted only from October, 1900, to June, 1901, when General Katsura Tarō's Cabinet took over. Itō never again entered a Cabinet. In 1903 he became President of the Privy Council and turned the party presidency over to his protégé, Saionji Kimmochi. During the next eighteen years sporadic efforts were made by various factions to weaken the bureaucracy and strengthen the position of political parties. In this period liberals like Ozaki and Inukai Tsuyoshi fought vigorously against the bureaucracy and the military. But party leaders at the top restored the neo-oligarchical system consisting of bureaucracy seasoned lightly with party influence. Between 1901 and 1913, for example, five governments were alternated between Katsura, the Chōshū clansman, and Saionji, leader of the *Seiyūkai* majority.

For sixteen years, 1898 to 1914, leaders of the *Shimpotō* (Progressives reassumed the former title under their president, Marquis Ōkuma) failed to receive an Imperial summons to take office. In 1910 the party moved through one reorganization (the *Kokumintō* or Nationalist Party under Inukai) into another in 1913 (the *Rikken Dōshikai,* Constitutional Fellow-Thinkers, under the arch-bureaucrat-militarist Katsura), and into still a third in 1915 (the *Kenseikai,* under Baron Katō Takaakira). It was during the last evolution that Katō made the connections with Mitsubishi which were characteristic of the Progressive party from then on. It was also under the *Kenseikai* flag that Ōkuma returned to the political stage as Premier from April 1914, to October, 1916. Ōkuma's cabinets, however, were never made up exclusively of party men, and internal squabbles, as well as machinations of the Yamagata clique, finally forced his resignation. The Progressives waited another thirteen years before coming to power.

It was not until September, 1918, when Hara Takashi (or Hara Kei) became Premier, that a true party government was established. Saionji had resigned as President of the Liberals in 1914 and had turned party reins over to Hara, perhaps the ablest party boss ever developed in Japanese political history. He was recommended by the *Genrō* and asked to form the old-type coalition cabinet of bureaucrats and *Seiyūkai* members. He boldly rejected the proposal and formed a single-party government. Hara was, on the one hand, "a man of the people"; untitled, former publisher of the *Ōsaka Mainichi,* he finally broke the monopoly of high office held by noble or military figures. And his rule did tend to democratize politics and to strengthen party rule. His Cabinet succeeded in improving higher education, in creating a jury system, in amending the election law (1919), and in reforming Korean and Formosan military government. On the other hand, within the party he was a bureaucrat of a new order and ruled with an iron hand. During his ministry, the influence of business began to supplant that of clan leadership. The *Seiyūkai* gradually associated itself primarily with Mitsui interests. On November 4, 1921, in Tokyo's Central Station, Hara met death at the hand of an assassin.[7]

After Hara's death, leadership of the *Seiyūkai* passed to Takahashi Korekiyo (Premier, November, 1921-June, 1922). A man of liberal principles, Takahashi found himself unable to hold the party in line, and he retired after only seven months in office. A revival of "transcendental" (this time, Peers') cabinets was effective for two years. Then dissolution of the Diet in February, 1924, by the Kiyoura (bureaucratic) cabinet temporarily brought the factions together again: the *Seiyūkai* under Takahashi, the *Kenseikai,* under Katō, and a reform group led by Inukai and Ozaki. In the general election of May 24, the anti-government forces dealt the final death blow to clan rule in Japan. Under a new coalition cabinet headed by Viscount Katō (June 24 to August 25), the long-fought-for Universal Manhood Suffrage Law was finally passed. But the coalition was soon dissolved. The *Seiyūkai* offered its presidency to Baron General Tanaka Giichi (of Tanaka Memorial fame) who retired from military life to accept and also persuaded the staunch liberal, Inukai, into its ranks. Thus, within a month an almost inconceivable alliance (from the Western point of view) was perfected between an arch-militarist and reactionary and a fighting liberal within the same inscrutable party folds. Tanaka became Premier in April, 1927.

The Progressives countered by enticing 90 members of a faction split off from the *Seiyūkai,* by combining these with the *Kenseikai,* and by organizing the *Minseitō* (the Party for Popular Government). This was Japan's second major pre-World War II party. This new group came under the leadership of Hamaguchi Osachi (or Hamaguchi Yūkō, often called "The Lion"), a civil service bureaucrat of iron will. By 1927 the *Minseitō* had 227 members in the House, almost a majority. Its platform was short and safely vague: a more accurate reflection of public opinion in the Diet, equalization of income distribution, racial equality, and the open door. Using Tanaka's foreign policy, specifically relations with China, and the Pact of Paris as issues, the *Minseitō* finally brought the downfall of Tanaka and the *Seiyūkai* in 1929. "The Lion" now replaced the General.

There followed in 1930 and 1931 a brief political honeymoon. Hamaguchi and his foreign minister, Shidehara Kijurō (destined to be Premier under the Occupation), were as sincerely patriotic as Tanaka had been. A popular reaction to Tanaka's "positive policy" in China, however, led naturally to support of Shidehara's "conciliatory" policy. Moreover, predominance of

[7] For a biography of Hara Takashi (1856-1921), see *Shinsen dai jimmei jiten* (Revised dictionary of selected biographies), Tōkyō, 1937-40, Vol. V, pp. 164-165.

Mitsubishi interests, better fitted to European concepts of world capitalism, had replaced the colonial and self-sufficient interests of the Mitsui bankers. Yet, although the public at large, liberals, and many business magnates favored the Cabinet, others deeply hated it. Signature of the London Naval Treaty, bitterly opposed by the growing class of young militarists and the old House of Peers, spelled the beginning of the end. Party government received a second crushing blow in November, 1930, when Hamaguchi was shot by a fanatic. "The Lion" died in April, 1931. In September the Mukden Incident gave the militarist clique its golden opportunity. From then on party governments tried only to rationalize the *faits accomplis* of the Army. In December, 1931, Inukai Tsuyoshi, then president of the *Seiyūkai,* was given a final opportunity to try party leadership. On May 15, 1932, Premier Inukai was assassinated by young officers. Party leadership was literally and figuratively dead. An era had closed.[8]

The Proletarian Parties. During the period when the power of parties flared up and just as suddenly died down, there appeared another trend of great significance in the political development of Japan. Although the life span of the so-called "proletarian" parties was even more brief, the forces symbolized by their very existence, in a hostile atmosphere, were important if only for the use to which they were put later on. (Such parties are shown genealogically in Chart 18.)

As early as 1882, the left-wing of the *Jiyūtō* had flirted intellectually with Socialism. By 1901, the Social Democratic Party (*Shakai-Minshutō*) had put in its appearance but was dissolved by the government on the same day it was founded. Its leaders included Kōtoku Shusui (condemned to death in 1911), Katayama Sen (died later in Moscow), and Abe Isoo (he alone survived). The Social Democratic platform was modeled on the *Communist Manifesto.* After suppression of their party, Socialists turned to active dissemination of their ideas and gained the support of many "social reformers," driven by government oppression into Socialist ranks.

Widespread disappointment over the Treaty of Portsmouth, 1905, could have brought vindication of Socialists' declaration that war never pays the masses. Actually it brought discord in Socialist ranks. Strangely enough, although Saionji's permission allowed the reorganization of a *Nihon Shakaitō* (Japanese Socialist Party) in 1906, members soon split into two factions, the "theorists" and the "direct actionists." The problem came to a head in February, 1907, when 60 delegates convened in Tokyo for the Second Congress of the Japanese Socialist Party. But the government had already

[8] In a thorough study, based on Japanese primary and secondary sources, Professor Robert A. Scalapino has analyzed the sociology of democratic organization from the Meiji era to 1940. In discussing the impact of modern industrial capitalism on Japan, he has concluded that timing was perhaps the most significant single factor in the failure of democracy in prewar Japan. See *Democracy and the Party Movement in Prewar Japan; The Failure of the First Attempt,* Berkeley, 1953.

solved the internal problem by dissolving the party in 1907.[9] There were two other brief attempts to revive the movement as a Socialist League (1920), with labor support; and as a Farmer-Labor Party (1925), but both were immediately dissolved by the government.

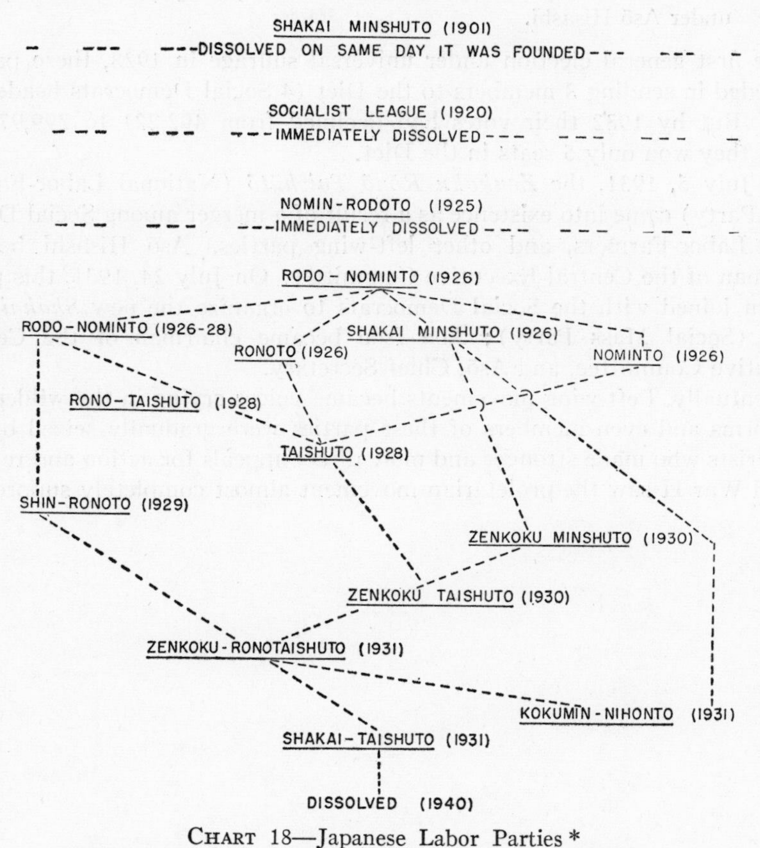

CHART 18—Japanese Labor Parties *

* Courtesy of Prof. H. S. Quigley, The University of Minnesota.

It was not until after the passage of the suffrage act in 1925 that proletarian parties had a chance, although the General Federation of Labor (originally *Yūaikai*, later *Rōdō Sōdōmei*) became active in promoting interests of workers. In 1925 four parties appeared almost simultaneously:

1. *Rōdō-Nōmintō* (Labor-Farm Party), Osaka, March 5, under Ōyama Ikuo (fled to the United States in 1932; returned to Japan in December, 1947);

[9] Hyman Kublin, "The Japanese Socialist Movement in the Meiji Era (1868-1912)," unpublished paper read before the American Historical Association, Chicago, December 29, 1950; also on this early period, see his "The Japanese Socialists and the Russo-Japanese War," *The Journal of Modern History*, Vol. XXII, No. 4 (December, 1950), pp. 322-339.

2. *Nihon Nōmintō* (Japan Peasant Party); Tokyo and Osaka, October 17, under Sugiyama Motojirō;
3. *Shakai Minshutō* (Social Democratic Party), Tokyo, December 5, under Abe Isoo;
4. *Nihon Rōnōtō* (Japan Labor-Farmer Party), Tokyo, December 9, under Asō Hisashi.

In the first general election under universal suffrage in 1928, these parties succeeded in sending 8 members to the Diet (4 Social Democrats headed by Abe). But by 1932 their votes had declined from 492,221 to 299,979 by which they won only 5 seats in the Diet.

On July 5, 1931, the *Zenkoku Rōnō Taishūtō* (National Labor-Farmer Mass Party) came into existence as a result of a merger among Social Democrats, Labor-Farmers, and other left-wing parties. Asō Hisashi became chairman of the Central Executive Committee. On July 24, 1931, this party in turn joined with the Social Democrats to organize the new *Shakai Taishūtō* (Social Mass Party); Abe Isoo became chairman of the Central Executive Committee, and Asō, Chief Secretary.

Eventually, Left-wing movements became voices crying in the wilderness. Platforms and even members of these parties were gradually seized by the militarists who made stronger and more direct appeals for action and reform. World War II saw the proletarian movement almost completely suppressed.

CHAPTER NINETEEN

Modern Militarist Japan

WITHIN the limits of the twentieth century itself it is almost impossible to explain the phenomenon of militarism in any one of the major nation-states. We Americans would certainly be hard put to explain the contribution made to our national existence by the recurrent crisis of war. By the middle of the twentieth century it is evident that our economy has become very characteristically a defense economy and that we, no less than any other of the great peoples in the modern world, find our prosperity and security, both of them, inextricably commingled with our long-range commitments to defense. The story of American militarism has scarcely begun; it would be a foolish person indeed who would attempt to predict: the long-range effect that the maintenance of massive and expensive armaments might have on our economy; the development of universal military training on our social habits; the pressure of almost uninterrupted international fears on our psychology; and the results upon our literature and our characteristic ways of thinking of all these factors put together.

The outbreak of the Korean war in 1950 marked a real milepost in the exchange of international roles between Japan and the United States. An American people who had fought World War II with the avowed commitment, so far as the Far East was concerned, of eliminating Japanese militarism, found itself involved in a strategic situation to which the only answer was American armament and American military effort on a scale never before known. The five years 1945 to 1950 marked a halcyon in Japan's power-political position. Japan down to 1945 had been defended by her own military establishments. For five years no serious attention was given to the defense of Japan until the beginning of Communist aggression in Korea, but as soon as the North Korean people's army moved, the defense of Japan once more became a requisite in international politics. And it was Americans, not Japanese, who had to defend Japan this time. We Americans had exterminated the Japanese militarists so thoroughly that when Japan needed militarists again we ourselves had to play that role.

Defense and Militarism. The entirely proper argument can be set forth that the possession of weapons does not of itself constitute militarism—that modern Sweden and Switzerland demonstrate well-armed countries which are in no sense militarist—that an armed democracy can exercise military power without having the institutional or cultural element which must be termed *militarist.*

This objection must be met if one is to understand the role of the military establishment in modern Japan. The argument can perhaps be clarified if *militarism* is defined.

A nation can be described as possessing militarism *if the military factors in its political, economic, social, educational, and religious life become important beyond the requirements of international defense and function as dynamic factors in the entire pattern of the nation's culture.*

In this sense America in the 1920's can scarcely be described as a militarist state, even of the most mild and innocent variety. The army was less than 200,000 men. The navy required only a tiny fraction of the total national income. By contrast the America of the 1950's might face catastrophic depression and revolutionary remedial experiment if the Soviet Union were to disappear altogether and if the elimination of foreign threats destroyed the *raison d'être* of our booming defense economy. In the 1950's a very substantial portion of the total American national production is expended for defense purposes. The greater part of the American national budget is either paying for past wars, guarding against current ones, or getting ready for future ones, and the American people find themselves in the situation in which the stimulus of war—while dangerous and unpleasant—is their most immediate assurance of the good things of life. It is entirely problematical whether Americans would be able in the 1950's or 1960's to find their way back to a demilitarized economy in the event that world peace were to strike all the nations like a white plague.

Militarism does not have to be purposeful or outward directed in order to contribute significantly to national life. The Swiss would not destroy their political system if they disarmed; their economy would be unimpaired. By contrast it was a tragedy of the Japan of the entire modern period, as well as of the United States of the present day, that the removal of all military factors in the national culture would lead to disorientation, partial collapse, and crisis.

Ironically enough, it was American detestation of militarism in German, Italian, and Japanese national life which helped to persuade American leaders to make militarism a vital factor in our own domestic life.

A definite theory of militarism does not explain the historical day-by-day necessities which lead some nations to depend on the military aspects of their own cultures. Japanese militarism cannot be understood merely by deploring it from the outside. The militarism which led to such unhappy consequences in World War II started with necessities no more pretentious than the necessities imposed upon the United States by the month-to-month politics of the 1950's. It was not a necessary malignity of character which made modern Japan militarist, but a malign necessity of her domestic and international fortunes.

The Modern Japanese Pattern of War. When the tiny squadron of Commodore Matthew Calbraith Perry came into Tokyo Bay in 1853 Japan felt the first effects of the *power* of modern Western culture. Something had happened in the world in the two hundred and more years of Japan's isolation. What was that something?

The industrial state had arisen together with its military counterpart—the national machine-supported conscript army and the steam-powered navy. Conscript armies and space-devouring navies had altered the space-and-time relationships throughout the world. Tokugawa Japan had gone to sleep strong and woke up feeble. China next door gave Japan a terrifying example of what happened to people who dared to pit traditional Asian weapons against an armed power supported by engineers.[1]

The modern Japanese pattern of war cannot be accommodated within the trite limits of the equation, *reaction equals militarism and militarism equals reaction.* As early as the period 1871-1873 it was the liberal opposition to clan government which demanded a military campaign against Korea.

Again in the 1890's Japan's shift toward a policy of armed expansion was supported by liberals as much as by military commanders. The soldiers of Japan had predicted the war; they had done little to precipitate it. It is significant that the Sino-Japanese War of 1894-95 followed the inauguration of the Meiji Constitution. The first modern war was *par excellence* the demonstration of Japan's modernization, the testing of investment of thirty years' hard work to make Japan into a nation-state with forces characteristically modern.

The course of the Sino-Japanese War surprised the world. The Chinese and Japanese had both experimented with modern land forces; they had both bought some modern steamships for the purpose of naval warfare; they had both raised the question of modernizing the mechanisms of their military and naval power. Yet when the test came, Japan's modernization was proved to be thoroughgoing and effective and China's a phantom. The Chinese steam warships went out to certain defeat because there were neither naval officials nor naval officers capable of manipulating the modern defenses which a Ch'ing dynasty China could purchase, but could not manipulate.

By April, 1895, the Chinese sued for peace and there ensued the notorious

[1] It is not necessary here to rewrite the history of modern Japanese diplomacy and war, since the field is ably covered. The best survey of modern international relations of the Far East is Harold M. Vinacke, *A History of the Far East in Modern Times,* New York, 1950 (5th edition); see especially chapters on Japan. In this chapter the emphasis will be *on the reciprocating influence* of war and Japanese politics.

international swindle celebrated among diplomatists as one of the most neatly contrived robberies in the international field when Japan, which had won Manchurian bases by her victory over Manchu China, was denied those bases by Germany, France, and Russia, forced to give them back to China, and then further forced to watch Russia take from China the very bases which Japan had had to give up.

Nevertheless the Sino-Japanese War had immense political and institutional consequences. Externally, it convulsed China and startled all of Asia: one Asian nation had become modern enough to fight with Western weapons. Could not the others do the same? Internally, the Japanese people reacted cordially to the recognition they obtained as a result of the show of military strength. The foreign powers began to consider abandoning their special privileges in Japan and the Japanese looked forward to being relieved of the burdensome humiliation of having foreign citizens under their own special jurisdiction within Japanese territory. The Chinese indemnity of 230 million taels (about $115 million) became the base for putting the Japanese currency on the gold standard. Japan became a full-fledged member of the Western family of nations. Japanese troops were the only Asian troops asked to join the "civilized" nations in the Boxer intervention of 1900. The Japanese acquisition of Formosa (Taiwan) set the pattern for an expanding modern colonial system. Finally, the promulgation of the Anglo-Japanese alliance of 1902 made the Japanese feel that they were not merely tolerated in the family of great nations, but were actually needed by a foreign great power.

Russian Militarism and Japanese Militarism. The competition in the early 1900's between Russia and Japan over Manchuria is strangely reminiscent of the competition a half century later between Russia and America over the world. By pressing for interests which in Russian eyes were entirely legitimate, the Russians followed under czarist leadership the same pattern of insolence, duplicity, and bad faith which they were to display fifty years later toward America. The Russian armed forces, for example, moved into Manchuria for the benevolent purposes of suppressing Boxers and of aiding the community of nations in suppressing China's frantic and holyless war against the outer world; but once in Manchuria the Russians refused to get out.

The Russo-Japanese War (1904-05), like the Sino-Japanese conflict, was partly a product of internal Japanese politics. The militarists had never forgotten the three-power intervention. They convinced themselves that Japan's position in the Orient could be maintained only by force. About the war itself, at first glance it seemed again like a boxer fighting out of his class. But the lightweight, Japan, was in good trim and the heavyweight, Russia, was soft. Immediately after the Treaty of Shimonoseki, Japan had concentrated on her navy, using part of the indemnity from the previous war to prepare for the next. Nor was the army neglected. Japan's seven divisions had been expanded to thirteen.

The last battle in the war was actually fought over the tables of diplomacy at Portsmouth, New Hampshire, where the American President, Theodore Roosevelt, offered "good offices." Despite disappointment within Japan over the Treaty of Portsmouth,[2] the Russo-Japanese War marked an advance of Japan's hegemony in East Asia. At long last she had a foothold on the continent. And once again, in 1905, mighty Britain recognized Japan's "paramount political, military, and economic interests in Korea." The mutual-aid pact was to prove important in the next war.

Korea was the second gem added to Japan's imperial necklace, by means of a treaty of annexation concluded in 1910. Thus, finally, the dream of Hideyoshi was realized. Much less figuratively, the acquisition of Korea (Chōsen) ended the international life of Korea until 1945; it brought to a close, from the Japanese point of view, dangerous foreign intrigue in the peninsula; and, of course, it produced more jobs for the bureaucrats.[3] By the end of the 1920's, ninety per cent of Chōsen's trade was with Japan.

Manchuria became even more vital to Japan and to her militarists. Technically, Japan acquired from Russia—with Chinese approval—only the Leased Territory (*Soshakuchi*) in Kwantung Province. The leased territory was 1,300 square miles in area and had a population of 800,000. Kwantung police jurisdiction, however, extended over the entire right of way of the South Manchurian Railway, adding approximately 100 square miles and 300,000 persons, two thirds of them Chinese. The Japanese Governor, responsible to the Minister of Overseas Affairs, had no control over the Commander, Kwantung Army (*Kantōgun*), who was subject to orders from the "Big Three" of the Army in Japan.

Parallel with Japanese administration of Kwantung was the South Manchurian Railway Company (S.M.R., *Minami Manshū Tetsudō K. K.*), typical of the semi-private, semi-official *Zaibatsu* technique exported overseas. In one sense, the S.M.R. was an agency of the Japanese government: the government controlled half the stock shares, valued at 440 million yen, and controlled blocks of stock held by directors, whom the government appointed. In another sense, the S.M.R. soon became one of the great independent corporate structures of the world. It operated over 700 miles of railroad, built and operated schools, maintained research, controlled vast mining

[2] Japan's point of view is presented by Roy H. Akagi, *Japan's Foreign Relations, 1542-1936*, Tokyo, 1936; and in the more scholarly work of Kanichi Asakawa, *The Russo-Japanese Conflict, Its Causes and Issues*, Boston, 1904.

[3] In creating the Ministry of Overseas Affairs in 1929, the Japanese government came to recognize the special status of both Taiwan and Chōsen. In terms of administration, both resembled British crown colonies; in terms of political development, both tended toward incorporation into the Japanese prefectural system. The Chōsen government was headed by a Governor-General (*shinnin* rank, seldom filled by other than an active or retired general or admiral). For a Japanese view of early administration, see Viscount Masatake Terauchi, "Reforms and Progress in Korea," in Angus Hamilton and Herbert H. Austin, *Korea: Its History, Its People, and Its Commerce*, Boston, 1910, Chaps. XVII-XXVI.

properties (at Fushun and Tentai), improved a harbor (at Dairen), and operated electric generating plants (at Dairen, Mukden, Changchun, and Antung). In the last analysis, these activities added to the prosperity of Manchuria and consequently to its value to Japan. The company's policies and profits were the policies and profits of the Japanese Government.[4]

Despite these evidences of wide-ranging Japanese power and influence, the most lasting and significant result of Japan's first two wars was felt internally. In 1896, *after* the Sino-Japanese War, the national budget had doubled and almost all the increase went into military expenditures. In 1897, half the total expenditures went to the military. With its control over such a large proportion of the budget, the army and navy worked ceaselessly toward self-sufficiency. And they also extended their influence from economics and industry into diplomacy.

Effects of the First "Big War." When World War I broke out in August 1914, "Japan in the spirit of *noblesse oblige,* and by virtue of the Anglo-Japanese Alliance, sided with the Allies."[5] Japan declared war on Germany on August 23, 1914.

In entering the war, Japan was actually moved less by a "spirit of *noblesse oblige*" than by ulterior motives. Although the war's outbreak in no way affected the special interests of Japan in East Asia, she used the conflict as a golden opportunity to secure hegemony on the continent. Captured German concessions in Shantung provided a foothold for later encroachments on China proper. Spearhead of expansion was the secret Black Dragon Society (*Koku-ryūkai*), which in part inspired Japan's Twenty-One Demands served on China. The Marshall Islands were occupied in September, 1914, and the Marianas and Carolines (all called *Nampō Shotō*), in October. Gradually, the islands sank into the obscurity of mandates, which veiled secret naval preparations. They sprang back into the headlines only after 1941.

Immediately after World War I, Japan also used the Allied intervention in Siberia as a cover for expansionist purposes. Japan proper, the island of Tsushima, the peninsula of Korea, occupied Shantung, and the South Manchurian concessions threw a Japanese net completely around the sea approaches to Manchuria. Japan thus emerged from the war the most powerful nation in the Far East. For a time, the Nine-Power Treaty concluded at Washington in 1922 reduced and balanced off Japan's spheres in the Orient with naval disarmament. Nevertheless, the Manchurian question was far from settled in Japanese minds. And the core of Sino-Japanese relations was

[4] The great bulk of official government research, of course, was undertaken later with the establishment of the puppet state of Manchukuo. Thereafter the official publications of the S.M.R. and Japan-sponsored developing companies were legion. See, for example, *Mammō Hakurankai Kinen* (Manchurian-Mongolian Exhibition), *Manshū no taikan* (General survey of Manchuria), Tōkyō, 1930; *Manchuria Today,* Hsinking: Manchukuo Foreign Office, 1940 (10 in series); Mantetsu (S.M.R.Co.) *Mantetsu sanjūnen shi* (Thirty years of the South Manchurian Railway Co.), Dairen, 1937; and Minami Tetsudō K. K. (South Manchurian Railway Co.), *Manshū dekasegisha iji kammin no sūteki kōsatsu* (A statistical survey of Chinese migrants to Manchuria), Dairen, May 10, 1931.

[5] So the *Japan Year Book, 1946-48* put it, p. 76.

the future of Manchuria. It is alleged that in 1927 Baron Tanaka prepared the blueprint for conquest, not only of Manchuria, but also of the world.[6]

Within Japan, the immediate effect of World War I was identical with that of previous conflicts, tremendously increasing the size and influence of militarism. The disarmament slashes of 1922-25 and the unpopular Siberian Expedition, it is true, cut in on the militarists' power, but the Army took a deep breath, studied the tactical lessons of World War I, and awaited its next chance. The Army, moreover, had changed in social character, as we shall soon see.

The most significant long-range effects of World War I were economic: Japan was catapulted into World Power status industrially, capital production mushroomed under government auspices, and financial control became concentrated in a few hands. The wartime munitions boom reduced the number of Japan's economic plutocracy; the Tokyo earthquake of 1923 shook out and the financial panic of 1927 squeezed out smaller capitalists. The chief firms (Mitsui, Sumitomo, and Mitsubishi) were left holding roughly one fourth the private capital. The "Big Eight" (the firms mentioned plus Yasuda, Asano, Kawasaki, Tanaka, and Furukawa) controlled one third of all bank deposits, four fifths of bankrupt properties, and one fourth of Japan's insurance company liabilities. The *Zaibatsu* became one of the major forces in Japanese political life.

Another force, the political parties—particularly the *Seiyūkai* and the *Minseitō*—became political instruments of the capitalists. A third, the bureaucracy, operated in the background, sometimes in alliance and sometimes in opposition to the parties, but always the lubricant for obvious parts of the political machine: militarists, capitalists, and parties.[7]

Deep, disturbing effects of World War I were felt in at least three large sectors of the Japanese economy. Small businessmen and retailers were caught in the squeeze between increased capital concentration and postwar depression. Industrial labor was also adversely affected. Squabbling within labor groups, the large proportion of cheap female labor, a paternalistic tradition, and, above all, the view of union activity as "dangerous thought" stunted labor organization. Yet the depth of dissatisfaction could be measured by the increase in number and in violence of strikes. Intense unrest was most marked, as usual, among the agrarian classes.[8]

[6] The Tanaka Memorial was first publicized in the fall of 1929, at the time of an Institute of Pacific Relations Conference in Kyoto. The presumed text appeared in the *China Critic,* a Shanghai English-language journal, in 1931. For a Japanese view of the Manchurian question, see Tōa Keizai Chōsakyoku, *Manshū tokuhon* (East Asia Economic Research Bureau, *Manchurian Yearbook),* Tōkyō, 1937, pp. 312 ff.

[7] The *Dai hyakka jiten,* cited, Vol. X, p. 340, defined *Zaibatsu:* "Persons of family or other special relationships or persons of capitalistic lineage who hold huge resources and, through influence, control and manage enterprises such as banks, concerns and companies. They are alleged to reign in financial and industrial circles." On the role of the bureaucracy, see John M. Maki, *Japanese Militarism, Its Cause and Cure,* New York, 1945, pp. 14-15. For the interconnection, see C. G. Allen, "The Concentration of Economic Control in Japan," *Economic Journal,* June 1937.

[8] Shidachi Tetsujirō, *The Depression of 1930 as It Affected Japan,* Tōkyō, 1931, which

Peasant Unrest. Despite rapid strides in industrialization, Japan in the 1920's and 1930's remained largely an agrarian nation. In a real sense, the Japanese peasant paid the bill for capitalization, as he had the bill for conversion of Japan into a modern state. Passage of the years saw no diminution in the peasant's dilemma of debt and tenancy. Each war boom and deflation left a larger mass of tenants. By 1930, full and partial tenants made up 70 per cent of Japan's agrarian population.

Neither completely proletarian, since the peasant thought he "owned" the land, nor completely *entrepreneur,* since he was gouged with high rents, the peasant was simultaneously deeply conservative and violently radical. Traditionally and unswervingly loyal to the *Tennō,* he thought not of complete revolution. Dimly he began to see the landlord, the giant *Zaibatsu,* founded on his own shoulders, and the corrupt parties as his enemies. The frustration and bitterness are clearly revealed in a proclamation drawn up by the Japanese Farmers Union, 1933:

1. Landlords must return land to the *Tennō.*
2. Capitalists and bourgeois political parties must be eliminated.
3. Rapacious landlords should be punished.
4. Rebellious Communists should be liquidated.
5. The revenues from Manchukuo should be nationalized.[9]

It took an old force, however, to harness these various deep dissatisfactions leading to a social crisis. This older force was the Army and, to a lesser extent, the Navy. But the Army itself, especially in the years after World War I, had felt the tremendous impact of social change. It was a case, as Toynbee would have it, of new wine in old bottles. The resultant brew was heady doctrine and eventually drunken rage.

The New Military Tunic. Of equal significance, and related to economic unrest, were the growing social effects of conscription in post-World War I Japan. Unlike the democratic and revolutionary heritage of conscription in France, universal military service in Japan was autocratic in its establishment and reactionary in its effects. The young conscript army was drawn from a wide social base, but especially from the peasants. The bulk of the Army's man power, even in recent times, came from families of low income.[10] Conscription rapidly assumed the character of a gigantic indoctrination

---

is cited among others with voluminous data in the comprehensive study of Jerome B. Cohen, *Japan's Economy in War and Reconstruction,* Minneapolis, 1949, Chap. I, "A Decade of Preparation."

[9] As cited in V. A. Yakhontoff, *Eyes on Japan,* New York, 1936, pp. 142-143. Wakukawa Seiyei, "The Japanese Farm-Tenancy System," in Douglas G. Haring, Editor, *Japan's Prospect,* Cambridge, Mass., 1946, Chap. V, presents data on growth of tenancy and farm debt. For a Japanese view, see Mayeda Shigeichi, "Our Stricken Agriculture," *Contemporary Japan,* Vol. I (September 1932), pp. 271 ff.

[10] The most complete study was made by Takata, translated by Ogawa Gotaro, *The Conscription System in Japan,* cited; distribution of conscripts according to tax payments is given on pp. 216-220. Briefer but more thoughtful is Norman's monograph, *Soldier and Peasant,* cited.

project under the autonomous Inspector General of Military Education.

The Army became a living symbol of equality for the underprivileged people of Japan. In this sense, clan rule of the Army, effective at least until until 1922, was an anachronism. For the Conscription Act made the Army the symbol of social equality for the underprivileged of Japan, as well as the legitimate heir of the *samurai* Code. It should also be noticed that the Japanese Army, like the state, was highly paternalistic, if a strict father to the conscript. A letter was always sent to the nearest relative of the young soldier before his induction. In the letter, the conscript's commanding officer promised to be a loving father and a stern elder brother to the conscript. The family was questioned closely as to the boy's home life. This interest sprang, in part at least, from the fact that the officers themselves increasingly were drawn from the lower classes.[11]

Especially after 1925, the old Chōshū clan clique gradually lost Army control in favor of a new group drawn from the ranks. Often called the Young Officers (or League of Imperial Young Officers, *Kōkoku Seinen Dōmei*), this new group came up from an entirely different social stratum of Japanese society. The Young Officers especially were determined to place the national defense on a more secure basis and to stabilize the nation's livelihood. They bitterly resented the exploitation of the peasantry for the purpose, they believed, of enhancing the swelling profits of the *Zaibatsu*. The ideology of this new officer class was colored by a bitter hatred of capitalistic standards, by advocacy of an amorphous but drastic program of economic reform, and by the need for expansion of Japan's armed forces.

The peasantry, in turn, began to look upon the Army as its savior. The corruption in political parties and the weakness of farmer-labor movements offered little hope for economic salvation through such normal means. There never developed a formal alliance among peasants, workers, and the Army, but there existed deep appreciation of their common interests. In attacking the *status quo* and spearheading the dissatisfaction, the Young Officers focussed their pressure on the entire parliamentary structure.

Above all, the Young Officers were dedicated to *Kōdō,* the Imperial Way; they were often called the *Kōdō-ha,* Followers of the Imperial Way. Popularized in the 1930's, *Kōdō* expressed the traditional morale of Japan, governed by a line of emperors unbroken for ages eternal. Anti-foreign, anti capitalist, it was presumably Japan's alternative to fascism and communism. Japan's mission, under *Kōdō,* was to extend the Imperial Way throughout the world. To most Japanese, the term's meaning was probably vague; they took *Kōdō* for granted, as many Englishmen did the "White Man's Burden."

The idol of the Young Officers and the high priest of *Kōdō* was General Araki Sadao. Born in 1877 of humble parentage, he had worked as a laborer in his youth. He rose through the Army to become President of the Imperial

[11] Hillis Lory, *Japan's Military Masters, the Army, in Japanese Life,* New York, 1943, carefully deals with this phase of militarism. See pp. 17-18, 24-27, 91.

Military Academy and finally, in 1931, Minister of War. His motives were considered pure, his personal habits almost monastic, and, above all, he was a Japanese soldier in true *samurai* tradition. Araki envisioned himself as the ideological leader of Japan. He represented, in fact, the modern personification of *bushidō, Zen* Buddhism, and peasant aspirations. Araki and the *Kōdō-ha,* like the lower *samurai* of the early Meiji, claimed they wished to restore power to the Emperor so that he might delegate it to incorruptible leaders. Thus they justified rebellion (but not revolution) as necessary to achieve the Shōwa Restoration. In other words, they were in true harmony with Japanese political traditions which looked to change through restoration rather than revolution.[12]

Secret Societies. Closely allied with the new *Gumbatsu* were the patriotic and secret societies. They, like the political parties and semi-public *Zaibatsu,* provided semi-private channels for public pressure which the militarists needed.

The most ramifying were centered around the services: the *Zaigō Gunjinkai* (Ex-Service Men's Association), with a membership of two and a half million; the *Nihon Seinendan* (Japan Youth Association), with 16,000 branches; and a women's auxiliary, numbering a million and a half members. Some were open to civilian as well as military personnel, for example, the secret *Genyōsha* (Black Ocean), *Kokuryūkai* (Black Dragon), and the *Yūzonsha* (Society that Criticizes). During the 1920's, the center of gravity of Japan's totalitarian movement settled in the Society for the Foundation of the State (*Kokuhonsha*). Its directors included Baron Hiranuma Kiichirō (later a premier), General Araki, and Finance Minister Ikeda Seihin.

During the 1930's there were societies for rural self-government and schools for love of the native soil. Other groups operated under the colorful, and sinister, names of House of the Cry of the Crane, the Golden Pheasant Institute, the Heavenly Action Club, and The Japanese Knot. There were even Oppose-Societies Societies.[13]

Direct Action at Home and Abroad. Backed by the swelling dissatisfaction in rural Japan, armed with the old immunity from civil interference granted in the Constitution itself, with a new determined leadership in its own ranks, and allied with a network of patriotic, terroristic societies, the

[12] See, for example, Tokutomi Iichirō, *Kōdō Nihon no sekaika* (The changed world of Japan of the Imperial Way), Tōkyō, 1938; for General Araki, *Shinsen dai jimmei jiten,* cited, Vol. VII, p. 22. Use of the term Shōwa (name of the reign from 1926) indicated an analogy with the Meiji Restoration.

[13] The HQ, Supreme Commander for the Allied Powers, must have had an enormous task in running down groups and societies after the war. The first directive (SCAPIN 548, January 4, 1946) listed twenty-seven proscribed societies; Appendix I of an Ordinance of January 4, 1947, Part III (Influential Members of Ultra-Nationalistic, Terroristic or Secret Patriotic Societies), listed 145 societies, prefecture by prefecture. The list occupies two and a half pages, five columns of SCAP, *Political Reorientation,* cited, Vol. II, Appendix B: 5R, pp. 511-513. On secret societies in general, see also Hugh Borton, *Japan Since 1931; Its Political and Social Developments,* New York, 1940, pp. 30-35; and Tanin and Yohan, *op. cit.,* pp. 33, 41, 63, 90.

military dominated Japanese politics in the 1930's and came close to establishing military fascism in Japan.

It is of little interest whether Japan entered her last war in 1931 with the conquest of Manchuria, or in 1937 with the invasion of North China, or in 1941 with the attack on Pearl Harbor. It is enough to say that the first two acts accelerated the plunge into the third. Politically, no effective, organized protest attended the Manchurian invasion: it seemed easy.

Long before the Manchurian Incident itself, the Army began to marshal its battle forces, as well as to plan its diplomacy, its economics, its thoughts. In the Army's bid for power, certain factors strengthened its command over policy. Direct access to the Emperor, already discussed, was primary. In the Cabinet, General Araki was a shrewd master. He rarely spoke on matters which did not concern the Army or national security. Yet when someone once asked Premier Inukai who his foreign minister was, he silently pointed to Araki. The Army's tools in the economic sphere were control of appropriations, by Imperial ordinance if necessary, and alliance with industrial interests, particularly in the sphere of armament supplies.[14]

The events in which the Japanese Army found, or made, its opportunity are too familiar to be repeated here. It was quite appropriate that Japan invaded Manchuria on September 18, 1931, the anniversary of the death of Hideyoshi. It was quite ominous that Manchuria in the Orient symbolized the failure of nation-states in the Occident to achieve collective security. It is more relevant here to note that the Manchurian Incident introduced dual diplomacy into Japan and allowed greater scope for Army activities on the continent. In New York, the *Times* of September 22 admitted lack of information and commented on the "extraordinary spectacle" of the Japanese War Office and Foreign Office "openly at odds." The *Trans-Pacific* editorialized that there was little doubt that "Army influence overshadowed the Foreign Office completely."

The Incident was climaxed by the creation of Manchukuo, actually a tool of the Japanese Army. Even the Japanese soon surrendered the hoax of independence. A S.M.R. research paper later admitted that in 1932 Japan not only began the "founding of a nation, by degrees, but recognized Manchukuo and led her to a premier appearance upon the international stage." Later during the war years, Manchukuo played several roles, all at the behest of Japan. The Japanese military hierarchy, topped by iron-fisted General Minami Jirō, seized control of the rail network in order to exploit the wealth of the region. In 1932, all banking assets were centered in the Central Bank of Manchukuo. After the second Chinese Incident in 1937, Manchukuo was

[14] An Army publication in the mid-1930's stated: "The remarkable development of science and technical knowledge, coupled with complexity in international relations, has inevitably enlarged the scope of war in which battles are fought along with diplomacy, economics, and thoughts." *Kokubō no hongi* (Fundamental principles of national defense), Tōkyō, War Ministry, Press Section, 1934, p. 2. Inukai's remark was quoted from *Sokoku* (Fatherland) by the *Japan Chronicle,* February 11, 1932, pp. 188-189.

prepared for another role: the first junior partner in the Greater East Asia Co-Prosperity Sphere. In the war against the West, Manchukuo was within the Inner Zone of the Japanese defense.[15]

Meanwhile, direct action took a more serious turn at home. Extremist militarists attempted two coups in late 1931 but were forestalled. Undaunted by initial failures, the Blood Brotherhood League (*Ketsumeidan*), in February and May, 1932, launched a bloody assault on the parliamentary regime. Victims included Premier Inukai, a former Finance Minister and the head of the Mitsui Corporation; bombs were hurled at the offices of the Lord Keeper of the Privy Seal, the Mitsubishi Bank, and the Metropolitan Police. Although the government was able to thwart a wide plan for military rule, party government finally collapsed.

Peculiar radical-reactionary undertones of the May 15 Incident were revealed by pamphlets, issued during the terror, by the courts-martial held for military personnel, and by the civil trials. On September 26, 1933, twenty civilian plotters with Tachibana Kozaburō, the ringleader, went on trial in Tokyo. Tachibana stressed the greed of capitalists and their lackeys, the parties. Under Japan of the Imperial Way (*Kōdō*), all men would return to the land. He completed his lecture with a bitter denunciation of communism. During the course of the civil trial, an orgy of sympathy for the defendants swept Japan. School boys sent notes to the courts, written in blood; youths committed suicide; and girls cut off their hair. Even the Union of Brothel Keepers was sufficiently moved to submit a petition, pleading leniency for those who defended the pristine national polity.[16]

Despite suppression of the 1932 uprising, a loosely knit front of pro-Araki militarists, agrarians, and politicians continued to harass the government. Determined to create an atmosphere of extreme crisis General Araki, still War Minister, began to bombard the country with patriotic pamphlets on the need for national defense. For example, *Kokubō no Hongi* (Fundamental Principles of National Defense, October 1934) pointed to great air fleets, built by the Soviets and Americans, and pled for a new order in Asia through *Kōdō*.

Two other major incidents of direct action, one at home and one abroad, were reproductions of earlier actions. On February 26, 1936, the Young Officers launched their boldest attempt to topple the government. In spite of assassination, terror, and the military seizure of a large part of Tokyo, the plot collapsed. The vigor of the government this time was in great contrast

[15] Tōa Keizei Chōsakyoku, *Manshū tokuhon,* cited, pp. 309 ff.; also Interrogation No. 155, United States Strategic Bombing Survey (Pacific War), Tokyo, October 28, 1945.

[16] Y. (Anonymous), "The May 15th Case," *Contemporary Japan,* Vol. II (September 1933), pp. 195-196. The coup of 1932, also 1936, called forth a mass of literature: *Trans-Pacific,* September 14, 21, October 5, 1933, covered the trials in detail; in Japanese, see Wada Hidekichi, *Ni-ni-roku igo* (Since the February 26th incident), Tōkyō, 1937; Hugh Byas, *Government by Assassination,* New York, 1942, is a popular account in English. On General Araki's "Crisis of 1935-1936" and the Army pamphlets, nothing in English is more complete than Kenneth C. Colegrove, *Militarism in Japan,* New York, 1936, based on Japanese sources.

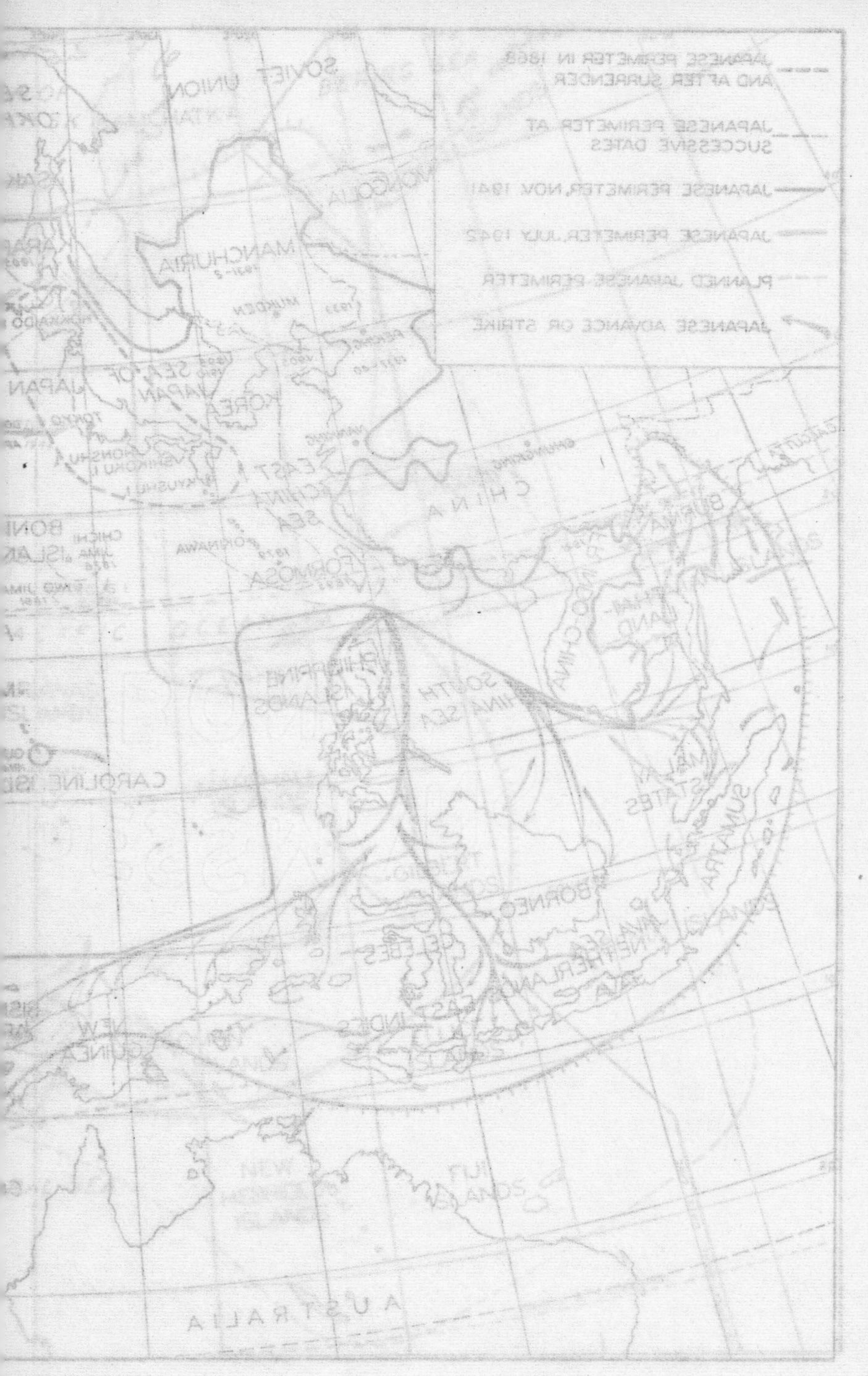

with leniency shown the 1932 conspirators. Even so, the *Kōdō-ha* had the last word.

On the night of July 7, 1937, at the Marco Polo Bridge, Lukouchiao, near Peiping, maneuvering Japanese troops were fired on. Another China Incident had begun. The War Ministry announced that reinforcements were on their way by July 13. A half million Ex-Soldiers began pressure on the government for action. In each step, Japanese Army demands were satisfied. For the second time in a decade, the military had used the war power to overshadow Japanese foreign relations. Japan had entered upon the road to Incident, the Big War, victory, and, in the end, defeat.

Blueprint for a Monolithic State. After 1937, Japan was in uninterrupted conflict for eight years. Two aspects of wartime Japan were significant. The larger pattern of the war, from 1937 to 1945, was striking testimony to the fact that this insular power was like a fault line running through the cultures of the East and the West. For Japan fought both China and the West in the larger war. Against China she pitted the new forces of the West; against America and the West she hurled the old forces of the East. Thus, as a nation, she was isolated from healthy interchange with either of the cultures these two regions represent.

Yet, although culturally isolated, the forces of inter-cultural penetration were still present, deep *inside* Japan. The war did not halt the process of adjustment; it merely hastened the tempo. Because of this need for adjustment, wartime Japan—presumably militaristic—was actually a nation still seeking compromises to ease internal conflict. They were never really found, and Japan's war effort was weakened as a result.

Based on such underlying instability, Japan's internal society saw a continuing struggle for control, even though at times some elements of the society appeared almost nonexistent. As a result, Japan was never completely united, either politically or economically. This caused a real problem of leadership. Coalitions acted more as places where differing viewpoints were focussed than as real attempts at unity. Those out of power contributed little, even though possessed of assets and abilities the sorely tried Empire desperately needed. The internal struggle at times appeared more important than the external one.

Japan did have a blueprint for a monolithic, war-dedicated state. Indeed, she had several, and thus the need again to adjust one to the other. The problem of leadership and the presence of disunity affected the harnessing of the economy, political adaptation to the changing needs of the war, and Japan's bid for leadership through the Greater East Asia Co-Prosperity Sphere. In short, characteristic diffusion of power was such as to throw doubt on the wisdom of applying the term *fascism,* like so many other Western political terms, even to wartime Japan.[17]

[17] Professor Charles B. Fahs, in his *Government in Japan: Recent Trends in Its Scope and Operation,* New York, 1940, published just before the United States was involved in

Japan's wartime economic scene was similar to the political picture. This was partly true because of inseparability of these two parts of a nation's life in total war. When political control was not strong, the economic effort was obviously weakened. Japan entered the war against the West with a small industrial machine, at least as compared with those of its enemies. In fact, the war should never have been fought since economically one side could not win and the other could not lose.[18] This, perhaps, is the best commentary of all on the dangers of economic determinism, as a formula to explain political behavior. It tends to throw the problem of political decision, including the decision to go to war, back to the social psychologist, where it belongs.

Indeed, some day, perhaps, the political scientists and the economists will formulate for us a theory of defeat in total war as a product of the *resistance* to total mobilization. All the major powers in World War II—democracies and totalitarian states alike—suffered from the disease. Japan was no exception. It is true that in the years 1931-1940, Japanese leaders realized the hard fact of shortage of raw materials. By cutting corners, they forged a very respectable industrial weapon. Abundant materials, trained labor force, and civilian amenities were, of course, still lacking. Because of insufficient stretch in the economy and because of early, exhilarating victories, Japan failed to take the strengthening steps in 1941-1942, which even her sketchy administrative control would allow. Too late, when dreams of conquest began turning into nightmares of defeat, urgent steps were taken toward industrial mobilization and economic administration.

In the too-late mobilization, deep within the intricacy of the war economy, lay the peculiar Japanese problem of compromise. Once again, a battle at home had to be won first. The opposing forces on the home front were the huge family-like *Zaibatsu* on one side and the uncompromising Army advocates of public ownership on the other. Remember, too, the farmer-peasant background of the Army leadership, and you will realize the gulf which continued to separate the two groups.

The *Zaibatsu* persistently feared and resented any encroachment on their vast preserves. Delighted they were, despite approaching national defeat, when Koiso succeeded Tōjō. Redistribution of governmental authority,

war with Japan, made a survey of early Japanese economic and political controls in this light. He emphasized that the growth of Japanese state power had as its objective the same security as that sought in the American New Deal, the Soviet Five-Year Plan, British measures for social security, or French experiments. For an earlier, exactly opposite view, see Sakuzo Yoshino, "Fascism in Japan," *Contemporary Japan,* September, 1932, pp. 185-197. Alas, as events were to prove, both erred in the extreme. Japan's "planned economy" became more and more dedicated to war. Yet Japan always kept her own unique "totalitarian" polity.

[18] So, neatly, Professor Jerome B. Cohen summed up the economic picture in 1941, in *op. cit.,* see especially Chap. 2," War Years—Overview." To compare the Japanese experience with the somewhat similar German failure to mobilize, see USSBS, Overall Economic Effects Division, *The Effects of Strategic Bombing on the German War Economy,* Washington, October 31, 1945.

regionalization, and decentralization of governmental control followed. Their struggle continued into peace and the Occupation, when they lost their first big battle.

These, in brief, are some of the main reasons why Japan prepared only a blueprint for a monolithic state. A New Structure was begun but never completed. Even so, in the attempt were characteristic Japanese methods for the governing of men. In some cases, the older structure was remodeled beyond recognition.

First changes in governmental structure after 1937 were a result of partial mobilization. The phrase, "quasi-wartime economic system" (*junsenji keizai*), was heard as early as the Hirota Cabinet (1936-37). Actually, Japan's pattern of control was first tested in the laboratories of overseas holdings, in such giant corporations as the Oriental Development Company (Korea), the Manchurian Industrial Development Company, and the various China development companies. Finally, back home in Japan the Diet passed the National General Mobilization Law (*Kokka Sōdōin Hō*).[19] Japan had begun a very interesting cycle: mobilization, as always, called forth new talents for production, particularly among younger industrialists; these young industrialists were quick to support the Army in its expansionist policies; young industrialists and the Army, particularly in Manchuria, built a model of a controlled economy, which in turn spurred further mobilization in Japan.

By 1940, Japan was caught in a bewildering network of "controls," "autonomous arrangements," independent ministry "orders," high prices, shortages, and delays. Continued Army dissatisfaction resulted in the resignation of the War Minister in July, 1940, thus precipitating the fall of the Yonai Cabinet (January-July, 1940). Its successor, the second Konoye Cabinet (July, 1940-July, 1941), had Tōjō as War Minister, Matsuoka Yōsuke as Foreign Minister, and Hoshino Naoki as Minister-without-Portfolio (concurrently, Chief, Cabinet Planning Board). The Cabinet thus marked the active entrance of the Kwantung Army, dedicated to a Total Defense State, into home affairs: Tōjō had come fresh from the Kwantung Army Command; Matsuoka, from Presidency of the S.M.R.; and Hoshino, from the Directorship of the General Affairs Bureau, Manchukuo.[20] The Cabinet also marked the last attempt, by Prince Konoye, to establish a balanced totalitarian state.

[19] The *Kokka Sōdōin Hō* consisted of fifty articles. The complete text, occupying ten pages, and the maze of succeeding legislation filled an entire volume: Tōsei Hōrei Kenkyūkai Hen (Control Laws and Ordinances Research Society, Editor), *Tōsei hōrei zensho* (Complete set of control laws and ordinances), Kyōto, 1942. Hugh Borton, *Japan Since 1931,* cited, Appendix II, gives a list of the articles invoked to March 1939.

[20] Both Hoshino and Vice Minister of Foreign Affairs Ōhashi had been leading planners of Manchukuo's state-controlled industrial structure and intimates of Kwantung Commander-in-Chief Tōjō and his Chief of Staff, General Umezu Yoshijirō. To the Kwantung Gang was added Baron Hiranuma as Home Minister, in December, 1940. Tōjō, of course, later became Premier; Hoshino, Chief Cabinet Secretary and Minister of State; Umezu, Chief of Staff. All, save Ōhashi, appeared later as major war criminals before the International Military Tribunal.

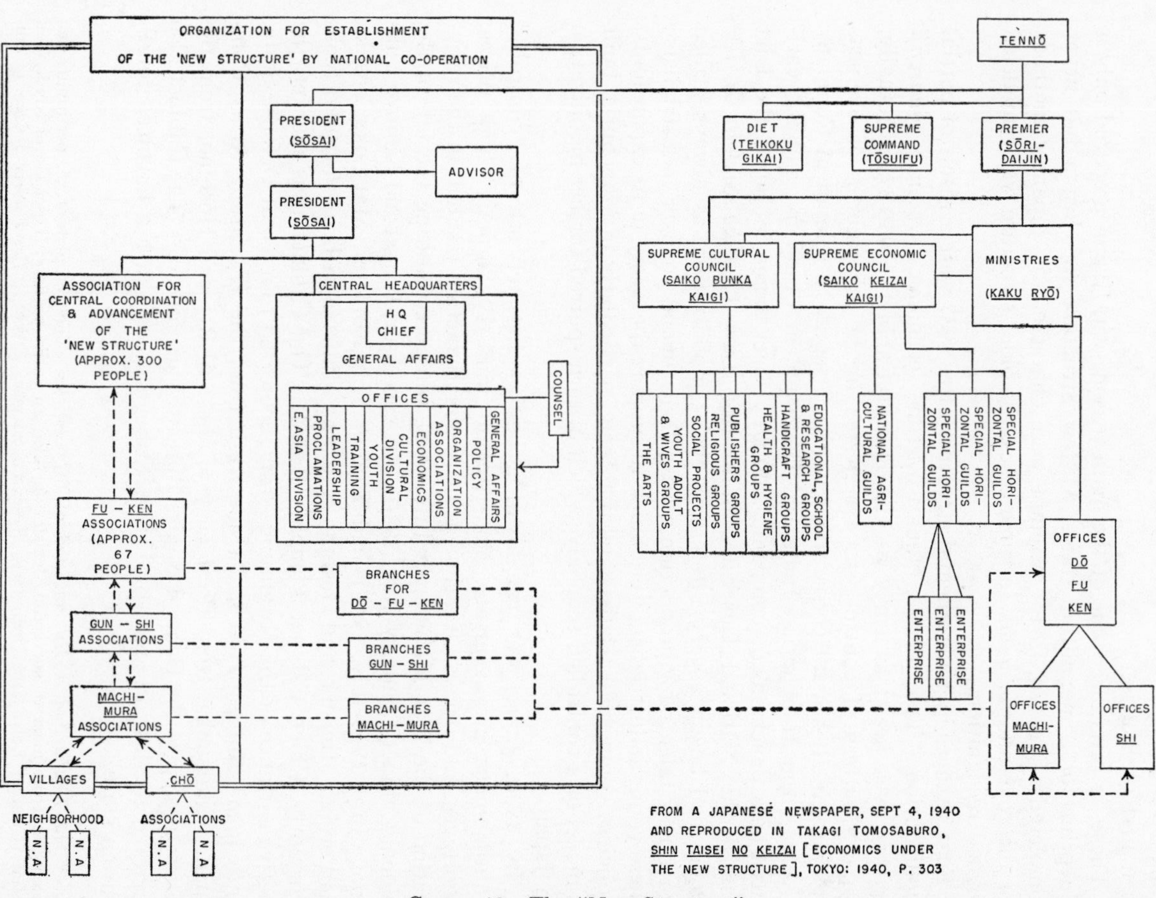

CHART 19—The "New Structure"

Prince Konoye Fumimaro, premier for a second time, was the logical man to form a new national government. Forty-seven years old when he had first formed a Cabinet in 1937, he brought a wealth of experience and wide contacts to the government. A member of one of Japan's oldest and most respected noble families, he developed rapidly under the venerable Saionji's tutorship. He was Vice-President of the House of Peers at the time of the May 15, 1932 Incident; he succeeded Prince Tokugawa as President in 1933. After the February 26, 1936 Incident he was urged to form a government superseding all political party leadership. After he resigned in 1939, the formation of a new party became a current topic of conversation. When he returned in 1940, he was one of the few men acceptable to all the cliques—the military, parties, bureaucrats, *Zaibatsu,* and aristocracy. The foreign press often erroneously spoke of him as the potential dictator of Japan, the Mussolini of *Dai Nihon.* Prince Konoye, however, was all things to all men: an aristocrat by tradition, a "liberal" by education, and a paternalistic authoritarian by experience. In short, Konoye was a Japanese.

Actually, when Konoye first resigned in 1939, he merely exchanged places with Baron Hiranuma (Premier, January-August, 1939). Konoye became President of the Privy Council and concurrent Minister-without-Portfolio. He continued to pull the Council and the government together during the interim cabinets of General Abe (August, 1939-January, 1940) and of Admiral Yonai (January-July, 1940). While still President of the Council, he began studies of a truly unified national administration. In late June, one month before his second premiership, he resigned from the Privy Council to devote all of his time to the establishment of a New Structure (*Shin Taisei*).[21] The chart on page 432, drawn from a Japanese source, shows the shape of *Shin Taisei.*

Hoshino, later Chief Cabinet Secretary under Tōjō, told American interrogators after surrender that a real "war economy" began only after the loss of Guadalcanal. To the control associations were added special wartime corporations, called *Eidan* Finally, in the first half of 1943, Premier Tōjō forced through legislation designed to concentrate administrative power in the hands of the Premier. Even so, he found it necessary to appoint business leaders to a Cabinet Advisory Board, to avoid the charge of dictatorship. The government was still trying to effect maximum efficiency of existing structure.

The last great shake-up came on November 1, 1943, when three new ministries appeared. The Ministry of Munitions (*Gunjushō*) assumed control over mobilization and control of production, raw materials allocation, prices, and wages. Its creation marked the abolition of the Cabinet Planning

[21] Discussion of the *Shin Taisei* caused a tidal wave of controversy. Typical were: Asahi Shimbun-sha (Asahi Newspaper Co.), *Shin Taisei kokumin kōza; keizai hen* (People's lectures on the New Structure; economics volume), Ōsaka, 1941; Ōtani Takeo, *Shin Taisei Nihon no seiji keizai bunka* (Japanese polity and economy under the New Structure), Tōkyō, 1940.

Board. Tōjō held the portfolio in addition to being Premier, War Minister, and Chief of Staff. Consumer goods and commerce went under the control of a Minister of Agriculture and Commerce; communications and railways, under a new Transportation Ministry. These changes marked the peak of wartime control of the economy. In theory, unification had been achieved. In practice, it was too late: by 1944-45, Allied measures had bitten deep into the Japanese economy. Incompetent planning merely hastened disaster.

The New Political Structure (Chart 19) was only little more successful. Two problems faced the architects of *Shin Taisei:* one was how to deal with the Diet—embodied in the Constitution—and the other was how to amalgamate the parties. The latter was easier to handle since parties were not embodied in the sacrosanct Constitution; indeed, they were quick to climb on the New Structure bandwagon. By August, 1940, the last party dutifully voted itself out of existence and, by September, preparatory meetings to establish the *Shin Taisei* were concluded. On October 12, the Imperial Rule Assistance Association (*Taisei Yokusan Kai*) made its bow.

The Diet proved much less tractable. First the government tried an oblique attack, tampering with election laws. The Diet, actually only a sounding board for hostile *Zaibatsu,* countered by celebrating its fiftieth anniversary with all possible pomp. Once the Diet was prorogued in March, 1941, the government breathed more easily.

After the Tōjō Cabinet was formed in October, 1941, the cycle of shabby, cut-rate political associations was rounded out by successive formation of the Imperial Rule Assistance Political Council, the I.R.A. Political Association, and finally, the Japan Political Party (*Nihon Seiji Kai*).

Several other changes in wartime administrative structure worthy of mention affected local government. In July, 1943, Japan Proper was divided into nine administrative regions (*chihō gyōsei*) designed to achieve centralization of policy-formulation and economic control but decentralization of administration. A regional administrative council (*chihō gyōsei kyōgikai*) consisted of all prefectural governors within the region; one was designated president. He was directly responsible to the Premier and was advanced from governors' *chokunin* to Cabinet *shinnin* rank. Major emphasis in the regions was placed on production of munitions and food, transport coordination, and organization of civilian defense. Even this plan had its compromise, however. Regional councilors, executive officers of the councils, remained responsible to the Home Minister.

In June, 1945, the entire regional structure was drastically reorganized to meet the threat of invasion. Regions became superintendencies-general (*sōkan-fu*); presidents, superintendents-general (*sōkan*); and councils, advisory councils (*sanyo-kai*). Vast grants of power, originally retained by the prefectures, were granted the *sōkan-fu* with the idea that areas might have to operate independently while other parts of the country were invaded.[22] Chart 20 shows the channels of local government authority at the end of the war.

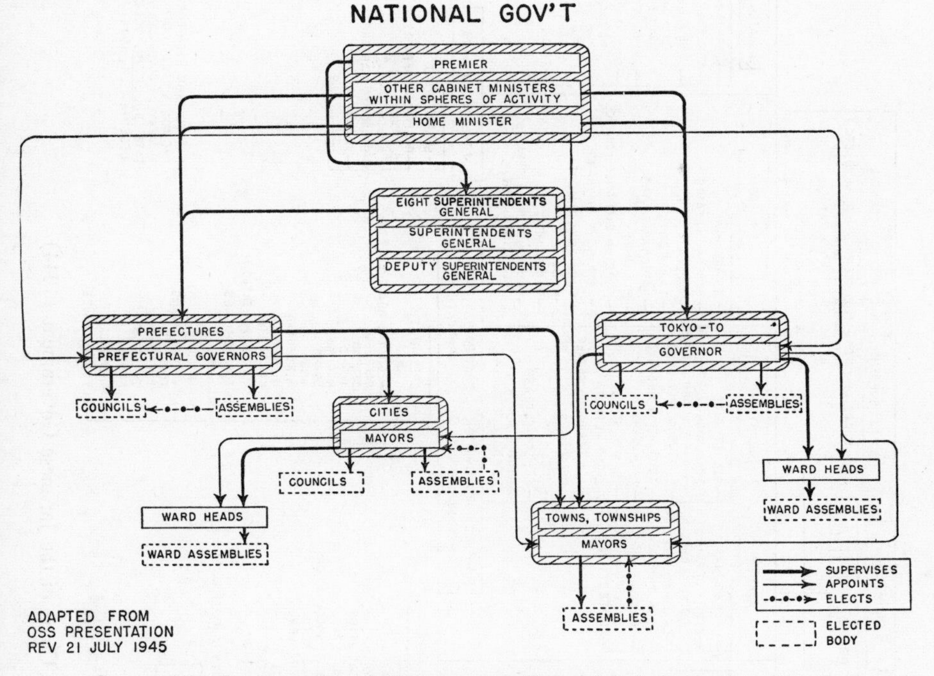

CHART 20—Japanese Local Government Channels of Authority (1945)

GEACPS. One other side of Japan's management of the war deserves special mention. Because it reflects so clearly the internal and external conflicts which robbed Japan of real unity, that country's bid for Asian leadership is perhaps one of the most significant political phenomena of the entire period.

When the Greater East Asia Co-Prosperity Sphere (GEACPS, or, in Japanese, *Dai Tōa Kyōei Ken*) was announced officially in 1940, the idea was not new. Japan had become the residium of Western-type power in the Orient. "Asia for the Asiatics" eloquently states how this nation began to think of an Asia freed from domination by Western states. Combine the two factors and the result was an Asia led by Japan; at least that is how the

[22] The chart on this page, which presents the channels of local government at the end of the war, is drawn from Office of Strategic Services, Research and Analysis 2760, *Local Government in Japan,* cited, 21 July 1945. The original regions were: (1) *Hokkai* (Hokkaidō, Karafuto); (2) *Tōhoku* (Aomori, Iwate, Miyagi, Akita, Yamagata, Fukushima); (3) *Kantō* (Ibaraki, Tochigi, Gumma, Saitama, Chiba, Kanagawa, Yamanashi, Tōkyō-*to*); (4) *Tōkai* (Gifu, Shizuoka, Aichi, Mie); (5) *Hokuriku* (Niigata, Toyama, Ishikawa, Fukui, Nagano); (6) *Kinki* (Shiga, Kyōto-*fu,* Ōsaka-*fu,* Hyōgo, Nara, Wakayama); (7) *Chūgoku* (Tottori, Shimane, Okayama, Hiroshima, Yamaguchi); (8) *Shikoku* (Tokushima, Kagawa, Ehime, Kōchi); (9) *Kyūshū* (Fukuoka, Saga, Nagasaki, Kumamoto, Ōita, Miyazaki, Kagoshima, Okinawa); *Japan Year Book, 1943-44,* p. 138.

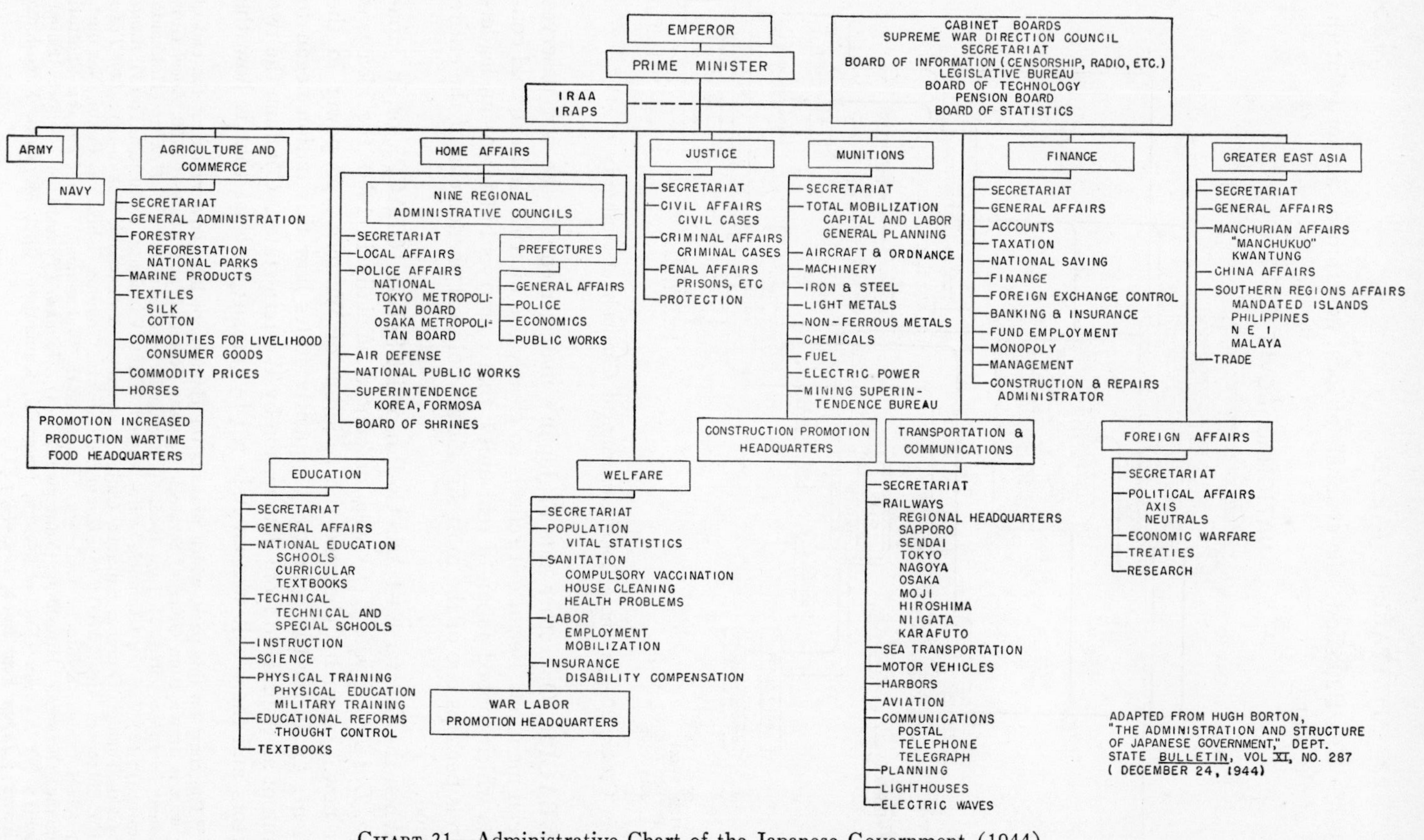

CHART 21—Administrative Chart of the Japanese Government (1944)

Japanese saw it. Much of their feeling came from the underlying ties which bound them to Oriental culture. The Confucian concept of the family of states, emphasis upon group rather than individual, and the stress on values —rather than materials—were all part of the idealism which bolstered this aim. Prince Konoye's *Hakkō Ichiu* was the equivalent of Wendell Willkie's phrase, "One World"; it was the Chinese concept of "eight corners of the universe under one roof."

One Japanese writer spoke of "the vital task of carrying through, with creative intelligence, the constructive duty which is Japan's." There should be a cooperative order with a world view as against the order of obsolete individualism. This new order would stand opposed to an international system of Communism, as well as to the domination of capitalism and banking.[23]

At its peak, Japan thought of GEACPS as including her own main islands, China, Manchukuo, Burma, Thailand, Indochina, Malaya, Sumatra, Java, Borneo, the Celebes, New Guinea, and the Philippines. At home she created the Greater East Asia Ministry (*Dai Tōashō*) in November, 1942, to handle these far-flung areas. From them she hoped to guarantee herself raw materials, markets, and political and military support.

Japan failed in this utterly and miserably. In this failure, Japan lost the chance of a nation's lifetime. Reasons for the fiasco are not hard to find.

When Japan launched her conquest of Asia, she started a prairie fire among the colonial peoples of that realm. Many were eager to extend and receive aid if it meant a chance for independence. This urge of Asia's millions to be free was a priceless asset to Japan's strategists. Used intelligently, such desires could have swept the West from Asia, denied it reentry, and gained for Japan undying gratitude of the area's peoples. Instead, Japan chose to supplant the West's mastery with her own, its exploitation with hers. There is the major reason for her failure.

In 1943, the First Assembly of Greater East Asiatic Nations met in Tokyo. The tawdry roll-call shows how unsuccessful Japan had been in enlisting the strong leadership of the realm. Wang Ching-wei of China, Wan Waithayakon of Thailand, Chang Ching-jui of Manchukuo, José Laurel of the Philippines, Ba Maw of Burma, Shubhas Chandra Bose of India—these were the opportunistic lemmings whom Japan lured by the *samisen*-diplomacy of the New Order. Chiang Kai-shek, Mao Tse-tung, Gandhi, Nehru, Osmeña, Quezon—these and others like them, the real leaders of independence, saw the design of plunder for what it was.

Japan was not even able to exploit Greater East Asia effectively. Internal dissensions among the Army, Foreign Office, GEA Ministry, and the *Zaibatsu* made a shambles of combined effort. (Chart 21 shows the complexity of the Japanese government.) Lack of leadership, disunity, and

[23] Sugihara Masanomi, *Tōa kyōdōtai no genri* (Principles of an East Asiatic Cooperative Order), Tōkyō, 1939.

special interests which rendered Japan ineffective internally also crippled external efforts. The prairie fire ignited by Japan turned against her in the end. By 1944, the Allies were enlisting and receiving support from these same areas.[24]

The Last "Big War." A war is lost if an inadequate estimate is made of the job to be done in order to win. A nation is headed toward defeat if it does not measure, with fair accuracy, its own capabilities and those of its enemies. The Japanese had built up, in the years since 1895, a historical justification for war. They thought they had adapted their political structure and their economy to modern conflict. They had become as familiar with war as monkeys are with trees. The Japanese themselves, however, have a saying: "Even monkeys fall from trees."[25]

Most objective observers now agree that the Empire of Japan was not brought to its knees in defeat by the fire-bomb raids of the B-29's, by the explosions of atomic bombs over Hiroshima and Nagasaki, or by the entry of the Soviet Union into the Pacific War. If these events had not occurred, it is altogether likely that the war would have ended within a matter of months. These dramatic events, then, marked the *occasion* for surrender, not the *cause* of defeat. The rhythm of events climaxed by the pounding of Japan's cities by fire and explosive can be shown to have begun in the fall of 1941 before hostilities with the West started.

It takes a brave, even a rather naïve, man who would sharpen another axe to try to cut away the jungle surrounding the causes of Japan's defeat. Too many axes have already been ground in publishing source material surrounding this highly complex matter. Too many special interests are involved. The event is still too contemporary for objectivity. For these reasons, no attempt will be made here to juggle the factors in Japan's defeat in any neat order of importance. Despite the dangers involved, however, we must make a reconnaissance of the jungle. For our purpose, only the factors which have a bearing on Japanese government and politics will be surveyed in any detail. Perhaps the excursion will be of some use: political aspects of the defeat have been largely overlooked.[26]

[24] A recent, very interesting description of the cycle is presented in David H. James, *The Rise and Fall of the Japanese Empire*, New York, 1951. Captain James, long a Far Eastern hand, describes the Malayan campaign and the fall of Singapore from personal experience; as a prisoner in Tokyo, he observed first-hand the exhilarating rise of the GEACPS and the giddy descent. With the personal account is reflective analysis of Japan's problems, based on intimate knowledge of Far Eastern languages, peoples, and culture.

[25] *Saru mo ki kara ochiru.*

[26] The basic source for evaluations, conjectures, and conclusions continues to be the mass of documents, interrogations, and published results of the U. S. Strategic Bombing Survey (Pacific). Representative documents are cited below. From personal experience, the author of this section soon realized that the survey, like the Japanese Cabinet, became a battleground for conflicting interests. With a shrewd eye on future appropriations, each branch of the U.S. Services—amazingly cooperative during the conflict—concluded that its contribution constituted the key blow. Such arguments must eventually be resolved by the military historian. The most thorough use of the evidence, from a scholarly viewpoint, is Jerome B. Cohen's monograph, already cited, which exhaustively covers the economic collapse. With his conclusion, that "the ever-enveloping American blockade of Japan, by

In this sense, Japan's collapse may be generally understood if the various reasons which have been cited are grouped, rather than rated, in order of importance. The first group, in time at least, were those which resulted from incorrect estimates of her own and her enemies' capabilities. In the longest view, these estimates were in turn partly a product of a rigid (in theory) and at the same time diffuse (in practice) policy-making mechanism. In the fall of 1941, the men gathered around the war-planning tables made several disastrous appraisals. From the beginning, leaders of Japan did not evaluate correctly the industrial potential of the United States. But then, who did? The gamble of war was also predicated on the concept of a war of limited objectives and in that appraisal, too, Japanese leaders made a basic error.[27]

A second group of reasons for defeat simply magnify the original miscalculations. The intermediate factors were not isolated: each individual failure compounded, and was compounded by, the others. There is little point, again, in listing them in any order of importance. For example, Japan's military strategists failed to understand the weapons of modern warfare. As some Japanese cried, late in the conflict, "Wars cannot be won by bamboo spears!" The increased capabilities of modern air power, in the broader sense, made a mockery of military frontiers. When command of the air was lost over Guadalcanal in the fall of 1942, it was lost forever. Every military defeat and supply problem was affected by this fact. Lack of economic mobilization was aggravated by an astounding failure of cooperation among the military services themselves. Interdiction of Empire supply lines, begun by inexpressibly brave American submariners, was completed by air bombing and mines by August, 1945. Nine tenths of Japan's total available merchant marine was put out of commission. The magnitude of this disaster was such as to deliver a blow from which there was no recovery. This the Japanese did not bungle. It was simply beyond their capacity to resist.

But somehow, amazingly, they continued to resist.

Among the secondary factors in defeat was another which the Japanese could not have expected to foresee. In retrospect, the island-hopping amphibious operations of Allied forces across the Pacific was a spectacular achievement. The speed of the onslaught staggered the Japanese and served

---

shutting off essential supplies . . . brought Japanese war production to a virtual standstill before the main weight of the strategic air attack was delivered . . ." (Author's Preface, p. xi) there can be little quarrel. Indeed, as Professor Cohen put it, Japan's basic incapability for a protracted struggle should have persuaded her never to enter it! For our purposes, however, this leaves psychological factors in Japan's stubborn continuation of the war, in governmental aspects of the "target," in the fascinating politics of the surrender decision, and in the political framework passed on to the Occupation—all unexplained. Here we are more concerned with the political end of all veiled force and outright violence—short of a war of annihilation—namely, how was Japan persuaded to surrender? And, What effect did her surrender have on the postwar political structure?

[27] Admiral Nomura, after the surrender, stated that the Privy Council "seemed to think that if we stood fast the people in the United States might, bye and bye, weary of the war"; that the Army "underestimated the speed of your reactions"; and that the High Command "thought that Germany would win." USSBS (Naval Analysis Division) *Interrogations of Japanese Officials,* Washington, 1946, Vol. II, pp. 384, 385, 387.

to chew up their naval and air forces. This cause of defeat can be considered with the sea blockade with which, in the words of the Strategic Bombing Survey, ". . . it formed a shears that scissored Japan's military potential into an ineffectual remnant." With the conquest of Iwo Jima in the spring of 1945, Japan's defeat became imminent.

Still the Japanese resisted. Okinawa, in the summer of 1945, proved the Japanese could still make Allied victory by invasion costly.

This brings up to a third group of reasons for defeat. Although they marked only the occasion for final defeat, they were politically significant in influence upon the conditions, the timing, and the lasting results of surrender.

First in influence were the incendiary and high-explosive bombing attacks of the B-29's on the Japanese home islands. True, the Japanese economy was staggering and the B-29 raids, as naval personnel liked to point out, were later regarded as duplicative destruction of Japan's industry. In terms of psychological warfare, however, here was *deed propaganda* of the grimmest variety. The refugee problem became enormous, especially because of the technique used by General Curtis LeMay of attacking widely separated areas. So firmly were Japanese impressed by the impunity of *B-san* (Mr. B-29) that it became necessary merely to warn cities of impending doom by means of leaflets to have them completely evacuated. Morale indices later showed that in December, 1944, only ten per cent of the people of the home islands believed victory impossible. By August, 1945, sixty-eight per cent believed defeat certain. One half of these believed that our attacks had cancelled the chance of avoiding defeat.

Two other factors which sealed Japan's defeat occurred at approximately the same time. On August 5 (Washington time), the low-lying, river-braided, humid, and morally wicked city of Hiroshima became the object of an attack. For the war's masterpiece of understatement, listen to a Japanese verbatim broadcast:

> Yesterday, August six, the city of Hiroshima suffered considerable damage due to attacks by a small number of enemy B-twenty-nines. In the above attack it appears that the enemy used a new type bomb. . . . In regard to its power, investigations are at present under way. However, we cannot be unconcerned.

The psychological effect of the atomic bombings of Hiroshima and Nagasaki was "remarkably localized" within the target cities. Possibly the bombs affected Japan's leaders more than her civilian population, for it was many days before the shroud of secrecy was lifted.

The man in the street was much more affected by Russia's entry into the Pacific War because he was better informed about it. The final hope for at least one secure flank was obviated by Russia's action. But in either case, as tools for use by those levering Japan into surrender, both Russia's attack and the atomic bombs were accelerators rather than prime movers.[28]

As in most wars and most surrenders, the last stage in Japan's defeat involved a political decision. In psychological warfare, however, the Allies had a self-imposed obstacle. The vague and impractical formula of unconditional surrender, originally laid down by Franklin Delano Roosevelt at Casablanca in December, 1942, had to be redefined. Because of uncertainty, great numbers of influential Japanese felt that unconditional surrender allowed die-hard militarists to incite the people to even greater sacrifices.

The Potsdam Proclamation, outlining the conditions of surrender, straightened out one of the last kinks in the chain of decision. The most effective broadcasts of Captain Ellis M. Zacharias, United States Navy, for example, were directed at a sympathetic segment of Japanese: influential leaders under the domination of militarists. The fourth broadcast exposed the military clique; the twelfth interpreted President Truman's "honorable conditional surrender." [29] Captain Zacharias' personal role in the defeat of Japan can be exaggerated; but the effect of definition of surrender conditions, which he and others explained to Japan, was crucial in the struggle to surrender.

The Internal Struggle to Surrender. Japan accepted defeat without invasion while still possessed of two and a half million combat troops and nine thousand *kamikaze* airplanes. This was a startling climax, both to the Allies and to the Japanese. There had been a fateful shift from the twisted and smoldering strategic target to the complex and interlocking mechanism of the political target. How was it decided that this too was no longer defensible?

The answer may be found in the period from the collapse of the Tōjō government in July, 1944, to the Imperial Rescript of August 15, 1945. For many Americans, the Emperor was the *only* actor in the drama. In truth, his role in the surrender *was* supreme. Since this was a Japanese political decision, however, there had to be others. Close to the *Tennō* were the *jūshin,* new elder statesmen like Marquis Kido, Lord Keeper and confidential adviser; Prince Konoye, who briefly re-entered the scene; Admirals Okada, Nomura, and Yonai, Navy men who early disagreed with Tōjō. Minor officials who played vital roles were Sakomizu Hisatsune, link between the Cabinet and his father-in-law, Okada; Colonel Matsutani, Suzuki's military secretary; Katō Masuo, former *Dōmei* American corro-

[28] See USSBS (Chairman's Office), *The Effects of Atomic Bombs on Hiroshima and Nagasaki,* Washington, 20 June 1946. Nothing in the above comments on *political* effects should be interpreted to detract from the *actual* effects of the A-bomb as a weapon. America's present flaccid civil defense could well use the USSBS study as a required text.

[29] The complete English text of the Potsdam Proclamation is given in Appendix 14 and is discussed in the next chapter. During the period of actual surrender, the Japanese radio said many times: "We are ending the war in accordance with Captain Zacharias' interpretation of unconditional surrender." An account of Captain Zacharias' career is presented in his autobiographical *Secret Missions,* New York, 1946.

spondent; Foreign Office officials; and university professors. Katō later wrote that long before Yalta, private meetings were being held to prepare Japan for defeat. The problem was to circulate among all leaders in retirement a true picture of the situation as viewed by the minority.[30]

On June 27, 1944, Admiral Okada, representing the *jūshin,* called on Tōjō and asked him to resign. For the time being, the General held fast. By mid-July advisers, the Navy, and members of the Imperial family had decided Tōjō must go. Only July 14 he called on the Emperor, expecting mediation. To Tōjō's surprise, the Emperor refused to support him. With the fall of Saipan, Tōjō resigned.

On July 22, 1944, General Koiso received the Imperial admonition to form a government and to start "a fundamental reconsideration" of the war. Almost his sole contribution, however, was the formation of a Supreme War Direction Council (*Gunreibu Saikō Sensō Shidōkaigi*), a body which later provided one vehicle for the approach to surrender. It had the effect of bringing the Chiefs of Staff into deliberations on national policy and the Premier into decisions of the high command.

After the Leyte debacle, the bloody defeat at Iwo Jima, and the fall of Okinawa, the Emperor on his own initiative held interviews with various *jūshin*. Prince Konoye particularly was obsessed by the ascendancy of the Soviet Union in world politics and revealed a deep fear of Russian interference in Japanese domestic affairs.[31]

He advised negotiation toward peace. On March 15, 1945, the Koiso government did try to approach China through its own puppet, the Provisional Government in Peiping. The Japanese Army, however, blocked serious compromise.

The Suzuki Cabinet was formed April 8, 1945, and may be characterized as representing the first direct expression of Imperial will in modern Japanese history. His responsibility, solely to the Emperor, was clear. As he explained it to interrogators after the war, "It was the Emperor's desire to make every effort to bring the war to a conclusion as quickly as possible, and that was my purpose."

After the collapse of Germany in May, the Army was willing to discuss alternatives. On June 8, the Supreme War Direction Council met with the

[30] The following account follows USSBS, *Japan's Struggle to End the War,* Washington, 1 July 1946; for a briefer summary, Ardath W. Burks, "Survey of Japan's Defeat," *Far Eastern Survey,* August 14, 1946. For an early post-surrender Japanese view, see Masuo Kato, *The Lost War; A Japanese Reporter's Inside Story,* New York, 1946. Toshikazu Kase, *Journey to the "Missouri,"* New Haven, 1950, is a more detailed, and shrewdly apologetic, account by a Foreign Office official. The most complete survey—covering available public and private, American and Japanese materials—is Robert J. C. Butow, *Japan's Decision to Surrender; A Study in Political Evolution,* Princeton (Ph.D. dissertation), planned for publication by the Stanford Univ Press.

[31] Konoye, in a memorandum addressed to the Emperor, wrote: "I think that there is no longer any doubt about our defeat. A defeat is, of course, a serious stain on our history, but we can accept it, so long as we can maintain our *Tennō* system. . . . What we have to fear, therefore, is not so much a defeat as a Communist revolution which might take place in the event of defeat." USSBS, *Japan's Struggle,* cited, Appendix A-5, p. 21.

Emperor to study a pessimistic report on Japan's capabilities, drawn up by Sakomizu.[32] In July, it was decided that Prince Konoye would go to Moscow to see what terms he could get. The first reply to a request for mediation had brought a simple answer: unconditional surrender. When the second reply came back, it was learned that Generalissimo Stalin and Commissar Molotov had left for Potsdam. Japanese officialdom awaited the outcome of the conference with great interest. Japanese naval leaders particularly hung on every word of Captain Zacharias' broadcasts. Then came the terms of the Potsdam Proclamation. The basic purpose was clear: "Japan shall be given an opportunity to end this war."

In discussions held July 26, Premier Suzuki, Foreign Minister Tōgō, and Navy Minister Yonai asked for compliance with the Potsdam terms. General Anami and the Staff Chiefs were opposed. Their minimum terms were: (1) no occupying troops in Japan proper; (2) Japan would draw back troops from overseas voluntarily; and (3) Japan would try her own war criminals. On July 29, Japan categorically rejected the Potsdam offer. Nevertheless, the first chink had appeared in Japan's will to resist.

The five days, August 5-9, 1945, brought the two atomic blasts, a declaration of war by Russia, the attack on Manchukuo. The military were caught flat-footed without a counter plan. Events now began to move on an hour-to-hour schedule.

At 7:00 A.M., on August 9, Premier Suzuki told the Emperor he had decided to accept the Potsdam Ultimatum. At 10:00 A.M. the Supreme War Direction Council met but ended in bitter dispute and a stalemate vote. In the full Cabinet, nine Ministers voted for unconditional acceptance, three for conditional, and three were on the fence. At 11:00 P.M. the Emperor met with the six members of the Supreme War Direction Council, their secretaries, and Baron Hiranuma, representing the Privy Council. The Imperial Council deadlocked and dissolved into an Inner Cabinet meeting. At about 2:30 A.M. the Emperor announced his desire to accept the Potsdam terms on one condition, that the prerogatives of the Imperial household be retained.

The drama had to be re-enacted, however, for the United States reply received on August 12 did not seem explicit. The Cabinet split again, but more strongly on the side of acceptance: 13-2. On the morning of the 13th, the War Minister, Munitions Minister and Chiefs of Staff remained opposed in a meeting of the Supreme War Direction Council. On the following morning, Emperor Hirohito himself reconvened the Council at 10:00 A.M. Each side again presented its case. The Emperor thanked his advisers and spoke as follows:

[32] Sakomizu has given us a grimly humorous picture of these hectic days. His own house was burned and he was living in his office building where he had set up a cot on a lower floor. Each morning he would arise, perform his ablutions, put on his hat, walk up through the building to his office, remove his hat, and go to work. This was "going-to-office." At night, the routine was reversed. This was "going-home-from-office."

> "Continuation of the war does not promise successful conclusion of the war no matter from what angle the situation is considered. Therefore, I have decided, without suggestions from anyone, to order the conclusion of the war, as I cannot endure the thought of having to kill tens, even hundreds of thousands of my subjects, and moreover to have to be called the disturber of world peace. . . . I have decided to endure what is unendurable and to accept the terms of the Potsdam Proclamation." [33]

General Anami, the War Minister, was deeply moved, retired, and later committed suicide. The Emperor, said the moderates, had come back to the people from his capture by the military. On August 15 the Emperor's voice, recorded for radio broadcast for the first time, read the Imperial Rescript accepting the Potsdam terms. It might be added that the word "surrender" was nowhere used in the rescript.

Two aspects of the decision to surrender were politically significant. As to public opinion, it is clear the will to resist collapsed first among political leaders before it crumbled among the people as a whole. One corollary was that the people felt, and feel today, little responsibility for the war or for their own defeat. They felt, and feel, resentment toward former militarist leaders. Some even said the last blows of the war were modern *kamikaze,* divine winds which blew in, saved Japan, and kept for Japan their *Tennō* system.

Once again, in a crisis in Japan's history, the Emperor played a central role. That the *Tennō* as person and institution would carry over and remain as asset or liability was equally apparent. For the moment Japan had escaped the horrors of the Big War. Whether she would also escape the tentacles of external and internal conflict now depended upon the Allies.

[33] USSBS, *Interrogations,* cited, Vol. II (13-14 November 1945, Nav 75), p. 233. It was not until December, four months later, that this scene was described for the Japanese people in the magazine *Yoron* (Public Opinion); see the *Nippon Times,* December 14, 1945, p. 1.

CHAPTER
TWENTY

The Scaffolding of Democracy (Occupation Government and Politics, I)

PERHAPS the strangest feature of the momentous occupation of the Japanese Empire by United States military and civil authority, cloaked though it was by the formality of international participation, was the fact that the American people as a whole never seemed to realize how revolutionary an act they and their government were committing. By accepting the occupation of Japan as a responsibility, by rejoicing in it as a consequence of victory, the Americans implicitly accepted the novel and disturbing assumption that a completely foreign culture could be modified in short order by the installation of democratic authority.

Generations subsequent to ours will speak with the voice of history. They, as men of the future, will be able to look back upon the consequences of the enterprise as well as upon the enterprise itself. They will be, as we are not, able to judge the consequences of this strange and hazardous political enterprise: the subjugation and occupation of one of the empires of the old world by a republic of the new.

The Occupation can be taken in a sense as the first forcible export, since Benedict Arnold's ill-starred campaign against Quebec in 1778, of the principles of American freedom. The American people, section for section, group for group, of all economic levels, saw nothing strange in our compelling Japan to become democratic. Generations of Americans have lived and died smugly superior to their old world neighbors, positive in their views that democracy of the American variety was a special and quite peculiar product of a new land, a new population, a new nation. The democratization which America had undertaken before the occupation of Japan were all of them casual by-products of strategic or naval necessity, the accidents of power politics. Even Wilson could not accept the mandate for Armenia. The proposal, had it been made at the Paris conference, that the Allies and the United States join in the forcible reconstruction of German society and redirection of the German spirit would have been denounced from Maine to California, from North Dakota to Texas. Twenty-five years later the American people as a whole and particularly the officers and officials among them had changed many of their basic assumptions about human society.

Whether they knew it or not, or even wished to know it or not, the Americans had accepted the basic practical lessons taught by the Bolshevik revolution in Russia and the National Socialist revolution in Germany—in at least one fundamental respect. Americans had come to believe in the reality of ideological politics.

Even if the Americans of 1945 did not say so forthrightly, the actions of their government occupying Japan can be argued to have demonstrated certain implicit assumptions: that there was justification for the initial use of forceful sanctions, both to punish and to teach; that, thereafter, dispositions of peoples could be modified by governmental action of a less forceful nature; and that, eventually, the freedom of the human spirit could be encouraged from the outside, through democratization. No American said, as his father might have said in 1918, "We've licked them. Now let's leave them alone, and go back to minding our own business."

Few political events have been ushered in with such a concurrent wave of shock and deep disquiet. The atomic bombs had fallen on Hiroshima and Nagasaki. The American community, already somewhat confused by a lack of long-range buoyancy or morale as to its own economic affairs, further disturbed by the decade-long nightmare of potential air war, was thrilled with guilt, triumph, and foreboding at the fearfulness of the weapons which the American government had completed with such consummate and amazing skill. The surrender of Japan occurred in the midst of an American psychological revolution, a very quiet revolution, but a revolution nonetheless, in that 1945 represented a redirection and revaluation of many things which most Americans then living had felt to be fundamental.

The Surrender Itself. What American today can name the greatest naval force ever assembled by mankind? It was our own, of course: the sea armada which on August 28, 1945, closed in upon the coast of Honshu. At Atsugi airfield on August 30, immense skytrains of C-54's flew in from Okinawa landing at four-minute intervals. While ten thousand sailors and marines landed at Yokosuka, an umbrella of fighters and dive bombers overhead guarded against acts of treachery. Shortly before noon, General of the Army Douglas MacArthur completed his long trip northward across the western littoral of the Pacific. He had started north from Melbourne, Australia, in 1942.

On a Yokohama factory roof some anonymous Japanese put up a sign which met with the ritual of Japanese etiquette. It read: "3 CHEERS FOR THE U. S. NAVY AND ARMY." The whole Japanese empire could assemble nothing more than a dilapidated convoy of hastily assembled passenger automobiles to meet the Americans at the end of the bad dirt roads which led to Atsugi airfield. Atsugi had been selected because it was one of the few airfields left operational. The Mayor of Yokohama blandly toasted President Harry S. Truman among the shattered and burned-over ruins of his city. For two days Americans and Japanese completed urgent and immediate plans for the arrival of Lieutenant General Robert L. Eichelberger and his Eighth Army—an Eighth Army which, unknown to Americans then, had further destinies awaiting it in Korea—and for the formalities of the surrender on board the USS *Missouri*.

Early in the morning of September 2 Allied plenipotentiaries began arriving on board the battleship which was by then anchored in Tokyo Bay. The Japanese delegation arrived at 8:55 A.M.; they drew themselves up at strict attention on the main deck.

They waited exactly four minutes.

General MacArthur came forth and started the ceremonies with a short humane address which impressed the Japanese as being touchingly merciful as well as magniloquent. The Japanese then signed. After them General MacArthur, the American representatives, then the Chinese, the British, the Russians, the Australians, the Canadians, the French, the Dutch, and the New Zealanders also signed in rapid succession. General MacArthur made another short speech and announced that the proceedings were finished.

A new age had opened for Japan.

The instruments of surrender contained eight basic provisions. The Japanese agreed:

> to accept all the provisions of the Potsdam Proclamation;
> to surrender unconditionally all forces;
> to cease hostilities and preserve all armed equipment;
> to command the Imperial Japanese General Headquarters to issue orders to field commanders to surrender unconditionally;
> to see that all civil and military officials obey and enforce the orders of the Supreme Commander;
> to carry out in good faith the Potsdam Proclamation so that freer institutions might be established leading to the restoration of sovereignty;
> to liberate all prisoners and see that they arrive safely at points of debarkation; and
> to acknowledge that the authority of the Emperor and the Japanese government was subject to the will of the Supreme Commander.

On the same day, September 2, the Shōwa Emperor, Hirohito, proclaimed the surrender by issuing an Imperial Rescript; the Japanese Central Government issued Japanese General Order No. 1, the first of a series of orders to the Japanese people from their government enforcing compliance with the surrender terms.[1]

Ceremonial completion of the surrender was rounded out on September 3 by the raising of the actual American flag which had happened to be flying over the Capitol in Washington on December 7, 1941, and which had subsequently been raised over Casablanca, over Rome, and over Berlin. The Japanese flag was nowhere to be seen. The Rising Sun emblem was prohibited. The surrender was complete.

Nature of the Occupation. Quite apart from the largely unrecognized deological character of the American occupation of Japan, the administrative and juridical aspects of the Occupation differed very sharply from the Occupation procedures and structures imposed on the other Axis powers.

Japan was not divided into zones as was Germany.

Japan was not placed under the direct military government of foreign forces, as was Italy.

Japan did not collapse into political anonymity and chaos, as did so much of Europe.

Finally, Japan won serious political victories in the weeks of surrender as did none of the other enemies of the United States. By supporting the independence movements of Indonesia, Indochina, and Korea, the Japanese left behind political successes which contrasted very sharply with the survival of Franco, and only Franco, from the whole family of Axis states in Europe. Most of all, the Japanese welcomed the permission of the victors to keep the Japanese Throne.[2] Surrender was unconditional in name only, since the Japanese had left themselves in something of a bargaining position.

Furthermore, the Japanese traditions of social and individual conflict stood them in good stead when it came to meeting the unprecedented requirements

[1] Texts of the Cairo Declaration (27 November 1943), announcing unconditional surrender *(mujōken kōfuku);* the exchange of notes leading to surrender—Japan's first offer (10 August 1945), the "Byrnes Note" (11 August 1945), Truman's statement on Japanese acceptance (14 August 1945), and surrender orders (15 August 1945)—the Instrument of Surrender (2 September 1945); and Directive No. 1 (including General Order No. 1, 2 September 1945) are all to be found conveniently (in Japanese) in Yokota Kisaburō, Editor, *Nihon kanri hōrei kenkyū* (Research in Japanese administrative directives), Tōkyō, Tōkyō Daigaku Hōgakubunai, Nihon Kanri Hōrei Kenkyū-kai (Tokyo University Law Department, Society for Research in Japanese Administrative Directives), Vol. I, No. 1 (April 1, 1946), pp. 1-26; and (in English) in Department of State, *Occupation of Japan; Policy and Progress* (Publication 2671, Far Eastern Series 17), Washington, 1946, Appendices 4-10; pp. 56-67 (hereafter the former will be cited *NKHK;* the latter, Dept. *Occupation*). President Truman's Statement (14 August 1945) was the only official announcement of the original appointment of U.S. General of the Army Douglas MacArthur as Supreme Commander for the Allied Powers (SCAP; in Japanese, Dagurasu Makkasa, *Rengōkoku Saikō Shireikan*). Appendix 15 gives a translated text of the Imperial Rescript Announcing Surrender to the Japanese People.

[2] The Japanese were quick to profit by the concession. Prince Higashi-kuni, who had formed the surrender cabinet (August 17-October 9, 1945), addressed the 88th Session of the Diet a few days after surrender: "The termination of the war has been brought about solely through the benevolence of our Sovereign. It was His Majesty himself, who, apologizing to the spirits of the Ancestors, decided to save the millions of His subjects from privation and misery, and to pave the way for an era of grand peace for generations to come. Never before have we been moved so profoundly as by this act of boundless benevolence." *Nippon Times,* September 6, 1945, p. 1, column 1.

of Occupation. It is part of the Japanese tradition to be wryly and controlledly realistic, even in the face of disaster—perhaps, it might be said, especially in the face of disaster. Once the Japanese surrendered, many of their more intelligent and sensitive leaders fell into a condition of apprehensiveness, gloom, or depression, but many of them accepted the Occupation not as the end of a world, but as the challenge of an even more difficult and even more interesting world than before. Never, it can be said, has an occupied nation met the process of occupation with so much curiosity and so much readiness to make the best of the actual state of affairs.

On the American side, the Occupation was singularly qualified by the unquestionable primacy of the United States among the victors. The only other power which had contributed substantially to the downfall of Japan in material terms was China, and the Chinese were in no position to do anything about Japan; quite the contrary, the Chinese Nationalists desperately needed the cooperation of the Japanese troops left in their country for the policing of railroad lines against Communists. Although the U.S.S.R. had made an important psychological contribution by attacking Japan in the last days and hours of the war, the Russians were in no position to extort from the Americans any concessions beyond the weighty territorial and strategic rewards already offered at Yalta. Although the British commonwealth nations had contributed very richly indeed to the war at the outer periphery of the Greater East Asia Co-Prosperity Sphere, their share in the final attacks upon metropolitan Japan was so negligible as to leave the United States under very little obligation toward them.

From one viewpoint, therefore, the Occupation can be seen as a series of minor compromises between the United States and the Allied Powers, who from beginning to end demanded, but rarely obtained, a greater measure of participation in the ruling of Japan. The final ignominious termination of this minor-partner role on the part of the other Allied powers was reached in May, 1952, when the Japanese government, shortly after the final ratification of the treaty of peace, coolly informed the Soviet Military Occupation group that the Japanese proposed to pay no attention to the Russian representatives and that if Russia had anything to say to Japan the Russians would be advised to communicate it through Stockholm.

From another viewpoint the re-emergence of Japan under Occupation encouragement was surprisingly shaped by the surrender. The Germans had made a desperate attempt to keep some kind of a juridical Germany intact by the tragi-comic horse opera of Flensburg, in which uniformed Nazis raced about a small town in forty Mercedes-Benz automobiles and quarreled with one another down to the last hours before they were arrested or committed suicide. The Japanese government remained an organized government; it did not move from Tokyo. The symbol of continuity was the institution of the Emperor. The Occupation of Japan subtly retained its Japanese stamp. From 1945 to 1952 Japan was governed through a *Japanese government.*

SCAP As News. These two factors, the continued Japanese government and the dominant position of America in the Occupation, are the points of departure in any attempt to understand the postwar politics of Japan.

Beyond them lie differing viewpoints and controversy. To the correspondent who had to turn out copy every day, the Occupation soon took on a different aspect. A steady flow of encouraging reports from Japan hardly warranted top-news rating. In the first stage the United States took the primary initiative, through the Supreme Commander for the Allied Powers (SCAP), in successfully carrying out the objective of demobilization. In this short-run objective, the Occupation was an unqualified and monotonous success. From time to time thereafter, there were truly big stories—the purges, the elections, the new Constitution, the Korean conflict, the removal of MacArthur himself—to write home about. In between, the correspondent tended to turn to personalities for his news.

The men of SCAP were certainly unique. They were a product of early operations in a theater with second priority. General MacArthur, once the youngest chief of staff (1930-1935) of the United States, ranked "with but after" General Marshall himself. Isolated, self-reliant, closely knit, SCAP Headquarters was—like the Tokugawa *Bakufu*—an outgrowth of a military command which brooked little interference. The legend of the MacArthur Command became well known through various kind and unkind interpretations by army men who fought under its order, by navy and marine corps personnel who cooperated with it in preparation for the final assault, and by inter-Allied officials who were attached to it during the Occupation. In these terms, the Occupation has been a human story of General MacArthur himself, who was Supreme Commander; of Generals Richard K. Sutherland, who was MacArthur's brilliant Chief of Staff, Charles A. Willoughby, his G2, and Courtney Whitney, Chief of Government Section, aide, and spokesman. It was also the doings, to a lesser extent, of volatile George Atcheson, United States political adviser to SCAP until his death in an airplane crash, August 17, 1947; of caustic Lieutenant General Kuzma Derevyanko, Soviet representative in Tokyo; of quiet Lieutenant General Chu Shih-ming, Chinese (Nationalist) delegate; and of critical W. MacMahon Ball, British Commonwealth spokesman. General MacArthur, of course, overshadowed them all.

To the technically trained military government expert, the pattern of the Occupation had a debatable significance from the beginning. When General MacArthur's staff (then in the Philippines) was faced with the fresh emergency of surrender, an important decision was made and aired frankly by General Sutherland. Orthodox military government plans and personnel, hastily assembled by Brigadier General W. E. Crist,[3] Chief of Military

[3] General Crist remained as first Chief, Government Section, GHQ, SCAP, from October 2 to December 13, 1945, when he returned to the United States. His place was taken by General Whitney.

Government Section, were to be dissolved. Extensive military government organization, modeled after the German and Italian experiences, would not evolve in Japan.

The Machinery of SCAP. The machinery would be more simple: it would consist of General MacArthur's own GHQ, supervising the Japanese government, which in turn would be responsible for its own housecleaning. The savings in resources and men have since been apparent. Nevertheless, discarded military government experts were quick to point out a fundamental issue involved, namely, efficiency (of military government) versus political reliability (of the Japanese government). When MacArthur publicly contemplated a reduction of Occupation force to 200,000 within six months, some observers concluded that military government would be conducted on the basis of expediency. Others warned that objectives outlined in the Potsdam Proclamation were in danger of abandonment. The then Acting Secretary of State, Dean Acheson, in a press interview which was prophetic in light of later events, issued a statement that "Occupation forces are the instruments of policy and not the determinants of policy." [4]

Temporarily, however, the Supreme Commander was the sole executive authority in Japan. And the Supreme Commander was General MacArthur. To understand how he actually became the determinant, rather than the instrument, of policy entails a description of the Occupation and Allied control machinery.

General MacArthur wore, as the saying goes, several hats. As Supreme Commander for the Allied Powers (SCAP; in Japanese *Rengōkoku Saikō Shireikan*) he exercised Allied sovereignty (*Rengōkoku no Kenryoku*) in Japan. As such, however, he at first received his authority in a policy decision prepared by the State, War, and Navy Departments, approved by the President of the United States on September 6, 1945, and transmitted through the Joint Chiefs of Staff.

For purposes of his administration and in order to separate outlying areas from Japanese authority, Japan was defined to include the four main islands (Hokkaido, Honshu, Kyushu, Shikoku); approximately one thousand adjacent islands, including the Tsushima group; and the Ryukyu (Nansei) Islands north of 30° N latitude. Until August 15, 1948, the United States had responsibility for the military government of Korea, south of 38° N latitude. The Deputy Chief of Staff, SCAP, acted as military government liaison between Tokyo and Seoul; after July, 1947, however, directives per-

[4] Department of State *Bulletin,* September 23, 1945, p. 427. On May 30, 1946, SCAP released statistics to show that the Occupation was being accomplished with a lower ratio of troops to population (190,000 men, controlling 75 million, or one fourth of one per cent) than the occupation of any other area (Austria, Soviet Zone, was highest: 6.6 per cent). For an early, critical view, see Merle Fainsod, "Military Government and the Occupation of Japan," *Japan's Prospect,* Douglas G. Haring, Editor, Cambridge, 1946, pp. 287-304. This volume, although published early in the Occupation, is of particular interest since it is a series of essays by the Faculty, School for Overseas Administration, Harvard University.

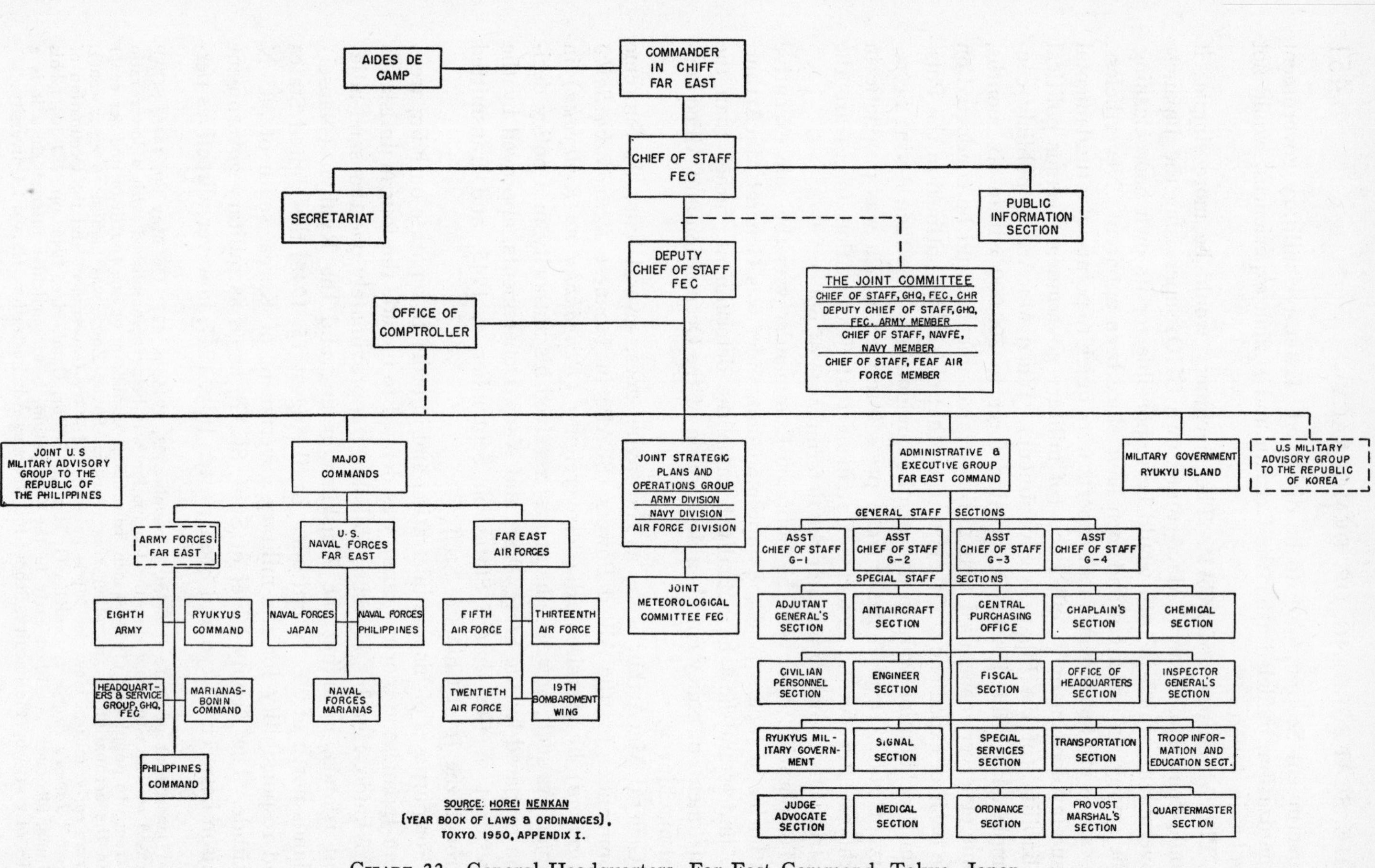

CHART 22—General Headquarters, Far East Command, Tokyo, Japan

taining to civil affairs in South Korea flowed direct from the Joint Chiefs to Generals Hodge and Dean in Korea. After July, 1946, the rest of the Ryukyus (including Okinawa) passed from U.S. Navy to U.S. Army administration but remained separate from that of Japan, since military government there had been established before the surrender.[5]

General MacArthur was also Commander in Chief, Far East (CINCFE), with command over all U.S. Army, Navy, and Air forces in the war-born Far East theater, as well as Commanding General, U.S. Army, Far East (see Chart 22). After July 8, 1950, as commander of forces in Korea, he was the first American general to fly the blue-and-white United Nations flag.[6] Although his international and national commands were distinct, in actual operations they tended to merge into GHQ, SCAP, the military command made up of many of the military officers who fought their way out of Bataan and from Brisbane to Japan.

To advise General MacArthur on nonmilitary activities, eight special Staff Sections were activated on October 2, 1945, and added to the normal General Staff Sections (G1, G2, G3, G4) in GHQ, SCAP. By August, 1947, these had been increased to fourteen; in November, 1949, the following were still active:

Government Section (Brig. Gen. C. Whitney)
Public Health and Welfare Section (Brig. Gen. C. F. Sams)
Office of Civil Property Custodian (Brig. Gen. J. F. Conklin)
Economic and Scientific Section (Maj. Gen. W. F. Marquat)
Natural Resources Section (Lt. Col. H. G. Schenck)
Civil Transportation Section (Col. H. T. Miller)
Statistics and Reports Section (Col. W. L. Mitchell)
Adjutant General's Section (Brig. Gen. K. B. Bush)
Civil Information and Education Section (Lt. Col. D. R. Nugent)
Civil Intelligence Section (Maj. Gen. C. A. Willoughby)
Legal Section (Mr. A. C. Carpenter)
Civil Communications Section (Brig. Gen. G. I. Back)
Office of General Procurement Agent (Col. D. T. Nelson)

[5] For the message designating General MacArthur's authority as Supreme Commander (SWNCC 21/6 (JCS 1467)) see Dept., *Occupation*, Appendix 16, pp. 88-89; and in Japanese, *NKHK*, Vol. I, No. 3 (June 15, 1946), pp. 1-2; Occupied Japan was originally defined in JCS 1380/15, "Basic Directive for Post-Surrender Military Government in Japan Proper," 3 November 1945, SCAP, *Political Reorientation*, Vol. II, Appendix A:13, pp. 428-439; General MacArthur's Directive (SCAPIN 677), "Governmental and Administrative Separation of Certain Outlying Areas from Japan," 29 January 1946 (in English and Japanese), *NKHK*, Vol. I, No. 8 (December 1, 1946), pp. 21-24; for Korea and the southern Ryukyus, Staff Memorandum No. 22 (SCAP and FEC), "Military Government in Korea and the Ryukyu Islands," 13 February 1946, SCAP, *ibid.*, Vol. II, Appendix G:8a(4), p. 799.

[6] One significant point is that MacArthur never had a deputy, either to SCAP or CINCFE. His chain of command always included a chief of staff. The Eighth Army, within Japan, had a field commander—General Eichelberger, and after August 4, 1948, Lieutenant General Walton H. Walker—and, in Korea, General Walker and, after his accidental death, Lieutenant General James H. Van Fleet. The whole world knew, of course, that General Ridgway succeeded to the commands in Tokyo after President Truman removed General MacArthur, April 11, 1951. Until then, however, there was never a *No. 2 Man* in the MacArthur organization.

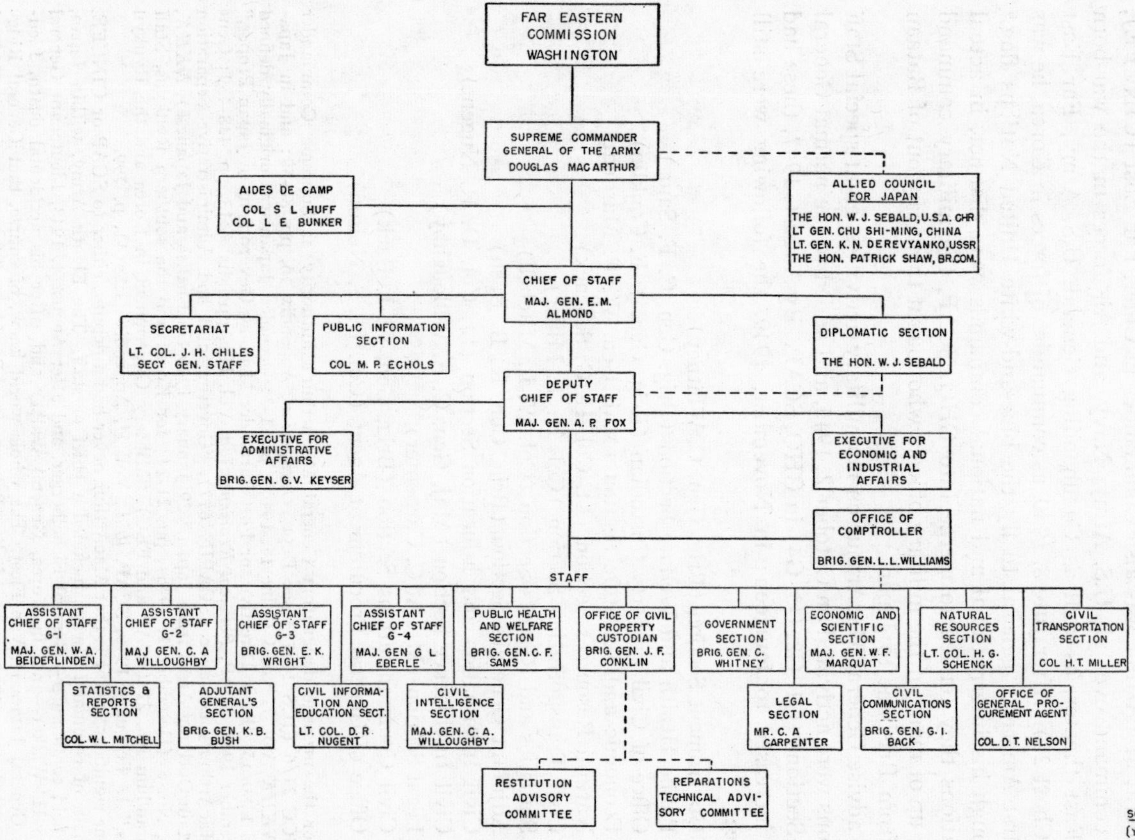

FAR EASTERN COMMISSION WASHINGTON

SUPREME COMMANDER GENERAL OF THE ARMY DOUGLAS MAC ARTHUR

ALLIED COUNCIL FOR JAPAN
THE HON. W. J. SEBALD, U.S.A. CHR
LT GEN. CHU SHI-MING, CHINA
LT. GEN. K. N. DEREVYANKO, USSR
THE HON. PATRICK SHAW, BR.COM.

AIDES DE CAMP
COL S L HUFF
COL L E BUNKER

CHIEF OF STAFF
MAJ. GEN. E. M. ALMOND

SECRETARIAT
LT. COL. J. H. CHILES
SECY GEN. STAFF

PUBLIC INFORMATION SECTION
COL M. P. ECHOLS

DIPLOMATIC SECTION
THE HON. W. J. SEBALD

DEPUTY CHIEF OF STAFF
MAJ. GEN. A. P. FOX

EXECUTIVE FOR ADMINISTRATIVE AFFAIRS
BRIG. GEN. G. V. KEYSER

EXECUTIVE FOR ECONOMIC AND INDUSTRIAL AFFAIRS

OFFICE OF COMPTROLLER
BRIG. GEN. L. L. WILLIAMS

STAFF

ASSISTANT CHIEF OF STAFF G-1
MAJ. GEN. W. A. BEIDERLINDEN

ASSISTANT CHIEF OF STAFF G-2
MAJ GEN. C. A WILLOUGHBY

ASSISTANT CHIEF OF STAFF G-3
BRIG. GEN. E. K. WRIGHT

ASSISTANT CHIEF OF STAFF G-4
MAJ. GEN G L EBERLE

PUBLIC HEALTH AND WELFARE SECTION
BRIG. GEN. C. F. SAMS

OFFICE OF CIVIL PROPERTY CUSTODIAN
BRIG. GEN. J. F. CONKLIN

GOVERNMENT SECTION
BRIG. GEN. C. WHITNEY

ECONOMIC AND SCIENTIFIC SECTION
MAJ. GEN. W. F. MARQUAT

NATURAL RESOURCES SECTION
LT. COL. H. G. SCHENCK

CIVIL TRANSPORTATION SECTION
COL H. T. MILLER

STATISTICS & REPORTS SECTION
COL. W. L. MITCHELL

ADJUTANT GENERAL'S SECTION
BRIG. GEN. K. B. BUSH

CIVIL INFORMATION AND EDUCATION SECT.
LT. COL. D. R. NUGENT

CIVIL INTELLIGENCE SECTION
MAJ. GEN. C. A. WILLOUGHBY

LEGAL SECTION
MR. C. A CARPENTER

CIVIL COMMUNICATIONS SECTION
BRIG. GEN. G. I. BACK

OFFICE OF GENERAL PROCUREMENT AGENT
COL. D. T. NELSON

RESTITUTION ADVISORY COMMITTEE

REPARATIONS TECHNICAL ADVISORY COMMITTEE

SOURCE: HOREI NENKAN (YEAR BOOK OF LAWS & ORDINANCES), TOKYO; 1950, APPENDIX I

CHART 23—General Headquarters, Supreme Commander for the Allied Powers, Tokyo, Japan

In addition to these special sections, there were, at the Chief-of-Staff level, a Diplomatic Section (The Hon. W. J. Sebald succeeded to the post of Ambassador Atcheson); and a Public Information Section (Col. M. P. Echols). Chart 23 shows the organization. By May, 1949, the predominantly military character of the administration was extended into the lower levels of SCAP personnel. By the end of the year, officials in Tokyo estimated that at least 40 per cent of the civilians on the Occupation staff would be replaced by army officers relieved of European duties.[7]

Government Section. Of greatest interest to us, in terms of the government and politics of Occupied Japan, is the Government Section (known to the Japanese as *Minsei-kyoku,* literally, "Democracy Section"). Its key position in the political reorientation of Japan is revealed by its primary mission which was

> to advise the Supreme Commander on the status of and policies pertaining to . . . the internal structure of civil government in Japan. Specifically, it was the function of the Section to make recommendations for: the demilitarization of the Japanese Government; the decentralization of government and the encouragement of local responsibility; the elimination therefrom of feudal and totalitarian practices which tended to prevent government by the people, and the elimination of those relationships between government and business which tended to continue the Japanese war potential and to hamper the achievement of Occupation objectives.

General Whitney, who became Chief of the Government Section on December 15, 1945, was convinced "that the highly fluid situation presented by post-surrender Japan would constantly demand the expeditious formulation of solutions to pressing political and governmental problems"; he therefore abolished an earlier planning group which he believed was separated from day-to-day issues. Even Government Section, then, apparently conducted "operations" as would a military staff section.

Such a characterization alone, however, would be unfair. Actually, although Government Section began as a section staffed with military personnel, a process of "civilianization" set in and brought to Tokyo skilled experts in government and politics. Special advisers—including Professors H. S. Quigley (University of Minnesota), K. C. Colegrove (Northwestern University), C. H. Peake (Columbia University)—who remained a long time—and

[7] As a result of transfer of authority in the U.S. Zone of Germany from the Army to the State Department. See Ardath W. Burks, "Occupied Japan," *American Year Book, 1949,* New York, 1950, p. 87. A Reparations Section was activated May 8, 1947, but was dissolved later in favor of Reparations Technical Advisory and Restitution Advisory Committees (under the Civil Property Custodian) in 1949. The International Prosecution Section was attached to the Chief of Staff until completion of the work of the International Military Tribunal, Far East. Formation of the original eight special sections was first announced in the *Nippon Times,* October 13, 1945. For the organization of SCAP in 1947, see Supreme Commander for the Allied Powers (SCAP), *Summation of Non-Military Activities in Japan,* No. 23 (August 1947), Appendix, Sec. 1, p. 313.

John M. Maki (University of Washington), to mention only a few—were occasionally brought in for consultantships. The amazing feature of the Section was its compactness: in January, 1948, at its peak strength, total personnel numbered only 120, of whom 68 were professionals; by mid-1948 this total had been reduced fifty per cent. In the hands of these few men lay responsibility for the political weaning of 75 million Japanese citizens.

Two specific projects handled by Government Section illustrated its characteristic flexibility. When, in early 1946, "it became evident that the Japanese government needed guidance and assistance" in producing a democratic constitution, Government Section took the primary responsibility for the task. The entire section became a Committee of the Whole, broken down into functional subcommittees on the Executive, the Legislature, the Judiciary, Finance, the Preamble, and Bill of Rights. So far, at least, no James Madison in Tokyo has been forthcoming to describe the inner workings of the Founding Fathers in Japan. Again, in Japan's first democratic elections of 1946-1947 virtually the entire Section, regardless of normal assignment, was formed into teams to go into the field to observe the balloting.[8]

Military Government. The newsworthy personalities at GHQ, SCAP in Tokyo and the use of the Japanese government to administer Occupation policy tended to eclipse more mundane activities at the local level. Nevertheless, military government at the prefectural level—or the lack of it—has been extremely significant in the Occupation. Although accounts of the Occupation have neglected this phase, their analyses based solely on SCAP activities are obviously inadequate. As the less accessible areas of Japan come under independent examination, there the lasting effect of the Occupation will doubtless be revealed.

The *power* behind the Occupation was, like SCAP itself, predominantly American. Occupation forces were grouped by function into three categories: tactical troops, having no official contact with Japanese; counterintelligence units, made up largely of Nisei; and military government personnel. The first group included the Sixth Army in southern Japan, until its withdrawal shortly after the beginning of the Occupation; and the Eighth Army in central and northern Japan. When the Eighth Army took over, it remained directly responsible for 11 prefectures in the Shikoku, Chūgoku, and Tokyo-Yokohama areas. Its I Corps in Kyoto held 20 prefectures in southern Japan; its IX Corps, at Sendai, 15 prefectures in northern Japan. Until 1948, about five thousand British Commonwealth Occupation Forces

[8] SCAP, *Political Reorientation of Japan,* two large volumes of 1,300 pages, cited above on numerous occasions, is, of course, in the narrower sense the official diary of Government Section. See particularly Appendix G, "History of the Government Section, GHQ, SCAP," and attached documents (specifically of interest: General Orders No. 8, 2 October 1945, General Orders No. 1, 13 February 1947, and General Orders No. 10, 13 June 1947—for mission; Document G:8b(1), organization chart early in the history of the Section; Document G:8b(4), organization, 4 December 1947; and Document G:8d, Directory of All Personnel, October 2, 1945-September 2, 1948). It should be noted here that no official histories of SCAP or its Sections, such as were produced to describe many wartime commands, have been written independent of SCAP itself.

(BCOF) were based in southern Honshu and Shikoku. By the end of 1948, they were reduced to one regiment and a small air force. Since no other power provided even a single regiment, the Occupation in force was almost entirely an American project.[9]

Since the responsibility for actual occupation of Japan was delegated, eventually to the Eighth Army alone, military government teams were technically nonexistent so far as SCAP was concerned. The Eighth Army and each corps had a military government section. Military government, then, was simply one staff activity at the tactical level. Between the corps and each prefectural team were military government regions, not linked with any tactical command; indeed, the eight regions were modeled on the abolished Japanese superintendencies-general! Prefectures were designated minor, intermediate, or major and each had its military government team. Osaka-*fu* was placed in a special category, as was the Tokyo-Kanagawa Military Government District. Under modifications of July 1, 1947, which allotted civil service personnel to field units, the military government teams consisted of 398 officers, 1,436 enlisted men, and 605 civilians (total, 2,439).[10]

With the skeleton of the Occupation in mind, we are now in a position to trace an instruction through the hierarchy and tentatively to characterize further the nature of the control. After research in special staff sections, GHQ transmitted to the Japanese government a SCAP directive, commonly called SCAPIN (officially, "Memorandum for the Imperial Japanese Government"). Copies of the directive went to the four lower echelons of military government through regular military channels. (Often the directive first reached lower Japanese administrative officers from whom teams would get their information!) The Eighth Army would add an "operational" or ancillary directive. Its administrative discretion was wide, but was procedural rather than substantive. Corps and Regional Headquarters simply transmitted, and delayed, directives. From a Japanese point of view, the path of such directives appeared [11] as shown in Chart 24.

At the American military government team level, administrative actions were discretionary but limited. Military government personnel could *watch.*

[9] Plans for the BCOF, under Lieutenant General Northcutt of Australia, were announced in Japan in the *Nippon Times,* February 2, 1946. A summary of the agreement between the U.S. and Australia, acting in behalf of the Commonwealth, may be found (in Japanese) in *NKHK,* Vol. I, No. 8 (December 1, 1946), pp. 25-30; and (in English) in Dept. *Occupation,* Appendix 17, pp. 89-94.

[10] A searchingly professional—and critical—description of local military government administration was made by Ralph J. D. Braibanti, "Administration of Military Government in Japan at the Prefectural Level," *American Political Science Review,* Vol. XLIII, No. 2 (April 1949), pp. 250-274. The key policy, wrote Professor Braibanti, was the exercise of SCAP authority through the Japanese Government. Technically, this process he called "administrative superintendence" or, at the local level, surveillance. For a highly interesting reportorial account—equally critical—see Mark Gayn, *Japan Diary,* New York, 1948. Mr. Gayn, an experienced correspondent for several publications, became *persona non grata* with SCAP because of his penchant for exploring the back areas remote from the Dai Ichi Building, Tokyo, seat of GHQ, SCAP.

[11] Yuhikaku, *Hōrei nempō,* cited, Appendix 1. The Ministry Liaison Bureau replaced the earlier Central Liaison Office.

Technically, they were not permitted to correct. They could *report* noncompliance, but a frustrating delay ensued while such reports climbed the American military ladder, crossed over to the Japanese government, and slowly descended the rickety ladder of Japanese administration. Hence, as

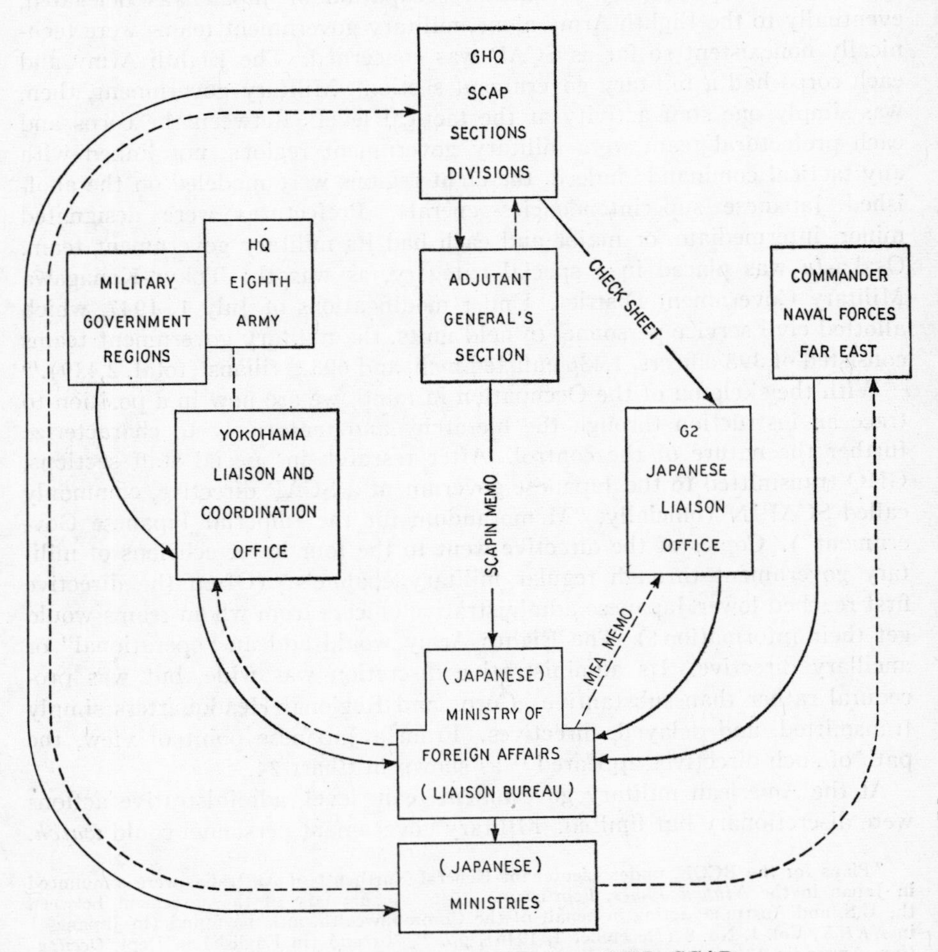

CHART 24—Flow of Directives from GHQ, SCAP

Professor Braibanti observed, local military government officers tended more and more to act first in a personal capacity. There were several by-products. Compliance to local orders, of course, was prompt. But regular failures to report noncompliance tended to give a rosy hue to SCAP summations of achievements of the Occupation, drawn up in Tokyo. Local enforcement techniques varied widely. And local Japanese administrators, rather than being weaned, were spoon-fed. They came to depend upon—there is even evidence they used—local military government teams. Again, local teams could *interpret* directives or *advise* on their implementation, but this action was explicitly proscribed by SCAP. Finally, military government teams could prosecute offenses committed by Japanese nationals, mainly against Occupation forces.

Limited in scope but willing as it was, military government at the local level was virtually wiped out by General MacArthur's Headquarters on July 28, 1949. An order disbanded Military Government Section of the Eighth Army, as well as subordinate sections of I Corps, IX Corps, and the prefectural teams.[12]

It is apparent that the Occupation, even viewed simply from within Japan itself, was not susceptible to easy definition. Beyond the predominance of Americans and the continuity of Japanese government, two other aspects may be mentioned and then one question asked. General MacArthur's authority as Supreme Commander and the Allied position was outlined in the Joint Chiefs' directive of September 6, 1945:

> Our relations with Japan do not rest on a contractual basis, but on unconditional surrender.[13]

The same directive, however, ordered General MacArthur to exercise control *through* the Japanese government, to the extent that such an arrangement produced satisfactory results. In one sense, then, GHQ, SCAP, was a *military government* and not a military occupation implementing an agency charged with *civil affairs.* In another sense, it was a cross between a military government and utilization of the Japanese government at national and local levels.

The administrative mixture had a reciprocal effect on the philosophy of the Occupation. General Whitney, in an explanation which was later to prove as intriguing as Acting Secretary of State Acheson's (mentioned previously), maintained that SCAP's policies bore witness to MacArthur's "devotion to the integrity of the civil process of government," even in Japan! In the beginning, SCAP issued a series of formal directives designed to establish the broad outlines of political reformation. Thereafter, the Supreme Commander "shifted the emphasis from the direction to leadership." SCAP personnel liked to call the process *induced revolution.* Expert public administrators would more accurately label it *administrative superintendence.*[14]

[12] Katayama Tetsu, first Premier under the new Constitution and later chairman of the Social Democratic Party, was visiting in the United States at the time. He told the author of this section that he interpreted the order to mean that the political reorientation of Japan was completed. Ardath W. Burks, "Occupied Japan," *American Year Book, 1949,* cited, p. 87.

[13] In Japanese: *"Ware-ware to Nihon to no kankei wa keiyakuteki kiso ni motozukazushite, mujōken kōfuku ni motozuku."*

[14] For the directive, JCS 1467, Dept., *Occupation,* Appendix 16, pp. 88-89; the Japanese text is from *NKHK,* Vol. I, No. 3 (June 15, 1946), pp. 1-2; General Whitney set forth "The Philosophy of the Occupation," in the Foreword, SCAP, *Political Reorientation,* cited, Vol. I, pp. xvii-xxii. The Japanese were presented with a text of General MacArthur's instructions to his commands, December 20, 1945: "Basic Aims of the Japanese Occupation," *NKHK,* Vol. I, No. 8 (December 1, 1946), pp. 1-4.

To answer the remaining question about the Occupation, we must go outside Japan. To whom was General MacArthur subject? Directives *to* SCAP were at first prepared and transmitted by the United States government. On the basis of recommendations submitted to its Far Eastern subcommitee, the State-War-Navy Coordinating Committee (SWNCC; after 1947, State-Army-Navy-Air Coordinating Committee, SANACC) formulated policy on questions of basic importance for the President's approval. The Joint Chiefs submitted their views on military issues. Directives carrying the approved policies were then drawn up, transmitted through the Joint Chiefs, the Department of the Army acting as executive agency, to General MacArthur. Ultimate implementation, of course, was in the hands of SCAP in Tokyo. The United States was thus playing a solitary role.

Internationally, however, the controlling position of the United States in Japan was a precarious one and soon became, along with other issues, an element of bargaining in world politics. In a move obviously designed to reduce Allied demands and to assume credit for taking the initiative, the United States had already, on August 21, 1945, officially invited Allied participation in the control of Japan.[15]

International Control Machinery. Almost before the ink was dry on the instrument of surrender, there were indications that the control of Japan could not long remain an exclusively American affair. Russia demanded a control commission in Tokyo; Australia began to criticize the mildness of American Occupation policy; the British, under Dominion pressure, devised a plan for an Allied commission in Tokyo. After an unscheduled debate at the London meeting of the Council of Foreign Ministers, Secretary of State James Byrnes released a communiqué which ignored Russian pressure and stated that the United Kingdom had consented to the American proposal to establish a Far Eastern commission.

Subsequently Russia, Great Britain, China, France, Australia, Canada, New Zealand, the Netherlands, the Philippines, and India were invited to a meeting in Washington on October 30, 1945. The Far Eastern Advisory Commission (FEAC: *Kyokutō Shimon Iinkai*) met regularly over the next two months, but without the U.S.S.R., which protested the advisory character of the FEAC. The problem of Russian participation was finally solved at the Council of Foreign Ministers meeting in Moscow, December, 1945. With the concurrence of China, the Ministers provided for establishment of a Far Eastern Commission (FEC: *Kyokutō Iinkai*) and an Allied Council for Japan (ACJ: *Rengoku Nihon Rijikai*).

The eleven-member FEC was originally composed of representatives of

[15] The so-called SWNCC directive, "Organization and Procedure for the Development and Promulgation of United States Policy With Respect to Occupied Areas," April 8, 1946; and the "United States Proposal for Establishment of Far Eastern Advisory Commission," August 21, 1945 (released October 10, 1945) are Appendices 14 and 11 of Dept., *Occupation,* pp. 82-84, 67-68; for a study of Allied pressures, see Werner Levi, "International Control of Japan," *Far Eastern Survey,* September 25, 1946, pp. 299-300.

the same powers which had been invited to the Washington meeting. To these, representatives of Pakistan and Burma were added on November 11, 1949. The major purpose of the FEC, according to its Terms of Reference, was "to formulate policies, principles, and standards in conformity with which the fulfillment by Japan of its obligations under the Terms of Surrender may be accomplished." Unlike the FEC, legally the policy-making organ for the control of Japan, the Allied Council was established for the purpose of "consulting with and advising the Supreme Commander." It consisted of representatives of the United States, the British Commonwealth, China, and the U.S.S.R. The ACJ was, then, an on-the-spot consultative body meeting in Tokyo. The FEC met appropriately in the former (and present) Japanese Embassy, Massachusetts Avenue, Washington, D.C. In summary, the result of the Moscow decisions altered the flow of policy into the following channels:

(1) The *FEC* in Washington initiated or reviewed directives communicated through—
(2) the *United States government,* the Joint Chiefs of Staff acting as a channel to—
(3) *SCAP,* which received advice from—
(4) the *ACJ,* before transmitting directives to—
(5) the Japanese government.[16]

In Toyko, the Japanese regarded with surprise and dismay the new control machinery and quickly noted that two of the four Council members represented nations which had publicly proposed elimination of the *Tennō* system. "People like and trust General MacArthur," said one Japanese newspaperman. "Now they feel some of his policies will be changed by Russians and Chinese. They have long been taught to fear and mistrust both countries."

General MacArthur himself soon made his own views clear. On December 30, 1945, his Public Relations Officer issued the following statement:

> The statement attributed to a Far Eastern Commission officer that I "did not object to the new Japan Control Plan before it was approved at Moscow" is incorrect. On October 31 my final dis-

[16] Students of international organization need not be reminded that Japan, like other occupied ex-enemy countries, was specifically excluded from the jurisdiction of the United Nations Organization (Charter of the United Nations, Article 107), although it was administered by certain members of the wartime united nations. Charts on pp. 462-463 showing "Relations between FEC and SCAP" and the internal "Organization of Far Eastern Commission" are drawn from official publications: Report by the Secretary General, *Activities of the Far Eastern Commission; February 26, 1946-July 10, 1947* (Department of State, Publication 2888, Far Eastern Series 24); Second Report by the Secretary General, *The Far Eastern Commission; July 10, 1947-December 23, 1948* (Department of State, Publication 3420, Far Eastern Series 29); and Third Report by the Secretary General, *The Far Eastern Commission; December 24, 1948-June 30, 1950* (Department of State, Publication 3945, Far Eastern Series 35), all Washington, 1947, 1949, 1950. For the FEC Terms of Reference, see Appendix 2, pp. 36-39, of the First Report; and (in Japanese) *NKHK,* Vol. I, No. 7 (October 15, 1946), pp. 1-8.

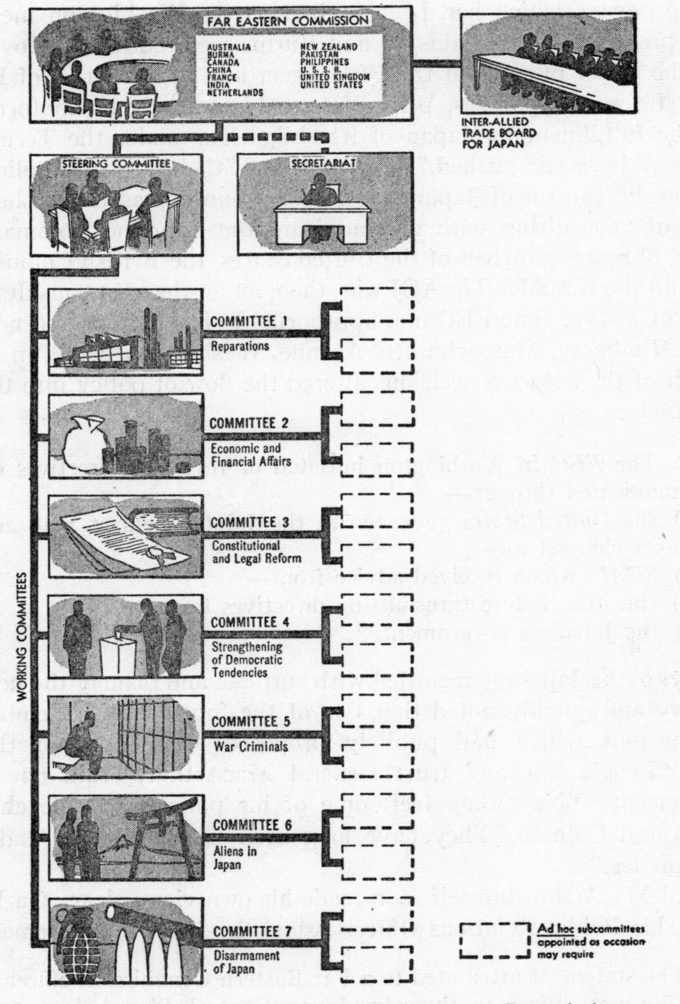

CHART 25A—Organization of Far Eastern Commission

> agreement was contained in my radio to the Chief of Staff for the Secretary of State, advising that the terms "in my opinion are not acceptable." Since that time, my views have not been sought. . . . I might add that whatever the merits or demerits of the plan, it is my firm intent within the authority entrusted to me, to try to make it work.

On January 10, 1946, a SCAP spokesman stated that the General had not dictated the type of membership of the Allied Council; he denied reports that MacArthur preferred to have army officers appointed.[17]

[17] See the *Nippon Times,* December 30, 1945, January 1 and January 12, 1946.

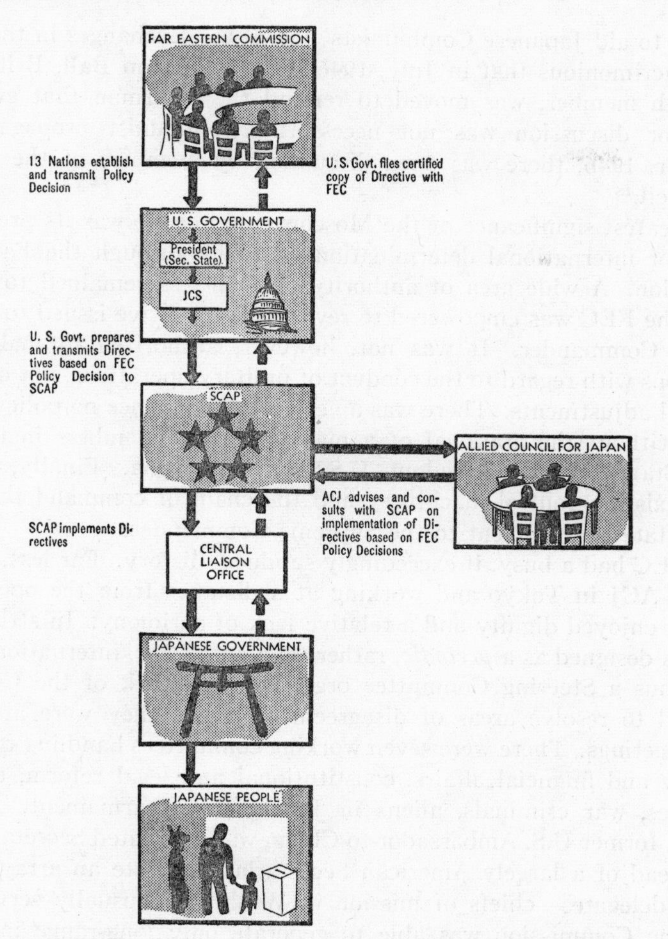

CHART 25B—Relations between FEC and SCAP: Normal Procedure for Policy Decisions

Source: The Far Eastern Commission, *Third Report by the Secretary General, December 24, 1948-June 30, 1950.*

Nevertheless, the Allied Council for Japan had a stormy history from its inception. General Whitney, representing SCAP, set the tone in the very first meetings in April, 1946. He demonstrated that a mere hint of criticism behind any inquiry was to be met by detailed, lengthy reports presented in gross and ill-mannered fashion. Apparently the Occupation was to be defended by filibuster. Under Ambassador Atcheson as Chairman, the Council became a sounding board for the natural American antipathy to communism. On the other side, General Derevyanko, the Soviet representative, used the forum to take pot-shots at SCAP's policy of utilizing the Japanese government. Russia in turn used the Soviet delegation as a core for a large mission in Tokyo to aid Japanese Communists' activities. Exchanges in the Council grew so acrimonious that in July, 1946, W. MacMahon Ball, British Commonwealth member, was moved to remind the chairman that every item offered for discussion was not necessarily Communist propaganda. By November, 1946, there was open discussion by members of the utility of the Council.[18]

The greatest significance of the Moscow compromise was its provision, in theory, for international determination of policy through the Far Eastern Commission. A wide area of authority nevertheless remained to be delineated. The FEC was empowered to review any directive issued to or by the Supreme Commander. It was not, however, authorized to make recommendations with regard to the conduct of military operations, nor concerning territorial adjustments. There was a veto provision, since no policy could be defined without the approval of a majority of its members including the United States, United Kingdom, U.S.S.R., and China. Finally, it was to respect existing control machinery and the chain of command through the United States government to the Supreme Commander.

The FEC had a busy, if exceedingly subdued, history. Far less publicized than the ACJ in Tokyo and working at a distance from the operations of SCAP, it enjoyed dignity and a relative lack of acrimony. In structure, the FEC was designed as a *periodic,* rather than an *ad hoc,* international conference. Thus a Steering Committee organized the work of the Commission and tried to resolve areas of disagreement before they were aired in the ormal meetings. There were seven working committees handling reparations, economic and financial affairs, constitutional and legal reform, democratic tendencies, war criminals, aliens in Japan, and disarmament. Nelson T. Johnson, former U.S. Ambassador to China, was appointed Secretary General at the head of a largely American Secretariat. Despite an array of distinguished delegates—chiefs of mission in Washington usually served on the FEC—the Commission was able to generate only long-range influence on the Occupation. Designed to be a policy-making body, it continued to be, in fact, advisory.[19]

Allied Policy for Japan. The Allies began in the unity bred of victory by expressing a desire for complete disarmament and demilitarization of Japan. They wanted a drastic curtailment of Japan's wartime economy.

[18] Professor Ball, after his resignation in August, 1947, loosed some of the critical arrows in the Australian and Commonwealth quiver. See his *Japan; Enemy or Ally?,* New York, 1949, especially Chap. 2 where he discusses the terms of reference and the work of the ACJ. There were three main reasons why American and other members found it difficult to make the Council a cooperative and constructive body, according to Ball: (1) the hostility between the U.S. and the U.S.S.R.; (2) the attendance of the press at all meetings; and (3) the extraordinary sensibility to criticism shown by GHQ, SCAP.

[19] General Whitney, for example, put it this way: "The Far Eastern Commission, because of its late start, its international composition, and the dispatch with which the Supreme Commander proceeded under his basic and *inherent* powers to realize Allied objectives, its policy decisions for the most part have been confirmatory of action already taken under the broad outline of the Potsdam requirements." (Italics added to) SCAP, *Political Reorientation,* cited, Vol. I, pp. xix, xx.

They were determined to punish war criminals. These were the negative and protective demands. Out of them, in some cases separate from them, were other objectives of a positive but controversial nature.

Allied war aims were expressed late in the conflict but, as we have seen, effectively in the Potsdam Proclamation. Potsdam at least showed Japan the path to surrender. It also purported to set out the fundamental objectives of the occupation. In the Proclamation the Allies demanded unconditional surrender; a military occupation would last until Allied objectives were secured; reparations and restitution of loot would be necessary. Japan would be permitted a peacetime economy and, eventually, could participate in world trade. Occupation forces would be withdrawn when Allied objectives were reached and when a responsible government was established in accordance with the freely expressed will of the Japanese people. One sentence was curiously phrased:

> The Japanese government shall remove all obstacles to the revival and strengthening of democratic tendencies among the Japanese people.[20]

Note the assumption that there had been democratic tendencies, in the Western sense, and the passive approach through removal of obstacles, rather than the encouragement of democracy.[21]

The Proclamation was, moreover, as striking for its omissions as for its declarative commitments on the Occupation. Wisely perhaps, the Allies had not expressed their faith in outsiders' ability to *democratize*—if there be such a word—Japan. The Emperor's status was not mentioned. The eventual *form* of responsible government was apparently left to the will of the Japanese. The dominant role of the United States in the Occupation was not officially forecast.

Before the United States reached a compromise with the Allies for control machinery, however, it had produced its own long-range statement of policy. It had done so because of the dominant role played by America in the Occupation and also because, in the interim, SCAP was already forming and implementing policy. Transmitted by radio on August 29, 1945, and by message on September 6, the United States Initial Post-Surrender Policy for Japan became the basis for all specific directives in the occupation. As such it was of the utmost importance.[22]

[20] In Japanese: *Nihonkoku seifu wa Nihonkoku Kokumin no aida ni okeru minshū shūgi-teki keikō no fukatsu kyōdai ni taisuru issai no shōgai wo jokyo subeshi.*

[21] The complete English text of the Potsdam Proclamation is given in Appendix 14. It was released July 26, 1945, by the Governments of the U.S., the U.K., and China; it was accepted by the Soviet Union at the time of its entry into the Pacific War. For the role of the Proclamation in leading Japan to surrender, see Chap. 19, p. 441. The Japanese text is from *NKHK*, Vol. I, No. 1 (April 1, 1946), pp. 1-6.

[22] The full text of the U.S. Initial Post-Surrender Policy for Japan is in Appendix 13, Dept., *Occupation,* pp. 73-84; and in Japanese, *NKHK,* Vol. I, No. 2 (June 1, 1946), pp. 17-30. As President Truman stated, in his message to Congress on January 14, 1946: "In this pattern of control, the United States, with the full approval of its partners, has retained

In general, the American policy statement spelled out United States interpretation of the earlier Potsdam terms. First, it recognized that "United States military policy and United States foreign policy must function as one"; it attempted to achieve a balance of participation—no mean feat in Washington—among American agencies. Every effort was to be made to satisfy the principal Allied powers, but if satisfaction did not result, the United States view would predominate. Second, it contained a clear statement of the authority of the Supreme Commander, his relation to the Japanese Emperor and government: "The policy is to use the existing form of Government in Japan, not to support it." The boundary line between *using* and *supporting* was not clearly delineated. Third, Japan was to be encouraged in developing individual freedom, democratic organizations, and an economy to meet the peacetime requirements of the population.

The primacy of the United States in the Occupation had both its advantages and disadvantages. It made for efficiency and almost unilateral interpretation of policy. It also allowed for a greater volume of criticism. There were plenty of back-seat drivers since the other powers were in an enviable position to attack American policy without the real responsibility to offer alternatives.

Actually, international carping was aimed mostly at SCAP in Tokyo. The first test of the Far Eastern Commission's authority, for example, came in an issue with General MacArthur. A SCAP directive of January 12, 1946, ordered the Japanese to hold an election for the old House of Representatives. On March 21, 1946, the Commission sent through an inquiry to General MacArthur expressing apprehension as to such early timing of the election. It was possible, the inquiry pointedly stated, that only the established reactionary parties would be organized; uncertainty in Japan's political future might work against an intelligent expression of popular will. The FEC asked for specific answers; it received pointed replies on March 29, 1946. The election was held as scheduled on April 10, 1946.[23]

---

primary authority and primary responsibility." Department of State *Bulletin,* February 3, 1946.

[23] MacArthur's replies were a monument to his own confidence in the progress of the Occupation and a further indication of impatience with interference. The text, appended to a longer message, is characteristic and worth quoting:

"*Q.* Does the Supreme Commander share the apprehensions expressed above?

"*A.* No.

"*Q.* If so, would he consider it possible to require a further postponement of the Japanese elections, and in that case, for what period?

"*A.* No.

"*Q.* If the Supreme Commander should not consider a further postponement desirable at this late date, would he express his views on the desirability, as an alternative, of publicly prescribing that the forthcoming election will be regarded as a test of the ability of Japan to produce a responsible and democratic government in full accordance with the wishes of the people and that further elections will be held at a later date?

"*A.* The suggested statement seems wholly unnecessary. The conditions it would announce are inherent in the situation and are completely understood, as I can require dissolution of the Diet and call for an election at any time." See Report of the Secretary General, *FEC* (1947), Appendices 6, 7, pp. 58-63.

Finally, on June 19, 1947, or almost two years after the appearance of the American policy statement, the FEC got around to adopting a Basic Post-Surrender Policy for Japan. It was an exact paraphrase—in places it borrowed the language exactly—of the United States Initial Post-Surrender Policy.[24]

The FEC and the ACJ were evolved in compromise of Big Power interests. They were not true examples of international cooperation, for the United States maintained its predominant position in policy formulation. Moreover, there was more than a quaint suspicion that the Japanese government, increasingly encouraged by the United States, was itself not entirely passive. The amenable Japanese often disconcerted Occupation authorities by anticipating policy decisions. Unkind critics of the Occupation traced the flow of policy from the Japanese to SCAP, back to the United States government, into a weighty FEC memorandum, back out to Tokyo, and into a directive ordering an action already accomplished! This is, of course, an exaggeration, for the Japanese persistently played the Oriental game of delay and planned confusion and had to be firmly prodded on numerous occasions. Nevertheless, the rehabilitation process was, to use the words of a SCAP officer, Brigadier General Ken R. Dyke, "like performing an appendicitis operation while the patient is walking around the room." In many aspects, the operation was a brilliant success. The patient will live. It remains to be seen if the surgeon thoughtlessly left some of the smaller instruments in the cavity.

Even today, after Japan has won her freedom, there are two partisan views of the Occupation experiment. Defenders of the Occupation, with SCAP itself foremost, set almost monthly milestones which purportedly marked Japan's progress along the road of political reorientation. Critics of SCAP—let it be emphasized here that Cominform recordings did not offer the sole sour note—claim there has been imperceptible change in Japanese political traditions. Neither view is, of course, correct. Somewhere in between lie an understanding of Japan's persistent political tradition, which has survived other crises; a sympathy for the Japanese people and with their attempts to be free from insecurity and the need for "uniqueness," a sympathy which tends to convert all students of Japan to Japanophiles; and a sincere attempt to describe objectively postwar changes.[25] Major changes

[24] See Appendix 5, pp. 49-58 of Report by the Secretary General, cited, 1947; the text in Japanese is available in *NKHK, "Nihon ni taisuru kōfukugo no kihon seisaku"* ("Basic Post-Surrender Policy for Japan"), No. 19 (April 25, 1948).

[25] The earlier, official source on occupied Japan to August 1948 was Supreme Commander for the Allied Powers, *Summation of Non-Military Activities in Japan,* General Headquarters, SCAP, Tokyo (monthly, numbered serially). The following is a sample list drawn from the sizable literature on the Occupation and representative of various points of view other than those already cited: for a broader view of the Occupation, placed in the setting of Japanese culture and affected by American policy, Edwin O. Reischauer, *The United States and Japan,* Cambridge, 1950; a factual account, from an American State Department official's point of view, Edwin M. Martin, *The Allied Occupation of Japan,* New York, 1948; and its companion volume, more critical of the Occupation, T. A. Bisson, *Prospects for Democracy in Japan,* New York, 1949, both under the auspices of the American Institute

affecting the form of government were two: the first was an attempt to eliminate aggressive elements from Japanese politics; the second, constitutional reform. Alteration of Japan's administrative structure, an attempt to introduce Western democracy in Japanese form, will be described in the next chapter. The results of these changes, in the short run, may be measured against the traditional and new working forces in Japanese politics. The long-run results, no Japanese, much less an outsider, can foresee.

First Stage: the Purges. One of the few steps all of the Allies agreed upon was the need for trial of some Japanese as war criminals. Although not considered technically part of the purge program, the Tokyo trials firmly expressed Allied determination to eliminate at least leading military and ultra-nationalist elements. In accordance with the Potsdam Proclamation and based on the legal precedence established at Nürnberg, there was established on January 19, 1946, an International Military Tribunal for the Far East (*Kyokutō Kokusai Gunji Saibansho*) and a charter for the Tribunal. Headquarters were in Tokyo.

Two years and three months—or 419 hearings, 452 witnesses, and 3,915 documents later—the Tribunal recessed. Some important evidence had been denied it. On Sunday morning, December 15, 1945, Prince Konoye had been found dead with a poison vial at his bedside. *Yomiuri Hōchi* predicted serious developments affecting the *Tennō* system; *Asahi* remarked that Konoye's name would always be clouded; the *Nippon Times* commented editorially: "By undergoing the trial and by revealing to the court all the important inside information which he knew so well, he would have been able to dispel the cloud which has hung too long over Japan's political history of the past few years." That fears for the Emperor were not unfounded was clearly illustrated in October, 1947, when testimony by Marquis Kido, former Lord Keeper, threatened to weaken the Throne itself. In May, 1948, the possibility of Hirohito's abdication was mentioned openly for the first time in the Japanese press.

Finally, on November 4, 1948, Sir William Webb, Australian Chief Justice, started reading the majority opinion. The Tribunal upheld ten general counts of the indictment against the twenty-five defendants, sustaining charges that they plotted and waged aggressive wars and were responsible for atrocities against Allied prisoners. After General MacArthur had upheld the sentences on November 24, two of the convicted appealed to the U.S. Supreme Court for a stay of execution under writ of *habeas corpus*. On December 20, six Justices held that because the Tribunal was international in character, no court of the United States could interfere in any way with

---

of Pacific Relations; from an entirely different, but equally critical point of view, Helen Mears, *Mirror for Americans,* Boston, 1948; for a cautiously optimistic viewpoint, Robert A. Fearey, *The Occupation of Japan; Second Phase: 1948-50,* New York, 1951; for somber reflection, Robert B. Textor, *Failure in Japan,* New York, 1951; among the best of the reportorial volumes, Russell Brines, *MacArthur's Japan,* Philadelphia, 1948; and on the lighter side but shrewdly intuitive, Lucy Herndon Crockett, *Popcorn on the Ginza; An Informal Portrait of Postwar Japan,* New York, 1949.

the convictions. On December 22, MacArthur's Public Relations Officer announced the hanging at Sugamo Prison of seven of the Japanese war criminals.[26]

While the International Military Tribunal was slowly cutting the top out of the militarist tree, the Supreme Commander meanwhile began chipping at growths on the trunk. The first steps were purely precautionary, breaking the power of the military to oppose the Occupation. Thus the Imperial General Headquarters was disbanded in September, 1945; the Japanese Cabinet abolished conscription in November. The War and Navy Ministries handled early stages of armed forces demobilization, but by June, 1946, civilian Demobilization Bureaus (*Fukuin-kyoku*) had taken over. By October, 1947, the once-powerful service ministries were completely abolished, all demobilization functions having been turned over to the Welfare Ministry.[27]

The housecleaning did not stop with the military. The Japanese themselves had taken a few halting steps toward what they thought was democracy, even before the arrival of the Supreme Commander. On August 22, 1945, the *Taisei Yokusan Kai* (Imperial Rule Assistance Association) and the *Taisei Yokusan Seiji Kai* (Imperial Rule Assistance Political Association) were publicly dissolved. After the arrival of the conquerors, one newspaper editorial had slyly drawn an analogy with the overthrow of the Tokugawa Shogunate. There, too, the military struggle was terminated before the process of liquidation of feudal elements was complete, yet the followers of the *Shōgun* ". . . except for a few extremists, were brought over eventually to the support of the new regime through persuasion and conversion." MacArthur's reply to this attitude was a rude shock and a foretaste of things to come. In September, he flatly vetoed the Japanese government's appointment of former Finance Minister Ikeda Seihin, one-time manager of Mitsui interests, to a liaison post.[28]

These first developments were, however, as nothing compared with what the Japanese government was to accomplish under the firm prodding from SCAP. The first phase in the purging of ultra-nationalists, begun early in 1946 and completed by the summer, resulted in the removal of one thousand incumbents and candidates for important positions. It included a preliminary screening of all candidates in the April, 1946, elections and final screening of the successful candidates before the Diet met for business in June of that year. The second phase, designed to remove undesirables from leadership positions down through local government, coincided with the

[26] Section II, Article 5, of the Tribunal's Charter listed the offenses: (a) Crimes against peace *(Heiwa ni taisuru Tsumi)*; (b) Conventional war crimes *(Tsurei no Sensō Hanzai)*; (c) Crimes against humanity *(Jindō ni taisuru Tsumi)*. See *NKHK*, Vol. I, No. 7 (October 15, 1946), pp. 67-86. For the list of judges, prosecution statement, and Indictment No. 1, Department of State, *Trial of Japanese War Criminals* (Publication 2613, Far Eastern Series 12), Washington, 1946. For a brief summary of the Tribunal's work, see Solis Horwitz, "The Tokyo Trial," *International Conciliation*, No. 465 (November, 1950).

[27] For successive directives concerning demobilization agencies, *NKHK*, No. 12 (August 1, 1947), pp. 48-49; No. 20 (June 1, 1948), pp. 9-14; and No. 22 (August 1, 1948), pp. 7-8.

[28] See the *Nippon Times*, September 10 and 26, 1945.

elections of April, 1947, when the Japanese elected local representatives and executives (for the first time) as well as Diet members. In this period, some seven thousand were removed or barred from offices, chiefly in local government. The third and last phase, late in 1947, invaded private financial and industrial enterprises and mass media of information (about eight hundred were barred in this period).

The scope of the purge program was, of course, so vast that a volume could be devoted to the careful and secretive plans for the operation, drawn up by Government Section mainly; to the directives, interpretations, and ordinances; to the concern expressed by the Japanese (and by some SCAP officials as well), occasional resistance, and effects.[29]

Confusion was soon converted into a Japanese plan—to delay. Hiding behind jargon which purported to convert the purge from an administrative to a judicial process, the government offered to substitute *individual inquiries* for *categorical removals.* SCAP's reply, given to Premier Shidehara himself, showed no patience with bargaining: "The directive must be complied with in letter as well as in spirit. . . ." With a long stretch of the imagination perhaps, one could agree with Government Section's claim that "General MacArthur consistently followed a policy of encouraging the Japanese government to act on its own initiative . . ." in effecting democratic reforms.

Once the government was given a clear outline of where it should show initiative, it fell over itself to implement the directives. Category by category, the scope of the removals was spelled out by Cabinet interpretation and Imperial Ordinances.

Even before the first directives were translated into Japanese law, the highest levels of Japanese politics were deeply affected. The *Nippon Times* summarized Japanese press comment:

> General of the Army MacArthur sliced off most of the Japanese government's top crust, deeply cauterized the Diet and political parties and possibly gave the Shidehara Cabinet a death blow in his twin "housecleaning" directives today.

The first purge phase hit the Minister of Imperial Household, the President of the Privy Council, and the Grand Chamberlain, thus leaving only the Premier the task of assisting the Emperor. Although five Cabinet members

[29] General MacArthur's basic authorization for the program was the Joint Chiefs of Staff Directive of November 3, 1945, already cited: JCS 1380/15, Appendix A:13, SCAP, *Political Reorientation,* Vol. II, pp. 428-439; for the January 4, 1946 Directives, "Removal and Exclusion of Undesirable Personnel from Public Office" (SCAPIN 550) and "Abolition of Certain Political Parties, Associations, Societies, and Other Organizations" (SCAPIN 548), *ibid.,* Appendices B:5b and B:5a, pp. 479-488; (in Japanese) *NKHK,* Vol. I, No. 7 (October 15, 1946), pp. 17-36, 37-42; for the earlier memorandum (SCAPIN 93), removing high officials in police administration, October 4, 1945, SCAP, *op. cit.,* Appendix B:2d, pp. 463-465; and (in Japanese) *NKHK,* Vol. I, No. 3 (June 15, 1946), pp. 29-38. The best brief but authoritative analysis, based on first-hand observation, is Harold S. Quigley, "The Great Purge in Japan," *Pacific Affairs,* Vol. XX, No. 3 (September 1947), pp. 299-308.

immediately tendered resignations, Premier Shidehara decided to reshuffle his post-surrender Cabinet (October 9, 1945-May 22, 1946) and ride out the crisis. It was a strange coincidence of fate, said *Yomiuri Hōchi* on January 22, 1946, that the decision to abolish the entire peerage system came under a government headed by a Baron, Shidehara.

By May of 1946, after the first elections, it became apparent that few were immune. Political circles were thrown into a dither when Hatoyama Ichirō, President of the new Liberal Party and leading candidate for Premier, was specifically forbidden to take office. As early as November, 1945, letters to editors had pointed to the irony in the fact that Hatoyama who, as Education Minister in the 1930's, had brought pressures to bear on university circles, was organizing the postwar Liberal Party. By December, Hatoyama stooped to answer press charges that he stood by, arms folded, while the war progressed. One week after the election of April 10, 1946, *Asahi Shimbun* picked up the charge (originally made by the American GI newspaper, *Stars and Stripes*) that Hatoyama had neglected to mention his pro-Axis book, *Face of the Earth* (*Sekai no Kao*), in filling out his qualifications questionnaire. On May 3, 1946, SCAP, in its only directive aimed at a single individual, ordered Premier Shidehara to remove and exclude Hatoyama Ichirō from public office, under provisions of category G of the basic SCAP directives.[30]

During the second phase of the purge, prior to the elections of 1947, Government Section again had to formulate plans to guide the Japanese in extending removals to local levels. General MacArthur's G2 (Civil Intelligence Section) had already warned that former personages of national importance, once purged, were drifting into local offices. Nevertheless, Premier Yoshida (May 23, 1946-June 1, 1947) argued that wartime regimentation had been engineered at the higher levels, and that lower ranks and local levels were merely the objects of that regimentation. This time General MacArthur himself told the Japanese government to get on with the job. In four Imperial Ordinances and a supplemental Cabinet order of January 4, 1947, removal categories were extended from national and Diet offices to prefectural offices, mayoralties, assembly memberships, neighborhood leadership, party directorships, and offices in industrial, commercial, and financial institutions. To void the possibility of "substitutional candidates" and pup-

[30] SCAPIN 919, 3 May 1946, listed points in the "indictment": Hatoyama had served: (a) as Chief Secretary, Cabinet of General Tanaka (1927-1929) and shared responsibility for the notorious Peace Preservation Law; (b) as Minister of Education (1931-1934), shared responsibility for mass dismissals, (c) participated in forced dissolution of farmer-labor parties; (d) as personal envoy of Prince Konoye in July 1937, acted as an apologist for Japanese aggression; (e) although he posed as an antimilitarist, in his election campaign of 1942 he justified expansion to his constituents. See SCAP *Political Reorientation,* cited, Vol. II, Appendix B:5f, pp. 494-495 and (in Japanese) *NKHK,* Vol. I, No. 12 (August 1947), pp. 178-181; for the background: *Nippon Times,* November 7, 1945, December 11, 1945; *Asahi Shimbun,* April 18, 1946. The Communists, using their bitter enemy as authority, cited the SCAP directive to prove the criminality not only of Hatoyama but also of the entire Liberal Party and the Shidehara Government; and the need for another election. See *Mainichi Shimbun,* May 5, 1946.

pets, even purgees' relatives by blood, marriage, or adoption were proscribed. The number of Japanese affected was conservatively estimated at one million. After the second and third phases, the pendulum began to swing the other way.

Criticism of the depth of the purges was inevitable. Even in SCAP, voices were heard protesting the loss of knowledgeable managers of industry producing for the Occupation. The Yoshida government, after delaying the administration of the purge, later used it effectively to hammer down political opposition. More serious, young unemployed officers trained only in violence sought outlet elsewhere for their talents. Their influence within the new labor unions, for example, was destructive. By August, 1949, Japanese officials began considering plans to reinstate approximately seventy thousand purgees. SCAP at first took the position that the basic purge ordinances could not be changed piecemeal, nor could individual appeals be acted upon. By January, 1950, the Japanese government was convinced the purge system could be reviewed only as a whole and rested its hopes on negotiation within the forthcoming peace terms.[31]

Second Stage: Constitutional Reform. Of all the steps ordered by SCAP the most important was the adoption imposed upon the Japanese government of a new Constitution. This may be looked at in several ways. Even a brief account of the drafting of the Constitution will reveal that the process was primarily an effect of surrender, an inevitable consequence to the creation of that singular political creature, MacArthur's Japan. Apart from its role as a result of the surrender, the new Constitution (*Shin Kempō*) can also be considered as a blueprint for intra-Japanese democratization, a logical and perhaps equally inevitable development in the assimilation of Japan in the modern world. In this rather long-range context the document raises some worrisome queries. Finally, the new Constitution necessarily serves as a cornerstone in the completely redesigned structure of Japan's legal codes. Allied policy declarations clearly revealed the basic dilemma concerning Japanese constitutional reform. At Potsdam the Allied Powers had demanded the establishment of "a peacefully inclined and responsible government." Yet the United States, speaking on behalf of the other Allies as well as itself, had officially stated that "the ultimate form of government shall . . . be established by the freely expressed will of the Japanese people." This raised a corollary question. How were the Japanese to obtain democracy, assuming that the Allies could agree upon the meaning of the term, in a Japanese political climate which had a traditional lack of political democracy?

Should the Allies have chosen to let constitutional reform develop in its

[31] Shortly after General Matthew B. Ridgway succeeded General MacArthur, an order permitted the Japanese government to review purge laws and ordinances. On June 19, 1951, the government announced the "depurge" of approximately 3,000 persons at national level and 67,000 in the prefectures, providing they had been banned only because of the category purged rather than personal guilt. *The New York Times,* June 20, 1951.

own Japanese way as a result of the reorganization of the Japanese economic structure, the reshaping of Japanese social life, and the placing of Japan among a family of democratic nations so that both internally and externally the Japanese citizenry would learn democracy by taking part in it? Or should the Allies have imposed the formal scaffolding of reform and expect that the everyday political habits would develop within the scaffolding and hope that the social, economic and related modes of behavior would in turn follow the political? [32]

The choice was made. The second alternative was selected. For one thing, the American mentality was prepared to understand practical problems of constitutional and legal reform, but neither Americans nor any other non-Communist democracies were prepared to describe what a social system, any social system, should be like. The non-Communist democracies did not have clear-cut enough models of social and economic democracy themselves to permit them to decide what the structure of Japanese life should be apart from political forms. The Communists could have "democratized" Japan in their own way. They would have known how to meet every social question from hospitalization and old-age relief through trade-union organization and questions of public ownership all the way to worship and ceremonial; they would have had a dogmatic Marxist answer for each topic. This was not true of the other Allies. The Americans could not prescribe a society in their own image because most Americans did not think beyond categorically political terms.

In a sense, therefore, the Americans did the utmost which Americans could do. They attempted to give the Japanese those political and constitutional guarantees to which American leaders and thinkers, rightly or wrongly, attributed most of the benefits of American life. It was clearly not possible to give the Japanese a vast new continent, immense natural resources, a different racial constitution, or even a new set of historical memories. The political factors could be reached, and these the Americans did indeed modify.

The choice, from a bystander's viewpoint, resembled nothing so much as the curious manner in which the Japanese themselves construct a new, large office building. With materials at hand, a very complex scaffolding of surplus bamboo and screening is first put up. Sidewalk superintendents are allowed only the most incomplete view of the shape or quality of foundation

[32] SCAP officials were fully aware of the basic dilemma, which is explained in SCAP, *Political Reorientation,* Vol. I, "The New Constitution of Japan," especially p. 90. It should be noted that constitutional reform was imposed by more subtle means than military fiat, a dubious process under international law and highly undesirable in any case (see p. 89, same essay). It should also be recalled that the Allies, through the FEC, had a further word to say on constitutional reform; and presumably, the Japanese will have the last word. See p. 479 and Report of Secretary General (February 26, 1946-July 10, 1947), cited, Appendix 12, p. 67. The entire dilemma of constitutional reform is carefully analyzed by David Nelson Rowe, "The New Japanese Constitution," *Far Eastern Survey,* January 29, 1947, and February 12, 1947.

and building behind the scaffolding. With the scaffolding removed, it is fervently hoped the real structure will stand.

The first sweep was against individuals themselves, by means of the purges. The second attack was upon institutions which the Americans deemed to be bad. On October 4, 1945, a directive, SCAPIN 93, was issued to establish a virtual Bill of Rights. Political prisoners were ordered released. Restrictions on political and religious liberty were forbidden. The doomed Ministry of Home Affairs (*Naimushō*) had most of its authority stripped away. Drastic modifications were made in Japan's police organization.[33]

Several times during the first four months of the Occupation General MacArthur informed the Japanese government that constitutional revision was of the utmost importance. The Japanese tried to receive these communications in their own way. According to *Dōmei* in October, 1945, "His Majesty the Emperor graciously proposed a revision of the Imperial Constitution." As an adviser to the Imperial household, Prince Konoye (who was soon to kill himself when he realized that his political role had reached the end of its dignity) first began to investigate the broad aspects of reform. Konoye managed to have several interviews with the Supreme Commander on several occasions and obtain access to the United States political representative, Mr. George Atcheson. For a while poor Konoye dreamed of himself as fulfilling the role of constitutional founding father and performing the kind of task which Prince Itō had carried out with such success sixty years before.[34] In mid-October, however, the Shidehara cabinet appointed Dr. Matsumoto Jōji, a corporation lawyer, to begin detailed drafting with the assistance of a Constitutional Problems Investigation Committee. Although the so-called Matsumoto Committee worked behind closed doors, constitutional revision received widespread press publicity and private groups did not hesitate to make their views public.

Three major problems faced the Committee, the Japanese public, and SCAP itself. These were:

[33] Louis J. Valentine, head of New York City's Police Department, was invited by General MacArthur to help with police reorganization. Texts of SCAPIN 93, "Removal of Restrictions on Political, Civil, and Religious Liberties," may be found (in English), in SCAP, *Political Reorientation,* Vol. II, Appendix B:2d, pp. 463-465; and (in Japanese) in *NKHK,* Vol. I, No. 3 (June 15, 1946), pp. 29-38. A few samples of laws swept out by the directive were: Peace Preservation Law *(Chian Iji Hō),* 1941; "Dangerous Thoughts" Law *(Shisō-han Hogo-kansatsu Hō),* 1936; Religious Bodies Law *(Shukyō Dantai Hō),* 1939.

[34] The confusion as to Konoye's precise role in the process doubtless arose because of an interview with the Prince by the AP correspondent in Japan, Russell Brines. When translated into English for Americans and then retranslated into Japanese, the story left the impression that Konoye was to *revise* the Constitution rather than to investigate revision; Konoye later corrected the impression and SCAP officially announced the Prince had not been singled out by Allied authorities to revise the Constitution. See *Nippon Times,* October 25, October 26, November 3, November 4, 1945. *Mainichi Shimbun,* December 22, 1945 (one week after Konoye's death) published the "Konoye Draft," which seemed to bear out the official announcement that the Prince was concerned only with broad principles. Nevertheless, the rumor persisted that the Constitution was originally written by Konoye and later revised by SCAP; see Noel Busch, *Fallen Sun: A Report on Japan,* New York, 1948, pp. 52-53.

(1) treatment of the *Tennō* within the *Kokutai;*
(2) maintenance of legal continuity; and
(3) the machinery of revision.[35]

The area of agreement was substantial. Only the Japanese Communists proposed abolition of the Imperial institution, and they themselves were not at this time vociferous in the demand for the establishment of a democratic republic. One minority group headed by Dr. Takano Iwasaburō proposed substitution of an elected president and a republic form of government, but this group, once heard from, never obtained the backing which it expected from the Social Democrats and lapsed into obscurity. All other Japanese groups suggested a retention in some form of the Japanese Imperial House and significant modifications of a constitutional parliamentary structure. Two major parties demanded a functional upper house. Other groups asked for an independent judiciary. Still others demanded extensive prescription of particular civil and economic rights. The Imperial Lawyers' Association prepared a draft which stressed a government operated jointly by the Emperor and the people. None of the private groups proposed guarantees against seizure and search; none insisted on women's suffrage; and none established a logical connection between democracy for Japan as a whole and local autonomy at the community or prefecture level.

In any event, these independent plans were radical as compared with the so-called Matsumoto draft. Although the official committee proceedings were never published, it is evident that Dr. Matsumoto himself guided the thinking of the committee. A conservative who believed devoutly in the Emperor system and in the maintenance of Japan's very special kind of "national constitution" (*Kokutai*), Matsumoto wanted to leave the Japanese state unchanged and went about the task of saving it by clouding over the whole issue of reconstitution with a swarm of words. Matsumoto submitted explanatory memoranda, but not a draft, to SCAP on February 1, 1946, and by the time that he was allowed a conference with the SCAP officials on February 13, 1946, General MacArthur had already instructed the Government Section to prepare a detailed rejection of the Matsumoto draft and to take up the task itself.[36]

[35] The *Nippon Times,* October 16, 1945, carried an interview with Dr. Minobe Tatsukichi, which may be considered representative of even enlightened views. After having stated that he thought the Meiji Constitution, properly interpreted, needed no revision, the following exchange regarding the Emperor occurred:

"*Q.* What is your view on Article III that declares the Emperor holy and inviolable?

"*A.* I think there is no harm in using those terms as even foreign constitutions have them. Personally, I interpret it to mean that the Emperor is inviolable, but Imperial Ordinances and other orders issued by the Emperor can be criticized. . . .

"*Q.* Do you think the position of the Emperor can be left as it is?

"*A.* Yes. In this regard too, if the Constitution is properly operated, I believe the democratization of politics as i Britain under the King is possible."

[36] Early in November 1945, *Asahi Shimbun* quoted Matsumoto as saying it was his policy not to go so far as to consider the question of whether the *Tennō* system should be abolished. The "Matsumoto Draft" was never officially released, although *Mainichi Shimbun,* February 1, 1946, carried a "Tentative Plan" attributed to the Committee (the Chief Secre-

Full discussion was allowed the Americans in Government Section in preparing the so-called Whitney draft except for three points which General MacArthur specifically required: first, the Emperor's powers were to be exercised only constitutionally and only according to the basic will of the people; second, Japan was to renounce war forever; third, the Japanese should abolish all vestiges of feudalism.* Behind closed American doors there was a conference on February 4, 1946, in which General Whitney and his chief staff officers (Colonel Charles Kades, Lieutenant Colonel Milo Rowell, and Commander Alfred Hussey) briefed the assembled personnel of the Section. A steering committee and a special committee of the Section set to work and submitted a draft for the Supreme Commander's approval on February 10.[37]

When the Japanese met the Americans on February 13, they were startled out of their wits by the complete rejection of their own draft and by the appearance of a SCAP draft. One member of the group, Shirasu Jirō, later wrote General Whitney his personal impression of the way the draft was received by Dr. Matsumoto and the Cabinet:

> . . . I must say your draft was more than a little shock to them. . . . He and his colleagues feel that yours and theirs aim at the same destination, but there is this great difference in the routes chosen. Your way is so American in the way that it is straight and direct. Their way must be Japanese in the way it is roundabout, twisted, and narrow. Your way may be called an Air Way and their way Jeep Way over bumpy roads (I know the roads are bumpy!).[38]

Once the Japanese got out of this shocking conference they transferred their side of the debate directly to the Cabinet. Yoshida Shigeru, then Foreign Minister and later Premier, supported Matsumoto and his die-hards; Premier Shidehara stood with the progressives who were willing to go along with liberalization. The two groups finally turned to the Emperor himself. Once again, as at the time of surrender, the Shōwa Emperor made the final decision himself. He supported revision. He even supported his own deprivation of political authority.

---

tary of the Cabinet promptly disowned the text). Texts of the "Tentative Plan," as well as the "Gist" and "Explanation" of the Matsumoto Draft submitted to SCAP, are reproduced in SCAP, *Political Reorientation,* Vol. II, Appendices C:5, C:6, pp. 611-621.

* Years later Americans and Japanese were still undertaking a veritable detective-story campaign to discover who had actually been the first to saddle Japan with an idealistic, hopeful, but incredibly impractical renunciation of war. Many SCAP officials assumed that it came from General MacArthur himself. Even at the time that the idea first appeared some Japanese swore it originated with the Emperor or with Prince Konoye. Dr. Kenneth Colton is currently preparing a study of personalities in the occupation period and is seeking by a process of cross-questioning to discover which Japanese to credit with the origination of this idea. It appears possible that the definitively original authorship of this concept will never be traced.

[37] Appendix 16 of this book presents the text of the instructions to Government Section, from General MacArthur's own notes. See SCAP, *Political Reorientation,* Vol. I, "SCAP's Answer to Matsumoto Draft," pp. 101-105.

[38] *Ibid.,* Vol. II, Appendix C:8, p. 624.

Early in March, 1946, the Cabinet draft was introduced to the Japanese public. It was accompanied by a statement from the Supreme Commander, an Imperial Rescript, and an announcement by Premier Shidehara. There had been some delay in the process of translating the Japanese text into English, retranslating the English back into Japanese, and comparing the net product in the two languages. The press reaction suggested that the Japanese people were surprised, but not dismayed, and that their reaction was as a whole quite favorable. The newspaper, *Jiji Shimpō,* of March 8, 1946, cautiously observed "it was the result of the closest consultations with SCAP officials. . . ." The *Asahi Shimbun* flatly commented that the Shidehara Cabinet could not by itself have been capable of producing such a good draft!

Five main features appeared in the Cabinet draft, none of which was fundamentally altered by subsequent revision. The major structural changes in Japanese government included: first, a redefinition of the Emperor's powers; second, a transfer of basic political powers to the Diet and the Cabinet, and replacement of the House of Peers by a House of Councilors; third, the establishment of a Bill of Rights; fourth, the alteration of the antiquated Japanese judicial system; and fifth, the total renunciation of war.

The administrative changes effected by the Constitution are described in the next chapter. The content of the Constitution can be readily comprehended from examining the actual English text given in Appendix 17.[39]

Peculiar to this Constitution are the features that it was quite probably written in Japanese from an original English basic draft prepared in Government Section and the further confusion concerning the mild discontinuity of this Constitution in relation to the Meiji Constitution.

The new Constitution is technically a revolutionary document in that the Meiji Constitution had been issued by the Japanese Emperor on his own divine authority, whereas the new Constitution is issued by the Japanese people beginning with the quite un-Japanese phrase, "*Nihon Kokumin wa* . . ." ("We, the Japanese people . . ."). In other words, the former Constitution had been issued by a recognizedly divine king and the new one by a reluctantly democratic people under the orders of a foreign occupation. What the Japanese people of the future may make of it is yet to be determined.[40]

[39] Published SCAP documents do not include the Government Section draft. Four Government Drafts are given in SCAP, *ibid.,* Vol. II, Appendices C:9a, C:9b, C:9c, C:9d, pp. 625-648. The English text in Appendix 17 of this book is taken from Department of State, *The Constitution of Japan* (Publication 2836, Far Eastern Series 22), Washington, 1947. A photostatic copy of the Japanese text was early made available to the author of this section, thanks to the Japanese Section, Division of Orientalia, Library of Congress. Much of the following analysis and Japanese terminology is taken from Yanagizawa Yoshio, *Nihonkoku Kempō chikujō kōgi* (An explanation of the Japanese constitution), Tōkyō, 1947.

[40] *Asahi Shimbun,* April 24, 1946, complained that the Preamble did not clarify the spirit of Japanese politics. Somewhat more objectively, a Japanese professor defined the origin in political theory: Kiyomiya S., "*Nihonkoku Kempō to Rokku no seiji shisō*" (The Japa-

Within the Constitution itself the *Bill of Rights* (*Kokumin no Kenri oyobi Gimu*), literally "Rights and Duties of the People," consists of 31 articles and is the longest single chapter in the Constitution. This section more than any other demonstrates the character of the democratization which Americans undertook in Japan; it is certainly the chapter most clearly reflective of American ideals. In fact, the inalienable privileges of a Japanese individual go according to this Constitution far beyond the first ten amendments of the American Constitution. In sharp contrast to the Meiji Constitution, which also contained a Bill of Rights, there are no qualifications or reservations by legislation. The rights granted are to life, liberty, and the pursuit of happiness. Juridical equality is assured. The recognition of the peerage is denied, on the perhaps vain assumption that the destruction of a long-established set of particular social courtesies somehow, in George Orwell's immortal phrase, make some people more equal than others.

Government Section did a good job of thinking up additional rights. Freedoms of thought, of conscience, of assembly, of speech, of academic teaching, of selection of residence, of choice of occupation, of collective bargaining in organization, and of property ownership are guaranteed. The right to work is included even though the Constitution does not provide an economic system or (by constitutional fiat) an international market for Japanese products which would make that right to work more than hypothetical. Husband and wife are given equal rights, even though the Constitution was unable to confer the right of motherhood on Japanese fathers; biology was at this point a little recalcitrant. Finally, Japanese citizens were assured the right of suing their own government for redress if they were acquitted after arrest and detention.

In the brave new world of 1946 these rights made sense; in the next decade they had become ludicrous if not pitiable. The right not to be a battlefield between American and Russian power, the right never to be bombed, the right to be the member of a respected and splendid nation, the right to take part in a stable and purposeful civilization, and the right to assure the effective working of a selected economic system, none of them were mentioned. The Americans, in other words, instigated the Japanese to set up a perfect catalogue of rights which Americans might wish, but they were not aware and, given their social and ideological backgrounds, were incapable of being aware of the kinds of problems which succeeding years would bring to Japan. An American such as Harold Lasswell might have raised the point that the social, psychological, and even psychiatric aspects of freedom and purpose in a defeated, wrecked, and humiliated nation might be more important to the patriotic citizens of that nation than their own rights against their own officials, but the Americans who had a share in

---

nese constitution and the political thought of Locke), *Kokka gakkai zasshi,* cited, Vol. LXII, No. 9 (September 1948), pp. 1-15.

making the Japanese Constitution and in guiding Japanese thought on this subject were lawyers rather than political scientists or sociologists.

Something was gained by making the Japanese list of rights exhaustive. The Japanese were given at least a model of one particular kind of government. Whether that government worked or not, it would certainly stand for a long time as the world's outstanding model of the conveying of political rights by constitutional fiat and the ignoring of the revolutionary challenges brought up against traditional democracy by the Bolshevik revolution of 1917, the Fascist revolution of 1922, and the National Socialist revolution of 1933. One can say with Anatole France that the new Constitution gives rich and poor equal rights to sleep under a bridge, but one cannot reproach the Japanese for accepting from the Americans the best that the Americans themselves thought they had to offer.

The new Constitution grants to the Supreme Court a new power in Japanese Government: *judicial review of constitutionality.* This unfamiliar concept the phrase-makers had to render in a cumbersome sentence. The Court (Article 81) has the power to determine whether a law, order, regulation, or official act literally ". . . is in conformity with the Constitution or not."[41]

Amendment (*Kaisei,* Chapter IX) may prove to be the most important feature of the new Constitution so far as the Japanese are concerned. Here there will be less procedural difficulty than is involved in changing the Constitution of the United States. Changes in Japan may be made by two-thirds vote of all members of each house, ratified by a majority of all Japanese casting a ballot in a special referendum or in an election designated by the Diet.

Renunciation of war (*Sensō no Hōki*) is the subject of Chapter II. It is the most idealistic and widely discussed section of the Constitution. It reads, in part:

> *Article 9.* Aspiring sincerely to an international peace based on justice and order, the Japanese people forever renounce war as a sovereign right of the nation and the threat or use of force as means of settling international disputes.[42]

In order to guarantee this pledge, the Japanese promise never to maintain land, sea, and air forces. To nail down the promise even more securely, Article 66 (Chapter V, the Cabinet) provides that the Premier and Ministers of State must be civilians (*bummin,* literally "civil affairs persons"). Of this provision, Professor Yanagizawa of Chūō University carefully writes:

[41] . . . *Kempō ni tekigō suru ka shinai ka.* After circling this power warily for two years, the Court voided a lower court judgment on the basis of constitutionality. For a learned discussion of *pouvoir constituant* and *pouvoir constitué,* with reference to comparative amendment processes, see Gyobu So, *"Saikin no kempō ni okeru kaisei tetsuzuki no minshūka"* (Democratization of the amendment process in recent constitutions), *Kokka gakkai zasshi,* cited, Vol. LX, No. 6 (June 1946), pp. 1-23.

[42] *Nihon Kokumin wa, seigi to chitsujo wo kichō to suru kokusai heiwa wo seijitsu ni kikyū shi, kokken no hatsudōtaru sensō to, buryoku ni yoru ikaku mata wa buryoku no kōshi wa, kokusai funjō wo kaiketsu suru shudan to shite wa eikyū ni kore wo hōki suru.*

> Although this provision was not in the original drafts nor in the version adopted by the House of Representatives, it was inserted in the House of Peers. It is believed the word *"bummin"* has never been used as legal terminology originating in our constitutional law. Consequently it is extremely difficult to understand, judging from traditional usage, and also dangerous. In the present context, the opposite of "civil" is "military" and within this paragraph the term must be understood to mean the equivalent of the English word *civilian,* to exclude those who by career are military men.[43]

In the early years of the Occupation, during the surge of idealism inspired by the resurrection of Hiroshima, the unique snubbing of things military perhaps made sense. The Japanese, this time by renouncing war, were still unique and superior morally. As signature of a peace treaty approached and Korea became once again a danger, the chill winds of world power politics blew in on Japan. Blissful and total security, wrapped in American power, might suddenly become less total. Revision of Chapter II, Article 9, became a central topic of discussion.

To go back to March, 1946, however, General MacArthur was obviously proud of the handiwork shown on the Government draft. He called it a "liberal charter" with frailties like all products of human endeavor. He claimed the draft demonstrated how far "we have come since hostilities ended." Actually proof of the progress claimed under the parental "we" was more realistically demonstrated in the reception accorded by Japanese to this phase of democratization.

With the basic dilemma of constitutional reform in mind, *we* should not be too dismayed that some official Japanese placed obstacles in the passage way of the Constitution. Premier Yoshida, whose first Cabinet was formed May 23, 1946, had openly praised the Meiji Constitution as "immutable for all ages"; clearly the Allies had "misinterpreted" the Constitution of 1889. Kanamori Tokujirō, Yoshida's Minister-without-Portfolio, spoke of the new Constitution as "full of flexibilities to respond to the new times as they come in the future." In reply to queries as to where sovereignty lay, under the new Constitution, he reiterated: "Sovereignty exists in the people in general, including the Emperor."[44]

Discussion of the draft by the political parties and the press was lively. The *Nippon Times* of March 9, 1946, set the tone by observing that the

[43] Yanagizawa Y., *Nihonkoku kempō chikujō kōgi,* cited, pp. 146-147. SCAP documents state flatly that the requirement was a result of FEC, particularly British Commonwealth, pressure; *Political Reorientation,* Vol. I, p. 111; Vol. II, Appendices C:14, C:16, pp. 661, 667. For an early comment on Chapter Two, see Yokota Y., *"Sensō no hōki"* (Abandonment of war), *Kokka gakkai zasshi,* Vol. LX, No. 10 (October, 1946), pp. 44-62; on the possibility of renouncing renunciation and its effects, Satō Isaō, *"Chōsen dōran to Kempō no zento"* (The Korean incident and the future of the new Japanese constitution), *Kaizō* (Reconstruction), Vol. XXXI, No. 10 (October, 1950), pp. 18-24. An excellent recent summary is Theodore McNelly, "American Influence and Japan's No-War Constitution," *Political Science Quarterly,* December, 1952.

[44] *Mainichi Shimbun,* June 28, 1946.

charter, whoever drafted it, had to be discussed by the Diet, ". . . which means that the role of the common man and his elected representatives in the process of constitution-making is not finished yet by any means." All of the political parties, with the exception of the Communists, received the draft with surprise and delight. They generally recognized it to be a practical compromise between retention of the *Tennō* and popular sovereignty, between national tradition and democratic principle. The press too, by and large, supported the draft.

There were some complaints, of course. *Tōkyō Shimbun* (April 22, 1946) said of the draft: ". . . Despite its good reputation we feel that something is wanting, for it provides only three articles concerning economics among the total of 100." The *Kahoku Shimpō* (Sendai, April 19, 1946) criticized many of the legal terms used for their lack of definiteness. The authority of the Emperor, not clearly outlined, might be far-reaching. *Mainichi Shimbun* (April 21, 1946) contrasted the emphasis on inviolability of private property in the Japanese draft with provisions in many modern constitutions placing obligations on the owner not to use property against the public interest. A completely new draft, simplified and less wordy in style, was drawn up by a group of Tokyo University professors. An amusing feature was their provision for a House of Councilors made up of intellectuals to check the radicalism of the lower House. More seriously, at a citizens' discussion meeting held May 2, 1946, a former Tokyo Imperial University professor charged the Japanese people with indifference to the problem of revision. "I think it is a significant fact," he said, "that this is the only meeting so far held in Japan to stimulate popular discussion of the Constitution."

A common note in much of the criticism of the Cabinet draft was complaint about the phraseology. The document abounded in redundancy and didactic passages, particularly in the Preamble; it preached too much. It was preoccupied with interests of the moment, for example, the unilateral renunciation of war. Much of the phrasing was so unfamiliar to the average Japanese as to defy comprehension. It should be added that the Legislative Bureau of the Cabinet did considerable redrafting before the Constitution was submitted to the government.[45]

The most significant technical criticism was offered by the noted constitutional lawyer, Dr. Minobe. On the whole, he supported the proposed constitution as one which "does provide Japan with the basis for the establishment of a democratic government." He felt the document went too far, however, in making the Emperor a mere symbol and he deplored failure to

[45] See the *Nippon Times,* March 21, 1946 (Editorial) and the *Asahi Shimbun,* April 18, 1946. The former newspaper on March 30 supplemented its criticism with a report from an elementary school teacher. Out of an entire class of sixth-grade pupils, only two were able to read and reasonably understand the draft. It is a question, the paper hastily added, as to how well even American sixth-grade pupils can read and understand the Constitution of the United States. Then again, perhaps the entire Japanese language needed to be redone for purposes of democracy!

copy the American system of checks and balances as safeguards against hasty legislative action.[46]

In the end, of course, the Japanese adopted the new organic law. On August 24, Ashida Hitoshi, speaking for the government, addressed an appeal to the world to reciprocate Japan's renunciation of war and laid a revised draft before the lower House. Leaders of the major parties followed with statements of support. Katayama Tetsu, soon to be Japan's first Socialist Premier, assented that his party had decided to give support on the basis of the newly asserted pledge that "sovereignty rests with the people." The final draft passed, 421-8. The House of Peers took a little over a month to consider it, and pass it, 298-2. The final version was adopted on October 7 by the House of Representatives, 432-5. After considerable debate in the Privy Council, it was approved at a special session of the Council on October 29 in the presence of the Emperor. On November 3, birthday of the Emperor Meiji, Emperor Hirohito formally promulgated the new Constitution in the Diet. Women legislators were disappointed that the Empress did not attend, but she made up for her absence that afternoon. Two hundred thousand Japanese pushed into the vast plaza between the palace and the Dai Ichi Building, SCAP Headquarters, and thundered welcome as the Imperial couple participated in a brief public ceremony.

Rain marred Constitution Day six months thereafter, when the basic law was formally put in effect. On the same day, May 3, 1947, General MacArthur showed his approval by granting the government once again the right to fly the flag of the Rising Sun without restriction over the nation's public buildings.

The new Constitution, in turn, demanded a complete revamping of Japanese legal codes. The greatest change in law was automatically provided by the Constitution itself, which unequivocally became the nation's supreme law (*saikō hōki;* Chapter X). Beyond that, the reform of Japan's legal system was an undertaking of tremendous scope. To free the Japanese completely, a thorough renovation of all laws was necessary. But the time available was so brief, as SCAP officials explained later, that errors, oversights, and deliberate omissions were inevitable. In the process of revision, Japanese lawyers showed eagerness to learn. They were so eager, in fact, that often they had to be dissuaded from copying Anglo-Saxon law, which would not fit Japan's society. On the other hand, to SCAP's credit, not a single formal directive was issued to the Japanese concerning revision of legal codes.[47]

[46] Minobe's views on fundamental problems of revision were carried in *Hōritsu shimpō* (Legal news), Tōkyō, April and May 1946, among many other journals. His statements, courageous even under the Occupation, were unfortunately his last. In honor of their late President (1873-1948), the *Kokka Gakkai* published *"Minobe sensei no tsuioku"* (Professor Minobe in retrospect) in the *Kokka gakkai zasshi,* cited, Vol. LXII, No. 6 (July 1948). Among colleagues who wrote for the commemorative issue were professors Miyazawa (on Minobe's contributions to legal science), Yanase (on Minobe's views of the new Constitution), and Ukai (Minobe and the study of comparative law).

[47] This statement should not obscure the fact that SCAPINS (SCAP directives) *were* domestic Japanese law. For discussion of constitutional law and legal codes under Meiji

The first priority was revision which would bear directly on Occupation objectives: protection of fundamental rights, guarantee against state interference except for the public welfare, and securing of equality before the law. Administratively, the judiciary had to be transformed into a truly independent branch of government.

Political objectives, and thus priority of revision, did not include improvements in awkward legislative techniques, unreasoning complexity, and strange economic theories, for example. Consequently the first three books of the Civil Code remained virtually unaltered; no over-all revision of the Commercial Code was attempted and here Japanese practices remained untouched. In contrast, some ancient and venerable practices had to be pinched out and subjected to surgery. Thus the House System, founded on centuries of Confucian tradition, on paper fell before new and strange concepts of written, contractual, individual rights. Likewise, the old system of family registration by *koseki*—easily misused for official purposes—legally, if not actually, gave way to new, impersonal, statistical census methods.

The Code of Criminal Procedure (400 articles) required the most backbreaking work. Since here the psychology of the police state was most deeply imbedded, strenuous advisory efforts by SCAP legal experts were necessary to shape a code better suited to the new civil liberties. The most startling, and contested, alteration was in the abolition of the whole chapter providing special penalities for *lèse majesté*. Offenders against the life and honor of the *Tennō*, although they are sure to be caught more efficiently, are now punishable under general provisions of murder, manslaughter, or defamation.[48]

The extent to which certain other legal reforms stick depends on how well a younger generation of judges interprets law in the spirit of the new Constitution. They will have help, of course, for powerful social forces will be at work to help block the vitiation of reforms by regarding them as mere paper statutes. This is particularly true of such statutes as the *Habeas*

government, see Chapter 16 of this book. The size of the postwar job of revision will be realized when it is recalled the previous codes took ten years to draft. Most wartime codes and regulations were suspended in September 1945, and later abolished with the sanction of the Diet. See *Nippon Times,* September 23, 1945. The 92d Diet passed eleven basic laws just prior to adoption of the new Constitution, including "Temporary Adjustments" in the old codes until new ones could be drafted. SCAP's method of collaboration in legal revision consisted of *ad hoc* conferences between Courts and Law Division (Government Section) personnel and various Japanese officials. The following summary is based largely on Government Section's excellent and detailed review, *Political Reorientation,* Vol. I, Section VI, "The Judicial and Legal System" and Vol. II, appropriate appendices.

[48] The Japanese at least never gave up trying to stay the surgeon's knife. Premier Yoshida wrote General MacArthur an eloquent letter on December 27, 1946, in which he pleaded for retention of the *lèse majesté* provisions. After all, even Britain retains special acts relating to violence against the person of the monarch, concluded Yoshida. But the General knew his history. In his reply, February 25, 1947, MacArthur pointed out that the Statute of Treasons, ordained under Edward III, "is a remnant of and derived from the age of Germanic feudalism" and has never been applied in modern times. As "symbol" of the state, made up of the people, it is particularly appropriate that the Emperor be accorded the same protection as is given each of his subjects, concluded the Supreme Commander. See SCAP, *ibid.,* Vol. II, Appendix C:23, pp. 679-680.

Corpus Act of July 1, 1948. Law itself—as Americans well know—can provide a legitimate vested interest among its practitioners. Lawyers and bar associations played an active part in Japanese constitutional reform and legal revision. And if the lawyers do not develop fast enough or slip back into the folds of bureaucracy, there is always the new Japanese Civil Liberties Union established in November, 1947, after a timely visit by Secretary-General Roger M. Baldwin of the American Union.

Profile of the Occupation. The Occupation of Japan began on September 2, 1945, and ended on April 28, 1952, on which occasion the Japanese Chargé d'Affaires in Washington, D.C., paid a formal call on the Department of State in symbolic demonstration of the fact that Japan had once again regained independent diplomatic access to the nations of the world and that the Japanese were no longer bound to communicate officially with the rest of mankind through the channels of SCAP. Not quite seven years in length, the Occupation was as important for what happened outside Japan as for what occurred within Japan.

Basically the Occupation started out as the attempted redesign of Japan to fit into a community of nations under a proposed United Nations system. The system as proposed did not materialize. The power-political conflict which had been trilateral among the democracies, the Axis states, and the Communist world, and which had finally degenerated into World War II, was replaced by an entirely comparable bilateral series of conflicts in which the Communist world gained enormous successes at the expense of its democratic allies and launched enough attacks on its democratic allies to compel the creation of an anti-Communist political and strategic system. In other words, the Japan of 1945 was designed to fit into one world, a single world in which Communists and democrats could coexist. The China of 1949 collapsed. The Korea of 1950 became a scene of war. All around the world, the one world of San Francisco planners was replaced by the two worlds of the Politburo and the Truman Doctrine.

Americans and Japanese have, as one of their few shared political traits, an undue respect for the legal formula and an extraordinary confidence in the power of law, even when law is unsupported by political behavior, social action, economic operations, or even common custom. Once Americans and Japanese had embarked upon the inexpressibly quaint and idealistic partnership of making Japan a tutelary democracy for a world destined never to exist, neither Americans nor Japanese were ready to give up the ideal formula and to create in its stead a formal legal system which would make Japan a flexible, tough, fighting member of the anti-Communist team of nations. To do so would have been to admit in form as well as in fact that there was a fight between Washington and Moscow. Tokyo certainly did not wish to get into any more conflicts than necessary, and neither General MacArthur overseas nor the American authorities at home were anxious to reverse the direction of Japanese political change in any sudden, humiliating, or reactionary-looking way.

Taken as a whole, the Occupation was an amazing success when measured against the political history of the times in which it occurred. Everywhere else in the world there was a downgrading of expectations, a relinquishment of high hopes, a retrogression from expected freedoms. In Japan, without much fanfare, the economic reconstruction of the country proceeded at a rapid pace—with massive American help, of course. Americans and Japanese, as far apart in the formal tenets of their thinking as Jesuits and Yogis, managed with good faith and practical sincerity to create an astonishing partnership. Under the Occupation, Americans and Japanese worked out financial and military questions very quietly and to common satisfaction.

Some of the credit for this must go to the remarkable personality of General of the Army Douglas MacArthur. It can be said that, for purposes of the military aspects of the Occupation, American society happened to produce a man fitted by temperament and experience to be a great viceroy at the one and only time in American history that the United States needed to export a viceroy. Much of the credit also must go to the Japanese themselves, who showed their usual resiliency and flexibility even in the face of unprecedented defeat. As to the long-run effects of the Occupation—political and economic—no one who has read the previous chapters should dare to predict the manner in which the Japanese themselves will absorb and reshape the influences of so-called democratization. A few trends, quite visible in the immediate post-treaty period, will be summarized below. Suffice it to say here that, fortunately or unfortunately, the Occupation affected the deep roots of Japanese society—as did the Meiji transformation—probably very little. In this light, the greatest fault of the men of SCAP—and it is perhaps a pardonable fault—was that, having performed a creditable military task, they claimed entirely too sweeping changes as a result of their "induced revolution." Perhaps no military occupation has ever been successful in that sense. Japan, with centuries' experience at absorption, was therefore both the most difficult country to reform and the easiest to occupy.

The international aspects of the Occupation faded slowly away. The increasing bitterness of the cold war and the weighty strategic responsibilities placed upon the United States for the defense of what was left of Free Northeast Asia reduced the amount of criticism heard from the other Allied powers. The Russians, abusive as always, were in no position to give legal, economic, or military weight to their criticisms of the policies in Japan.

By and large the Occupation demonstrated an astonishing American capacity to come to grips with Japanese problems as long as these problems were simple, humane, and tangible in character. On the Japanese side, the Occupation demonstrated very clearly that Japanese with high professional qualifications could deal with Americans less well educated, less experienced, and with less knowledge than themselves, without injuring American self-esteem and without allowing themselves to become cynical or bitter in the process. After the first year or so of the Occupation, many of the most talented Americans went home. These were the men who had serious civilian careers awaiting them. The men who stayed on were impelled, sometimes by patriotism, in that they were first-class men who rejected the far better career opportunities in the continental United States for the sake of their duty to the army or their duty, as they saw it, to the Japanese people. A far greater number consisted of Americans who were capable, but far from outstanding; such men discovered that with modest experience and reasonable capabilities they were capable of playing a very grand role in Japan when a return home would have meant serious demotion. Curiously enough, even the less qualified American did fairly well, and the Occupation ended without a single bloody clash between Americans and Japanese and with neither nation considering itself the victim of atrocities or deception practiced by the other. To put it in an unfamiliar context, the Occupation can be said to be as admirable for the misfortunes which did not occur as for the practical results which were accomplished. Any nation with a big army and navy can find some other nation to occupy; few nations can get out of an occupation with so much good-will on both sides as did the Americans of 1945-1952.

CHAPTER TWENTY-ONE

The Western Democracy in Japanese Form (Occupation Government and Politics, II)

THE government of Japan under the Occupation followed the great tradition of adaptation, importation, and consolidation, which the Japanese have followed on other occasions in their history. The Japanese had a Western democracy, a democracy which possessed many links with the parliamentary empire which Japan imported in the Meiji period, but one which had even more resemblance to America. The America which provided the model for this Japan was not the real-life America in which the citizens of the United States actually lived; it was, rather, a projection of America—a dream-America which might have come to being had the United Nations system worked out as it was originally planned.

The Western democracy set forth to Japanese eyes by the Occupation was indeed a remarkable country, full of American paradoxes, far more subtle and mysterious than anything which the Japanese mind could have worked out by itself. A social democracy by profession of constitutional clauses, it made no provision for the implementation of the economic, social, and extra-political democracy of the proposed new Japanese society. It can be said that, in a sense, Japan under MacArthur represented the high-water mark of the New Deal in world affairs, and that the democratization of Japan involved attacks on big business, prejudice against capitalism, the encouragement of labor unions, the juridical attack on social inequalities, and other New Deal features to an extent to which neither President Roose-

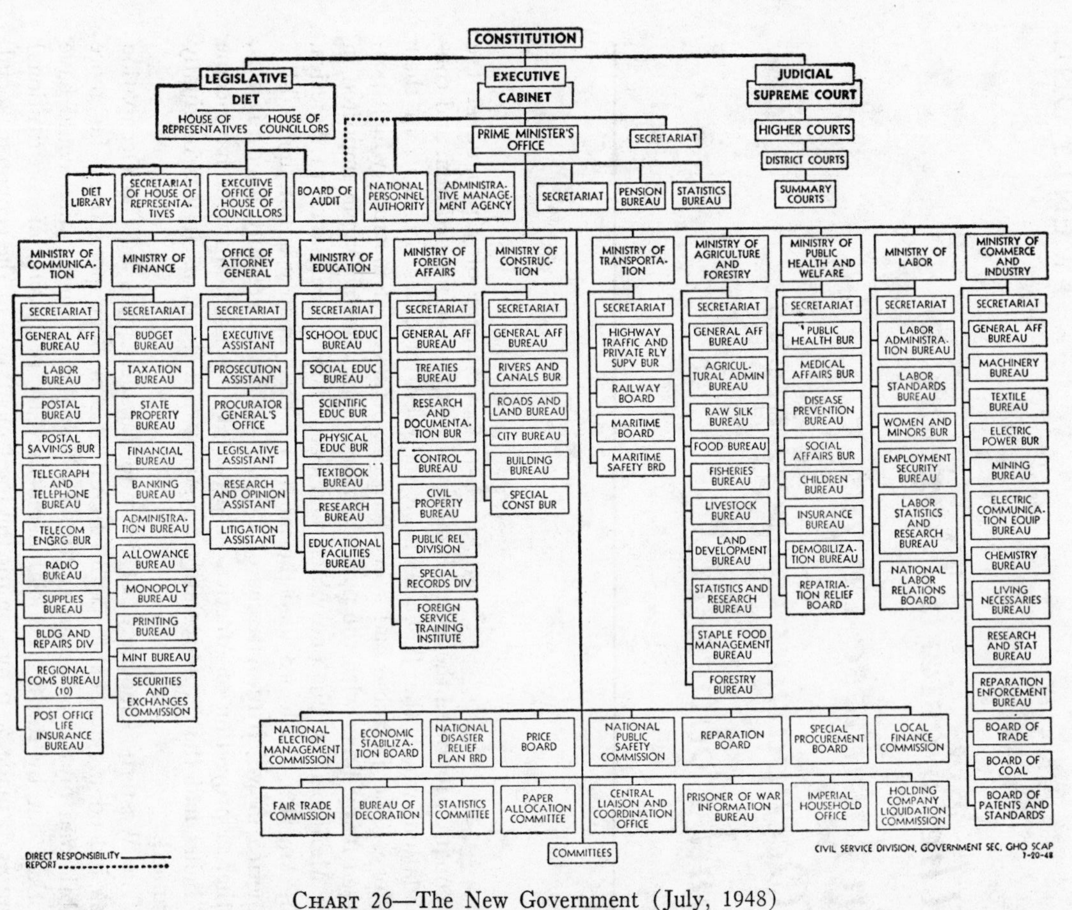

CHART 26—The New Government (July, 1948)

Source: Govt. Sec., SCAP, *Political Reorientation*, Vol. I, cited, p. viii.

velt nor President Truman ever carried the prototypical New Deal. These American forms cannot be taken as a meaningless mimicry of a conqueror's institutions, at the one extreme, nor as familiar and long-tested political features of a going government, at the other extreme.

As so often before in their history, the Japanese have allowed their own ways of doing things and their own institutional structures with which to do them to flow fluidly into new channels, retaining a singular Japanese vitality, absorbing much of the good of the new system, but giving it a nature which is still quite essentially Japanese. Preposterous though it may have been, for example, to destroy the most ancient nobility in the world (*kuge*) while retaining an Emperor whose pretensions to monarchical authority were little better grounded than the *kuge* pretensions to aristocratic prestige, the Japanese accepted American paradoxes and, having resolved to "endure the unendurable," they did what they had to do whether it seemed to make sense or not. Out of this curious mélange of Japanese and Western institutions the Japanese have come forth with a composite which enjoys a vitality far beyond rational explanation. In recent decades it was often said in the West that China as a political entity was almost immortal because the Chinese had the capacity to absorb and survive the processes of foreign conquest; it can be said, perhaps no less provocatively, that the Japanese in the past have learned the talents of absorbing exterior political challenges with the result that Japan can change its political forms over and over again, but still end up with an implicit continuity of political tradition. Putting the matter another way, one can say that the patterns of Japanese statecraft change, but that the basic design of Japanese culture remains.

The Japan that was an Anglophile monarchy forty years ago and a pseudo-Hitlerite dictatorship (at least in appearance) a decade ago is today a characteristic Western democracy, no farther distant from American patterns than is Belgium or Denmark. Yet, somehow, it *is* still Japanese.[1]

The Unofficially Divine Emperor. Constitutionally the Emperor has been deprived of all the powers of government which he previously enjoyed. Indeed, Hirohito wrote his own preamble to democratization in a famous Imperial Rescript of January 1, 1946. In this amazing message he rejected his own Imperial Divinity; only the future can tell whether this rejection may not have confirmed in the minds of many Japanese the very special invulnerability of Japanese monarchy to verbal or logical attack. He further declared to be false the doctrine that the Japanese were superior to other peoples or destined to rule the world.

The Constitution carried the process further. The Meiji Constitution of 1889 had declared the Emperor to be "sacred and inviolable," but the new

[1] The chart on page 488 presents an interesting view of the new government, drawn by the Information Division of the new National Personnel Authority *(Jinji-in)*, January 1949. Two features of the chart should be noted. First, the Emperor was omitted entirely; second, the branches were arranged in such a way as to reflect the American principle of separation of powers, absent in any parliamentary-cabinet regime.

Constitution specifically described the Emperor as "the symbol of the state and of the unity of the people, deriving his position from the will of the people with whom resides sovereign power." The immense reserve powers left to the Emperor by the Meiji Constitution were withdrawn and, like the King of the Belgians and other European monarchs, the Japanese Emperor is to perform all state functions only on the basis of the advice and approval of the Cabinet.

The duties changed. The title remained. The new Constitution used the same term for Emperor as had the Meiji Constitution: *Tennō,* or "Heavenly Lord."

Even preceding the redefinition of Imperial prerogatives, the Japanese eliminated old inner circles of advisory influence which before Pearl Harbor transmitted itself mysteriously from outside the Imperial palace through unchallengeable and unmentionable Imperial channels and back into the workaday government. The most conspicuous political institution to go was, of course, the Privy Council, but with it went the *jūshin,* the Lord Privy Seal, the Imperial Household Ministry, the Ministry of War, the Ministry of the Navy, and the elaborate hierarchy of half-independent service government. The Imperial Household Ministry became a mere subdivision of the Premier's office. A new Imperial Family Council (*Kōshitsu Kaigi*) consists of a mere two members of the Imperial family, the President and Vice-President of each house of the Diet, the Premier, the Chief of the New Imperial Household Office, the Chief Judge and one other Judge of the Supreme Court.

The Shōwa Emperor is a long way from the phantom monarchy enjoyed with such obvious impotence as the Annamite role of Bao Dai or the Manchukuoan role of that ill-fated emperor, "Mr. Henry Pu Yi." The adaptability of the Imperial institution itself was nowhere better illustrated than in the fact that Mrs. Elizabeth Vining, a Quaker lady of irreproachable manners and intelligence, who possessed a purity of democratic outlook which made her *persona grata* to the State Department, General MacArthur, and the Japanese Government all at once, trained the Crown Prince Akihito in how to be a Western democratic boy, Imperial Japanese model. Father, mother, and son in the Imperial family all act as though they were mere du Ponts or Bourbons instead of being the descendants of kings once contemporary with the Ptolemies and the heirs of men who fought off Kublai Khan.

Similarly, the Japanese Emperor today has lost the support of a formal state religion, but the very fact that he exists in terms of a diffuse and historically well-grounded tradition implies that, given luck for the nation and talent for the world's only uninterrupted dynasty, the Japanese monarchy may survive past this age as it has survived through so many other ages of mankind. If one accepts the kind of approach to culture so brilliantly set forth by Ruth Benedict in her *Patterns of Culture* and *The Chrysanthemum and the Sword,* Japan's revolution will have to reach psychiatric depths before the subsurface convulsions of Japanese everyday life change the meaning of authority so thoroughly as to make the Emperor meaningless or unneeded.

The Emperor, Society, Politics. One feature in Japanese life may be construed as an ultra-long-range threat to the Imperial power. This is the legal emancipation of women, a change in the status of a class which is, for the purposes of world history, perhaps comparable to the Emancipation Proclamation of 1863. While liberation of American slaves affected all the whites by removing the concealed uncertainties of American political philosophy and affected all the Negroes by making them insecure citizens instead of hopelessly secure bondmen, the emancipation of Japanese women will involve not only all the women of Japan, but all the men as well. The political emancipation of women, their juridical enablement to own property, the formal legal change in their own status—all these mean that the Japanese are going to have subsequent generations of their people grow up with a different pattern of family authority and a new diagram of deference. The extraordinary stratification which applied even in the smallest household could be broken at its source. Quietly, though resolutely, Japanese women are beginning to respond to the liberation. The right to vote is the least of the changes involved in the emancipation of Japanese women. Far more important is the gradual change in the attitude of men toward women, the lessening of the responsibility of men for authority over women, the relaxation of the intra-family controls, and the general loosening of Japanese behavior.

The Japanese Emperor has been the genuinely potent capstone of an elaborate human pyramid. The secularization of the Imperial Office did little more than to change the luster of that capstone, but the legal emancipation of women may have shaken the very base of the pyramid.

Interconnections of Japanese society and politics are demonstrated nowhere more vividly than by two points, which can be selected from among thousands of others for purposes of illustration, as follows: first, the ethics taught in the schools; second, the use of the Emperor's portrait in the educational scheme.

Before Pearl Harbor the ethics taught in Japanese elementary schools were authoritarian and loyalist. In modern times these ethics had been ultra-nationalist and militarist in flavor. Under the Tokugawa they had been feudal and loyalist. Before the Tokugawa they had been loyally feudal and still loyalist, and so on all the way back to the very beginnings of Japan. After surrender, ethics were not taught in the schools. Japanese teachers could not conscientiously teach the ethics of American grade schools, and they were afraid of being purged if they taught the traditional *bushidō* of the Japanese. Throughout the Occupation and even after Japan resumed diplomatic relations with other nations, ethics was simply left out of the curriculum and parents taught their children any way they dared. Without a divine Emperor as an object of loyalty, without a striking past as a topic for veneration, without a disciplined and patriotic future as a subject for training, how could small Japanese boys be inculcated with the very special ethics of Japan?

Down to the time of surrender, the picture of the Emperor was the focal point of every Japanese school building. In the event of fire it was the duty of the school principal to remove the Emperor's picture first and to save the children's lives later. To avoid such embarrassing dichotomies of loyalty, the Emperor's portrait was often put in a specially built shrine in the school yard, but no matter how cheap the picture, it was always treated as the most valuable single possession of the school. Under Occupation, Japanese schools were forbidden to have ceremonial pictures of the Emperor, although "mere" pictures of the Emperor were treated like any other artistic portrait. Americans living out among the Japanese population away from the sophisticated cosmopolitan centers would be wise to observe the minutiae of Japanese behavior in relation to these pictures and to see whether ordinary Japanese teachers and children in everyday life show a propensity to treat these pictures as being once again divine.

Amid cultural stimuli such as these, multiplied a millionfold, the future of the Japanese Empire must be found. It is unlikely that the *Tennō* himself is certain of the future of his dynasty. The one sure thing about the Japanese Throne is that the Japanese traditionalists made a point of the monarchy at the moment of surrender, that the surrender was carried out largely through the good offices of the monarchy, that the monarchy has cut itself free of formal religion and is in a sense able to start with clear books.

The unofficial divinity of the Japanese Emperor will obviously not be decided by political decisions which specifically allude to the Throne itself. The future of the Empire is tied in most closely with the evolution or decline of the Western democracy in Japanese form and with the compromises which Japanese are going to have to make between the deep well of their ideographic literature, their cultural tradition, the religious, political, and philosophical demands placed upon their sense of "sharing in the destinies of mankind" which the near future will bring. If the Western democracy now operating in Japan remains the prevailing political system with a slight tendency to gravitate toward the renewed exercise of the full rights of sovereignty, including such rights as armed national self-defense, of patriotic self-esteem, and of confidence in the mission of one's nation—all of them rights *not* enumerated in the Constitution—it is entirely possible that the Throne will rise in importance. If, on the other hand, Japan undergoes the slow inward collapse of all morality other than the transparently rational, as did so much of Germany under the Weimar Republic, it is possible that the Imperial institution will move along with the rest of Japan into what can be termed a state of active decay, that state epitomized by

Sebastian de Grazia when he resurrected the fine old Renaissance term *anomie* to describe peoples in a condition of "governedlessness."

Particulars of the Imperial role were evident even in the Occupation period. The *Minshū Kyōiku* (Democratic Education) for April, 1946, summed up the Japanese feeling neatly: "Devotion to the Emperor transcends logic. It is a tradition."

The Imperial Institution. Because the tradition of Imperial rule is in truth the all-encompassing "symbol of the state and of the unity of the people," the postwar Emperor can be observed from several different angles. It is impossible even for purposes of evaluation to slice up so complex a social, religious, and political institution and to subdivide ideological phenomena which are as important emotionally as they are rationally, if not more so. Nevertheless, that is precisely what the logical Western conquerors of Japan did do, and Hirohito, who in this respect (as in so many others) authentically represented most Japanese, did what he was told by the Occupation authorities.

Economic and financial holdings of the Imperial family were easiest to handle. The Family Council, like the *Zaibatsu,* was completely reorganized. Even in dissolution, however, the Imperial wealth was dedicated to public welfare in practice rather than in theory. The household holdings—which had been estimated by SCAP officials at a value of one and a half billion yen—became state property. The fabulous Imperial crown jewelry was made the base for a revolving fund to finance desperately needed imports. In their first joint press conference on June 3, 1947, the Imperial couple proudly described their food as being the same as that granted other Japanese under existing rationing conditions.

The social (or, in the Western sense, religious) aspects of the *Tennō* system were a little harder to deal with. Some authorities, even including some Japanese writers, have never conceded that the concept of Emperor-God was ever wholly accepted by the Japanese people. Sir George Sansom has said that he never met a Japanese who believed that the Emperor was really and truly of divine descent. In common with the Chinese of old, the modern Japanese have regarded their *Tennō* as a sort of ever-present intercessor between them and the world of spirits or, in modern terms, the world of the unknown. The role of the Emperor in the surrender lessened their formal dependence and may have increased their psychological dependence on the Throne. At its very worst the Japanese Imperial tradition is a socio-psychological phenomenon larger than, but not qualitatively different from, the complex body of good and bad luck superstitions which can be found more or less subject to practice in almost all strata of American society.

The informal divinity of the post-surrender Emperor meant that the Throne was not seriously damaged by the SCAP directive which disestablished State Shintō (*Kokka Shintō*). Courses in morals were suspended at all levels of the educational system. The new pictures of Hirohito for the schools did not show him in uniform and were not put in the role of shrine centers. The last Japanese premier to make the pilgrimage to the Grand Shrine of Japan at Ise (that is, the last before signature of the peace treaty) was Baron Shidehara who reported to the Sun Goddess on October 24, 1945. SCAP ran a frustrating succession of minor skirmishes with Japanese communities which continued to support Shintō shrines and festivals informally and in other undemocratic ways attempted to maintain their most ancient social traditions.[2]

The postwar British have come through with a George VI and an Elizabeth II; they have kept up their national morale by salvaging as much as they can from the disappointments of their Imperial tradition. The Russians, who became atheists in order to avoid a czardom which was as heavy-handed in religious matters as it was in the political field, came forth with the late Comrade Stalin, whose ego transcended that of any czar and whose ceremonial demands far exceeded the liturgical requirements of even a church-infatuated reactionary like Pobiedonostsev. The Japanese find solace with the symbolism of their Emperor; as long as the *Tennō* fills the emotional needs of the Japanese considered as a single mass group, Japan may be protected from some of the more gross psychological temptations offered by fanatical aspirants to dictatorship.

The third phase of the Imperial institution, the political, has undergone substantial change.

It is apparent from earlier chapters that Japanese emperors have often been shields behind which ruling oligarchies fashioned the nation for their own purposes. The significant political characteristic of the *Tennō* is not, therefore, that the Emperor has really controlled Japanese government, but that the ordinary Japanese people have always *thought* it was controlled in his name. The Occupation did not actually do much to disturb this concept. The question of retaining the Emperor lapsed into silence in Western forums; Japanese debaters followed suit.

The Occupation at first retained the Emperor because of his utility in speeding the surrender. He was later retained for reasons foreign to the original policy of the United States, namely, for the purpose of stabilizing Japan against wholesale or violent renovation which might favor the Communists. When the Americans used the Emperor, they were doing nothing which Japanese politicians had not done before them.

The role of the Emperor under the Occupation cannot be described with any accuracy as a reflection of the desire of the Allies to be in accord with the wishes of the people of Japan. While the Japanese at large would undoubtedly still have voted to keep the Emperor, they were not so unanimous in their interpretation of his role that the Allied policy can be regarded as

[2] The original SCAP disestablishment directive is reproduced in Japanese in *NKHK*, Vol. I, No. 6 (September 1, 1946), pp. 29-34, as is the Memorandum suspending Courses in *Shūshin*, pp. 42-43. SCAP's recognition of continued support of *Shintō* is embodied in a directive of November 6, 1946, *ibid.*, No. 16 (January 20, 1948), pp. 9-11.

acquiescence and nothing more. The Allied policy is perhaps best described as one of inertia—an inertia prompted by the increasing threats from the Communist world near by.[3]

The Japanese themselves were often willing to reappraise and reorganize the *Tennō* system. In May, 1946, the press was highly critical of Hirohito's first experiment with live radio broadcasting. In August, 1946, the Emperor's constitutional role was frankly debated and the *Yomiuri Shimbun* predicted that sooner or later the *Tennō* system would have to be liquidated. (That particular editorial staff of the *Yomiuri Shimbun* was liquidated two years later by the bloodless process of being fired from their jobs; the Emperor remained.) On December 6, 1948, a Japanese Emperor was publicly rebuked for the first time in the history of Japan. The Diet criticized him for having represented himself abroad as the symbol of the nation because he had dared to send a private congratulatory message to President-elect Truman.

The Japanese Emperor in the new Western democracy of Japan has voluntarily assumed a role similar to that of the British King. The Japanese Emperor does not even have the support offered to the British monarchy by the social prestige of the aristocracy.[4] The Imperial tradition remains, and it is an open question as to whether bureaucrats or politicians will get the chief lead in doing that which had been done throughout Japanese history: cloaking practical power in the all-inspiring prestige of the Imperial cult.

Tone and Morale of the Postwar Government. It was not only the Imperial institution of occupied Japan which, while remaining Japanese, took on a new form. The Western democracy which the Japanese attempted to incorporate into their body politic was singularly hedged about by imponderables more massive in their effect than the sharp distinctions of public law which define the government's responsibilities to the people, to other governments, and to the community of nations at large.

Chief, of course, among these imponderables was the strange power-political situation of Japan in world affairs. If the Japanese were capable of attaching immense tugboats to their islands and of pulling the entire empire across the Pacific so that Japan could lie safely anchored off the

[3] In February of 1946, *Asahi Shimbun* took a poll of the intelligentsia, probably the most anti-*Tennō* group in Japan, and found that 80 per cent favored retention of the Imperial institution, with modifications. A modern, sophisticated view of the tradition was presented previously in Chapter One, pp. 264-266; a good survey of postwar opinion is contained in Genji Okubo, *The Problems of the Emperor System in Postwar Japan,* cited. For an earlier, non-Western view of the necessity for abolition of the Emperor, see Sun Fo [the son of Dr. Sun Yat-sen], "The Mikado Must Go," *Foreign Affairs,* October 1944, p. 23.

[4] Eventually Japan's *Kazoku* may lapse into the status of White Russian counts; their descendants, into "Sons of the Satsuma Secession." According to an *Asahi Shimbun* story of February 7, 1946, the blue-blooded scion of one illustrious family, a viscount, opened a prosperous delicatessen store dealing in pickles and dried fish. "Clad in a white apron and *soroban* in hand, he is in efficient charge, from stocking up on merchandise to a courteous and diplomatic management of customers and shop girls in his simple shop of only about 10 *tsubo.*"

coast of Chile, they would undoubtedly remove themselves from a critical and dangerous strategic position and could aspire under such circumstances to the role of a Switzerland. The islands were, alas, immovable; the Japanese, whether they liked it or not, lived encamped at the mid-point of one of the world's greatest highways of destruction. Japan in terms of latitude, longitude, relation to the continent, relation to the pattern of world sea power, and juxtaposition to the land forces of the Asiatic portion of the U.S.S.R., could either become Russia's chief channel for a major break-through of Soviet power into the Pacific Ocean area or, alternatively, could remain what Japan is in fact today—America's permanent beachhead in the Western Pacific. No domestic consideration of Japanese politics could possibly have been as portentous as this. Japan's strategic position was subject to modification by the Japanese themselves only if they wished to undertake some of the riskiest and most dangerous gambles in the history of modern international relations. It was difficult to be pro-Soviet without being devoured by Soviet ideological control and enclosed by the real Iron Curtain, the Iron Curtain which Russia called her "strategic requirements for a safe outer perimeter."

Both for the present and for the longer-range future the Japanese can accept the benefits of membership in a free world system at the price of strategic affiliation with the anti-Communist nations, or Japan can essay the extraordinary hazards of trying to go a lonely national way between the two competing power-political systems. In this respect, Japan's position is entirely different from that of Indonesia. The Indonesian cabinet can view the world from the vantage point of geographical remoteness from the major battlegrounds of any possible war between the American and Russian blocs of nations; the Indonesians have a seller's market for their raw materials and, although they may not always get the price they expect, they can come very close to autarchy without any serious risk of general famine. An Indonesian foreign minister can therefore allow himself the privilege of talking and thinking in neutralist terms while a Japanese foreign minister cannot.

The tone of Japanese postwar government was, therefore, necessarily flavored by Japan's diplomatic orientation and by Japan's relationship to the semi-wars which were likely to recur in the foreseeable future or the general war which hangs like a threat over the heads of all mankind. It would be unrealistic in the extreme for the Japanese to devise a pattern of government which was hopelessly at variance with the realities of world power. The Japanese were obligated, so long as a pattern of sovereign states existed, to insure the survival of their own people by maintaining a viable role in one of the several economic systems which were available. And of these economic systems the only one which offered the Japanese serious promise of maintaining a reasonable standard of living was the free enterprise system supported and maintained by the power and wealth of the United States.

The limits of Japanese domestic politics were therefore bounded in terms of policies which fell short of alienating or antagonizing American opinion; at the very worst, extreme Right-wing policies might lead to a temporary short-run common interest of the U.S. and the U.S.S.R. in getting rid of Japanese neo-militarists who were so unfortunate as to arouse the wrath of Moscow and Washington at the same time. By contrast, the limits on the Left of Japanese domestic policy were measured by how much the United States could stand before a policy of economic abandonment, rejection, or reprisal was undertaken. It was unimaginable that the Japanese should, short of recovering strategic and economic control of Manchuria or a comparable area elsewhere in the world (and there seemed to be no comparable areas available), become economically self-sufficient enough to pay their own way.[5]

There was a middle ground in Japanese affairs delimited by the dangerous extremes of Right and Left within which the issues of Japanese domestic and foreign policy were fought out. No Japanese cabinet or prime minister could go far outside this ground without imperiling the permanent security of the nation and without risking the fall of his own cabinet, not to mention the finish of his personal political career. A Fascist Japan was therefore almost unimaginable; so too was an ultra-Leftist Japan short of surrender to and absorption in the Soviet system. A neutralist Japan would have involved wild hazards, since some kind of United States underwriting of the Japanese economy appeared to be a requisite for Japanese survival.

It must be admitted that nations learn not only from their own experience, but from the experience of their neighbors. The Japanese have learned the extraordinary expensiveness of aggressive war in terms of their own disasters of 1941-1945. As witnesses, rather than as participants, they may have learned the dreadful price which must be paid by any Asian nation so hastily bent upon achieving economic democracy as to receive Communist

[5] The most detailed study has already been cited, Jerome B. Cohen's *Japan's Economy in War and Reconstruction,* especially Chap. 7, "The Economy under Occupation." To add to his already wide experience in so few years, Dr. Cohen served on the United States (Shoup) Tax Mission to Japan, April-August 1949. More recently, for the Center of International Studies, Princeton University (Frederick S. Dunn, Director), Dr. Cohen has taken a second and, on the whole, more optimistic look at Japan's economy: *Economic Problems of Free Japan,* Princeton, 1952. For example, "If Japanese rice yields could be raised to the levels attained by Spain, Italy and Australia in the thirties, Japan's present dependence upon imports for 20 per cent of its food consumed could be largely eliminated" (p. 11). Again (pp. 80-84), Dr. Cohen comes close to abandoning his former view that Japan *must* trade with China.

Among numerous specialized studies issued by SCAP, the series issued by Natural Resources Section on Japan's resources and industries is excellent. For specific aspects of the economics of the Occupation, see issues of *Pacific Affairs,* for example: Miriam Farley, "Labor Policy in Occupied Japan" (June 1947); Andrew J. Grad, "Land Reform in Japan" (June 1948); Shigeto Tsuru, "Toward Economic Stability in Japan" (December 1949). Both Miss Farley and Mr. Grad served briefly with the Occupation. Mr. Tsuru, Harvard-educated and reputed economic brain behind the Socialist "White Paper" of 1947, is presently Professor of Economics, Tokyo University of Commerce.

dictatorship along with the democracy in a package deal. The Japan of 1945 or of 1946 might have been tempted to the folly of the kind of chimerical Communist-and-anti-Communist coalition so attractively urged upon China at the time of the Marshall mission, but the Japan of the 1950's saw that "coalition" with Communists meant extinction for all political leadership and all intellectual and social groups which were not abjectly servile in terms of Communist dogma.

Beneath their glaze of heroism and romance, Japanese national policies in the past have often been earthy, practical, and realistic. The Japanese would like to have the combined pleasures of an admirable ideological role, a fitting part in the drama of nations, together with an adequate livelihood in terms of mere production, crudely practical imports and exports, and humdrum cash balances. The Japanese are no more fools than are the Scots and English; they like their pageantry, but they like everyday life equally. The Japanese are not likely to give up concessions which are essential to their everyday well-being for the sake of attaining a flamboyant effect in international politics. They can leave to the Indians, the Indonesians, the Iranians, and other Asian nations the achievements of the grand effects and can themselves concentrate on being prosperous.

Japan could return to the world of international affairs with a high degree of vitality only by breaking through the ceiling or floor of Japan's relations with the United States. Japan might have hoped to perform so superlatively well as to become a real working member of the free nation system, a great power in its own right once again, a positive and esteemed contributor to the economic welfare and strategic security of the free world. At the other extreme, Japan might have feared bankruptcy or near bankruptcy by short-sighted American tariff policies, or an unintelligent aid program which did not keep the Japanese economy vigorous and effective; Japan might have been driven into drama through sheer desperation; the leaders of such a Japan might have tried to play a power-political role among nations simply because the desperate position of their country gave them no alternative. Neither of these choices was immediate.

The Rule of Sobriety. The functioning, therefore, of the Diet and of the Cabinet was framed by policies which were far narrower than the imaginable range of Japanese choices. Minor groups at Right and Left, from time to time, made it appear that the Japanese were willing to undertake radical or serious experimentation with their domestic structure or with their strategic position. This did not happen. Instead, the major parties of Japan represented serious, sober interests of the Japanese people as seen by the successive combinations of bureaucrats, businessmen, labor officials, intellectuals, and a few re-emergent defense officials.[6]

[6] Appendix 18 presents a chronological list of premiers, with the dates of their cabinets, down to surrender; and a complete roster of cabinets in the postwar era. The author of this section would like to acknowledge here his use of material on the first two years of the Occupation, drawn from Robert Braden and Ardath Burks, Editors, in collaboration

The last year of the Occupation and the beginning of the post-treaty period were certainly marked by an extreme of sobriety. The Yoshida cabinet reflected not merely the personality of Mr. Yoshida himself; it represented Japanese national attitudes. The Japanese did virtually nothing in world affairs except to espouse the most irreproachable international causes. They issued few policy pronouncements. They swung to no extreme at home. They put up with the world as they found it. While the Diet remained rather sharply outspoken about the security agreement between the United States and Japan, there was something not far from unanimity among Japanese when it came to the belief that Japan could not afford the luxuries of controversy whenever the controversy involved alienating powerful friends, making dangerous enemies, or risking actual money. The Socialists objected to various provisions in the final treaty, for example, but they did not carry their objections to the point of an attempted filibuster in the Diet or a really major party political crisis for the country at large.

Diet and Cabinet. Under the *Shin Kempō* (see pages 477-480), the Diet consists entirely of elected representatives of the people, acts as the "highest organ of state power," constitutes the "sole law-making organization of the state," and thus legally inherits the powers stripped from the Emperor (Chapter IV of the new Constitution, especially Article 41). Members of the House of Representatives (*Shūgi-in*) hold office for four years unless the house is dissolved. Those in the House of Councilors (*Sangi-in*) hold office for six years, with half of the membership coming up every three years. The two houses together comprise the Diet (*Kokkai*) and must be convoked at least once in every year; extraordinary sessions may be called. When the House of Representatives is dissolved, there must be a general election within forty days and the new Diet must be convoked within a month of the election.[7]

In the new parliamentary system the upper house is clearly subordinated to the lower. A bill becomes law upon passage by both houses; when proposed legislation is passed by the Representatives and rejected by the Councilors it still becomes law when repassed by two thirds of the lower house.[8]

---

with John Allen, Donald Jordan, Gordon King, and Betty Stein, *Japan—Two Years After,* Washington: School of Advanced International Studies, 1947 (typescript), a seminar project under the direction of Professor Paul M. A. Linebarger.

[7] The 1947 elections, most significant in Japan's post-surrender politics short of the end of the Occupation, were exhaustively studied by the Division of Research for Far East (DRF), Office of Intelligence Research, Department of State: *An Analysis of the 1947 Japanese House of Representatives Election* (OIR Report No. 4310), Washington, September 1, 1947; and *The 1947 Japanese House of Councillors Election* (OIR Report No. 4334), Washington, January 15, 1948 (both Restricted; declassified March 14, 1949). OIR pointed to the following trends: (1) a marked growth of absenteeism, in contrast with previous enthusiastic voter participation; (2) emergence of fresh, if untried, leadership; (3) a decline in Communist influence; and (4) the emergence of the first Socialist leadership in Japan's history.

[8] There is an interesting disagreement at this point between two of the three authors of this text, Dr. Djang remaining neutral. Professor Burks believes that the Japanese parliamentary system, while far from perfect, represents at least a scaffolding for a democracy in our own time. Professor Linebarger regards the present constitution of the House of Coun-

Under the new Constitution the fifth chapter (especially Article 66) clearly demonstrates the subordination of executive power to legislative authority. This chapter provides for the Cabinet (*Naikaku*). Within the *Naikaku* the Premier (*Sōri-daijin*) is very distinctly the most important single individual—with the test of practical experience making the Premier even more important perhaps than the American and Japanese drafters of the new Constitution themselves anticipated.

The elimination of the multiple quasi-executive agencies which were mysteriously conglomerated around the pre-surrender Throne leaves the Cabinet and the Premier in a sharply clean-cut position. Although the Premier is considerably less powerful than his wartime predecessor was in terms of his strength *against* the wishes of the Diet, he is, on the other hand, considerably more powerful, in terms of his independence of any *other* executive official. The Emperor's executive powers have been, from a legalistic point of view, completely nullified, although it is up to the test of time for the Japanese to determine what the implicit powers of the Emperor may be and how these may be exercised without definite reference to constitutional or statutory requirements.

The lack of a strong continuing executive is obviously borrowed from the Third French Republic and is in marked contrast to the older Japanese system. Under the Occupation Constitution, the Premier and Cabinet both were responsible to the Diet. The Premier himself was appointed by the Diet and he, subject to the approval of the Diet, appointed the other members of the Cabinet. Under the precedents developed under the significant premiership of Mr. Yoshida, the Premier established his own personal primacy within the Cabinet in unmistakable terms; Yoshida held the portfolio of Foreign Affairs concurrently with the premiership during the most critical period in which he negotiated and signed the treaty of peace with the United States.

The role of the Premier is constitutionally prescribed by the requirement that if the House of Representatives passes a no-confidence resolution the Cabinet must resign *en masse* or dissolve the house within ten days. Once dissolved the house is elected anew, as described previously, and then a new Cabinet is appointed.

Prewar Japanese cabinets were *always* responsible to the definers of Imperial will, *usually* beholden to the military services, and *occasionally*

---

cilors as verging upon the absurd when one considers that Japan is socially, psychologically, and constitutionally still an Imperial state. Professor Linebarger holds that if the upper house has so little power that a simple repassage of a proposed Act by two-thirds vote of the House of Representatives is enough to overrule the upper house totally and forever, the Japanese would have been well advised to retain the House of Peers *(Kizoku-in)* provided by the Meiji Constitution and to have modified the House of Peers enough to make the upper house representative of Japan by professions, occupational groups, and the representation of intellectual and cultural organizations. These could have been added to a purged and reconstituted body of nobility with considerable profit to the security of Japan as an Imperial state. With this Professor Burks disagrees. The authors at this point leave the issue to the readers and to the future for decision.

responsible to the Diet.[9] Now the old competitive agencies, which used to interfere with direct Diet-Cabinet channels, have been abolished altogether. The semi-independent War and Navy Ministries are gone, the old Home Ministry (*Naimushō*), which used to control all local governments on behalf of a central government, is also gone, and the rest of the conservative and militarist apparatus shows no sign of early reappearance.

The entire trend from 1947, when the new Constitution was put into effect, to the end of the Occupation in 1952 was for the Japanese executive to grow in two marked manners. The Cabinet acquired a complex of nonministerial bureaus, offices, and boards as administrative offshoots. The Japanese, quick to learn from foreign patterns, not only set up their own version of a Western democracy, but promptly encumbered it with independent agencies as promptly as they could. (For example, see Chart 27, which shows the new Ministry of Construction (*Kensetsushō*).) Along with this centrifugal tendency there has been a centripetal pull of power toward the Premier himself.[10]

The continued presence of United States military installations in Japan to the end of the Occupation, and even after, and the little-noted fact that many of the most important financial and economic decisions in Japan required close coordination with the American defense system and therewith involved confidential information, meant that there was a pull on the Japanese from the Americans for a responsible small group of Japanese with whom the American commanding officer could deal. A many-faceted or irresponsible cabinet would scarcely be in position to retain effective bargaining authority with the Americans. Since it is extremely likely that continued American economic and strategic aid will be channeled through the readily accepted structure and semantics of a going military command, rather than by being thrown into the more complicated, less efficient, and more controversial channel of bilateral international economic negotiations, it is probable that for the foreseeable future the American military along with the American State Department will continue to be prime negotiators of on-the-spot Japanese policy. This kind of relationship lends itself very strongly to a corresponding concentration and continuation of responsibility on the part of the other party to such negotiation.

Finance (*Zaisei*) is the subject of an entire section (Chapter VII) of the new Constitution. Drafters thus clearly realized the controlling position enjoyed by those who hold the purse strings in government. Although the Cabinet prepares, submits, and executes the budget and reports to the Diet

[9] Paul M. A. Linebarger, "Government in Japan," p. 584 of Fritz Morstein Marx, Editor, *Foreign Governments; the Dynamics of Politics Abroad,* New York, 1949. A useful chart showing the old and new Japanese government in juxtaposition is shown on p. 578 of the Morstein Marx volume

[10] The old Ministry of Justice, bureaucratic master of the courts, was replaced by a streamlined, American-type Attorney General's Office *(Hōmuchō),* independent of the courts (later this name was abandoned). Two new portfolios reflected postwar concern for economic reconstruction: a full-fledged Ministry of Labor *(Rōdōshō),* established on September 1, 1947; and a Ministry of Construction *(Kensetsushō),* on July 10, 1948. See page 502 for sample organization chart of the Construction Ministry.

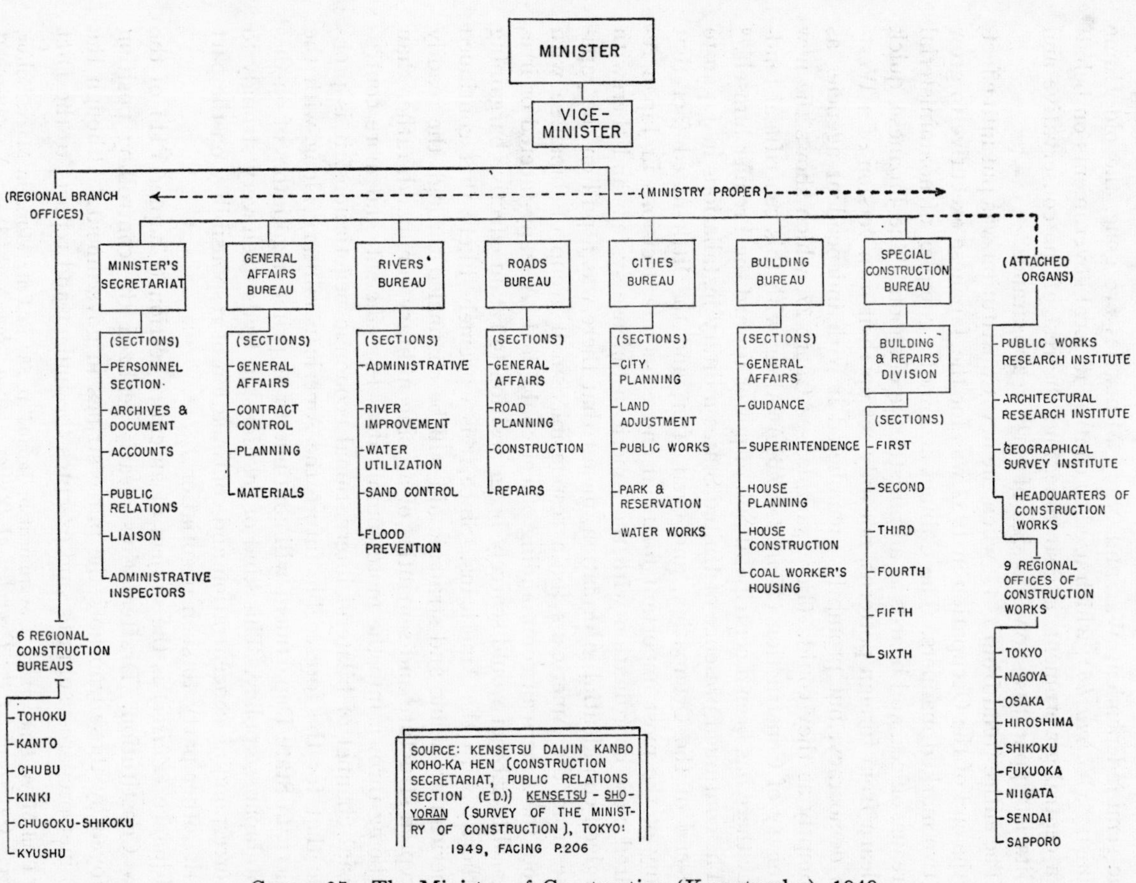

CHART 27—The Ministry of Construction (Kensetsusho), 1949

and to the people on the state of national finances, all public expenditures, revenues, and obligations must be authorized by the Diet. The lower house holds the advantage here, for (Chapter IV, Article 60) the budget is initiated in the House of Representatives and if a joint committee of both houses cannot reconcile budgetary differences of opinion, the decision of the lower house is the decision of the Diet.

The Judiciary. In any government, the judiciary must always be the last line of defense of the legal gains which constitute greater democracy. The new Constitution (Chapter VI, especially Article 76) eliminates former bureaucratic control of the judiciary (*Shihō*). Judicial power is vested in a Supreme Court (*Saikō Saibansho*) and in such inferior courts as are established by law. The Emperor, guided by the Cabinet, appoints the Chief Judge (*Chōtaru Saibankan*); all other judges (*Hanji*) are directly appointed by the Cabinet. Unlike the American federal system, the Japanese provided a review by the people of all such appointments at the first general election after appointment, and every ten years thereafter.[11]

Civil Service and Local Government. Civil service as we understand it—that is, public servants operating under law rather than bureaucrats armed with legalistic weapons—was an alien concept in prewar Japan. Nor could the postwar Constitution, a charter for the people at large, deal minutely with the legitimate boundaries of bureaucracy. Constitutionally, it is true, public officials became "servants of the whole community" (Chapter III, Article 15); Japanese citizens have been granted redress in case of illegal acts by any public official (Article 17); and the "civil service" is to be administered by the Cabinet, in accordance with standards established by law (Chapter V, Article 73).[12] Beyond these provisions, initial phases in the actual reform of bureaucracy had to await prodding by a high-level Personnel Advisory Mission from the United States, passage of a national public service law, and establishment of an American-type, semi-independent National Personnel Authority (*Jinji-in*). Excision of the most insidious influence working for authoritarian government, the *kanryō*, did not therefore anticipate or automatically follow the new Constitution. Grave doubts have been expressed that the grip of the *kanryō* on the vital organs of the state has been broken, even today. A description of the attempts to break that grip provides an interesting test case and is presented below.

Self-government at local levels (*Chihō Jiji*), along the lines of home rule within an American state, constituted one of the most drastic alterations of

[11] I am indebted to Professor Robert E. Ward for pointing out that the referendum is, however, distinctly American in origin. Public administration experts refer to it as the "Missouri System."

[12] The difficulties of translating a concept from one language into another is illustrated in these provisions. Although the Americans used the words "civil service" (Article 73) in the official English text of the new Constitution, the Japanese had to be more roundabout, less abstract, characteristically more personal in referring to Cabinet supervision of *kanri ni kansuru jimu,* literally "affairs concerning government officials." In the other provisions, the term *kōmuin,* "public officials," is used.

prewar Japan. Divorce of the prefectures from central authority was symbolized by the absence of the old Home Ministry (*Naimushō*), abolished December 31, 1947; it has been effected by conversion from a highly unitary police-type state to a decentralized grouping of self-governing prefectures. Even the most progressive reformers could not, however, successfully advocate a federal structure for a nation so small and so compact.[13] Thus Japan still fits closer the British unitary, rather than the American federal, pattern. Under the 1947 Constitution (Chapter VIII) and the supplemental Local Autonomy Law (*Chihō Jichi Hō,* April 17, 1947), the National Diet fixes by statute: (1) local public entities with their own deliberative assemblies; (2) local elections for chief executives, assemblymen, and other officials; and (3) general regulations for management of local affairs, property, and administration.

Old Wine in New Bottles. Constitutionally, the postwar Emperor assumed a role similar to that of the British Crown. The aristocracy was leveled. The other powerful, unseen, inner circles of influence around the Throne were legally abolished. The big question remained: What organs would inherit the role formerly played by those who spoke in the Imperial name?

There was real danger that the bureaucracy (*kambatsu*) would fill the vacuum. Part of the difficulty in controlling bureaucracy in Japan arose out of the traditional reliance of the Japanese on men, rather than law, for their administration. Unfortunately, part arose out of the nature of the Occupation itself. Government by directive, either open and by fiat or induced and subtle, is a poor school for training self-reliant public servants or courageous legislators. Finally, part of the difficulty arose out of the world-wide dilemma of increasing controls by government versus individual freedom. Japan's leading commercial newspaper put its finger on this aspect of the problem in an editorial entitled, "Bureaucracy and Official Machinery":

> The two are quite different. If we abolish or reform the former and establish the latter, we have democracy. Socialistic policy, inevitable in the present crisis, requires various official agencies and extension of their powers.[14]

It was no accident, then, that the attempt by Japanese to control the bureaucracy, in its traditional prerogatives, reached a crisis under the Socialist Katayama government; and that by and large the Socialists too failed to curb bureaucracy, in both the traditional and the more modern sense. Kata-

[13] One of the few such suggestions was on an even broader scale. *Jiji Shimpō,* January 18, 1946, reported that Matsumoto Jiichirō, leader of a "leveling movement" for abolition of discrimination against Japan's *Eta* outcasts, conceived of a Japanese Union of Republics. Four republics in Japan—Kyūshū, Kansai, Kantō, Tōhoku—would become units in a "Union of East Asiatic Nations" and eventually join a "World Union of Nations."

[14] *Nihon Keizai Shimbun* (The Japan Economist), June 5, 1946.

yama could find company in disappointment, for his efforts capped the most earnest efforts by Allied officials.

As early as November, 1945, a few SCAP Government Section officials had surveyed the problem of civil service reform but had laid aside plans for a detailed revision of Japanese bureaucracy, in favor of more pressing and fundamental tasks. In February, 1946, the powerful Japanese Cabinet Bureau of Legislation submitted to SCAP a plan to "reform" the civil service. The Bureau was frank in admitting that the plan embodied no fundamental changes, but constituted a precedent for more basic changes. Actually the plan merely led to some simplification of hopelessly complex pay scales and personal ranks. By April of 1946, impatient SCAP officials were considering once again a directive on civil service reform. At this juncture, the cause received unexpected support from within the Japanese government.

A typical Japanese Cabinet crisis occurred on May 14, 1946. The issue was over an unsolicited request, submitted by the Finance Minister to SCAP, for a commission of American experts to make a thorough-going revision of the Japanese pay and allowance system. Although the Finance Minister apologized to the Director of the Legislative Bureau for failure to clear his request, an "understanding" was reached whereby the Cabinet went officially on record inviting the assistance of American experts. SCAP responded quickly, and the United States Personnel Advisory Mission to Japan was sent out from the United States in November, 1946.[15] The Mission, working closely with SCAP and Japanese officials, drafted a national public service law and submitted it in the form of an interim report through SCAP to the Japanese government in July of 1947. In summary, the Mission recommended the establishment of a central personnel agency and enactment of a law providing a democratically oriented merit service.

Socialist Premier Katayama pledged his government to the reform of bureaucracy in the opening sessions of the 1st Diet Session under the new Constitution:

> . . . The government must, I consider, embark upon the reorganization of the administrative structure and the reform of the civil service system. The essential motive of these reorganizations is in the elimination of the bureaucratic concept.

Mr. Kitamura Tokutarō, representing the Democratic opposition, took up the same theme. Japan, he said, is regarded as having proportionately the largest number of government officials of any country in the world: there are

[15] Mr. Blaine Hoover, President, Civil Service Assembly of the U.S. and Canada, was chairman of the group made up of planning, classification, and personnel experts. The preparatory work of SCAP and the Mission is described in SCAP, *Political Reorientation,* cited, Vol. I, sec. VII, pp. 246-259 See also Vol. II, Appendix B:8b, "Correspondence from Japanese Government Regarding Request for Civil Service Mission," pp. 579-580.

two and a half million government employees who, with their families, account for twelve and a half million of the population, or one for every six Japanese. Mr. Kimura Kōhei, speaking for the Liberals, sounded a familiar theme. Bureaucracy, he said, is a product of controlled economy; there is no need for a big bureaucracy in a free economy.[16]

Despite apparent agreement among majority and minority parties, the National Public Service Law (*Kokka Kōmuin Hō*), promulgated in October and enforced July 1, 1948, left much to be desired. It was found to have been considerably altered in coherence and content from the painstaking draft provided by the Advisory Mission. Revision of the law, directly encouraged by the Supreme Commander in a letter to the Premier, July 22, 1948, awaited further guidance by the newly created Civil Service Division, Government Section, SCAP; real reform depended upon strengthening of the new Japanese National Personnel Authority (*Jinji-in*). Above all, reform of bureaucracy depended upon the emergence of a virile, independent Diet, constitutionally the "highest organ of state power."

Indeed, much of the success of the entire democratization experiment in postwar Japan rests in the hands of the new National Diet (*Kokkai*), successor to the old Imperial Diet (*Teikoku Gikai*). Its responsibilities under the new Constitution are thrown into bold relief when it is noted that the Diet has legally assumed the policy-making powers once exercised by the Privy Council, Cabinet, Imperial Household Ministry, senior statesmen, service staffs, and the Imperial conferences. Its postwar membership is probably not as bad as one editorial characterization:

> . . . The new Diet is not much different from the old one and we will even go so far as to say that we have killed the tiger at the front door in the form of the old militaristic Diet, but a wolf, which is the new disposition of the Diet, is waiting for us at the back door.[17]

Certainly the opening of the first session of the new Diet in 1947 was on a higher plane than the convocation of its predecessor, described previously. For one thing, the public was admitted without official order (there were only 250 seats). The entire inside of the Diet building had been cleaned. Elevator girls, guards, and doorkeepers were all newly employed. All had been subjected to disinfection with DDT. Seats on the floor of the lower

[16] *The Official Gazette,* Extra No. 8 (Wednesday, July 2, 1947), p. 5; Extra No. 9 (Thursday, July 3, 1947), p. 13; Extra No. 27 (Friday, August 27, 1947), p. 13.

[17] *Tōkyō Shimbun,* June 20, 1946. The Diet Law, successor to Itō's Law of the Houses, was promulgated April 28, 1947, and put into force, along with the new Constitution, May 3, 1947. An English text is available in *Japan Year Book, 1946-48,* Appendix, pp. 38-44. Japanese terminology used here is drawn from Ōike Makoto, *Shin kokkai kaisetsu* (An explanation of the new Diet), Tōkyō, 1947 (Ōike was then Chief Clerk of the Diet). In English, see Justin Williams, "The Japanese Diet under the New Constitution," and "Party Politics in the New Japanese Diet," two articles in a symposium edited by Harold S. Quigley, *American Political Science Review,* Vol. XLII, No. 5 (October 1948) and No. 6 (December 1948), pp. 927-939 and 1163-1180.

House were arranged according to party affiliation, left to right. A special seat was arranged down front for Japan's professional liberal, Ozaki Yukio, who was hard of hearing. Men members wore cutaways, the national Diet uniform (*kokuminfuku*), or sack cloth; women wore *mompei,* the loose-fitting ankle-tied trousers which became so popular during the war. At 10:55 A.M., Monday, June 23, 1947, the officers of both Houses and members, Premier and ministers, representatives of the Supreme Court and Board of Audit entered the Assembly Hall of the Diet. After princes of the blood were seated, at 11:01 A.M., His Imperial Majesty was conducted to the Throne by the President of the House of Representatives, who then spoke:

> Today we hold in the August presence of His Majesty the Emperor the opening of the First Session of the Diet. . . . The Diet is, under our Constitution, the supreme organ of state and the sole law-making body of the land. . . .

In his Imperial Rescript in reply, the Emperor stated simply that "the foundation for the development of future Japan lies solely in right management of the Diet." [18]

When the new Diet got down to business, it too found it necessary to fit old political factions and the normal Japanese parliamentary pattern to a new order of things. The Diet Law alone, of all statutes paralleling the new Constitution, had already been drafted and introduced in March, 1947, by the old House of Representatives, rather than the government. In fact, the Law was passed without the approval of the Cabinet or the old House of Peers.

Superseding Itō's Law of the Houses, the new Diet Law of 132 articles made radical alterations in the houses' structure. The term of ordinary sessions was increased from three to five months; extension of sessions was no longer determined by Imperial order but by the houses themselves. Diet finances were released from the grip of the Ministry of Finance. Members received a salary not less than that of vice-ministers. Other omissions from the Imperial Law of the Houses included committees of the whole house; prorogation of the houses; schedules reported in advance to the government; and representations to the government. Moreover the new Diet was equipped with facilities found in most modern legislatures: allowances, use of the frank, clerical assistance, a Diet Library, bill-drafting and research services.

The most important single chapter in the new Diet Law (Chapter V, especially Article 42) established standing committees, closely patterned after those provided Congress in the United States Legislative Reorganization Act of 1946. Whether the Diet truly becomes the engine of state power depends in large measure upon the skill with which the twenty-one standing com-

[18] In his Rescript opening the Second Session, January 21, 1948, the Emperor dropped the *chin* of formal court language, and referred to himself as a member of "we, the Japanese people." For the first session see *Official Gazette,* Extra No. 6 (June 24, 1947), p. 1.

mittees, one for each field of administration, are used.[19] Public participation in the law-making process, a strange new privilege, was introduced into committees by procedures long familiar to us in the West, namely, open hearings, legislative junkets, and the power to summon witnesses.

Plenary sessions of the new Japanese Diet are, alas, like those of almost any legislature, used primarily to give formal approval to matters settled in committee; to embarrass the government; and to filibuster. "Free discussion," provided under Diet Law in at least one plenary session every two weeks, has been a complete disappointment and has been openly criticized on the floor of the Diet itself.[20]

The chief difficulties faced by Japan's new Diet have been unprecedented economic crisis, its own unfamiliarity with Western concepts written into the Diet Law, and the mysteries of the ubiquitous Japanese bureaucracy. Its own shortcomings have so far been the prevalence of rowdyism on the floor, which the Japanese Diet has perfected as a fine art; and cynical tolerance of lobbying, which once again threatens to discredit the legislature in the eyes of the public. Japanese lobbying consists of regular contact between special interests and members, a function of hack errand-boys (*ingaidan,* literally "bullies"); more formal but surreptitious instruction by "wirepullers" (*kuromaku*); or direct intervention by representatives of special interests in the Diet caucus rooms. The height of lobbyist brashness came with the organized campaign against coal nationalization in 1947. Lobbying in Japan, as is so often the case elsewhere, is intimately tied up with the party boss system, to be discussed later.

The strong point of the postwar Japanese Diet, aside from Cabinet responsibility, is the promise that the new standing committees will become powerful weapons in the hands of politicians in their assault on the barri-

[19] The twenty-one committees in each house, with the number of lower house members on each in parentheses (1st Session, 1947), are as follows:

1. Foreign Affairs *(Gaimu Iinkai)* (20)
2. Public Order and Local Government *(Chian oyobi Chihō Seido Iinkai)* (30)
3. National Land Planning *(Kokudō Keikaku Iinkai)* (30)
4. Judicial *(Shihō Iinkai)* (25)
5. Education *(Bunkyō Iinkai)* (25)
6. Cultural Affairs *(Bunka Iinkai)* (25)
7. Welfare *(Kōsei Iinkai)* (30)
8. Labor *(Rōdō Iinkai)* (30)
9. Agriculture and Forestry *(Nōrin Iinkai)* (30)
10. Fisheries *(Suisan Iinkai)* (25)
11. Commerce *(Shōgyō Iinkai)* (25)
12. Mining and Industry *(Kōkōgyō Iinkai)* (25)
13. Electric Industry *(Denki Iinkai)* (25)
14. Transportation *(Unyu oyobi Kōtsū Iinkai)* (25)
15. Communications *(Tsūshin Iinkai)* (25)
16. Finance and Banking *(Zaisei oyobi Kinyū Iinkai)* (30)
17. Budget *(Yosan Iinkai)* (50)
18. Audit *(Kessan Iinkai)* (25)
19. House Management or "Steering Committee" *(Giin Unei Iinkai)* (25)
20. Library Management *(Toshokan Unei Iinkai)* (10)
21. Discipline *(Chōbatsu Iinkai)* (25)

[20] The House of Representatives held its first "free discussion" on the technique of "free discussion," Friday, July 11, 1947. Mr. Tanaka Kakukei, Democratic Party spokesman, bewailed the poor reception accorded the Diet's debates by the press. Originally speakers were chosen in the Steering Committee; eventually they were recognized by the Speaker, which meant selection of party spokesman by inter-party compromise. *Official Gazette,* Extra No. 15 (Friday, July 11, 1947), pp. 1-5.

caded bureaucracy. The Diet, through its committees, very early challenged the Katayama Cabinet's right to appoint members as vice-ministers or councilors in the ministries. The Cabinet has found it necessary, as never before, to consult the steering committees to obtain an extension of session. The Diet has made steady encroachment on the Finance Minister's hitherto exclusive preserve, the budget. Like all good parliamentarians anywhere, Diet members have even successfully competed with the bureaucrats for official residences and public vehicles.

Finally, the inherent danger in the new Diet's rise to power lies in the fact that, faced with a policy vacuum to fill and vast new privileges to enjoy, it has gradually built a legislative bureaucracy of its own. In one sense, this is a normal development in all legislatures. Political parties manage the Diet; every move is a party move; every vote is a party vote.[21] Perhaps more quickly and more naturally than in politics elsewhere, a neo-feudal party cohesion has rapidly reduced the individual Diet members to a nonentity. In short, the quality of the new Diet depends upon the quality of the postwar parties. And the parties, although changed to some extent, in turn give a clue to the postwar succession of weak, coalition cabinets and the failure of Japan to produce imaginative leadership. Here, with a vengeance, is a case of using new bottles for old wine.

Postwar Parties. The Japanese have a saying: "With too many captains, the ship climbs the mountain." This would seem to apply to postwar Japanese political parties. As a matter of fact, although there were over one thousand registered political groups according to a recent count, Japan has a paucity of true political parties. Even the three or four major ones have had a bewildering shift of names, symbolic of bland transfer of members' allegiance, and an almost total lack of actual political principles. The confusing details need not detain us, but a brief survey of the postwar parties will serve to illustrate their major characteristics.[22]

The two conservative parties which have contended, merged, and split off again are the Liberal (direct descendant of the postwar Democratic-Liberal

[21] Even the great authority granted the *Gichō* (Speaker) by Diet Law and House Rules is completely controlled by the traditional and extra-legal Inter-party Negotiating Conference, representing each party with 25 or more Diet members. The new "unseen" government is nowhere better "seen" than in the new, and almost equally arduous, process for selecting a premier. Katayama, the first under the new Constitution, was "elected" by the Diet only after weeks of private compromise. Delay in selecting his cabinet was publicly attacked in the House. *Official Gazette,* Extra No. 10 (Friday, July 4, 1947), pp. 5-6.

[22] There are few good analyses of postwar parties as yet in Japanese. The best reference is Asahi Shimbun Seitō Kishadan (Asahi Newspaper, Political Staff) *Seitō nenkan* (Party yearbook), Tōkyō, 1948 (1949 edition); in English, Yutaka M., Editor, *Political Handbook,* cited, is brief but useful; searching articles were written by experienced former SCAP officials in the Symposium edited by Professor Quigley; Kenneth E. Colton, "Pre-war Political Influences in Post-war Conservative Parties"; John Saffell, "Japan's Post-war Socialist Party," *American Political Science Review,* cited, pp. 940-969; a very useful, up-to-date reference paper is Department of State, Office of Intelligence Research, *Major Political Parties of Japan* (DRF Information Paper No. 402), Washington, February 27, 1951 (dittoed, unclassified). Appendix 19 in this book presents data on the party composition of the postwar Diets under the new Constitution.

[*Minshu Jiyūtō*], and earlier Liberal Party) and the People's Democratic (direct descendant of the postwar Progressive [*Shimpotō*] and Democratic Party [*Minshutō*]). Both are grandsons, at least by marriage, of the old prewar *Seiyūkai* and *Minseitō*. The great purges beginning in 1946, however, effectively ended the possibility and advisability of direct lineal inheritance.

The first of these conservative parties to leave the starting-gate after surrender was what is now once again called the Liberal Party (*Jiyūtō*). It was born of the ambitions of the experienced Hatoyama Ichirō, who had dreams of a united front of all anti-military, conservative forces cutting across party lines. As leader of the old Kuhara branch of the prewar *Seiyūkai,* the Liberals reflected Hatoyama's staunch support of the Meiji Constitution, nineteenth-century liberalism, and the more corrupt side of Japanese politics. Not only in platform but also in membership and tactics, the party at first inherited *Seiyūkai* characteristics.[23]

The initial purge directive of January 4, 1946, hit mainly at Liberal Diet membership (reduced from 46 to 18); a relatively large proportion of the leadership, including Hatoyama, was left intact. But the quality of leadership changed measurably, the machine politicians stepping into the shoes of the already thin parliamentarians. The tendency was greatly accelerated with the elimination of Hatoyama himself, and the selection of Yoshida, untrained in political mechanics, as President. Only with the rescreenings of 1947 did the parliamentarians begin to displace the machine faction. Meanwhile, in the elections of 1946-47, the Liberals continued to cultivate prewar *Seiyūkai* districts despite the complete break in continuity of personnel. The machine elements also gave the Liberal Party the old *Seiyūkai* stamp of dictatorial discipline.

The Liberal Party was the first in postwar Japan to obtain an absolute majority in the lower house. In the elections of 1949 (as the Yoshida Democratic-Liberal coalition), it placed 268 out of the 466 seats. Entrance into its ranks of the coalition Democrats during 1950 increased its seats to 286. As a result, the Liberals had no serious opposition in the lower house and would have had even less if the long-sought merger with the People's Democrats could have been effected. In the upper house, with only a bare Liberal plurality, the party has had rough sailing. Within the party, Yoshida Shigeru did well to consolidate his leadership, although there were rumors that he

[23] The *Seiyūkai* had finally split in 1939, after bitter internecine strife. Kuhara Fusanosuke, a wealthy mine operator, joined forces with Hatoyama's Constitutional Parliamentarians. Nakajima Chikuhei, aircraft producer, led the larger pro-militarist faction. The postwar *Jiyūtō* was formally inaugurated November 9, 1945. Its platform, in brief, advocated: (1) adherence to Potsdam terms, in letter and spirit; (2) protection of the national polity, with an admixture of democracy; (3) strengthening of national finance and the economy; (4) enhancement of political and social ethics "to brighten national life"; (5) respect for human rights, promotion of the status of women, and active support for social policies. *Nippon Times,* November 11, 1945.

would retire after the peace treaty. Then Hatoyama Ichirō, founder of the party, was presumably to be depurged and to accept the presidency.

Despite its name, the Liberal Party is far to the Right of the conservative groups. Generally, it enjoys the support of new industrial and business interests, as well as the votes of conservative, rural Japan.

In January, 1951, one major, if ineffective, force in opposition to the Liberals was provided by the People's Democratic Party (*Kokumin Minshutō;* sometimes National Democrats or simply Democrats). The Democrats had a confused postwar origin, a brief disastrous tenure in government, and they now suffer a dim future as an independent party. Inexperienced compared with Hatoyama's Liberals, the party's leadership emerged in November, 1945, from the odoriferous *Nippon Seiji Kai* (Japan Political Party), the prewar Nakajima *Seiyūkai,* and the old *Minseitō.*[24]

As first constituted, the Democrats (then called Progressives) made a perfect rogues' gallery of those who had served wartime bureaucracy and militarism. It should have come as no surprise, then, that the first purge of 1946 all but abolished the party. Yet that was the major blow and strangely served to give the party a temporary lease on life by eliminating the worst elements. From then on the party carried the *Minseitō* stamp. This tendency was increased with the purge extensions of 1947. Meanwhile, the party picked up new leadership—when Ashida Hitoshi, a co-founder of the Liberals, bolted—and a new name, Democratic Party, in March of 1947. Again despite a break in the continuity of personnel, the Democrats cultivated the old *Minseitō* spheres of influence. Partially because of *Minseitō* background in the urban areas, the Democratic Party allied with the Socialists and cooperative parties in the Katayama government and later in a Cabinet under its own President, Ashida Hitoshi. Of the conservative parties, the Democrats have been most influenced by the rise of socialism.

On the other hand, the desire to recultivate *Minseitō* influences in rural Japan led the Democrats to flirt with the Cooperative Democratic Party (*Kyōdō Minshutō*), founded in May, 1946, and reorganized as the People's Cooperative Party (*Kokumin Kyōdōtō*) in 1947. Finally in the spring of 1950, the anti-coalition Democrats (still opposed to the Liberals largely on personal grounds) joined the People's Cooperatives to control 67 seats in the lower and 29 seats in the upper House.

The Democratic Party was only a little less conservative than its Liberal rival, and whatever principles it possessed differed only on minor points from those of the Liberal Party. Nevertheless, it took an opposition stand

[24] For the split of the *Seiyūkai,* see Footnote 23. The *Nippon Seiji Kai* formally dissolved September 14, 1945, the last of the wartime "assistance" associations. The Democrats were formally organized November 16, 1945, under the noncommittal name, Progressive Party *(Shimpotō).* It had no president, although the name of retired General Ugaki Kazushige was frequently mentioned. It had no real platform, save the basic desire of its members to be elected. In fact, one editorial acidly remarked that the choice of its first name was not too subtle an indication that the party wished to progress, but did not know where. *Nippon Times,* September 16, November 18 and 19, 1945.

in the Diet on most domestic issues and agreed with the Liberal government only on signature of a Japanese peace treaty. There were repeated rumors of amalgamation of the remaining party members into the Liberal cause, but depurgings of former Democratic leaders probably postponed union.

The other major, and somewhat more effective, opposition was the Japan Socialist Party (*Nihon Shakaitō*), formally organized in November, 1945. Especially in the formative process, divergent elements such as were represented by Kagawa Toyohiko, famed Christian leader; Abe Isoo, old-line Socialist from the early 1900's; and Takano Iwasaburō, former adviser to the Social Mass Party, came together under one roof.[25] Indeed, the Socialists were a conglomeration of the vaguely and sharply Left; repeated forays were made by some Socialists to form a united front with the Communists. The most important single characteristic of the postwar Socialists was intra-party cleavage.

Although the Socialists also did not go unscathed in the first purge, by April, 1946, they demonstrated that they had become a major political force by capturing 18 per cent of the votes cast in the general election of that year and seating 92 members in the lower house. Having rejected bids by the Communists to join forces against the Yoshida government, the party nevertheless rapidly rose to become the major opposition in late 1946. They led the "Down with Yoshida" rallies of December. In April, 1947, they became the leading party with 143 seats in the lower house.

The first Socialist government in Japan's history began operations with much untested strength, much more weakness—especially in leadership—and the misfortune of catching postwar Japan at low economic ebb. Katayama Tetsu, who had been elected chairman of the party's central executive committee in 1946, was neither a dynamic person nor an astute politician. *Mainichi Shimbun* (May 7, 1946) compared him with Attlee, "who has no characteristic personality, but is a man of gentleness and endurance." Unfortunately for the party, management of affairs fell to Nishio Suehiro, the Socialists' shrewdest politician, and Right-wing Socialist. Failure to pass a real coal production control law brought waning Socialist prestige. Food shortages, inflation, and intense intra-party conflict brought brief Socialist tenure to a close in 1948. Socialist popularity was a result not of Japanese mass belief in socialism, but of mass disappointment in conservative leadership.

Socialist leadership still consists largely of old-time, moderate Left-wingers, although the farther Left faction has drawn new leadership from

[25] As Katō Kanju, *Shakaitō* leader, explained to Mr. John Saffell (whose article is cited above), the title literally means "Social Party." The translation, "Social Democratic," is often used abroad to indicate the party similarity to other such-named parties; but never the Japanese *Shakai Minshutō,* which would link the new party to an older intellectual group. The *Nihon Shakaitō* was formally launched November 2, 1945. Its platform, presented by a Preparatory Committee, included: (1) political liberty and establishment of a democratic structure of government; (2) socialism to advance the people's livelihood: (3) opposition to militarism. *Nippon Times,* October 17 and 20, 1945.

Japan's postwar trade unions.[26] Intra-party conflict continues over tactics and, lately, over international issues.

The Green Breeze Society (*Ryōkufukai*), that organization of the delightful name, is not really a party at all. A loosely organized group of independent Councilors, the society includes many famous nonprofessional politicians, has no clear platform, and generally lacks party discipline. Although it could generally be counted on to support conservative policy, the Liberals with a slight plurality always require the support of the Society for a majority.

The extreme Left is occupied, of course, by the Japanese Communist Party (*Nihon Kyōsantō*). Japanese Communists, like Communists everywhere, were immensely aided by the proximity and fear of Soviet power and the direct encouragement of a large Russian mission in Tokyo. Although the Supreme Commander early ordered the release of Japanese political prisoners, including Communists, the party was hampered by hostility from SCAP. It has, on the one hand, been aided by the hue and cry raised by the conservatives. It hampered its own growth, on the other hand, by its stand against the Emperor system. Like Communists in Yugoslavia and in Italy, it has had trouble in straightening out an acceptable party line to fit both the Cominform and Japanese ideology. More recently it has been torn by expulsion or defection from party ranks.[27]

That the so-called Orthodox Faction, led by Nozaka Sanzō and Tokuda Kyūichi, at first dictated Communist tactics was revealed by the Manifesto of the Fifth Party Convention, issued early in 1946:

> The Japanese Communist Party, for the time being, aims chiefly at carrying out the bourgeois, democratic revolution, which is now in progress in our country, by peaceful and democratic methods.

Nozaka spoke of his party as a group of "sincere patriots." In the 1st Session of the Diet, 1947, Tokuda argued for a check on inflation, control of the black market, and a united front with the Social Democrats. That the moderate tactics paid off was shown by the spectacular gain by the Com-

[26] The Central Executive Committee, elected January 1951, consisted of 30 members (Katayama, centrist, remained as supreme adviser); 5 were centrists, 15 were from the left wing (including Katō Kanju, Nomizo Masaru, and Wada Hiroo), and 10 from the right (including Suzuki Yoshio, Hatano Kanae, and Mizutani Chosaburō).

[27] See Awa Tokusaburō, Naboyama Sadakichi, and Naruhashi Wataru *"Senryō chika no Nihon Kyōsantō,"* (The Japanese Communist Party under the Occupation), *Kaizō* (Reconstruction), Vol. 31, No. 61 (June 1950), pp 58-73. Tokuda Kyūichi, Shiga Yoshio and other Japanese Communists were released from jail on October 10, 1945. Nozaka Sanzō, experienced in the Communist strategy of Mao Tse-tung and absent from Japan for sixteen years, returned on January 15, 1946, and the next day announced an "understanding" with his Comrades. Shortly thereafter the *Nippon Times* predicted weakness and division in Communist ranks and ridiculed the apoplectic alarm over the Red menace, exploited by the conservatives. "The newspapers also, by giving to the Communist activities far more publicity than their actual strength warrants, are artificially bolstering up the Communists." *Nippon Times,* March 8, 1946.

munists, after the collapse of the Socialists, in the elections of 1949.[28] During 1950, however, the brethren were hit from three sides. The blow below the belt was dealt by the Cominform, which poked fun at the party for toadying to Japanese traditions. Despite immediate recantation, the moderate faction tended to be overshadowed thereafter by the Internationalists, led by Shiga Yoshio and Miyamoto Kenji. Meanwhile, repeated body blows in the form of officially supported measures of the Japanese government cut the registered membership of the party from a peak of 108,000 early in 1950 to 69,000 by December.

SCAP dealt the blow to the head in June, 1950. Having consistently jabbed at the Soviet Union through the local party in sessions of the Allied Council for Japan and in threatening communiqués, the Supreme Commander finally ordered all 24 members of the Central Committee purged. There remained only a Temporary Central Guidance Committee (*Rinji Chūō Shidōbu*) of five, none members of the elite of the party. It was overtly suggested that Nozaka and Tokuda, having compromised in the direction of militant activity and while still in hiding, continued to control the party.[29]

The more immediate danger in postwar Japan was not, however, from a powerful Communist underground. It was rather from the basically undemocratic character of all the "respectable" parties, their consequent degradation of the Diet, and the eventual channels of the new "unseen" government of Japan. The major parties actually had little in the way of grass-roots support; they had to do little to plow up and stimulate competing principles. No individual voter had the faintest say in the formulation of party policies or the direction of party organization. All decisions were made in Tokyo headquarters. No Diet member dared flout party discipline, for fear of losing party privileges. This characteristic, of course, was not unique to Japan. The American Kefauver Committee could have found points in common between local organization of politics in Kanagawa Prefecture and that of Bergen County, New Jersey.

[28] See *Akahata* (Red Flag), Editorial, May 26, 1946 (the Communist paper was banned by order of SCAP in 1950); *Official Gazette,* Extra No. 11, (Saturday, July 5, 1947), pp. 18-19. That Nozaka was following Mao Tse-tung principles of New Democracy is suggested by Rodger Swearingen, "Nosaka and the Cominform," *Far Eastern Survey,* May 17, 1950. What the 1950 Cominform denunciation of Nozaka meant for Mao Tse-tung, somewhat more successful, is hard to fathom.

[29] The extreme Right in the form of ultra-nationalism has been slow to re-emerge in Japan. Dr. Nobutaka Ike, now with the Hoover War Library, Stanford, California, believes, however, that one organization is worth watching. The *Nihon Kakumei Kikuhata Dōshikai* (Japan Revolutionary Chrysanthemum Flag Association), headquarters in traditionally militant Kyushu, boasts a political philosophy and a program. *Kiku-,* of course, suggests the Imperial house, symbolized by the chrysanthemum; *-hata,* the banned *Akahata.* Needless to say, the Association is anti-Communist; *Kikuhata*-ism is national, "democratic," and socialist. The group has been affected, like all else in Japan, by the Occupation, for it renounced force and stressed mass democracy. In view of the ignominy of defeat, the fumbling of the postwar Diet, and the pusillanimity of the political parties, neo-Japanese totalitarianism may well develop along German Nazi or Italian Fascist lines. Nobutaka Ike, "'National Socialism' in Japan," *Pacific Affairs,* Vol. XXIII, No. 3 (September 1950), pp. 311-314.

The Japanese Diet and Japan's postwar parties, however, have inherited immense power and grave responsibilities. Therein lies the danger. And Japan's new "unseen" government does have characteristics peculiar to Japan. The force of tradition guarantees that much.

The so-called *oyabun,* a powerful pressure group at all levels of government, demonstrates one outstanding and not altogether evil characteristic. The *oyabun,* a wire-pulling boss or mugwump, is a modern throw-back to the security of feudal hierarchy and control. The system has wide ramifications. *Oyabun* in the cities control construction projects, labor, scarce materials, gambling, gangs of hoodlums, street-stalls, and, through the power of a *nouveau riche,* political party organization. In rural areas, the system reflects an almost undisturbed feudal landlord-tenant relationship. So powerful and complex is the *oyabun* network of organizations that Charles Kades of Government Section, SCAP, using words befitting our American Senatorial committee, called it a vast underground government extending from the smallest village to the capital city itself.[30] The essential difference between Japanese *oyabun* and American crime organizations is that the former are often far from amoral, even in political influence. They pull out all the stops on the organ of loyalty to the Throne; they stress ethics and discipline; they fancy themselves the modern counterparts of Japan's epic "wave-men," *rōnin.*

SCAP officials, often not too well versed in Japanese psychology, mistook a basic way of doing things for a specific evil. For example, on March 31, 1947, they legally abolished the old *tonari-gumi,* or neighborhood association, believing this ancient system to be the seat of gang politics. Certainly the *tonari-gumi* as used during the war and as a potential channel for "unseen" government in the future was a danger. But the neighborhood association, out in the open and under progressive leadership, could have been a powerful counter-weapon against corruption, not unlike the youth gangs organized to suppress other youth gangs in New York City. Nor in the end did SCAP actually abolish this Japanese method of association.

Field studies have shown that, despite the edicts against *tonari-gumi* and for local self-government, rural Japanese politics continued in the old channels. The family, not the individual, continued to be the core of society. *Sonraku* or more popularly *buraku* (the rural equivalent of urban *tonari-gumi*), based not on kinship but on proximity, continued not sub-legally but entirely illegally. Local leadership was in the hands of *buraku* elders, enjoying status by experience. Without national identification or broad principle, these groups were suspicious of central government. Headless, they were fair game, usually, for the conservative parties who "drive stakes" among the village elders.[31]

[30] As cited by the very knowledgeable ex-SCAP official, Harry Emerson Wildes, "Underground Politics in Post-War Japan," in the Quigley symposium, cited, *American Political Science Review,* Vol. XLII, No. 6 (December 1948), pp. 1149-1162.

[31] The SCAP Directive which first investigated *Tonari-gumi* was issued November 4,

A second characteristic of postwar parties, an unfortunate carry-over from prewar Japan, was political corruption. The massive Shōwa Denkō case, which brought down Ashida and his Democratic Cabinet in 1948, is illustrative if somewhat on a grand scale. Briefly, the major charges involved State Minister Kurusu Takeo, Director of the new Economic Stabilization Board; Nishio Suehiro, former Deputy Premier; and several other prominent politicians and businessmen. Kurusu (also Finance Minister under Katayama) exercised policy influence over the Japanese Reconstruction Finance Bank. Monetary contributions to the Democratic Party, after Kurusu's entry, were repaid via an excessive loan of a billion *yen* to the Shōwa Electric Industry Company. Although a Democratic Liberal member of the lower house originated the investigation, his own party as well as the Socialists were eventually implicated. Ashida himself was never linked with the Shōwa case, but he was indicted on December 8, 1948, for receiving bribes to facilitate parallel loans to contractors. The only bright spot in the sordid affair was that the press credited the House of Representatives itself with breaking the scandal.[32]

A third characteristic of Japan's postwar parties was a new test of eligibility for leadership, the ability to tap new sources of party funds. Two major changes in the Japanese scene have made this need a real challenge to the ingenuity of political bosses. Within the Japanese government, abolition of the service ministries and the old Home Ministry destroyed the former major sources of patronage and influence. Party leaders turned first to the Foreign Ministry, which channeled all manna from the all-powerful Supreme Commander. Later, each agency built its own liaison bureau. Lucrative sources of income included *oyabun,* supervising the vast reconstruction of Japan; dealers in scarce commodities and outright black marketeers; and hoarders of the unmeasured amount of surplus Japanese military supplies. In addition, as Japan began to get on its feet, government control of industrial loans through new postwar agencies became a battleground of influence and potential party revenue. These last-named characteristics, corruption and party finance, will serve to introduce a few words about the economic working forces in postwar Japan.

Economic Bases of Politics. Within Japan, the economics of the Occupation left an indelible stamp on Japanese government. The effects have

---

1945; see *NKHK,* Vol. 1, No. 5 (August 15, 1946), pp. 7-10. The first independent field studies carried out in occupied Japan were managed by the new Center for Japanese Studies, University of Michigan, which maintains a station in Okayama Prefecture. The reconnaissance conclusions summarized were based on an article by Dr. Robert E. Ward, "Some Observations on Local Autonomy at the Village Level in Present-day Japan," *Far Eastern Quarterly,* Vol. XII, No. 2 (February, 1953). Dr. Ward's findings at least show the danger of generalizing on the effects of the Occupation from cement buildings or newspaper offices in Tokyo.

[32] Four years later, the courts got around to disposing of the Shōwa Denkō defendants. Five of the six-man Kurusu group, including Kurusu himself, were found guilty of bribery. Ashida was acquitted by the Tokyo District Court from all charges. Nishio was also found guilty of bribery. *Mainichi,* October 21, 1952; *Nippon Times,* October 23, October 28, 1952.

been both positive and negative. Inside the government *qua* government the effects were shown clearly by the creation of new, semi-independent agencies like the Economic Stabilization Board (*Keizai Antei Hombu*), attached to the executive offices of the Premier; and the Board of Trade (*Bōeki-chō*), an offshoot of the Ministry of Commerce and Industry. Cabinets revolved around programs for economic planning, designed to meet economic crisis. "The Report on the Economic Situation" (White Paper) drawn up under the Katayama Cabinet, is an outstanding example.[33]

Creation of the Labor Ministry (*Rōdōshō*) in 1947 symbolized the potentially strongest new political and economic force in Japan outside the government *qua* government. It paralleled and implemented new legislation dealing with union organization, labor-management relations, labor standards, labor insurance and compensation. In October, 1945, there had been only five labor unions in Japan with a total membership of 5,300. By March, 1949, there were almost seven million workers organized in 36,500 unions representing 38 per cent of all nonagricultural labor. Largest organizations were the Japanese Federation of Labor (JFL; *Nihon Sōdōmei*) and the National Congress of Industrial Unions (NCIU; in Japanese, *Sambetsu* for short). The real dilemma, wrestled with by the government and SCAP, was how to treat central and local government employees, nearly 40 per cent of all Japanese labor. As demonstrated several times during the Occupation, Japanese labor had become a powerful political pressure group. Despite sporadic alliances with both the Socialists and the Communists on the Left, no political party has as yet proved its ability to hang on to the tail of the tiger.[34]

In two spheres of politico-economic activity, the effects of the Occupation were largely negative. In one of the most necessary and important steps in the elimination of aggressive influence, SCAP ordered dissolution of major financial and industrial combines. Certainly the giant *Zaibatsu*—specifically the Mitsui, Mitsubishi, Sumitomo, and other finance trusts—had unsupportable war records and, even more important, a long record of callous disregard for the welfare of the Japanese people. However, here again, as in the case of neighborhood associations, the specific evil and its elimination were probably confused with a basic method of ordering Japanese economic life. The point is that the *Zaibatsu* is also a familiar Japanese way of doing things, the ordering of business according to the family system. Properly directed and with the technical know-how of the manager class harnessed to legitimate economic objectives, the *Zaibatsu* method—certainly not the *Zaibatsu* clique—could well supply the long-sought-for formula of maximum

[33] SCAP Memoranda approving establishment of the *Bōeki-chō* and the *Keizai Antei Hombu* are to be found in *NKHK*, cited, Vol. I, No. 10 (February 15, 1947), pp. 23-28 and Vol. I, No. 11 (April 20, 1947), pp. 35-36. The free discussion in the Diet on the White Paper is covered in the *Official Gazette*, Extra No. 13 (Tuesday, July 8, 1947), pp. 1-19.

[34] Debate on establishment of the *Rōdōshō*, and implemented labor legislation, is covered in the *Official Gazette*, Extra No. 22 (Friday, August 8, 1947), pp. 1-17.

individual security balanced against controlled social activity within a typically Japanese democratic socialism.

The other major neglected area, as always in Japan's controlled revolutions, was the agrarian base. It is significant that, despite induced land reform on paper under the Occupation, the Japanese peasant is still not actually represented in the major political parties of Japan. His latent, conservative-radical wrath must as usual be taken into account by all governments and by all parties. The significance and precise nature of the Japanese agrarian problem are a part of the whole picture of backward areas everywhere, and Oriental countries in particular. The pressing need for some sort of solution, at the base, contradicts the tendency both domestically and outside countries like Japan to approach the problem through the economic and political elite.[35] Land reform as a political vested interest held by individuals, on the other hand, was a positive gain under the Occupation. It should be trumpeted to the international skies. (Land reform is discussed further in Chapter Twenty-Two.)

The Peace Treaty Issue. Quite naturally the last major working force in Occupation politics was the issue of when the Occupation itself would come to a close. It will always stand to the credit of the former Supreme Commander, General Douglas MacArthur, that he was among the first to predict diminishing returns from a military occupation. In his first formal press conference since early in the Pacific War, General MacArthur on March 17, 1947, divided the Occupation into three phases. The military purpose of the Occupation, he thought, had been accomplished. Democratization, the political phase, he admitted was incomplete but must be accomplished by the Japanese themselves. Only removal of military control would provide the ultimate test. "The process of democratization is one of continual flux. It takes years." The third phase, the economic, was scarcely begun. With a peace treaty, which he advocated immediately, Japan could exercise her right to establish an independently managed economy.

Governmentally, Japan had long since been prepared for her re-entry into the family of nations. This fact in itself is surprising and a tribute to Japanese ingenuity, for early in the Occupation, Japan was as isolated from normal international intercourse as she had been under the Tokugawa. All foreign contact with Japan was channeled through SCAP. The Supreme Commander, exerciser of Japan's sovereignty, received all chiefs of mission —including American diplomats—in Tokyo. Behind the screen of isolation, however, the Japanese managed to keep up on diplomatic techniques and etiquette. Her trained and experienced diplomatic personnel were simply transferred to the very important, if subdued, agency called the Central

[35] Memoranda concerning dissolution of the *Zaibatsu* and establishment of Liquidation Commissions are contained in *NKHK,* Vol. I, No. 5 (August 15, 1946), pp. 9-14; concerning rural land reform, *ibid.,* Vol. I, No. 6 (September 1, 1946), pp. 11-14.

Liaison Office (CLO; *Shūsen Renryaku Chūō Jimu-kyoku*).[36] With SCAP increasingly dependent on technical liaison direct with appropriate ministries, the CLO was abolished on February 1, 1948. Thereafter, as signature of the peace treaty approached, the *Gaimushō* proper came back into its own (see Chart 28).

The roadblock to a peace treaty, then, was neither SCAP nor the Japanese government. Delay was occasioned by larger world factors, such as maneuvers in the cold war. On July 11, 1947, the United States followed the Supreme Commander's suggestion and proposed a preliminary conference of *all* Far Eastern Commission members to draft a treaty outside the structure of the FEC. Such a draft would then be submitted to the Foreign Ministers of all FEC member states and finally to all states at war with Japan. All states approached, except one, approved the conference; eight agreed to the American voting formula; the Soviet Union objected, insisting that preliminary drafts had to be drawn by a Pacific Council of Foreign Ministers, including only the United States, the Soviet Union, the United Kingdom, and China.

Real progress toward a peace treaty began to be made during 1950, although there were many obstacles in addition to Soviet intransigeance and the appearance of a new factor, the Chinese People's Republic. In Washington the Defense Department, harried by responsibilities of the Korean conflict, continued to oppose the MacArthur-State Department plan for an early Japanese peace. Late in the year, an interdepartmental compromise involving the expressed intention to retain bases in Japan cleared the way in Washington. On May 18 President Truman assigned the treaty problem to Special Adviser (Republican, and later Secretary of State) John Foster Dulles; in September he ordered the State Department to begin conversations with willing FEC members.

Within Japan, the peace treaty curiously became a real political issue in the House of Councilors elections of June 4. Earlier, the Liberal government had formally announced its willingness to sign a separate treaty with any nation prepared to recognize Japan's independence. On May 1, the Administration beat down an opposition resolution of censure concerning the statement, 251-143. Censure was generally supported by Democrats, Socialists, and cooperative groups who demanded a treaty signed by the U.S.S.R. and Chinese Communists as well as the other Allies. Nevertheless, the opposition parties were badly split over the issue and the Liberals were united. The elections of June 4 gave the Liberals a gain in the upper house. By mid-1951, amid talks of a Korean truce, the Japanese were informed even

[36] Cutting of all Japanese overseas contacts is covered in SCAP, *Political Reorientation*, cited, Vol. I, Section 1, "Control of Japanese External Affairs," pp. 1-7. The ordinance establishing the CLO was reproduced in the *Nippon Times*, October 2, 1945. *Tōkyō Shimbun* (Editorial), September 11, 1945, carried a biting criticism of the entrenchment of the elite of bureaucracy in the CLO.

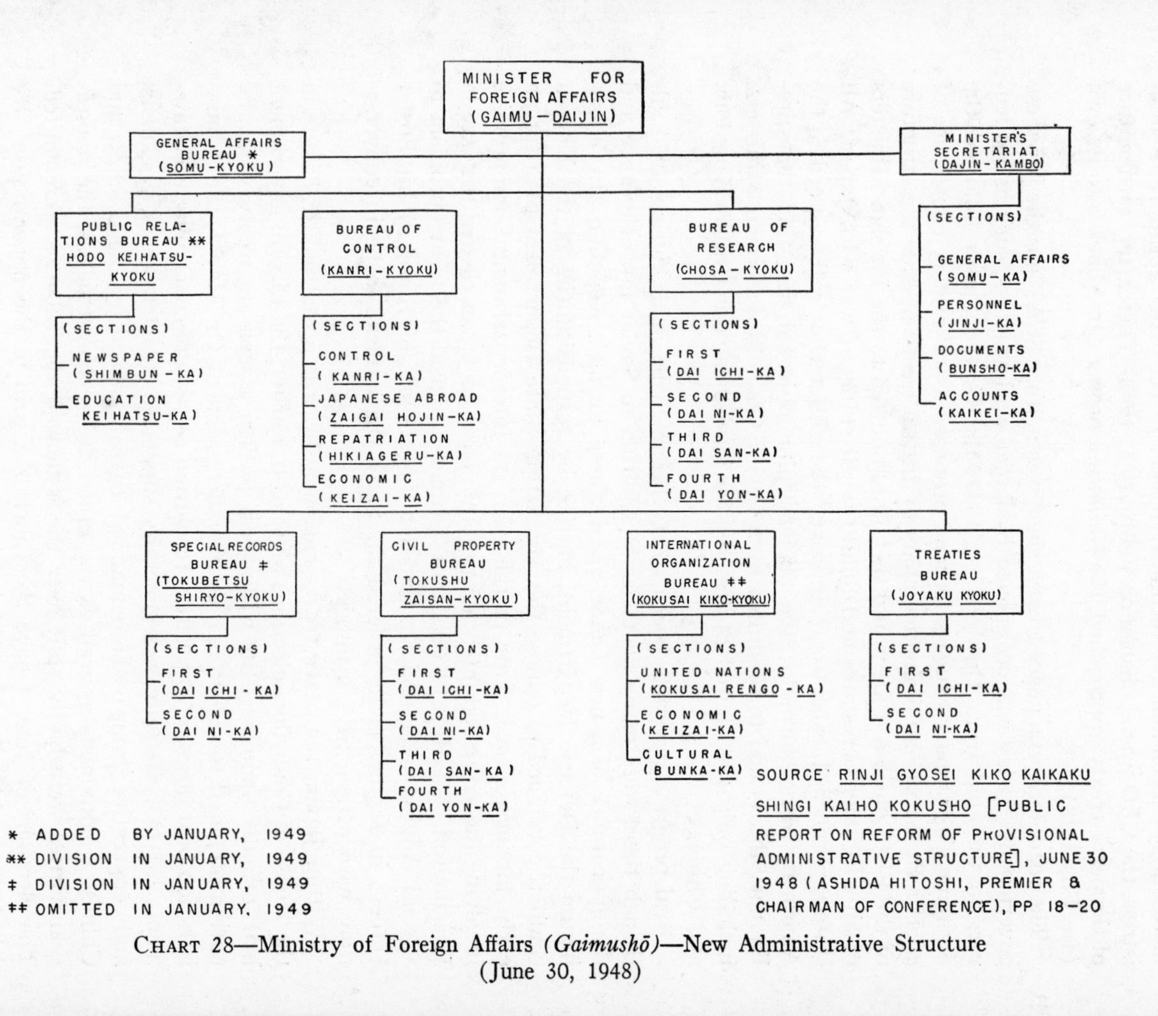

CHART 28—Ministry of Foreign Affairs *(Gaimushō)*—New Administrative Structure (June 30, 1948)

of the site of their liberation. The treaty was to be signed in San Francisco, birthplace of the United Nations.[37]

Someday, long after the peace treaty and Japan's new-found freedom, an elderly professor in mellow mood may well reflect on the Occupation, in all of its better aspects. In thoughts thoroughly Japanese, no more adroit than revealing, no more prudent than wise, he may say:[38] We Japanese found it difficult to be a model conquered people, seeing that for two thousand years of our national life we had never been conquered. You Americans, on the other hand, were in a position only a little less embarrassing, for you found it difficult to be conquerors, seeing that in your one hundred and fifty years of national life you never formed the habit of conquering other peoples. Both of our intentions, however, were honorable. We were utterly inexperienced, needed coaching. You often made the same mistake we made, in the heyday of conquest, trying to thrust bodily upon the conquered your way of life. There we could coach you. All in all, through mutual aid and many mistakes we did not do too badly giving the world a pattern of conduct for those mutually embarrassed.

[37] *Conference for the Conclusion and Signature of the Treaty of Peace with Japan; Record of Proceedings,* Washington, 1951 (Publication 4392, International Organization and Conference Series II, Far Eastern 3).

[38] With all due apologies to the Japanese Minister of Education, Mr. Takahashi Seiichirō, and acknowledgment of his reported interview with T. V. Smith, summer, 1947.

CHAPTER
TWENTY-TWO

The Japanization of American Democracy

A NEW and subtly different period of Japanese government and politics came into effect at 10:30 P.M. Tokyo time, April 28, 1952. Japan was once more at peace almost seven years after the surrender; the Japanese once again took up the burdens of independence.

Once again the Japanese have begun a process of Japanizing massive imports of alien culture. This time, unlike the previous experiences following the Taika reforms or the Westernization of the Meiji period, Japan's development must be paced to the severe demands of international strategic threats and the inward requirements for economic survival in an unpromising setting.

All three of the authors of this work have visited Tokyo within recent months before the final printing of this book. One of the authors (Burks) spent the academic year 1952-1953 in Japan.[1]

The post-treaty period started off with a Communist-directed mob disturbance in the Imperial palace plaza on May Day, 1952. The Communists displayed the truculent bullying and the reckless disregard of public dignity and safety which have won them enemies in so many other places; apart from the distant but real Communist threat to Japan, Japan's post-treaty absorption of American democracy is characterized by its dryness of spirit, mildness of enthusiasm, and matter-of-factness of practical development.

A return to Japanization, in the form of "rectification of Occupation direc-

[1] The author did, of course, visit Tokyo for extended periods. Although during the year he traveled south to Shimane-ken and Shikoku, through the Kansai (Kyōto-Osaka-Kobe), the Kantō Plain, and north into Tōhoku, many of his specific impressions and observations are limited to "his" prefecture. He is grateful for the year's opportunity, made possible by an Area Research Training Fellowship, Social Science Research Council; by a supplemental grant from the Calm Foundation, Rutgers University; and by his affiliation, first as Research Associate and then Director of Research, University of Michigan Center for Japanese Studies, with the Field Station, Okayama-shi, Okayama-ken, Japan.

tives," was almost inevitable. Both history and logic predicted a Japanese reexamination of the massive reforms of 1945-1952. They had been carried out under an alien military occupation.[2] They had assumed for Japan a level of (Western) political sophistication which had not been achieved in prewar days. Japan's post-treaty leaders consistently demonstrated a tendency toward reversal of Occupation reforms and a majority of the electorate consistently voted conservative.[3] By mid-1956, constitutional revision—at least incorporating the symbols of Japan's new-found sovereignty—was a sure thing. Less certain, because they were tactically fought step by step by the increasingly powerful Socialists, were constitutionally legal rearmament, centralization of control over education, the conservatives' political attempt to gerrymander Japan's electoral districts, and certain legal and administrative changes.

Reverse Course. The ebb tide of a moderate reversal was marked by a bill which conservative parties finally pushed through both houses of the Diet in 1956. This legislation provided for a Constitution Research Council within the Cabinet "to carry out a complete examination of the Constitution of Japan from a national viewpoint."[4] A Government statement pointed to the fact that the Constitution had been drafted in a short period, on the request of SCAP: "It is an undeniable fact that the Constitution which came into force under such circumstances does not represent the freely expressed will of the nation." Socialists denounced the whole scheme as leading to "a constitution prepared and enforced by the Liberal-Democratic Party." The *Asahi Shimbun* of February 17, 1956, warned, "We have been opposed to a hasty revision of the Constitution." The *Mainichi Shimbun*, of the same date, supported revision of the Constitution, but questioned placement of the Research Council under the Cabinet rather than under the Diet.

As the Research Council went to work, these were the proposed amendments to the Constitution most often mentioned: to convert the Emperor

[2] For an illuminating discussion of this point, explaining the probable results in constitutional revision, see Kazuo Kawai, "Sovereignty and Democracy in the Japanese Constitution," *American Political Science Review*, Vol. XLIX, No. 3 (September 1955), pp. 663-673.

[3] Hugh Borton, "Past Limitations and the Future of Democracy in Japan," *Political Science Quarterly*, Vol. LXXX, No. 3 (September 1955), pp. 410-420. The author was privileged to join professor Borton and others in a Council on Foreign Relations seminar on Japan in New York during the spring of 1956. The study project, under the directorship of Dr. Philip E. Mosely of the Council and the able chairmanship of former ambassador Ernest A. Gross, is scheduled for publication in the autumn of 1956 under the title, *Japan Between East and West*. See Dr. Borton's forthcoming chapter, "Democracy in Postwar Japan."

[4] First submitted to the 22d special session in June, 1955, the bill passed the House of Representatives by a vote of 238 to 129, but later died in the House of Councillors. Introduced again, the bill passed the lower houses on March 29, 1956, by a vote of 239 to 139, and the upper house in the last strife-torn days before the summer elections for the upper house. Although the Council was to be established under the Cabinet, it was to operate without Government intervention. The membership is set at a maximum of 50, including 30 Diet members and 20 nonpolitical experts. See Consulate General of Japan, *Japan Report, New York* (mimeograph), Vol. II, No. 7 (Apr. 17, 1956).

from "the symbol of the state" to the chief of state; to redraft Article 9; to clarify Chapter III (Rights and Duties of the People) in order to allow restrictions in the public welfare; to clarify Article 7 concerned with the right of the Cabinet to dissolve the House of Representatives; and to reexamine the role of the House of Councillors.

The Economics of Sovereignty. As compared with reexamination of Occupation reforms, economic independence was a wraith far more difficult to grasp. Here the facts of life were far less flexible. Despite a peace treaty to which many referred as soft, Japan nevertheless emerged land-poor, resources-poor, and overpopulated.

By the mid-1950's the problem of economic viability had become essentially a foreign trade puzzle. The dollar trade gap, it is true, had been steadily cut back from $514 million in 1951 to $103 million in 1955. Yet the United States remained a dominant factor in Japanese foreign trade, supplying almost one-third of Japan's imports and taking about one-fourth of her exports in 1955. Discouragingly, Japan remained a relatively unimportant factor in American foreign trade, taking but 5 per cent of our exports and providing only 4 per cent of our total imports.[5]

Furthermore, the economic umbilical cord which had so long pumped life into the Japanese economy was always in danger of being severed. Large deficits in trade with the United States in the postwar period could not have been incurred, had it not been for abnormal outlays for aid to the ex-enemy, special procurement during the Korean conflict, and most recently disposal of American food surpluses to provide yen debt funds for Japanese industrial modernization. The economic utility of this last step, taken unselfishly from our point of view, was obscured by political opposition in Japan to continued dependence.

Post-treaty Japan had the highest density of population per cultivable area of any country in the world. Gloomily but authoritatively, the Population Problem Research Office of the Welfare Ministry had estimated that a 1953 population of 85 million would increase by 1955 to 89 million and by 1960 to 95 million. Tentative figures based on the census of October 1, 1955, showed how accurate the prediction had been: Japan had almost 18 million households and a population of over 89 million. Moreover, hopes for rising agricultural production in the underdeveloped countries of Asia were not to be shared by Japan. Japanese rice yields per acre, using age-old agrarian engineering and hard labor, were already among the highest in the world. In 1955 Japan's rice output reached a new all-time high; yet she spent $524 million for imported foods. To maintain minimum Japanese stand-

[5] The authors are grateful for these data to Dr. Jerome Cohen, who also participated in the Council on Foreign Relations seminar mentioned above. During 1956 Professor Cohen was preparing a revised edition of his authoritative *Japan's Economy,* cited above. See also The Chemical Corn Exchange Bank, *International Economic Survey,* "Japan," No. 106 (February 1956). Most recent population statistics may be found in Embassy of Japan, *Japan Report, Washington* (mimeograph), Vol. I, No. 9 (Dec. 14, 1955), p. 9.

ards judged by the depression levels of 1930-34, the Japanese had to import one fifth of their food consumption, nine tenths of their petroleum products, half of their vital chemical fertilizers, and a substantial majority of the industrial raw materials.

Considering this grim environment the Japanese—with American aid—had performed miracles in rebuilding their worn-out, bombed-out, and burned-out economy. By 1953, for example, this economy had already surpassed the goals of the 1945 five-year plan; these goals had, in their turn, planned a 130 per cent rise in production and a restoration of 90 per cent of the prewar levels of consumption. Some observers felt that by the mid-1950's the Japanese economy was reaching the margin of reconstruction. Even the Japanese Foreign Office was blunt in its description of the Japanese economic position:

> The economy of Japan is unique in that it is unbalanced, with modernism shackled to feudalism, as the result of the superimposition of a highly developed modern industrial system upon a semi-feudal agricultural and handicraft society. Unless Japan shares in the world economy, her economic development will be restricted to her own boundaries, which will necessarily limit its scale and reduce the living standards of the Japanese people.

In order to share in the world economy, continued the *Gaimushō,* Japan must (1) develop resources, modernize industry, accumulate capital at home, and (2) promote trade abroad.[6]

Some Japanese observers and some Western ones as well had fallen captive to the delusion that, because of the proximity of the Asian land mass and the density of the Asian populations, Japan should trade with Asia. The 1949 plan assumed this. By the middle 1950's the practical results were unrewarding. Both Japanese and foreigners were beginning to realize that, in terms of ton-yen costs, Japan was closer to the coast of Africa than to the interior of China, closer to Brazil than to Mongolia, and that apart from the difficulties of dealing with Communist-controlled states the Japanese simply did not have available the kind of *laissez-faire* market which they had had under the old unequal treaties with China. Asia figured largely in the Japanese economic future, but no one knew how to reconcile the rational and apparent requirements of that future with the practical necessities imposed by the Washington-Moscow competition for power and safety.

The Healing of the Scars. Neither the surrender itself nor the Occupation policies had as much visible effect in Japanese life as their designers

[6] In a brace of pamphlets, the *Gaimushō* was as frank about economic prospects as it had been about the strategic danger. See Gaimushō, Jōhō Bunkakyoku, *Saikin no Nihon seiji-keizai jijō* (Ministry of Foreign Affairs, Bureau of Public Information & Cultural Affairs, Recent Japanese political and economic status), Tōkyō, March, 1953, espec. pp. 77-90 and 91-104; *Present Conditions of Japan, Economic Section,* Tokyo, August, 1951, pp. 29-32; and *Economic Rehabilitation and Foreign Commerce of Japan,* Tokyo, April, 1953. The quotation is from the latter, p. 12.

might have planned. The Japanese showed themselves perfunctorily but sincerely appreciative of America's magnanimous role as victor, but by the 1950's Japan's role in a possible World War III was a far more burning issue than Japan's responsibility for World War II. Now and then an outspoken revisionist, such as the famous and eloquent journalist, Tokutomi ("Soho") Ichirō, broke through the screen of Japanese politeness and spoke out of the depths of his Japanese patriotism. The Japanese got over 1945 by forgetting it.[7]

More often the Japanese turn to the future. It is perhaps safe to say of the MacArthur era that the Occupation changed Japan far less than the authors of *induced revolution* had claimed, that Japanese life was nevertheless altered far more by the Occupation than most Japanese themselves realized, and that the Occupation *qua* military government had run its course with less friction than its critics would admit.

Superficial traces remain. The Tokyo streets retain their American military nomenclature of A, B, C, or 1st, 2nd, or 3rd, and the like because the Japanese themselves found the new names, in contrast to the old ward names, useful. The railway system originally planned on the German model still had American sanitary inspection forms and station names in Roman letters. In the *kenchō* offices of almost all prefectures the appendage of *shōgaigakari* or *renraku-shitsu* (liaison office) remained, useful to foreign travelers, businessmen, and scholars.

Deep underneath these surface changes, the significant, final judgment on Occupation revolution was being recorded in the minds of the Japanese, just as previous importations in Japanese history had been mentally sorted. In one prefecture, a sample of city and prefectural assemblymen were asked their opinions on good and bad features of the Occupation. These men and women were open and specific on disliked features, which outnumbered those they liked. Educational reform, the new tax system, and the commission in government were criticized; health measures, welfare plans, and land reform were often praised. Among a mass panel of voters from the same prefecture, 45 per cent could think of no good results of the Occupation; 44 per cent could think of no bad ones. Those who believed the overall effect of the Occupation was good for Japan were vague, speaking in generalities of "democratization." About 40 per cent felt a few, strong leaders in post-

[7] Sometimes the roles of prosecutor and defender were curiously reversed. A volume by former Ambassador Joseph C. Grew drew widespread attention in the Japanese press. He went further than any other outstanding American in charging that the United States, more specifically President Roosevelt and Secretary of State Hull, substantially shared the responsibility for the failure to avert war with Japan. In an interview in Tokyo on the eleventh anniversary of Pearl Harbor, Japan's wartime Ambassador to Washington Nomura Kichisaburō, by implication, absolved Roosevelt and Hull. Lack of able leadership in Japan capable of unifying public opinion and controlling hot-headed militarists prevented settlement with Washington. The late Prince Konoye, whom Grew trusted, could not provide that leadership, Nomura concluded. Tokutomi Ichirō, *Shōrisha no hiai* (Sorrows of the victor), Tōkyō, 1953. Joseph C. Grew, *Turbulent Era,* New York, 1952, received spreads in three successive issues of the *Nippon Times* (November 22, 23, 24, 1952), which also carried (December 9, 1952) Nomura's story of Pearl Harbor.

treaty Japan would do more to solve problems than definition of issues, political talk, or parties.[8]

The purges had come to a close. The Occupation itself had de-purged most of the persons originally excluded from public life by the Allied military authorities. Japanese public opinion generally reflected the view that the sentences on war criminals were exorbitantly heavy. The war criminals became heroes, but half-forgotten heroes. The de-purgees did not become a significant, solid bloc. In the general election of 1952 they were scattered among all parties and were not ultra-nationalist as a group.

The process of healing was so quiet that a great deal of talk concerning the amendment of the new Constitution centered on the one issue of rearmament rather than on the constitutional profile of Japan as a whole. An attempt on the part of the Administration to raise the issue of constitutional change was met by a largely negative public opinion in 1953 and 1954. Two of the Japanese who actually helped draft the new organic law, Dr. Kanamori Tokujirō of the National Diet Library and ex-Premier Ashida Hitoshi of the Progressive Party, claimed rearmament did not require amendment of the existing Constitution. Yet political party candidates who sponsored rearmament—constitutionally or otherwise—discovered ruefully in the 1953 elections that views in that direction were political dynamite.

The Empire and Shintō. The Japanese Imperial family showed both deftness and good taste in retaining their archaic prestige and adding modern popularity to it. On November 10, 1952, Akihito, the Crown Prince, rode in a horse-drawn carriage from his temporary residence in Shibuya to the Imperial palace, marking his own coming of age and investiture as heir to the Throne. The Emperor stayed out of politics, but made himself felt in the Japanese press and public opinion as a modest spokesman of the new Japan and a quiet civilian who shared the experience of defeat and the hope of reconstruction with his people.

The Imperial family ventured on dangerous ground when the Crown Prince visited London to attend the coronation of Queen Elizabeth II. Residua of wartime resentment might have inflamed foreign opinion, Japanese opinion, or both. The worldwide reaction was smooth and friendly; Akihito himself contributed to making it so.

Shintō, the national cult, continued despite disestablishment as a state faith. The great Shrine of Ise, traditionally dedicated five years before the

[8] The author of this section is indebted for these estimates to his colleague in research and former fellow-language officer, Douglas H. Mendel, Jr. During 1952-53 Mr. Mendel, also based at the Michigan Center for Japanese Studies, conducted mass and leadership public opinon surveys to get at Japanese political opinion and behavior. Samples were chosen from metropolitan Ōsaka-fu, balanced Okayama-ken, and rural Shimane-ken for comparison. Results, such as those summarized from Okayama data, were obtained in intensive, personal interviews. Analysis was checked against findings of Japanese political scientists, such as the distinguished Dr. Rōyama Masamichi. The sifted, invaluable data will be available soon, it is hoped, in Mr. Mendel's dissertation for the University of Michigan. Such field studies will do more to pass judgment on the Occupation than all the journalistic descriptions and official releases combined.

birth of Christ to the Sun Goddess, Amaterasu Ōmikami, became a mere corporation supported by the Ise Shrine Worshippers' Association. The number of Ise pilgrims dropped from a 1940 high of eight million to a low point in 1947 of 780,000 and then rose again to two million in 1950 and to three and a half million in 1952. Columns of school children led by their teachers lined up outside the shrine to fulfill their obligations as Japanese. Few dreamt of exercising the new freedom of religion by refusing to pay homage to the divine mother-goddess of their own country, even when the teachers asked them—under the new laws—how many wished to go and how many to stay away.[9]

Development of Public Administration. Bureaucracy, along with the Empire, is both old and Japanese. The complexity, diffuseness, and indirection of Japan's prewar bureaucracy survived war, defeat, Occupation, and post-treaty reform. Pitted against this inertia of the old bureaucracy were Japanese attempts, sustaining previous Occupation attempts, to modernize the bureaucracy for the sake of efficiency and to reform the bureaucracy for the sake of democracy. A third force in bureaucratic development was the treaty structure existing between the United States and Japan.[10]

Japanese attempts in 1949 and 1950 to put reform plans into practice fell far short of success. The Cabinet then borrowed an American technique, the appointment of a Japanese "Hoover commission" of prominent citizens. Their report on reform was submitted in August, 1951, released by the Cabinet two months later, and put into effect, for the greater part, in 1952. Briefly the report advocated: termination of Occupation administration (*senryō gyōsei*); further democratization by simplifying personnel, auditing, and accounting procedures; regrouping of ministries, offices, and agencies, particularly external organs and agencies concerned with administrative control; reduction and consolidation of administration.[11]

[9] The Society for *Shintō* Culture began a difficult venture, attempting to explain the mysticism of *Shintō* in English to foreigners in Noritake Tsuda, Editor, *The Shintō Bulletin,* Tokyo, quarterly. Vol. I, No. 1 (March, 1953) carried a Shintō Message, articles on the status of shrines, Shintō and Nationalism, Faith in the Ise Shrine, and excellent pictures. Chief Priest Takatsukasa Nobusuke of Meiji Shrine set the tone for post-treaty *Shintō:* "It is our greatest regret that Japanese Shintō was severely criticized in the world before and after the war and that it was bitterly misunderstood and consequently oppressed so much during the Occupation period in a manner that Japanese people never expected. . . . All that we entreat is to do our best to establish a new positive culture hand in hand with other countries of the world."

[10] These estimates were carried in "A Note on the Emerging Structure of the Post-Treaty Japanese National Government," *Occasional Papers, Center for Japanese Studies,* No. 3 (1952), pp. 47-58. The author again would like to express his appreciation to Mr. Nakagawa Toru, then Deputy Chief of the Gyōsei Kanrichō (Administrative Management Agency), under the Prime Minister's Office. Mr. Nakagawa is representative of postwar public servants who are members of, and have a stake in the reform of, administrative structure. (Mr. Nakagawa later took over the sensitive post of Japanese Minister to the Philippine Republic.) Legally, the A.M.A. was authorized to (a) study administration; (b) plan structure and operations; (c) recommend creation, abolition, and reorganization of organs; and (d) inspect activities. *Gyōsei Kanrichō setchi hō* (Law establishing the Administrative Management Agency), Tōkyō, rev. to 31 July 1952 (mimeograph).

[11] Naikaku Kambō (Cabinet Secretariat) *Gyōsei seido no kaikaku ni kansuru tōshin* (Report on reform of the administrative system), Tōkyō, August 14, 1951, 22 pp.

The 1952 reforms survived. Amalgamation was marked among commissions, agencies, and their divisions. Reduction in number was matched by the attempt to make consistent the internal structure of all organs. As before, the major subdivisions of government were ministries, with one office (the Prime Minister's Office), and one authority (the National Personnel). Each ministry was subdivided into a secretariat, bureaus, and sections; commissions, into an executive office and divisions. Each chief of department (Minister of State) was aided by a permanent vice-minister and had the option of establishing one additional post of parliamentary vice-minister.[12]

A valiant effort had been made to eliminate independent agencies or to include them under the Prime Minister's Office, which would then become the equivalent of the Executive Office of the President in American government. The National Personnel Authority (*Jinji-in*), often called the "Fourth Power" (in addition to Cabinet, Diet, and courts), was the major exception. Destined to become a commission, like others under the Prime Minister's Office, it survived and gave rise to suspicion that it was a screen for traditional bureaucracy.

The Prime Minister's Office (*Sōrifu*), although cut down, was strengthened. The Office proper consisted of a Secretariat, the Pensions Bureau, and Statistics Bureau. Gone was the Occupation-born Economic Stabilization Board and, in its place, an Economic Investigation Agency became an external organ of the Prime Minister's Office. The Procurement Agency, the funnel for American purchases in Japan, doubtless gave room for new-style politico-economic patronage. Other reduced agencies and commissions dealt with fair trade, land, local autonomy, Hokkaido development, and administrative management.

A new *National Safety Agency* (*Hoanchō*), under the Prime Minister's Office, reflected the transitional method of handling the explosive problem of rearmament. Existing law provided that the post of chief, the "Security Minister," be held by a civilian. Prime Minister Yoshida delicately held the portfolio concurrently for a time before turning it over to State Minister Kimura Tokutarō, Director-General of *Hoanchō.* After October, 1952, the corps of the National Police Reserve became a Security Force (*Hoantai*). There was as well a National Public Safety Commission, also under the Prime Minister's Office, with Headquarters, National Rural Police—the police were actually split up among the prefectures—and National Fire Defense.

The revived *Ministry of Foreign Affairs* (*Gaimushō*) was, of course, the most obvious addition to the post-treaty Cabinet. Under plans for reform drawn up in 1951, of all agencies only the *Gaimushō* was recommended for

[12] For statistics on amalgamation, see Appendix II; and for a glossary of selected administrative terms, with English equivalents, Appendix I of "Structure of Japanese Government," cited.

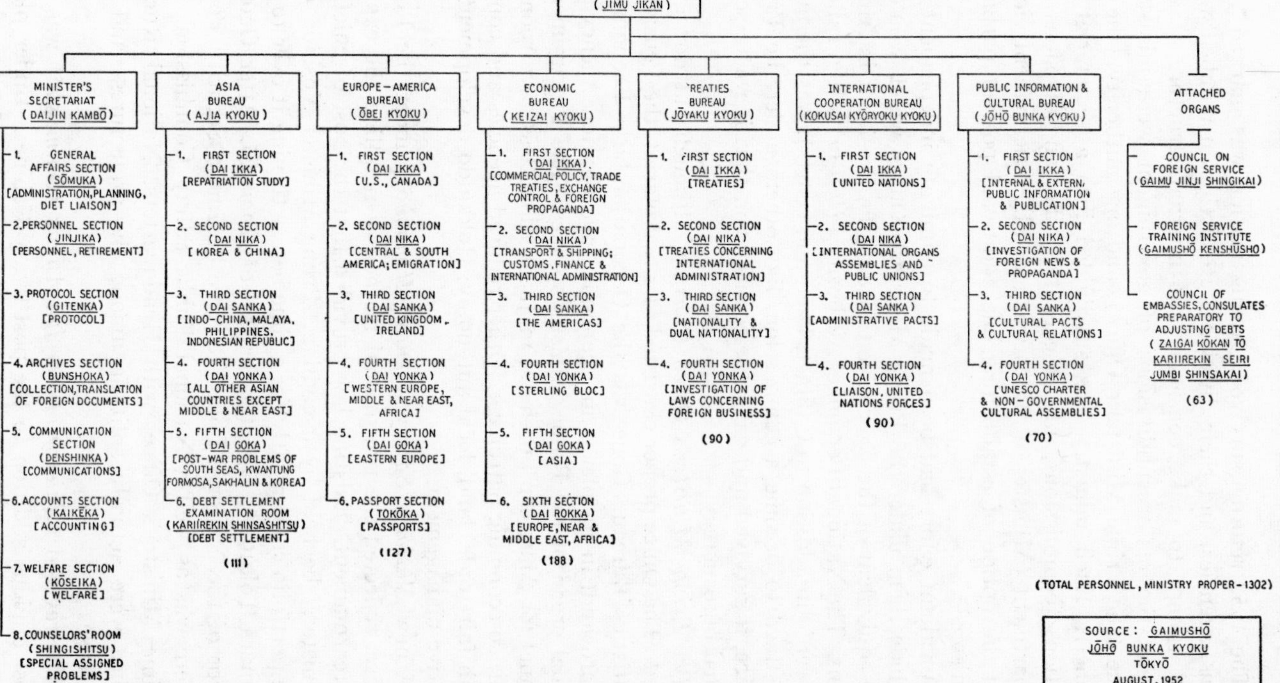
MINISTER (GAIMU DAIJIN)
PARLIAMENTARY VICE-MINISTER (SEIMU JIKAN)
MINISTRY ADVISOR (GAIMUSHŌ-KOMON)
MINISTRY COUNSELOR (GAIMUSHŌ-SANYŌ)
PERMANENT VICE-MINISTER (JIMU JIKAN)
MINISTER'S SECRETARIAT (DAIJIN KAMBŌ)
1. GENERAL AFFAIRS SECTION (SŌMUKA) [ADMINISTRATION, PLANNING, DIET LIAISON]
2. PERSONNEL SECTION (JINJIKA) [PERSONNEL, RETIREMENT]
3. PROTOCOL SECTION (GITENKA) [PROTOCOL]
4. ARCHIVES SECTION (BUNSHOKA) [COLLECTION, TRANSLATION OF FOREIGN DOCUMENTS]
5. COMMUNICATION SECTION (DENSHINKA) [COMMUNICATIONS]
6. ACCOUNTS SECTION (KAIKĒKA) [ACCOUNTING]
7. WELFARE SECTION (KŌSEIKA) [WELFARE]
8. COUNSELORS' ROOM (SHINGISHITSU) [SPECIAL ASSIGNED PROBLEMS]
(563)
ASIA BUREAU (AJIA KYOKU)
1. FIRST SECTION (DAI IKKA) [REPATRIATION STUDY]
2. SECOND SECTION (DAI NIKA) [KOREA & CHINA]
3. THIRD SECTION (DAI SANKA) [INDO-CHINA, MALAYA, PHILIPPINES, INDONESIAN REPUBLIC]
4. FOURTH SECTION (DAI YONKA) [ALL OTHER ASIAN COUNTRIES EXCEPT MIDDLE & NEAR EAST]
5. FIFTH SECTION (DAI GOKA) [POST-WAR PROBLEMS OF SOUTH SEAS, KWANTUNG FORMOSA, SAKHALIN & KOREA]
6. DEBT SETTLEMENT EXAMINATION ROOM (KARIIREKIN SHINSASHITSU) [DEBT SETTLEMENT]
(111)
EUROPE-AMERICA BUREAU (ŌBEI KYOKU)
1. FIRST SECTION (DAI IKKA) [U.S., CANADA]
2. SECOND SECTION (DAI NIKA) [CENTRAL & SOUTH AMERICA; EMIGRATION]
3. THIRD SECTION (DAI SANKA) [UNITED KINGDOM, IRELAND]
4. FOURTH SECTION (DAI YONKA) [WESTERN EUROPE, MIDDLE & NEAR EAST, AFRICA]
5. FIFTH SECTION (DAI GOKA) [EASTERN EUROPE]
6. PASSPORT SECTION (TOKŌKA) [PASSPORTS]
(127)
ECONOMIC BUREAU (KEIZAI KYOKU)
1. FIRST SECTION (DAI IKKA) [COMMERCIAL POLICY, TRADE TREATIES, EXCHANGE CONTROL & FOREIGN PROPAGANDA]
2. SECOND SECTION (DAI NIKA) [TRANSPORT & SHIPPING; CUSTOMS, FINANCE & INTERNATIONAL ADMINISTRATION]
3. THIRD SECTION (DAI SANKA) [THE AMERICAS]
4. FOURTH SECTION (DAI YONKA) [STERLING BLOC]
5. FIFTH SECTION (DAI GOKA) [ASIA]
6. SIXTH SECTION (DAI ROKKA) [EUROPE, NEAR & MIDDLE EAST, AFRICA]
(188)
TREATIES BUREAU (JŌYAKU KYOKU)
1. FIRST SECTION (DAI IKKA) [TREATIES]
2. SECOND SECTION (DAI NIKA) [TREATIES CONCERNING INTERNATIONAL ADMINISTRATION]
3. THIRD SECTION (DAI SANKA) [NATIONALITY & DUAL NATIONALITY]
4. FOURTH SECTION (DAI YONKA) [INVESTIGATION OF LAWS CONCERNING FOREIGN BUSINESS]
(90)
INTERNATIONAL COOPERATION BUREAU (KOKUSAI KYŌRYOKU KYOKU)
1. FIRST SECTION (DAI IKKA) [UNITED NATIONS]
2. SECOND SECTION (DAI NIKA) [INTERNATIONAL ORGANS ASSEMBLIES AND PUBLIC UNIONS]
3. THIRD SECTION (DAI SANKA) [ADMINISTRATIVE PACTS]
4. FOURTH SECTION (DAI YONKA) [LIAISON, UNITED NATIONS FORCES]
(90)
PUBLIC INFORMATION & CULTURAL BUREAU (JŌHŌ BUNKA KYOKU)
1. FIRST SECTION (DAI IKKA) [INTERNAL & EXTERN. PUBLIC INFORMATION & PUBLICATION]
2. SECOND SECTION (DAI NIKA) [INVESTIGATION OF FOREIGN NEWS & PROPAGANDA]
3. THIRD SECTION (DAI SANKA) [CULTURAL PACTS & CULTURAL RELATIONS]
4. FOURTH SECTION (DAI YONKA) [UNESCO CHARTER & NON-GOVERNMENTAL CULTURAL ASSEMBLIES]
(70)
ATTACHED ORGANS
COUNCIL ON FOREIGN SERVICE (GAIMU JINJI SHINGIKAI)
FOREIGN SERVICE TRAINING INSTITUTE (GAIMUSHŌ KENSHŪSHO)
COUNCIL OF EMBASSIES, CONSULATES PREPARATORY TO ADJUSTING DEBTS (ZAIGAI KŌKAN TŌ KARIIREKIN SEIRI JUMBI SHINSAKAI)
(63)
(TOTAL PERSONNEL, MINISTRY PROPER-1302)
SOURCE: GAIMUSHŌ JŌHŌ BUNKA KYOKU TŌKYŌ AUGUST, 1952

CHART 29—Ministry of Foreign Affairs *(Gaimushō)*

expansion. After the treaty, the Foreign Minister had a difficult role in relations with other ministries. He and his staff had to press claims of other agencies with the United Nations and their security forces; they represented the Justice Ministry in the campaign for court jurisdiction over U.N. forces off bases; they represented the Agriculture and Forestry Ministry in complaints against the limitation of fishing in Korean waters.

In numbers, the *Gaimushō* remained small (in 1952, 1581 employees worked in the rented upper three floors of the substantial Nissan Building). At the end of the Occupation, experienced diplomats who had been purged had never regained their seniority status. Yet once again commanding the elite of young personnel, the *Gaimushō,* its 18 embassies, 14 legations, 16 consulates-general, and one mission were rapidly regaining prestige. Certainly the Ministry was a model of administrative neatness (the organization is presented in Chart 29) and could have been envied by those who periodically despaired over the intricacies of the U.S. Department of State.

Other ministries showed less internal reorganization. The Ministry of Justice (*Hōmushō*), in its new name, reflected reversion from a brief experience with the American-type office of Attorney General.

The powerful Finance Ministry (*Ōkurashō*) was further strengthened, budgetary and therefore administrative management still lying in the hands of its Budget Bureau. Reformist public administrators frankly hoped for the bureau's transfer to the Prime Minister's Office, where it could work closely with the Administrative Management Agency. With continued separation of personnel (N.P.A.), budgetary (Finance), and administrative (A.M.A.) control, the forces in opposition to the intrenched *kambatsu* were badly split.

The Ministries of Welfare, Agriculture and Forestry, International Trade and Industry, Transportation, Education, Postal Services, Labor, and Construction remained unchanged. The Japan Telegraph and Telephone Company, Ltd., absorbed duties of the Ministry of Telecommunications.

All this reshuffling and consolidation resulted in a reduction of total personnel. Even after the first phase of reform, however, the national government employed almost a million and a half public servants. The government plan to carry out a further 10 per cent personnel cut in February, 1953, ran into opposition of parties with eyes on the elections.

If anyone thought the *kambatsu* would disappear under the new Constitution, he was mistaken. Dr. Rōyama Masamichi, Japan's most distinguished political scientist, wrote that, if there was a mortal enemy of democracy in post-treaty Japan, it was the bureaucrats. The effects of strong Occupation controls, weakness of party cabinets, and ignorance of legislators left the bureaucrats intrenched despite all efforts to root them out.[13]

It is nevertheless encouraging that two excursions of bureaucracy into the

[13] Dr. Masamichi Rōyama, "Bureaucrats—Enemy of Democracy," a summary of an article in *Kaizō,* in *Nippon Times,* September 29, 1953.

public's new-found freedom raised a storm of protest. Chief Cabinet Secretary Ōgata, wartime head of the Cabinet Information Bureau and former editor of *Asahi,* let it be known in late 1952 that the government was considering the establishment of an information agency. He almost lost his political life in the attacks from the public, the opposition, and even government circles. Japanese newspapers, who seldom used U.S. Information Service handouts, simply revolted against releases such as had been forced down their throats for ten years. In January, the controversial chamber was blueprinted to collect information useful in formulation of policy, to provide analytical intelligence, and to release information which public media could voluntarily use in reporting.

The other proposed change included revision of the Police Law and Code of Criminal Procedure, and possibly even centralization of police control in the hands of a State Minister. Although flaws in drafting were linked with other budget difficulties in Diet hearings, still both the police measures and the information plan provided goads to the opposition in its successful campaign to drive the Yoshida Administration to a vote of non-confidence and general elections in April, 1953.[14]

Parliamentary Vitality. Many Americans and some Japanese hoped during the Occupation that the post-war National Diet would assume political leadership. In the period following signature of the peace treaty of Japan with the Allies, this did not happen; the Diet slipped back. Instead of becoming the "highest organ of state power," it became a cockpit for debate and nothing more than the supporting facility for the executives.

Parties and party splinters fought one another in sham battles which were not unreal enough to reveal a basic patriotism underneath nor real enough, as the alternative possibility, to precipitate decisiveness in the Japanese nation. The bitter but shallow party battles of the post-treaty period were not seriously discommoded by an anti-parliamentary Left or an anti-parliamentary Right. Only the mild preponderance of the Liberals and the personal survival capacity of Mr. Yoshida kept Japanese parliamentarism from verging upon ruin.

Even the House of Councilors got away from the role assigned to it by the new Constitution and had become a house with strong partisan coloring. The national constituency had not worked out well.[15]

[14] Nagato Masaji, an editor of *Mainichi,* cleverly pointed out that, in Britain, the Prime Minister was an outstanding source of information, working closely with the great, free English press; in America, the President effectively used the weekly press conference to co-operate with independent reporters. The editor thus got back at Premier Yoshida for his notorious disregard of Japanese newsmen (*Mainichi,* December 4, 1952). *Nihon Keizai* and *Sangyō Keizai* (both February 28, 1953) warned that revision of criminal procedure might lead to a police state, and dictatorial power in the hands of the Premier. *Tōkyō Shimbun* (March 1, 1953) shuddered at the government handling both procurators and police, in a manner in which the Tokugawa *Bakufu* controlled both judicial and police machinery.

[15] Fifty-three of the total of 128 candidates standing in the election of April 24, 1953 were national; 75 were prefectural. Only 63.2 per cent of the eligible electorate turned out, a low figure in contrast with the voting rate in lower House elections. Former Secretary

Party politics in post-treaty Japan, despite maneuvers and mergers, demonstrated recurrent instability fed by independent and uncooperative factions. These trends were exaggerated, not obscured, by polarization into what appeared to be a two-party system. Continued prosperity favored the conservatives, but time smiled on the rising Socialists.

Conservative Competition to Coalition. For two years beyond the peace, Yoshida Shigeru did give the Japanese nation leadership. Denounced as a testy and autocratic politician and as a pro-American "stooge," he was among the first to throw the Occupation reforms into reverse gear. Although his leadership saw the assimilation of many reforms into everyday life, he remained an uncompromising traditionalist, opposed to extremes of both the Right and the Left. Five times Premier of Japan, he broke the fifty-year-old record of Prince Itō, premier four times between 1885 and 1889.

The Liberals (Jiyūtō) were actually the first to propose conservative coalition, in April, 1954. Yoshida's plans for control of education, centralization of police (which passed after riots in the Diet), and a Defense Council had set the pattern of polarization of Right and Left. The majority Yoshida Liberals meanwhile became practically a party in their own right when the Premier expelled two party leaders who would not bow to his unqualified leadership, Ishibashi Tanzan and Kono Ichirō.

Led by Hatoyama Ichirō, the famed depurgee, the minority faction became in many ways more conservative than the Yoshida group. Hatoyama himself openly advocated constitutional amendment, a self-defense army, and diplomacy above party.

The Progressives (Kaishintō) except for the label did not differ very much from the Liberals. Each was a moderate, constitutionalist, and capitalist party. Two of the most prominent Progressive leaders were ex-Premier Ashida Hitoshi and the future and ex-Foreign Minister, Shigemitsu Mamoru, both diplomats, both men of extensive literary gifts, and neither one afire with the glories of the future.[16]

The Democrats (Minshutō) eventually embraced the dissident Hatoyama Liberals and succeeded the Progressive Party, which was dissolved in November, 1954. Faced with certain defeat, Yoshida resigned on December 7. Although he did not control a majority of the Diet, Hatoyama was elected

---

General Kondō Hideaki of the House of Councillors (whom the author met in his Diet office in May, 1953) summed up the disadvantages of the national constituency as (1) making it difficult for capable independents to campaign and (2) making it difficult for the voting public to know national candidates. Observers eagerly awaited elections in the summer of 1956 for clues as to the future of the upper house.

[16] The editor of this book interviewed Mr. Ashida in 1951 and had the opportunity of discussing Japanese politics with him for a very pleasant and extended conversation. Mr. Ashida reminded the editor not so much of the interwar world as of that world lost in August, 1914, in which sensitive intellectuality, refinement of manners, and a confidence in the world-as-it-is were touchstones of political success. Incidentally, the postwar genealogy of Mr. Ashida's party ran as follows: *Shimpotō, Minshutō, Kokumin Minshutō, Kaishintō;* later, *Minshutō* and *Jiyū-Minshutō*. For a recent study of parties and politics, see Harold S. Quigley and John E. Turner, *The New Japan: Government and Politics,* Minneapolis, 1956.

Premier on December 9 over Yoshida's successor, Ogata Taketora. Ironically Hatoyama won the support of the Left Socialists, in return for the promise of a spring election. Kishi Nobusuke, Secretary General of the new party, now became the architect of conservative coalition. Although the February, 1955, elections gave the Democrats a majority in the lower house, and Hatoyama was reelected Premier, it was widely assumed that he would rule temporarily and would give way before Ogata.

The Liberal-Democratic (Jiyū-Minshutō) coalition of November 15, 1955 actually occurred when the conservatives paused to look over their right shoulders at the Socialists, who merged on October 13. Fusion gave the Liberal-Democrats 64 per cent of lower-house seats, as against 33 per cent for the Socialists, and Hatoyama his third premiership. The new party went on record for revision of the Constitution and reform of administrative structure, against autocracy of power *(kenryoku)* and class-ism *(kaikyūshugi)*.

Socialist Misunderstandings to Merger. The *Socialists (Shakaitō)* had been even more impracticably divided than their conservative colleagues.[17] The right wing *(u-ha)* split off from the left wing *(sa-ha)* because they supported both the peace treaty and limited rearmament, while the left opposed both. The right wing continued as a mild opposition under the direction of ex-Premier Katayama and Asanuma Inejiro, and with the support of the moderate Japan Trade Union Congress *(Zenro,* 670,000 members). The left attracted the younger, theoretical Marxists, under Suzuki Mosaburō, and with the backing of the militant General Council of Trade Unions *(Sōhyō)*, 3 million members).

After a working agreement applied in the campaign of February, 1955, a complex organization scheme was completed by mid-October; Suzuki became Chairman, and Asanuma Secretary General. In the hodgepodge platform, leftists significantly seemed to have given way on more points than did rightists, specifically on the advisability of direct action. The new unified Socialist Party stood for "independent diplomacy, opposition to rearmament, stabilization of the people's livelihood, and the establishment of democracy." The Socialists pinned hopes on Japanese neutralism, new voters, and the unstable nature of their opponents' coalition.

The Japan Communist Party *(Nihon Kyōsantō)*. The Communists had emerged in the early days of the Occupation, surged to prominence before the outbreak of the Korean conflict (35 lower-house seats in 1949), and then had all but disappeared underground. When they reemerged, they found many Japanese strangely attracted more by a vision of "new China" than the presence of native Japanese Communists. The party was bewildered by factionalism,

[17] The background of ideological squabbles which have always denied the Socialists unified strength is told in detail in Evelyn S. Colbert, *The Left Wing in Japanese Politics,* New York, 1952. Left, right, and unified platforms may be conveniently found in Uyehara, Royama, and Ogata, *Comparative Platforms of Japan's Major Political Parties,* Medford, Mass. (mimeograph), 1955, part of a study of social democracy being directed by Professor Allan B. Cole and Dr. George Totten.

badgered by the shifts of both the Russian Communists and Chinese Communist Party lines, and harassed by the Japanese police. Their leader, Mr. Nozaka Sanzō,[18] was a shrewd, modest, determined, dry Communist. He belonged to the age of Malenkov even before Malenkov came to power.

The Japanese Rightists. Although it is easy to see a Rightist bogey under even the most innocent organization of Japanese veterans, only a small number of ultra-Nationalists were elected to the post-Occupation parliament. Typical of such Rightists were Kimura Takeo and the fanatical ex-Colonel Tsuji Masanobu. Tsuji, the author of two thrillers about his escape from British-captured Siam, was once chief of staff to the hanged General Yamashita, the so-called Tiger of Malaya. Tsuji derided the United States, advocated an impractical form of armed neutralism, and predicted that the Soviet Union would have the advantage in World War III. He expected America and Russia to destroy one another in that war.[19]

Election Techniques. Japan's eighty-odd years of more or less open elections, first local and then national, were amply demonstrated by the authenticity and vigor of Japanese election behavior. The Occupation did not have to tell the Japanese how to conduct elections: they remembered. It is probably true that no man now living in Japan can remember the time in which there were no elections whatever. This is completely unlike the experience of any other Asian country and must be kept in mind as a significant but not predominant factor in assessing the political maturity of Japan.

Japanese political campaigns are quite different from the American version of sound-and-fury. Even shorter than the American counterpart, electioneering is marked by severe restrictions on fund collections, posters, number of radio appearances, and newspaper advertising. The universal method is to hire a small truck, often only a trimobile, and load it with workers. On top is a loudspeaker tuned to the maximum volume Japanese electronics can produce. Farmers' ears eventually become conditioned to the sound effect, first heard in the distance, gradually increasing to the peak of proximity, and gradually fading away—in favor of the next truck. Partisan rallies as such are infrequent. Radio stations and newspapers sponsor in-

[18] One of the authors of this book met Nozaka in the Chinese *Communist* capital of Yenan during the war. He was much impressed with Nozaka's capacity to adjust himself to a Chinese peasant environment and by Nozaka's brilliant political leadership, which kept the Chinese Communist military leaders thoroughly aware of the temperament and political limitations of the common Japanese soldier in North China. Nozaka's having come from Yenan led to early speculation that his supporters in the Japanese Communist movement would follow Peking when and if Peking turned "Titoite" in the way that some Americans both expected and desired. This eventuality has not come to pass. A recent analysis of the Japanese Communist Party is presented by Rodger Swearingen and Paul Langer, *Red Flag in Japan; International Communism in Action, 1919-1951,* Cambridge, Mass., 1952.

[19] One of the authors heard Colonel Tsuji speak in the Kokaidō, Okayama City, on February 16, 1953. His disarming, personal-experience approach was intriguing and puzzling. Anti-American barbs were humorously and subtly hidden. He had the audience with him all the way. Tsuji's confused but dangerous views were expounded in *Kono Nippon wo* (For this Japan), Tōkyō, 1953.

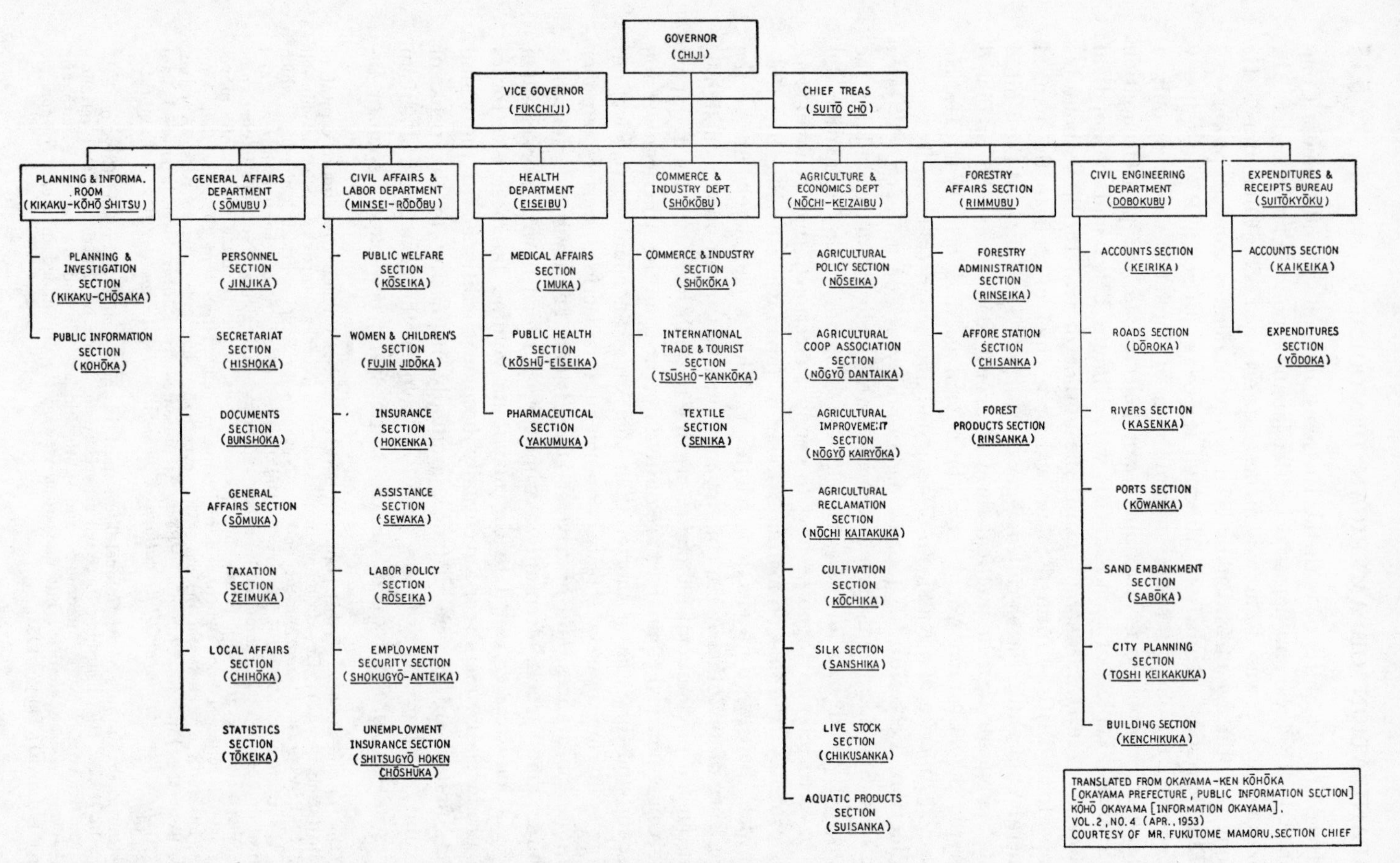

CHART 30—Okayama-Ken Revised Organization of Kenchō Proper *(Honchō Shin Kikō)*

stead one or two 3- to 4-hour panels, presenting as many competitors as possible. Still, the gay hand wave, the boutonniere, the decorations, the repetition of the name (clearly reproduced in easily read *kana*), the hangers-on, and the fireworks of debate put the Japanese politician in a universally recognized species.

The campaign for the election of the fall of 1952 was vigorous, but fortunately without violence. Altogether 1200 candidates sought 466 seats; more than 45,300,000 voters took part. The spring campaign of 1953, in contrast, fought lethargy. Meetings drew small crowds. The voting rate, although lower than that of 1952, was surprisingly high for the circumstances.[20] Analysis of the 1955 election results revealed five basic trends: (1) a revival of interest and a large turnout (75.84 per cent of the 50 million voters); (2) the decline of the Liberals; (3) the advance of the Democrats; (4) solid gains by the Socialists, especially the left wing; and (5) no visible improvement of position by the Communists. By shrewd campaigning, both Democrats and Socialists gained a greater percentage of seats in the House of Representatives than their earned percentage of the total number of votes cast in the general election.

Recentralization of Local Government. One of the great pendulum swings fostered by a great push from the Occupationaires was the introduction of elective governorships for the *ken* of Japan. Before surrender the local governments of Japan, except for elective advisory councils, had been pretty strictly the civilian extensions of the central government to the outer areas.

The Local Autonomy Law and the new Constitution went into effect on the same day: May 3, 1947. The Government Section of SCAP obviously believed that local democracy was the foundation of national democracy. Japanese press reaction was, in large part, favorable, and Japanese political behavior in the five years following decentralization showed that local politicians very soon obtained a vested interest in the autonomy of the *ken*. Only in the post-treaty period did the Japanese leaders and people begin to realize that decentralization might not be the best way of dealing with the problems of a country under chronic and severe pressure. The immediate crisis was caused by the shaky condition of prefectural finance.[21]

[20] For the resulting line-up in the lower house after each of these, as well as the 1955 election, see Appendix 19, p. 617. The election of 1953 marked a sad parliamentary milepost: the nonagenarian Ozaki Yukio, who had been elected to every single session of the Diet since parliamentary government began in Japan, was defeated for the first time. He died in 1954. For a brilliant profile, based partly on conversations with the statesman in 1952-53, see Douglas H. Mendel, Jr., "Ozaki Yukio: Political Conscience of Japan," *Far Eastern Quarterly,* Vol. XV, No. 3 (May 1956).

[21] Chart 30 presents an organization chart of a typical prefecture. In 1949, the American Government had sent a study group under Dr. Carl Shoup as head of what has become popularly identified as the Shoup Tax Mission. The mission made a study of Japanese local finance and attempted to work out an equalization law which would bring all *ken* up to a national standard. By 1953 this system was working rather unevenly. The monthly *Tō-shi mondai kenkyū* (Research on municipal problems), Ōsaka, discussed the

Recentralization in the post-treaty period took on two forms. At the top the national government undertook a review of the issues of decentralization and recentralization, establishing under the Cabinet a Local Government System Investigation Council (*Chihō Seido Chōsa Kai*). Locally, villages and towns in widely scattered areas across the country accepted recentralization by the merger (*gappei*) of local governments, usually for the immediate purpose of increasing local government credit.

Press and Pressures. The Japanese press survived the Occupation well. Editors and newspapermen became in the post-Occupation period a vested interest for freedom; they firmly resisted any attempt of the government to control news or even to undertake foreign propaganda. Tough and realistic men who had grown up under a system of clumsy patriotic controls showed no disposition to trust government officials on press matters more than themselves.

The Japanese newspaper world returned to its prewar competitive position. Newspapers such as the *Asahi, Mainichi,* and *Yomiuri* returned fully to their prewar prominence. The Occupation-sponsored cooperative news service, Kyōdō, lost the great newspapers as members.

If governmental pressure was pretty well extinguished in the Japanese press scene, there was no serious evidence that undue pressure was being exercised by special groups, such as particular capitalists or particular unions, when it came to the reporting and printing of news. The Japanese press was, in great part, to the Left of the public as a whole and still carrying on something of a crusading job. The Communists regarded the entire press, with the exception of their own publications, as reactionary and capitalist-controlled: to do otherwise would have been to violate Communist dogma. From an American point of view, the fact remained that the Japanese press was one of the freest in Asia.

Strangely enough the war itself did not create particularly powerful blocs of politically vested interests. Although the number of Japanese returned to Japan from Japan's old overseas empire was approximately half the size of the Germans driven from their homes by Communist transfers of population, Japan (unlike West Germany) did not have a special repatriates' party. Ex-servicemen made mild demands upon the government; these demands were not reinforced by tight-knit political aggroupations.

Even Japanese businessmen got into a new form of political pressure. They resembled neither the prewar *Zaibatsu* nor American capitalists. The

---

Shoup Mission recommendations in every issue during 1949-50. Early in 1953, the author discussed prefectural finance problems with Mr. Araki Eietsu, Chief, General Affairs Section, Okayama Prefecture. His lucid summary of problems appeared in *Jiji Tsūshin, "Fu-ken zaizesei seido no mondai ten to kaikaku no hōkō wo ronzu,"* (Problems of finance and tax system of prefectures and their reform), November 18, 1952, pp. 6143-6145; November 19, 1952, pp. 6152-6154. It should be added that the larger, richer prefectures were quick to demand reform. Officers of poor prefectures (like Yamagata-ken) were equally quick to defend the Equalization Grants.

trust-busting measures of the Occupation had created a new group of highly paid salaried corporate executives, who were managers rather than shareholders. In a way this development precipitated in Japan a more rapid maturation of what James Burnham calls "the managerial revolution" than would otherwise have occurred. Japanese companies in the post-war period were often managed by a coalition of board and union with the stockholders looking on wanly from the outside. Japanese managers and executives soon organized their own Japan Federation of Employers' Associations (*Nikkeiren*) and linked it with the Liberal Party.

On the labor side, Japanese unionism lost ground in the last period of the Occupation and the early post-treaty period; it still remained relatively strong. About 5,000,000 union members were organized in almost 30,000 unions. Only a few dozen of the unions were large by American standards. The Japanese Communists established a strong foothold in the union movement. Much, but not all of this, was lost when the Korean war broke out and the government found itself justified in applying security measures.

Much more important than the change in the situation of labor was the appearance of the new vested interest in land reform. The fact remained that the land—and land, one must remember, is the most visible form of property—*had* already been divided. The landlords had little more chance of recapturing their estates than the haciendados of Porfirio Diaz's Cientifico period would have in reinstating their great estates in present-day Mexico.[22]

All the statistics in the world could not substitute for the facts, observed in rural Japan. The little hamlets looked the same. Lives revolved around the same crop cycle. Age and respect still chose the leadership. One chain of tradition, however, had been broken. In many fine old houses the collection of documents, signifying descent from *samurai* or magistrate status through village chief to modern elective post, was still intact. The distinctive signature in cursive script of a prominent Meiji political boss still dominated the largest room of the house. His political stakes, driven into Japan's soil, had once marked out the circle of influence subtly mixed with the system of landholding. But the documents—and sometimes even the political memento—were for sale. For the land surrounding the fine house now belonged to the neighbors.

On the other hand, one had to go into rural Japan also to see the vast gap between law and fact in regard to the status of women. Economically and technologically, the militarists themselves had set the stage for the emancipation of women by dragging them off farms to fill Japan's manpower needs in the years of Pacific War. The Occupation gave legal standing to this change of role by providing for the political emancipation of women.

[22] In Yamagata Prefecture, the following results of land reform speak for themselves: (1) before reform—owner-farmer land, 46.7%; tenant-farmer land, 53.3%; (2) after reform—owner-farmer land, 95%; tenant-farmer land, 5%. Liaison Section, Yamagata Prefecture, *Yamagata,* Yamagata City, 1951, p. 11.

Yet women, like Japan's labor class, had been handed privileges with scarcely a struggle for it. In large cities, women dressed as smartly as meager budgets allowed and as far as confused standards of beauty led. In medium-sized cities, women dutifully turned out in the traditional *kimono* to celebrate National Women's Week. But most Japanese women were born, educated, married, and reared children in rural Japan. On the farm, as usual, Japanese women had little time except for work.[23]

The Rice Roots. One also had to go to rural Japan to observe the persistent gap between national political theory—whether it was of the new structure, of democratization, or of the reverse course—and political facts as the people knew them. Even in Japan, which was regarded as a relatively developed Asian nation, 62 per cent of the people were rural in character and agrarian in social organization. Not even legally recognized, the folk village *(buraku)* continued to be the mediator between the Japanese people and the political village *(mura)* the lowest rung of the national bureaucracy.[24]

It is true that the folk village, with its extended family and sense of community, was reluctantly giving way before the paraphernalia of modernization, industrialization, and democratization. Railroads, bicycles, telephones, the tracts of political parties, and the more subtle effects of migration, equal inheritance, and expanded educational facilities were making inroads on self-sufficiency. And yet, one hundred years after the opening of Japan, real as compared with formal political leadership was still chosen on the basis of traditional qualifications. Age, ancestral status, and family connections still helped mark the ballots. Popular consensus was accepted in place of mathematical voting divisions, which were regarded as distinctly bad form and socially dangerous. Settlement of disputes had little or nothing to do with the formal judiciary. Taxes were dutifully recorded in the village's *yakuba* or town hall, as collected from individuals; in most folk villages taxes were spread upon the community. Certainly the persistent rule by consensus, if it was not Western democracy, did avoid authoritarianism. No one—not a Konoye, not a Tojo, not a MacArthur, neither a Yoshida nor a Hatoyama—was able to disrupt the rural

[23] The Labor Ministry recently published a study of five villages in prefectures in different parts of Japan: 82% of the women of these villages, as against 77% of the men, were engaged in agricultural labor. No mother interrupted household duties during pregnancy; 86% continued farm labor until the very day of delivery. Few had ever been outside the immediate neighborhood of their villages. Rōdōshō, Fujinshōnenkyoku, *Nōson fujin no seikatsu* (Labor Ministry, Women and Children's Bureau, The life of farm women), Tōkyō, 1952.

[24] Western political scientists were realizing this fact more and more in their studies of post-treaty Japan. For a fascinating survey of comparative rural politics, see Robert E. Ward's introduction to "Village Government in Eastern and Southern Asia: A Symposium," *Far Eastern Quarterly*, Vol. XV, No. 2 (February 1956); also in the same issue, Kurt Steiner, "The Japanese Village and Its Government." For other aspects, see Paul S. Dull, "The Political Structure of a Japanese Village," *Far Eastern Quarterly*, Vol. XIII, No. 2 (February 1954); and "Two Japanese Villages," *Occasional Papers, Center for Japanese Studies*, No. 5 (1956).

village's ability to delay, to ignore, to misinterpret, or to reinterpret. Sometimes in Japanese history this had been a most unfortunate and sometimes a most fortunate aspect of the real Japan.

The Old Peace and the Cold War. The most realistic Japanese knew that Japan's position in the mid-1950's was unrealistic. They knew that it had to be unrealistic. The peace of 1945 was already an old one, out of keeping with the strategic needs of a sovereign state. Far more important than any problem of where the Japanese might *wish* their country to go, was Japan's position—geographically between America and mainland China and Russia, and politically on the American side in the cold and later cool wars which had replaced the sought but unsound peace of 1945.[25]

Even had she wanted to, Japan could not follow the ephemeral "Asian bloc" in the U.N. As late as 1955 Japan's hopes for admission were dashed on the rocks of a paired veto of Outer Mongolia (by the Nationalist Chinese), Russian hopes for admission of her ally (Communist China), and sheer Soviet blackmail (dangling a Russo-Japanese peace treaty as a price).

The Japanese perforce had to tag along with the United States. The peace treaty specifically gave the Japanese Government the right to defend itself, within the limits of self-defense mentioned in the United Nations Charter; nevertheless Article 6 recognized Japan's right to have foreign troops stationed in Japanese territory for the defense of Japan. The Japanese then concluded two fundamental accommodations with the United States—a security treaty signed along with the peace treaty on September 9, 1951, and an administrative agreement signed February 28, 1952.[26] The latter was supplemented in March, 1954, by a Mutual Defense Assistance Agreement. The Japanese were realistic enough to know that their only safety lay in association with America. They did not like the situation very much.

Most Japanese knew that even rearmament would not give Japan strategic autonomy and that the cost of genuine independence would be economic ruin. As of the end of 1955, Japan's Self-Defense Force numbered about 200,000

[25] One of the authors has evaluated the so-called cold war with extensive reference to the Far East: Paul M. A. Linebarger, *Psychological Warfare,* Washington, 1954. For surveys of postwar Far Eastern international relations see: Harley F. MacNair and Donald F. Lach, *Modern Far Eastern International Relations,* New York (second edition), 1955; Harold M. Vinacke, *Far Eastern Politics in the Postwar Period,* New York, 1956; Franz H. Michael and George E. Taylor, *The Far East in the Modern World,* New York, 1956.

[26] Art. 5(c) was regarded as consistent with Art. 9 of the new Constitution, renouncing aggressive war. Art. 6(a) was regarded as consistent with Art. 51 of the U.N. Charter. For the text of the treaty see *Conference Proceedings,* cited above. The text of the peace treaty between the Republic of China and Japan signed in Taipeh, April 28, 1952, is included in "Documentary Material," *Contemporary Japan,* Vol. XXI, Nos. 1-3 (1952), pp. 160-163. The Japanese text of the treaty may be found conveniently in *Asahi nenkan* (The Asahi yearbook), Tōkyō, 1952, pp. 31-32. Texts of the administrative agreement is included in *Contemporary Japan,* cited above, pp. 152-158. The *Gaimushō* went to some pains to explain the need for these arrangements to the public. The significance of the peace and security treaties, of the Administrative Agreement, and of psychological warfare of Communism was ably explained in a pair of pamphlets: *Japan, Her Security and Mission* and *Japan in the World Today,* both Tokyo: Ministry of Foreign Affairs, Public Information and Cultural Affairs Bureau, April 28, 1952.

men in six district corps (and two mixed battalions), with trainer aircraft (jets yet to come) and with light vessels. Beyond these meager forces, both the Liberal-Democrats and the Americans faced a real dilemma. Every insistence that Japan follow the American foreign-policy line seemed to increase the power of the Socialists. And the Socialists were outspoken in their desire to main Occupation reforms, in their attachment to the American-inspired Constitution, especially Article 9, and in their dream or nightmare of a Japan constructed on the old MacArthur model of a neutral "Switzerland of the Far East."[27]

Yet if the history of governments in Japan teaches us anything, it is this: the Japanese, as much as any people on earth, know how to put up with the inevitable and to adjust themselves shrewdly and realistically. In this sense, Hatoyama's foreign policy took the form of a reassertion of Japanese independence through a return to symbols of the past. To the opposition he spoke of rearmament softly, and for the Americans began to carry a moderately big stick. To the Russians he offered patient conversations throughout 1955 toward normalization of relations, but without sacrifice of honor. Meanwhile, the more power and influence Japan could develop, the greater her ability to act independently vis-à-vis either America or Russia.

A new decade of realism would be refreshing and certainly not un-Japanese. Perhaps Japan had been pleasantly Americanized, in the best sense of the term; or perhaps American democracy had been more quietly Japanized than the people of either country realized.

[27] Neutralism of the pacifist variety gained ground tremendously after the treaty; witness the tone of the three popular magazines for intellectuals: *Chūō Kōron, Kaizō,* and *Sekai* (combined circulation, three to four hundred thousand). *Chūō Kōron,* in a January, 1953 panel discussion, did carry the view that the anti-American "struggle" arose mainly out of a post-treaty inferiority complex, which could and should be erased by forthright diplomatic negotiation. See *"Konnichi no fuan"* (Present uneasiness), *Chūō Kōron,* Vol. XLVIII, No. 1 (January, 1953). pp. 192-200. To be sure, not all Japanese intellectuals adopted naïve neutralist theories. Among those intellectuals whom the author met and talked with, for example, two expounded interesting Japanese viewpoints. Dr. Koizumi Shinzō, economist, former Dean of Keio University, member of the Academy of Japan, and sometime tutor to Crown Prince Akihito, supported the peace treaty and preparedness from the beginning. He welcomed, however, different opinions as to Japan's best road to peace (see his radio address, NHK, translated in *Tokyo Evening News,* September 2, 1952). Dr. Ōuchi Hyōe, also a distinguished economist and now President, Hosei University, discussed economics with the author in historic Kamakura in the summer of 1952. He was concerned mainly with Japan's economic independence, and awaited the day Japan would have the strength to join an "Asian Third Force" (for a condensation of his views, drawn from a background paper for the Institute of Pacific Relations Conference on Japanese-American Relations, Honolulu, January, 1953, see *Nippon Times,* April 1, 1953).

Appendices

CHINA

Appendix 1

FAR EASTERN CHRONOLOGY
(With Some Comparative Western Dates)

CHINA		JAPAN		THE WEST	
The Legendary Period	ca. 2679-2205 B.C.				
Hsia	ca. 2205-1766 B.C.				
Shang (Yin)	ca. 1766-1122 B.C.				
Chou	1122-255 B.C.	Legendary Period	ca. 660 B.C.-A.D. 530	Rome founded (traditional)	753 B.C.
Chin	255-206 B.C.			Birth of Alexander the Great	356 B.C.
Han (Former)	206 B.C.-A.D. 25			Birth of Jesus Christ	0
Han (Later)	A.D. 25-220				
Wei (One of the Three Kingdoms)	A.D. 220-265				
Tsin (Chin)	A.D. 265-420				
The Southern and Northern Dynasties					
Southern Dynasties:		Foundation Period	A.D. 530-709	Deposition of Romulus Augustulus	A.D. 476
Sung, Ch'i, Liang Ch'en	A.D. 420-589			Birth of Mohammed	A.D. 570
Northern Dynasties:					
Northern Wei, Western Wei, Eastern Wei, Northern Ch'i, Northern Chou	A.D. 386-581				
Sui	A.D. 581-618				
T'ang	A.D. 618-907	Taika Era	A.D. 645-654	Conquest of Spain by Saracens	A.D. 713
Five Dynasties: Later Liang, Later T'ang, Later Tsin, Later Han, Later Chou	A.D. 907-960	Nara Era	A.D. 710-793	Charlemagne crowned Emperor	A.D. 800
		Heian Era	A.D. 794-1192	Battle of Hastings	A.D. 1066
Sung	A.D. 960-1279	Kamakura Era	A.D. 1193-1333	Magna Charta	A.D. 1215
Yüan (Kublai seated on Chinese throne from A.D. 1280)	A.D. 1206-1368			Travels of Marco Polo	A.D. 1271-1295
		Muromachi Era	A.D. 1334-1602	Diaz rounds Cape of Good Hope	A.D. 1487
Ming	A.D. 1368-1644	Edo (Tokugawa) Era	A.D. 1603-1867	Philippines taken by Spanish	A.D. 1565
				Thirty Years' War	A.D. 1618
				Treaty of Westphalia	A.D. 1648
Ch'ing	A.D. 1644-1912	Meiji Era	A.D. 1868-1912	Declaration of Independence	A.D. 1776
				Marx' *Das Kapital*, Vol. I, published	A.D. 1867
The Republic	A.D. 1912- —	Taishō Era	A.D. 1913-1925	World War I	A.D. 1914-1918
(People's Republic)	A.D. 1949- —	Shōwa Era	A.D. 1926- —	World War II	A.D. 1939-1945

Appendix 2

PRINCIPLES OF CONSTITUTION (*HSIEN-FA TA-KANG*), PROMULGATED BY THE MANCHU COURT ON 27 AUGUST 1908*

THE POWERS OF THE SOVEREIGN

1. The Ta Ch'ing Emperor will rule supreme over the Ta Ch'ing Empire for one thousand generations in succession and be honored forever.

2. The sacred majesty of the sovereign may not be offended against.

3. Laws shall be made and promulgated by the sovereign and he has the power to determine what may be assigned to others for deliberation. (Laws which have been passed by the National Assembly shall not become operative until approved and promulgated by the sovereign.)

4. The sovereign has the power to convoke, to open and to close, to suspend and to extend the time of and to dissolve the National Assembly. (On the dissolution of the National Assembly the people shall be called upon to elect a new National Assembly. The members of the old National Assembly shall be classed with the common people. If any of them commit offenses, they shall be punished by the proper court according to circumstances.)

5. The sovereign has power to appoint all officials and fix their salaries and to degrade or promote them. (The power to use men rests with the Emperor. The National Assembly may not interfere with this.)

6. The sovereign has supreme command over the army and navy, with power to make all regulations concerning them. (The sovereign may dispatch armies and fix the number of soldiers. In this his power is absolute. The National Assembly may not interfere in military affairs.)

7. The sovereign has power to declare war and to make peace, to make treaties, to appoint and receive ambassadors. (Foreign relations will be controlled by the sovereign, without the advice of the National Assembly.)

8. The sovereign has the power to take repressive measures and, in times of emergency, to deprive officials and people of their personal liberty.

9. The sovereign has the power to confer distinctions and to issue pardons. (Mercy is from above. Officials, below, may not arrogate it to themselves.)

10. The sovereign has supreme power over the administration of the laws and the appointment of judges, but he will act in accordance with the imperially sanctioned laws, and not make changes arbitrarily. (Power to administer the law rests with the sovereign. Judges are appointed by the sovereign to act for him in the administration of the laws. Changes will not be made by the sovereign arbitrarily, because the interests at stake in law cases are important, so that imperially settled laws must be treated as final to avoid confusion.)

11. The sovereign has powers to issue "imperial orders" or to cause them to be issued, but, in the matter of laws which have already received the imperial

* U. S. Department of State, *Papers Relating to the Foreign Relations of the United States, 1908* (Washington, 1912), pp. 194-195. The words "the National Assembly" have been substituted throughout for the word "Parliament."

sanction, he will not change or abrogate laws which already received the imperial sanction without first obtaining the advice of the National Assembly and acting on its memorial. (Statutes proceed from the power of the sovereign to administer the laws. Imperial orders proceed from the power of the sovereign to carry on government. The two powers are distinguished. Therefore "imperial orders" must not be used to abrogate statutes of law.)

12. When the National Assembly is not in session, in case of urgent necessity, the sovereign may issue emergency orders to raise funds which may be necessary. But the next year, when the National Assembly meets, he shall refer such matters to the National Assembly.

13. The expenses of the Imperial Household shall be fixed by the sovereign and taken from the national treasury without reference to the National Assembly.

14. In the great ceremonies of the Imperial Household, the sovereign shall have supreme authority over the imperial clan and shall appoint ministers to settle such affairs. The National Assembly may not interfere.

POWERS, PRIVILEGES AND DUTIES OF THE OFFICERS AND PEOPLE

1. All officers and people who have the qualifications prescribed by law are eligible for appointment as civil or military officials and members of the National Assembly.

2. Officers and people who keep within the law will have freedom of speech, of the press and of assembly.

3. Officers and people shall not be liable to arrest, restrictions or punishments except as prescribed by law.

4. Officers and people may appeal to the judiciary officials to judge their cases.

5. Officers and people can be judged only by those specially appointed to act as judges.

6. Officers and people shall not be disturbed without cause in their possession of property nor interfered with in their dwellings.

7. Officers and people have the obligation to pay taxes and render military service as the law may prescribe.

8. Officers and people shall continue to pay taxes at the rate now assessed until the law has been changed.

9. Officers and people have the duty of obedience to the law of the land.

Appendix 3

PROVISIONAL CONSTITUTION OF THE REPUBLIC OF CHINA (*CHUNG-HUA MIN-KUO LIN-SHIH YÜEH-FA*), PROMULGATED BY THE COUNCIL OF REPRESENTATIVES OF THE PROVISIONAL GOVERNMENT ON 11 MARCH 1912 *

CHAPTER I. GENERAL PROVISIONS

Art. 1. The Republic of China is composed of the Chinese people.

Art. 2. The sovereignty of the Chinese Republic is vested in the people.

Art. 3. The territory of the Chinese Republic consists of 22 Provinces, Inner and Outer Mongolia, Tibet and Chinghai.

Art. 4. The sovereignty of the Chinese Republic is exercised by the Advisory Council, the Provisional President, the Cabinet and the Judiciary.

CHAPTER II. CITIZENS

Art. 5. Citizens of the Chinese Republic are all equal and there shall be no racial, class or religious distinctions.

Art. 6. Citizens shall enjoy the following rights:

(1) The persons of the citizens shall not be arrested, imprisoned, tried or punished except in accordance with law.

(2) The habitations of citizens shall not be entered or searched except in accordance with law.

(3) Citizens shall enjoy the right of the security of their property and the freedom of trade.

(4) Citizens shall have the freedom of speech, of composition, of publication, of assembly and of association.

(5) Citizens shall have the right of the secrecy of their letters.

(6) Citizens shall have the liberty of residence and removal.

(7) Citizens shall have the freedom of religion.

Art. 7. Citizens shall have the right to petition the National Assembly.

Art. 8. Citizens shall have the right of petitioning the executive officials.

Art. 9. Citizens shall have the right to institute proceedings before the judiciary and to receive its trial and judgments.

Art. 10. Citizens shall have the right of suing officials in the administrative courts for violation of law or against their rights.

Art. 11. Citizens shall have the right of participating in civil examinations.

Art. 12. Citizens shall have the right to vote and to be voted for.

Art. 13. Citizens shall have the duty to pay taxes according to law.

Art. 14. Citizens shall have the duty to enlist as soldiers according to law.

Art. 15. The rights of citizens as provided in the present chapter shall be limited or modified by laws, provided such limitation or modification shall be

* U. S. Department of State, *Papers Relating to the Foreign Relations of the United States, 1914* (Washington, 1922), pp. 38-41. The words "the National Assembly" have been substituted throughout for the word "Parliament."

deemed necessary for the promotion of public welfare, for the maintenance of public order or on account of extraordinary exigency.

CHAPTER III. THE ADVISORY COUNCIL

Art. 16. The legislative power of the Chinese Republic is exercised by the Advisory Council.

Art. 17. The Advisory Council shall be composed of members elected by the several districts as provided in Article 18.

Art. 18. The Provinces, Inner and Outer Mongolia, and Tibet shall each elect and depute five members to the Advisory Council, and Chinghai shall elect one member.

The election districts and methods of election shall be decided by the localities concerned.

During the meeting of the Advisory Council each member shall have one vote.

Art. 19. The Advisory Council shall have the following powers:

(1) To pass all bills.
(2) To pass the budgets of the Provisional Governments.
(3) To pass laws of taxation, of currency and of weights and measures for the whole country.
(4) To pass measures for the calling of public loans and to conclude contracts affecting the National Treasury.
(5) To give consent to matters provided in Articles 34, 35, and 40.
(6) To reply to injuries from the Provisional Government.
(7) To receive and consider petitions of citizens.
(8) To make suggestions to the Government on legal or other matters.
(9) To introduce interpellations to members of the Cabinet and to insist on their being present in the Council in making replies thereto.
(10) To insist on the Government investigating into any alleged bribery and infringement of laws by officials.
(11) To impeach the Provisional President for high treason by a majority vote of three fourths of the quorum consisting of more than four fifths of the total number of the members.
(12) To impeach members of the Cabinet for failure to perform their official duties or for violation of the law, by majority vote of two thirds of the quorum consisting of over three fourths of the total number of the members.

Art. 20. The Advisory Council shall itself convoke, open and adjourn its own meetings.

Art. 21. The meetings of the Advisory Council shall be conducted publicly, but secret meetings may be held at the instigation of members of the Cabinet or by the majority vote of its quorum.

Art. 22. Matters passed by the Advisory Council shall be communicated to the Provisional President for promulgation and execution.

Art. 23. If the Provisional President should veto matters passed by the Advisory Council, he shall, within ten days after he received such resolutions, return the same with stated reasons to the Council for reconsideration. If the same matter should again be passed by a two thirds vote of the quorum of the Council, it shall be dealt with in accordance with Article 22.

Art. 24. The President of the Advisory Council shall be elected by ballots signed by the voting members and the one who receives more than one half of the total number of the votes cast shall be elected.

Art. 25. Members of the Advisory Council shall not, outside the Council hall, be responsible for their opinions expressed and votes cast in the Council.

Art. 26. Members of the Council shall not be arrested without the permission of the President of the Council except for crimes committed at the time of arrest and for crimes pertaining to civil and international warfare.

Art. 27. Procedures of the Advisory Council shall be decided by its own members.

Art. 28. The Advisory Council shall be dissolved on the day of the convocation of the National Assembly and its powers shall be exercised by the latter.

CHAPTER IV. THE PROVISIONAL PRESIDENT AND VICE PRESIDENT

Art. 29. The Provisional President and Vice President shall be elected by the Advisory Council and he who receives two thirds of the total amount of votes cast by a sitting of the Council consisting of over three fourths of the total number of members shall be elected.

Art. 30. The Provisional President represents the Provisional Government as the fountain of all executive powers and for promulgating all laws.

Art. 31. The Provisional President may issue or cause to be issued orders for the execution of laws and of powers delegated to him by the laws.

Art. 32. The Provisional President shall be Commander-in-Chief of the army and navy of the whole of China.

Art. 33. The Provisional President shall ordain and establish the administrative system and official regulations, but he must first submit them to the Advisory Council for its approval.

Art. 34. The Provisional President shall appoint and remove civil and military officials, but in the appointment of members of the Cabinet, ambassadors and ministers he must have the concurrence of the Advisory Council.

Art. 35. The Provisional President shall have power, with the concurrence of the Advisory Council, to declare war and conclude treaties.

Art. 36. The Provisional President may, in accordance with law, declare a state of siege.

Art. 37. The Provisional President shall, representing the whole country, receive ambassadors and ministers of foreign countries.

Art. 38. The Provisional President may introduce bills into the Advisory Council.

Art. 39. The Provisional President may confer decorations and other insignia of honor.

Art. 40. The Provisional President may declare general amnesty, grant special pardon, commute a punishment and restore rights, but, in the case of a general amnesty, he must have the concurrence of the Advisory Council.

Art. 41. In case the Provisional President is impeached by the Advisory

Council, he shall be tried by a special court consisting of nine judges, elected among the justices of the Supreme Court of the realm.

Art. 42. In case the Provisional President vacates his office for various reasons or is unable to discharge the powers and duties of the said office, the Provisional Vice President shall take his place.

CHAPTER V. MEMBERS OF THE CABINET

Art. 43. The Premier and the Chiefs of the Government Departments shall be called Members of the Cabinet (literally, Secretaries of State Affairs).

Art. 44. Members of the Cabinet shall assist the Provisional President in assuming responsibilities.

Art. 45. Members of the Cabinet shall countersign all bills introduced by the Provisional President and all laws and orders issued by him.

Art. 46. Members of the Cabinet and their deputies may be present and speak in the Advisory Council.

Art. 47. After Members of the Cabinet have been impeached by the Advisory Council, the Provisional President may remove them from office, but such removal shall be subject to the reconsideration of the Advisory Council.

CHAPTER VI. THE JUDICIARY

Art. 48. The Judiciary shall be composed of those judges appointed by the Provisional President, and the Chief of the Department of Justice. The organization of the courts and the qualifications of judges shall be determined by law.

Art. 49. The Judiciary shall try civil and criminal cases, but cases involving administrative affairs or arising from other particular causes shall be dealt with according to special laws.

Art. 50. The trial of cases in the law courts shall be conducted publicly, but those affecting public safety and order may be in camera.

Art. 51. Judges shall be independent and shall not be subject to the interference of higher officials.

Art. 52. Judges during their continuance in office shall not have their emoluments decreased and shall not be transferred to other offices, nor shall they be removed from office except when they are convicted of crimes or of offenses punishable according to law by removal from office.

Regulations for the punishment of judges shall be determined by law.

CHAPTER VII. SUPPLEMENTARY ARTICLES

Art. 53. Within ten months after the promulgation of this Provisional Constitution the Provisional President shall convene a National Assembly, the organization of which and the laws for the election of whose members shall be decided by the Advisory Council.

Art. 54. The Constitution of the Republic of China shall be adopted by the National Assembly, but before the promulgation of the Constitution the Provisional Constitution shall be as effective as the Constitution itself.

Art. 55. The Provisional Constitution may be amended by the assent of two thirds of the members of the Advisory Council or upon the application of the Provisional President and being passed by over three fourths of the quorum of the Council consisting of over four fifths of the total number of its members.

Art. 56. The present Provisional Constitution shall take effect on the date of its promulgation and the fundamental articles for the organization of the Provisional Government shall cease to be effective on the same date.*

Appendix 4

PROVISIONAL CONSTITUTION OF THE REPUBLIC OF CHINA FOR THE PERIOD OF POLITICAL TUTELAGE (*CHUNG-HUA MIN-KUO HSÜN-CHÊNG SHIH-CH'I YÜEH-FA*), PROMULGATED BY THE NATIONAL GOVERNMENT OF THE KUOMINTANG ON 1 JUNE 1931 †

PREAMBLE

The National Government, in order to rebuild the Republic of China on the bases of *The Three Principles of the People* and the Constitution of Five Powers, which forms the underlying principle of the Revolution, having now brought the Revolution from the Military to the Political Tutelage Period, deems it necessary to promulgate a Provisional Constitution (*Yüeh-fa*) for general observance, so that the realization of constitutional government may be accelerated and political power restored to a popularly-elected Government and, further, in pursuance of the Last Will of our late Leader, has called at the national capital the National People's Convention (*Kuo-min hui-i*).

The said National People's Convention do hereby enact and ordain the following Provisional Constitution for enforcement during the Political Tutelage Period:

[CHAPTER] I. GENERAL PRINCIPLES

Art. 1. The territory of the Republic of China consists of the various Provinces and Mongolia and Tibet.

Art. 2. The sovereignty of the Republic of China is vested in the people as a whole.

All persons who, according to law, enjoy the nationality of the Republic of China shall be citizens (*Kuo-min*) of the Republic of China.

Art. 3. The Republic of China shall be a unified Republic forever.

Art. 4. The national flag of the Republic of China shall have a red background with a blue sky and white sun in the upper left corner.

Art. 5. Nanking shall be the national capital of the Republic of China.

[CHAPTER] II. RIGHTS AND DUTIES OF THE PEOPLE

Art. 6. All citizens of the Republic of China shall be equal before the law, irrespective of sex, race, religion or caste.

* Sealed by the Advisory Council, 11 March, 1st year of the Republic of China (1912).
† H. G. W. Woodhead (editor), *The China Year Book, 1935*, (Shanghai, 1935), pp. 63-66.

Art. 7. Citizens of the Republic of China shall, according to the stipulation of Article 8 of *The Fundamentals of National Reconstruction,* enjoy in all completely autonomous districts (*Hsien*) the rights of election, initiative, recall and referendum as provided by Article 9 of *The Outline of National Reconstruction.*

Art. 8. Except in accordance with law, no person shall be arrested, detained, tried or punished.

When a person is arrested or detained on a criminal charge, the organ responsible for his [or her] arrest or detention shall send him [or her] to the competent court for trial not later than 24 hours. The party concerned may himself petition, or some other person may petition on his behalf, that he be brought [before the court] for trial within 24 hours.

Art. 9. Except in accordance with law, no person other than those in active military service shall be subject to trial by a military court.

Art. 10. Except in accordance with law, no private houses of the people shall be subject to forcible entry, search or sealing.

Art. 11. All persons shall have liberty of conscience.

Art. 12. All persons shall be free to choose and change their residence; such freedom shall not be denied or restricted except in accordance with law.

Art. 13. All persons shall have the right to the privacy of correspondence and telegraphic communications; such freedoms shall not be denied or restricted except in accordance with law.

Art. 14. All persons shall have the freedom of assembly and formation of associations; such freedom shall not be denied or restricted except in accordance with law.

Art. 15. All persons shall have the liberty of speech and publication; such liberty shall not be denied or restricted except in accordance with law.

Art. 16. Except in accordance with law, no private property shall be sealed or confiscated.

Art. 17. The exercise of the right of ownership by any private owner of property, insofar as it does not conflict with the public interest, shall be protected by law.

Art. 18. Where public interest necessitates, the property of the people may be expropriated in accordance with law.

Art. 19. All persons shall have the right to inherit property in accordance with law.

Art. 20. All persons shall have the right of petition [to the government].

Art. 21. All persons shall have the right to institute judicial proceedings in the courts of justice, in accordance with law.

Art. 22. All persons shall have the right to submit petitions and institute administrative proceedings [in the Administrative Court] in accordance with law [for the redress of wrongs done by Government administrative organs].

Art. 23. All persons shall have the right to compete in civil service examinations in accordance with law.

Art. 24. All persons may, according to law, hold public posts.

Art. 25. All persons shall have the duty of paying taxes in accordance with law.

Art. 26. All persons shall have the duty of performing military service and compulsory labor [for the State] in accordance with law.

Art. 27. All persons shall have the duty to obey the measures adopted by Government organs in performance of their duties according to law.

[CHAPTER] III. ESSENTIALS OF POLITICAL TUTELAGE

Art. 28. The political policies and programs during the Period of Political Tutelage shall be in accordance with the *Fundamentals of National Reconstruction.*

Art. 29. The system of district autonomy shall be enforced in accordance with the provisions of the *Outline of National Reconstruction* and the *Law Governing the Institution of District Autonomy.*

Art. 30. During the Period of Political Tutelage, the National Congress of Kuomintang delegates (*Kuo-min-tang ch'üan-kuo tai-piao ta-hui*) shall exercise the governing powers on behalf of the National People's Congress (*Kuo -min ta-hui*). During the Period of Political Tutelage, the National Congress of Kuomintang delegates, the Central Executive Committee of the Kuomintang shall exercise the said powers.

Art. 31. The National Government shall train and guide [the citizens] in the exercise of the four political rights of election, initiative, recall and referendum.

Art. 32. The National Government shall exercise the five governing powers, namely, executive, legislative, judicial, examination and supervisory.

[CHAPTER] IV. PEOPLE'S LIVELIHOOD

Art. 33. In order to develop the people's economic welfare, the State (*Kuo-chia*) shall afford every encouragement and protection to the productive enterprises of the people.

Art. 34. In order to develop rural economy, to improve the living conditions of farmers and to promote the well-being of peasants, the State shall take active steps for the carrying out of the following measures:

(1) Reclamation of all waste land in the country and development of farm irrigation;

(2) Establishment of agricultural banks and encouragement of cooperative enterprises in the rural communities;

(3) Enforcement of the [public] granary system for the prevention of famine and other calamities and replenishment of the people's food supplies;

(4) Development of agricultural education with special emphasis on scientific experiments, extensive development of agricultural enterprises and increase of agricultural produce;

(5) Encouragement of road-building in the rural villages to facilitate the transportation of agricultural products.

Art. 35. The State shall open and develop all coal, gold and iron mines; and shall also encourage and protect private mining enterprises.

Art. 36. The State shall undertake and inaugurate State shipping enterprises; and shall also encourage and protect private shipping enterprises.

Art. 37. All persons shall be free to choose their profession or occupation. But when it is contrary to the public interest, the State may, by law, restrict or deny such freedom.

Art. 38. All persons shall be free to make contracts; such freedoms, insofar as it is not in conflict with the public interest or with good morals, shall be protected by law.

Art. 39. In order to better the economic well-being and to promote closer cooperation between capital and labor, the people may form occupational organizations in accordance with law.

Art. 40. Both capital and labor shall develop productive enterprises in accordance with the principle of cooperation and mutual benefit.

Art. 41. In order to improve the living conditions of labor, the State shall put into effect various laws for the protection of labor and shall afford special protection to children and women workers in respect to their age and health.

Art. 42. In order to safeguard and relieve peasants as well as workers, who shall be unable to work on account of accidents, sickness, disability or old age, the State shall put into effect a labor insurance system.

Art. 43. In order to promote the economic interests of the people, the State shall encourage and promote various cooperative enterprises.

Art. 44. The State may control or regulate the production or sale as well as the market price of daily necessities of the people.

Art. 45. Laws shall be enacted for the prohibition of usury and exorbitant rents for the use of immovable properties.

Art. 46. The State shall give appropriate relief to those members of the national forces who are disabled in the course of active service.

[CHAPTER] V. EDUCATION OF THE CITIZENS

Art. 47. *The Three Principles of the People* shall be the basic principles of education in the Republic of China.

Art. 48. Both sexes shall have equal opportunity for education.

Art. 49. All public and private educational institutions in the country shall be subject to the supervision of the State and shall also be responsible for the carrying out of the educational policies adopted by the State.

Art. 50. All children of school age shall receive free education. Details shall be separately provided by law.

Art. 51. Those who have not had free education [in their youth] shall receive special adult education. Details shall be separately provided by law.

Art. 52. The Central and local governments shall provide adequate funds for necessary educational expenses and shall also safeguard the security of funds which are by law specially set apart [for educational purposes].

Art. 53. The State shall give encouragement or grants to private educational institutions which have achieved particularly satisfactory results.

Art. 54. Encouragement and grants shall be given for the education of overseas Chinese.

Art. 55. The State shall encourage and safeguard members of the administrative or teaching staffs of schools who hold satisfactory records and have been long in service.

Art. 56. All public and private educational institutions in the country shall establish scholarships and prizes for the encouragement of deserving, but needy students.

Art. 57. The State shall encourage and protect research and discoveries in science and the arts.

Art. 58. The State shall protect and preserve historic remains and ancient relics which have historical, cultural or artistic value.

[CHAPTER] VI. DIVISION OF POWER BETWEEN THE CENTRAL AND LOCAL GOVERNMENTS

Art. 59. The principle of equilibrium shall be adopted in the divisions of power between the Central and local governments, as stipulated in Article 17 of *The Fundamentals of National Reconstruction*.

Art. 60. The various local governments may, within their respective spheres of authority, enact and ordain local laws and regulations. Where such laws and regulations are in conflict with those promulgated by the Central Government, they shall be null and void.

Art. 61. The demarcation between Central and local revenues shall be separately determined by law.

Art. 62. The Central Government may by law restrict any local tax, when—

(1) It is contrary to public interest;
(2) It encroaches upon the source of Central revenue;
(3) It constitutes overlapping taxation;
(4) It is detrimental to communications;
(5) It is unjustifiably imposed upon goods imported from other localities for the sole benefit of the locality concerned;
(6) It is in the nature of a transit duty on commodities in circulation among various localities.

Art. 63. The power of granting patents and monopolies is vested in the Central Government.

Art. 64. When one of the Provinces reaches the period of constitutionalism, the division of power between the Central and the local governments shall be defined in detail by law in accordance with *The Fundamentals of National Reconstruction*.

[CHAPTER] VII. ORGANIZATION OF THE GOVERNMENTS

SECTION 1. THE CENTRAL GOVERNMENT

Art. 65. The National Government shall exercise all the governing powers of the Republic of China.

Art. 66. The National Government shall have supreme command over the land, naval and air forces.

Art. 67. The National Government shall have the power to declare war, to negotiate peace and to conclude treaties.

Art. 68. The National Government shall exercise the power of granting amnesties, pardons, reprieves and restitutions of civic rights.

Art. 69. The National Government shall exercise the power of conferring medals and decorations of honor.

Art. 70. The National Government shall compile and publish a budget and financial statement of the national revenues and expenditures for each fiscal year.

Art. 71. The National Government shall be composed of the five Yüan: the Executive Yüan, the Legislative Yüan, the Judicial Yüan, the Examination Yüan and the Control Yüan, as well as various Ministries and Commissions.

Art. 72. The National Government shall have a President and an appropriate number of State Councilors, who shall be selected and appointed by the Central Executive Committee of the Kuomintang. The number of State Councilors shall be separately determined by law.

Art. 73. The President of the National Government shall represent the nation both internally and internationally.

Art. 74. The Presidents of the five Yüan and the heads of the various Ministries and Commissions shall be appointed or dismissed in accordance with law by the National Government at the instance of the President of the National Government.

Art. 75. All laws shall be promulgated and mandates issued upon the signature of the President of the National Government according to law.

Art. 76. The various Yüan, Ministries or Commissions shall, according to law, issue orders.

Art. 77. The organization of the National Government and of the various Yüan, Ministries and Commissions shall be separately determined by law.

SECTION 2. THE LOCAL GOVERNMENTS

Art. 78. In each Province, a Provincial Government shall be established, which shall attend to the administration of provincial affairs under the direction of the National Government. Its organization shall be separately determined by law.

Art. 79. When, as stipulated in Article 16 of *The Fundamentals of National Reconstruction,* a Province reaches the period of constitutionalism, the [Provincial] Assembly of People's Delegates may elect a Provincial Governor (*Shêng-chang*).

Art. 80. The system of local government in Mongolia and Tibet shall be determined separately by law in the light of the local conditions.

Art. 81. In each district (*Hsien*), a district government shall be established, which shall attend to the administration of district affairs under the direction of the Provincial Government. Its organization shall be separately determined by law.

Art. 82. In each of the districts, a District Autonomy Preparatory Committee shall be organized to carry out the preparations as provided in Article 8 of *The Fundamentals of National Reconstruction.* Its organization shall be separately determined by law.

Art. 83. Municipalities may be established in localities where industry and commerce, population or other special conditions warrant. The organization of such municipalities shall be separately determined by law.

[CHAPTER] VIII. ANNEX

Art. 84. All laws which are in conflict with this Provisional Constitution shall be null and void.

Art. 85. The power of interpreting this Provisional Constitution shall be exercised by the Central Executive Committee of the Kuomintang of China.

Art. 86. A draft of the Permanent Constitution (*Hsien-fa*) shall be prepared by the Legislative Yüan on the basis of *The Fundamentals of National Reconstruction* as well as the achievements during the Political Tutelage and Constitutional Periods. The said draft shall be duly made known to the people at large in preparation for its adoption and enforcement at the opportune moment.

Art. 87. When a majority of the Provinces in the country reach the period of constitutionalism, that is, when district autonomy has been completely instituted throughout each of such Provinces, then the National Government shall immediately summon a National People's Congress (*Kuo-min ta-hui*) to decide upon the adoption and promulgation of the Permanent Constitution.

Art. 88. The present Provisional Constitution shall be enacted by the National People's Convention (*Kuo-min hui-i*) and forwarded to the National Government for promulgation.

Art. 89. The present Provisional Constitution shall come into force from the date of promulgation.

Appendix 5

CONSTITUTION OF THE REPUBLIC OF CHINA (*CHUNG-HUA MIN-KUO HSIEN-FA*), ADOPTED BY THE NATIONAL ASSEMBLY ON 25 DECEMBER 1946 AND PROMULGATED BY THE NATIONAL GOVERNMENT ON 1 JANUARY 1947 *

PREAMBLE

The National Assembly of the Republic of China, by virtue of the mandate received from the whole body of citizens, and acting in accordance with the teachings of Dr. Sun Yat-sen, Founder of the Republic of China, and in order to consolidate the authority of the State, safeguard the rights of the people, ensure social tranquility and promote the welfare of the people, hereby adopts this Constitution and causes it to be promulgated for faithful and permanent observance by all in the country.

CHAPTER I. GENERAL PROVISIONS

Art. 1. The Republic of China, founded on the basis of the *San Min Chu I* (Three People's Principles), shall be a democratic republic of the people to be governed by the people and for the people.

Art. 2. The sovereignty of the Republic of China shall reside in the whole body of citizens.

* *China Handbook, 1951,* Taipeh, 1951, pp. 551-570.

Art. 3. Persons possessing Chinese nationality shall be citizens of the Republic of China.

Art. 4. The territory of the Republic of China, as represented by her existing geographical areas, shall not be altered except by resolution of the National Assembly.

Art. 5. All component racial groups in the Republic of China shall enjoy equal rights.

Art. 6. The National Flag of the Republic of China shall have a red background with a blue sky and a white sun in the upper left corner.

CHAPTER II. RIGHTS AND OBLIGATIONS OF THE PEOPLE

Art. 7. All citizens of the Republic of China, irrespective of sex, religion, race, class or party affiliation, shall be equal before the law.

Art. 8. The people shall be guaranteed freedom of person. Except in case of apprehension *flagrante delicto* as otherwise provided for by law, no person shall be arrested or detained except by a judicial or a police organ in accordance with procedure prescribed by law. No person shall be tried or punished except by a law court in accordance with procedure prescribed by law. Any arrest, detention, trial or punishment not in accordance with procedure prescribed by law may be contested.

When a person is arrested or detained on suspicion of having committed a crime, the organ making the arrest or detention shall in writing inform the said person and his designated relative or friend of the reason for his arrest or detention, and shall, within twenty-four hours, turn him over to a competent court for trial. The said person, or any other individual, may petition the competent court that a writ be served within twenty-four hours on the organ making the arrest for the surrender of the said person for trial.

The court may not reject the petition mentioned in the preceding paragraph, nor may it order the organ concerned to make an investigation and report first. The organ concerned may not refuse or delay to execute the writ of the court for the surrender of the said person for trial.

When a person is arrested or detained illegally, he, or any other person, may petition the court for an investigation. The court may not reject such a petition, and shall, within twenty-four hours, pursue the investigation with the organ concerned, and proceed with the matter in accordance with law.

Art. 9. Except those in active military service, no person shall be subject to trial by a military court.

Art. 10. The people shall have freedom of domicile and of changing their domicile.

Art. 11. The people shall have freedom of speech, academic instruction, writing and publication.

Art. 12. The people shall have freedom of secret correspondence.

Art. 13. The people shall have freedom of religious belief.

Art. 14. The people shall have freedom of assembly and freedom to form associations.

Art. 15. The people's right to life, right to work and right to property shall be inviolate.

Art. 16. The people shall have the right to present petitions, file complaints or institute legal proceedings.

Art. 17. The people shall have the rights of election, recall, initiative and referendum.

Art. 18. The people shall have the right to take civil service examinations and to hold public offices.

Art. 19. The people shall have the obligation to pay taxes in accordance with law.

Art. 20. The people shall have the obligation to perform military service in accordance with law.

Art. 21. The people shall have the right as well as the obligation to receive public education.

Art. 22. All other freedoms and rights of the people that do not jeopardize the social order or general welfare shall be guaranteed under the Constitution.

Art. 23. All the freedom and rights enumerated in the preceding Articles may not be restricted by law, except for reasons of preventing infringement upon the freedoms of other persons, averting an imminent crisis, maintaining social order or advancing general welfare.

Art. 24. Any public functionary who, in violation of the law, infringes upon the freedoms or rights of any person shall, in addition to being subject to disciplinary measures in accordance with the law, be held accountable under the criminal and civil laws. The injured person may, in accordance with the law, ask the State for indemnity.

CHAPTER III. THE NATIONAL ASSEMBLY

Art. 25. The National Assembly shall, in accordance with the provisions of the Constitution, exercise political powers on behalf of the whole body of citizens.

Art. 26. The National Assembly shall be organized with the following components:

(1) One delegate to be elected from every *hsien,* municipality or area of an equivalent status. In case its population exceeds 500,000, one additional delegate shall be elected for each additional 500,000. Areas of an equivalent status with the *hsien* or the municipality shall be prescribed by law.

(2) Delegates of Mongolia shall be elected four for each league and one for each special banner.

(3) The number of delegates to be elected from Tibet shall be prescribed by law.

(4) The number of delegates to be elected by various racial groups in the border regions shall be prescribed by law.

(5) The number of delegates to be elected by Chinese nationals residing abroad shall be prescribed by law.

(6) The number of delegates to be elected by occupational groups shall be prescribed by law.

(7) The number of delegates to be elected by women's organizations shall be prescribed by law.

Art. 27. The functions and powers of the National Assembly shall be as follows:

(1) Election of the President and the Vice-President.

(2) Recall of the President or the Vice-President.

(3) Amendment of the Constitution.

(4) Referendum on amendments to the Constitution proposed by the Legislative Yüan.

With respect to the exercise of the powers of initiative and referendum, in addition to the authority stipulated in Sections (3) and (4) of this Article, the National Assembly shall formulate measures pertaining thereto and enforce them, after the said two powers shall have been exercised in one-half of the *hsien* and municipalities of the whole country.

Art. 28. Delegates to the National Assembly shall be elected every six years.

The term of office of the delegates to the National Assembly shall terminate on the day of convocation of the next National Assembly.

Incumbent Government officials may not be elected delegates to the National Assembly in electoral areas where they hold office.

Art. 29. The National Assembly shall be summoned by the President to meet ninety days prior to the date of expiration of each presidential term.

Art. 30. The National Assembly may, in any of the following circumstances, convene an extraordinary session:

(1) When in accordance with the provisions of Article 49 of the Constitution, a new President and a new Vice-President are to be elected.

(2) When, in accordance with a resolution of the Control Yüan, an impeachment of the President or the Vice-President is to be instituted.

(3) When, in accordance with a resolution of the Legislative Yüan, an amendment to the Constitution is to be proposed.

(4) When a meeting is requested by over two-fifths of the delegates to the National Assembly.

When an extraordinary session is to be called in accordance with Sections (1) and (2) of this Article, the President of the Legislative Yüan shall issue the notice of convocation; when it is to be called in accordance with Sections (3) and (4) of this Article, it shall be convened by the President of the Republic.

Art. 31. The National Assembly shall meet at the seat of the Central Government.

Art. 32. No delegate to the National Assembly shall be held responsible outside the Assembly for opinions expressed or votes cast in the Assembly.

Art. 33. While the Assembly is in session, no delegate to the National Assembly shall, except in case of apprehension *flagrante delicto,* be arrested or detained without the permission of the National Assembly.

Art. 34. The organization of the National Assembly, the election and the recall of delegates to the National Assembly, and the procedure whereby the National Assembly is to carry out its functions shall be prescribed by law.

CHAPTER IV. THE PRESIDENT

Art. 35. The President shall be the Head of the State and shall represent the Republic of China in foreign relations.

Art. 36. The President shall command the nation's land, sea and air forces.

Art. 37. The President shall, in accordance with law, promulgate laws and issue mandates with the counter-signature of the President of the Executive Yüan, or with the counter-signature of both the President of the Executive Yüan and of the heads of ministries or commissions concerned.

Art. 38. The President shall, in accordance with the provisions of the Constitution, exercise the powers of concluding treaties, declaring war and making peace.

Art. 39. The President may, in accordance with law, declare martial law with the approval or confirmation of the Legislative Yüan. When the Legislative Yüan deems it necessary, it may, by resolution, request the President to terminate martial law.

Art. 40. The President shall, in accordance with law, exercise the powers of granting general amnesty, pardons, remission of sentences and restitution of civil rights.

Art. 41. The President shall, in accordance with law, appoint and remove civil and military officers.

Art. 42. The President may, in accordance with law, confer honors and award decorations.

Art. 43. In case of a natural calamity, an epidemic or a national financial or economic crisis that calls for emergency measures, the President, during the Legislative Yüan's recess, may, by resolution of the Executive Yüan Council and in accordance with the Emergency Decrees Act, issue an emergency decree proclaiming such measures as are necessary to cope with the situation. Such decree shall, within one month after issuance, be presented to the Legislative Yüan for confirmation; in case the Legislative Yüan withholds confirmation, the said decree shall immediately become null and void.

Art. 44. In case of any dispute between the various Yüan, unless there are relevant stipulations in the Constitution, the President may call a meeting of the Presidents of the Yüan concerned for consultation with a view to reaching an agreement.

Art. 45. Any citizen of the Republic of China having attained the age of forty years shall be eligible to the office of the President or Vice-President.

Art. 46. The election of the President and the Vice-President shall be prescribed by law.

Art. 47. The term of office of the President and of the Vice-President shall be six years. They may be elected for a second term.

Art. 48. The President shall, at the time of his inauguration, take the following oath:

"I do solemnly and sincerely swear before the people of the whole country that I shall observe the Constitution, faithfully perform my duties and strive to promote the people's welfare and defend the country. Under no circumstances shall I betray the people's trust. Should I break my oath, I shall submit myself to severe punishment by the State."

Art. 49. In the event of the President's office becoming vacant, the Vice-President shall succeed to the Presidency until the expiration of the original presidential term. In case the Presidency and the Vice-Presidency should both become vacant, the President of the Executive Yüan shall exercise the functions of the President and, in accordance with the provisions of Article 30 of the Constitution, convene an extraordinary session of the National Assembly to elect a new President and a new Vice-President, who shall hold office until the completion of the term left unfinished by the preceding President.

In case the President should, due to any cause, become incapacitated, the Vice-President shall exercise the functions of his office. In case both the President and the Vice-President should become incapacitated, the President of the Executive Yüan shall exercise the functions of the President.

Art. 50. The President shall vacate his office on the day his term expires. If by that time the succeeding President has not yet been elected, or if the President-elect and the Vice-President-elect have not yet assumed office, the President of the Executive Yüan shall exercise the functions of the President.

Art. 51. The period during which the President of the Executive Yüan may exercise the functions of the President shall not exceed three months.

Art. 52. The President shall not, without having been recalled or having vacated his office, be liable to criminal prosecution unless he is charged with having committed acts of rebellion or treason.

CHAPTER V. ADMINISTRATION

Art. 53. The Executive Yüan shall be the highest administrative organ of the State.

Art. 54. The Executive Yüan shall have a President, a Vice-President, a number of heads of ministries and commissions and a number of ministers of state without portfolio.

Art. 55. The President of the Executive Yüan shall be nominated and appointed by the President of the Republic with the consent of the Legislative Yüan.

If the President of the Executive Yüan should resign or otherwise vacate his office during the recess of the Legislative Yüan, the Vice-President of the Yüan shall exercise his functions, but the President of the Republic shall, within forty days, request a meeting of the Legislative Yüan to confirm his nominee.

Pending such confirmation by the Legislative Yüan, the Vice-President of the Executive Yüan shall exercise the functions of the President of the Yüan.

Art. 56. The Vice-President of the Executive Yüan, the heads of the various ministries and commissions and the ministers of state without portfolio shall be appointed by the President of the Republic upon the recommendation of the President of the Executive Yüan.

Art. 57. The Executive Yüan shall be responsible to the Legislative Yüan in accordance with the following provisions:

(1) The Executive Yüan has the obligation to present to the Legislative Yüan its administrative policies and its administrative reports. Members of the Legislative Yüan have, during sessions of the Legislative Yüan, the right to interpellate the President and the heads of the various ministries and commissions of the Executive Yüan.

(2) If the Legislative Yüan does not concur in any important policy of the Executive Yüan, it may, by resolution, ask the Executive Yüan to alter such a policy. With respect to such resolution, the Executive Yüan may, with the approval of the President of the Republic, request the Legislative Yüan to reconsider it. If, after reconsideration, two-thirds of the attending Members

of the Legislative Yüan uphold the original resolution, the President of the Executive Yüan shall either abide by the same or resign.

(3) If the Executive Yüan deems a statutory, budgetary or treaty bill passed by the Legislative Yüan difficult to carry out, it may, with the approval of the President of the Republic, request, within ten days after the delivery of the said resolution to the Executive Yüan, that the Legislative Yüan reconsider the same. If, after reconsideration, two-thirds of the attending Members of the Legislative Yüan uphold the original resolution, the President of the Executive Yüan shall either abide by the same or resign.

Art. 58. The Executive Yüan shall have an Executive Yüan Council to be composed of its President, Vice-President, heads of the various ministries and the commissions and ministers of state without portfolio, with the President of the Yüan as Chairman.

Prior to submission to the Legislative Yüan of any statutory or budgetary bill or any bill concerning martial law, general amnesty, declaration of war, conclusion of peace, treaties or other important affairs, or concerning matters of common concern to the various ministries and commissions, the President and heads of the various ministries and commissions of the Executive Yüan shall present the said bill to the Executive Yüan Council for discussion and decision.

Art. 59. The Executive Yüan shall, three months before the beginning of every fiscal year, present to the Legislative Yüan the budget for the following fiscal year.

Art. 60. The Executive Yüan shall, within four months after the end of every fiscal year, present the budget statement to the Control Yüan.

Art. 61. The organization of the Executive Yüan shall be prescribed by law.

CHAPTER VI. LEGISLATION

Art. 62. The Legislative Yüan shall be the highest legislative organ of the State to be composed of popularly elected Members to exercise the legislative power on behalf of the people.

Art. 63. The Legislative Yüan shall have the power to decide upon any statutory or budgetary bill or any bill concerning martial law, general amnesty, declaration of war, conclusion of peace, treaties and other important affairs of the State.

Art. 64. Members of the Legislative Yüan shall be elected in accordance with the following provisions:

(1) Those elected from provinces and by municipalities under the direct jurisdiction of the Executive Yüan shall be five for each province or municipality with a population of less than 3,000,000. In case of a population exceeding 3,000,000, one additional Member shall be elected for each additional 1,000,000 persons.

(2) Those elected from Mongolian leagues and banners.

(3) Those elected from Tibet.

(4) Those elected by various racial groups in the border regions.

(5) Those elected by Chinese nationals residing abroad.

(6) Those elected by occupational groups.

The election of Members of the Legislative Yüan and the number of those to be elected in accordance with Sections (2) to (6) in this article shall be prescribed by law.

The number of women to be elected in the above-mentioned categories shall be prescribed by law.

Art. 65. Members of the Legislative Yüan shall serve a term of three years, and shall be eligible for re-election. The election of Members of the Legislative Yüan shall be completed not later than three months prior to the expiration of each term of office.

Art. 66. The Legislative Yüan shall have a President and a Vice-President to be elected by and from among the Members.

Art. 67. The Legislative Yüan may organize various committees.

Such committees may invite government officials and private individuals concerned to be present at their meetings for consultation.

Art. 68. The Legislative Yüan shall hold two sessions every year, to be convened by itself. The first session shall last from February to the end of May, and the second session from September to the end of December. When necessary, a session may be extended.

Art. 69. In any of the following circumstances, the Legislative Yüan may hold an extraordinary session:

(1) At the request of the President of the Republic.

(2) Upon the request of more than one-fourth of its Members.

Art. 70. The Legislative Yüan shall not make proposals to increase expenditures listed in the budget presented by the Executive Yüan.

Art. 71. At meetings of the Legislative Yüan, the Presidents of the various Yüan and the heads of the various ministries and commissions concerned may be in attendance to present their opinions.

Art. 72. Statutory bills passed by the Legislative Yüan shall be sent to the President of the Republic and to the Executive Yüan. The President may proceed with them in accordance with provisions of Articles 57 of the Constitution.

Art. 73. No Member of the Legislative Yüan shall be held responsible outside the Yüan for any utterances made or votes cast in the Yüan.

Art. 74. No Member of the Legislative Yüan may, except in case of apprehension *flagrante delicto,* be arrested or detained without the permission of the Legislative Yüan.

Art. 75. No Member of the Legislative Yüan may concurrently hold a government post.

Art. 76. The organization of the Legislative Yüan shall be prescribed by law.

CHAPTER VII. JUDICIARY

Art. 77. The Judicial Yüan shall be the highest judicial organ of the State and shall have jurisdiction over civil, criminal and administrative cases and over cases concerning disciplinary punishment of public functionaries.

Art. 78. The Judicial Yüan shall have the power to interpret the Constitution and also the power to unify the interpretation of laws and decrees.

Art. 79. The Judicial Yüan shall have a President and a Vice-President, who shall be nominated and appointed by the President of the Republic with the consent of the Control Yüan.

The Judicial Yüan shall have a number of Grand Justices to attend to matters stipulated in Article 78 of the Constitution, who shall be nominated and appointed by the President of the Republic with the consent of the Control Yüan.

Art. 80. Judges shall be above party affiliations and shall, in compliance with the law, hold trials independently and free of any interference.

Art. 81. Judges shall hold office for life. No judge may be removed from office unless he has been found guilty of criminal offenses or subjected to disciplinary punishment, or declared legally incompetent. No judge may, except in accordance with the law, be suspended, transferred or have his salary reduced.

Art. 82. The organization of the Judicial Yüan and of the law courts of various grades shall be prescribed by law.

CHAPTER VIII. EXAMINATION

Art. 83. The Examination Yüan shall be the highest examination organ of the State and shall attend to matters such as examination, appointment, registration and ranking, checking of records, salary scales, promotion and transfer, safeguarding of tenures, commendation, compensation, retirement and pension.

Art. 84. The Examination Yüan shall have a President and a Vice-President and a number of Members who shall be nominated and appointed by the President of the Republic with the consent of the Control Yüan.

Art. 85. In the selection of public functionaries, a system of competitive examination shall be enforced, quotas of candidates shall be prescribed severally according to provinces and areas, and examinations shall be held by regions. No person may be appointed to a public office unless he has qualified through examination.

Art. 86. The following qualifications shall be determined through examinations to be held by the Examination Yüan in accordance with law:

(1) Qualifications for appointment as public functionaries.

(2) Qualifications for practice in specialized professions and as technicians.

Art. 87. The Examination Yüan may, with respect to matters under its charge, present statutory bills to the Legislative Yüan.

Art. 88. Members of the Examination Yüan shall be above party affiliations and shall, in accordance with law, independently carry out their functions.

Art. 89. The organization of the Examination Yüan shall be prescribed by law.

CHAPTER IX. CONTROL

Art. 90. The Control Yüan shall be the highest organ of control of the State and shall exercise the powers of consent, impeachment, censure and auditing.

Art. 91. The Control Yüan shall be composed of Members to be elected by provincial and municipal councils, the local councils of Mongolia and Tibet and Chinese nationals residing abroad. Their numbers shall be determined in accordance with the following provisions:

(1) Five Members from every province.

(2) Two members from every municipality under the direct jurisdiction of the Executive Yüan.

(3) Eight Members from Mongolian leagues and banners.

(4) Eight Members from Tibet.

(5) Eight Members from Chinese nationals residing abroad.

Art. 92. The Control Yüan shall have a President and a Vice-President, to be elected by and from among its Members.

Art. 93. Members of the Control Yüan shall serve a term of six years and shall be eligible for re-election.

Art. 94. When the Control Yüan exercises the power of consent in accordance with the Constitution, it shall do so by resolution of a majority of the attending Members.

Art. 95. The Control Yüan, in the exercise of its powers, may send for orders issued by the Executive Yüan and its ministries and commissions and for other relevant documents for perusal.

Art. 96. The Control Yüan, taking into account the functions of the Executive Yüan and its various ministries and commissions, may accordingly set up a number of committees to investigate their measures with a view to ascertaining whether they have violated any law or have been derelict in the performance of their duties.

Art. 97. The Control Yüan may, on the basis of the investigations and resolutions of its committees, propose corrective measures and forward them to the Executive Yüan and its appropriate ministries and commissions with request that improvements be effected.

When the Control Yüan deems a public functionary in the Central or a local government derelict in the performance of duty or when it deems there has been violation of law, it may institute an indictment or an impeachment. If it is a criminal offense, the case shall be turned over to a law court.

Art. 98. Any impeachment by the Control Yüan of a public functionary in the Central or a local government shall be instituted upon the proposal of more than one Member of the Control Yüan and the endorsement, after due consideration, of more than nine other Members.

Art. 99. In instituting impeachments of the personnel of the Judicial Yüan or of the Examination Yüan for dereliction in the performance of duty or for violation of law, the provisions of Articles 95, 97 and 98 of the Constitution shall be applicable.

Art. 100. Any impeachment of the President or the Vice-President of the Republic by the Control Yüan shall be instituted upon the proposal of more than one-fourth, and the endorsement, after due consideration, of the majority of the Members of the Control Yüan, and the same shall be presented to the National Assembly.

Art. 101. No Member of the Control Yüan shall be held responsible outside the Yüan for opinions expressed or votes cast in the Yüan.

Art. 102. No Member of the Control Yüan may, except in case of apprehension *flagrante delicto,* be arrested or detained without the permission of the Control Yüan.

Art. 103. No Member of the Control Yüan may concurrently hold a public office or engage in professional practices.

Art. 104. In the Control Yüan, there shall be an Auditor-General, who shall be nominated and appointed by the President of the Republic with the consent of the Legislative Yüan.

Art. 105. The Auditor-General shall, within three months after the presentation of the budget statement by the Executive Yüan, complete the auditing thereof in accordance with law, and submit an auditing report to the Legislative Yüan.

Art. 106. The organization of the Control Yüan shall be prescribed by law.

CHAPTER X. POWERS OF THE CENTRAL AND LOCAL GOVERNMENTS

Art. 107. The following matters shall be legislated upon and executed by the Central Government:

(1) Foreign affairs
(2) National defense and military affairs concerning national defense
(3) Nationality law, and criminal, civil and commercial laws
(4) Judicial organization
(5) Aviation, national highways, State-owned railways, navigation, postal telegraph services
(6) Central Government finance and national revenues
(7) Demarcation of national, provincial and *hsien* revenues
(8) State-operated economic enterprises
(9) Currency system and State banks
(10) Weights and measures
(11) Foreign trade policies
(12) Financial and economic matters affecting foreigners or foreign countries
(13) Other matters of the Central Government as stipulated in the Constitution.

Art. 108. The following matters shall be legislated upon and executed by the Central Government, which may delegate their execution to the provincial and *hsien* governments:

(1) General rules governing provincial and *hsien* self-government
(2) Division of administrative areas
(3) Forestry, industry, mining and commerce
(4) Educational system
(5) Banking and stocks and commodities
(6) Navigation and deep sea fishing enterprises
(7) Public utilities
(8) Cooperative enterprises
(9) Water and land communication and transportation affecting two or more provinces
(10) Water conservancy, waterways, agriculture and pasture affecting two or more provinces
(11) Registration and ranking, appointment, supervision and protection of officials in the Central and local governments
(12) Land legislation
(13) Labor legislation and other social legislation

(14) Eminent domain
(15) Census-taking and compilation of statistics
(16) Immigration and land reclamation
(17) Police system
(18) Public health
(19) Ordinary relief, compensation and unemployment relief
(20) Preservation of ancient books, articles and monuments of cultural value.

With respect to the above-mentioned matters, the provinces may enact separate laws and rules, provided these do not contravene the national laws.

Art. 109. The following matters shall be legislated upon and executed by the provinces, which may delegate their execution to the *hsien:*

(1) Provincial education, public health, industries and communications
(2) Management and disposal of provincial property
(3) Administration of municipalities under provincial jurisdiction
(4) Province-operated enterprises
(5) Provincial cooperative enterprises
(6) Provincial agricultural, forestry, water conservancy, fishery, animal husbandry and public works
(7) Provincial finance and revenue
(8) Provincial debts
(9) Provincial banks
(10) Enforcement of provincial police administration
(11) Provincial charitable and public welfare enterprises
(12) Other matters delegated to the provinces in accordance with national legislation.

Except as otherwise provided for by law, any of the above-mentioned matters which concern two or more provinces may be undertaken jointly by the provinces concerned.

When any province, in undertaking matters in Section (1) of this Article experiences financial difficulties, it may, by resolution of the Legislative Yüan, receive a subsidy from the National Treasury.

Art. 110. The following matters shall be legislated upon and executed by the *hsien:*

(1) *Hsien* education, public health, industries and communications
(2) Management and disposal of *hsien* property
(3) *Hsien*-operated enterprises
(4) *Hsien* cooperative enterprises
(5) *Hsien* agriculture and forestry, water conservancy, fishery, animal husbandry and public works
(6) *Hsien* finance and revenue
(7) *Hsien* debts
(8) *Hsien* banks
(9) Administration of *hsien* police and defense
(10) *Hsien* charitable and public welfare enterprises
(11) Other matters delegated in accordance with national legislation and the Provincial Self-Government Law.

Any of the above-mentioned matters covering more than two *hsien* may, except as otherwise provided for by the law, be undertaken jointly by the *hsien* concerned.

Art. 111. Should there occur any matter not enumerated in Articles 107, 108, 109, and 110, the same shall fall within the jurisdiction of the Central Government if it is national in nature; of the province, if it is provincial in nature; and of the *hsien,* if it is *hsien* in nature. Any dispute over jurisdiction shall be settled by the Legislative Yüan.

CHAPTER XI. LOCAL GOVERNMENT

SECTION 1. THE PROVINCE

Art. 112. A province may convene a Provincial Assembly to enact, in accordance with the "General Principles of Provincial and *Hsien* Self-Government," a "Provincial Self-Government Law," provided the same does not contravene the Constitution.

The organization of the Provincial Assembly and the election of the Representatives shall be prescribed by law.

Art. 113. The "Provincial Self-Government Law" shall, *inter alia,* provide for the following:

(1) In each of the provinces, there shall be a Provincial Council. Members of the Provincial Council shall be elected by the people of the province.

(2) In each of the provinces there shall be a Provincial Government with a Provincial Governor, to be elected by the people of the province.

(3) Relationship between the province and the *hsien* shall be defined.

The legislative power of the province shall be exercised by the Provincial Council.

Art. 114. The Provincial Self-Government Law shall, when enacted, be subject to review by the Judicial Yüan, which shall, if it deems any part thereof unconstitutional, declare such part null and void.

Art. 115. If during the enforcement of the Provincial Self-Government Law, there should arise any serious obstacle in the application of one or more of the articles contained therein, the Judicial Yüan shall first summon the various parties concerned to present their views; and on the basis of the findings, the Presidents of the Executive Yüan, the Legislative Yüan, the Judicial Yüan, the Examination Yüan and the Control Yüan shall form themselves into a committee, with the President of the Judicial Yüan as its Chairman, to propose a formula for solution.

Art. 116. Provincial laws and regulations that are in contravention of national laws shall be null and void.

Art. 117. When doubt arises as to whether or not a law is in contravention of the Constitution, the Judicial Yüan shall render its opinion thereon.

Art. 118. The self-government of municipalities under the direct jurisdiction of the Executive Yüan shall be prescribed by law.

Art. 119. The local self-government system of the Mongolian leagues and banners shall be prescribed by law.

Art. 120. The self-government system of Tibet shall be safeguarded.

SECTION 2. THE *hsien*

Art. 121. The *hsien* shall enforce *hsien* self-government.

Art. 122. The *hsien* may convene a *hsien* assembly and enact, in accordance with the "General Principles of Provincial and *Hsien* Self-Government," a "*Hsien* Self-Government Law," provided the same does not contravene the Constitution or "Provincial Self-Government Law."

Art. 123. The people of the *hsien* shall, in accordance with law, exercise the rights of initiative and referendum in matters pertaining to *hsien* self-government, as well as the rights of election and recall of the magistrate and other *hsien* self-government officers.

Art. 124. In each *hsien,* there shall be a *hsien* council. Members of the *hsien* council shall be elected by the people of the *hsien.*

The legislative power of the *hsien* shall be exercised by the *hsien* council.

Art. 125. *Hsien* laws and regulations that are in contravention of national laws or provincial laws and regulations shall be null and void.

Art. 126. In each *hsien* there shall be a *hsien* government with a *hsien* magistrate, to be elected by the people of the *hsien.*

Art. 127. The *hsien* magistrate shall attend to the enforcement of *hsien* self-government and to the execution of matters delegated by the Central and provincial governments.

Art. 128. The provisions governing the *hsien* shall apply *mutatis mutandis* to the municipality.

CHAPTER XII. SUFFRAGE, RECALL, INITIATIVE AND REFERENDUM

Art. 129. The elections stipulated in the Constitution, except as otherwise provided for by the Constitution, shall be by universal, equal, and direct suffrage and by secret ballot.

Art. 130. Any citizen of the Republic of China having attained the age of twenty years shall have the right of suffrage in accordance with law. Except as otherwise provided for by law and by the Constitution, any citizen having attained the age of twenty-three years shall have the right to be elected to office in accordance with the law.

Art. 131. All candidates in the elections prescribed in the Constitution shall openly campaign for election.

Art. 132. Intimidation and material inducements shall be strictly forbidden in elections. Disputes of election shall be settled by the courts.

Art. 133. After being elected, a person may, in accordance with law, be recalled by his constituency.

Art. 134. In the elections, the minimum number of women to be elected shall be decided upon, and measures pertaining thereto shall be prescribed by law.

Art. 135. Regarding the number and election of Representatives for interior areas where a different mode of living obtains, necessary measures shall be prescribed by law.

Art. 136. The exercise of the rights of initiative and referendum shall be prescribed by law.

CHAPTER XIII. FUNDAMENTAL NATIONAL POLICIES

SECTION 1. NATIONAL DEFENSE

Art. 137. The national defense of the Republic of China shall have as its object the safeguarding of national security and the preservation of world peace.

The organization of national defense shall be prescribed by law.

Art. 138. The land, sea and air forces of the whole country shall be above personal, regional or party affiliations and shall be loyal to the State and protect the people.

Art. 139. No political party or faction or private individual may make use of the armed forces as an instrument in the struggle for political power.

Art. 140. No person in active military service may concurrently hold a civil office.

SECTION 2. FOREIGN POLICY

Art. 141. In its external relations, the Republic of China shall, in keeping with the spirit of independence and on the basis of the principles of equality and reciprocity, cultivate good neighborliness with other nations, respect treaties and the United Nations Charter, protect the rights and interests of Chinese nationals residing abroad, promote international cooperation and advance the cause of righteousness among nations and of world peace.

SECTION 3. NATIONAL ECONOMY

Art. 142. National economy shall be based on the Principle of the People's Livelihood and seek to effect equalization of land ownership and control over private capital in order to attain fair distribution and sufficiency in national economy.

Art. 143. All the land within the territory of the Republic of China shall belong to the whole body of citizens. Private ownership of land, acquired by the people in accordance with the law, shall be protected and restricted by law. Land owned by private individuals shall be liable to taxation, or government purchase, according to its value.

Mineral deposits and natural power which may be economically utilized for the public benefit shall belong to the State and shall in no way be affected by the people's acquisition of the right of ownership over the land in question.

If the value of any piece of land shall have increased not through the exertion of labor or the employment of capital, the State shall levy thereon an increment tax, the proceeds of which shall be used for public welfare.

In the distribution of land and adjustment of title deeds the State shall, as a matter of principle, assist tiller-owners and persons who make use of the land themselves, and shall also regulate the size of land appropriate for cultivation and other purposes.

Art. 144. Public utilities and other enterprises of a monopolistic nature shall, as a matter of principle, be under public operation. They may, if permitted by the law, be operated by the people.

Art. 145. With respect to private wealth and privately operated enterprises, the State shall restrict them by law if they are deemed prejudicial to a balanced development of the national economy.

Cooperative enterprises shall receive the encouragement and assistance of the State.

Private productive enterprises and foreign trade shall receive the encouragement, guidance and protection of the State.

Art. 146. The State shall, by the use of scientific technique, undertake water conservancy projects, increase the productivity of land, improve agricultural conditions, plan the utilization of land and develop agricultural resources in order to hasten the industrialization of agriculture.

Art. 147. The Central Government, in order to attain a balanced economic development of the provinces, shall give appropriate aid to economically poor provinces.

The provinces, in order to attain a balanced economic development of the *hsien,* shall give appropriate aid to economically poor *hsien.*

Art. 148. Within the territory of the Republic of China, goods of all kinds shall be permitted to move freely from place to place.

Art. 149. Financial institutions shall, in accordance with the law, be subject to State control.

Art. 150. The State shall establish throughout the country special financial institutions to aid the unemployed.

Art. 151. With respect to Chinese nationals residing abroad, the State shall foster and protect the development of their economic enterprises.

SECTION 4. SOCIAL SECURITY

Art. 152. The State shall give adequate opportunity of employment to people who are capable of work.

Art. 153. The State, in order to improve the livelihood of laborers and farmers and to improve their productive skill, shall enact laws and carry out policies for their protection.

Women and children engaged in labor shall, according to their age and physical condition, be accorded special protection.

Art. 154. Capital and labor shall, in accordance with the principle of harmony and cooperation, promote productive enterprises. Mediation and arbitration of disputes between capital and labor shall be prescribed by law.

Art. 155. The State, in order to promote social welfare, shall put into operation a Social Insurance System. To the aged, the infirm and the disabled among the people who are unable to earn a living and to victims of natural calamities, the State shall give appropriate assistance and relief.

Art. 156. The State, in order to consolidate the foundation of national existence and development, shall protect motherhood and carry out the policy of promoting the welfare of women and children.

Art. 157. The State, in order to improve national health, shall extend throughout the country public health and medical services and the State Medicine System.

SECTION 5. EDUCATION AND CULTURE

Art. 158. The nation's educational and cultural services shall have as their aim the development among the citizens of national characteristics, a democratic spirit, traditional morality, good physique, scientific knowledge and the ability to earn a living.

Art. 159. All citizens shall have an equal opportunity to receive education.

Art. 160. All children of school age, to wit, those from six to twelve years, shall receive free primary education. Those from poor families shall be supplied with textbooks at the expense of the Government.

All citizens above school age who have not received primary education shall receive such education free of charge and shall likewise be supplied with textbooks at the expense of the Government.

Art. 161. The National, provincial, and local governments shall create scholarships to assist students of good scholastic standing and of exemplary conduct who lack the means to continue their school education.

Art. 162. All public and private educational and cultural institutions in the country shall, in accordance with law, be subject to State supervision.

Art. 163. The State shall pay due attention to the balanced development of education in different regions and shall promote social education in order to raise the cultural standard of the citizens in general. The National Treasury shall give cash grants to border regions and economically poor areas to help them meet their educational and cultural expenses. The Central Government may itself undertake the more important educational and cultural enterprises in such regions or give them financial assistance.

Art. 164. Expenditures for educational programs, scientific studies and cultural services shall be, in respect of the Central Government, not less than 15 per cent of the total national budget; in respect of the provinces, not less than 25 per cent of the total provincial budget; and in respect of the municipality or *hsien*, not less than 35 per cent of the total municipal or *hsien* budget. Educational and cultural foundations established in accordance with the law shall, together with their property, be protected.

Art. 165. The State shall safeguard the livelihood of those who work in the fields of education, sciences and arts and shall, in accord with the development of the national economy, increase their remuneration from time to time.

Art. 166. The State shall encourage scientific discoveries and inventions and shall protect monuments and articles of historical, cultural or artistic value.

Art. 167. The State shall give encouragement or subsidies to the following enterprises or individuals:

(1) Private educational enterprises in the country which have a good record;

(2) Chinese educational enterprises abroad which have a good record;

(3) Persons who have made discoveries or inventions in the fields of learning and technology;

(4) Persons who have rendered long and meritorious service to the cause of education.

Art. 168. The State shall accord legal protection to the status of racial groups in the border regions and shall give them special assistance in their local self-government undertakings.

Art. 169. The State shall positively undertake and foster the development of education, cultural services, communications, water conservancy, public health and other economic and social enterprises for the benefit of racial groups in the border regions. With respect to the utilization of land, the State shall, after taking into account local climatic conditions and the nature of the soil and in the light of the living habits of the local people, adopt measures to protect the land and to assist in its development.

CHAPTER XIV. ENFORCEMENT AND AMENDMENT OF THE CONSTITUTION

Art. 170. The term "Law," as used in the Constitution, denotes any legislative bill that shall have been passed by the Legislative Yüan and promulgated by the President.

Art. 171. Laws that are in contravention of the Constitution shall be null and void.

When doubt arises as to whether or not a law is in contravention of the Constitution, the Judicial Yüan shall render its opinion thereon.

Art. 172. Ordinances that are in contravention of the Constitution or laws shall be null and void.

Art. 173. Interpretation of the Constitution shall be undertaken by the Judicial Yüan.

Art. 174. Amendments to the Constitution shall be made in accordance with one of the following procedures:

(1) An amendment may be made upon the proposal of one-fifth of the total number of the delegates to the National Assembly and by a resolution of three-fourths of the delegates present at a meeting having a quorum of two-thirds of the entire Assembly.

(2) An amendment may be drawn up and submitted to the National Assembly for referendum upon the proposal of one-fourth of the Members of the Legislative Yüan and by a resolution of three-fourths of the Members present at a meeting having a quorum of three-fourths of the Members of the entire Yüan.

Such a proposed amendment to the Constitution shall be published at least six months before the National Assembly convenes.

Art. 175. Whenever necessary, enforcement procedures in regard to any matter prescribed in the Constitution shall be separately provided by law.

The preparatory procedure for the enforcement of the Constitution shall be decided upon by the same National Assembly which shall have adopted the Constitution.

Appendix 6

ORGANIC LAW OF THE CENTRAL PEOPLE'S GOVERNMENT OF THE PEOPLE'S REPUBLIC OF CHINA (*CHUNG-HUA JÊN-MIN KUNG-HO-KUO CHUNG-YANG JÊN-MIN CHÊNG-FU TSU-CHIH-FA*), PASSED BY THE FIRST SESSION OF THE CHINESE PEOPLE'S CONSULTATIVE CONFERENCE ON 27 SEPTEMBER 1949 *

CHAPTER I. GENERAL PRINCIPLES

Art. 1. The People's Republic of China is a State of the People's Democratic Dictatorship, led by the working class, based on the alliance of workers and peasants, and rallying all democratic classes and various nationalities within the country.

Art. 2. The Government of the People's Republic of China is a government of the people's congress system based on the principle of democratic centralism.

Art. 3. Prior to the convocation of the All-China People's Congress through universal suffrage, the first session of the Chinese People's Political Consultative Conference shall exercise the functions and powers of the All-China People's Congress, enact the Organic Law of the Central People's Government of the People's Republic of China, elect the Central People's Government Council of the People's Republic of China and vest this Council with the power of exercising State authority.

Art. 4. The Central People's Government Council represents the People's Republic of China in international relations and assumes leadership of the State authority at home.

Art. 5. The Central People's Government Council shall set up the State Administration Council as the highest executive organ for State administration; shall set up the People's Revolutionary Military Council as the supreme military command of the State; and shall set up the Supreme People's Court and the People's Procurator-General's Office as the highest judicial and supervisory organs of the country.

CHAPTER II. THE CENTRAL PEOPLE'S GOVERNMENT COUNCIL

Art. 6. The Central People's Government Council shall consist of a chairman and six vice-chairmen of the Central People's Government and 56 Council members elected by the first session of the Chinese People's Political Consultative Conference and a secretary general elected by and from the Central People's Government Council.

Art. 7. The Central People's Government Council exercises the following jurisdiction in accordance with the Common Programme enacted by the first session of the Chinese People's Political Consultative Conference:

(1) Enactment and interpretation of the laws of the State, promulgation of decrees and supervision of their execution.

* Published in *China Digest*, Vol. VII, No. 2, Hongkong, (Oct. 19, 1949).

(2) Determination of the administrative policies of the State.
(3) Annulment or amendment of the decisions and orders of the State Administration Council, which do not conform to the laws and decrees of the State.
(4) Ratification, abrogation or amendment of treaties and agreements concluded by the People's Republic of China with foreign countries.
(5) Dealing with the question of war and peace.
(6) Approval or revising of the State budget and final accounts.
(7) Promulgation of the acts for general amity and pardon.
(8) Instituting and awarding of orders and medals and conferring of titles of honour of the State.
(9) Appointment or dismissal of the following government personnel:
a. Appointment or dismissal of the premier and deputy premier and members of the State Administration Council; secretary general and assistant secretaries general of the State Administration Council; chairman, vice-chairman, and members of the various committees and commissions; ministers and vice-ministers of the various ministries; president and vice-presidents of the academy of sciences; director and assistant directors of various administrations; and manager and assistant-managers of the bank.
b. Appointment or dismissal or ratification of the appointment or dismissal on the recommendation of the State Administration Council, the chairman, vice-chairman and main administrative personnel of various administrative areas and various provincial, municipal people's governments.
c. Appointment or recall of the ambassadors, ministers and plenipotentiary representatives to foreign states.
d. Appointment or dismissal of the chairman, vice-chairman and members of the People's Revolutionary Military Council, the commander-in-chief, deputy commander-in-chief, chief of staff and deputy chief of staff of the People's Liberation Army, and the director and vice-director of the general political department.
e. Appointment or dismissal of the chief justice, vice chief justice and committee members of the Supreme People's Court, the procurator-general, vice-procurators-general and committee members of the People's Procurator-General's Office.
(10) Preparation for and convocation of the All-China People's Congress.

Art. 8. The chairman of the Central People's Government shall preside over the meetings of the Central People's Government Council and direct the work of the Central People's Government Council.

Art. 9. The vice-chairmen and secretary general of the Central People's Government shall assist the chairman in the discharge of his duties.

Art. 10. The Central People's Government Council shall hold bi-monthly meetings convened by the chairman. The chairman may convene the meeting earlier or postpone it when necessary or upon the request of more than one third of the members of the Central People's Government Council or upon the request of the State Administration Council. More than half of the Council members are required to form a quorum and all resolutions shall be passed with the concurrence of over one half of the members present at the meeting.

Art. 11. The Central People's Government Council shall have a general office and may set up other subordinate working organs when necessary.

Art. 12. The organization regulations of the Central People's Government Council shall be enacted by the Central People's Government Council.

CHAPTER III. THE STATE ADMINISTRATION COUNCIL

Art. 13. The State Administration Council shall consist of a premier, a certain number of deputy premiers, a secretary general and a certain number of members appointed by the Central People's Government Council.

Members of the State Administration Council may concurrently hold posts as chairmen of the various committees or commissions or as the ministers of ministries.

Art. 14. The State Administration Council is responsible and accountable to the Central People's Government Council. When the Central People's Government Council adjourns, the State Administration Council shall be responsible and accountable to the chairman of the Central People's Government.

Art. 15. The State Administration Council shall exercise the following jurisdiction on the basis and in pursuance of the Common Programme of the Chinese People's Political Consultative Conference, laws and decrees of the State and the administrative policies stipulated by the Central People's Government Council:

1. Issue decisions and orders and verify their execution; 2. Annul or amend the decisions and orders of committees, ministries, commissions, academy, administrations, and bank, and all levels of governments which do not conform to the laws and decrees of the State and the decisions and orders of the State Administration Council; 3. Submit bills to the Central People's Government Council; 4. Coordinate, unify and direct the inter-relations, the internal organization and the general work of committees, ministries, commissions, academy, administrations and bank and other subordinate organs; 5. Direct the work of local people's governments throughout the country; 6. Appoint or dismiss, confirm the appointment or dismissal of the main administrative personnel of the county and municipal level and above, not included in Article 7 (9), b.

Art. 16. The premier of the State Administration Council shall direct the affairs of the Council. The deputy premiers and the secretary general of the State Administration Council shall assist the premier in the discharge of his duties.

Art. 17. The State Administration Council shall hold weekly meetings convened by the premier. The premier may convene the meeting earlier or postpone it when necessary, or upon the request of over one third of its members. Over half of the members of the State Administration Council are required to form a quorum, and resolutions shall be passed with the concurrence of over one half of the members present at the meeting.

The decisions and orders of the State Administration Council shall come into force with the signature of the premier or with the counter signatures of the heads of the committees, ministries, commissions, academy, administrations, and bank concerned.

Art. 18. The State Administration Council shall set up a Committee of Political and Legal Affairs, a Committee of Finance and Economics, a Committee of Culture and Education, a Committee of People's Supervision, and the following ministries, commissions, academy, administrations and bank, which shall direct their respective department of State administration:

Ministry of Interiors, Ministry of Foreign Affairs, Information Administration, Ministry of Public Security, Ministry of Finance, People's Bank, Ministry of Trade, Maritime Customs Administration, Ministry of Heavy Industry, Ministry of Fuel Industry, Ministry of Textile Industry, Ministry of Food Industry, Ministry of Light Industries (not belonging to the above-mentioned four industries), Ministry of Railways, Ministry of Post and Telegraph, Ministry of Communications, Ministry of Agriculture, Ministry of Forestry and Land Reclamation, Ministry of Water Conservancy, Ministry of Labour, Ministry of Culture, Ministry of Education, Academy of Sciences, News Administration, Publication Administration, Ministry of Public Health, Ministry of Justice, Commission of Law, Commission of the Affairs of Nationalities, and Commission of Overseas Chinese Affairs.

The Committee of Political and Legal Affairs shall direct the work of the Ministry of Interiors, the Ministry of Public Security, the Ministry of Justice, the Commission of Law, and the Commission of the Affairs of Nationalities.

The Committee of Finance and Economics shall direct the work of the Ministry of Finance, the Ministry of Trade, the Ministry of Heavy Industry, the Ministry of Fuel Industry, the Ministry of Textile Industry, the Ministry of Food Industry, the Ministry of Light Industries, the Ministry of Railways, the Ministry of Post and Telegraph, the Ministry of Communications, the Ministry of Agriculture, the Ministry of Forestry and Land Reclamation, the Ministry of Water Conservancy, the Ministry of Labour, the People's Bank, and the Maritime Customs Administration.

The Committee of Culture and Education shall direct the work of the Ministry of Culture, the Ministry of Education, the Ministry of Public Health, the Academy of Sciences, the News Administration, and the Publication Administration.

In order to carry out their work, the Committees may issue decisions and orders to the Ministries, the Commissions, the Academy, the Administrations, the Bank under their direction and other subordinate organs, and verify their execution.

The Committee of People's Supervision is responsible for the supervision of the execution of duties by government institutions, and government functionaries.

Art. 19. The Ministries, Commissions, Academy, Administrations, and Bank may issue decisions and orders within their jurisdiction and verify their execution.

Art. 20. The State Administration Council shall have a Secretariat to deal with day-to-day work and take charge of the files, archives and seal of the State Administration Council etc.

Art. 21. The organization regulations of the State Administration Council and the Committees, the Administrations, Bank and the Secretariat shall be enacted or ratified by the Central People's Government Council.

Art. 22. The Central People's Government Council may, when necessary, decide on the increase or reduction of the number or merging of the Committees, Ministries, Commissions, Academy, Administrations, People's Bank and the Secretariat.

CHAPTER IV. THE PEOPLE'S REVOLUTIONARY MILITARY COUNCIL

Art. 23. The People's Liberation Army and other people's armed forces throughout the country shall come under the unified control and command of the People's Revolutionary Military Council.

Art. 24. The People's Revolutionary Military Council shall have a chairman and a certain number of vice-chairmen, and a certain number of council members.

Art. 25. The organization of the People's Revolutionary Military Council, and its administration and command shall be determined by the Central People's Government Council.

CHAPTER V. THE SUPREME PEOPLE'S COURT AND THE PEOPLE'S PROCURATOR-GENERAL'S OFFICE

Art. 26. The Supreme People's Court is the highest judicial organ of the country, and is responsible for the directing and supervising of the judicial work of all the judicial organs of the country.

Art. 27. The Supreme People's Court shall have a chief justice and a certain number of vice chief justices and a number of committee members.

Art. 28. The People's Procurator-General's Office has the greatest responsibility for the strict observance of the laws by all government institutions and government functionaries as well as nationals of the country.

Art. 29. The People's Procurator-General's Office shall have a procurator-general, a certain number of vice-procurators-general and a certain number of committee members.

Art. 30. The organization regulations of the Supreme People's Court and the Office of the People's Procurator-General shall be enacted by the Central People's Government Council.

CHAPTER VI. RIGHTS OF AMENDMENT AND INTERPRETATION OF THIS ORGANIC LAW

Art. 31. The right of amendment of the Organic Law of the Central People's Government belongs to the plenary session of the Chinese People's Political Consultative Conference, or to the Central People's Government Council when the People's Political Consultative Conference is not in session. The right of interpretation of the Organic Law belongs to the Central People's Government Council.

Appendices

JAPAN

Appendix 7

THE JAPANESE: ORIGINS *

THE MYTHOLOGICAL STORY OF ORIGIN

Like most insular peoples, the Japanese regard themselves as a race apart. This idea of uniqueness is carried to the extreme of claiming lineal descent from the gods who first created Nippon,† the sacred land wherein they dwell. Some understanding of Japanese attitudes toward the world may be gained by a read-

* From John F. Embree, *The Japanese,* Washington: Smithsonian Institution War Background Studies Number Seven (Publication 3702), January 23, 1943, pages 1-4.

† The name Japan is a modification of a Chinese reading of the characters [for] *Jihpen.* The Japanese pronounce these characters Nihon or Nippon.

ing of their myths of origin, myths which to many Japanese are fundamental articles of faith.

In the beginning there was nothingness. Then a series of gods were born "in the Plain of High Heaven" who did little but exist until the advent of a male and female pair called Izanagi and Izanami. Izanagi dipped a heavenly jeweled spear into the deeps, and the drops that fell from it as he withdrew it formed the islands of Japan.

. . . . .

During the age of the gods thousands of deities came into existence, thus providing deities as ancestors for most of the important tribes and clans of early Japan, spirits for the mountains and streams, and patron gods for the villages. It is this myriad pantheon of deities and the rituals associated with them that makes up what is today called Shinto.

The transition period between myth and history is the arrival on the scene of Jimmu Tennō as the first historical ruler of Japan and the man who first succeeded in bringing together under one rule a number of separate tribes. Jimmu was born in Kyushu in 660 B.C. according to Japanese orthodox history, or about A.D. 1 according to more critical historians. After conquering the tribes of northern Kyushu and southern Honshu, he established a permanent imperial line that has existed unbroken, if occasionally tangled, from his day to the present.

Appendix 8

CHRONOLOGICAL TABLE OF MAJOR STEPS IN THE TAIKA REFORMS *

A.D. 645,	6th month	Emperor Kōtoku ascends throne.
	. . . . .	The Three Ministers appointed.
	. . . . .	The Oath of allegiance.
	. . . . .	Naming of first reign period *(nengō)*, Taika.
	8th month	Eastern governors appointed and instructed.
	. . . . .	Status of free and unfree defined.
	. . . . .	Buddhist Church organized and established.
	9th month	Counterrevolt of Soga (Prince Furuhito) suppressed.
	. . . . .	Arms collected and stored by Government.
	. . . . .	Private sale of land forbidden.
A.D. 646,	1st month	The Decree of the Reform: four articles of the new civil law *(ryō)* promulgated.

* Based on Asakawa K., *The Early Institutional Life of Japan,* cited, pp. 267-268; and R. K. Reischauer, *Early Japanese History (c.40 B.C.—A.D. 1167),* Part A, "A Chronicle of Events," pp. 145-165.

	3rd month	Conduct of Eastern governors reviewed.
		Certain popular evil customs of burial and marriage outlawed.
A.D. 646,	8th month	Intention of establishing a new hierarchy of rank and office announced.
A.D. 647,	1st month	
	10th month	System of thirteen cap ranks *(Kan-i)* of seven colors established.
A.D. 649,	2nd month	System of nineteen cap ranks established.
		Eight departments, numerous offices established.
A.D. 652,	4th month	Census and register of households *(koseki)* made.
		Households grouped in fives; fifty households grouped in township *(sato)*.
A.D. 655,	2nd month	Empress Kōkyoku reascends throne (as Saimei *Tennō)*.
A.D. 661,	1st month	Saimei *Tennō* died during Korean Expedition (Naka-no-Oye began rule as Crown Prince).
A.D. 666,	1st month	Naka-no-Oye returned to Yamato, and moved his capital to Omi-no-Kuni (the Omi Civil and Penal Codes were drawn up here).
A.D. 668,	2nd month	Coronation of Tenchi *Tennō* (formerly Prince Naka-no-Oye).
A.D. 669,	11th month	Nakatomi Kamatari given family name of Fujiwara (Fujiwara Kamatari); he died the next day.
A.D. 673,	3rd month	Coronation of Temmu *Tennō.*
A.D. 681,	4th month	Compilation of records of Sovereigns and ancient matters (led to writing of *Kojiki* and *Nihon shoki*).
A.D. 690,	2nd month	Coronation of Jito *Tennō.*
A.D. 697,	8th month	Coronation of Mommu *Tennō.*
A.D. 700,	4th month	Princes and officials ordered to study civil codes and penal laws (led to compilation of Taihō Civil Code and Taihō Penal Code, completed in 701 and promulgated in 702).

Appendix 9

THE CHARTER OATH OF FIVE ARTICLES, 1868
(*GOKAJŌ NO GOSEIMON*)

A. Older Forms

(1) We will call councils and rule the nation according to public opinion;
(2) Men of upper and lower classes without distinction shall be united in all enterprises;
(3) Civil officials and military officers shall be in one accord and all the common people shall be so treated that they can attain their aims and feel no discontent;
(4) Old unworthy ways and customs shall be destroyed and the people shall walk along the highway of heaven and earth; and
(5) Knowledge shall be sought among the nations of the world and the Empire shall be led up to the zenith of prosperity.

To accomplish this unprecedented reformation, We go before the people, and proclaim the fundamental national principles even in the presence of the gods of heaven and earth, to establish the way for the public welfare. Ye, Our subjects, shall be united all together, according to these principles.

The Japan Year Book, 1946-48

Public councils shall be organized and all governmental affairs shall be decided by general discussion.

All classes, both rulers and ruled, shall with one heart devote themselves to the advancement of the national interests.

All the civil and military officials and all the common people shall be allowed to realize their own aspirations and to evince their active characteristics.

All base customs of former times shall be abolished, and the justice and equity as they are universally recognized shall be followed.

Knowledge shall be sought for throughout the world and thus the foundations of the Empire shall be extended.

Ukita Version, from Ōkuma S. (Editor),
Fifty Years of New Japan

B. Modern Form

I. An Assembly widely convoked shall be established, and thus great stress shall be laid upon public opinion.
II. The welfare of the whole nation shall be promoted by the everlasting efforts of both the governing and the governed classes.
III. All subjects, civil and military officers, as well as other people shall do their best, and never grow weary in accomplishing their legitimate purposes.
IV. All absurd usages shall be abandoned; justice and righteousness shall regulate all actions.
V. Knowledge shall be sought for all over the world, and thus shall be strengthened the foundations of the Imperial Polity.

McLaren, *Japanese Government Documents*

Appendix 10

THE CONSTITUTION OF THE EMPIRE OF JAPAN (MEIJI CONSTITUTION, 1889)

PREAMBLE

Having, by virtue of the glories of Our Ancestors, ascended the Throne of a lineal succession unbroken for ages eternal; desiring to promote the welfare of, and to give development to the moral and intellectual faculties of Our beloved subjects, the very same that have been favoured with the benevolent care and affectionate vigilance of Our Ancestors; and hoping to maintain the prosperity of the State, in concert with Our people and with their support, We hereby promulgate, in pursuance of Our Imperial Rescript of the 12th day of the 10th month of the 14th year of Meiji, a fundamental law of State, to exhibit the principles, by which We are to be guided in Our conduct, and to point out to what Our descendants and Our subjects and their descendants are forever to conform.

The rights of sovereignty of the State, We have inherited from Our Ancestors, and We shall bequeath them to Our descendants. Neither We nor they shall in future fail to wield them, in accordance with the provisions of the Constitution hereby granted.

We now declare to respect and protect the security of the rights and of the property of Our people, and to secure to them the complete enjoyment of the same, within the extent of the provisions of the present Constitution and of the law.

The Imperial Diet shall first be convoked for the 23rd year of Meiji and the time of its opening shall be the date when the present Constitution comes into force.

When in the future it may become necessary to amend any of the provisions of the present Constitution, We or Our successors shall assume the initiative right, and submit a project for the same to the Imperial Diet. The Imperial Diet shall pass its vote upon it, according to the conditions imposed by the present Constitution, and in no otherwise shall Our descendants or Our subjects be permitted to attempt any alteration thereof.

Our Ministers of State, on Our behalf, shall be held responsible for the carrying out of the present Constitution, and Our present and future subjects shall forever assume the duty of allegiance to the present Constitution.

CHAPTER I. THE EMPEROR

Art. I. The Empire of Japan shall be reigned over and governed by a line of Emperors unbroken for ages eternal.

Art. II. The Imperial Throne shall be succeeded to by Imperial male descendants, according to the provisions of the Imperial House Law.

Art. III. The Emperor is sacred and inviolable.

Art. IV. The Emperor is the head of the Empire, combining in Himself the rights of sovereignty, and exercises them, according to the provisions of the present Constitutions.

Art. V. The Emperor exercises the legislative power with the consent of the Imperial Diet.

Art. VI. The Emperor gives sanction to laws and orders them to be promulgated and executed.

Art. VII. The Emperor convokes the Imperial Diet, opens, closes and prorogues it, and dissolves the House of Representatives.

Art. VIII. The Emperor, in consequence of an urgent necessity to maintain public safety or to avert public calamities, issues, when the Imperial Diet is not sitting, Imperial Ordinances in the place of law.

Such Imperial Ordinances are to be laid before the Imperial Diet at its next session, and when the Diet does not approve the said Ordinances, the Government shall declare them to be invalid for the future.

Art. IX. The Emperor issues or causes to be issued, the Ordinances necessary for the carrying out of the laws, or for the maintenance of the public peace and order, and for the promotion of the welfare of the subjects. But no Ordinance shall in any way alter any of the existing laws.

Art. X. The Emperor determines the organization of the different branches of the administration, and salaries of all civil and military officers, and appoints and dismisses the same. Exceptions especially provided for in the present Constitution or in other laws, shall be in accordance with the respective provisions (bearing thereon).

Art. XI. The Emperor has the supreme command of the Army and Navy.

Art. XII. The Emperor determines the organization and peace standing of the Army and Navy.

Art. XIII. The Emperor declares war, makes peace, and concludes treaties.

Art. XIV. The Emperor declares a state of siege.

The conditions and effects of a state of siege shall be determined by law.

Art. XV. The Emperor confers titles of nobility, rank, orders and other marks of honor.

Art. XVI. The Emperor orders amnesty, pardon, commutation of punishments and rehabilitation.

Art. XVII. A Regency shall be instituted in conformity with the provisions of the Imperial House Law.

The Regent shall exercise the powers appertaining to the Emperor in His name.

CHAPTER II. RIGHTS AND DUTIES OF SUBJECTS

Art. XVIII. The conditions necessary for being a Japanese subject shall be determined by law.

Art. XIX. Japanese subjects may, according to qualifications determined in laws or ordinances, be appointed to civil or military or any other public offices equally.

Art. XX. Japanese subjects are amenable to service in the Army or Navy, according to the provisions of law.

Art. XXI. Japanese subjects are amenable to the duty of paying taxes, according to the provisions of law.

Art. XXII. Japanese subjects shall have the liberty of abode and of changing the same within the limits of law.

Art. XXIII. No Japanese subject shall be arrested, detained, tried or punished, unless according to law.

Art. XXIV. No Japanese subject shall be deprived of his right of being tried by the judges determined by law.

Art. XXV. Except in the cases provided for in the law, the house of no Japanese subject shall be entered or searched without his consent.

Art. XXVI. Except in the cases mentioned in the law, the secrecy of the letters of every Japanese subject shall remain inviolate.

Art. XXVII. The right of property of every Japanese subject shall remain inviolate.

Measures necessary to be taken for the public benefit shall be provided for by law.

Art. XXVIII. Japanese subjects shall, within limits not prejudicial to peace and order, and not antagonistic to their duties as subjects, enjoy freedom of religious belief.

Art. XXIX. Japanese subjects shall, within the limits of law, enjoy the liberty of speech, writing, publication, public meetings and associations.

Art. XXX. Japanese subjects may present petitions, by observing the proper forms of respect, and by complying with the rules specially provided for the same.

Art. XXXI. The provisions contained in the present Chapter shall not affect the exercise of the powers appertaining to the Emperor, in times of war or in cases of a national emergency.

Art. XXXII. Each and every one of the provisions contained in the preceding Articles of the present Chapter, that are not in conflict with the laws or the rules and discipline of the Army and Navy, shall apply to the offices and men of the Army and of the Navy.

CHAPTER III. THE IMPERIAL DIET

Art. XXXIII. The Imperial Diet shall consist of two Houses, a House of Peers and a House of Representatives.

Art. XXXIV. The House of Peers shall, in accordance with the Ordinance concerning the House of Peers, be composed of the members of the Imperial Family, of the orders of nobility, and of those persons who have been nominated thereto by the Emperor.

Art. XXXV. The House of Representatives shall be composed of Members elected by the people, according to the provisions of the Law of Election.

Art. XXXVI. No one can at one and the same time be a Member of both Houses.

Art. XXXVII. Every law requires the consent of the Imperial Diet.

Art. XXXVIII. Both Houses shall vote upon projects of law submitted to it by the Government, and may respectively initiate projects of law.

Art. XXXIX. A Bill, which has been rejected by either the one or the other of the two Houses, shall not be again brought in during the same session.

Art. XL. Both Houses can make representations to the Government, as to laws or upon any other subject. When, however, such representations are not accepted, they cannot be made a second time during the same session.

Art. XLI. The Imperial Diet shall be convoked every year.

Art. XLII. A session of the Imperial Diet shall last during three months. In case of necessity, the duration of a session may be prolonged by Imperial Order.

Art. XLIII. When urgent necessity arises, an extraordinary session may be convoked, in addition to the ordinary one.

The duration of an extraordinary session shall be determined by Imperial Order.

Art. XLIV. The opening, closing, prolongation of session and prorogation of the Imperial Diet, shall be effected simultaneously for both Houses.

In case the House of Representatives has been ordered to dissolve, the House of Peers shall at the same time be prorogued.

Art. XLV. When the House of Representatives has been ordered to dissolve, Members shall be caused by Imperial Order to be newly elected, and the new House shall be convoked within five months from the day of dissolution.

Art. XLVI. No debate can be opened and no vote can be taken in either House of the Imperial Diet, unless not less than one third of the whole number of the Members thereof is present.

Art. XLVII. Votes shall be taken in both Houses by absolute majority. In the case of a tie vote, the President shall have the casting vote.

Art. XLVIII. The deliberations of both Houses shall be held in public. The deliberations may, however, upon demand of the Government or by resolution of the House, be held in secret sitting.

Art. XLIX. Both Houses of the Imperial Diet may respectively present addresses to the Emperor.

Art. L. Both Houses may receive petitions presented by subjects.

Art. LI. Both Houses may enact, besides what is provided for in the present Constitution and in the Law of the Houses, rules necessary for the management of their internal affairs.

Art. LII. No Member of either House shall be held responsible outside the respective Houses, for any opinion uttered or for any vote given in the House. When, however, a Member himself has given publicity to his opinions by public speech, by documents in print or in writing, or by any other similar means, he shall, in the matter, be amenable to the general law.

Art. LIII. The Members of both Houses shall, during the session, be free from arrest, unless with the consent of the House, except in cases of flagrant delicts, or of offenses connected with a state of internal commotion or with a foreign trouble.

Art. LIV. The Ministers of State and the Delegates of the Government may, at any time, take seats and speak in either House.

CHAPTER IV. THE MINISTERS OF STATE AND THE PRIVY COUNCIL

Art. LV. The respective Ministers of State shall give their advice to the Emperor, and be responsible for it.

All Laws, Imperial Ordinances and Imperial Rescripts of whatever kind, that relate to the affairs of the State, require the countersignature of a Minister of State.

Art. LVI. The Privy Councillors shall, in accordance with the provisions for the organization of the Privy Council, deliberate upon important matters of State, when they have been consulted by the Emperor.

CHAPTER V. THE JUDICATURE

Art. LVII. The Judicature shall be exercised by the Courts of Law according to law, in the name of the Emperor.

The organization of the Courts of Law shall be determined by law.

Art. LVIII. The judges shall be appointed from among those who possess proper qualifications according to law.

No judge shall be deprived of his position, unless by way of criminal sentence or disciplinary punishment.

Rules for disciplinary punishment shall be determined by law.

Art. LIX. Trials and judgments of a Court shall be conducted publicly. When, however, there exists any fear that such publicity may be prejudicial to peace and order, or to the maintenance of public morality, the public trial may be suspended by provision of law or by the decision of the Court of Law.

Art. LX. All matters that fall within the competency of a special Court shall be specially provided for by law.

Art. LXI. No suit at law, which relates to rights alleged to have been infringed by the illegal measures of the administrative authorities, and which shall come within the competency of the Court of Administrative Litigation specially established by law, shall be taken cognizance of by a Court of Law.

CHAPTER VI. FINANCE

Art. LXII. The imposition of a new tax or the modification of the rates (of an existing one) shall be determined by law.

However, all such administrative fees or other revenue having the nature of compensation shall not fall within the category of the above clause.

The raising of national loans and the contracting of other liabilities to the charge of the National Treasury, except those that are provided in the Budget, shall require the consent of the Imperial Diet.

Art. LXIII. The taxes levied at present shall, in so far as they are not remodelled by a new law, be collected according to the old system.

Art. LXIV. The expenditure and revenue of the State require the consent of the Imperial Diet by means of an annual Budget.

Any and all expenditures overpassing the appropriations set forth in the Titles and Paragraphs of the Budget, or that are not provided for in the Budget, shall subsequently require the approbation of the Imperial Diet.

Art. LXV. The Budget shall be first laid before the House of Representatives.

Art. LXVI. The expenditures of the Imperial House shall be defrayed every year out of the National Treasury, according to the present fixed amount for the same, and shall not require the consent thereto of the Imperial Diet, except in case an increase thereof is found necessary.

Art. LXVII. Those already fixed expenditures based by the Constitution upon the powers appertaining to the Emperor, and such expenditures as may have arisen by the effect of law, or that appertain to the legal obligations of the government, shall be neither rejected nor reduced by the Imperial Diet, without the concurrence of the Government.

Art. LXVIII. In order to meet special requirements, the Government may ask the consent of the Imperial Diet to a certain amount as a Continuing Expenditure Fund, for a previously fixed number of years.

Art. LXIX. In order to supply deficiencies, which are unavoidable, in the Budget, and to meet requirements unprovided for in the same, a Reserve Fund shall be provided in the Budget.

Art. LXX. When the Imperial Diet cannot be convoked, owing to the external or internal condition of the country, in case of urgent need for the maintenance of public safety, the Government may take all necessary financial measures, by means of an Imperial Ordinance.

In the case mentioned in the preceding clause, the matter shall be submitted to the Imperial Diet at its next session, and its approbation shall be obtained thereto.

Art. LXXI. When the Imperial Diet has not voted on the Budget, or when the Budget has not been brought into actual existence, the Government shall carry out the Budget of the preceding year.

Art. LXXII. The final account of the expenditures and revenue of the State shall be verified and confirmed by the Board of Audit, and it shall be submitted by the Government to the Imperial Diet, together with the report of verification of the said Board.

The organization and competency of the Board of Audit shall be determined by law separately.

CHAPTER VII. SUPPLEMENTARY RULES

Art. LXXIII. When it has become necessary in future to amend the provisions of the present Constitution, a project to the effect shall be submitted to the Imperial Diet by Imperial Order.

In the above case, neither House can open the debate, unless not less than two-thirds of the whole number of Members are present, and no amendment can be passed, unless a majority of not less than two-thirds of the Members is obtained.

Art. LXXIV. No modification of the Imperial House Law shall be required to be submitted to the deliberation of the Imperial Diet.

No provision of the present Constitution can be modified by the Imperial House Law.

Art. LXXV. No modification can be introduced into the Constitution, or into the Imperial House Law, during the time of a Regency.

Art. LXXVI. Existing legal enactments, such as laws, regulations, Ordinances, or by whatever names they may be called, shall, so far as they do not conflict with the present Constitution, continue in force.

All existing contracts or orders, that entail obligations upon the Government, and that are connected with expenditure, shall come within the scope of Art. LXVII.

Appendix 11

THE IMPERIAL HOUSE LAW
(1889)

CHAPTER I. SUCCESSION TO THE IMPERIAL THRONE

Art. I. The Imperial Throne of Japan shall be succeeded to by male descendants in the male line of Imperial Ancestors.

Art. II. The Imperial Throne shall be succeeded to by the Imperial eldest son.

Art. III. When there is no Imperial eldest son, the Imperial Throne shall be succeeded to by the Imperial eldest grandson. When there is neither Imperial eldest son nor any male descendant of his, it shall be succeeded to by the Imperial son next in age, and so on in every successive case.

Art. IV. For succession to the Imperial Throne by an Imperial descendant, the one of full blood shall have precedence over descendants of half blood. The succession to the Imperial Throne by the latter shall be limited to those cases only in which there is no Imperial descendant of full blood.

Art. V. When there is no Imperial descendant, the Imperial Throne shall be succeeded to by an Imperial brother and by his descendants.

Art. VI. When there is no such Imperial brother or descendant of his, the Imperial Throne shall be succeeded to by an Imperial uncle and his descendants.

Art. VII. When there is neither such Imperial uncle nor descendant of his, the Imperial Throne shall be succeeded to by the next nearest member among the rest of the Imperial Family.

Art. VIII. Among the Imperial brothers and the remoter Imperial relations, precedence shall be given, in the same degree, to the descendants of full blood, and to the elder over the younger.

Art. IX. When the Imperial heir is suffering from an incurable disease of mind or body, or when any other weighty cause exists, the order of succession may be changed in accordance with the foregoing provisions, with the advice of the Imperial Family Council and with that of the Privy Council.

CHAPTER II. ASCENSION AND CORONATION

Art. X. Upon the demise of the Emperor, the Imperial heir shall ascend the Throne and shall acquire the Divine Treasures of the Imperial Ancestors.

Art. XI. The ceremonies of Coronation shall be performed and a Grand Coronation Banquet (*Daijōsai*) shall be held at Kyōto.

Art. XII. Upon an ascension to the Throne, a new era shall be inaugurated, and the name of it shall remain unchanged during the whole reign in agreement with the established rule of the 1st year of Meiji.

CHAPTER III. MAJORITY, INSTITUTION OF EMPRESS AND OF HEIR-APPARENT

Art. XIII. The Emperor, the *Kōtaishi,* and the *Kōtaison* shall attain their majority at eighteen full years of age.

Art. XIV. Members of the Imperial Family, other than those mentioned in the preceding article, shall attain their majority at twenty full years of age.

Art. XV. The son of the Emperor who is Heir-apparent, shall be called *"Kōtaishi."* In case there is no *Kōtaishi,* the Imperial grandson who is Heir-apparent shall be called *"Kōtaison."*

Art. XVI. The Institution of Empress and that of *Kōtaishi* or of *Kōtaison* shall be proclaimed by an Imperial Rescript.

CHAPTER IV. STYLES OF ADDRESS

Art. XVII. The style of address for the Emperor, the Grand Empress Dowager, the Empress Dowager, and of the Empress shall he "His," or "Her," or "Your Majesty."

Art. XVIII. The *Kōtaishi* and his consort, the *Kōtaison* and his consort, the Imperial Princes and their consorts, and the princesses shall be styled "His," "Her," "Their," or "Your Highness" or "Highnesses."

CHAPTER V. REGENCY

Art. XIX. When the Emperor is a minor a Regency shall be instituted. When he is prevented by some permanent cause from personally governing, a Regency shall be instituted, with the advice of the Imperial Family Council and with that of the Privy Council.

Art. XX. The Regency shall be assumed by the *Kōtaishi* or the *Kōtaison,* being of full age of majority.

Art. XXI. When there is neither *Kōtaishi* nor *Kōtaison,* or when the *Kōtaishi* or *Kōtaison* has not yet arrived at his majority, the Regency shall be assumed in the following order:

1. An Imperial Prince or a Prince.
2. The Empress.
3. The Empress Dowager.
4. The Grand Empress Dowager.
5. An Imperial Princess or a Princess.

Art. XXII. In case the Regency shall be assumed from among the male members of the Imperial Family, it shall be done in agreement with the order of succession to the Imperial Throne. The same shall apply to the case of female members of the Imperial Family.

Art. XXIII. A female member of the Imperial Family chosen to assume the Regency shall be exclusively one who has no consort.

Art. XXIV. When on account of the minority of the nearest related member of the Imperial Family, or for some other cause, another member has to assume the Regency, the latter shall not, upon the arrival at majority of the above mentioned nearest related member, or upon the disappearance of the aforesaid cause, resign his or her post in favour of any person other than of the *Kōtaishi* or of the *Kōtaison*.

Art. XXV. When a Regent or one who should become such, is suffering from an incurable disease of mind or body, or when any other weighty cause exists therefor, the order of the Regency may be changed, with the advice of the Imperial Family Council and with that of the Privy Council.

CHAPTER VI. THE IMPERIAL GOVERNOR

Art. XXVI. When the Emperor is a minor, an Imperial Governor shall be appointed to take charge of his bringing up and of his education.

Art. XXVII. In case no Imperial Governor has been nominated in the will of the Preceding Emperor, the Regent shall appoint one, with the advice of the Imperial Family Council and with that of the Privy Council.

Art. XXVIII. Neither the Regent nor any of his descendants can be appointed Imperial Governor.

Art. XXIX. The Imperial Governor cannot be removed from his post by the Regent, unless upon the advice of the Imperial Family Council and upon that of the Privy Council.

CHAPTER VII. THE IMPERIAL FAMILY

Art. XXX. The term "Imperial Family" shall include the Grand Empress Dowager, the Empress Dowager, the Empress, the *Kōtaishi* and his consort, the *Kōtaison* and his consort, the Imperial Princes and their consorts, the Imperial Princesses, the Princesses and their consorts, and the Princesses.

Art. XXXI. From Imperial sons to Imperial great-great-grand-sons, Imperial male descendants shall be called Imperial Princes; and from Imperial daughters to Imperial great-great-grand-daughters Imperial female descendants shall be called Imperial Princesses. From the fifth generation downwards, male descendants shall be called Princes and females Princesses.

Art. XXXII. When the Imperial Throne is succeeded to by a member of a branch line, the title of Imperial Prince or Imperial Princess shall be specially granted to the Imperial brothers and sisters, being already Princes or Princesses.

Art. XXXIII. The births, namings, marriages, and deaths in the Imperial Family shall be announced by the Minister of the Imperial Household.

Art. XXXIV. Genealogical and other records relating to the matters mentioned in the preceding Article shall be kept in the Imperial archives.

Art. XXXV. The members of the Imperial Family shall be under the control of the Emperor.

Art. XXXVI. When a Regency is instituted, the Regent shall exercise the power of control referred to in the preceding Article.

Art. XXXVII. When a member, male or female, of the Imperial Family is a minor and has been bereft of his or her father, the officials of the Imperial Court shall be ordered to take charge of his or her bringing up and education.

In certain circumstances, the Emperor may either approve the guardian chosen by his or her parent, or may nominate one.

Art. XXXVIII. The guardian of a member of the Imperial Family must be himself a member thereof and of age.

Art. XXXIX. Marriages of members of the Imperial Family shall be restricted to the circle of the Family, or to certain noble families specially approved by Imperial Order.

Art. XL. Marriages of the members of the Imperial Family shall be subject to the sanction of the Emperor.

Art. XLI. The Imperial writs sanctioning the marriages of the members of the Imperial Family shall bear the countersignature of the Minister of the Imperial Household.

Art. XLII. No member of the Imperial Family can adopt any one as his son.

Art. XLIII. When a member of the Imperial Family wishes to travel beyond the boundaries of the Empire, he shall first obtain the sanction of the Emperor.

Art. XLIV. A female member of the Imperial Family, who has married a subject, shall be excluded from membership of the Imperial Family. However, she may be allowed, by the special grace of the Emperor, to retain her title of Imperial Princess or Princess, as the case may be.

CHAPTER VIII. IMPERIAL HEREDITARY ESTATES

Art. XLV. No landed or other property, that has been fixed as the Imperial Hereditary Estates, shall be divided up and alienated.

Art. XLVI. The landed or other property to be included in the Imperial Hereditary Estates shall be settled by Imperial writ with the advice of the Privy Council, and shall be announced by the Minister of the Imperial Household.

CHAPTER IX. EXPENDITURES OF THE IMPERIAL HOUSE

Art. XLVII. The expenditures of the Imperial House of all kinds shall be defrayed out of the National Treasury at a certain fixed amount.

Art. XLVIII. The estimates and audit of accounts of the expenditures of the Imperial House and all other rules of the kind, shall be regulated by the Finance Regulations of the Imperial House.

CHAPTER X. LITIGATIONS, DISCIPLINARY RULES FOR MEMBERS OF THE IMPERIAL FAMILY

Art. XLIV. Litigation between members of the Imperial Family shall be decided by judicial functionaries specially designated by the Emperor to the Department of the Imperial Household, and execution issued after Imperial sanction thereto has been obtained.

Art. L. Civil actions brought by private individuals against members of the Imperial Family shall be decided in the Court of Appeal in Tokyo. Members of the Imperial Family shall, however, be represented by attorneys, and no personal attendance in the Court shall be required of them.

Art. LI. No members of the Imperial Family can be arrested, or summoned before a Court of Law, unless the sanction of the Emperor has been first obtained thereto.

Art. LII. When a member of the Imperial Family has committed an act derogatory to his (or her) dignity, or when he has exhibited disloyalty to the Imperial House, he shall, by way of disciplinary punishment and by order of the Emperor, be deprived of the whole or a part of the privileges belonging to him as a member of the Imperial Family, or shall be suspended therefrom.

Art. LIII. When a member of the Imperial Family acts in a way tending to the squandering of his (or her) property, he shall be pronounced incapable by the Emperor, prohibited from administering his property, and a manager shall be appointed therefor.

Art. LIV. The two foregoing Articles shall be enforced upon the advice of the Imperial Family Council.

CHAPTER XI. THE IMPERIAL FAMILY COUNCIL

Art. LV. The Imperial Family Council shall be composed of the male members of the Imperial Family who have reached the age of majority. The Lord Keeper of the Privy Seal, the President of the Privy Council, the Minister of the Imperial Household, the Minister of State for Justice, and the President of the Court of Cassation shall be ordered to take part in the deliberations of the Council.

Art. LVI. The Emperor personally presides over the meetings of the Imperial Family Council, or directs one of the members of the Imperial Family to do so.

CHAPTER XII. SUPPLEMENTARY RULES

Art. LVII. Those of the present members of the Imperial Family of the fifth generation and downwards, who have already been invested with the title of Imperial Prince, shall retain the same as heretofore.

Art. LVIII. The order of succession to the Imperial Throne shall in every case relate to the descendants of direct lineage. There shall be no admission to this line of succession to any one, as a consequence of his now being an adopted Imperial son, *Koyushi* or heir to a princely house.

Art. LIX. The grades of rank among the Imperial Princes and Princesses shall be abolished.

Art. LX. The family rank of Imperial Princes and all usages conflicting with the present law shall be abolished.

Art. LXI. The property, annual expenses, and all other rules concerning the members of the Imperial Family shall be specially determined.

Art. LXII. When in the future it shall become necessary either to amend or make addition to the present law, the matter shall be decided by the Emperor, with the advice of the Imperial Family Council and with that of the Privy Council.

ADDITIONAL RULES

(Promulgated February 11, 1907)

Art. I. The Princes may be created peers, either by order of the Emperor or at their own wishes, with family names to be granted by the Emperor.

Art. II. The Princes may, with the sanction of the Emperor, become heirs of peers or be adopted as their sons with a view to becoming their heirs.

Art. III. The consorts, lineal descendants and their wives, of the Princes who have been excluded from membership of the Imperial Family for the reason stated in the two foregoing Articles are also excluded from membership in the Imperial Family as members of the families of the Princes who have become subjects. The rule does not, however, apply to those female members of the Imperial Family who have married other members of the Imperial Family or their lineal descendants.

Art. IV. A member of the Imperial Family who has been deprived of the privileges belonging to him as a member of the Imperial Family may be excluded from membership of the Imperial Family and placed in the rank of subjects by order of the Emperor. The consort of a member of the Imperial Family who has been excluded from membership of the Imperial Family and placed in the rank of subjects in accordance with the foregoing Article is also excluded from membership of the Imperial Family and placed in the rank of subjects.

Art. V. In the cases mentioned in Arts. I, II and IV (of the present additional rules), the matter shall be decided with the advice of the Imperial Family Council and that of the Privy Council.

Art. VI. Those members of the Imperial Family who have been excluded from membership of the Imperial Family cannot be reinstated as members of the Imperial Family.

Art. VII. Regulations pertaining to the legal status of the members of the Imperial Family and the limits of their competence, other than those provided for elsewhere in the present law, shall be defined separately. Regarding the affairs in which are involved the interests of a member of the Imperial Family and a subject or subjects and in which different regulations apply to the respective parties, such regulations shall apply.

Art. VIII. Those provisions of laws and ordinances designated as applicable to the members of the Imperial Family shall apply to them only in cases where no particular regulations are specifically provided for in the present law or such regulations as are issued in accordance with the present law.

ADDITIONAL RULE

(Promulgated November 28, 1908)

A female member of the Imperial Family can marry a male member of Ozoku or Kozoku (former Royal Family of Korea).

Appendix 12

THE JAPANESE EXECUTIVE: STRUCTURE AND FUNCTIONS UNDER THE PARLIAMENTARY EMPIRE *

Office	*Composition and Appointment*	*Powers and Functions*
CIVIL OFFICES		
Lord Keeper of the Privy Seal *(Nai-daijin)*	Appointed by Emperor, on advice of Premier; customarily, not necessarily, for life.	Highest personal advisor; custodian of Imperial, State seals, affixed to all Imperial ordinances and laws; with Imperial Household Minister, makes all appointments for Imperial audiences; advises Emperor on appointment of Premier; participates in Imperial Family Council.
Imperial Household Minister *(Kunai-daijin)*	Appointed by Emperor, on advice of Premier; customarily, not necessarily, for life.	Advises Emperor on all matters re: Imperial Family; advises Emperor on appointment of Premier; advises Emperor on conferring of titles of nobility and rank; with Lord Keeper of the Privy Seal, makes all appointments for Imperial audiences; directs, supervises Imperial Household Ministry.
Privy Council *(Sumitsu-in)*		
President *(Gichō)*	Appointed by Emperor on advice of Premier, for life.	Advises Emperor in re: appointment of Premier; presides over Privy Council, determines time of meeting and order of business; appoints special committees for Government measures; casts vote in event of tie; signs all Council documents; consents to appointment of new members.
Vice-President *(Fuku-Gichō)*	Appointed by Emperor on advice of Premier and President; for life.	Assists President in functions; presides in absence of President.
Secretary-General *(Shokikanchō)*	Appointed by Emperor on advice of Premier and President; for life.	Attends meetings, no vote; manages ordinary business under President; investigates reports on Council matters.

* Based on Department of State, Interim Research & Intelligence Service, Research & Analysis Branch. *The Japanese Executive: Structure and Functions* (R. & A. No. 3407), Washington: 18 October 1945, Restricted (Declassified), Appendix A, pp. 27-34.

Office	*Composition and Appointment*	*Powers and Functions*
Councilors *(Komonkan)*	25 appointed by Emperor on advice of Premier and President; for life. All members of Cabinet *ex officio* members of Privy Council.	Council as a whole: advises as to institution of Regency; as to changes in succession; and, on Emperor's submission, important matters of state.
THE CABINET *(Naikaku)*		
Premier *(Naikaku Sōri-daijin)*	Appointed by Emperor, on advice of Imperial Household Minister, Lord Keeper of the Privy Seal, President of the Privy Council.	Selects members of Cabinet; convenes, presides over, draws up agenda for Cabinet meetings; presents Cabinet views to Emperor; advises on appointment of Lord Keeper of the Privy Seal, Imperial Household Minister, President and members of Privy Council; countersigns laws, ordinances affecting administration as whole; general control over administration; may give instructions to any branch or suspend its orders, pending Imperial decision; advises on appointment of *chokunin* and *shinnin* officials (highest civil service ranks).
Ministers *(Daijin)*	Heads of Ministries and Ministers w/o Portfolio appointed by Emperor, on advice of Premier.	Cabinet meets as group under Premier to determine general policy; as individuals, administratively responsible for respective Ministries; countersign affecting ordinances; instructions to local officials under jurisdiction; issue ordinances implementing laws within sphere of activity; appoint and discipline subordinates within civil service regulations.
MILITARY OFFICES		
Imperial Headquarters *(Senji Daihonei)*	In time of war or national emergency; chiefs of Army, Navy General Staffs; Army and Navy Ministers; selected high-rank officers; (March, 1945: the Premier).	Exercises supreme military command.

Office	*Composition and Appointment*	*Powers and Functions*
Supreme War Council *(Gunji Sangi-in)*	Board of Field Marshals and Fleet Admirals; Chiefs of Army, Navy General Staffs; Army, Navy Ministers; high-rank officers appointed by Emperor.	Meets on summons of Emperor to discuss, advise on military problems; advises on correlation of functions between services; Army members recommend Generals and Lt. Generals on active list for position of Army Minister; Navy members similarly on Admirals and Vice Admirals, active; Army, Navy members may meet separately to discuss respective business.
Board of Field Marshals and Fleet Admirals *(Gensui-fu)*	Composed of rank of Field Marshal, Fleet Admiral; in peacetime, small number of Imperial Princes; in war, larger number by appointment.	Advises Emperor on military affairs.
Chiefs, Army and Navy General Staffs *(Rikugun Sambō-sōchō)* *(Kaigun Gunreibu-sōchō)*	Appointed by Emperor from among Generals, Admirals, Lt. Generals, Vice Admirals on active list.	Direct access to Emperor on matters concerning supreme command; direct General Staffs, planning of operations, national defense, size and disposal of armed forces; countersign Imperial ordinances issued in exercise of supreme command; members of Imperial Headquarters and Supreme War Council.
Army and Navy Ministers *(Rikugun-daijin)* *(Kaigun-daijin)*	General or Lt. General/ Admiral or Vice Admiral on active list, appointed by Emperor, after selection by Premier, approval respectively of Army or Navy members of Supreme War Council.	Direct access to Emperor on matters concerning supreme command; major administrative responsibility for conduct of Army and Navy affairs; members of Imperial Headquarters and Supreme War Council.

Appendix 13

COMPARATIVE SUFFRAGE QUALIFICATIONS *

Election Law Revision Dates	Electors			
	Sex	Age	Property Requirement	Residence Requirement
1889	Male	25	To have paid more than ¥15 Direct National Tax for more than one year, or To have paid an income tax for more than three years.	1889: To have official residence as well as actual residence within prefecture for more than one year.
1902	Male	25	To have paid more than: 1. ¥10 Land Tax for more than one year. 2. ¥10 Direct National Tax, other than Land Tax for more than two years. 3. ¥10 of Land Tax and other Direct National Taxes for more than two years.	
1919	Male	25	To have paid more than ¥3 Direct National Tax for more than one year.	1919: Period reduced to six months.
1925	Male	25	None	1925: To register on elector list actual address within city, town, or village from which he voted for more than one year. (Period reduced to six months in 1934.)

* SCAP, *Political Reorientation,* Vol. I, p. 342.

Appendix 14

PROCLAMATION DEFINING TERMS FOR JAPANESE SURRENDER (THE POTSDAM PROCLAMATION)*

July 26, 1945

(1) WE—THE PRESIDENT of the United States, the President of National Government of the Republic of China, and the Prime Minister of Great Britain, representing the hundreds of millions of our countrymen, have conferred and agree that Japan shall be given an opportunity to end this war.

(2) The prodigious land, sea and air forces of the United States, the British Empire and of China, many times reinforced by their armies and air fleets from the west, are poised to strike the final blows upon Japan. This military power is sustained and inspired by the determination of all the Allied Nations to prosecute the war against Japan until she ceases to resist.

(3) The result of the futile and senseless German resistance to the might of the aroused free peoples of the world stands forth in awful clarity as an example to the people of Japan. The might that now converges on Japan is immeasurably greater than that which, when applied to the resisting Nazis, necessarily laid waste to lands, the industry and the method of life of the whole German people. The full application of our military power, backed by our resolve, *will* mean the inevitable and complete destruction of the Japanese armed forces and just as inevitably the utter devastation of the Japanese homeland.

(4) The time has come for Japan to decide whether she will continue to be controlled by those self-willed militaristic advisers whose unintelligent calculations have brought the Empire of Japan to the threshold of annihilation, or whether she will follow the path of reason.

(5) Following are our terms. We will not deviate from them. There are no alternatives. We shall brook no delay.

(6) There must be eliminated for all time the authority and influence of those who have deceived and misled the people of Japan into embarking on world conquest, for we insist that a new order of peace, security and justice will be impossible until irresponsible militarism is driven from the world.

(7) Until such a new order is established *and* until there is convincing proof that Japan's war-making power is destroyed, points in Japanese territory to be designated by the Allies shall be occupied to secure the achievement of the basic objectives we are here setting forth.

(8) The terms of the Cairo Declaration shall be carried out and Japanese sovereignty shall be limited to the islands of Honshu, Hokkaido, Kyushu, Shikoku and such minor islands as we determine.

(9) The Japanese military forces, after being completely disarmed, shall be permitted to return to their homes with the opportunity to lead peaceful and productive lives.

(10) We do not intend that the Japanese shall be enslaved as a race or destroyed as a nation, but stern justice shall be meted out to all war criminals, including those who have visited cruelties upon our prisoners. The Japanese

* Department of State, *Occupation of Japan; Policy and Progress*, Appendix 3, pp. 53-55.

Government shall remove all obstacles to the revival and strengthening of democratic tendencies among the Japanese people. Freedom of speech, of religion, and of thought, as well as respect for the fundamental human rights shall be established.

(11) Japan shall be permitted to maintain such industries as will sustain her economy and permit the exaction of just reparations in kind, but not those which would enable her to re-arm for war. To this end, access to, as distinguished from control of, raw materials shall be permitted. Eventual Japanese participation in world trade relations shall be permitted.

(12) The occupying forces of the Allies shall be withdrawn from Japan as soon as these objectives have been accomplished and there has been established in accordance with the freely expressed will of the Japanese people a peacefully inclined and responsible government.

(13) We call upon the government of Japan to proclaim now the unconditional surrender of all Japanese armed forces, and to provide proper and adequate assurances of their good faith in such action. The alternative for Japan is prompt and utter destruction.

Appendix 15

IMPERIAL RESCRIPT ANNOUNCING SURRENDER TO THE JAPANESE PEOPLE *

(SEPTEMBER 2, 1945, TOKYO TIME)

"Proclamation. Accepting the terms set forth in the Declaration issued by the heads of the Governments of the United States, Great Britain and China on July 26th, 1945 at Potsdam and subsequently adhered to by the Union of Soviet Socialist Republics, we have commanded the Japanese Imperial Government and the Japanese Imperial General Headquarters to sign on Our behalf the Instrument of Surrender presented by the Supreme Commander for the Allied Powers and to issue General Orders to the Military and Naval Forces in accordance with the direction of the Supreme Commander for the Allied Powers. We command all Our people forthwith to cease hostilities, to lay down their arms and faithfully to carry out all the provisions of the Instrument of Surrender and the General Orders issued by the Japanese Imperial Government and the Japanese Imperial General Headquarters hereunder.

This second day of the ninth month of the twentieth year of Shōwa.

Signed: HIROHITO

Countersigned: Naruhiko-o

Countersigned by other Cabinet Ministers"

* Yokota, Kisaburō [Ed.], *Nihon Kanri Hōrei Kenkyū* [Research in Japanese Administrative Directives], Vol. I, No. 1 (April 1, 1946), pp. 11-14.

Appendix 16

MAJOR POINTS INCORPORATED IN GOVERNMENT SECTION DRAFT OF THE NEW CONSTITUTION *

(FROM GENERAL MACARTHUR'S NOTES, FEBRUARY 3, 1946)

I

The Emperor is at the head of the State.

His succession is dynastic.

His duties and powers will be exercised in accordance with the Constitution and responsible to the basic will of the people as provided therein.

II

War as a sovereign right of the nation is abolished. Japan renounces it as an instrumentality for settling its disputes and even for preserving its own security. It relies upon the higher ideals which are now stirring the world for its defense and its protection.

No Japanese Army, Navy, or Air Force will ever be authorized and no rights of belligerency will ever be conferred upon any Japanese force.

III

The feudal system of Japan will cease.

No rights of peerage except those of the Imperial family will extend beyond the lives of those now existent.

No patent of nobility will from this time forth embody within itself any National or Civic power of Government.

Pattern budget after British system.

Appendix 17

THE CONSTITUTION OF JAPAN †

(EFFECTIVE MAY 3, 1947)

We, the Japanese people, acting through our duly elected representatives in the National Diet, determined that we shall secure for ourselves and our posterity the fruits of peaceful cooperation with all nations and the blessings of liberty throughout this land, and resolved that never again shall we be visited with the horrors of war through the action of government, do proclaim that sovereign power resides with the people and do firmly establish this Constitution. Government is a sacred trust of the people, the authority for which is derived from the people, the powers of which are exercised by the representatives of the people, and the benefits of which are enjoyed by the people. This is a universal principle of mankind upon which this Constitution is founded. We reject and revoke all constitutions, laws, ordinances, and rescripts in conflict herewith.

We, the Japanese people, desire peace for all time and are deeply conscious of

* SCAP, *Political Reorientation,* Vol. I, p. 102.

† Department of State, Publication 2836, Far Eastern Series 22.

the high ideals controlling human relationship, and we have determined to preserve our security and existence, trusting in the justice and faith of the peace-loving peoples of the world. We desire to occupy an honored place in an international society striving for the preservation of peace, and the banishment of tyranny and slavery, oppression and intolerance for all time from the earth. We recognize that all peoples of the world have the right to live in peace, free from fear and want.

We believe that no nation is responsible to itself alone, but that laws of political morality are universal; and that obedience to such laws is incumbent upon all nations who would sustain their own sovereignty and justify their sovereign relationship with other nations.

We, the Japanese people, pledge our national honor to accomplish these high ideals and purposes with all our resources.

CHAPTER I. THE EMPEROR

Art. 1. The Emperor shall be the symbol of the State and of the unity of the people, deriving his position from the will of the people with whom resides sovereign power.

Art. 2. The Imperial Throne shall be dynastic and succeeded to in accordance with the Imperial House Law passed by the Diet.

Art. 3. The advice and approval of the Cabinet shall be required for all acts of the Emperor in matters of state, and the Cabinet shall be responsible therefor.

Art. 4. The Emperor shall perform only such acts in matters of state as are provided for in this Constitution and he shall not have powers related to government.

The Emperor may delegate the performance of his acts in matters of state as may be provided by law.

Art. 5. When, in accordance with the Imperial House Law, a Regency is established, the Regent shall perform his acts in matters of state in the Emperor's name. In this case, paragraph one of the preceding article will be applicable.

Art. 6. The Emperor shall appoint the Prime Minister as designated by the Diet.

The Emperor shall appoint the Chief Judge of the Supreme Court as designated by the Cabinet.

Art. 7. The Emperor, with the advice and approval of the Cabinet, shall perform the following acts in matters of state on behalf of the people:

Promulgation of amendments of the constitution, laws, cabinet orders and treaties.

Convocation of the Diet.

Dissolution of the House of Representatives.

Proclamation of general election of members of the Diet.

Attestation of the appointment and dismissal of Ministers of State and other officials as provided for by law, and of full powers and credentials of Ambassadors and Ministers.

Attestation of general and special amnesty, commutation of punishment, reprieve, and restoration of rights.

Awarding of honors.

Attestation of instruments of ratification and other diplomatic documents as provided for by law.

Receiving foreign ambassadors and ministers.

Performance of ceremonial functions.

Art. 8. No property can be given to, or received by, the Imperial House, nor can any gifts be made therefrom, without the authorization of the Diet.

CHAPTER II. RENUNCIATION OF WAR

Art. 9. Aspiring sincerely to an international peace based on justice and order, the Japanese people forever renounce war as a sovereign right of the nation and the threat or use of force as means of settling international disputes.

In order to accomplish the aim of the preceding paragraph, land, sea, and air forces, as well as other war potential, will never be maintained. The right of belligerency of the state will not be recognized.

CHAPTER III. RIGHTS AND DUTIES OF THE PEOPLE

Art. 10. The conditions necessary for being a Japanese national shall be determined by law.

Art. 11. The people shall not be prevented from enjoying any of the fundamental human rights. These fundamental human rights guaranteed to the people by this Constitution shall be conferred upon the people of this and future generations as eternal and inviolate rights.

Art. 12. The freedoms and rights guaranteed to the people by this Constitution shall be maintained by the constant endeavor of the people, who shall refrain from any abuse of these freedoms and rights and shall always be responsible for utilizing them for the public welfare.

Art. 13. All of the people shall be respected as individuals. Their right to life, liberty, and the pursuit of happiness shall, to the extent that it does not interfere with the public welfare, be the supreme consideration in legislation and in other governmental affairs.

Art. 14. All of the people are equal under the law and there shall be no discrimination in political, economic or social relations because of race, creed, sex, social status or family origin.

Peers and peerage shall not be recognized.

No privilege shall accompany any award of honor, decoration or any distinction, nor shall any such award be valid beyond the lifetime of the individual who now holds or hereafter may receive it.

Art. 15. The people have the inalienable right to choose their public officials and to dismiss them.

All public officials are servants of the whole community and not of any group thereof.

Universal adult suffrage is guaranteed with regard to the election of public officials.

In all elections, secrecy of the ballot shall not be violated. A voter shall not be answerable, publicly or privately, for the choice he has made.

Art. 16. Every person shall have the right of peaceful petition for the redress of damage, for the removal of public officials, for the enactment, repeal or amendment of laws, ordinances or regulations and for other matters; nor shall any person be in any way discriminated against for sponsoring such a petition.

Art. 17. Every person may sue for redress as provided by law from the State or a public entity, in case he has suffered damage through illegal act of any public official.

Art. 18. No person shall be held in bondage of any kind. Involuntary servitude, except as punishment for crime, is prohibited.

Art. 19. Freedom of thought and conscience shall not be violated.

Art. 20. Freedom of religion is guaranteed to all. No religious organization shall receive any privileges from the State, nor exercise any political authority.

No person shall be compelled to take part in any religious act, celebration, rite or practice.

The State and its organs shall refrain from religious education or any other religious activity.

Art. 21. Freedom of assembly and association as well as speech, press and all other forms of expression are guaranteed.

No censorship shall be maintained, nor shall the secrecy of any means of communication be violated.

Art. 22. Every person shall have freedom to choose and change his residence and to choose his occupation to the extent that it does not interfere with the public welfare.

Freedom of all persons to move to a foreign country and to divest themselves of their nationality shall be inviolate.

Art. 23. Academic freedom is guaranteed.

Art. 24. Marriage shall be based only on the mutual consent of both sexes and it shall be maintained through mutual cooperation with the equal rights of husband and wife as a basis.

With regard to choice of spouse, property rights, inheritance, choice of domicile, divorce and other matters pertaining to marriage and the family, laws shall be enacted from the standpoint of individual dignity and the essential equality of the sexes.

Art. 25. All people shall have the right to maintain the minimum standards of wholesome and cultured living.

In all spheres of life, the State shall use its endeavors for the promotion and extension of social welfare and security, and of public health.

Art. 26. All people shall have the right to receive an equal education correspondent to their ability, as provided by law.

All people shall be obligated to have all boys and girls under their protection receive ordinary education as provided for by law. Such compulsory education shall be free.

Art. 27. All people shall have the right and the obligation to work.

Standards for wages, hours, rest and other working conditions shall be fixed by law.

Children shall not be exploited.

Art. 28. The right of workers to organize and to bargain and act collectively is guaranteed.

Art. 29. The right to own or to hold property is inviolable.

Property rights shall be defined by law, in conformity with the public welfare.

Private property may be taken for public use upon just compensation therefor.

Art. 30. The people shall be liable to taxation as provided by law.

Art. 31. No person shall be deprived of life or liberty, nor shall any other criminal penalty be imposed, except according to procedure established by law.

Art. 32. No person shall be denied the right of access to the courts.

Art. 33. No person shall be apprehended except upon warrant issued by a competent judicial officer which specifies the offense with which the person is charged, unless he is apprehended, the offense being committed.

Art. 34. No person shall be arrested or detained without being at once informed of the charges against him or without the immediate privilege of counsel; nor shall he be detained without adequate cause; and upon demand of any person such cause must be immediately shown in open court in his presence and the presence of his counsel.

Art. 35. The right of all persons to be secure in their homes, papers and effects against entries, searches and seizures shall not be impaired except upon warrant issued for adequate cause and particularly describing the place to be searched and things to be seized, or except as provided by Article 33.

Each search or seizure shall be made upon separate warrant issued by a competent judicial officer.

Art. 36. The infliction of torture by any public officer and cruel punishments are absolutely forbidden.

Art. 37. In all criminal cases the accused shall enjoy the right to a speedy and public trial by an impartial tribunal.

He shall be permitted full opportunity to examine all witnesses, and he shall have the right of compulsory process for obtaining witnesses on his behalf at public expense.

At all times the accused shall have the assistance of competent counsel who shall, if the accused is unable to secure the same by his own efforts, be assigned to his use by the State.

Art. 38. No person shall be compelled to testify against himself.

Confession made under compulsion, torture or threat, or after prolonged arrest or detention shall not be admitted in evidence.

No person shall be convicted or punished in cases where the only proof against him is his own confession.

Art. 39. No person shall be held criminally liable for an act which was lawful at the time it was committed, or of which he has been acquitted, nor shall he be placed in double jeopardy.

Art. 40. Any person, in case he is acquitted after he has been arrested or detained, may sue the State for redress as provided by law.

CHAPTER IV. THE DIET

Art. 41. The Diet shall be the highest organ of state power, and shall be the sole law-making organ of the State.

Art. 42. The Diet shall consist of two Houses, namely the House of Representatives and the House of Councillors.

Art. 43. Both Houses shall consist of elected members, representative of all the people.

The number of the members of each House shall be fixed by law.

Art. 44. The qualifications of members of both Houses and their electors shall be fixed by law. However, there shall be no discrimination because of race, creed, sex, social status, family origin, education, property or income.

Art. 45. The term of office of members of the House of Representatives shall be four years. However, the term shall be terminated before the full term is up in case the House of Representatives is dissolved.

Art. 46. The term of office of members of the House of Councillors shall be six years, and election for half the members shall take place every three years.

Art. 47. Electoral districts, method of voting and other matters pertaining to the method of election of members of both Houses shall be fixed by law.

Art. 48. No person shall be permitted to be a member of both Houses simultaneously.

Art. 49. Members of both Houses shall receive appropriate annual payment from the national treasury in accordance with law.

Art. 50. Except in cases provided by law, members of both Houses shall be exempt from apprehension while the Diet is in session, and any members apprehended before the opening of the session shall be freed during the term of the session upon demand of the House.

Art. 51. Members of both Houses shall not be held liable outside the House for speeches, debates or votes cast inside the House.

Art. 52. An ordinary session of the Diet shall be convoked once per year.

Art. 53. The Cabinet may determine to convoke extraordinary sessions of the Diet. When a quarter or more of the total members of either House makes the demand, the Cabinet must determine on such convocation.

Art. 54. When the House of Representatives is dissolved, there must be a general election of members of the House of Representatives within forty (40) days from the date of dissolution, and the Diet must be convoked within thirty (30) days from the date of the election.

When the House of Representatives is dissolved, the House of Councillors is closed at the same time. However, the Cabinet may in time of national emergency convoke the House of Councillors in emergency session.

Measures taken at such session as mentioned in the proviso of the preceding paragraph shall be provisional and shall become null and void unless agreed to by the House of Representatives within a period of ten (10) days after the opening of the next session of the Diet.

Art. 55. Each House shall judge disputes related to qualifications of its members. However, in order to deny a seat to any member, it is necessary to pass a resolution by a majority of two-thirds or more of the members present.

Art. 56. Business cannot be transacted in either House unless one-third or more of total membership is present.

All matters shall be decided, in each House, by a majority of those present, except as elsewhere provided in the Constitution, and in case of a tie, the presiding officer shall decide the issue.

Art. 57. Deliberation in each House shall be public. However, a secret meeting may be held where a majority of two-thirds or more of those members present passes a resolution therefor.

Each House shall keep a record of proceedings. This record shall be published and given general circulation, excepting such parts of proceedings of secret session as may be deemed to require secrecy.

Upon demand of one-fifth or more of the members present, votes of the members on any matter shall be recorded in the minutes.

Art. 58. Each House shall select its own president and other officials.

Each House shall establish its rules pertaining to meetings, proceedings and internal discipline, and may punish members for disorderly conduct. However, in order to expel a member, a majority of two-thirds or more of those members present must pass a resolution thereon.

Art. 59. A bill becomes a law on passage by both Houses, except as otherwise provided by the Constitution.

A bill which is passed by the House of Representatives, and upon which the House of Councillors makes a decision different from that of the House of Representatives, becomes a law when passed a second time by the House of Representatives by a majority of two-thirds or more of the members present.

The provision of the preceding paragraph does not preclude the House of Representatives from calling for the meeting of a joint committee of both Houses, provided for by law.

Failure by the House of Councillors to take final action within sixty (60) days after receipt of a bill passed by the House of Representatives, time in recess excepted, may be determined by the House of Representatives to constitute a rejection of the said bill by the House of Councillors.

Art. 60. The budget must first be submitted to the House of Representatives.

Upon consideration of the budget, when the House of Councillors makes a decision different from that of the House of Representatives, and when no agreement can be reached even through a joint committee of both Houses, provided for by law, or in the case of failure by the House of Councillors to take final action within thirty (30) days, the period of recess excluded, after the receipt of the budget passed by the House of Representatives, the decision of the House of Representatives shall be the decision of the Diet.

Art. 61. The second paragraph of the preceding article applies also to the Diet approval required for the conclusion of treaties.

Art. 62. Each House may conduct investigations in relation to government, and may demand the presence and testimony of witnesses, and the production of records.

Art. 63. The Prime Minister and other Ministers of State may, at any time, appear in either House for the purpose of speaking on bills, regardless of whether they are members of the House or not. They must appear when their presence is required in order to give answers or explanations.

Art. 64. The Diet shall set up an impeachment court from among the members of both Houses for the purpose of trying those judges against whom removal proceedings have been instituted.

Matters relating to impeachment shall be provided by law.

CHAPTER V. THE CABINET

Art. 65. Executive power shall be vested in the Cabinet.

Art. 66. The Cabinet shall consist of the Prime Minister, who shall be its head, and other Ministers of State, as provided for by law.

The Prime Minister and other Ministers of State must be civilians.

The Cabinet, in the exercise of executive power, shall be collectively responsible to the Diet.

Art. 67. The Prime Minister shall be designated from among the members of the Diet by a resolution of the Diet. This designation shall precede all other business.

If the House of Representatives and the House of Councillors disagree and if no agreement can be reached even through a joint committee of both Houses, provided for by law, or the House of Councillors fails to make designation within ten (10) days, exclusive of the period of recess, after the House of Representatives has made designation, the decision of the House of Representatives shall be the decision of the Diet.

Art. 68. The Prime Minister shall appoint the Ministers of State. However, a majority of their number must be chosen from among the members of the Diet.

The Prime Minister may remove the Ministers of State as he chooses.

Art. 69. If the House of Representatives passes a non-confidence resolution, or rejects a confidence resolution, the Cabinet shall resign en masse, unless the House of Representatives is dissolved within ten (10) days.

Art. 70. When there is a vacancy in the post of Prime Minister, or upon the first convocation of the Diet after a general election of members of the House of Representatives, the Cabinet shall resign en masse.

Art. 71. In the cases mentioned in the two preceding articles, the Cabinet shall continue its functions until the time when a new Prime Minister is appointed.

Art. 72. The Prime Minister, representing the Cabinet, submits bills, reports on general national affairs and foreign relations to the Diet and exercises control and supervision over various administrative branches.

Art. 73. The Cabinet, in addition to other general administrative functions, shall perform the following functions:

Administer the law faithfully; conduct affairs of state.

Manage foreign affairs.

Conclude treaties. However, it shall obtain prior or, depending on circumstances, subsequent approval of the Diet.

Administer the civil service, in accordance with standards established by law.

Prepare the budget, and present it to the Diet.

Enact cabinet orders in order to execute the provisions of this Constitution and of the law. However, it cannot include penal provisions in such cabinet orders unless authorized by such law.

Decide on general amnesty, special amnesty, commutation of punishment, reprieve, and restoration of rights.

Art. 74. All laws and cabinet orders shall be signed by the competent Minister of State and countersigned by the Prime Minister.

Art. 75. The Ministers of State, during their tenure of office, shall not be subject to legal action without the consent of the Prime Minister. However, the right to take that action is not impaired hereby.

CHAPTER VI. JUDICIARY

Art. 76. The whole judicial power is vested in a Supreme Court and in such inferior courts as are established by law.

No extraordinary tribunal shall be established, nor shall any organ or agency of the Executive be given final judicial power.

All judges shall be independent in the exercise of their conscience and shall be bound only by this Constitution and the laws.

Art. 77. The Supreme Court is vested with the rule-making power under which it determines the rules of procedure and of practice, and of matters relating to attorneys, the internal discipline of the courts and the administration of judicial affairs.

Public procurators shall be subject to the rule-making power of the Supreme Court.

The Supreme Court may delegate the power to make rules for inferior courts to such courts.

Art. 78. Judges shall not be removed except by public impeachment unless judicially declared mentally or physically incompetent to perform official duties. No disciplinary action against judges shall be administered by any executive organ or agency.

Art. 79. The Supreme Court shall consist of a Chief Judge and such number of judges as may be determined by law; all such judges excepting the Chief Judge shall be appointed by the Cabinet.

The appointment of the judges of the Supreme Court shall be reviewed by the people at the first general election of members of the House of Representatives following their appointment, and shall be reviewed again at the first general election of members of the House of Representatives after a lapse of ten (10) years, and in the same manner thereafter.

In cases mentioned in the foregoing paragraph, when the majority of the voters favors the dismissal of a judge, he shall be dismissed.

Matters pertaining to review shall be prescribed by law.

The judges of the Supreme Court shall be retired upon the attainment of the age as fixed by law.

All such judges shall receive, at regular stated intervals, adequate compensation which shall not be decreased during their terms of office.

Art. 80. The judges of the inferior courts shall be appointed by the Cabinet from a list of persons nominated by the Supreme Court. All such judges shall hold office for a term of ten (10) years with privilege of reappointment, provided that they shall be retired upon the attainment of the age as fixed by law.

The judges of the inferior courts shall receive, at regular stated intervals, adequate compensation which shall not be decreased during their terms of office.

Art. 81. The Supreme Court is the court of last resort with power to determine the constitutionality of any law, order, regulation or official act.

Art. 82. Trials shall be conducted and judgment declared publicly.

Where a court unanimously determines publicity to be dangerous to public order or morals, a trial may be conducted privately, but trials of political offenses, offenses involving the press or cases wherein the rights of people as guaranteed in Chapter III of this Constitution are in question shall always be conducted publicly.

CHAPTER VII. FINANCE

Art. 83. The power to administer national finances shall be exercised as the Diet shall determine.

Art. 84. No new taxes shall be imposed or existing ones modified except by law or under such conditions as law may prescribe.

Art. 85. No money shall be expended, nor shall the State obligate itself, except as authorized by the Diet.

Art. 86. The Cabinet shall prepare and submit to the Diet for its consideration and decision a budget for each fiscal year.

Art. 87. In order to provide for unforeseen deficiencies in the budget, a reserve fund may be authorized by the Diet to be expended upon the responsibility of the Cabinet.

The Cabinet must get subsequent approval of the Diet for all payments from the reserve fund.

Art. 88. All property of the Imperial Household shall belong to the State. All expenses of the Imperial Household shall be appropriated by the Diet in the budget.

Art. 89. No public money or other property shall be expended or appropriated for the use, benefit or maintenance of any religious institution or association, or for any charitable, educational or benevolent enterprises not under the control of public authority.

Art. 90. Final accounts of the expenditures and revenues of the State shall be audited annually by a Board of Audit and submitted by the Cabinet to the Diet, together with the statement of audit, during the fiscal year immediately following the period covered.

The organization and competency of the Board of Audit shall be determined by law.

Art. 91. At regular intervals and at least annually the Cabinet shall report to the Diet and the people on the state of national finances.

CHAPTER VIII. LOCAL SELF-GOVERNMENT

Art. 92. Regulations concerning organization and operations of local public entities shall be fixed by law in accordance with the principle of local autonomy.

Art. 93. The local public entities shall establish assemblies as their deliberative organs, in accordance with law.

The chief executive officers of all local public entities, the members of their assemblies, and such other local officials as may be determined by law shall be elected by direct popular vote within their several communities.

Art. 94. Local public entities shall have the right to manage their property, affairs and administration and to enact their own regulations within law.

Art. 95. A special law, applicable only to one local public entity, cannot be enacted by the Diet without the consent of the majority of the voters of the local public entity concerned, obtained in accordance with law.

CHAPTER IX. AMENDMENTS

Art. 96. Amendments to this Constitution shall be initiated by the Diet, through a concurring vote of two-thirds or more of all the members of each House and shall thereupon be submitted to the people for ratification, which shall require the affirmative vote of a majority of all votes cast thereon, at a special referendum or at such election as the Diet shall specify.

Amendments when so ratified shall immediately be promulgated by the Emperor in the name of the people, as an integral part of this Constitution.

CHAPTER X. SUPREME LAW

Art. 97. The fundamental human rights by this Constitution guaranteed to the people of Japan are fruits of the age-old struggle of man to be free; they have survived the many exacting tests for durability and are conferred upon this and future generations in trust, to be held for all time inviolate.

Art. 98. This Constitution shall be the supreme law of the nation and no law, ordinance, imperial rescript or other act of government, or part thereof, contrary to the provisions hereof, shall have legal force or validity.

The treaties concluded by Japan and established laws of nations shall be faithfully observed.

Art. 99. The Emperor or the Regent as well as Ministers of State, members of the Diet, judges, and all other public officials have the obligation to respect and uphold this Constitution.

CHAPTER XI. SUPPLEMENTARY PROVISIONS

Art. 100. This Constitution shall be enforced as from the day when the period of six months will have elapsed counting from the day of its promulgation.

The enactment of laws necessary for the enforcement of this Constitution, the election of members of the House of Councillors and the procedure for the convocation of the Diet and other preparatory procedures necessary for the enforcement of this Constitution may be executed before the day prescribed in the preceding paragraph.

Art. 101. If the House of Councillors is not constituted before the effective date of this Constitution, the House of Representatives shall function as the Diet until such time as the House of Councillors shall be constituted.

Art. 102. The term of office for half the members of the House of Councillors serving in the first term under this Constitution shall be three years. Members falling under this category shall be determined in accordance with law.

Art. 103. The Ministers of State, members of the House of Representatives and judges in office on the effective date of this Constitution, and all other public officials who occupy positions corresponding to such positions as are recognized by this Constitution shall not forfeit their positions automatically on account of the enforcement of this Constitution unless otherwise specified by law. When, however, successors are elected or appointed under the provisions of this Constitution, they shall forfeit their positions as a matter of course.

Appendix 18

JAPANESE PREMIERS (1885-1953)*

From	*To*	*Premier*	
Dec. 22, 1885	Apr. 29, 1888	ITŌ, Hirobumi	(First Cabinet)
Apr. 30, 1888	Dec. 23, 1889	KURODA, Kiyotaka	
		(SANJO, Sanetomi, Oct., 1889)	
Dec. 24, 1889	May 5, 1891	YAMAGATA, Aritomo	(First)
May 6, 1891	Aug. 7, 1892	MATSUKATA, Masayoshi	(First)
Aug. 8, 1892	Sept. 17, 1896	ITŌ, Hirobumi	(Second)
		(KURODA, Kiyotaka, June, 1896)	
Sept. 18, 1896	Jan. 11, 1898	MATSUKATA, Masayoshi	(Second)
		(KURODA, Kiyotaka, Apr., 1897)	
		(MATSUKATA, Masayoshi, June, 1897)	
Jan. 12, 1898	June 29, 1898	ITŌ, Hirobumi	(Third)
June 30, 1898	Nov. 7, 1898	ŌKUMA, Shigenobu	(First)
Nov. 8, 1898	Oct. 18, 1900	YAMAGATA, Aritomo	(Second)
Oct. 19, 1900	June 1, 1901	ITŌ, Hirobumi	(Fourth)
June 2, 1901	Jan. 6, 1906	KATSURA, Tarō	(First)
Jan. 7, 1906	July 13, 1908	SAIONJI, Kimmochi	(First)
July 14, 1908	Aug. 29, 1911	KATSURA, Tarō	(Second)
Aug. 30, 1911	Dec. 20, 1912	SAIONJI, Kimmochi	(Second)
Dec. 21, 1912	Feb. 19, 1913	KATSURA, Tarō	(Third)
Feb. 20, 1913	Apr. 15, 1914	YAMAMOTO, Gombei	(First)
Apr. 16, 1914	Oct. 8, 1916	ŌKUMA, Shigenobu	(Second)
Oct. 9, 1916	Sept. 28, 1918	TERAUCHI, Seiki	
Sept. 29, 1918	Nov. 12, 1921	HARA, Takashi	
		(UCHIDA, Yasuya, Nov., 1921)	
Nov. 13, 1921	June 11, 1922	TAKAHASHI, Korekiyo	
June 12, 1922	Sept. 1, 1923	KATŌ, Tomosaburō	
Sept. 2, 1923	Jan. 6, 1924	YAMAMOTO, Gombei	(Second)
Jan. 7, 1924	June 10, 1924	KIYOURA, Keigo	
June 11, 1924	Aug. 1, 1925	KATŌ, Takaakira	(First)
Aug. 2, 1925	Jan. 29, 1926	KATŌ, Takaakira	(Second)
Jan. 30, 1926	Apr. 19, 1927	WAKATSUKI, Reijirō	(First)
Apr. 20, 1927	July 1, 1929	TANAKA, Giichi	
July 2, 1929	Apr. 13, 1931	HAMAGUCHI, Osachi	
		(SHIDEHARA, Kijurō, Nov., 1930)	
		(HAMAGUCHI, Osachi, Mar., 1931)	
Apr. 14, 1931	Dec. 12, 1931	WAKATSUKI, Reijirō	(Second)
Dec. 13, 1931	May 25, 1932	INUKI, Tsuyoshi	
May 26, 1932	July 7, 1934	SAITŌ, Makoto	

* *The Japan Year Book, 1946-48.*

From	*To*	*Premier*	
July 8, 1934	Mar. 8, 1936	OKADA, Keisuke (GOTŌ, Fumio, Feb., 1936) (OKADA, Keisuke, Feb., 1936)	
Mar. 9, 1936	Feb. 1, 1937	HIROTA, Koki	
Feb. 2, 1937	June 3, 1937	HAYASHI, Senjurō	
June 4, 1937	Jan. 4, 1939	KONOYE, Fumimaro	(First)
Jan. 5, 1939	Aug. 29, 1939	HIRANUMA, Kiichirō	
Aug. 30, 1939	Jan. 15, 1940	ABE, Nobuyuki	
Jan. 16, 1940	July 21, 1940	YONAI, Mitsumasa	
July 22, 1940	July 17, 1941	KONOYE, Fumimaro	(Second)
July 18, 1941	Oct. 17, 1941	KONOYE, Fumimaro	(Third)
Oct. 18, 1941	July 21, 1944	TŌJŌ, Hideki	
July 22, 1944	Apr. 7, 1945	KOISO, Kuniaki	
Apr. 7, 1945	Aug. 17, 1945	SUZUKI, Kantaro	
Aug. 17, 1945	Oct. 9, 1945	HIGASHIKUNI, Naruhiko	
Oct. 9, 1945	May 22, 1946	SHIDEHARA, Kijurō	
May 23, 1946	June 1, 1947	YOSHIDA, Shigeru	(First)
June 1, 1947	Feb. 10, 1948	KATAYAMA, Tetsu	
Mar. 10, 1948	Oct. 7, 1948	ASHIDA, Hitoshi	
Oct. 19, 1948	Feb. 10, 1949	YOSHIDA, Shigeru	(Second)
Feb. 16, 1949	Oct. 23, 1952*	YOSHIDA, Shigeru	(Third)
Oct. 24, 1952	May 17, 1953	YOSHIDA, Shigeru	(Fourth)
May 18, 1953	Dec. 7, 1954	YOSHIDA, Shigeru	(Fifth)
Dec. 9, 1954	Mar. 17, 1955	HATOYAMA, Ichirō	(First)
Mar. 18, 1955	Nov. 21, 1955	HATOYAMA, Ichirō	(Second)
Nov. 22, 1955	———	HATOYAMA, Ichirō	(Third)

Appendix 19

CHANGING COMPOSITION OF THE HOUSE OF REPRESENTATIVES UNDER THE NEW CONSTITUTION, 1947-1953.†

Parties	Apr. 25 1947 [1]	Jan. 1948
Socialists	143	128
Hirano Faction (Socialists)	—	12
Liberals	132	120
Democrats	126	106
People's Cooperatives	31	32
Communists	4	4
Minor Parties	17	23
Independents	13	1
Dōshikai (followers of former Premier Shidehara, Kijurō)	—	22

* The Cabinet of Yoshida was reshuffled in May, 1950.

† *American Year Book, 1947; 1948; 1949; 1950;* Paul S. Dull, "The Japanese General Election of 1952," *The American Political Science Review,* Vol. XLVII, No. 1 (March, 1953); *Nippon Times,* May 18, 1953.

[1] First general election for the House under the new Constitution.

Parties	Dec. 1, 1948 [2]
Democratic Liberals	153
Socialists	110
Democrats	90
People's Cooperatives	30
Labor-Farmers (former Left-wing Socialists)	20
New Liberals (former Democrats and Liberals)	11
Social Renovationists (former Right-wing Socialists)	11
Communists	4
Minor Parties	17
Independents	4

Parties	Jan. 23, 1949 [3]	Dec. 15, 1949
Democratic Liberals	268	266
Democrats	68	70
Socialists	48	47
Communists	35	36
People's Cooperatives	14	—
Minor Parties	24	42
Independents	9	2
Vacancies	—	3

Parties	Nov. 20, 1950 [4]
Liberals	286
Democrats	67
Socialists	45
Communists	27
Farm Cooperatives	9
Minor Parties	12
Independents	3
Vacancies	14

[2] After the collapse of the Yoshida Government and prior to the second general election.
[3] Result of the general election of January 23, 1949.
[4] After the merger of Democratic Liberals and "Coalition" Democrats.

Parties	Oct. 1, 1952	May 18, 1953 [5]
(Yoshida) Liberals	240	202
(Hatoyama) Liberals	—	35
Progressives	85	77
Right-wing Socialists	57	66
Left-wing Socialists	54	72
Communists	0	1
Minor and Independent	30	13

Parties	Dec. 10, 1954 [6]	Feb. 27, 1955 [7]
Democrats [8]	121	185
Liberals	185	112
Left-wing Socialists	72	89
Right-wing Socialists	61	67
Communists	1	2
Minor and Independent	20	12
Vacancies	7	—

Parties	Nov. 22, 1955 [9]
Liberal-Democrats	300
Socialists	154
Farmer-Labor	4
Communists	2
Minor and Independent	4
Vacancies	3

[5] Opening day of 16th Diet, result of general election of April 19, 1953.
[6] After the election of the first Hatoyama Cabinet.
[7] Result of the general election of February 27, 1955.
[8] Coalition of Progressives and (Hatoyama) Liberals.
[9] After the installation of the third Hatoyama Cabinet, the merger of Liberals and Democrats (Nov. 15), and the merger of left- and right-wing Socialists (Oct. 13).

Appendix 20

CONSTITUTION OF THE PEOPLE'S REPUBLIC OF CHINA ADOPTED SEPTEMBER 20, 1954, BY THE FIRST NATIONAL PEOPLE'S CONGRESS *

PREAMBLE.—In the year 1949, after more than a century of heroic struggle, the Chinese people, led by the Communist Party of China, finally achieved their great victory in the people's revolution against imperialism, feudalism and bureaucrat-capitalism; and so brought to an end a long history of oppression and enslavement and founded the People's Republic of China, a people's democratic dictatorship. The system of people's democracy—new democracy—of the People's Republic of China guarantees that China can in a peaceful way banish exploitation and poverty and build a prosperous and happy Socialist society.

From the founding of the People's Republic of China to the attainment of a Socialist society is a period of transition. During the transition the fundamental task of the State is, step by step, to bring about the Socialist industrialization of the country and, step by step, to accomplish the Socialist transformation of agriculture, handicrafts and capitalist industry and commerce. In a few short years our people have successfully carried out a series of large-scale struggles: the reform of the agrarian system, resistance to American aggression and aid to Korea, the suppression of counter-revolutionaries and the rehabilitation of the national economy. As a result, the necessary conditions have been created for planned economic construction and gradual transition to Socialism.

The first National People's Congress of the People's Republic of China, at its first session held in Peking, the Capital, solemnly adopted the Constitution of the People's Republic of China on September 20, 1954. This Constitution is based on the Common Programme of the Chinese People's Political Consultative Conference of 1949, and is an advance on it. It consolidates the gains of the Chinese people's revolution and the victories won in the political and economic fields since the founding of the People's Republic of China; and, moreover, it reflects the basic needs of the State in the period of transition, as well as the general desire of the people as a whole to build a Socialist society.

In the course of the great struggle to establish the People's Republic of China, the people of our country forged a broad people's democratic united front, composed of all democratic classes, democratic parties and groups, and popular organizations, and led by the Communist Party of China. This people's democratic united front will continue to play its part in mobilizing and rallying the whole people in common struggle to fulfill the fundamental task of the State during the transition and to oppose enemies within and without.

All nationalities of our country are united in one great family of free and equal nations. This unity of China's nationalities will continue to gain in strength, founded as it is on ever-growing friendship and mutual aid among themselves, and on the struggle against imperialism, against public enemies of

* *New China News Agency,* Peking, October 5, 1954.

the people within the nationalities and against both dominant-nation chauvinism and local nationalism. In the course of economic and cultural development, the State will concern itself with the needs of the different nationalities, and, in in the matter of Socialist transformation, pay full attention to the special characteristics in the development of each.

China has already built an indestructible friendship with the great Union of Soviet Socialist Republics and the People's Democracies; and the friendship between our people and peace-loving peoples in all other countries is growing day by day. Such friendship will be constantly strengthened and broadened. China's policy of establishing and extending diplomatic relations with all countries on the principle of equality, mutual benefit and mutual respect for each other's sovereignty and territorial integrity, which has already yielded success, will continue to be carried out. In international affairs our firm and consistent policy is to strive for the noble cause of world peace and the progress of humanity.

Chapter I: GENERAL PRINCIPLES.—1. The People's Republic of China is a people's democratic State led by the working class and based on the alliance of workers and peasants.

2. All power in the People's Republic of China belong to the people. The organs through which the people exercise power are the National People's Congress and the local people's congresses. The National People's Congress, the local people's congresses and other organs of state without exception practise democratic centralism.

3. The People's Republic of China is a unified, multi-national State. All the nationalities are equal. Discrimination against, or oppression of, any nationality, and acts which undermine the unity of the nationalities are prohibited. All the nationalities have freedom to use and foster the growth of their spoken and written languages, and to preserve or reform their own customs or ways. Regional autonomy applies in areas entirely or largely inhabited by national minorities. National autonomous areas are inalienable parts of the People's Republic of China.

4. The People's Republic of China, by relying on the organs of state and the social forces, and by means of Socialist industrialization and Socialist transformation, ensures the gradual abolition of systems of exploitation and the building of a Socialist society.

5. In the People's Republic of China the ownership of the means of production today mainly takes the following forms: state ownership, that is, ownership by the whole people; cooperative ownership, that is, collective ownership by the working masses; ownership by individual working people; and capitalist ownership.

6. State-owned economy is Socialist economy owned by the whole people; it is the leading force in the national economy and the material basis on which the State carried out Socialist transformation. The State ensures priority for the development of state-owned economy. All mineral resources and waters, as well as forest, undeveloped land and other resources which the State owns by law, are the property of the whole people.

7. Cooperative economy is either Socialist economy collectively owned by the working masses, or semi-Socialist economy in part collectively owned by the working masses. Such partial collective ownership by the working masses is a transitional form by means of which individual peasants, individual handicraftsmen and other individual working people organize themselves in their advance towards collective ownership by the working masses. The State protects the property of the cooperatives, encourages, guides and helps the development of cooperative economy. It regards the promotion of producers' cooperatives as the chief means for the transformation of individual farming and individual handicrafts.

8. The State protects peasant ownership of land and other means of production according to law. The State guides and helps individual peasants to increase production and encourages them to organize producers', supply and marketing, and credit cooperatives voluntarily. The policy of the State towards rich-peasant economy is to restrict and gradually eliminate it.

9. The State protects the ownership of the means of production by handicraftsmen and other non-agricultural individual working people according to law. The State guides and helps individual handicraftsmen and other non-agricultural individual working people to improve the management of their affairs and encourages them to organize producers', and supply and marketing cooperatives voluntarily.

10. The State protects the ownership by capitalists of the means of production and other capital according to law. The policy of the State towards capitalist industry and commerce is to use, restrict and transform them. The State makes use of the positive qualities of capitalist industry and commerce which are beneficial to national welfare and the people's livelihood, restricts their negative qualities which are not beneficial to national welfare and the people's livelihood, encourages and guides their transformation into various forms of state-capitalist economy, gradually replacing capitalist ownership with ownership by the whole people; and this it does by means of control exercised by administrative organs of state, the leadership given by state-owned economy, and supervision by the workers. The State forbids any kind of illegal activity by capitalists which endangers the public interest, disturbs the social economic order, or undermines the economic plan of the State.

11. The State protects the right of citizens to ownership of lawful income, of savings, houses and the means of life.

12. The State protects the right of citizens to inherit private property according to law.

13. The State may, in the public interest, buy, requisition or nationalize land and other means of production both in cities and countryside according to provisions of law.

14. The State forbids any person to use his private property to the detriment of the public interest.

15. By economic planning, the State directs the growth and transformation of the national economy to bring about the constant increase of productive forces, in this way enriching the material and cultural life of the people and consolidating the independence and security of the country.

16. Work is a matter of honor for every citizen of the People's Republic of

China who is able to work. The State encourages initiative and creative activity of citizens in their work.

17. All organs of state must rely on the masses of the people, constantly maintain close contact with them, heed their opinions and accept their supervision.

18. All persons working in organs of state must be loyal to the people's democratic system, observe the Constitution and the law and strive to serve the people.

19. The People's Republic of China safeguards the people's democratic system, suppresses all treasonable and counter-revolutionary activities and punishes all traitors and counter-revolutionaries. The State deprives feudal landlords and bureaucrat-capitalists of political rights for a specific period of time according to law; at the same time it provides them with a way to live, in order to enable them to reform through work and become citizens who earn their livelihood by their own labor.

20. The armed forces of the People's Republic of China belong to the people; their duty is to safeguard the gains of the people's revolution and of national construction, and to defend the sovereignty, territorial integrity and security of the country.

Chapter II. THE STATE STRUCTURE.—Section I. The National People's Congress.—21. The National People's Congress of the People's Republic of China is the highest organ of state power.

22. The National People's Congress is the only organ exercising the legislative power of the State.

23. The National People's Congress is composed of deputies elected by provinces, autonomous regions, municipalities directly under the central authority, the armed forces and Chinese resident abroad. The number of deputies to the National People's Congress, including those representing national minorities, and the manner of their election, are prescribed by Electoral Law.

24. The National People's Congress is elected for a term of four years. Two months before the term of office of the National People's Congress expires, its Standing Committee must carry to completion the election of deputies to the next National People's Congress. Should exceptional circumstances arise preventing such an election, the term of office of the sitting National People's Congress may be prolonged until the first session of the next National People's Congress.

25. The National People's Congress meets once a year, convened by its Standing Committee. It may also be convened whenever its Standing Committee deems this necessary or one-fifth of the deputies so propose.

26. When the National People's Congress meets, it elects a presidium to conduct its session.

27. The National People's Congress exercises the following functions and powers: (1) to amend the Constitution; (2) to enact laws; (3) to supervise the enforcement of the Constitution; (4) to elect the Chairman and the Vice-Chairman of the People's Republic of China; (5) to decide on the choice of the Premier of the State Council upon recommendation by the Chairman of the People's Republic of China, and of the component members of the State

Council upon recommendation by the Premier; (6) to decide on the choice of the Vice-Chairmen and members of the Council of National Defense upon recommendation by the Chairman of the People's Republic of China; (7) to elect the President of the Supreme People's Court; (8) to elect the Chief Procurator of the Supreme People's Procuratorate; (9) to decide on the national economic plan; (10) to examine and approve the state budget and the financial report; (11) to ratify the status and boundaries of provinces, autonomous regions, and municipalities directly under the central authority; (12) to decide on general amnesties; (13) to decide on questions of war and peace; and (14) to exercise such other functions and powers as the National People's Congress considers necessary.

28. The National People's Congress has power to remove from office: (1) the Chairman and the Vice-Chairman of the People's Republic of China; (2) the Premier and Vice-Premiers, Ministers, Heads of Commissions and the Secretary-General of the State Council; (3) the Vice-Chairmen and members of the Council of National Defence; (4) the President of the Supreme People's Court; (5) the chief Procurator of the Supreme People's Procuratorate.

29. Amendments to the Constitution require a two-thirds majority vote of all the deputies to the National People's Congress. Laws and other bills require a majority vote of all the deputies to the National People's Congress.

30. The Standing Committee of the National People's Congress is the permanent body of the National People's Congress. The Standing Committee of the National People's Congress is composed of the following persons, elected by the National People's Congress: the Chairman; the Vice-Chairmen; the Secretary-General; Members.

31. The Standing Committee of the National People's Congress exercises the following functions and powers: (1) to conduct the election of deputies to the National People's Congress; (2) to convene the National People's Congress; (3) to interpret the laws; (4) to adopt decrees; (5) to supervise the work of the State Council, the Supreme People's Court and the Supreme People's Procuratorate; (6) to annul decisions and orders of the State Council where these contravene the Constitution, laws or decrees; (7) to revise or annul inappropriate decisions of organs of state power of provinces, autonomous regions, and municipalities directly under the central authority; (8) to decide on the appointment or removal of any Vice-Premier, Minister, Head of Commission or the Secretary-General of the State Council when the National People's Congress is not in session; (9) to appoint or remove the Vice-Presidents, judges, and members of the Judicial Committee of the Supreme People's Court; (10) to appoint or remove the Deputy Chief Procurators, Procurators, and members of the Procuratorial Committee of the Supreme People's Procuratorate; (11) to decide on the appointment or recall of plenipotentiary envoys to foreign states; (12) to decide on the ratification or abrogation of treaties concluded with foreign states; (13) to institute military, diplomatic and other special title and ranks; (14) to institute and decide on the award of state orders, medals and titles of honor; (15) to decide on the granting of pardons; (16) to decide, when the National People's Congress is not in session, on the proclamation of a state of war in the event of armed attack against the

State or in fulfillment of international treaty obligations concerning common defence against aggression; (17) to decide on general or partial mobilization; (18) to decide on the enforcement of martial law throughout the country or in certain areas; and (19) to exercise such other functions and powers as are vested in it by the National People's Congress.

32. The Standing Committee of the National People's Congress exercises its functions and powers until the next National People's Congress elects a new Standing Committee.

33. The Standing Committee of the National People's Congress is responsible to the National People's Congress and reports to it.

The National People's Congress has power to recall members of its Standing Committee.

34. The National People's Congress establishes a Nationalities Committee, a Bills Committee, a Budget Committee, a Credentials Committee and other necessary committees. The Nationalities Committee and the Bills Committee are under the direction of the Standing Committee of the National People's Congress when the National People's Congress is not in session.

35. Investigation committees may be constituted to enquire into specific questions when the National People's Congress, or its Standing Committee if the National People's Congress is not in session, deems it necessary. All organs of state, people's organizations and citizens concerned are obliged to supply necessary information to these committees when they conduct investigations.

36. Deputies to the National People's Congress have the right to address questions to the State Council, or to the Ministries and Commissions of the State Council, which are under obligation to answer.

37. No deputy to the National People's Congress may be arrested or placed on trial without permission of the National People's Congress or, when the National People's Congress is not in session, of its Standing Committee.

38. Deputies to the National People's Congress are subject to the supervision of the units which elect them. These electoral units have power to replace at any time the deputies they elect, according to the procedure prescribed by law.

Section 2. The Chairman of the People's Republic of China.—39. The Chairman of the People's Republic of China is elected by the National People's Congress. Any citizen of the People's Republic of China who has the right to vote and stand for election and has reached the age of thirty-five is eligible for election as Chairman of the People's Republic of China. The term of office of the Chairman of the People's Republic of China is four years.

40. The Chairman of the People's Republic of China, in accordance with decisions of the National People's Congress or the Standing Committee of the National People's Congress, promulgates laws and decrees; appoints or removes the Premier, Vice-Premiers, Ministers, Heads of Commissions and the Secretary-General of the State Council; appoints or removes the Vice-Chairmen and members of the Council of National Defence; confers state orders, medals and titles of honor; proclaims general amnesties and grants pardons, proclaims martial law; proclaims a state of war; and orders mobilization.

41. The Chairman of the People's Republic of China represents the People's

Republic of China in its relations with foreign states, receives foreign envoys and, in accordance with decisions of the Standing Committee of the National People's Congress, appoints or recalls plenipotentiary envoys to foreign states and ratifies treaties concluded with foreign states.

42. The Chairman of the People's Republic of China commands the armed forces of the country, and is Chairman of the Council of National Defence.

43. The Chairman of the People's Republic of China convenes a Supreme State Conference whenever necessary and acts as its Chairman. The Vice-Chairman of the People's Republic of China, the Chairman of the Standing Committee of the National People's Congress, the Premier of the State Council and other persons concerned take part in the Supreme State Conference. The Chairman of the People's Republic of China submits the views of the Supreme State Conference on important affairs of state to the National People's Congress, its Standing Committee, the State Council, or other bodies concerned for their consideration and decision.

44. The Vice-Chairman of the People's Republic of China assists the Chairman in his work. The Vice-Chairman may exercise such part of the functions and powers of the Chairman as the Chairman may entrust to him. The provisions of Article 39 of the Constitution governing the election and term of office of the Chairman of the People's Republic of China apply also to the election and term of office of the Vice-Chairman of the People's Republic of China.

45. The Chairman and the Vice-Chairman of the People's Republic of China exercise their functions and powers until the new Chairman and Vice-Chairman elected by the next National People's Congress take office.

46. Should the Chairman of the People's Republic of China for reasons of health be unable to perform his duties over a long period, the Vice-Chairman exercises the functions and powers of Chairman on his behalf. Should the office of Chairman of the People's Republic of China fall vacant, the Vice-Chairman succeeds to the office of Chairman.

Section 3. State Council.—47. The State Council of the People's Republic of China, that is, the Central People's Government, is the executive of the highest organ of state power; it is the highest administrative organ of state.

48. The State Council is composed of the following persons: the Premier; the Vice-Premiers; the Ministers; the Heads of Commissions; the Secretary-General. The organization of the State Council is determined by law.

49. The State Council exercises the following functions and powers: (1) to formulate administrative measures, issue decisions and orders and verify their execution, in accordance with the Constitution, laws and decrees; (2) to submit bills to the National People's Congress or its Standing Committee; (3) to coordinate and lead the work of Ministries and Commissions; (4) to coordinate and lead the work of local administrative organs of state throughout the country; (5) to revise or annul inappropriate orders and directives of Ministers or of Heads of Commissions; (6) to revise or annul inappropriate decisions and orders of local administrative organs of state; (7) to put into effect the national economic plan and provisions of the state budget; (8) to control foreign and domestic trade; (9) to direct cultural, educational and public health work; (10) to administer affairs concerning the nationalities; (11) to administer affairs concerning Chinese resident abroad; (12) to protect the interests of the State, to maintain public order and to safeguard the rights of citizens; (13) to direct the conduct of external affairs; (14) to guide the building up of the defence forces; (15) to ratify the status and boundaries of autonomous Chou, counties, autonomous counties, and municipalities; (16) to appoint or remove administrative personnel according to provisions of law; and (17) to exercise such other functions and powers as are vested in it by the National People's Congress or its Standing Committee.

50. The Premier directs the work of the State Council and presides over its meetings. The Vice-Premiers assist the Premier in his work.

51. The Ministers and Heads of Commissions direct the work of their respective departments. Ministers and Heads of Commissions may issue orders and directive within the jurisdiction of their respective departments and in accordance with laws and decrees, and decisions and orders of the State Council.

52. The State Council is responsible to the National People's Congress and reports to it, or, when the National People's Congress is not in session, to its Standing Committee.

Section 4. The Local People's Congresses and Local People's Councils.— **53.** The Administrative division of the People's Republic of China is as follows: (1) The country is divided into provinces, autonomous regions, and municipalities directly under the central authority; (2) provinces and autonomous regions are divided into autonomous Chou, counties, autonomous counties, and municipalities; (3) counties and autonomous counties are divided into Hsiang, nationality Hsiang, and towns. Municipalities directly under the central authority and other large municipalities are divided into districts. Autonomous Chou are divided into counties, autonomous counties, and municipalities. Autonomous regions, autonomous Chou and autonomous counties are all national autonomous areas.

54. People's congresses and people's councils are established in provinces, municipalities directly under the central authority, counties, municipalities. municipal districts, Hsiang, nationality Hsiang, and towns. Organs of self-government are established in autonomous regions, autonomous Chou and autonomous counties. The organization and work of organs of self-government are specified in Section 5 of Chapter II of the Constitution.

55. Local people's congresses at all levels are the local organs of state power.

56. Deputies to the people's congresses of provinces, municipalities directly under the central authority, counties, and municipalities divided into districts are elected by the people's congresses of the next lower level; deputies to the people's congresses of municipalities not divided into districts, municipal districts, Hsiang, nationality Hsiang and towns are directly elected by the voters. The number of deputies to local people's congresses and the manner of their election are prescribed by Electoral Law.

57. The term of office of the provincial people's congresses is four years. The term of office of the people's congresses of municipalities directly under the central authority, counties, municipalities, municipal districts, Hsiang, nationality Hsiang, and towns is two years.

58. The local people's congresses at every level ensure the observance and execution of laws and decrees in their respective administrative areas; draw up plans for local economic and cultural development and for public works; examine and approve local budgets and financial reports; protect public property; maintain public order; safeguard the rights of citizens and the equal rights of national minorities.

59. The local people's congresses elect, and have power to recall, members of the people's councils at corresponding levels. The people's congresses at county level and above elect, and have power to recall, the presidents of people's courts at corresponding levels.

60. The local people's congresses adopt and issue decisions within the limits of the authority prescribed by law. The people's congresses of nationality Hsiang may, within the limits of the authority prescribed by law, take specific measures appropriate to the characteristics of the nationalities concerned. The local people's congresses have power to revise or annul inappropriate decisions and orders of people's councils at corresponding levels. The people's congresses at county level and above have power to revise or annul inappropriate decisions of people's congresses at the next lower level as well as inappropriate decisions and orders of people's councils at the next lower level.

61. Deputies to the people's congresses of provinces, municipalities directly under the central authority, counties, and municipalities divided into districts are subject to supervision by the units which elect them; deputies to the people's congresses of municipalities not divided into districts, municipal districts, Hsiang, nationality Hsiang, and towns are subject to supervision by their electorates. The electoral units and electorates which elect the deputies to the local people's congresses have power at any time to recall their deputies according to the procedure prescribed by law.

62. Local people's councils, that is, local people's governments, are the executive organs of local people's congresses at corresponding levels, and are the local administrative organs of state.

63. A local people's council is composed according to its level, of the Provincial Governor and Deputy Provincial Governors; or the Mayor and Deputy Mayors; or the County Head and Deputy County Heads; or the District Head and Deputy District Heads; or the Hsiang Head and the Deputy Hsiang Heads; or the Town Head and Deputy Town Heads, as the case may be; together with council members. The term of office of a local people's council is the same as that of the people's congress at corresponding level. The organization of local people's councils is determined by law.

64. The local people's councils administer their respective areas within the limits of the authority prescribed by law. The local people's councils carry out the decisions of people's congresses at corresponding levels and decisions and orders of administrative organs of state at higher levels. The local people's councils issue decisions and orders within the limits of the authority prescribed by law.

65. The people's councils at county level and above direct the work of all their subordinate departments and of people's councils at lower levels, as well as appoint or remove personnel of organs of state according to provisions of law. The people's councils at county level and above have power to suspend the execution of inappropriate decisions by people's congresses at the next lower level; and to revise or annul inappropriate orders and directives issued by their subordinate departments, and inappropriate decisions and orders issued by people's councils at lower levels.

66. The local people's councils are responsible to the people's congresses at corresponding levels and to the administrative organs of state at the next higher level, and report to them. The local people's councils throughout the country are administrative organs of state which are under the unified leadership of, and subordinate to, the State Council.

Section 5. The Organs of Self-government of National Autonomous Areas.—67. The organs of self-government of all autonomous regions, autonomous Chou and autonomous counties are formed in accordance with the basic principles governing the organization of local organs of state as specified in Section 4 of Chapter II of the Constitution. The form of each organ or self-government may be determined in accordance with the wishes of the majority of the people of the nationality or nationalities enjoying regional autonomy in a given area.

68. In all autonomous regions, autonomous Chou and autonomous counties where a number of nationalities live together, each nationality is entitled to appropriate representation on the organs of self-government.

69. The organs of self-government of all autonomous regions, autonomous Chou and autonomous counties exercise the functions and powers of local organs of state as specified in Section 4 of Chapter II of the Constitution.

70. The organs of self-government of all autonomous regions, autonomous Chou and autonomous counties exercise autonomy within the limits of the authority prescribed by the Constitution and the law. The organs of self-government of all autonomous regions, autonomous Chou and autonomous counties administer their own local finances within the limits of the authority prescribed by law. The organs of self-government of all autonomous regions, autonomous Chou and autonomous counties organize their local public security forces in accordance with the military system of the State. The organs of self-government of all autonomous regions, autonomous Chou and autonomous counties may draw up regulations governing the exercise of autonomy and other special regulations suited to the political, economic and cultural characteristics of the nationality or nationalities in a given area and submit any such regulations to the Standing Committee of the National People's Congress for approval.

71. In performing their duties, organs of self-government of all autonomous regions, autonomous Chou and autonomous counties employ the spoken and written language or languages commonly used by the nationality or nationalities in a given area.

72. The higher organs of state should fully safeguard the right of organs of self-government of all autonomous regions, autonomous Chou and autonomous counties to exercise autonomy, and should assist the various national minorities in their political, economic and cultural development.

Section 6. The People's Courts and the People's Procuratorate.—73. In the Peoples Republic of China judicial authority is exercised by the Supreme People's Court, local people's courts and special people's courts.

74. The term of office of the President of the Supreme People's Court and presidents of local people's courts is four years. The organization of people's courts is determined by law.

75. The system of people's assessors applies, in accordance with law, to judicial proceedings in the people's courts.

76. Cases in the people's courts are heard in public unless otherwise provided for by law. The accused has the right to defence.

77. Citizens of all nationalities have the right to use their own spoken and written languages in court proceedings. The people's courts are to provide interpretation for any party unacquainted with the spoken or written language commonly used in the locality. In an area entirely or largely inhabited by a national minority or where a number of nationalities live together, hearings in people's courts are conducted in the language commonly used in the locality, and judgments, notices and all other documents of the people's courts are made public in such language.

78. In administering justice the people's courts are independent, subject only to the law.

79. The Supreme People's Court is the highest judicial organ. The Supreme People's Court supervises the judicial work of local people's courts and special people's courts; people's courts at higher levels supervise the judicial work of people's courts at lower levels.

80. The Supreme People's Court is responsible to the National People's Congress and reports to it; or, when the National People's Congress is not in session, to its Standing Committee. Local people's courts are responsible to the local people's congresses at corresponding levels and report to them.

81. The Supreme People's Procuratorate of the People's Republic of China exercises procuratorial authority over all departments of the State Council, all local organs of state, persons working in organs of state, and citizens, to ensure observance of the law. Local organs of the People's Procuratorate and special people's procuratorates exercise procuratorial authority within the limits prescribed by law. Local organs of the People's Procuratorate and the special people's procuratorates work under the leadership of the people's procuratorates at higher levels, and all work under the unified leadership of the Supreme People's Procuratorate.

82. The term of office of the Chief Procurator of the Supreme People's Procuratorate is four years. The organization of people's procuratorates is determined by law.

83. In the exercise of their authority local organs of the People's Procuratorate are independent and are not subject to interference by local organs of state.

84. The Supreme People's Procuratorate is responsible to the National

People's Congress and reports to it; or, when the National People's Congress is not in session, to its Standing Committee.

Chapter III. FUNDAMENTAL RIGHTS AND DUTIES OF CITIZENS.—85. Citizens of the People's Republic of China are equal before the law.

86. Citizens of the People's Republic of China who have reached the age of eighteen have the right to vote and stand for election whatever their nationality, race, sex, occupation, social origin, religious belief, education, property status, or length of residence, except insane persons and persons deprived by law of the right to vote and stand for election. Women have equal rights with men to vote and stand for election.

87. Citizens of the People's Republic of China have freedom of speech, freedom of the press, freedom of assembly, freedom of association, freedom of procession and freedom of demonstration. By providing the necessary material facilities, the State guarantees to citizens enjoyment of these freedoms.

88. Citizens of the People's Republic of China have freedom of religious belief.

89. Freedom of the person of citizens of the People's Republic of China is inviolable. No citizen may be arrested except by decision of a people's court or with the sanction of a people's procuratorate.

90. The homes of citizens of the People's Republic of China are inviolable and privacy of correspondence is protected by law. Citizens of the People's Republic of China have freedom of residence and freedom to change their residence.

91. Citizens of the People's Republic of China have the right to work. To guarantee enjoyment of this right, the State, by planned development of the national economy, gradually creates more employment, and better working conditions and wages.

92. Working people in the People's Republic of China have the right to rest and leisure. To guarantee enjoyment of this right, the State prescribes working hours and holidays for workers and office employees; at the same time it gradually expands material facilities to enable working people to rest and build up their health.

93. Working people in the People's Republic of China have the right to material assistance in old age, illness or disability. To guarantee enjoyment of this right, the State provides social insurance, social assistance and public health services and gradually expands these facilities.

94. Citizens of the People's Republic of China have the right to education. To guarantee enjoyment of this right, the State establishes and gradually extends the various types of schools and other cultural and educational institutions. The State pays special attention to the physical and mental development of young peoples.

95. The People's Republic of China safeguards the freedom of citizens to engage in scientific research, literary and artistic creation and other cultural activity. The State encourages and assists citizens engaged in science, education, literature, art and other fields of culture to pursue their creative work.

96. In the People's Republic of China women enjoy equal rights with men in all spheres—political, economic, cultural, social and domestic. The State protects marriage, the family, and the mother and child.

97. Citizens of the People's Republic of China have the right to bring complaints against any person working in organs of state for transgression of law or neglect of duty by making a written or verbal statement to any organ of state at any level. People suffering loss as a result of infringement by persons working in organs of state of their rights as citizens have the right to compensation.

98. The People's Republic of China protects the proper rights and interests of Chinese resident abroad.

99. The People's Republic of China grants the right of asylum to any foreign national persecuted for supporting a just cause, taking part in the peace movement or engaging in scientific activity.

100. Citizens of the People's Republic of China must abide by the Constitution and the law, uphold discipline at work, keep public order and respect social ethics.

101. The public property of the People's Republic of China is sacred and inviolable. It is the duty of every citizen to respect and protect public property.

102. It is the duty of citizens of the People's Republic of China to pay taxes according to law.

103. It is the sacred duty of every citizen of the People's Republic of China to defend the homeland. It is the honorable duty of citizens of the People's Republic of China to perform military service according to law.

Chapter IV. NATIONAL FLAG, STATE EMBLEM, CAPITAL.–104. The national flag of the People's Republic of China is a red flag with five stars.

105. The state emblem of the People's Republic of China is: in the center, Tien An Men under the light of five stars, framed with ears of grain, and with a cogwheel at the base.

106. The capital of the People's Republic of China is Peking.

Index

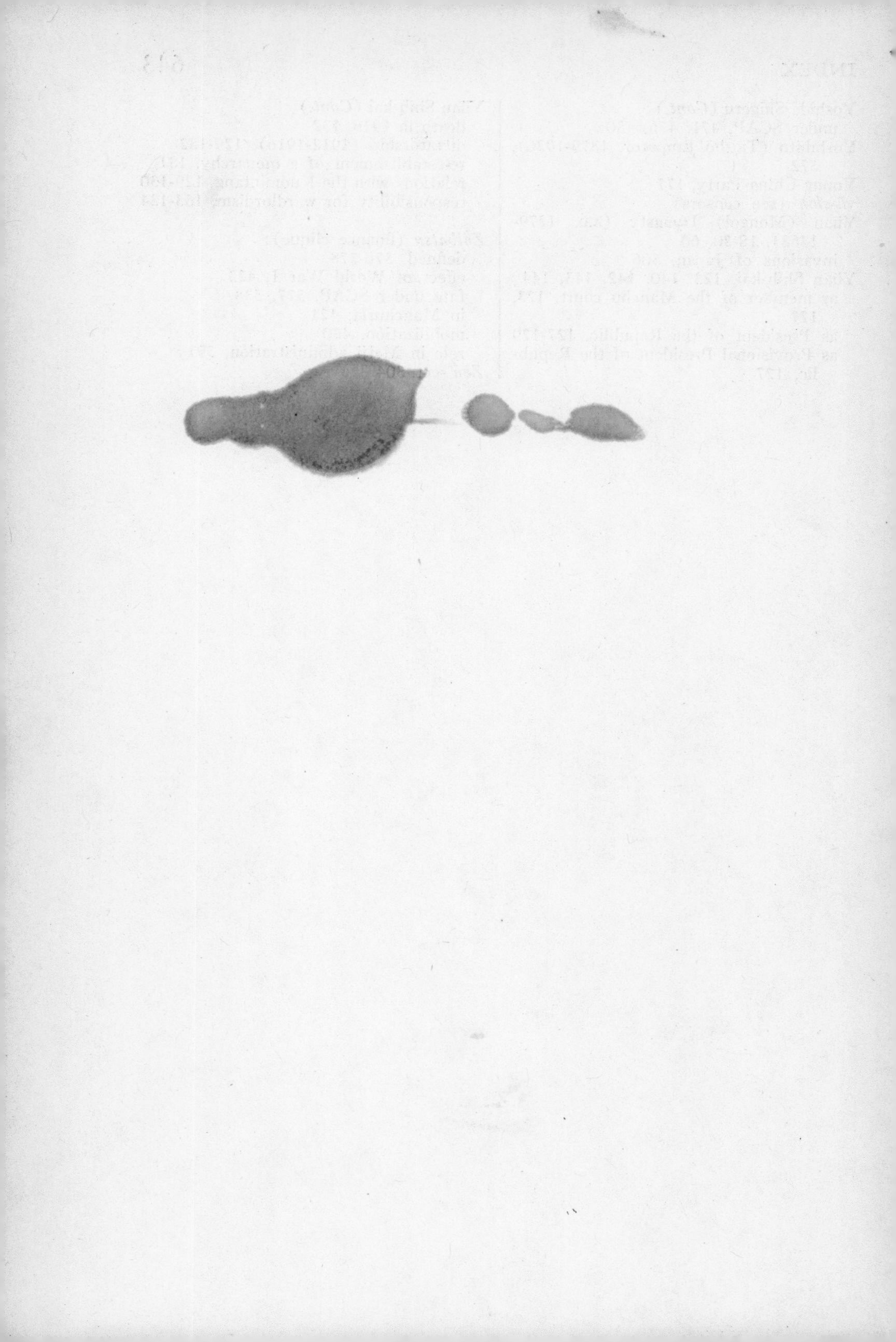

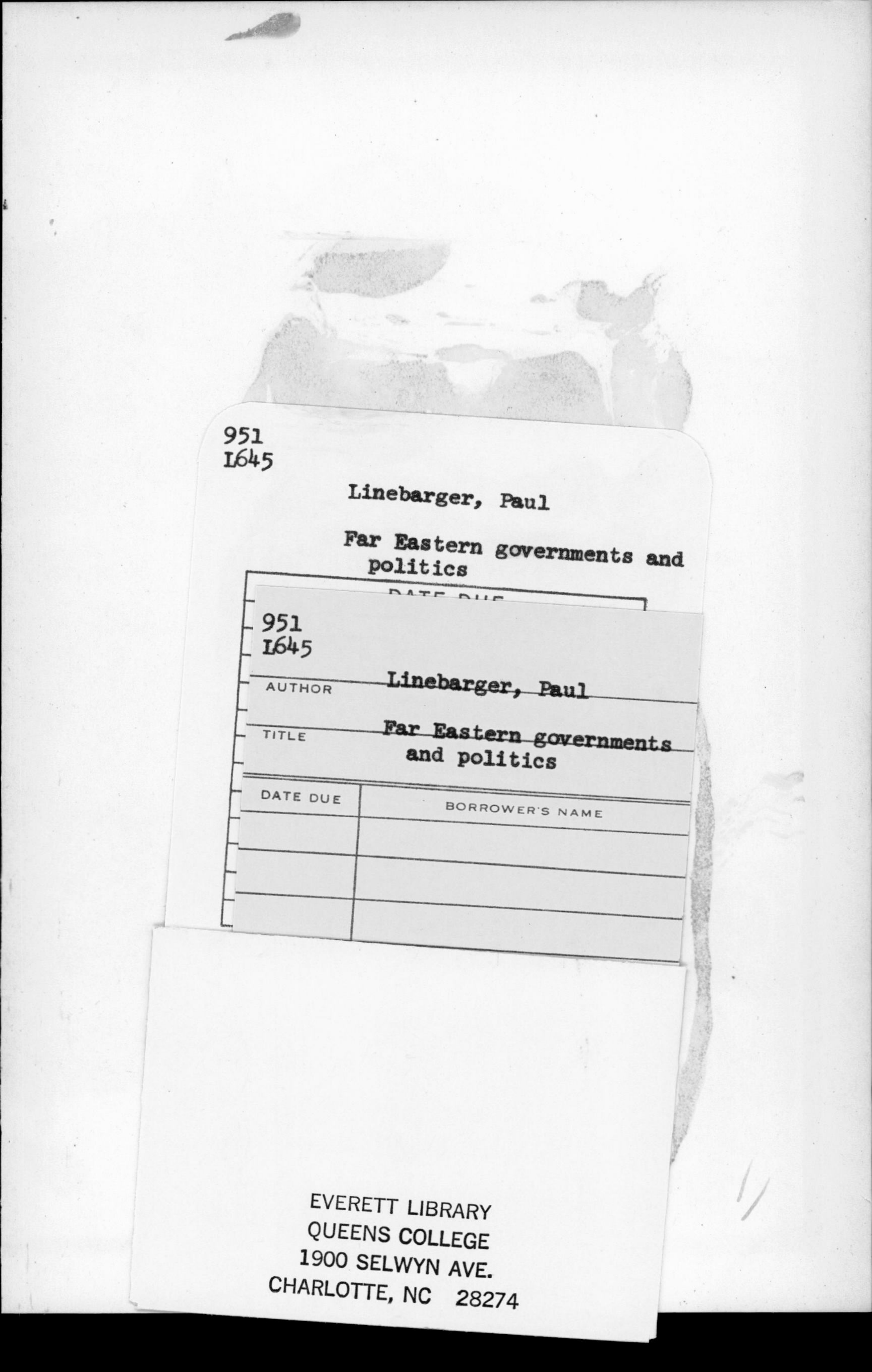
951
L645
Linebarger, Paul
Far Eastern governments and politics
DATE DUE
951
L645
AUTHOR
Linebarger, Paul
TITLE
Far Eastern governments and politics
DATE DUE
BORROWER'S NAME
EVERETT LIBRARY
QUEENS COLLEGE
1900 SELWYN AVE.
CHARLOTTE, NC 28274

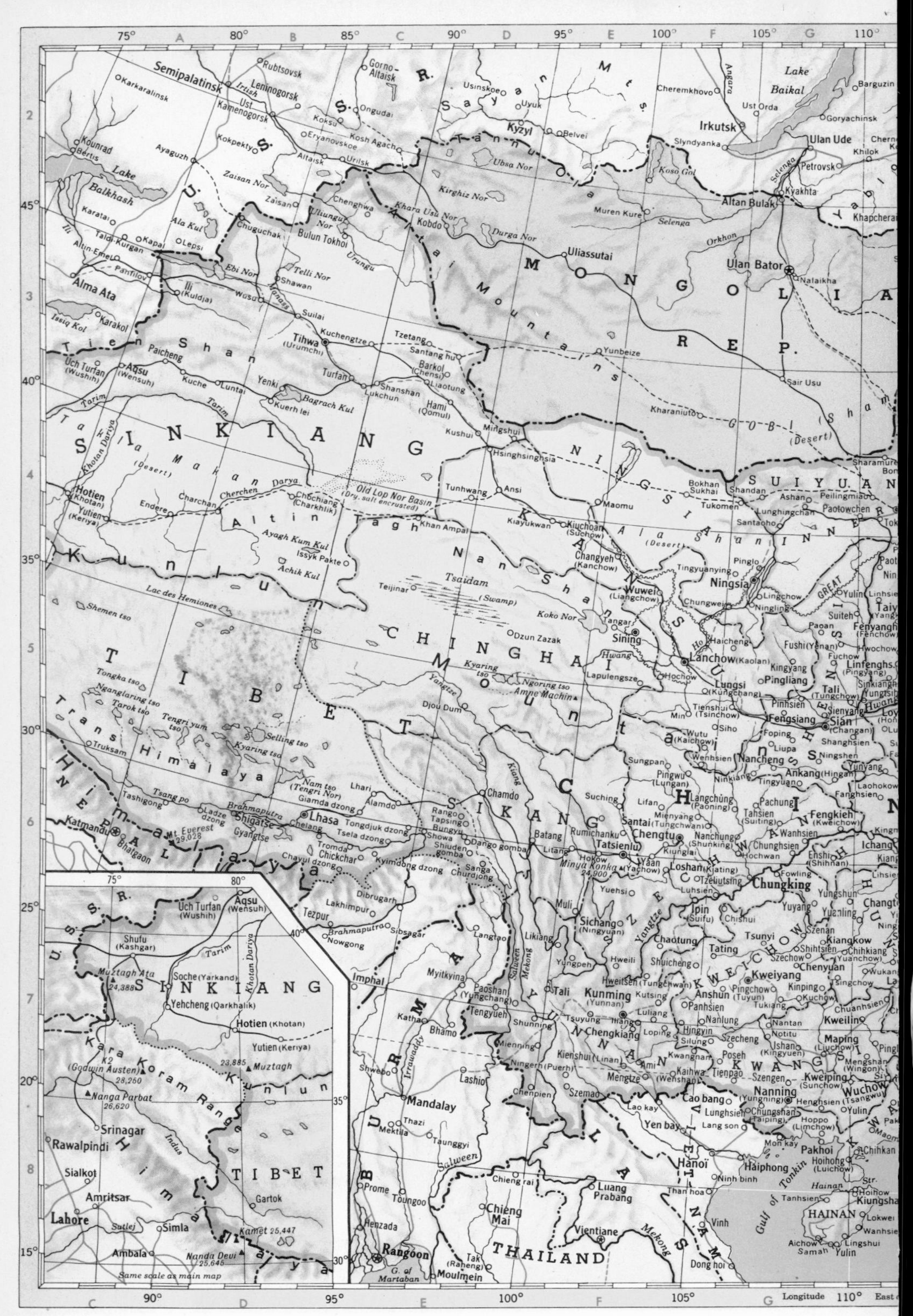

75°
80°
85°
90°
95°
100°
105°
110°
A
B
C
D
E
F
G
Semipalatinsk
Rubtsovsk
Leninogorsk
Ust Kamenogorsk
Irtish
Karkaralinsk
Gorno-Altaisk
Ongudai
Koksu
Eryanovskoe
Kosh Agach
Altaisk
Urilsk
Kokpekty
Ayaguzh
Zaisan Nor
Zaisan
Kounrad
Bertis
Lake Balkhash
Karatai
Ala Kul
Taldi Kurgan
Kapal
Lepsi
Altin Emel
Panfilov
Alma Ata
Issiq Kol
Karakol
Ili
Ili (Kuldja)
Ebi Nor
Chuguchak
Chenghwa
Uliungur Nor
Bulun Tokhoi
Urungu
Telli Nor
Shawan
Wusu
Manass
Suilai
Kuchengtze
Tihwa (Urumchi)
Tzetang
Santang hu
Barkol (Chensi)
Turfan
Shanshan
Lukchun
Liaotung
Hami (Qomul)
Kushui
Mingshui
Tien Shan
Uch Turfan (Wushih)
Paicheng
Aqsu (Wensuh)
Kuche
Luntai
Yenki
Bagrach Kul
Kuerh lei
Tarim
SINKIANG
Takla Makan (Desert)
Khotan Darya
Hotien (Khotan)
Yutien (Keriya)
Endere
Charchan
Cherchen
Cherchen Darya
Chochiang (Charkhlik)
Old Lop Nor Basin (Dry, salt encrusted)
Tunhwang
Ansi
Hsinghsinghsia
Altin Tagh
Khan Ampal
Ayagh Kum Kul
Issyk Pakte
Achik Kul
Kunlun
Lac des Hemiones
Shemen tso
Teijinar
Tsaidam (Swamp)
Nan Shan
CHINGHAI
Koko Nor
Dzun Zazak
Tangar
Sining
Hwang Ho
Kyaring tso
Ngoring tso
Amne Machin
Yangtze
Djou Dum
TIBET
Tongka tso
Nganglaring tso
Tarok tso
Tengri yum tso
Selling tso
Kyaring tso
Trans Himalaya
Truksam
Tashigong
Tsang po
Brahmaputra
Ladze dzong
Shigatse
Chelang
Lhasa
Nam tso (Tengri Nor)
Giamda dzong
Lhari
Alamdo
Tongdjuk dzong
Tsela dzong
Gyangtse
Mt. Everest 29,028
Katmandu
NEPAL
Bhatgaon
Himalaya
Tromda
Chickchar
Chayul dzong
Kyimdong dzong
Rango
Tapsing
Bungyu
Showa
Shiuden gomba
Dango gomba
Sanga Churdjong
Chamdo
SIKANG
Kiang
Batang
Litang
Rumichanku
Tatsienlu
Hokow
Minya Konka 24,900
Yaan (Yachow)
U. S. S. R.
Sayan Mts.
Usinskoe
Uyuk
Kyzyl
Belvei
Tannu Ola
Ubsa Nor
Kirghiz Nor
Khara Usu Nor
Kobdo
Durga Nor
Altai Mountains
Uliassutai
MONGOLIAN REP.
Yunbeize
Kharaniuto
GOBI (Desert)
Sair Usu
Cheremkhovo
Angara
Irkutsk
Ust Orda
Lake Baikal
Barguzin
Goryachinsk
Slyndyanka
Ulan Ude
Khilok
Petrovsk
Selenga
Kyakhta
Altan Bulak
Khapcheranga
Koso Gol
Muren Kure
Orkhon
Ulan Bator
Nalaikha
NINGSIA
Bokhan Sukhai
Shandan
Maomu
Kiayukwan
Kiuchoan (Suchow)
Ala Shan (Desert)
Changyeh (Kanchow)
Tingyuanying
Wuwei (Liangchow)
Ningsia
Chungwei
Lanchow
Hochow
Haicheng
Lapulengsze
KANSU
SUIYUAN
Ashan
Peilingmiao
Lunghingchan
Paotowchen
Tukomen
Santaoho
INNER
Pinglo
Lingchow
Ningling
GREAT
Yulin
Suiteh
Paoan
Fenyang
Fushi (Yenan)
Kingyang
Pingliang
Lungsi (Kungchang)
Kaolan
Tali
Linfenghs
Tienshui (Tsinchow)
Min
Pinhsien
Fengsiang
Sian (Changan)
Shanghsien
Wutu (Kaichow)
Siho
Foping
Liupa
Wenhsien
Nancheng
Ankang (Hingan)
Ningshen
Yunyang
Sungpan
Pingwu (Lungan)
Tingyuen
Ninkiang
Suching
Langchung (Paoning)
Pachung
Fengkieh
Lifan
Mienyang (Tungchwan)
Tahsien (Suiting)
Santai
Chengtu
Nanchung (Shunking)
Wanhsien
Chunghsien
Kiunglai
Hochwan
Ichang
Enshi (Shihnan)
Loshan (Kiating)
Tzeliutsing
Chungking
Fowling
Lunhsien
Yuehsi
Muli
Sichang (Ningyuan)
Ipin (Suifu)
Chishui
SZECHWAN
Yungshun
Yuyang
Changteh
Tsunyi
Chaotung
Tating
Likiang
Yungpeh
Hweili
Shuicheng
Szechow
Chenyuan
KWEICHOW
Kweiyang
Hweitsen (Tungchwan)
Tali
Kunming (Yunnan)
Kutsing
Anshun
Panhsien
Pingchow (Tuyun)
Kinping
Tukiang
Nanlung
YUNNAN
Tsuyung
Shunning
Luliang
Chengkiang
Loping
Hingyin
Silung
Szecheng
Ishan (Kingyuen)
Nantan
Notitu
Kweilin
Maping (Liuchow)
Kienshui (Linan)
Kwangnan
Poseh
Tienpao
KWANGSI
Mengtze
Kaihwa (Wenshan)
Szengen
Nanning (Yungning)
Kweiping (Sunchow)
Wuchow
Hengshsien
Lao kay
Cao bang
Lungshsien
Chungshan (Taiping)
Hoppo (Limchow)
Yulin
Yen bay
Lang son
Mon kay
Pakhoi
Hoihong (Luichow)
Chihkan
Hanoi
Haiphong
Ninh binh
Than hoa
Gulf of Tonkin
Hainan Str.
Hoihow
Kiungshan
HAINAN
Tanhsien
Lokwei
Wanhsien
Lingshui
Aichow
Samah
Yulin
Vinh
Dong hoi
VIET NAM
Mekong
Vientiane
Luang Prabang
LAOS
THAILAND
Chieng rai
Chieng Mai
Tak (Raheng)
Moulmein
G. of Martaban
Rangoon
Henzada
Prome
Toungoo
Salween
Taunggyi
Thazi
Meiktila
Mandalay
Shwebo
Lashio
BURMA
Irrawaddy
Katha
Bhamo
Myitkyina
Paoshan (Yungchang)
Tengyueh
Mienning
Ningerh (Puerh)
Szemao
Chenpien
Salween
Mekong
Langtao
Imphal
Tezpur
Sibsagar
Nowgong
Dibrugarh
Lakhimpur
Brahmaputra
Longitude 110° East
75°
80°
U. S. S. R.
Aqsu (Wensuh)
Uch Turfan (Wushih)
Shufu (Kashgar)
Tarim
Khotan Darya
Muztagh Ata 24,388
SINKIANG
Soche (Yarkand)
Yehcheng (Qarkhalik)
Hotien (Khotan)
Yutien (Keriya)
Kara Koram Range
K2 (Godwin Austen) 28,250
Muztagh 23,885
Kunlun
Nanga Parbat 26,620
Srinagar
Rawalpindi
Indus
Sialkot
Himalaya
TIBET
Amritsar
Gartok
Lahore
Sutlej
Simla
Kamet 25,447
Ambala
Nanda Devi 25,645
Same scale as main map
35°
40°
30°
45°
40°
35°
30°
25°
20°
15°
2
3
4
5
6
7
8
90°
95°
100°
105°